GEORGE BERNARD SHAW

HIS LIFE AND WORKS

A CRITICAL BIOGRAPHY
(Authorized)

By

ARCHIBALD HENDERSON, M.A., Ph.D.
Of the University of North Carolina

With 33 Illustrations, including two Plates in Colour (one from an autochrome by Alvin Langdon Coburn, the other from a water-colour by Bernard Partridge), two Photogravures (Coburn and Steichen), and numerous facsimiles in the text

STEWART & KIDD COMPANY
CINCINNATI
1911

AUTHOR'S INTRODUCTION

MORE than six years ago I conceived the idea of writing a book about Bernard Shaw. The magnitude of the undertaking and the elusiveness of the subject, had I realized them then in their full significance, might well have made me pause. My earliest interest in his work, aroused by his thoughtful laughter and piqued by his elfish impudence, convinced me that this remarkable talent was like no other I had known.

In characteristic style, Mr. Shaw once gave the following fantastic account of the evolution of the present work. A young American professor, Shaw explained, wished to write a book about him. Originally, he thought of beginning his task by writing an article for a daily newspaper. But so rapidly did the material grow that he soon saw the necessity of expanding the newspaper article into a long essay for a monthly review. When the essay was completed, in view of the mass of material in his hands, it appeared totally inadequate to express what he really wished to say about Bernard Shaw. It then occurred to him to write a short book entitled " G. B. S." Alas! This plan had also to be relinquished, for it was now manifest that in no such small compass was it possible to do justice to his subject. At last he hit upon the brilliant scheme of his final adoption: he would write a history of modern thought in twenty volumes. After considering the forerunners of his hero in the first nineteen volumes, he would devote the twentieth solely to the treatment of George Bernard Shaw.

Such is the history of the genesis of this book—as narrated by Shaw in the well-known Milesian manner. His whimsicalities find gay expression in the invention of such fantastic stories, which delight his auditors and exasperate only the persons concerning whom the invention is concocted. For example, Mr. Shaw once laughingly declared that " Henderson began by hailing me as an infant prodigy, and ended by pronouncing me a genius." And he delights in retailing the story of my chiv-

v

alrously coming to his rescue under the impression that he was an unknown and struggling dramatist who sorely needed, and greatly deserved, enthusiastic championship.

The real history of this biography, if not so interesting or amusing, at least possesses the merit of greater accuracy. I was first drawn to Shaw, not because he was a Socialist, a publicist, an economist. I was concerned with neither his fame nor his obscurity. I had seen his plays produced in America, had followed the ups and downs of his career as a dramatist, and was marking the rise of his star successively in Austria and Germany. The Shaw who caught and held my interest was the dramatist of a new type. I planned writing a brief study of Bernard Shaw and his plays less comprehensive in scope even than the subsequent studies of Holbrook Jackson, Gilbert Chesterton and Julius Bab. Mr. Shaw furnished me with a brief outline of his career and I set to work. After studying his works for some months, I sent a series of queries to Mr. Shaw. Fear fell upon me when, some time later, I received from him a card saying that he had only come to the forty-first page of his reply; and he assured me that if this business was to come off, it might as well be done thoroughly. Fear was turned to consternation when the big budget finally arrived. " I knew that you thought you were dealing simply with a new dramatist," wrote Mr. Shaw, " whereas, to myself, all the fuss about Candida was only a remote ripple from the splashes I made in the days of my warfare long ago. I do not think what you propose is important as *my* biography, but a thorough biography of any man who is up to the chin in the life of his time as I have been is worth writing as a historical document; and, therefore, if you still care to face it, I am willing to give you what help I can. Indeed, you can force my hand to some extent, for any story that you start will pursue me to all eternity; and if there *is* to be a biography, it is worth my while to make it as accurate as possible."

In this way my original plan was developed and expanded. Mr. Shaw's abundant sympathy and encouragement; the overflowing measure of material afforded me; the insight into a life and a period of tremendous significance and vitality; all these combined to offer an opportunity not to be neglected. My interest in the subject deepened with my knowledge. It became my aim to write—not a Rougon-Macquart history of modern thought in twenty volumes—but an account of the movements of a most interesting period, the last quarter of the nineteenth and the opening decade of the twentieth centuries, à propos of Bernard Shaw. As the work progressed, Shaw warned me— and the reporters—that in attempting his biography I had undertaken a " terrific task," an opinion endorsed by others. I remember one day being introduced to Mr. Bram Stoker as Bernard Shaw's biographer; whereupon he remarked with genuine feeling in his tone: " I can only say that you have my profoundest sympathy!" Soon after I had fairly embarked upon the undertaking, in fact, Shaw pointed out to me its magnitude. " I want you to do something that will be useful to yourself and to the world," he wrote in February, 1905; " and that is, to make me a mere peg on which to hang a study of the last quarter of the nineteenth century, especially as to the collectivist movement in politics, ethics and sociology; the Ibsen-Nietzschean movement in morals; the reaction against the materialism of Marx and Darwin; the Wagnerian movement in music; and the anti-romantic movement (including what people call realism, materialism and impressionism) in literature and art."

During the progress of the work I beheld Shaw conquer America, then Germany, then England, and, lastly, the Scandinavian countries and Continental Europe. I realized that my subject, beginning as a somewhat obscure Irish author, had thrown off the garb of submerged renown, taken the public by storm, and become the most universally popular living dramatist, and the most frequently paragraphed man in the world. No British dramatist—not even Shakespeare!—had conquered the world during his lifetime; yet Shaw, just past fifty, had succeeded in turning this cosmic trick. Clippings, pictures, journals and books poured in upon me from every quarter of the globe. I discovered that Shaw was a man with a past as well as a genius with a future, and I realized the truth of his cryptic boast that he had lived for three centuries.

Now and then, to relieve the burden of my thoughts, I would write an essay for some German, French, or American review. But I only met with base ingratitude from the subject of the essay. " Your articles have been a most fearful curse to me," Mr. Shaw wrote me on one occasion, after the appearance of an article in which I had referred to his unobtrusive philanthropy. " For instance, the day before yesterday I got a typical letter. The writer has nine children; has lost his wife suddenly, and was on the point of shooting himself in desperation for want of fifteen pounds to get him out of his difficulties, when he happened to come on a copy of your article. He instantly felt that here was the man to give him the fifteen pounds and save his life. He is only one out of a dozen who have had the same idea. I shall refer them all to you with assurances that you have read your own character into mine, and are a man with a feeling heart, a full pocket, and a ready hand to give to the afflicted."

When the book was well under way, I came to Engand, at Mr. Shaw's invitation, to " study my subject." My views of his work and genius remained fundamentally the same, though the personal contact with one of the most vivid and remarkable personalities of our time, quite naturally brought about some marked modifications of my more remote impressions, and corrected some of the minor misunderstandings which are inevitable in the absence of a personal acquaintance. Many passages in his works, many phases of his personality, hitherto obscure or incomprehensible, became clear to me. I learned the meaning of his plays, the purport of his philosophy, and the objects of his life not from my viewpoint alone, but from his own. In the quiet of Ayot, we read and discussed together the portion of the biography then written. With frequent criticism and comment Mr. Shaw helped me to a new and larger comprehension of his life and work.

On my return to America I once more approached my task— this time with the illumination of personality, and with the deeper knowledge of his own interpretation of his life and works, even though Mr. Shaw's views might not, and often did not, entirely

SHAW AND THE BIOGRAPHER.

Ayot St. Lawrence, Hertfordshire. July, 1907.

From a photograph taken by Mrs. Bernard Shaw.

[*Facing p.* x.

tally with my own. The biography was now written finally, from the first chapter to the last.

One who has pursued the errant course of a Will-o'-the-wisp may understand somewhat of my effort to follow the devious route of G. B. S. With interest, though I confess at times with dwindling patience, I have followed the lure of that occasionally somewhat impishly un-kindly light, " o'er moor and fen, o'er crag and torrent," till after the fashion of his kind, he abandoned me, wayfaring, on the brink of the abyss to save my neck as best I might. Which things are a parable.

Characteristically, and, it must be admitted, in a sense justly, he remarks that a biography of a living man cannot be finished till he is dead, or words to that effect. But the chances there are against the Biographer as well as the Biographed; and I have no fancy, I confess, that the book should be, as he once maliciously prophesied, " a posthumous work for both of us," nor that he should be justified in his presentiment that we should " both die the moment we finished it."

While nothing but death can fitly end a man's life, being no Boswell, and having my own life to attend to as well as his, I have brought these " twenty volumes " to a close. A man who has already, by his own account, " lived three centuries," is as likely to live three more; but it is less probable that I shall see the end of them. So I take Time by the forelock and write *finis* to a contribution which can only hope to cover the first three centuries.

" Who is to tackle Mr. Bernard Shaw," Mr. Augustine Birrell once asked, " and assign to him his proper place in the providential order of the world? " This work is in no sense an effort to assign to Bernard Shaw his " proper place in the providential order of the world." Such a task it is impossible to accomplish so long as Shaw lives to belie it. No more is it possible to say the final word about any genius in mid-career with limitless possibilities before him. Shaw's masterpiece— even a series of masterpieces!—perhaps remains to be written. His career may have only just begun.

This book is designed to give an authoritative account, biographical and critical, of Bernard Shaw's work, art, philosophy and life up to the present time. Perhaps its appearance is not premature. Shaw has suffered no little from the Shavians. He has served more than once as an excuse for propaganda and counter-propaganda. But save for one or two glaring exceptions, the fatuities of the cult, and the image of the shrine and burning candles have in large measure vanished—it is hoped, to return no more. The time seems ripe for conscientious and thoughtful consideration of the man and his work, in relation to the thought movement of our time—irrespective of political bias and personal prejudice. Perhaps the portrait, though neither " disparaging " nor " unflattering," may present the " real Shaw," if more " unexpectedly," perhaps no less truly, in that I am " a stranger to the Irish-British environment."

If I have succeeded in removing a legendary figure from the atmosphere of contemporary mythology, and in portraying the real man in the light of common day, then an earnest search for the *aurea media* of true criticism will not have proved wholly fruitless. I hope I may have succeeded, in some adequate degree, in exhibiting, in their true colours, what Mr. Gilbert Chesterton once justly described to me in a letter as " that humour and that courage which have cleansed so much of the intellect of to-day."

PREFACE

I HAVE neither space nor words to express, in full measure, my gratitude and indebtedness to the many friends, critics, scholars and men of letters who have aided me in the preparation of this work. First of all I wish to thank Mr. Shaw himself for his assistance. The voluminous correspondence filled with criticism, exposition and reminiscence; the immense trouble taken in placing ample materials at my disposal; the personal assistance in detailed discussion of the work—will have made this work possible. For the views expressed in this biography Mr. Shaw is in no sense responsible. On many points we are in hearty disagreement. At this place, I take pleasure in expressing my indebtedness to Mrs. Shaw, for kind assistance and helpful suggestions.

Valuable assistance, especially in connection with the earlier stages of Shaw's career as a dramatist, was derived from Mr. William Archer's collection of Shaviana, which he freely and most generously placed at my disposal. The chapter on Shaw as a critic of music I could not have written without the articles lent me by Mr. Archer. I am likewise greatly indebted to Mr. Holbrook Jackson, who gave me free access to his collection of Shaviana, and lent me valuable material hitherto unknown to me, or inaccessible. During the entire course of the preparation of the present work, I have received the counsel and aid of that scholarly student of the drama, Mr. James Platt White, of Buffalo, New York, who freely placed the services of himself and his fine library of dramatic literature at my disposal.

To certain able students of Shaw's work, some of them not known to me personally, and also to a few personal friends, I am also especially indebted. To Mr. John Corbin, Professor William Lyon Phelps and Professor E. E. Hale, Jr., in connection with the chapters treating of the plays; to Mr. James Huneker, in connection with the chapter treating of Shaw as a critic of music; to the late Mr. Samuel L. Clemens and to Dr. C. Alphonso Smith in connection with other critical and biographical chapters—for reading these portions of the work, for helpful criticism in some instances, for the loan of material in others, to all my thanks are gratefully accorded. Needless to say, they are in no wise responsible for any faults or errors of mine. In various ways, in lesser degree, I am indebted to Miss Sally Fairchild, Mr. Henry George, Jr., Mr. J. T. Grein and Mr. Austin Lewis.

Of foreign critics, I wish especially to thank M. Augustin Hamon, the French translator of Shaw's works, for his interesting suggestions, his numerous acts of kindness, and for the rich mass of documents embodying the continental criticism of Shaw with which he has kept me supplied; and Herr Siegfried Trebitsch, of Vienna, the German translator of Shaw's works, for detailed information in regard to Shaw's position and recognition in German Europe. I cannot permit myself to omit from the list of those to whom I am especially indebted the names of M. Jean Blum, formerly Professor at the Lycée, Oran, Algeria; Herr Heinrich Stümcke, editor of *Bühne und Welt;* Professor Paul Haensel, of the University of Moscow; Dr. Julius Broutá, of Madrid, the Spanish translator of Shaw's works; Herr Hugo Vallentin, the Swedish translator of Shaw's works; Mr. J. M. Borup, the Danish translator of Shaw's works; Baron Reinhold von Willebrand, editor of the *Finsk Tidskrift*, Helsingfors, Finland; M. Auguste Filon, now resident in England, I believe; and Dr. Georg Brandes, of Copenhagen. In the text of the present work, or in footnotes, I trust I have not failed to express my indebtedness to everyone, not heretofore mentioned, who, in one way or another, has aided me in the present work. I should, however, like to acknowledge here my indebtedness to the officials of the Library of Congress, Washington, D. C., of the British Museum, and of the Cambridge University Library, for their unfailing courtesy and helpfulness.

I have taken the utmost pains to include among the illustrations the most notable representations ever made of Shaw—sculpture, portrait, photograph and cartoon. Moreover, the thought of presenting Shaw to the eye in the most characteristic and representative way, as he appeared at various stages in his career, has been constantly borne in mind. My thanks are now expressed to M. Auguste Rodin for permission to reproduce a photograph of his bronze bust of Shaw, the marble replica of which, presented by Mr. Shaw, now stands in the Municipal Gallery of Modern Art, Dublin; to Prince Paul Troubetzkoy, Paris, for a photograph of his remarkable plaster bust of Shaw, said to have been made in forty minutes; to the Hon. Neville S. Lytton, for permission to reproduce his unique portrait of Mr. Shaw, after the Innocent X. of Velasquez; to Mr. Bernard Partridge for the loan of his admirable water-colour of Shaw; to Miss Jessie Holliday for the loan of her striking water-colour of Shaw, her photo-drawing of Mr. Webb, and her sketch of Mr. Archer; to Mr. Max Beerbohm and Mr. E. T. Reed for permission to reproduce cartoons of Shaw; to Mr. H. G. Wells for permission to reproduce his drawing of six Socialists; to Mr. Joseph Simpson, the artist, and Mr. J. Murray Allison, the owner, for the loan of a black-and-white wash drawing—all the best of their kind. I was so fortunate as to enlist the interest and co-operation of those two great American artist-photographers, Alvin Langdon Coburn (London) and Éduard J. Steichen (Paris). Notable portraits and pictures were taken by them especially for this work—one Lumière autochrome and four monochromes by Mr. Coburn, and two monochromes by Mr. Steichen. For permission to photograph the first and last pages of the original manuscript of *Love Among the Artists*—and also for supplying me with much other valuable material—I am indebted to Mr. D. J. Rider. I wish to express my thanks to Dr. M. L. Ettinghausen, of Munich, who secured for me many playbills of the productions of Shaw's plays in German Europe. I wish to express my thanks also to Mr. Roger Ingpen, for his assistance in the matter of illustrations. My thanks are likewise extended to the proprietors of *Punch* and *Vanity Fair* for permission to reproduce certain cartoons which originally appeared in those publications. In especial, I wish to thank Mrs. Shaw for her intelligent aid in the selection of likenesses of Mr. Shaw from his own large collection.

PREFACE

In accordance with the original plan for the biography of Mr. Shaw, the present volume was to contain an appendix, treating chronologically and critically of the production of Shaw's plays throughout the world, from the inception of his career as a dramatist. It has proved advisable to publish this appendix later in a separate, souvenir volume, embodying the history of the dramatic movement inaugurated by Bernard Shaw. Consequently, the chapters in the present volume dealing with Shaw's plays are concerned primarily with critical discussion of the genesis and art of the plays, touching upon their production only in the most casual and adventitious way.

Mr. Shaw is fond of saying: " I am a typical Irishman; my family came from Hampshire." His lineal ancestor, Captain William Shaw, was of Scotch descent; lived in Hampshire, England; and in 1689 went to Ireland, where the family has since lived. The strains in Mr. Shaw's ancestry are so complicated and interwoven, that it has seemed important to publish a genealogical chart of the Shaw family. The researches were conducted by the expert genealogist, Rev. W. Ball Wright, M.A., Osbaldwick Vicarage, York, at the instance and under the direction of Mr. Shaw himself. The chart, compiled from the data of Mr. Wright, was prepared by the experts of the Grafton Genealogical Press, New York.

To my wife, for her untiring assistance and inestimably valuable criticism, I cannot cancel my debt of gratitude by any expressions, however eloquent. I could not have written this book without her aid. It is to her intellectual directness and to her genius for suggestive criticism, that the present volume owes very much of whatever merit it may possess.

ARCHIBALD HENDERSON.

CAMBRIDGE, ENGLAND.
November 30th, 1910.

PREFACE TO THE AMERICAN EDITION

THE association of America and Bernard Shaw connotes, at the first glance, incongruity if not mutual antipathy. There is at once a suggestion of conflict between the most individualistic personality of the day and the most individualistic nation of the world. One of America's deplorable, if amiable, weaknesses is the predilection for inviting estimates of herself from supercilious people who know nothing about her. And one of Shaw's amusing idiosyncracies is his fancy for discoursing freely upon subjects of which he is pathetically ignorant. Bull-baiting is his daily pastime; but now and then he eagerly yields to the tempting invitation to take a new fling at America. So from time to time we have the diverting spectacle of a remarkably clever and shrewd Irishman making quaintly stupid and delightfully inapposite strictures upon a country he has never visited and upon a people among whom he has never lived or even sojourned.

Imagine a Martian making his first studies of the United States through the sole intermediary of the writings and discourses of Mr. Bernard Shaw. What a lurid and shocking picture would be presented to his view! The United States, thus portrayed, is a " nation of villagers," suburban in instinct and parochial in moral judgments, " overridden with old-fashioned creeds and a capitalistic religion." The Americans are an " appalling, horrible, narrow lot," and America is a " land of unthinking, bigoted persecution." The American woman is attractive, beautiful, and well-dressed—but has no soul. The American man is a machine of voluble activity without progressive impetus, whose single aim is the acquisition of wealth. America is a semi-barbaric country, incessantly shocking the world with its crass exposures of political corruption and industrial brigandage, murders, manslaughters, and lynchings, peonage, sweat-shops, child-labor, and white slavery. It is fifty years behind England, and a hundred years behind Europe, in art, literature, science, religion, and government—in a word, in civilization.

This lurid chromo, painted in crude and primary colors, is clearly the Shavian reflection of English press-opinion of America and the Americans—if it is not one of Mr. Shaw's most successful comic fictions. In whatever proportion jest and earnest may be commingled in such a comic fiction, certainly it is disappointing to find a man who has often proven himself an exceedingly clear-sighted observer and astute thinker with respect to subjects upon which he is fully informed, betray so pathetic an ignorance of the realities of American life. Mr. Shaw has been content to acquire his notions concerning America at second hand, and often at third and fourth—a method of acquiring information which is to be recommended for ease rather than for accuracy.

The English newspaper is, actually, a standing menace to perfectly equable relations between England and America. There is a yellowness of sensationalism, and there is a yellowness of deliberate misrepresentation. There is a deeper, more subtle inaccuracy than that which inheres in the distortion of facts; it is the inaccuracy which inheres in the suppression of facts; The picture of America daily presented to English eyes through the medium of the English press is a caricature—a broad, crude caricature. It is so flagrant as to lead to the lurid chromo of America achieved by Mr. Shaw. The English visitor to the United States, who gets no further than the hotels of the great cities and the rear platform of an observation car, catches only the most superficial of impressions—chiefly of the hurried metropolitan search for wealth and of the natural, still almost primitive, wildness of the landscape. England means censoriousness; and English curiosity and inquisitiveness are more than often misguided—searching into and accentuating those phases of American life and character which are most open to adverse criticism, and overlooking or ignoring those indicative features and attributes which are most suggestive in their utility and value.

In reality, England and America have much to learn from each other that will be mutually helpful and beneficial. That spirit of generosity which characterizes America in her relations

to all the world is the significant deficiency in the English
national character. America is the supreme exemplar of inter-
nationalism. America is open-mindedness, enterprise, acquisitiveness. England, as instanced most signally in her splendid
public institutions, is unsparingly generous—liberally sharing
her treasures with all the rest of the world. But she is deplora-
bly retrograde, as a nation, through declining to utilize the best
that is to be found in other nationalities and other civilizations.
It is, perhaps, sometimes more generous to receive than to give.
England austerely plays the *rôle* of model to other nations;
but she cannot abide to " sit at the feet of wisdom," to appropriate for her own advancement the good and the useful in
others, whosoever those others may be. England's besetting sin
of national vanity is the canker in the flower of her civilization,
the ominous source of her progressive relinquishment of international supremacy.

On the other hand, America has much to learn from England,
and from that phase of English spirit signally exemplified in
the person of Bernard Shaw. For if he is anything, Shaw is
a free thinker—in the original and entirely uncorrupted meaning of that term. His is that boundless naïveté so fertile for
truth's own discovery. Not only is he free thinker: he is equally
free writer and free speaker. He says exactly what he thinks—
and a good deal more. He coats the pill of the satirist with
the sugar of the artist; his wit stands sponsor for his irreverence. In Nietzschean phrase, Shaw is a " good European." He
is fully abreast of the most advanced thought of Europe, and
consistently maintains relations with the latest developments in
the fine arts, philosophy, and sociology. For many years, he has
served as a channel for the influx into English-speaking countries of the streams of European consciousness. As an original
thinker, Shaw has independently arrived at many conclusions
which have been more rigorously elaborated by numerous modern
thinkers, from Stirner, Nietzsche and Ibsen to Maeterlinck,
Bergson and James. As the literary popularizer of contemporary philosophic ideas, Bernard Shaw is one of the heralds of
that steadily evolving spirit of cosmopolitan culture which bids
fair to give the intellectual note of the twentieth century.

In this hour of America's great national resurgence in the

effort to purge the body politic of glaring social evils, it is helpful to study Bernard Shaw and to discover that his most distinctive and noteworthy service as a public character has been his splendid struggle for the inculcation of the highest ideals of unselfish public service. England far surpasses America in the relative amount of public service rendered by individuals and public organizations in behalf of the general welfare, without remuneration or the hope of remuneration. " I am of the opinion that my life belongs to the whole community," Bernard Shaw has finely declared, " and as long as I live it is my privilege to do for it whatsoever I can." Only when individual leaders of opinion in America, of which there is now no dearth, are supported everywhere by an awakened public conscience and a universally functioning spirit of individual responsibility, shall we secure throughout our country, from hamlet to metropolis, the much desiderated remedy for social abuse and the progressive perfecting of popular government.

ARCHIBALD HENDERSON.

Salisbury, N. C., September 4, 1911.

CONTENTS

CHAPTER   PAGE

AUTHOR'S INTRODUCTION v

PREFACE xi

PREFACE TO THE AMERICAN EDITION . . . xv

I.—DUBLIN DAYS 3

II.—LONDON 31

III.—THE NOVELIST 59

IV.—THE FABIAN SOCIETY 89

V.—THE CART AND TRUMPET 121

VI.—SHAVIAN SOCIALISM 151

VII.—THE ART CRITIC 195

VIII.—THE MUSIC CRITIC 231

IX.—THE DRAMATIC CRITIC 261

X.—THE PLAYWRIGHT—I 293

XI.—THE PLAYWRIGHT—II 335

XII.—THE PLAYWRIGHT—III 363

XIII.—THE TECHNICIAN 409

XIV.—THE DRAMATIST 431

XV.—ARTIST AND PHILOSOPHER 453

XVI.—THE MAN 491

APPENDIX.—A GENEALOGY OF THE SHAW FAMILY.

ILLUSTRATIONS

COVER DESIGN

A Satyric Mask. *From an original in the Department of Greek and Roman Antiquities, British Museum.*

COLOURED PLATES

George Bernard Shaw. *Lumière autochrome, by Alvin Langdon Coburn* . . . . . . *Frontispiece*

Ahenobarbus at Rehearsal. *Water-colour of G. B. Shaw, by J. Bernard Partridge* . . . . *facing p.* 246

PHOTOGRAVURE PLATES

George Bernard Shaw. "The Diabolonian." *Monochrome by Éduard J. Steichen* . . . . . *facing p.* 80

George Bernard Shaw. "The Philosopher." *Monochrome by Alvin Langdon Coburn* . . . . *facing p.* 468

OTHER ILLUSTRATIONS

Shaw and the biographer. *Photo by Mrs. Bernard Shaw*
           facing p. viii
Lucinda Elizabeth Shaw, George Carr Shaw, etc. "   18
Shaw at the age of twenty-three . . . . "   46
Sidney Webb . . . . "   92
Henry George . . . . "   96
Karl Marx . . . . "   96
Cover of Fabian Tract, No. 2 . . . . *p.* 103
The Socialist (George Bernard Shaw in 1891) . *facing p.* 116
The Cart and Trumpet . . . . . . "   144
A Study of Six Socialists . . . . . "   164
Cover design of Fabian Essays, 1890. *By Walter Crane*   *p.* 179
Fitzroy Square, London . . . . . . *facing p.* 196
William Morris . . . . "   211
George Bernard Shaw. A Cartoon. *By Max Beerbohm* . . . . . . "   232
Pope Innocent X. . . . . "   262
The Modern Pope of Wit and Wisdom. *By Neville S. Lytton* . . . . "   262
John Bull's other Playwright. A Cartoon. *By E. T. Reed* . . . . "   270

ILLUSTRATIONS

William Archer. *By Jessie Holliday* . . . *facing p.* 276

Bernard Shaw. *Black-and-white wash sketch by Joseph Simpson* . . . . . . " 294

In Consultation (G. B. S. and the author). *By É. J. Steichen* . . . . " 336

H. Granville Barker. *By A. L. Coburn* . . " 372

Shaw's House at Ayot St. Lawrence . . . " 422

George Bernard Shaw. *Photo by Histed* . . " 436

Shaw's present home in London (10, Adelphi Terrace) " 446

A plaster bust of Shaw. *By Troubetzkoy* . . " 480

G. B. S. (*A Cartoon*). *By Joseph Simpson* . . *p.* 497

A bust of Shaw. *By Rodin* . . . . *facing p.* 500

A Prophet, the Press, and Some People. *From a water-colour by Jessie Holliday* . . . " 506

FACSIMILES

MANUSCRIPTS

A page of a letter from Bernard Shaw to the biographer . . . . . . *facing p.* vi

The first and last pages of original MS. of *Love Among the Artists* . . . . . *pp.* 65-66

PLAYBILLS, ETC.

PAGE

Sunday Afternoon Lectures. March, 1886 . . . 126

The Philanderer. Berlin 301

Mrs. Warren's Profession. Munich 301

Arms and the Man. London. First performance . . 311

You Never Can Tell. Stockholm 326

The Man of Destiny. Frankfort 326

Candida. Paris 349

Candida. Brussels 352

Man and Superman. New York 365

Candida. New York 379

The Doctor's Dilemma. Cologne 395

Arms and the Man. Frankfort 395

Press Cuttings. London 403

A GENEALOGICAL CHART . . . . . *facing p.* 514

xxii

DUBLIN DAYS

"If religion is that which binds men to one another, and irreligion that which sunders, then must I testify that I found the religion of my country in its musical genius and its irreligion in its churches and drawing-rooms." —*In the Days of My Youth.* By Bernard Shaw. *Mainly About People,* 1898.

GEORGE BERNARD SHAW:

HIS LIFE AND WORKS

CHAPTER I

IT is a circumstance of no little significance that Bernard Shaw and Oscar Wilde, two dramatists whose plays have achieved so notable a success on the European stage, should both have been born in Dublin within two years of one another. It has been the good fortune of no other living British or Irish dramatist of our day to receive the enthusiastic acclaim of the most cultured public of continental Europe. What more fitting and natural than this sustention, by the countrymen of Swift and Sheridan, of the Celtic reputation for brilliancy, cleverness and wit?

George Bernard Shaw was born on July 26th, 1856—well-nigh a century later than his countryman and fellow-townsman, Richard Brinsley Sheridan. Only one year before, in 1855, was born Shaw's sole rival to the place of the foremost living dramatist of the United Kingdom, Arthur Wing Pinero. It is an interesting coincidence that the year which saw the demise of that "first man of his century," Heinrich Heine, also witnessed the birth of the brilliant and original spirit who is, in some sense, his natural and logical successor: Bernard Shaw. There is some suggestion of the workings of that wonderful law of compensation, which Emerson preached with such high seriousness, in this synchronous relation of birth and death, connecting Heine and Shaw. The circumstance might be said to proclaim the unbroken continuity of the comic spirit.

Bernard Shaw possesses the unique faculty of befuddling the brains of more sane writers than any other living man. The critic of conventional view-point is dismayed by the discovery that Shaw is bound by no conventions whatever, with the possible exception of the mechanical conventions of the stage. Shaw is essentially an intellectual, not an emotional, talent; the critic of large imaginative sympathy discovers in him one who on occasion disclaims the possession of imagination. Unlike the idealist critic, Shaw is never a hero-worshipper: he derides heroism and makes game of humanity. To the analytic critic, with his schools, his classifications, his labellings, Shaw is the elusive and unanalyzable quantity—a fantastic original, a talent wholly *sui generis*. With all his realism, he cannot be called the exponent of a school. It would be nearer the truth to say that he is himself a school.

It is futile to attempt to measure Shaw with the foot-rule of prejudice or convention. Only by placing oneself exactly at his peculiar point of view and recording the impressions received without prejudice, preference or caricature, can one ever hope to fathom the mystery of this disquieting intelligence. Most mocking when most serious, most fantastic when most earnest; his every word belies his intent. The antipode to the farcicality of pompous dulness, his gravity is that of the masquerader in motley, the mordant humour of the licensed fool. Contradiction between manner and meaning, between method and essence, constitutes the real secret of his career. The truly noteworthy consideration is not that Shaw is incorrigibly fantastic and frivolous; the alarming fact is that he is remarkably consistent and profoundly in earnest. The willingness of the public to accept the artist at his face value blinds its eyes to the profound, almost grim, seriousness of the man. The great solid and central fact of his life is that he has used the artistic mask of humour to conceal the unswerving purpose of the humanitarian and social reformer. The story of the career of George Bernard Shaw, in whom is found the almost unprecedented combination of the most brilliantly whimsical humour with the most serious and vital purpose, has already, even in our time, taken on somewhat of the character of a legend. It might become a fairy story, in very fact, if we did not finally determine to relate it, to associate it in printed form with the life of our time.

4

How to write the biography of so complex a nature? The greatest living English dramatic critic once confessed that he never approached a more difficult task than that of interpretation of Shaw's plays. One of Shaw's most intimate friends once suggested that the title of his biography would probably be " The Court Jester who was Hanged."

A few years ago, in discussing with me the plan of his biography, Mr. Shaw suggested for it the euphonious if journalistic title—*G. B. S. Biography and Autobiography*. Though the book as a whole is not developed along the lines originally suggested sufficiently to render that title truly applicable, for this first chapter surely none could be more suitable. These " Dublin Days " have been reproduced by Shaw with much amplitude, and more or less precision; so that, accepting Shaw's definition of Autobiography and mine of Biography, the result will be a narrative of much falsehood and perhaps a little truth.

" All autobiographies are lies," is Shaw's fundamental thesis. " I do not mean unconscious, unintentional lies: I mean deliberate lies. No man is bad enough to tell the truth about himself during his lifetime, involving, as it must, the truth about his family and friends and colleagues. And no man is good enough to tell the truth in a document which he suppresses until there is nobody left alive to contradict him." The true, the real autobiography will never be written; no man, no woman—Rousseau, Marie Bashkirtseff?—ever dared to write it. Were one to attempt to write the book entitled, *My Heart Laid Bare*, as Poe says somewhere in his *Marginalia*, " the paper would shrivel and blaze at every touch of the fiery pen." Shaw once " tried the experiment, within certain limits, of being candidly autobiographical." He produced no permanent impression, because nobody ever believed him; but the extent to which he stood compromised with his relations may well be imagined. His few confidential reminiscences won him the reputation of being the "most reckless liar in London "; they reeked too strongly of the diabolism mentioned by Poe. And yet we must accept Shaw's comically irreverent autobiographical details, in view of his assertion that they are attempts at genuine autobiography.

In the autobiographical accounts of his youth and early life, as well as in many conversations on the subject with Mr. Shaw, I have discovered ample explanation of his scepticism concerning the binding ties of blood, of the strangely unsympathetic, even hostile, relations between parents and children displayed throughout his entire work. These autobiographical accounts reveal on his part less filial affection than a sort of comic disrespect for the mistakes, faults and frailties of his parents and relatives.

Mr. Shaw's grandfather was a Dublin notary and stockbroker, who left a large family unprovided for at his death. George Carr Shaw, his son and Bernard Shaw's father, was an Irish Protestant gentleman; his rank—a very damnable one in his son's eyes—was that of a poor relation of that particular grade of the *haute bourgeoisie* which makes strenuous social pretensions. He had no money, it seems, no education, no profession, no manual skill, no qualification of any sort for any definite social function. Moreover, he had been brought up " to believe that there was an inborn virtue of gentility in all Shaws, since they revolved impecuniously in a sort of vague second cousinship round a baronetcy." His people, who were prolific and numerous, always spoke of themselves as " the Shaws " with an intense sense of their own importance—as one would speak of the Hohenzollerns or the Romanoffs. An amiable, but timid man, the father's worst faults were inefficiency and hypocrisy. His son could only say of him that he might have been a weaker brother of Charles Lamb. Proclaiming, and half believing, himself a teetotaller, he was in practice often a furtive drinker. The one trait of his which was reproduced in his son, his antithesis in almost every other respect, was a sense of humour, an appreciation of the comic force of anti-climax. " When I was a child, he gave me my first dip in the sea in Killiney Bay," writes his son. " He prefaced it by a very serious exhortation on the importance of learning to swim, culminating in these words : ' When I was a boy of only fourteeen, my knowledge of swimming enabled me to save your Uncle Robert's life.' Then, seeing that I was deeply impressed, he stooped, and added confidentially in my ear : ' And, to tell the truth, I never was so sorry for anything in my life afterwards.' He then plunged into the

6

ocean, enjoyed a thoroughly refreshing swim, and chuckled all the way home."

All the Shaws, because of that remote baronetcy, Mr. Shaw once gravely assured me, considered it the first duty of a respectable Government to provide them with sinecures. After holding a couple of clerkships, Shaw's father, by some means, finally asserted his family claim on the State with sufficient success to attain a post in the Four Courts—the Dublin Courts of Justice. This post in the Civil Service must have been a gross sinecure, for by 1850 it was abolished, and he was pensioned off. He then sold his small pension and went into business as a wholesale dealer in corn, a business of which he had not the slightest knowledge. " I cannot begin, like Ruskin, by saying that my father was an entirely honest merchant," said his son in one of his autobiographical confidences. " I don't know whether he was or not; I do know that he was an entirely unsuccessful one." In addition to a warehouse and office in the city, he had a flour mill at a place called Dolphin's Barn, a few miles out. This mill, attached to the business as a matter of ceremony, perhaps paid its own rent, since the machinery was generally in motion. But its chief use, according to Bernard Shaw, " was to amuse me and my boon companions, the sons of my father's partner."

When he was about forty years of age, Shaw's father married Lucinda Elizabeth Gurly, the daughter of a country gentleman. Students in eugenics might find in their disparity in age—a difference of twenty years—some explanation of the singular qualities and unique genius of their son. The estate in Carlow, now owned by Mr. Shaw, descended to him from his maternal grandfather, Walter Bagnal Gurly, through his mother's brother. Miss Gurly was brought up with extreme severity by her maternal aunt, Ellen Whitcroft, a sweet-faced lady, with a deformed back and a ruthless will, who gave her niece the most rigorous training, with the intention of subsequently leaving her a fortune. The result of this course of education upon Miss Gurly was ignorance alike of the value of money and of the world; her marriage, hastily contracted when her home was made uncomfortable for her by her father's second marriage, gave her a sufficient knowledge of both. Her aunt, angered by this unexpected and vexatious conduct on the part of this absurdly inexperienced young woman, her erstwhile paragon and *protégée*, summarily disinherited her. In many ways, Miss Gurly's marriage proved a disappointment. Her husband, one of the most impecunious of men, was far too poor to enable her to live on the scale to which she had been accustomed. Indeed, he was anything but a satisfactory husband for a clever woman. It was in her music that Mrs. Shaw found solace and comfort—a refuge from domestic disappointment.

The formative influences of Shaw's early life were of a nature to inculcate in him that disbelief in popular education, that disrespect for popular religion, and that contempt for social pretensions which are so deeply ingrained in his work and character. Is it any wonder, after his youthful experience with orthodox religion, that, like Tennyson, he cherished a contempt for the God of the British: " an immeasurable clergyman "? In his own perverse and brilliant way, he has told us the history of his progressive revolt against the religious standards of his family:

" I believe Ireland, as far as the Protestant gentry are concerned, to be the most irreligious country in the world. I was christened by my uncle; and as my godfather was intoxicated and did not turn up, the sexton was ordered to promise and vow in his place, precisely as my uncle might have ordered him to put more coals on the vestry fire. I was never confirmed, and I believe my parents never were either. The seriousness with which English families take this rite, and the deep impression it makes on many children, was a thing of which I had no conception. Protestantism in Ireland is not a religion; it is a side in political faction, a class prejudice, a conviction that Roman Catholics are socially inferior persons, who will go to hell when they die, and leave Heaven in the exclusive possession of ladies and gentlemen. In my childhood I was sent every Sunday to a Sunday school where genteel children repeated texts, and were rewarded with little cards inscribed with other texts. After an hour of this, we were marched into the adjoining church, to fidget there until our neighbours must have wished the service over as heartily as we did. I suffered this, not for my salvation, but because my father's respectability demanded it. When we went to live in the country, remote from social criticism, I broke with the observance and never resumed it.

"What helped to make this ' church ' a hot-bed of all the social vices was that no working folk ever came to it. In England the clergy go among the poor, and sometimes do try desperately to get them to come to church. In Ireland the poor are Catholics—' Papists,' as my Orange grandfather called them. The Protestant Church has nothing to do with them. Its snobbery is quite unmitigated. I cannot say that in Ireland every man is the worse for what he calls his religion. I can only say that all the people I knew were."

One must beware of the error of exaggerating the influence of Puritanism upon Shaw's character in his youth. Mr. Shaw has laughed consumedly at Mr. Chesterton for speaking of his " narrow, Puritan home." A little incident may serve to reflect the tone of the heated religious controversies that went on in Mr. Shaw's home when he was a lad. Shaw's father, one of his maternal uncles, and a visitor engaged one day in a discussion over the raising of Lazarus. Mr. Shaw held the evangelical view: that it took place exactly as described. The visitor was a pure sceptic, and dismissed the story as manifestly impossible. But Shaw's uncle described it as a put-up job, in which Jesus had made a confederate of Lazarus—had made it worth his while, or asked him for friendship's sake to pretend he was dead and at the proper moment to pretend to come to life. " Now imagine me as a little child," said Shaw in narrating the story, " in my ' narrow, Puritan home,' listening to this discussion. I listened with very great interest, and I confess to you that the view which recommended itself most to me was that of my maternal uncle, and I think, on reflection, you will admit that that was the right and healthy point of view for a boy to take, because my maternal uncle's view appealed to a sense of humour, which is a very good thing and a very human thing, whereas the other two views—one appealing to my mere credulity and the other to mere scepticism—really did not appeal to anything at all that had any genuine religious value. . . . Now that was really the tone of religious controversy at that time, and it almost always showed us the barrenness on the side of religion very much more than it did on the side of scepticism." This anecdote brings irresistibly to mind Mark Twain's story of the old sea-captain who declared that Elijah had won out in the altar contest, not because of his superiority over the other prophets, or of his God to theirs, but because, under the pretence that it was water, he had had the foresight to inundate his altar with—petroleum!

A short while after he entered a land office in Dublin as an employee, a position secured for him by his uncle, Frederick Shaw, a high official in the Valuation Office, it was discovered that the young Shaw, then in his teens, instead of being an extremely correct Protestant and churchgoer, was actually what used to be known in those days as an " infidel." Many were the arguments, on the subject of religion and faith, that arose among the employees of the firm, arguments that usually went hard for young Shaw, the novice, untrained in dialectic. " What is the use of arguing," one of the apprentices, Humphrey Lloyd, said to Shaw one day, " when you don't know what a syllogism is? " As he once told me, Mr. Shaw promptly went and found out what it was, learning, like Molière's hero, that he had been making syllogisms all his life without knowing it. Mr. Uniacke Townshend, Shaw's employer, a pillar of the church —and of the Royal Dublin Society—so far respected his freedom of conscience as to make no attempt to reason with him, only imposing the condition that the subject be not discussed in the office. Although secretly chafing under the restraint, young Shaw for a time honourably submitted to the stern limitation; but an outbreak of some sort was inevitable. The immediate occasion of his first alarming appearance in print was the visit of the American evangelists, Moody and Sankey, to Dublin. Their arrival in Great Britain created a considerable sensation, and young Shaw went to hear them when they came to Dublin.

Not only was he wholly unmoved by their eloquence, but he actually felt bound to inform the public that, if this were Religion, then he was, on the whole, an Atheist. Imagine the extreme horror of his numerous uncles when they read his letter, solemnly printed in *Public Opinion*.* These evangelistic services, he maintained, " were not of a religious, but a secular, not to say profane, character." Further, he said: " Respecting the effect of the revival on individuals I may mention that it has a tendency to make them highly objectionable members of society, and induces their unconverted friends to desire a speedy reaction, which either soon takes place or the revived one relapses slowly into his previous benighted condition as the effect fades; and although many young men have been snatched from careers of dissipation by Mr. Moody's exhortations, it remains doubtful whether the change is not merely in the nature of the excitement rather than in the moral nature of the individual."

The complete story of his " honest doubts," and his conscientious revolt against the hollowness and inhuman frigidity of the religion he saw practised around him, he has related in the most ludicrously irreverent vein:

" When I was a little boy, I was compelled to go to church on Sunday; and though I escaped from that intol-

---

* This letter, signed " S," appeared in *Public Opinion* on April 3d, 1875. It is a criticism of the methods adopted by Messrs. Moody and Sankey, and an attempt to show that the enormous audiences drawn to the evangelistic services were not proof of their efficacy. Shaw then proceeds to explain the motives which induced many people to attend, predominant among them being " the curiosity excited by the great reputation of the evangelists and the stories, widely circulated, of the summary annihilation by epilepsy and otherwise of sceptics who had openly proclaimed their doubts of Mr. Moody's divine mission." This letter has been reprinted in *Public Opinion*, November 8th, 1907.

In his monograph on Shaw (pp. 42-3), Mr. Holbrook Jackson has pointed out that this was not Shaw's first bid for publicity. In the *Vaudeville Magazine* of September, 1871, there appeared among the Editorial Replies the following: " G. B. Shaw, Torca Cottage, Torca Hill, Dalkey, Co. Dublin, Ireland.—You should have registered your letter; such a combination of wit and satire ought not to have been conveyed at the ordinary rate of postage. As it was, your arguments were so weighty, we had to pay *twopence* extra for them."

erable bondage before I was ten, it prejudiced me so violently against church-going that twenty years elapsed before, in foreign lands and in pursuit of works of art, I became once more a church-goer. To this day, my flesh creeps when I recall that genteel suburban Irish Protestant church, built by Roman Catholic workmen who would have considered themselves damned had they crossed its threshold afterwards. Every separate stone, every pane of glass, every fillet of ornamental ironwork—half dog-collar, half-coronet—in that building must have sowed a separate evil passion in my young heart. Yes; all the vulgarity, savagery, and bad blood which has marred my literary work, was certainly laid upon me in that house of Satan! The mere nullity of the building could make no positive impression on me; but what could, and did, were the unnaturally motionless figures of the congregation in their Sunday clothes and bonnets, and their set faces, pale with the malignant rigidity produced by the suppression of all expression. And yet these people were always moving and watching one another by stealth, as convicts communicate with one another. So was I. I had been told to keep my restless little limbs still all through the interminable hours; not to talk; and, above all, to be happy and holy there and glad that I was not a wicked little boy playing in the fields instead of worshipping God. I hypocritically acquiesced; but the state of my conscience may be imagined, especially as I implicitly believed that all the rest of the congregation were perfectly sincere and good. I remember at the time dreaming one night that I was dead and had gone to Heaven. The picture of Heaven which the efforts of the then Established Church of Ireland had conveyed to my childish imagination, was a waiting-room with walls of pale sky-coloured tabbinet, and a pew-like bench running all round, except at one corner, where there was a door. I was, somehow, aware that God was in the next room, accessible through the door. I was seated on the bench with my ankles tightly interlaced to prevent my legs dangling, behaving myself with all my might before the grown-up people, who all belonged to the Sunday congregation, and were either sitting on the bench as if at church or else moving solemnly in and out as if there were a dead person in the house. A grimly-handsome lady, who usually sat in a corner seat near me in church, and whom I believed to be thoroughly conversant with the arrangements of the Almighty, was to introduce me presently into the next room—a moment which I was supposed to await with joy and enthusiasm. Really, of course, my heart sank like lead within me at the thought; for I felt that my feeble affectation of piety could not impose on Omniscience, and that one glance of that all-searching eye would discover that I had been allowed to come to Heaven by mistake. Unfortunately for the interest of this narrative, I woke, or wandered off into another dream, before the critical moment arrived. But it goes far enough to show that I was by no means an insusceptible subject; indeed, I am sure, from other early experiences of mine, that if I had been turned loose in a real church, and allowed to wander and stare about, or hear noble music there instead of that most accursed ' Te Deum ' of Jackson's and a senseless droning of the ' Old Hundredth,' I should never have seized the opportunity of a great evangelical revival, which occurred to me when I was still in my teens, to begin my literary career with a letter to the Press, announcing with inflexible materialistic logic, and to the extreme horror of my respectable connections, that I was an atheist. When, later on, I was led to the study of the economic basis of the respectability of that and similar congregations, I was inexpressibly relieved to find that it represented a mere phase of industrial confusion, and could never have substantiated its claims to my respect, if, as a child, I had been able to bring it to book. To this very day, whenever there is the slightest danger of my being mistaken for a votary of the blue tabbinet waiting-room or a supporter of that morality in which wrong and right, base and noble, evil and good, really mean nothing more than the kitchen and the drawing-room,

I hasten to claim honourable exemption, as atheist and socialist, from any such complicity." *

The lesson of the selfishness and insincerity of society ineradicably impressed upon Ibsen's mind in his childhood days is paralleled by a similar experience in the youth of Shaw. The ingrained snobbery of society as he saw it, the contempt for those lower in social pretensions, if not in social station, revolted the lad's whole nature. He soon became animated with a Carlylean contempt for the snobbery of " respectability in its thousand gigs." As in the case of the disconsolate Stendhal, Shaw was not long in discovering that his family revered what he despised, and detested what he enthusiastically admired. An incident he relates, in illustration of this trait in his father, serves in great measure to explain Shaw's scorn, in after life, of the blandishments of the drawing-room, his intolerance of fashionable society.

" One evening I was playing on the street with a school-fellow of mine, when my father came home. He questioned me about this boy, who was the son of a prosperous ironmonger. The feelings of my father, who was not prosperous and who sold flour by the sack, when he learned that his son had played on the public street with the son of a man who sold nails by the pennyworth in a shop are not to be described. He impressed on me that my honour, my self-respect, my human dignity, all stood upon my determination not to associate with persons engaged in retail trade. Probably this was the worst crime my father ever committed. And yet I do not see what else he could have taught me, short of genuine republicanism, which is the only possible school of good manners.

"Imagine being taught to despise a workman, and to respect a gentleman, in a country where every rag of excuse for gentility is stripped off by poverty! Imagine being

---

* *On Going to Church.* This essay appeared originally in the *Savoy Magazine,* January, 1896; it is now published in book form by John W. Luce and Co., Boston, Mass.

taught that there is one God—a Protestant and a perfect gentleman—keeping Heaven select for the gentry; and an idolatrous impostor called the Pope, smoothing the hellward way for the mass of the people, only admissible into the kitchens of most of the aforesaid gentry as 'thorough servants' (general servants) at eight pounds a year! Imagine the pretensions of the English peerage on the incomes of the English lower middle-class. I remember Stopford Brooke one day telling me that he discerned in my books an intense and contemptuous hatred for society. No wonder! though, like him, I strongly demur to the usurpation of the word 'society' by an unsocial system of setting class against class and creed against creed." *

As to education, in the ordinary sense, the lad had none: he never learned anything at school. He found no incentive to study under the tutelage of people who put *Cæsar* and *Horace* into the hands of small boys and expected the result to be an elegant taste and knowledge of the world. His first teacher was his uncle, the Rev. William George Carroll, Vicar of St. Bride's, Dublin—reputed the first Protestant clergyman in Ireland to declare for Home Rule. We have one brief but comprehensive glimpse of his school life at this period of immaturity: " The word education brought to my mind four successive schools where my parents got me out of the way for half a day. In these *crèches*—for that is exactly what they were—I learned nothing. How I could have been such a sheep as to go to them, when I could just as easily have flatly refused, puzzles and exasperates me to this day. They did me a great deal of harm, and no good whatever. However, my parents thought I ought to go, being too young to have any confidence in my own instincts. So I went. And if you can in any public way convey to these idiotic institutions my hearty curse, you will relieve my feelings infinitely. . . . As a schoolboy I was incorrigibly idle and worthless. And I am proud of the fact." In the preface to *John Bull's Other Island*, Shaw has referred in par-

* *In the Days of My Youth.* By Bernard Shaw. *Mainly About People,* 1898.

ticular to the Wesleyan Connexional School, now Wesley College, Dublin. Here the Wesleyan catechism was taught without protest to pupils, the majority of whom were Church (Protestant Irish) boys! So long as their sons were taught genuine Protestantism, the parents didn't bother about the particular brand. The school's most famous alumni are Sir Robert Hart and Bernard Shaw. In the school roll-book Shaw is entered for the first time as attending on April 13th, 1867. Unfortunately, only a bare record of his class marks is given. " He seems to have been generally near or at the bottom of his classes," said the principal, the Rev. William Crawford, in a letter to me of date August 6th, 1909; " but, perhaps typically of the man, he jumped up suddenly to second place once in his first quarter, and does not seem to have aspired again. He was entered in the ' First Latin Class,' I suppose the most junior division on the classical side." Shaw sat in class between a classic and a mathematician, both in after years distinguished scholars. Each did his appropriate share of young Shaw's work. In return Shaw would narrate for their delectation, according to the account of one of the twain, numerous stories from the *Iliad* and *Odyssey*, in his own peculiar and inimitable vein. Shaw was only in his tenth year when he entered the Wesleyan Connexional School; and in that year Dr. H. R. Parker, of Trinity College, Dublin, was head master and Rev. T. A. McKee was governor. Apparently, no picture of the old school now exists; the new building stands near, but not on, the site of the old school.*

It might be imagined, from the evidence of Shaw's own confessions just detailed, that it was impossible for a boy who " took refuge in idleness " at school to acquire any sort of an education; but such a supposition is very wide of the mark. The discipline he received at home, the discipline of *laissez faire et laissez aller*, which might have spoiled the average boy, had just the opposite effect upon this strangely inquisitive, alarmingly self-assertive child. If he lost somewhat in youthful gentleness and tenderness, he gained greatly in manly determination and

* Compare *Jubilee of Wesley College, Dublin,* December, 1895—being a special number of the *Wesley College Quarterly.*

16

independence. If he was never treated as a child, at least he was let do what he liked. Thus the habit of freedom, which, as he once assured me, most Englishmen and Englishwomen of his class never acquire, came to him naturally.

One might say of Shaw's mother that she was the antithesis of Candida on the domestic plane. In many respects she was a forerunner of the " new woman " of our own day—independent, self-reliant, indifferent to public opinion. She was, in her son's phrase, " constitutionally unfitted for the sentiment of wifehood and motherhood "; her genuine energy and talents were bestowed almost undividedly upon music. Not long after her marriage to Mr. Shaw, she became the right hand of an energetic genius, who had formed a musical society and an orchestra in Dublin. These organizations were composed wholly of amateurs—and unavoidably so—in view of the state of musical activity in Dublin at the time. By all the local professors of music this energetic genius and man of successful ambitions, George John Vandaleur Lee, was held in the greatest contempt, even hatred, because he had repudiated their traditions, and thereby actually trained himself to become an effective teacher of singing. Through actual dissection, as well as by practical singing, he studied the anatomy of the throat until he was able, by watching and hearing a singer, to state with certainty the exact nature of the physical processes going on. From Badeali, an Italian opera singer, who preserved a splendid voice to a great age, he learned the secret of voice preservation. This method he taught to Mrs. Shaw so successfully that when she gave up singing, late in life, it was not because her voice failed her, but because her age made singing ridiculous.*

---

* Lee continued steadily to advance in his profession, becoming successively music-teacher, opera-conductor, festival conductor, and finally fashionable teacher of singing in Park Lane, London. He accomplished everything that he undertook, even conducting a Handel Festival in Dublin, participated in by Tietjens, Agnesi, and other leading singers of the day. For several years he enjoyed great popularity in London as a teacher of music. When he died, quite suddenly, at his home in Park Lane, it was discovered, Shaw afterwards remarked, that he had exhausted his stock of health in his Dublin period, and that the days of his vanity in London were days of progressive decay.

Lee's twofold influence upon the young Shaw—indirectly through Mrs. Shaw's musical activities, and directly through the inspiration of his personal character, one of phenomenal competence and unswerving determination—is very markedly visible in the Shaw of after years, the brilliant musical critic and the doggedly persistent seeker after worthy success and merited fame. Mrs. Shaw studied singing under Lee, and thorough bass under Logier. She assisted Lee in all his various and varied enterprises, copying orchestral parts and scoring songs for him. She led the chorus for him at the musical society; and at different times she appeared in operas produced and directed by Lee, playing Azucena in *Il Trovatore*, Donna Anna in *Don Giovanni*, Margaret in Gounod's *Faust*, and Lucrezia Borgia in Donizetti's opera of that name. Finally, in order to facilitate matters, Mrs. Shaw kept house for Lee by setting up a joint household, a sort of " blameless *ménage à trois* "—the phrase her son used in speaking of it to me—which lasted until 1872, the year of Lee's departure for London.

As all these operas were rehearsed at his home, it was only natural that Bernard Shaw should pick up, quite unconsciously, indeed, a knowledge of that extraordinary literature of modern music, from Bach to Wagner, with which his mother and Lee were so familiar. While he was yet a small boy, he whistled and sang, from the first bar to the last, not only the operas he frequently heard, but also the many oratorios rendered from time to time by the musical society. Indeed, Mr. Shaw once remarked that, besides their respectability, the chief merit of his family was a remarkable aptitude for playing all sorts of wind instruments by ear, even his father playing " Home, Sweet Home " upon the flute. Before he was fifteen, Bernard Shaw knew at least one important work by Handel, Mozart, Beethoven, Mendelssohn, Rossini, Bellini, Donizetti, Verdi and Gounod from cover to cover. Not only did he whistle the themes to himself as a street boy whistles music-hall songs, but he also sang incessantly, to himself and for himself, opera and oratorio, in an " absurd gibberish which was Italian picked up by ear—and Irish Italian at that." No one ever taught him music in his youth, but when he grew up, although he had a

18

Lucinda Elizabeth
(Gurly) Shaw.

George Carr
Shaw.

George John Vandaleur Lee.

Reproduced from a copy, by Bernard Shaw, of the original photograph by Richard
Pigott, forger of the Parnell letters. Taken in 1863.

[Facing p. 18

very indifferent voice, he took some singing lessons under his mother. At first, he found that he could not make a rightly produced sound that was audible two yards off. But he learned readily, under the competent instruction of his mother, and now his voice, " a commonplace baritone of the most ordinary range, B flat to F, and French pitch preferred for the F," is distinguished rather by audibility than in any other respect. It is noteworthy that the lessons he learned from his mother— the secrets of breathing and enunciation—proved of incalculable value to him afterwards on the platform, in the strenuous days of his dialectical warfare.

Although Bernard Shaw idled away his time at school, the very real education he received through other broader and deeper channels has since saved him, he stoutly maintains, from being " at the smallest disadvantage with men who only know the grammar and mispronunciation of the Greek and Latin poets and philosophers." The other great motor of educational influence in his youth was the National Gallery of Ireland; to that cherished asylum, which he haunted in the days of his youth, he has often expressed his unmeasured gratitude. Whenever he had any money, he bought volumes of the Bohn translation of Vasari; and at fifteen he knew enough of a considerable number of Italian and Flemish painters to recognize their work at sight. His communion with the masterpieces preserved in the Dublin Gallery was so solitary that he was once driven to say, with comically extravagant egoism, that he believed he was the only Irishman, except the officials, who had ever been there. This acquaintance with art and the history of art " did more for him," he once asserted, than the two cathedrals in Dublin so magnificently " restored " out of the profits of the drink trade. I think we must conclude, with the ever modest autobiographer, that, thanks to communism in pictures, he was really a very highly educated boy.

Through lack of means, the Shaws were unable to give their son a university education; perhaps no regret need be felt on this score, since it is not unlikely, in view of his attitude towards a university education, that he would have taken refuge in idleness at Oxford, Cambridge, or Dublin, just as he had done at the schools he had already attended. Unlike his future colleagues in dramatic criticism, William Archer and Arthur Bingham Walkley, graduates of Edinburgh and Oxford respectively, Shaw despised, half ignorantly, half penetratingly, the thought of a university education, for it seemed to him to turn out men who all thought alike and were snobs. So in 1871, at the age of fifteen, he entered the office of an Irish land agent, Mr. Charles Uniacke Townshend, and remained there until March, 1876. Perhaps the Ibsenite, the Nietzschean of after years was thus beginning a course of preliminary training: Henri Beyle used to say that to have been a banker was to have gone through the best preparatory school for philosophy. During this period Bernard Shaw lived in lodgings in Dublin with his father, who had by this time given up that furtive drinking, of which his son in after life spoke with such frank levity. The lad's salary at first was eighteen pounds a year, his position that of junior clerk. He had no fondness for his work, and took no interest in land agency; nevertheless, he made a very satisfactory clerk. At the end of about a year, a sudden vacancy occurred in the most active post in the office, that of cashier. As this involved a sort of miniature banking business for the clients, and the daily receipt and payment of all sorts of rents, interests, insurances, private allowances and so on, it was a comparatively busy post, and a position of trust besides. The junior clerk was temporarily called upon to fill the sudden vacancy pending the engagement of a new cashier of greater age and experience. He performed his numerous duties so successfully that the engagement of the new man was first delayed and then dropped. The child of fifteen, laboriously and successfully struggling to change his sloped, straggly, weak-minded handwriting into a fair imitation of his predecessor's, father of the man of forty, carefully drawing up elaborate contracts with theatre managers, who never kept them. By this initial exhibition of enterprise, young Shaw's salary, now twenty-four pounds a year, was doubled, which meant a considerable step ahead. The clear-cut chirography of the Shaw of to-day and the neatness of arrangement so noticeable in his apartments at Adelphi Terrace are the results of his early training; indeed, he was a remarkably correct cashier and accountant, as one of Mr. Shaw's colleagues in the office once told me. While he was always ignorant of the state of his own finances, and to-day troubles little about his personal accounts, he was never a farthing out in his accounts at the office.

Land agency in Ireland was, and is still, a socially pretentious business. Although the position Shaw held was regarded as a very genteel sort of post, yet to him this was no gratification, but quite the reverse. It was saturated with a class feeling for which, even at that time, he had an intense loathing. The position carried with it, nevertheless, certain obvious advantages. It secured for him the society of a set of so-called apprentices, who were, in fact, idle young gentlemen who had paid a big premium to be taught a genteel profession. Though the premium was not paid to Shaw, still he took delight in teaching his co-workers various operatic *scenas*, which were occasionally in full swing when the principal or a customer would enter the office unexpectedly. On one occasion, Mr. Shaw once told me gleefully, a certain apprentice sang: *"Ah, che la morte "* in his tower—standing on the washstand with his head appearing over a tall screen—with such feeling and such obliviousness to all external events, that the whole office force was suddenly struck busy and silent by the arrival of Mr. Townshend, the senior partner, who stared, stupended, at the bleating countenance above the screen and finally fled upstairs, completely beaten by the situation. The young clerk thus found plenty of fun and diversion in his association with young men of culture and education; this did not make him hate his work any the less. His natural antipathy to respectability asserted itself very early in his career: he once said that land agency was too respectable for him. Moreover, the enforced repression concerning his religious beliefs bred in him a spirit of discontent and revolt. Although he realized that silence on the subject was undoubtedly an indispensable condition of sociability among people who disagreed strongly on such a matter, yet he chafed under the restraint. To such a restraint he felt he could never permanently submit. This incident alone would have had the ultimate effect of making him a bad employee. Fortunately for the world, it put land agency and business as a serious career out of the question for him. The author of *Widowers' Houses* collecting rents as a lifelong profession is a ludicrous, an incredible incongruity. Shaw retained his place simply for the sake of financial independence. When he gave up his position, his employer was sorry to lose him, and, at the request of Shaw's father, readily gave him a handsome testimonial. In speaking of the circumstance one day, Mr. Shaw told me that he was furious that such a demand should have been made. Nothing could have shown more clearly his distaste for the position he held. "Once or twice," commented Mr. Shaw, "my employer showed himself puzzled and annoyed when some accident lifted the veil for a moment and gave him a glimpse of the fact that his excellent and pecuniarily incorruptible clerk's mind and interest and even intelligence were ten thousand leagues away, in a region foreign, if not hostile." Surely this was another age of "inspired office boys." *

In 1872, Mr. Lee left Dublin for London, the joint household broke up, and all musical activity ceased. The return to a single household on Mr. Shaw's income was all but impossible, for his affairs were as unprosperous as ever. At this time there was even some question of Bernard Shaw's two sisters becoming professional singers. With characteristic energy and decisiveness, Mrs. Shaw boldly cut the Gordian knot by going to London and becoming a professional teacher of singing. This domestic *débâcle* robbed young Shaw of his mother's influence, which was always stimulating and inspiring, if somewhat indirectly and impersonally so. It deprived him also of music, which, up to that time, had been his daily food. This sudden deprivation of the solace of music came to him as a distinct surprise. He had never dreamed of such a contingency. Fortunately the piano

* In speaking of his apprenticeship as a clerk in the land office, Shaw declares: "I should have been there still if I had not broken loose in defiance of all prudence, and become a professional man of genius—a resource not open to every clerk. I mention this to show that the fact that I am not still a clerk may be regarded for the purposes of this article as a mere accident. I am not one of those successful men who can say, 'Why don't you do as I do?'"—From *Bernard Shaw as a Clerk. By Himself* in *The Clerk*, January, 1908.

remained. Although he had never until then touched it except to pick out a tune with one finger, he now set to work in earnest to learn the art of piano playing. It was in a spirit of desperation that he went out and bought a technical handbook of music, containing a diagram of the keyboard. No finger exercises, no *études de vélocité* for Shaw: he at once got out *Don Giovanni* and tried to play the overture! It took him ten minutes to arrange his fingers on the notes of the first chord. " What I suffered, what everybody in the house suffered, whilst I struggled on, labouring through arrangements of Beethoven's symphonies, of *Tannhäuser*, and of all the operas and oratorios I knew, will never be told." It was in vain now, he said, merely to sing: " my native wood-notes wild—just then breaking frightfully— could not satisfy my intense craving for the harmony which is the emotional substance of music, and for the rhythmic figures of accompaniment which are its action and movement. I had only a single splintering voice, and I wanted an orchestra." This musical starvation it was that drove him to the piano in disregard of the rights of his fellow-lodgers.

" At the end of some months I had acquired a technique of my own, as a sample of which I may offer my fingering of the scale of C major. Instead of shifting my hand by turning
$$\overline{C\ D\ E\ F\ G\ A\ B\ C}$$
the thumb under and fingering $1\ 2\ 3\ 1\ 2\ 3\ 4\ 5$, I passed my fourth finger over my fifth,
$$\overline{C\ D\ E\ F\ G\ A\ B\ C}$$
and played $1\ 2\ 3\ 4\ 5\ 4\ 5\ 4$.
This method has the advantage of being applicable to all scales, diatonic or chromatic, and to this day I often fall back on it. Liszt and Chopin hit on it too, but they never used it to the extent I did. I soon acquired a terrible power of stumbling through pianoforte arrangements and vocal scores; and my reward was that I gained penetrating experiences of Victor Hugo and Schiller from Donizetti, Verdi, and Beethoven; of the Bible from Handel; of Goethe from Schumann; of Beaumarchais and Molière from

Mozart; and of Merimée from Bizet, besides finding in Berlioz an unconscious interpreter of Edgar Allan Poe. When I was in the schoolboy adventure vein, I could range from Vincent Wallace to Meyerbeer; and if I felt piously and genteelly sentimental, I, who could not stand the pictures of Ary Scheffer or the genteel suburban sentiment of Tennyson and Longfellow, could become quite maudlin over Mendelssohn and Gounod. And, as I searched all the music I came across for the sake of its poetic or dramatic content, and played the pages in which I found poetry or drama over and over again, whilst I never returned to those in which the music was trying to exist ornamentally for its own sake and had no real content at all, it soon followed that when I came across the consciously perfect art work in the music dramas of Wagner, I ran no risk of hopelessly misunderstanding it as the academic musicians did. Indeed, I soon found that they equally misunderstood Mozart and Beethoven, though, having come to like their tunes and harmonies, and to understand their mere carpentry, they pointed out what they supposed to be their merits with an erroneousness far more fatal to their unfortunate pupils than the volley of half-bricks with which they greeted Wagner (who, it must be confessed, retaliated with a volley of whole ones fearfully well aimed)." *

Although he did a good deal of accompanying, especially in the days of his intimacy with the Salt family, he never really mastered the instrument. Once, in a desperate emergency, he supplied the place of the absent half of the orchestra at a performance of *Il Trovatore* at a People's Entertainment evening at the Victoria Theatre—and, luckily, came off without disaster. To-day he goes to his little Bechstein piano, a relic of the first Arts and Crafts Exhibition, and fearlessly attacks any opera or symphony. He is his own Melba, his own Plançon, too, thanks, as his wife pathetically explains, to " a remarkable power of making the most extraordinary noises with his throat." He

* *The Religion of the Pianoforte,* in the *Fortnightly Review,* February, 1894.

even revels in the pianola! And I have shared his enjoyment in his own rendition of a Chopin nocturne upon that remarkable mechanical toy.

Bernard Shaw would have been a model young man at the desk but for the fact that, like Nathaniel Hawthorne at the Boston Custom House, like Ibsen at the apothecary's shop in Grimstad, his heart was not in the thing. " I never made a payment," he once frankly confessed to me, " without a hope or even a half resolve that I should never have to make it again. In spite of which, I was so wanting in enterprise and so shy and helpless in worldly matters (though I believe I had the air of being quite the reverse), that six months later I found myself making the payment again."

There gradually came to him a consciousness of the futility of his life, the consciousness of one who has been freed of illusion. In this young boy was none of the soft-blarney, the winning and dulcet melancholy, of the proverbial Irishman. He escaped that mystic influence of Roman Catholicism, which produces the phantast, the dreamer and the saint. Calvinism had taught him that " once a man is born it is too late to save him or damn him; you may ' educate ' him and ' form his character ' until you are black in the face; he is predestinate, and his soul cannot be changed any more than a silk purse can be changed into a sow's ear." In the atmosphere of the Island of the Saints— " that most mystical of all mystical things "—he learned to realize the barrenness of all else in comparison with the supreme importance of realizing the purpose of his existence on this earth.

Hence it was that his work and position finally became unbearably irksome, unendurable. London imperatively beckoned to him. That way, perhaps, lay freedom from the obsession of hated respectability, freedom from repression of his convictions, freedom for self-development and spiritual expansion. At the age of twenty, this raw Irish lad, wholly ignorant of the great world, walked out of his office, and threw himself recklessly into London. There, immediately after the death of his sister Agnes in the Isle of Wight, in 1876, he joined his mother in *la lutte*

pour la vie.* There he was to set the crystalline intellectual
clarity, the philosophic consciousness of the brilliant Celt, into
sharp juxtaposition with the plodding practicality, the dogged
energy of the complacent Briton. There he was to find the
arena for his championship of those advanced movements in art,
music, literature and politics, which give significance and character to the closing quarter of the nineteenth century.

In these early years we may discern in Shaw the gradual birth
of the social consciousness, the slow unfolding of deep-rooted
impulses toward individualism and self-expression. Like other
boys of his day and time, Shaw melted lead on Holieve, hid
rings in pancakes, and indulged in the conventional mummeries
of Christmas. But to him these were dreary, silly diversions,
against which his nature rebelled. He once refused to celebrate
Shakespeare's birthday—for the very good reason that he had
never celebrated his own. In the conventional sense, he was
never " reared " at all: he simply " grew up wild." No effort
was made to form his character: he developed from within,
strangely aloof in spirit from the healthy gaieties of the normal
lad. Thus was bred in him, even at an early age, a sort of
premature asceticism which left its indelible mark upon his
character. The puritanic convictions which have animated his
entire life find their origin in the half-instinctive, half-enforced
aloofness of his childhood days.

Shaw was not brought up, as we might expect, a Nonconformist; he was a member of the Irish Protestant Church. He
rebelled against the inhuman repression, the meaningless ritual-
ism of his church; but the influences of his home, nevertheless,
left their impress upon his nature. His whole long life is an
outcry of soaring individualism against repressive authority;
and yet the puritan intensity in condemnation of self-indulgence,
the ascetic revolt from alcoholism, speaks forth unmistakably
in the humanitarian, the vegetarian, the teetotaller of a later
epoch.

* Mr. Shaw's other sister, Miss Lucy Carr Shaw, was the immediate
cause of her mother's settling in London. She became a professional
singer, and, later, a writer. Her best known book is entitled *Five Letters
of the House of Kildonnel.*

The ingrained and constitutional protestantism of his forbears found expression in his boyish, yet rigorously atheistic protest against the religion of Moody and Sankey. In this audacious protest we can scarcely expect to find any sort of matured conviction; it is the first bold denial of his life. Thus early we observe the workings of polemic, of criticism and analysis— before he had ever left Irish soil. Even then, I fancy, he felt faint stirrings of a deeper religious protestant faith. In that protest, we may discern a forecast of the *Plays for Puritans* and *The Showing-up of Blanco Posnet*.

Thrown upon his own resources, sharing with his fellows none of the wholesome and joyous foolhardiness of youth, he developed a maturity of judgment, a detachment in observation, out of all proportion to his years. His puritanism expressed itself in silent condemnation of the social self-righteousness he saw around him, the distinctions so sharply drawn on lines, not of individual worth, but of social station and respectability. That arresting passage in *Man and Superman* in which he describes the birth of the social passion is a piece of spiritual autobiography: it changed the child into the man. There was already at work within him the leaven of the later social revolution of our own day. Intensity of political conviction was a family tradition and heritage. In the eighteenth century a Shaw had been leader of the " Orangemen "; and in the nineteenth century one of Shaw's uncles was the first Protestant priest in Ireland who, contrary to the convictions of his companions in creed, declared himself in favour of Home Rule. By heritage, by environment, by temperament, Bernard Shaw was destined to display throughout his life that intensity of political conviction, that depth of humanitarian concern, that passion for social service which will for ever remain associated with his name.

LONDON

" My destiny was to educate London, but I had neither studied my pupil nor related my ideas properly to the common stock of human knowledge."—*George Bernard Shaw: an Interview*, in *The Chap-Book*, November, 1896.

CHAPTER II

"WHEN did you first feel inclined to write?" Shaw was once asked. "I never felt inclined to write, any more than I ever felt inclined to breathe," was his perverse reply. "I felt inclined to draw: Michael Angelo was my boyish ideal. I felt inclined to be a wicked baritone in an opera when I grew out of my earlier impulse towards piracy and highway robbery. You see, as I couldn't draw, I was perfectly well aware that drawing was an exceptional gift. But it never occurred to me that my literary sense was exceptional. I gave the whole world credit for it. The fact is, there is nothing miraculous, nothing particularly interesting, even, in a natural faculty to the man who has it. The amateur, the collector, the enthusiast in an art, is the man who lacks the faculty for producing it. The Venetian wants to be a cavalry soldier; the Gaucho wants to be a sailor; the fish wants to fly, and the bird to swim. No, I never wanted to write. I know now, of course, the value and the scarcity of the literary faculty (though I think it over-rated); but I still don't want it." And he added: "You cannot want a thing and have it, too."

That Shaw did want to write, however, is clearly shown by the early outpourings of the artistic mood in the imaginative boy. When he was quite small, he concocted a short story and sent it to some boys' journal—something about a man with a gun attacking another man in the Glen of the Doons. In after years, spiritual adventures fired his soul; at this time, the gun was the centre of interest. The mimetic instinct of childhood in his case, however, found incentives to the development of almost every artistic faculty other than writing. His hours spent in the National Gallery of Ireland, his study of the literature of Italian art, filled him with the desire to be another Michael Angelo; but he couldn't draw. Like Browning, Shaw wished to be an artist, and, like Browning also, he wished to

31

be a musician. He heard music from the rising of the sun unto the going down of the same; he knew whole operas and oratorios. He wanted to be a musician, but couldn't play; to be a dramatic singer, but had no voice. The facile conqueror of every literary domain, mocked in later life with the accusation of being a sort of literary Jack-of-all-trades, was only puzzled as a youth to discover in himself a single promising potentiality.

A casual remark of an acquaintance first startled Shaw, then in his teens, into recognition of the fact that he lacked any sort of final consciousness in regard to his own position and destiny. The apprentice in the land agency office, eight or ten years Shaw's senior, who sang, " *Ah, che la morte* " with such deadly effect, one day happened to observe that every young fellow thinks that he is going to be a great man until he is twenty. " The shock that this gave me," Mr. Shaw once confessed to me with perfect naïveté, " made me suddenly aware that this was my own precise intention. But a very brief consideration reassured me—why, I don't know; for I could do nothing that gave me the smallest hope of making good my calm classification of myself as one of the world to which Shelley and Mozart and Praxiteles and Michael Angelo belonged, and as totally foreign to the plane on which land agents laboured."

In *Cashel Byron's Profession*, the hero, a prize-fighter, remarks that it is not what a man would like to do, but what he can do, that he must work at in this world. Naturally enough, Bernard Shaw, the young lad in his teens, had not yet come to any sort of artistic self-consciousness. Shaw may be said to have spent half of his life in the search for the Ultima Thule of what he *could* do. And it is by no means certain, judging from the lesson of his career, that he has yet discovered all of his capabilities. Certain it is that, at this formative stage in his career, he had found only one: the ability to keep—not to write—books. Mr. Shaw once pictured for me his state of dejection at this time over his inefficiency and incompetence. " What was wrong with me then was the want of self-respect, the diffidence, the cowardice of the ignoramus and the duffer. What saved me was my consciousness that I must learn to do something—that nothing but the possession of skill, of efficiency,

32

of mastery, in short, was of any use. The sort of aplomb which my cousins seemed to derive from the consciousness that their great-great-grandfather had also been the great-great-grandfather of Sir Robert Shaw, of Bushy Park, was denied to me. You cannot be imposed on by remote baronets if you belong to the republic of art. I was chronically ashamed and even miserable simply because I couldn't do anything. It is true that I could keep Mr. Townshend's cash, and that I never dreamt of stealing it; and riper years have made me aware that many of my artistic feats may be less highly estimated in the books of the Recording Angel than this prosaic achievement; but at this time it counted for less than nothing. It was a qualification for what I hated; and the notion of my principal actually giving me a testimonial to my efficiency as a cashier drove me to an exhibition of rage that must have seemed merely perverse to my unfortunate father."

In these days of inarticulate revolt against current religious and social ideals, Shaw somehow found an outlet for that seething lava of his spirit, which was one day to burst forth with such alarming effect. This, Shaw's first published work, was the forthright letter in *Public Opinion*, in which he sought to stem the force of the first great Moody and Sankey revival by the announcement that he, personally, had renounced religion as a delusion! Besides this single public vent for his insurgency, he had found, in the friendship of a kindred spirit of imaginative temperament, the opportunity for the expression of all the doubts, hopes and aspirations of his eager and revolutionary intelligence. With one of his schoolfellows, Shaw struck up a curious friendship: this young fellow, Edward McNulty, was afterwards known as the author of *Misther O'Ryan*, *The Son of a Peasant*, and *Maureen*,* three very original and very remarkable novels of Irish life. Both boys possessed imaginative temperaments, and their association gave promise of ripening into close and lasting friendship. But circumstances separated them so effectually that, after their schooldays, they saw very little of each other. McNulty was an official in the Bank of

* These books were published by Edward Arnold.

Ireland, and had been drafted to the Newry branch of the institution, while Shaw, as we know, was in Mr. Townshend's land office in Dublin. During the period of their separation, between Shaw's fifteenth and twentieth years, they kept up a tremendous correspondence. In this way they probably worked off the literary energy which usually produces early works. The immense letters, sometimes illustrated with crude drawings and enlivened by brief dramas, which came and went with each post, served as " exhausts " for the superfluous steam of their literary force. It was understood between them that the letters were to be destroyed as soon as answered, as their authors did not relish the possibility of such unreserved soul histories falling into strange hands.

I believe that Shaw perpetrated one more long correspondence, this time with an unnamed English lady, whose fervently imaginative novels would have made her known, Shaw once asserted, had he been able to persuade her to make her name public, or at least to stick to the same pen name, instead of changing it for every book. Shaw also made one valuable acquaintance at this time through the accident of coming to lodge in the same house with him. This was Chichester Bell, of the family of that name distinguished for its inventive genius, a cousin of Graham Bell, the inventor of the telephone, and a nephew of Melville Bell, the inventor of the phonetic script known as Visible Speech. The author of the *Standard Elocutionist,* Chichester Bell's father, whom Shaw has described as by far the most majestic and imposing looking man that ever lived on this or any other planet, was the elocution professor in one of the schools attended by Shaw in his youth, the Wesleyan Connexional, now Wesley College, attendance at which, we may be sure from Shaw's case, by no means implied Methodism.*
Although a qualified physician, Chichester Bell did not care for medical practice, and had gone to Germany, where he devoted himself to the study of chemistry and physics in the school of Helmholtz. Shaw's intercourse with Bell proved to be of great value to him. They studied Italian together, and while

* Cf. *John Bull's Other Island;* Preface for Politicians, p. xvii.

Shaw did not learn Italian with any final thoroughness, he learned a great deal else, chiefly about physics and pathology. It was through his association with Bell that he had come to read Tyndall and Trousseau's " Clinical Lectures." But Bell is to be remembered chiefly in relation to Shaw, as first calling his serious attention to Wagner. When Shaw discovered that Bell, whose judgment he held in high regard, considered Wagner a great composer, he at once bought a vocal score of *Lohengrin*, which chanced to be the only sample to be had at the Dublin music shops. From this moment dates the career of the remarkable music critic, who, in after life, swept Max Nordau off the field with his brilliant and unanswerable defence of the master-builder of modern music. For the first few bars of *Lohengrin* completely converted him. He immediately became, and ever afterwards remained, the " Perfect Wagnerite."

The days of Shaw's youth before he went to London, as we have seen, were poisoned because he was taught to bow down to proprietary respectability. But even in his " unfortunate childhood," as he calls it, his heart was so unregenerate that he secretly hated, and rebelled against, mere respectability. In after life, he found it impossible to express the relief with which he discovered that his heart was all along right, and that the current respectability of to-day is " nothing but a huge inversion of righteous and scientific social order weltering in dishonesty, uselessness, selfishness, wanton misery, and idiotic waste of magnificent opportunity for noble and happy living." Not the evangelist's but the true reformer's zeal was always Shaw's. He had too much insight not to recognize the futility of the effort to reform individuals; his humanitarian spirit was impersonal and found its freest manifestation in fulmination and revolt against social institutions. Concerning the unsocial system of setting class against class, and creed against creed, he has mordantly expressed himself:

> " If I had not suffered from these things in my childhood, perhaps I could keep my temper about them. To an outsider there is nothing but comedy in the spectacle of a forlorn set of Protestant merchants in a Catholic country, led

35

by a miniature plutocracy of stockholders, doctors and land agents, and flavoured by that section of the landed gentry who are too heavily mortgaged to escape to London, playing at being a court and an aristocracy with the assistance of the unfortunate exile who has been persuaded to accept the post of lord-lieutenant. To this pretence, involving a prodigious and continual lying, as to incomes and the social standing of relations, are sacrificed citizenship, self-respect, freedom of thought, sincerity of character, and all the realities of life, its votaries gaining in return the hostile estrangement of the great mass of their fellow countrymen, and in their own class the supercilious snubs of those who have outdone them in pretension and the jealous envy of those whom they have outdone."

The power which he found in Ireland religious enough to redeem him from this abomination of desolation was, fitly enough, the power of art. "My mother, as it happened, had a considerable musical talent. In order to exercise it seriously she had to associate with other people who had musical talent. My first childish doubt as to whether God could really be a good Protestant was suggested by my observation of the deplorable fact that the best voices available for combination with my mother's in the works of the great composers had been unaccountably vouchsafed to Roman Catholics. Even the divine gentility was presently called in question, for some of these vocalists were undeniably connected with retail trade."

The situation in which Mrs. Shaw found herself offered no alternative. "There was no help for it; if my mother was to do anything but sing silly ballads in drawing-rooms she had to associate herself on an entirely republican footing with people of like artistic gifts, without the smallest reference to creed or class. Nay, if she wished to take part in the masses of Haydn and Mozart, which had not then been forgotten, she must actually permit herself to be approached by Roman Catholic priests and even, at their invitation, to enter that house of Belial, the Roman Catholic chapel (in Ireland the word church, as applied to a place of worship, denotes the Protestant denomination),

36

and take part in their services. All of which led directly to the discovery, hard to credit at first, that a Roman Catholic priest could be as agreeable and cultivated a person as a Protestant clergyman was supposed, in defiance of bitter experience, always to be; and, in short, that the notion that the courtly distinctions of Dublin society corresponded to any real human distinctions was as ignorant as it was pernicious. If religion is that which binds men to one another, and irreligion that which sunders, then must I testify that I found the religion of my country in its musical genius and its irreligion in its churches and drawing-rooms."

It was unerring common sense on the domestic plane, acquiescence in the sole solution of a flinty problem of life, which reveals Shaw's mother to us as the parent from whom he derived his determination, and his firm grip on practical affairs. In marked contradistinction to Lee, Mrs. Shaw made no concessions to fashion, firmly adhering to her master's old method in all its rigour. She behaved with complete independence of manner and speech in the mode of an Irish lady confronted with English people openly describing themselves as " middle-class." On account of this characteristic independence her first experiences in London were unfortunate and disheartening. Not until she began to teach choirs in schools did she enter upon the road of complete success. The results she produced in these undertakings so pleased the inspectors—and more particularly the parents at the prize distributions—that the head mistresses were sensible enough to let her go her own way. Quite a conclusive proof of her ability is found in the fact that this remarkable woman, vigorous and young-minded to-day although now in the seventies, worked at that famous modern institution, the North Collegiate School for Girls, until quite recently. For some years she sought to retire for the same reason that she stopped singing: to her Irish sense of humour there was an element almost of the ridiculous in a first-rate school having an old woman of between seventy and eighty wave a stick and conduct a choir. But D. Sophia Bryant, the principal and an old friend of hers, could not see her way to change for the better, and it was only within the last year or two that Mrs. Shaw retired from her post. No doubt Mrs. Bryant was right; for Mr. Shaw once remarked to me that it was not an easy matter to find a woman in England who perfectly combines the ability to take command in music with the knowledge of music as an artist, and not as a school-mistress who has superficially studied the subject for the sake of the certificates and the position.

Mr. Shaw's mother is the most remarkably youthful person for her years I have ever known, with the possible exception of Mark Twain. I remember with vivid pleasure taking tea with her and her son one afternoon at her attractive little " retreat " in West London. Her eyes danced with suppressed mirth as she talked, and it was quite easy to see from whom her son derived his strong sense of humour. Mrs. Shaw told several delightful stories, one of which deserves repetition here. It seems that Mrs. Shaw is quite a medium and spiritualist, and takes a great deal of interest in communicating with " spirits " from the other world. One day she " called up " Mr. Shaw's sister and asked her what she thought of George being such a distinguished man. The spirit expressed surprise to hear the news. " But aren't you very proud of George? " queried his mother disappointedly. " Oh, yes," replied the spirit; " it's all very well in its way. But," she added, " that sort of thing doesn't count for anything up here "!

Many of Mr. Shaw's very distinctive traits are a direct inheritance from his mother, modified, to be sure, by the differences in education, temperament and views of life. In her teaching of music, Mrs. Shaw deliberately displayed total insensibility to the petty dignities so cherished in English school-life. Upon visiting rectors, head mistresses, local " personages," and, in fact, upon all those who wished things done their own way, she made what her son called " perfectly indiscriminate onslaughts." This aggressive assertion of her authority would often have made her position untenable, had it not been for her patent ability and unquestioned power of leadership. Her outspoken frankness of manner and conduct, reproduced with such comically extravagant excess in her son, always won her the support of the discriminating: it was always the real " bigwigs " who understood her manners. Mr. Shaw once said: "From my mother I derive my brains and character, which do her credit." I remember asking Mr. Shaw's mother one day to what she attributed her son's remarkable success in the world of letters. "Oh," she said, without a moment's hesitation, her eyes twinkling merrily the while, "the answer is quite simple. Of course, he owes it all to me."

To his parents, his mother in particular, Mr. Shaw is also indebted for actual financial support during several years of an able-bodied young manhood. But he has warned us against supposing, because he is a man of letters, that he never tried to commit that "sin against his nature" called earning an honest living. We have followed his struggles from his fifteenth to his twentieth year—a period marking a social and spiritual growth on his part, he maintains, of several centuries. "I was born on the outskirts of an Irish city, where we lived exactly as people lived in the seventeenth century, except that there were gas-lamps and policemen in tall hats. In the course of my boyhood literature and music introduced me to the eighteenth century; and I was helped a step further through the appearance in our house of candles that did not need snuffing, an iron-framed pianoforte and typhoid sanitation. Finally, I crossed St. George's Channel into the decadence of the mid-nineteenth-century England of Anthony Trollope, and slowly made my way to the forefront of the age—the period of Ibsen, Nietzsche, the Fabian Society, the motor-car, and my own writings." Very slowly indeed did he make his way to the forefront of the age of Shavianism. He felt that he was a man of genius, and coolly classified himself as such. With no effort of the imagination, and, likewise, with no prevision of his subsequent oft-repeated failures and the position of pecuniary dependence he was temporarily to occupy, he found himself looking upon London as his destiny. There is something at once amusing, inspiring, and pathetic in the spectacle of this bashful, raw, inexperienced boy, fortified only by the confident consciousness of his yet unproved superiority to the "common run" of humanity, throwing himself thus headlong into London.

Little of romantic glamour, fittingly enough, attaches to

39

Shaw's early struggles in London. No rapt listening to the songs of rival nightingales, Keats and Shelley, as with Browning; no impetuous and clandestine marriage, as with Sheridan; no roses and raptures of *la vie Bohème*, as with Zola. It is, instead, for the most part a tale of consistent literary drudgery, rewarded by continual and repeated failures. The rare and individual style of the satirist, the deft fingering of the dramatist were wholly undeveloped, and even unsuspected, during this tentative period in his career. He turned his hand to various undertakings—to musical criticism, to versifying, to blank-versifying, to novel-writing; but all equally to no purpose. Asked once what was his first real success, he replied: " Never had any. Success in that sense is a thing that comes to you and takes your breath away. What came to me was invariably failure. By the time I wore it down I knew too much to care about either failure or success. Life is like a battle; you have to fire a thousand bullets to hit one man. I was too busy firing to bother about the scoring. As to whether I ever despaired, you will find somewhere in my works this line: ' He who has never hoped can never despair.' I am not a fluctuator." His self-sufficiency, even at this time, was proof against all discouragement. Perhaps he found consolation also in the saying: " He who is down need fear no fall."

Shaw never experienced any poverty of spirit, of determination, or of will; his poverty was pecuniary only. Until the time of his marriage he remained secure from the accusation of being the mould of fashion or the glass of form. While the Shaw of matrimonial respectability bears all the marks of his wife's civilizing influence in the matter of a *costume de rigueur* —fashionable clothes, patent-leather boots, and even, on rare occasions, a " stiff " collar—his dress in the late seventies and for twenty years thereafter was usually, like that of Marchbanks, strikingly anarchic. His outward appearance, as someone unkindly remarked, suggested that he might be a fairly respectable plasterer! " Now," said Shaw in 1896, " when people reproach me with the unfashionableness of my attire, they forget that to me it seems like the raiment of Solomon in all his glory by contrast with the indescribable seediness of those days, when

I trimmed my cuffs to the quick with scissors, and wore a tall hat and *soi-disant* black coat, green with decay." But the poverty of which this attire was the outward, visible sign was " shortness of cash," as numerous personal reminiscences show. From the depressing and devitalizing effects of " real poverty " he was strong enough to free himself, as the following autobiographical confidence clearly evidences:

" Whilst I am not sure that the want of money lames a poor man more than the possession of it lames a rich one, I am quite sure that the class which has the pretensions and prejudices and habits of the rich without its money, and the poverty of the poor without the freedom to avow poverty—in short, the people who don't go to the theatre because they cannot afford the stalls and are ashamed to be seen in the gallery—are the worst-off of all. To be on the down grade from the *haute bourgeoisie* and the landed gentry to the nadir at which the younger son's great-grandson gives up the struggle to keep up appearances; to have the pretence of a culture without the reality of it; to make three hundred pounds a year look like eight hundred pounds in Ireland or Scotland; or five hundred pounds look like one thousand pounds in London; to be educated neither at the Board School and the Birkbeck nor at the University, but at some rotten private adventure academy for the sons of gentlemen; to try to maintain a select circle by excluding all the frankly poor people from it, and then find that all the rest of the world excludes you—that is poverty at its most damnable; and yet from that poverty a great deal of our literature and journalism has sprung. Think of the frightful humiliation of the boy Dickens in the blacking warehouse, and his undying resentment of his mother's wanting him to stay there—all on a false point of genteel honour. Think of Trollope, at an upper-class school with holes in his trousers, because his father could not bring himself to dispense with a man-servant. Ugh! Be a tramp or be a millionaire—it matters little which: what *does* matter is being a poor relation of

41

~ the rich; and that is the very devil. Fortunately, that sort of poverty can be cured by simply shaking off its ideas—cutting your coat according to your cloth, and not according to the cloth of your father's second cousin, the baronet. As I was always more or less in rebellion against those ideas, and finally shook them off pretty completely, I cannot say that I have much experience of real poverty— quite the contrary." *

With that comic seriousness which always passes for outrageous prevarication, Shaw has related that during the nine years from 1876 to 1885 his adventures in literature netted him the princely sum of exactly six pounds. At first he " devilled " for a musical critic; but his notices " led to the stoppage of all the concert advertisements and ruined the paper "—" which died—partly of me." He also began a Passion Play in blank verse, with the mother of the hero represented as a termagant. Ah, if that play had only been finished! But Shaw never carried through these customary follies of young authors, unless we agree with those who classify his novels as follies of a green boy. " I was always, fortunately for me," Mr. Shaw once remarked, " a failure as a trifler. All my attempts at Art for Art's sake broke down; it was like hammering tenpenny nails into sheets of notepaper."

One finds it an easy matter to believe him when he tells us, not only that he was provincial, unpresentable, but, more broadly speaking, that he was in an impossible position. " I was a foreigner—an Irishman, the most foreign of all foreigners when he has not gone through the University mill. I was . . . not uneducated; but, unfortunately, what I knew was exactly what the educated Englishman did not know, and what he knew—I either didn't know or didn't believe." Six pounds was a very small allowance for a growing young man, even a struggling author, to live on for nine years. Even if we match him with equal scepticism, at least we can discover, as will be seen, no

* *Who I Am, and What I Think,* by G. Bernard Shaw. Part I.—In the *Candid Friend,* May 11th, 1901.

error in his arithmetical calculations. After Shaw had hounded the musical critic and his paper to the grave, London absolutely refused to tolerate him on any terms. As the nine years progressed, he had one article accepted by Mr. G. R. Sims, who had just started a short-lived paper called *One and All.* "It brought me fifteen shillings. Full of hope and gratitude, I wrote a really brilliant contribution. That finished me." During this period, he received his greatest fee—five pounds—for a patent medicine advertisement, a circumstance which may give some colour to Dr. Meyerfeld's early denunciation of Shaw as a "quacksalver." On another occasion, a publisher asked Shaw for some verses to fit some old blocks which he had bought up for a school prize book. "I wrote a parody of the thing he wanted and sent it as a joke. To my stupefaction he thanked me seriously, and paid me five shillings." Shaw was so much touched by the gift of five shillings for his parody that he wrote the generous publisher a serious verse for another picture. With the startling result that the publisher took it as a joke in questionable taste! Is it any wonder that Shaw's career as a versifier abruptly ended?

The analysis of the artistic temperament which Shaw puts in the mouth of John Tanner—an analysis which Mr. Robert Loraine finds to smack more of mania than of insincerity— is a cynical and distorted picture at best. And yet it gives us a refracted glimpse of the position which Shaw himself deliberately assumed. "The true artist," Tanner rattles on, "will let his wife starve, his children go barefoot, his mother drudge for his living at seventy, sooner than work at anything but his art. To women he is half vivisector, half vampire. He gets into intimate relations with them to study them, to strip the mask of convention from them, to surprise their inmost secrets, knowing that they have the power to rouse his deepest creative energies, to rescue him from his cold reason, to make him see visions and dream dreams, to inspire him, as he calls it. He persuades women that they may do this for their own purpose, whilst he really means them to do it for his." After various attempts "to earn an honest living," Shaw gave up trying to commit that sin against his nature, as he puts it.

His last attempt was in 1879, we are told, " when a company was formed in London to exploit an ingenious invention by Mr. Thomas Alva Edison—a much too ingenious invention, as it proved, being nothing less than a telephone of such stentorian efficiency that it bellowed your most private communications all over the house instead of whispering them with some sort of discretion." His interest in physics, his acquaintance with the works of Tyndall and Helmholtz, and his friendship with Mr. Chichester Bell, of which mention has been made, gave him, he asserts, the customary superiority over those about him which he is in the habit of claiming in all the relations of life. While he remained with the company only a few months, he discharged his duties in a manner, which, according to his own outrageous and comically prevaricative assertion, " laid the foundation of Mr. Edison's London reputation."

After this experience, he began, as he says, to lay the foundations of his own fortune " by the most ruthless disregard of all the quack duties which lead the peasant lad of fiction to the White House, and harness the real peasant boy to the plough until he is finally swept, as rubbish, into the workhouse." Far from being a " peasant lad," who climbed manfully upward from the lowest rung of the social ladder, he was in reality the son of a gentleman who had an income of at least three figures (four, if you count in dollars instead of pounds), and was second cousin to a baronet. " I never climbed any ladder: I have achieved eminence by sheer gravitation; and I hereby warn all peasant lads not to be duped by my pretended example into regarding their present servitude as a practicable first step to a celebrity so dazzling that its subject cannot even suppress his own bad novels."

Shaw seems intent upon convincing us that, like the artist of his own description, he was an atrocious egotist in his disregard of others; but we must take his confessions with the customary grain of salt. " I was an able-bodied and able-minded young man in the strength of my youth; and my family, then heavily embarrassed, needed my help urgently. That I should have chosen to be a burden to them instead was, according to all the conventions of peasant fiction, monstrous. Well, without a blush

I embraced the monstrosity. I did not throw myself into the struggle for life: I threw my mother into it. I was not a staff to my father's old age: I hung on to his coat tails. His reward was to live just long enough to read a review of one of these silly novels written in an obscure journal by a personal friend of my own (now eminent in literature as Mr. John Mackinnon Robertson) prefiguring me to some extent as a considerable author. I think, myself, that this was a handsome reward, far better worth having than a nice pension from a dutiful son struggling slavishly for his parents' bread in some sordid trade. Handsome or not, it was the only return he ever had for the little pension he contrived to export from Ireland for his family. My mother reinforced it by drudging in her elder years at the art of music which she had followed in her prime freely for love. I only helped to spend it. People wondered at my heartlessness: one young and romantic lady had the courage to remonstrate openly and indignantly with me, ' for the which,' as Pepys said of the shipwright's wife who refused his advances, ' I did respect her.' Callous as Comus to moral babble, I steadily wrote my five pages a day and made a man of myself (at my mother's expense) instead of a slave."

In Shaw's opinion, his brain constituted the sum and substance of his riches. The projection and exposition of his experience came to be the most urgent need and object of his life. He recognized a higher duty than merely earning his living: the fulfilment of his individual destiny. He resolved to become a writer. In this resolve to dedicate all his powers to the art of self-expression, lies the explanation of his strange words: " My mother worked for my living instead of preaching that it was my duty to work for hers; therefore, take off your hat to her and blush." *

Although it was a " frightful squeeze " at times, Shaw was not wholly destitute. A suit of evening clothes and the knack of playing a " simple accompaniment at sight more congenially to a singer than most amateurs," gave him " for a fitful year

* *The Irrational Knot,* Preface to the American edition of 1905, Brentanos, N. Y.

or so," the *entrée* into the better circle of musical society in London.

In this latter day of his assertion that money controls morality, Shaw is perfectly consistent in speaking of his poverty and quotidian shabbiness as the two " disgusting faults " of his youth. But at the time he did not recognize them as faults, because he could not help them. " I therefore tolerated the gross error that poverty, though an inconvenience and a trial, is not a sin and a disgrace: and I stood for my self-respect on the things I had: probity, ability, knowledge of art, laboriousness, and whatever else came cheaply to me." A certain pride of birth, a consciousness of worthy ancestry, also sustained him, and helped him to triumph over circumstance. It was this same feeling which gave him suavity and poise during the later campaigns of his revolutionary Socialism, and saved him from the excesses, the blind fury, of the mere proletarian. He had a magnificent library in Bloomsbury, a priceless picture-gallery in Trafalgar Square, and another at Hampton Court, without any servants to look after or rent to pay. During these years Shaw's gain in the cultivation of his musical and artistic tastes more than compensated for his lack of the advantages of wealth. Nor were his essays in literature and criticism—I do not refer to his playful dilettantism—profitless in any real sense. It is true that innumerable articles were consistently returned to him; and yet he went his way undismayed, slowly saturating himself with Italian art from Mantegna to Michael Angelo, with the best music from London to Bayreuth. And while London had not " caught his tone," musical or otherwise, at this time, the day was to come in which he should reap the reward for his critical knowledge of art and music, for the rare and individual style which he was slowly perfecting.

To the student of Shaw as the *littérateur*—the highwayman who " held up " so many different forms of art—the chief interest of this period is to be found in the five novels which he wrote during the five years from 1879 to 1883—an average of one a year. His first novel, written in 1879, and called, " with merciless fitness " as Shaw says, *Immaturity*, was never published; and we are told that even the rats were unable to finish

SHAW AT THE AGE OF TWENTY-THREE.

From a photograph taken in London, July 4th, 1879.

[Facing p. 46

it. George Meredith, the novelist, who was a reader and literary adviser for the publishing firm of Chapman and Hall, London, from 1860 to 1897, rejected the manuscript of *Immaturity, sans phrase*—quickly disposing of it with a laconic " No." The remaining four have all been published, in magazines and in book-form, either in England or America. Shaw " turned them out," one each year, with unvarying regularity and also with unvarying result: refusal by the publishers. That six pounds which Shaw earned in nine years must certainly have gone a long way—as postage stamps.

Mr. Shaw has carefully explained to us why his works were refused by publisher after publisher. And I find no reason to question his explanation to the effect that it was the world-old struggle between literary conscience and public taste. The more he progressed towards his own individual style, and ventured upon the freer expression of his own ideas, the more he disappointed the " grave, elderly lovers of literature." As to the regular novel-publishing houses, whose readers were merely on the scent of popularity, they gave him, we are told, no quarter at all. " And so between the old stool of my literary conscientiousness and the new stool of a view of life that did not reach publishing point in England until about ten years later, when Ibsen drove it in, my novels fell to the ground."

We may omit for the present any discussion of the validity of Mr. Shaw's claims as a " fictionist." But the story of the circumstances under which the novels finally found their way into print is certainly worthy of narration. It was in 1882 that Henry George, by a speech during one of the public meetings at the Memorial Hall, Farringdon Street, London, fired Shaw to enlist, in Heine's phrase, " as a soldier in the Liberative War of Humanity." * About this time a body, styling itself the Land Reform Union, which still survives as the English Land Restoration League, was formed to propagate Georgite Land Nationalization. The official mouthpiece of this body was called, if memory serves, the *Christian Socialist*, which did not last long, owing, as Shaw said, to a lack of Christians. Shaw made

* *Cf.* Chapter IV., *The Fabian Society.*

a number of lifelong friends through his connection with this organization, which he joined soon after its formation. Chief among these may be mentioned James Leigh Joynes, Sydney Olivier and Henry Hyde Champion; other acquaintances were two Christian Socialist clergymen—Stewart Headlam and Symes of Nottingham. Shaw and Symes frequently indulged in wordy warfare over the respective merits of Socialism and Land Nationalization as universal panaceas for social evils. Symes argued that Land Nationalization would settle everything, to which Shaw cleverly and characteristically replied, as he once told me, that if capital were still privately appropriated Symes would remain " the chaplain of a pirate ship." It is proof of Shaw's fundamental Socialism that he still regards this as a very fair description of the position of a clergyman under our present system.

Through his association with James Leigh Joynes and the Salt family it is not difficult to trace Shaw's initial feeling for Shelley, and the origin and growth of his humanitarian and vegetarian principles. At this time Joynes had just been deprived of his Eton post because he had made a tour in Ireland with Henry George and been arrested with him under the Coercion Act by the police, who did not understand Land Nationalization and supposed the two to be emissaries of the Clan na Gael. Henry Salt, another Eton master, to whom Joynes' sister was married, was not only, like Joynes, a vegetarian, a humanitarian, a Shelleyan, but a De Quinceyite as well. Being a born revolutionist, he loathed Eton; and as soon as he had saved enough to live with a Thoreau-like simplicity in a labourer's cottage in the country, he threw up his post and shook the dust of Eton from his feet. In company with Joynes, Shaw visited the Salts once before they left Eton. It is interesting in this connection to read an absurdly amusing description, written by Shaw, of his first visit to them in the country at Tilford—an article entitled *A Sunday on the Surrey Hills.**

There were no children in the family; and one of Shaw's chief amusements while visiting the Salts was to play endless piano-

* The *Pall Mall Gazette,* April 28th, 1888.

forte duets with Mrs. Salt, on what he called "the noisiest grand piano that ever descended from Eton to a Surrey cottage." Salt found his *métier*, not in Socialism, but in humanitarianism. He founded the Humanitarian League, of which he is still secretary. This association of Shaw with the Salt family eventuated in close and warm mutual friendship. Many were the visits Shaw paid them at this time and in later years. It was in the heather on Limpsfield Common, during his visits to them at Oxford, that he wrote several of the scenes of his *Plays, Pleasant and Unpleasant.*

In this association may be discovered the real link between Shaw and the Humanitarians. For twenty-five years Shaw was a "cannibal," according to his own damning verdict. For the remainder of his life he has been a strict vegetarian, professing his principles with a comic force equalled only by the rigour with which he puts them into practice. While the most of men in their boyhood have walked about with a cheap edition of Shelley in their pockets, it is a tiresome trait in Shaw, someone has slightingly remarked, that he has never taken this cheap edition out. Shelley it was, certainly, who first called Shaw's attention to the "infamy of his habits." And it is also true that Shaw has never discarded his vegetarian principles, never repudiated Shelley's humane views and ideals of life. "It may require some reflection," Shaw once wrote, "to see that high feeling brings high thinking; but we already know, without reflection, that high thinking brings what is called plain living. In this century the world has produced two men—Shelley and Wagner—in whom intense poetic feeling was the permanent state of their consciousness, and who were certainly not restrained by any religious, conventional or prudential considerations from indulging themselves to the utmost of their opportunities. Far from being gluttonous, drunken, cruel or debauched, they were apostles of vegetarianism and water-drinking; had an utter horror of violence and 'sport'; were notable champions of the independence of women; and were, in short, driven into open revolution against the social evils which the average sensual man finds extremely suitable to him. So much is this the case that the practical doctrine of these two arch-voluptuaries always presents itself to ordinary persons as a saint-like asceticism." *

At the time of the mutual intimacy of Joynes, Shaw, and the Salts, and their unhesitating approval and admiration of Shelley, early in the eighties, vegetarian restaurants began to be established here and there throughout the country. These scattered restaurants, Mr. Shaw once remarked in connection with his own conversion to the faith of Shelley, " made vegetarianism possible for a man too poor to be catered for." † It is hardly open to doubt that, while Shelley first called Shaw's attention to vegetarianism, it was Joynes and Salt who first confirmed him in the belief, which soon became solidified into a hard-and-fast principle, that " the enormity of eating the scorched corpses of animals—cannibalism with its heroic dish omitted—becomes impossible the moment it becomes consciously instead of thoughtlessly habitual."

Another member of this coterie, in which there was no question of Henry George and Karl Marx, but a great deal of Walt Whitman and Thoreau, was the now well-known Socialist and author, Edward Carpenter, whose *Towards Democracy* and other works are a faithful reflex of the man. It became the habit of these early apostles of " the simple life " to wear sandals; Carpenter even wore his out of doors. He had taught the secret of their manufacture to a workman friend of his at Millthorpe, a village near Sheffield, where he resided. Not unfittingly, the habitual wearer of moccasins, Carpenter, was always called The Noble Savage by the members of this congenial and delightful circle. The noisy grand piano grew noisier than ever when Shaw and Carpenter visited the Salts— Carpenter, like Shaw, revelling in pianoforte duets with Mrs. Salt.

The death of Joynes was a great grief to these close friends,

* *The Religion of the Pianoforte.* In the *Fortnightly Review,* February, 1894.

† Mr. Shaw's confessions in regard to his change from " cannibalism " to vegetarianism are perhaps best given in an article in the *Pall Mall Gazette* for January 26th, 1886, entitled, *Failures of Inept Vegetarians. By an Expert.*

especially to Shaw. I am convinced that those mordantly incisive and penetrating attacks which Shaw, in after life, made upon modern surgery and modern medicine find their animus in his resentment of the manner of Joynes' death. Certain passages from *The Philanderer* and *The Conflict of Science and Common Sense* thus become more humanly comprehensible. The literary activities of this circle, so sadly broken up by the death of Joynes, were by no means confined solely to Carpenter and Shaw. Joynes himself left a volume of excellent translations of the revolutionary songs of the German revolutionists of 1848 —Herwegh, Freiligrath and others.* Salt, whom Shaw has occasionally quoted, has published several monographs, his tastes and predilections revealing themselves in the names of Shelley, James Thomson, Jeffries and De Quincey.

The Socialist revival of the eighties is responsible for the final publication of Shaw's novels. As long as he kept sending them to the publishers, " they were as safe from publicity as they would have been in the fire." But as soon as he flung them aside as failures, with a strange perversity, " they almost instantly began to show signs of life." Among the crop of propagandist magazines which accompanied the Socialistic revival of the eighties was one called *To-Day*—not the present paper of that name, but one of the many " To-Days which are now Yesterdays." It was printed by Henry Hyde Champion, but there were several joint editors, of brief tenure, among whom were Belfort Bax, the well-known Socialist, and James Leigh Joynes. Although publishing his novels in this magazine, which it seems paid nothing for contributions, " seemed a matter of no more consequence than stuffing so many window-panes with them," Shaw nevertheless offered up *An Unsocial Socialist* and *Cashel Byron's Profession* on this unstable altar of his political faith.†

---

* For a brief and illuminative biographical sketch of James Leigh Joynes, compare Shaw's review of his book, *Songs of a Revolutionary Epoch,* in the *Pall Mall Gazette,* April 16th, 1888.

† The first instalment of *An Unsocial Socialist* appeared in *To-Day,* a " monthly magazine of Scientific Socialism," New Series, Vol. I. (January-June, 1884), March number, pp. 205-220. The final instalment appeared in New Series, Vol. II., of the same magazine (July-December, 1884), December number, pp. 543-579. The novel appeared under Shaw's name,

With one noteworthy exception, there were no visible results from the serial publications of these two novels. Shaw's novels, not uncharacteristically, appeared in inverse order of composition; and number five, *An Unsocial Socialist*, made Shaw acquainted with William Morris, an acquaintance which, as we shall see, ripened later into genuine and sincere friendship. To Shaw's surprise, as he tells us, William Morris had been reading the monthly instalments with a certain relish—a proof to Shaw's mind " how much easier it is to please a great man than a little one, especially when you share his politics."

Another propagandist magazine, created after the passing of *To-day*, and called *Our Corner*, was published by Mrs. Annie Besant, with whom Shaw had become acquainted about the time he joined the Fabian Society. " She was an incorrigible benefactress," Shaw says, " and probably revenged herself for my freely expressed scorn for this weakness by drawing on her private account to pay me for my jejune novels." Up to this time, all Shaw's literary productions seemed to have the deadly effect of driving their media of circulation to an early grave. After *The Irrational Knot* and *Love Among the Artists* had run through its pages in serial form, *Our Corner* likewise succumbed to the inevitable.*

To Shaw's expressed regret, *Cashel Byron's Profession* found one staunch admirer at least. This was Henry Hyde Champion, who had thrown up a commission in the Army at the call of Socialism. This admiration for Shaw's realistic exposure of pugilism—Mr. Shaw once told me that he always considered admiration of *Cashel Byron's Profession* the mark of a fool!

and is marked at the close (page 579), " The End," and dated beneath, " London, 1883," the date of composition. *Cashel Byron's Profession* ran in the same magazine through the years 1885 and 1886, beginning in New Series, Vol. III. (January-June, 1885), April number, pp. 145-160, and concluding in Vol. V. (January-June, 1886), March number, pp. 67-73.

* *The Irrational Knot* began in Vol. V. (January-June, 1885), pp. 229-240, ran through Vols. VI., VII. and VIII., and was concluded in Vol. IX. (January-June, 1887), ending on page 82. *Love Among the Artists* opened in Vol. X. (July-December, 1887) of the same magazine, ran through Vol. XI., and was concluded in Vol. XII. (July-December, 1888), on page 352. It is marked at the close (page 352), " The End, London, 1881 "—the date of composition.

—had very momentous consequences. Champion, it seems, had an " unregenerate taste for pugilism "—a pugnacious survival of his abdicated adjutancy. " He liked ' Cashel Byron ' so much that he stereotyped the pages of *To-Day* which it occupied, and in spite of my remonstrances, hurled on the market a misshapen shilling edition. My friend, Mr. William Archer, reviewed it prominently; the *Saturday Review*, always susceptible in those days to the arts of self-defence, unexpectedly declared it the novel of the age; Mr. W. E. Henley wanted to have it dramatized; Stevenson wrote a letter about it . . . ; the other papers hastily searched their waste-paper baskets for it and reviewed it, mostly rather disappointedly; the public preserved its composure and did not seem to care." This letter of Stevenson's to William Archer,* written at Saranac Lake in the winter of 1887-8, contains some very interesting criticism, as a quotation will show:

"What am I to say? I have read your friend's book with singular relish. If he has written any other, I beg you will let me see it; and if he has not, I beg him to lose no time in supplying the deficiency. It is full of promise, but I should like to know his age. There are things in it that are very clever, to which I attach no importance; it is the shape of the age. And there are passages, particularly the rally in the presence of the Zulu King, that show genuine and remarkable narrative talent—a talent that few will have the wit to understand, a talent of strength, spirit, capacity, sufficient vision, and sufficient self-sacrifice, which last is the chief point in a narrative."

And at the end of his next letter to Mr. Archer (February, 1888), he says " Tell Shaw to hurry up. I want another."

Neither Shaw nor Champion earned anything from that first shilling edition, " which began with a thousand copies, but proved immortal." Shortly after this first edition was exhausted, the publishing house of Walter Scott and Company

* Published, in part, in *The Letters of Robert Louis Stevenson,* Vol. II., edited by Sidney Colvin.

placed a revised shilling edition on the market; and the book was also published in New York at about the same time (Harper and Brothers, New York, 1887). Brentanos, New York, brought out an edition in 1897, and this was followed in 1899 by an edition of *An Unsocial Socialist.*

The immediate cause of these editions was the temporary interest in the works of Mr. Shaw, occasioned by Mr. Richard Mansfield's notable productions of *Arms and the Man* and *The Devil's Disciple*. The publication of *Plays, Pleasant and Unpleasant*, in two volumes, by H. S. Stone and Company, of Chicago, followed shortly afterwards. In 1904, when Mr. Daly's production of *Candida* created such a stir in America, Mr. Volney Streamer, of the firm of Brentanos, a Shaw enthusiast of many years' standing, used his influence to have these two books reprinted. None of Shaw's novels are copyright in America, so that he has never, it appears, reaped the reward of the moderate, although intermittent, vogue which his novels have enjoyed in that country. It is a fact of common knowledge that Shaw prefers to be judged by his later work; but the demand in America for these novels has been so large that they are likely to be published for years yet to come. In 1889 or 1890, it must have been, Shaw happened to notice that his novels were " raging in America," and that the list of book sales in one of the United States was headed by a novel entitled *An Unsocial Socialist*. In the preface to the " Authorized Edition " of *Cashel Byron's Profession*, which contains the history of the life and death of the novels, Mr. Shaw says, " As it was clearly unfair that my own American publishers (H. S. Stone and Company) should be debarred by delicacy towards me from exploiting the new field of derelict fiction, I begged them to make the most of their inheritance; and with my full approval Opus 3, called ' Love Among the Artists ' (a paraphrase of the forgotten line ' Love Among the Roses ') followed." †

* The *New York Herald* contained the statement that " Brentanos have done a service to literature in reprinting two of Shaw's novels that are strangely unfamiliar to the American public."

† This book was published in 1900, followed in 1901 by the " Authorized Edition " of *Cashel Byron's Profession* (also published by H. S. Stone and

This third act of Shaw's "tragedy," as he calls it, is by no means the end of the play; as with Thomas Hardy's endless dramas, the curtain may never be rung down. One might imagine that Shaw, the Socialist, required the patience of a Job and the self-repression of a stoic to enable him to restrain his anger over the diversion of the rewards of his talent from his own to the pockets of Capitalist publishers, free of all obligation to the author. But he accepts his fate with breezy philosophy.

"I may say," he wrote to Harper and Brothers (who had published his *Cashel Byron's Profession*) in November, 1899, "that I entirely disagree with the ideas of twenty years ago as to the 'piratical' nature of American republications of non-copyright books. Unlike most authors, I am enough of an economist to know that unless an American publisher acquires copyright he can no more make a profit at my expense than he can at Shakspere's by republishing *Hamlet*. The English nation, when taxed for the support of the author by a price which includes author's royalties, whilst the American nation escapes that burden, may have a grievance against the American nation, but that is a very different thing from a grievance of the author against the American publisher." *

"Suffice it to say here that there can be no doubt now that the novels so long left for dead in the forlorn-hope magazines of the eighties have arisen and begun to propagate themselves

Co.), which contains the above-quoted remark. In the autumn of 1901, Grant Richards, at the time the English publisher of almost all of Mr. Shaw's works, also brought out a revised edition of *Cashel Byron's Profession*. In the autumn of 1904 *The Irrational Knot* was for the first time published in book form by Archibald Constable and Co., Mr. Shaw's English publishers at present. In 1905 *The Irrational Knot* was published in America by Brentanos.

* On publishing his *Cashel Byron's Profession*, Harper and Brothers sent Mr. Shaw ten pounds in recognition of his moral right as an author to share any profits the book might yield. There were then no international copyright laws in force, and the works of foreign authors were not protected in America. When Mr. Shaw learned that this same book had been republished by another American house, he sent back to Harper and Brothers the ten pounds, with thanks for its use, explaining that since the book had been republished by another firm, even his moral claim to recognition by the original American publishers had lapsed.

vigorously throughout the New World at the rate of a dollar and a half per copy, free of all royalty to the flattered author." He begs for absolution from blame " if these exercises of a raw apprentice break loose again and insist on their right to live. The world never did know chalk from cheese in the matter of art; and, after all, since it is only the young and old who have time to read—the rest being too busy living—my exercises may be fitter for the market than my masterpieces."

In 1883, when the last of the novels of his nonage was completed, Shaw was still striking in the dark. He had not yet found the opening into the light, the portal giving out from the stuffy world of imaginative lying into the great world of real life—a life of pleasurable activity, strenuous endeavour, and high achievement. He found his way out by following an insistent summons—the clarion call of Henry George. And when, having doffed the swaddling clothes of romance, he emerged from the dim retreat of his imagination, it was to find himself standing in the dazzling light of a new day—the day of Socialism, of the Fabian Society, and—of George Bernard Shaw.

THE NOVELIST

"London was not ripe for me. Nor was I ripe for London. I was in an impossible position. I was a foreigner—an Irishman, the most foreign of all foreigners when he has not gone through the University mill. I was . . . not uneducated; but, unfortunately, what I knew was exactly what the educated Englishman didn't know or didn't believe."—*George Bernard Shaw: an Interview.* In *The Chap-Book,* November, 1896.

CHAPTER III

AS a young man of twenty-four, Bernard Shaw began to evolve a moral code. He perceived in those phases of contemporary existence which either intimately touched his life or daily challenged his critical scrutiny, a shocking discrepancy between things as they are and things as they should be. He has never been a " whole hogger," like Pope or Omar Khayyam: he neither believed that whatever is is right nor wished to shatter this sorry scheme of things *entire*. The arch-foe of idealism, he paradoxically prefaced his attack by hoisting the banner of an ideal. Shaw has spent more than a quarter of a century in formulating his ideal, in attempting to concretize his individual code into a universal ethical system.

Let us not fall into the crass error of supposing that Shaw has never come under the spell of the fascination of idealism and romance. Shaw the realist paid his toll to Romance before the moral passion ever dawned upon his soul. Just as Zola always bore the brand of Hugo, just as Ibsen worked his way through romance to real life, so Shaw found his feet in realism only after tripping several times over the novels of a romantic imagination. Shaw's novels are the products of a riotous and fanciful imagination, if not, as he dubs them, the compounds of ignorance and intuition. In a celebrated discussion with Mr. W. H. Mallock, we have Shaw's frank confession:

" We are both novelists, privileged as such to make fancy pictures of Society and individuals, and to circulate them as narratives of things that have actually been; and the critics will gravely find fault with our fictitious law, or our fictitious history, or our fictitious psychology, if we depart therein from perfect verisimilitude. Why have we this extraordinary privilege? Because, I submit, we are both natural-born tellers of the thing that is not. Not, observe, vulgar impostors who lie for motives of gain, to extort alms, to conceal or excuse discreditable facts in our history, to glorify ourselves, to facilitate the sale of a horse, or to avoid unpleasantness. All humanity lies like that, more or less. But Mr. Mallock and I belong to those who lie for the sheer love of lying, who forsake everything else for it, who put into it laborious extra touches of art for which there is no extra pay, whose whole life, if it were looked into closely enough, would be found to have been spent more in the world of fiction than of reality." *

Shaw has somewhere placed on record his boast that such insight as he had in criticism was due to the fact that he exhausted romanticism before he was ten years old. " Your popular novelists," he contemptuously declared, " are now gravely writing the stories I told to myself before I replaced my first set of teeth. Some day I will try to found a genuine psychology of fiction by writing down the history of my imagined life, duels, battles, love-affairs with queens and all. They say that man in embryo is successively a fish, a bird, a mammal, and so on, before he develops into a man. Well, popular novel-writing is the fish stage of your Jonathan Swift. I have never been so dishonest as to sneer at our popular novelists. I once went on like that myself. Why does the imaginative man always end by writing comedy if only he has also a sense of reality? Clearly because of the stupendous irony of the contrast between his imaginary adventures and his real circumstances and powers. At night, a conquering hero, an Admirable Crichton, a Don Juan; by day, a cowardly little brat cuffed by his nurse for stealing lumps of sugar. . . . My real name," he added, " is Alnaschar." †

As a matter of fact, Shaw has anticipated his exhaustion of romanticism by some seventeen years. It was not until he finished the novels of his nonage that he could justly boast of

* *On Mr. Mallock's Proposed Trumpet Performance.* In the *Fortnightly Review,* April, 1894.

† *Who I Am, and What I Think.* Part I. In the *Candid Friend,* May 11th, 1901.

having " worked off " that romanticism which always appears to be latent in every creative imagination in the stage of incipiency. Remember what Stevenson wrote to William Archer of *Cashel Byron's Profession:*

" As a whole, it is (of course) a fever dream of the most feverish. . . . It is all mad, mad and deliriously delightful; the author has a taste in chivalry like Walter Scott's or Dumas's, and then he daubs in little bits of Socialism; he soars away on the wings of the romantic griffon—even the griffon, as he cleaves air, shouting with laughter at the nature of the quest—and I believe in his heart he thinks he is labouring in a quarry of solid granite realism.

" It is this that makes me—the most hardened adviser now extant—stand back and hold my peace. If Mr. Shaw is below five-and-twenty, let him go his path; if he is thirty, he had best be told that he is a romantic, and pursue romance with his eyes open; perhaps he knows it; God knows!—my brain is softened." *

It is all very well for Shaw to say that he used Bizet's *Carmen* as a safety valve for his romantic impulses. But the testimony of his own novels flatly contradicts his complacent assertion that he was romantic enough to have come to the end of romance before he began to create in art for himself.

These novels, in spite of their youthful romanticism, nevertheless constitute the record of the adventures of an earnest and anarchic young man, with a knack of keen observation and terse protraiture, striving to give voice to and interpret the spirit of the century. When someone, in 1892, suggested that Shaw was, of course, a follower of Ibsen, Shaw replied with a great show of indignation: " What! *I* a follower of Ibsen! My good sir, as far as England is concerned, Ibsen is a follower of mine. In 1880, when I was only twenty-four, I wrote a book called ' The Irrational Knot,' which reads nowadays like an

* *The Letters of R. L. Stevenson,* Vol. II. Edited by Sidney Colvin, pp. 107 *et seq.*

Ibsenite novel." And in the postscript to the preface to the
new edition of that novel, after having declared with familiar
Shavian wiliness in the preface that he " couldn't stand " his
own book, he makes a sudden *bouleversement* as follows: " Since
writing the above I have looked through the proof-sheets of
this book, and found, with some access of respect for my youth,
that it is a fiction of the first order. . . . It is one of those
fictions in which the morality is original and not ready-made.
. . . I seriously suggest that ' The Irrational Knot ' may be
regarded as an early attempt on the part of the life force to
write ' A Doll's House ' in English by the instrumentality of
a very immature writer aged twenty-four. And though I say
it that should not, the choice was not such a bad shot for a
stupid instinctive force that has to work and become conscious
of itself by means of human brains."

With all its immaturity, *The Irrational Knot* is undoubtedly
in the " tone of our time." It is the ill-chosen title, however,
rather than the contents which recalls Nora and Torvald. The
institution of marriage is not shown to be irrational; Shaw's
shafts were aimed at the code of social morality which renders
marriages such as the one described inevitable failures. Shaw
not only seeks to expose the fatal inconsistencies of this social
code, but also damns the feeble shams with which Society attempts to bolster up those inconsistencies.

Endowed with much of the bluntness of Bluntschli, but with
an added sensitiveness, the " hero " of this novel may be described as the crude and repellent prototype of the later Shavian
males. Believing more in force than in *savoir faire*, in brutal
sincerity than in conventional graces, Conolly stands out for
literal truth and violent tactlessness as against social propriety
and observance of *les convenances*. He is acting with perfect
validity to himself when he says, in answer to the question as
to what he is going to do about his wife's elopement with a
former lover: " Eat my supper. I am as hungry as a bear."
After Marian's desertion by her lover, Conolly urges her to
return to him, assuring her that now she is just the wife he
wants, since she is at last rid of " fashionable society, of her
family, her position, her principles, and all the rest of her chains

for ever." Marian refuses, because she cannot " respect herself for breaking loose from what is called her duty." Their definitive words epitomize the failure of their life together.

" ' You are too wise, Ned,' she said, suffering him to replace her gently in the chair.

" ' It is impossible to be too wise, dearest,' he said, and unhesitatingly turned and left her."

The subjects which inspired Shaw's maturer genius are the same subjects which so actively, if crudely and imperfectly, struggle for expression in this early work. Much acuteness is exhibited by the young man of twenty-four in spying out the weak points in the armour of " that corporate knave, Society." When the " high-bred " wife of the " self-made " man elopes with a " gentleman," Society's dismay is only feigned. Like Roebuck Ramsden, Marian's relatives are quite willing to forgive, and even to thank, the cur if he will only marry her: by ousting a rank outsider like Conolly, Douglas appears to Society almost in the light of a champion of its cause. Shaw was too close an observer of life, even at twenty-four, to attempt to make out a case against matrimony by celebrating the success of an unblessed union. His point is turned against Society, less for upholding traditional morality than for making the preservation of its class distinctions its highest laws. Society is ready enough to forgive Douglas; but Marmaduke Lind, in setting up an unblessed union with Conolly's sister, Mademoiselle Lalage Virtue, of the Bijou Theatre, places himself beyond the pale. For she is socially " impossible " ; and, consequently, there can be no relenting towards Marmaduke until he return, and, in the odour of sanctity and respectability, marry Lady Constance Carberry!

The Irrational Knot cannot be called novel on account of its rather commonplace thought that " a girl who lives in Belgravia ought not to marry with a man who is familiar with the Mile End Road." But as Mr. W. L. Courtney suggestively remarks: "What is novel is the illustration, in clever and mordant fashion, of the absurd folly and wastefulness of social conditions which obstinately make intelligence subservient to aristocratic prestige. Even in our much-abused country there is, and has been for a long time, a career open for talent; but the aspiring male must not encumber himself by taking a partner out of ranks to which he does not belong. Thus, ' The Irrational Knot ' is nothing more nor less than an early tract in defence of Socialism or Communism, or whatever other term should be applied to theories which seek to equalize the chances and opportunities of human beings." In *The Irrational Knot* are found the marks of that individual mode of observing and reflecting life, which is popularly denominated " Shavian." Here is the first clear testimony to that rationalistic mood in Shaw which permeates so much of his subsequent work. And yet this book contains intimations of that deeper philosophy of life which conceives of rationality merely as an instrumentality for carrying out its designs. This knot is irrational only because it is too rational. Marian shrinks from reconcilement with Conolly: she cannot breathe in the icy atmosphere of his rationalistic cocksureness. Conolly expresses Shaw's fundamental protestantism in his assertion that Marian's ill-considered flight with Douglas was the first sensible action of her whole life. It was admirable in his eyes because it was her first vigorous assertion of will, of vital purpose. The human being can and will find freedom only in overriding convention, repudiating " duty," and solving every problem in terms of its own factors. The book, indeed, is marked less by immaturity of thought than by crudeness of execution. The characters are deficient in the flexibility and pliancy of human beings, and the book lacks suggestion of " the slow, irregular rhythm of life," of which Henry James somewhere speaks. To Shaw, the depiction of Conolly was evidently a labour of love; and, consequently, we have an execution of force, if not always of convincing veracity. Elinor McQuinch, shrewd, sharp-tongued, acid—the familiar *advocatus diaboli*, and Shaw in petticoats of the later Shavian drama—is delightfully refreshing in her piquancy, and truly Ibsenic in her determination to " be herself." The nascent dramatist often speaks out in this book— note the melodramatic Lalage Virtue—but nowhere more characteristically than in the trenchant deliverance of the justly-vexed Elinor:

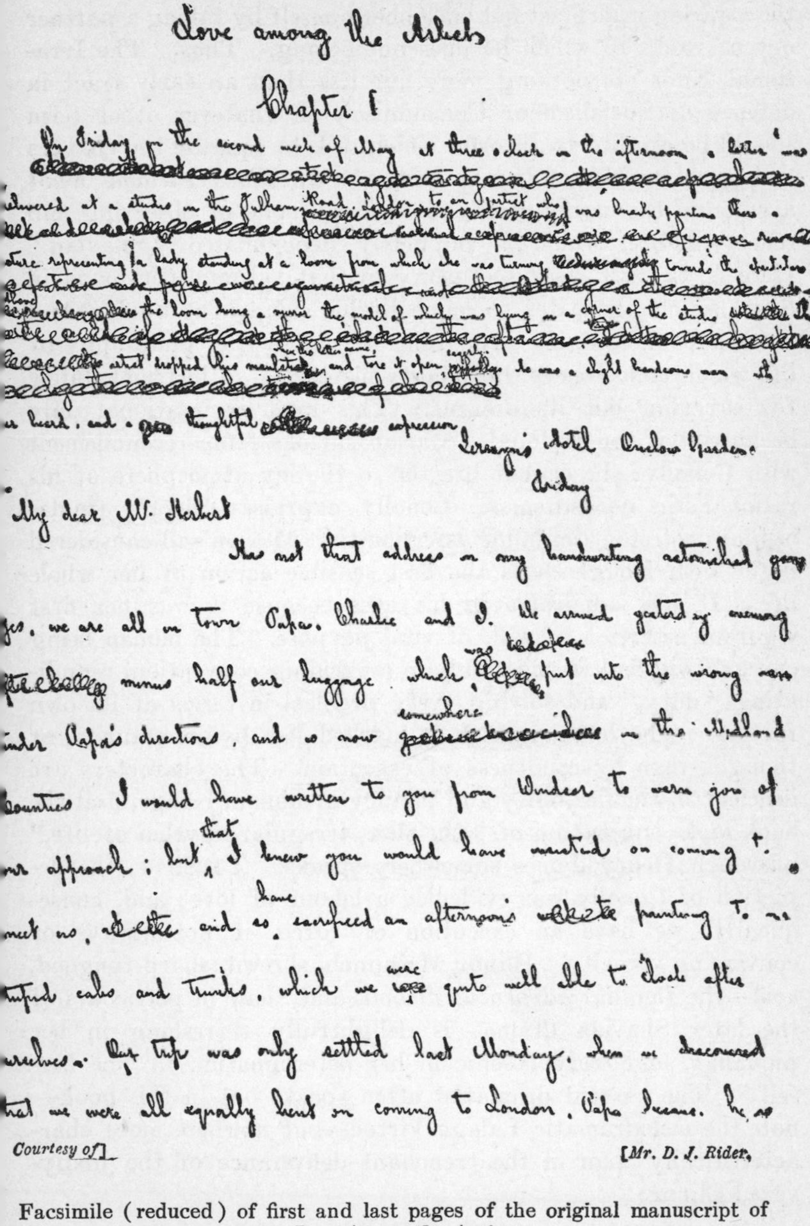
Love among the Artists

Chapter I

On Friday in the second week of May at three o'clock in the afternoon a letter was delivered at a studio in the Fulham Road, London, to an artist who was busily painting there a picture representing a lady standing at a loom from which she was turning towards the spectator. The loom being a ... the model of which was lying in a corner of the studio. The artist dropped his maulstick, took the letter, came, and tore it open eagerly. He was a slight handsome man with a beard, and a grave thoughtful expression.

Lorraine's Hotel Onslow Gardens.
Friday

My dear Mr. Herbert

Has not that address in my handwriting astonished you? Yes, we are all in town Papa, Charles and I. We arrived yesterday evening ... minus half our luggage which was taken put into the wrong van under Papa's directions, and is now somewhere in the Midland counties. I would have written to you from Windsor to warn you of our approach; but that I knew you would have insisted on coming to meet us, and so have sacrificed an afternoon's painting to our stupid cabs and trunks, which we were quite well able to look after ourselves. Our trip was only settled last Monday, when we discovered that we were all equally bent on coming to London. Papa became he so

Courtesy of] [Mr. D. J. Rider.

Facsimile (reduced) of first and last pages of the original manuscript of *Love Among the Artists.*

…offolding. they re-entered the drawing-room

"Dear Adrian, I am ready."

"Yes"; and Robert "Good-night, Mary."

"I think I heard that you say that Mr Robert is going off on a long tour"; said Charlie, coming forward, and speaking boldly, though this was very red

"Yes"; said Adrian. "And a very long tour, though, thank goodness."

"Then I shall not see him again — at least not for some time. I have made up my mind to go to that post in the locally Company's branch at Leeds"; and I shall be off before Mr Robert returns from the continent"

"This is a sudden resolution"; said Mary, in some astonishment

"I hope Mr Robert thinks it — wiser one"; said Charlie. "He has often made fun of my attempts setting myself in the world"

"Yes"; said Charlie; "it is very nice, and quite right… Good-night and Bon voyage, Monsieur ... …

 … Good-bye"; they then went downstairs into the garden; but he turned back into the room, and watched their departure from the window.

Love went no further among the … these among other people, after all.

<u>London 1886</u>

— The End

"Henceforth Uncle Reginald is welcome to my heartiest detestation. I have been waiting ever since I knew him for an excuse to hate him; and now he has given me one. He has taken part—like a true parent—against you with a self-intoxicated young fool whom he ought to have put out of the house. He has told me to mind my own business. I shall be even with him for that some day. I am as vindictive as an elephant: I hate people who are not vindictive; they are never grateful either, only incapable of any enduring sentiment. . . . I am thoroughly well satisfied with myself altogether; at last I have come out of a scene without having forgotten the right thing to say!"

Imagination lingers fondly, as Mr. Hubert Bland once remarked, over the spectacle of Elinor standing in the middle of the stage, three-quarters face to the audience, and firing off those acute generalizations about people who are not vindictive. Shaw's cleverness has begun thus early to betray him; a number of the characters are smart, but quite unnatural. The "Literary Great-grandfather" of the present Shaw unerringly pointed out many of the weak spots of Society; but his fundamental Socialism, impatient of class distinctions and social barriers, leads him occasionally into crude caricature. The book's greatest fault lies, perhaps, in the fact that his characters employ, not the natural, ductile speech of to-day, but the stilted diction of Dumas and Scott.

Commonplace as is the characterization, Shaw's next novel, *Love Among the Artists*, is a tract—less a novel than a critical essay with a purpose, in narrative form. Shaw confesses that he wrote this book for the purpose of illustrating "the difference between that enthusiasm for the fine arts which people gather from reading about them, and the genuine artistic faculty which cannot help creating, interpreting, or, at least, unaffectedly enjoying music and pictures."

I have often wondered if it might not be possible for one who did not know Shaw personally to construct a quite credible biography by making a composite of the peculiarly Shavian types presented in his novels and plays. Without carrying the analogy to extremes, I think it mediately true that Shaw has one by one exhibited, in semi-autobiographic form, the distinguishing hall-marks of his individual and many-sided character. To what extent Owen Jack is a projection of the Shaw of this period, how graphically, if unconsciously, Shaw has revealed in this droll original his own ideals of music and his defence of a certain impudently exasperating assertiveness of manner in himself, is difficult to decide. Shaw insists that Jack is partly founded on Beethoven. And yet there is an undoubted resemblance between the real Irishman and the imagined Welshman who plays the Hyde of Jack to the Jekyll of Shaw. Like " C. di B." and G. B. S., Jack is the first of the " privileged lunatics." He scorns the pedantry of the schools, sneers at mechanical music of academic origin, jibes at " analytic criticism," and fiercely denounces the antiquated views of the musical organizations of England, with their old fogeyism, their cowardice in the face of novelty, their dread of innovation, and their cringing subservience to obsolescent and outworn models. Like Shaw, Jack is always tolerant of sincerity, always sympathetic with true effort, unrestrainedly enthusiastic over any vital outpouring of the creative spirit; rebuking tyranny wherever he sees it, exposing falsehood whenever he hears it, eternally vigilant in exposing frauds and unmasking shams. And yet, with all his offensive brusqueness, fierce intolerance, and colossal self-sufficiency, gentle-hearted, compassionate, and, in the presence of beauty, deeply humble.

Shaw once called *Love Among the Artists* a novel with a purpose. Viewed from another standpoint, it is a collection of types, a study in temperaments. The author preaches the arrogance of genius as opposed to a false humility in the presence of great art works. The shallow artist, Adrian Herbert, " spends whole days in explaining to you what a man of genius is and feels, knowing neither the one nor the other "; Mary Sutherland never surpasses mediocrity as an artist because her knowledge is based upon hearsay instead of upon experience. She stands in sharp contrast to Madge Brailsford, who tersely puts her case to Mary—the case, one might say, of the whole book—" If you don't like your own pictures, depend upon it no one else will.

I am going to be an actress because I think I can act. You are going to be a painter because you think you can't paint." Mr. Huneker declares that Mary Sutherland, " lymphatically selfish and utterly unsympathetic," is his prime favourite in the story. " Her taste in flaring colours, her feet, her habit of breathing heavily when aroused emotionally, her cowardices, her artistic failures, her eye-glasses, her treacly sentiment—what a study of the tribe artistic! And truly British withal." The only other noteworthy figure in the book is the evasive, elusive Mademoiselle Szczympliça—a study searching in the closeness and delicacy of its observation. This charming and piquant Polish pianist, although emanating poetry and romance, has, as she puts it, the " soul commercial " within her. She cannot see why, even if she does love her husband, she should therefore dispense with her piano practice!

Unlike the classic model for a play, this novel has neither beginning, middle, nor ending; and yet it has many brilliantly executed scenes. Who could ever forget the street fight in Paris, the humorous " love-scene " between Madge Brailsford and Owen Jack, and the rehearsal, so acute in its satire—fitting companion-piece to the Wagner lecture in *Cashel Byron's Profession?*

It is noteworthy that *Love Among the Artists* heralds a favourite thesis of Shaw's—the natural antipathy between blood relations—a thesis expounded many years later by John Tanner in the rather leaden epigram " I suspect that the tables of consanguinity have a natural basis in a natural repugnance." Cashel Byron is always catching himself in the act of " shying " when his mother is around—she used to throw things at him when he was a boy! Blanche Sartorius is quite ready to hate her father at a moment's notice; no love is lost between Julia and Colonel Craven; Vivie Warren stands out determinedly against her mother's authority; and Frank, with nauseating levity, takes great delight in " jollying " his reprobate father upon the indiscretions of his youth. Phil and Dolly are breezily disrespectful of parental rule; and Anne uses her maudlin mother as an excuse to do just whatever she wants. The thesis is part of Shaw's stock-in-trade, and might be regarded as a mere comic *motif*, were it not for the " damnable iteration " of the thing. Adrian Herbert avows his positive dislike for his mother, because, as he affirms, their natures are antagonistic, their views of life and duty incompatible—because they have nothing in common. We must take Shaw's insistence upon incompatibility of temperament between blood-relations with a good many grains of salt. It is not even half true that every mother tries to defeat every cherished project of her sons " by sarcasms, by threats, and, failing these, by cajolery "; that everyone's childhood has been " embittered by the dislike of his mother and the ill-temper of his father "; that every man's wife soon ceases to care for him and that he soon tires of her; that every man's brother goes to law with him over the division of the family property; and that every man's son acts in studied defiance of his plans and wishes. These things are only true enough to be funny; just enough of them happen in real life to give Shaw's thesis a sort of comic plausibility. It is the phrases, " love is eternal," and " blood is thicker than water," rather than the facts themselves, which make the iconoclastic Shaw see red. I find some explanation of his view in pardonable revolt, as a dramatist, against that persistent superstition of French melodrama—the *voix du sang*. Some explanation of Shaw's views in the matter may possibly be found in the facts of his own personal experience; at any rate, he once said that the word education brought to his mind four successive schools where his parents got him out of the way for half a day. Indeed, his campaign against the modern system of education springs from his recently expressed disgust with educators for *concealing* the fact that " the real object of that system is to relieve parents from the insufferable company and anxious care of their children." Continuing in the same strain, he says:

" Until it is frankly recognized that children are nuisances to adults except at playful moments, and that the first social need that arises from the necessary existence of children in a community is that there should be some adequate defence of the comparative quiet and order of adult life against the comparative noise, racket, untidiness, inquisitiveness, restlessness, fitfulness, shiftlessness, dirt, destruction and mischief, which are healthy and natural for children, and which are no reason for denying them the personal respect without which their characters cannot grow and set properly, we shall have the present pretence of inexhaustible parental tenderness, moulding of character, inculcation of principles, and so forth, to cloak the imprisoning, drilling, punishing, tormenting, brigading, boy and girl farming, which saves those who can afford it from having to scream ten times every hour, ' Stop that noise, Tommy, or I'll clout your head for you.' " *

With gradual, yet unhalting steps, Shaw works his way to those startling and topsy-turvy theories which are so delightfully credible to the *intellectuels* and so bewilderingly exasperating to the Philistines. In *Love Among the Artists*, Madge Brailsford's open avowal to Owen Jack of her love for him gives a hint that the theory of woman as the huntress and man as the quarry is upon us. But quite the contrary course is taken in *Cashel Byron's Profession*, Shaw's next novel. Cashel Byron, the perfect pugilist, fights his way into the good graces of the " high-born " heiress, Lydia Carew, by the straight exhibition of his physical prowess. The whole book is conceived in such broadly satirical vein that it is impossible for me to accept it as anything except a boyishly irrepressible pasquinade. Fortunately, the " little bits of Socialism that were daubed in " here and there at first, were afterwards deleted; the current version is a novel, pure and simple, with no discoverable Socialistic thesis behind it. Shaw's explanation that the book was written as an offset to the " abominable vein of retaliatory violence " that runs all through the literature of the nineteenth century need not detain us here; Shaw has made out his own case with sufficiently paradoxical cleverness in the inevitable preface. He spends one-half of his time in explaining his actions during the other half; and it has even been unkindly hinted that each new book of

* *Does Modern Education Ennoble?* In *Great Thoughts*, October 7th, 1905.

71

his serves merely as an excuse for writing another preface. And it should be remembered that the preface to *Cashel Byron's Profession* was written some eighteen years later than was the book itself—ample time for Shaw to devise any excuse for representing his book as a deliberate challenge to British ideals. Suffice it to say that a comparison of *Cashel Byron's Profession* with *Rodney Stone,* for example, will make plain the distinction between the realism and the romance of pugilism. And while Byron's exhibitions of physical prowess are the most " howlingly funny " incidents in the book, it is nevertheless true that Shaw has done nothing to surround the " noble art of *sluggerei* " with any halo of fictitious romance.* " Its novelty," as Shaw himself maintains, " consists in the fact that an attempt is made to treat the art of punching seriously, and to detach it from the general elevation of moral character with which the ordinary novelist persists in associating it."

The real novelty, and, indeed, the chief charm, of the book consists rather in the fact that no attempt is made to treat anything seriously. So far as the prize-ring is concerned, the book's realism is veracious; the rest is the frankest of popular melodrama. What appeals more strongly to the popular heart than a low-born but invincible slugger fighting his way, round after round, to the side of a noble and fabulously wealthy heroine! What more oracularly Adelphic in its melodrama than the " finger of fate " upon the " long arm of coincidence " directing Cashel's mother to the mansion of Miss Lydia Carew! And what an exquisite fulfilment of poetic justice—the ultimate discovery that Cashel is a scion of one of the oldest county families in England, and heir to a great estate! The thing that makes the book go, of course, is its peculiarly Shavian cast— the combination of what Stevenson called " struggling, overlaid original talent " and " blooming gaseous folly." Shaw's sense of dramatic situation continually foreshadows the future play-

---

* A dramatization of the novel, by Mr. Stanislaus Stange, was produced with moderate success in New York several years ago. Unique interest attached to the production because the part of Cashel Byron was taken by Mr. James J. Corbett, some time pugilistic champion of the world—and incidentally quite a clever actor. There is much of Cashel in Mr. Corbett, whose popular sobriquet is " Gentleman Jim."

wright. The abounding humour of the exquisitely ludicrous scene at the reception—the devastating comicality of the brute, with his native " mother-wit," turned rough-and-ready philosopher! When Cashel is set down in the midst of this ethical-artistic circle, he breezily excels all the professors—for he discusses art *positively*, in the terminology of his own profession, in which he is a past master. The sublime hardihood of elucidating Beethoven and Wagner in terms of the pugilistic art of Jack Randall! And Bashville, over whom Stevenson howled with derision and delight, what a brief for democratic Socialism is Bashville—prototype for the Admirable Crichton and 'Enry Straker—keenly conscious of his own absurdity, yet zealously standing out in defence of his mistress and in insistence upon the truly democratic doctrine of " equal rights for all, special privileges for none." Who cannot sympathize with Stevenson: " I dote on Bashville—I could read of him for ever; *de Bashville je suis le fervent*—there is only one Bashville, and I am his devoted slave; *Bashville est magnifique, mais il n'est guère possible*." Or when he says: " Bashville—O Bashville! *j'en* chortle (which is finely polyglot)." Service is as sacred to Bashville as pugilism is to Cashel. Each is the " ideal " professional man, who magnifies his office and measures up to the height of his own profession. Each demands recognition for fulfilling to the best of his ability his own special function in life. Shaw insists that the real worth of a man is not to be measured by the social standing of his profession, but in terms of his professional efficiency.

Shaw's mastery of the portrayal of striking contrasts is exhibited in the case of Cashel Byron and Lydia Carew. There is a strong hint of the " female Yahoo " in Lydia's avowal to her aristocratic suitor: " I practically believe in the doctrine of heredity; and as my body is frail and my brain morbidly active, I think my impulse towards a man strong in body and untroubled in mind is a trustworthy one. You can understand that; it is a plain proposition in eugenics." This was fun to Stevenson—but " horrid fun." His postscript is laconically eloquent: "(I say, Archer, my God! what women!)" William Morris seems to have had the rights in the matter in describing Lydia, to Shaw privately, as a " prig-ess." Shaw grandiloquently speaks of her as " superhuman all through," a " working model " of an " improved type " of womanhood. " Let me not deny, however . . . ," he remarks, " that a post-mortem examination by a capable critical anatomist—probably my biographer—will reveal the fact that her inside is full of wheels and springs." The book closes on a mildly Shavian note—the romance has dwindled to banality. " Cashel's admiration for his wife survived the ardour of his first love for her; and her habitual forethought saved her from disappointing his reliance on her judgment."

All that was needed to expose the threadbare plot of *Cashel Byron's Profession* was *The Admirable Bashville: or Constancy Unrewarded*—Shaw's blank-verse stage version of the novel. This delightful jest was perpetrated in defence of the stageright of the novel, which threatened to pass into unworthy hands through the malign workings of that " foolish anomaly," the English Copyright Law. In Shaw's celebrated lecture on Shakespeare, at Kensington Town Hall, section 10, as given in his abstract, reads as follows:

" That to anyone with the requisite ear and command of words, blank verse, written under the amazingly loose conditions which Shakespeare claimed, with full liberty to use all sorts of words, colloquial, technical, rhetorical, and obscurely technical, to indulge in the most far-fetched ellipses, and to impress ignorant people with every possible extremity of fantasy and affectation, is the easiest of all known modes of literary expression, and that this is why whole oceans of dull bombast and drivel have been emptied on the heads of England since Shakespeare's time in this form by people who could not have written *Box and Cox* to save their lives. Also (this on being challenged) that I can write blank verse myself more swiftly than prose, and that, too, of full Elizabethan quality plus the Shakespearian sense of the absurdity of it as expressed in the lines of Antient Pistol. What is more, that I have done it, published it, and had it performed on the stage with huge applause." *

Liking the " melodious sing-song, the clear, simple, one-line and two-line sayings, and the occasional rhymed tags, like the half-closes in an eighteenth-century symphony, in Peele, Kid, Greene, and the histories of Shakespeare," Shaw quite naturally " poetasted *The Admirable Bashville* in the rigmarole style." After illustrating how unspeakably bad Shakespearean blank verse is, Shaw ludicrously claims that his own is " just as good." Nor is it possible to deny that his own blank verse positively scintillates with the Shakespearean—or is it Shavian?—sense of its absurdity. The preface to *The Admirable Bashville* has the genuine Shavian *timbre*, with its solemn fooling, its portentous levity, its false premisses and ludicrous conclusions. In that preface, as Mr. Archer puts it, Shaw " defends the woodenness of his blank verse by arguing that wooden blank verse is the best. That, at any rate, is the gist of his contention, though he does not put it in just that way."

The play—for despite Shaw's prefaces, the play's the thing— is a truly admirable burlesque of rhetorical drama. Not Bashville, but Cashel only is admirable; it is Cashel's constancy that is rewarded. The piece is couched in a tone of the most delicious extravagance—a hit, a palpable hit, in every line. I cannot resist the temptation to quote from the scene in which Lydia, Lucian, and Bashville, fast locked against intrusion, debate the question of admitting Cashel, the presumably infuriated ruffian, who has just been successfully tripped up by Bashville as he is trying to enter the Carew mansion.

LYDIA: We must not fail in courage with a fighter.
        Unlock the door.
LUCIAN: Like all women, Lydia,
        You have the courage of immunity.
        To strike *you* were against his code of honour;
        But *me*, above the belt, he may perform on
        T' th' height of his profession. Also Bashville.

* *Bernard Shaw Abashed.* In the *Daily News*, April 17th, 1905.

BASHVILLE: Think not of me, sir. Let him do his worst.
Oh, if the valour of my heart could weigh
The fatal difference 'twixt his weight and mine,
A second battle should he do this day:
Nay, though outmatched I be, let but my mistress
Give me the word: instant I'll take him on
Here—now—at catchweight. Better bite the
    carpet
A man, than fly, a coward.

LUCIAN: Bravely said:
I will assist you with the poker.

And well worth remembering is the naïve autobiography, delivered at the request of the Zulu king, of that celestially denominated " bruiser " concerning whom Cashel once said: " Slave to the ring I rest until the face of Paradise be changed."

CETEWAYO: Ye sons of the white queen:
Tell me your names and deeds ere ye fall to.

PARADISE: Your royal highness, you beholds a bloke
What gets his living honest by his fists.
I may not have the polish of some toffs
As I could mention on; but up to now
No man has took my number down. I scale
Close on twelve stun; my age is twenty-three;
And at Bill Richardson's " Blue Anchor " pub
Am to be heard of any day by such
As likes the job. I don't know, governor,
As ennythink remains for me to say.

Those who witnessed the original production of the play by the London Stage Society in 1903, and also the later production in 1909 at the " Afternoon Theatre " (His Majesty's), unhesitatingly gave it that " huge applause " of which Shaw speaks so frankly. " The best burlesque of rhetorical drama in the language," is Mr. Archer's sweeping dictum. Even the most hardened of Philistines might find it easy to agree with his statement: " Fielding's ' Tom Thumb ' and Carey's ' Chrononhotonthologos ' are, it seems to me, not in the running."

THE NOVELIST

Not until the appearance of *An Unsocial Socialist*, fifth of the novels of his nonage, is the Pandora's box of Shavian theories opened. There now begin to troop forth those startling and anarchic views with which the name of Shaw is popularly associated. This modern "*École des Maris*" heralds the reign of the "literature of effrontery"; Shaw is beginning to take his stride. With all its extravagance and waywardness, *An Unsocial Socialist* has been declared by at least one critic of authority to be as brilliant as anything George Meredith ever wrote. Let us recall Stevenson's warning to Shaw: "Let him beware of his damned century; his gifts of insane chivalry and animated narration are just those that might be slain and thrown out like an untimely birth by the Daemon of the Epoch." Gone are the chivalry and romance—the winds of Socialism have blown them all away. But the book fairly reeks of the "damned century," with its mad irresponsibility, its exasperating levity, its religious and social revolt. Written in 1883, it seethes and bubbles with the scum of the Socialist brew just then beginning to ferment. Shaw's original design, he tells us, was to "produce a novel which should be a gigantic grapple with the whole social problem. . . . When I had finished two chapters of this enterprise—chapters of colossal length, but containing the merest preliminary matter—I broke down in sheer ignorance and incapacity." Eventually the two prodigious chapters of Shaw's *magnum opus* were published as a complete novel, in two "books," under the title *An Unsocial Socialist*. Shaw begins fiercely to sermonize humanity, to deride all customs and institutions which have not their roots sunk in individualism and in social justice. The Seven Deadly Sins are: respectability, conventional virtue, filial affection, modesty, sentiment, devotion to woman, romance. Sidney Trefusis is the philosopher of the New Order, revolted by the rottenness of present civilization and resolved, by any means, to set in motion some schemes for its reformation. Discovering too late that marriage to him, as to Tanner, means "apostasy, profanation of the sanctuary of his soul, violation of his manhood, sale of his birthright, shameful surrender, ignominious capitulation, acceptance of defeat," Trefusis deliberately deserts his wife, *not* because, as with Falk and Svanhild in Ibsen's *Love's Comedy*, love seems too exquisite, too ethereal to be put to the illusion-shattering test of marriage, but because marriage involves the triumph of senses over sense, of passion over reason. Even after he has ceased to love Henrietta, her love for him continues to set in motion the mechanism of passion, and he is revolted by the fact that she is satisfied so long as " the wheels go round."

The millionaire son of a captain of industry, Trefusis has, by a strange freak of fate, drunk deep of the Socialist draught of the epoch. Respecting his dead father for his energy and bravery among unscrupulous competitors in the struggle for existence, Trefusis curses his memory for the inhuman means employed in his business dealings and the social crimes concealed by the shimmer of his " ill-gotten gold."

His most significant utterance—an outburst before the wealthy landowner, Sir Charles Brandon—gives us a clear picture of Shaw's Socialist views at this time:

> " A man cannot be a Christian: I have tried it, and found it impossible both in law and in fact. I am a capitalist and a landholder. I have railway shares, mining shares, building shares, bank shares, and stock of most kinds; and a great trouble they are to me. But these shares do not represent wealth actually in existence: they are a mortgage on the labour of unborn generations of labourers, who must work to keep me and mine in idleness and luxury. If I sold them, would the mortgage be cancelled and the unborn generations released from its thrall? No. It would only pass into the hands of some other capitalist; and the working classes would be no better off for my self-sacrifice. Sir Charles cannot obey the command of Christ: I defy him to do it. Let him give his land for a public park: only the richer classes will have leisure to enjoy it. Plant it at the very doors of the poor, so that they may at least breathe its air; and it will raise the value of the neighbouring houses and drive the poor away. Let him endow a school for the poor, like Eton or Christ's Hospital; and the rich will take it for their own children

as they do in the two instances I have named. Sir Charles does not want to minister to poverty, but to abolish it. No matter how much you give to the poor, everything but a bare subsistence wage will be taken away from them again by force. All talk of practising Christianity, or even bare justice, is at present mere waste of words. How can you justly reward the labourer when you cannot ascertain the value of what he makes, owing to the prevalent custom of stealing it? . . . The principle on which we farm out our national industry to private marauders, who recompense themselves by blackmail, so corrupts and paralyses us that we cannot be honest even when we want to. And the reason we bear it so calmly is that very few of us really want to."

A Marx in Shaw's clothing, Trefusis devotes all his energies, all his wealth, to the task of forming an international association—" The International," history gives it—of men pledged " to share the world's work justly; to share the produce of the work justly; to yield not a farthing—charity apart—to any full-grown and able-bodied idler or malingerer, and to treat as vermin in the commonwealth persons attempting to get more than their share of wealth or give less than their share of work." Whole-souledly committed to Socialism in its iconoclastic aspects, Trefusis defies convention, prudery, delicacy, good-taste, and tact in all his actions, convinced beyond reclaim that " vile or not, whatever is true is to the purpose." His philosophy holds it a short-sighted policy to run away from a mistake or a misunderstanding, instead of " facing the music " and clearing the matter up. A licensed eccentric like his prototypic creator in real life, Trefusis is permitted to take liberties granted to no one else; and by the " exercise of a certain considerate tact (which, on the outside, perhaps, seems the opposite of tact)," but which in reality consists in the most ingenious double-dealing, he somehow or other contrives to have his way and go scot-free.

In the early part of the story, disguised as that " terrific combination of nerves, gall, and brains," Smilash, he dexterously philanders to his heart's content with several young girls at the boarding-school where his wife was educated. The verisimilitude of the portraits, the acute psychology exhibited in the portrayal of the feelings, sentiments, and sentimentalities of young girls in the boarding-school stage of evolution, testify to Shaw's remarkable gifts as a genuine realist. That forerunner of Julia Craven, the romantic little Henrietta Jansenius, is portrayed with insight, and not without delicacy and restraint. The most unreal, most unhuman scene in the book is that in which Trefusis apostrophizes the body of his dead wife. His reflections impress me as both flippant and callous in their solemn setting. It is with a sense of profound shock that we hear him rudely flout the " funereal sanctimoniousness " of the family physician, mock at the " harrowing mummeries " of religious and social observance, and " damn the feelings " of a father and mother who regarded their daughter as their chattel and showed no true feeling for her when she was alive. Trefusis is devoured with the conviction that the first, if the hardest, of all duties is one's duty to one's self. His fine Italian hand is betrayed in his later philanderings with the whilom loves of Smilash, now grown up into disagreeable, hard, calculating women. Trefusis's trickery of Sir Charles Brandon, his unfeeling deception of Gertrude Lindsay, his base flattery of Lady Brandon, his misleading promise to Erskine, are all exhibitions of his Jesuitical policy. The exponent of Socialism and the New Morality, Trefusis has no scruples in employing unfair means to secure whatsoever he wants—for the cause of labour and for himself.*

Mr. W. L. Courtney has somewhere called attention to the curious triumph achieved by " our only modern dramatist," as he calls Bernard Shaw, in view of the fact that Shaw has never hesitated at interpreting women as beasts of prey. In the novels we find premonitions of Shaw's later attitude toward

---

* " The hero is remarkable because, without losing his pre-eminence as hero, he not only violates every canon of propriety, like Tom Jones or Des Grieux, but every canon of sentiment as well. In an age when the average man's character is rotted at the core by the lust to be a true gentleman, the moral value of such an example as Trefusis is incalculable."—*Mr. Bernard Shaw's Works of Fiction. Reviewed by Himself.* In the *Novel Review,* February, 1892.

George Bernard Shaw.

From a photograph by Edward J. Steichen, made at 10 Adelphi Terrace, London, W.C. August, 1907.

women. Some suspicion of Shaw's theory that woman "takes the initiative in sex business" dawns upon us when Madge Brailsford openly courts Owen Jack; but Lydia Carew, that bloodless Ibsen type, is anything but the huntress. *An Unsocial Socialist* opens our eyes; for Henrietta shamelessly pursues the mocking Trefusis and exhausts every feminine wile in the effort to induce him to return to the chains of wedlock. The idea is also uppermost in the final scene, in which Trefusis, by means of a little diabolically-concocted sentiment, persuades the pursuing Gertrude to give him up, and, " for his sake," to marry Erskine. When Shaw came to erect his theory into a system in *Man and Superman*, he threw a flood of light upon all his former work. There is a keynote to the philosophy of every great or pioneer thinker: Shakespeare had his Hamlet, Wagner his Free-willing of Necessity, Schopenhauer his Will to Live, and Nietzsche his Will to Power. So Shaw is the apostle of the Life Force, as he calls it; and woman is incarnate life force— potent instrument of that irresistible, secret, blind impulse which Nature wields for her own transcendent purposes, heedless of the feelings, welfare, or happiness of individuals. Recognizing woman as the primal vital agency in the fulfilment of Nature's laws, he has not unnaturally come to regard her as " much more formidable than man, because she is, as it were, archetypal, belonging to the original structure of things, and has behind her activity, sometimes benevolent and more often malevolent, the great authority of Nature herself." * Under the spell of this plausible conviction, Shaw endows woman with all the attributes of a blind, unreasoning, unscrupulous force of nature. And for his faith he can find ample support in the literature of an age which produced Schopenhauer's *Essay on Woman*, *The Master Builder*, *Little Eyolf*, *The Triumph of Death*, *Gräfin Julie*, *Erdgeist*, *The Confounding of Camellia*. With great adroitness, but with a curious inconsistency in one who has spent years of his life in " blaming the Bard," Shaw finds the chief support for his claim in the plays of Shakespeare himself. By blandishment, Rosalind accomplishes her purpose; Miranda

* The words are those of Mr. W. L. Courtney.

ensnares Ferdinand with the words, "I would not wish any companion in the world but you. I am your wife if you will marry me." Juliet scales Romeo's defences one by one, and there is Desdemona with her fond "hint"; Mariana, the strategist; Helena, pursuing the recreant Bertram; Olivia, powerless to hide her passion; and poor, mad, melancholy Ophelia.

One has only to pass in review Shaw's work, from *An Unsocial Socialist* to *Man and Superman*, to discover that persistent exemplification of his theory that " woman is the pursuer and contriver, man the pursued and disposed of." Indeed, in his very first play, we find Shaw's concrete illustration of Don Juan's statement that " a woman seeking a husband is the most unscrupulous of all the beasts of prey." All the men in Shaw's plays seem to suffer, not from Prossy's, but from Charteris's complaint: " At no time have I taken the initiative and pursued women with my advances as women have persecuted me." All seem to labour under the conviction that the woman's need of a man " does not prevail against him until his resistance gathers her energy to a climax, at which she dares to throw away her customary exploitations of the conventional affectionate and dutiful poses, and claim him by natural right for a purpose that far transcends their mortal personal purposes." The quintessence of the Shavian woman is Ann Whitefield, that " most gorgeous of all my female creatures," as Shaw calls her— incarnation of fecundity in Nature, wilful, unscrupulous, immodest, aggressive, dominant—compelling Tanner to obey her biological imperative.

The appearance of Shaw's theory in *An Unsocial Socialist* is responsible for this divagation of mine from the theme of the novels, this anticipation of the feminine psychology of the plays. It is highly unreasonable to suppose that the exploitation of such a theory on Shaw's part is a perverse and impish trick, designed solely *épater le bourgeois:* Shaw has driven home his theory in countless deliberate statements. As a philosophic concept, as an interpretation of woman by an a-priorist, little fault can be found with Shaw in the matter. No one can question Shaw's right to his opinion. Even as an effort to make the natural attraction of the sexes the mainspring of the action in modern English drama, Shaw's delineation of woman is far from being unworthy of consideration, though it has swung wide of the mark in exaggerative reaction against the romantic sentimentalities of the English stage. Shaw's women are full of purpose and vitality—the most " advanced " of women in assertion of their rights, in resolute determination to override all the barriers of current respectability and " prurient prudery," in perfect readiness to forego all considerations of good taste, tact, delicacy, modesty, conventional virtue. They ruthlessly repudiate all those qualities which have led man to dub her his " better half." Shaw's mistake consists in painting woman, not as she really, normally is, but as his preconceived philosophic system requires her to be. He planks down for our inspection less a life-like portrait of the eternal feminine than a philosophic interpretation of the " superior sex." Shaw is a remarkable critic of life. Certain phases of human nature, unnoticed or unaccented by others, he has depicted with a veracity, a cleverness, a sparkling brilliancy beyond all praise. But it is one thing to portray an individual, a totally different thing to announce a universal type. A soldier like Bluntschli, a dare-devil like Dudgeon, a minister like Gardner, a hero like Cæsar or Napoleon, a wooer like Valentine, a Socialist like Trefusis, a pugilist like Byron—all these may have lived. Shaw doubtless can—indeed, sometimes does—point to their counterparts, if not in literature, certainly in real life. But to say that all soldiers are like Bluntschli, for example, is little more foolish than to say that all women are like Blanche, like Julia, like Ann. The vital defect in Shaw's women is that they are too blatant, too obvious, too crude. They are lacking in mystery, in finer subtlety, in the subconscious and obscurer instincts of sex, in the arts of exquisite seduction, of keenly-felt yet only half-divined allurement.* The Life Force goes about its business, one would fain remind Mr. Shaw, not openly and with a blare of trumpets, but by a thousand devious and hidden paths. Of course, there is always the danger of taking

---

* There are exceptions to this generalization, of course—Lady Cicely, Candida, Nora, Jennifer, Barbara.

Shaw too seriously. Mr. Archer wittily, but, above all, entirely truthfully, dubbed Ann a "mythological monster." As a pendant to Everyman of the Dutch morality, Ann may be the Everywoman of the Shavian morality. But even Shaw himself admits, with wily fairness, that while, philosophically, Ann may be Everywoman according to the Shavian dispensation, yet in practical, every-day existence there are countless women who are not Ann.

If faith is to be placed in M. Émile Faguet's dictum that no exceptional work of art is ever written by anyone before reaching the age of thirty, then Shaw's novels are debarred by the Statute of Limitations. The "ineptitude" of his novels, of which Mr. Shaw once spoke to me, is attributable to the fact that during this early period he fed upon his imagination. He had not yet come into any deep or really vital communion with humanity. Produced in that impressionable period when dreaming seems preferable to living, the novels bristle with faults—immaturities of form, crudenesses of expression, blatant didactics. They are often loose and disjointed, generally lacking in closely articulated structure. With all his pretended effort at realism, Shaw has failed to impart to his novels that one quality without which no modern work of fictive art can take the very highest rank—inevitableness. To Shaw, as to Zola, art is life seen through a temperament. And I often receive the impression that Shaw's novels are less faithful records of contemporary existence than documents revelative of Bernard Shaw. Shaw is lacking in artistic self-restraint; like the true propagandist, he seems almost unwilling to accept facts as they are, so eager is he to impose upon them the stamp of his individual predilections. It is the strangest of paradoxes that one who claims for himself that rare and priceless gift—the abnormally normal eyesight of the realist—should have spent his life in the endeavour to fix the mask of Shaw upon the face of life.

"The gods know that Bernard Shaw has many sins of omission to answer for when he reaches the remotest peak of Parnassus," writes Mr. Huneker; "but for no one of his many gifts will he be so sternly taken to task as the wasted one of novelist. . . . There is more native talent for sturdy, clear-visioned, character-creating fiction in the one prize-fighting novel of Bernard Shaw than in the entire cobweb work of the stylistic Stevenson! . . . Shaw could rank higher as a novelist than as a dramatist—always selecting for judgment the supreme pages of his tales, pages wherein character, wit, humour, pathos, fantasy, and observation are mingled with an overwhelming effect." * While there is much of truth in what Mr. Huneker says, I should hold quite the opposite opinion concerning Shaw's relative merits as novelist and dramatist. Not the least significant feature of the novels, to my mind, is their foreshadowing of the future dramatist.† Turning over the pages of the novels, from first to last one cannot but observe this recurrent trait: Shaw always sees his characters in a " situation." It is difficult to read one of Shaw's novels without unconsciously looking for the stage directions. Proud as he is of his gifts as a " fictionist," no one is more conscious than is Shaw himself of his deficiencies in this *rôle*. With his customary succinctness, he once put the case to me as it really is: " My novels are very green things, very carefully written."

* *Bernard Shaw and Woman.* In *Harper's Bazaar,* June, 1905.

† It is worthy of remark that the conclusion of *Love Among the Artists,* as Julius Bab has pointed out, accurately prefigures the conclusion of *Candida.* The situation, the very words, are almost identical.

THE FABIAN SOCIETY

"If ever there was a society which lived by its wits, and by its wits alone, that society was the Fabian."—*The Fabian Society*. Tract No. 41. By G. B. Shaw.

CHAPTER IV

FOR the student of Shaw's work and career, there is no escape from the resemblance, superficial or vital, between Shaw himself and the numerous comic figures he has projected upon the stage. Like that Byronic impostor, Saranoff, Shaw has gone through life afflicted with a multiplicity of personalities. In *The Autocrat of the Breakfast Table,* Oliver Wendell Holmes said that when two people meet, there are always six persons present. But Shaw needs no party of the second part to sum up the total of personalities: he is eternally dogged with his own ubiquitous *aliases.* Bernard Shaw, the " fictionist "; Corno di Bassetto, the music critic of admirable fooling and pungent criticism; G. B. S., the apostle of comic *intransigéance* in criticism of art, music, and drama—and life; " P-Shaw," the Gilbertian topsy-turvyist of essay and drama; George Bernard Shaw, Fabian, economist, public speaker, borough councillor, reformer—all these distinct characters is Shaw, in Maeterlinckian phrase, constantly meeting upon the highway of fate. It is the province of the biographer to detect, among this confusing cloud of *aliases,* the real man.

In 1883, the career of Bernard Shaw the " fictionist " came to an abrupt and final conclusion. While this first and introductory chapter in the book of Shaw's multiplex life was being written, the material for another and infinitely more important chapter was slowly being collected and arranged. With this second chapter begins the life of the real Shaw.

As he himself has told us, his parents pulled him through the years in which he earned nothing. But he was perpetually " grinding away " at something, perpetually feeling his way towards confidence and efficiency. The diversity of his interests was remarkable: nothing he touched proved banal or unfruitful. This universality of interests—the determination to grasp, the effort to master, every subject that came to his hand—is little

89

less than conclusive as an explanation of his many-sidedness. "I did not start life with a programme. I simply accepted every job offered to me, and I did it the best way I could." In this simple and straightforward statement is found the key to that diversity of talent, that range of ability, which is perhaps the most striking and noteworthy characteristic of this rare and eccentric genius.

The decisive and revolutionary changes in Shaw's truly "chequered" career were due, in almost all cases, to the adventitious or deliberate influence of some dominant personality in literature or in life. The crucial conjunctures in his career are closely associated with the names of Shelley, Ibsen, Nietzsche, Marx, Wagner, Mozart and Michael Angelo, in art, music, literature and philosophy; with the names and personalities, among others, in life of James Leigh Joynes, the Salt family, Henry George, Sidney Webb, William Morris and William Archer.

In Shaw's acquaintance with the late James Lecky * is found the germ of that strenuous propagandist activity which may be called the most definitive expression of Shaw's life. It was in 1879 that Shaw first became intimate with Lecky and with those various subjects, connected with music and languages on the scientific side, to which Lecky devoted so much of his energy and attention. Once interested in some pursuit, Lecky would become so enthused that he would demand of his friends an interest therein commensurate with his own. This pestiferously altruistic spirit of Lecky's proved of great value to Shaw, who set his critical brain to work upon many of the problems which Lecky brought to his attention. Through Lecky, Shaw acquired a working knowledge of Temperament, concerning which he once boasted that he was probably the only living musical critic who knew what it meant; and a due appreciation of Pitman's Shorthand—which he could write at the rate of twenty words per minute and could not read afterwards on any terms!—as probably the worst system of shorthand ever

---

* Author of the article on Temperament (systems of tuning keyed instruments) in the first edition of Grove's *Dictionary of Music*.

invented, yet the best pushed on its business side. Together Lecky and Shaw studied and discussed Phonetics, and while Shaw's knowledge of the subject was by no means exhaustive, his interest in it has since served as a permanent protection against such superficial catch-penny stuff as the reformed spellings that are invented every six months by faddists. Shaw's individual mode of punctuation, his use of spaced letters in place of italics, his almost total rejection, on Biblical authority, which he accepted for once, of quotation marks, and those numerous original rules of punctuation and phonetics which he has from time to time formulated in magazine and daily press,* find their *raison d'être* in Shaw's early association with Lecky and subsequent acquaintance, through Lecky's instrumentality, with the late Alexander Ellis and Henry Sweet, of Oxford. As readers of the notes to *Captain Brassbound's Conversion* may gather, Shaw accepts Sweet as his authority; indeed, he highly values his acquaintance with that " revolutionary don," as he calls him, and once said that, in any other place or country in the world, Sweet would be better known than even Shaw himself. The knowledge of phonetics, the interest in language-reform acquired through his acquaintance with men like Lecky, Ellis and Sweet is the explanation, Mr. Shaw once told me, of the fact that the Cockney dialect, which so befuddles and astounds the readers of *Captain Brassbound's Conversion*, is far more scientific in its analysis of London coster lingo than anything that had previously occurred in fiction.

In the winter of 1879, Lecky joined a debating club, called The Zetetical Society, numbering among its members Mr. Sidney Webb, Mr. Emil Garcke, and Mr. J. G. Godard. It was a sort of " junior copy " of the once well-known Dialectical Society, which had been founded to discuss Stuart Mill's essay on Lib-

* Among Shaw's many articles on these topics, may be cited the following: *A Plea for Speech Nationalization*, in the *Morning Leader*, August 16th, 1901; *Phonetic Spelling: a Reply to Some Criticisms*, *ibid.*, August 22d, 1901; *Notes on the Clarendon Press Rules for Compositors and Readers*, in *The Author*, April, 1902, pp. 171-2. See also Mr. William Archer's two articles: *Spelling Reform v. Phonetic Spelling*, in the *Daily News*, August 10th, 1901; and *Shaw's Phonetic World-English*, in the *Morning Leader*, August 24th, 1901.

erty not long after its appearance in print. Both societies were
strongly Millite; in both there was complete freedom of discussion, political, religious and sexual. Women took a prominent
part in the debates, which often dealt with subjects concerning
their rights, interests and welfare. A noteworthy feature of
these debates, particularly in relation to Shaw's future development as a public speaker, and a critic as well, was that each
speaker, at the conclusion of his speech, might be cross-exam-
ined on it by any one of the others in a series of questions
In this society Malthus, Ingersoll, Darwin and Herbert Spencer
were held in especial reverence. The works of Huxley, Tyndal
and George Eliot were on the shelves of all the members. The
tone of the society was very " advanced "—individualistic
atheistic, evolutionary. Championship of the Married Woman's
Property Act was scarcely silenced by the Act itself. The fact
that Mrs. Besant's children were torn from her like Shelley's
aroused hot indignation, as did the prosecutions for " blasphemy " then going on. It is not without significance that, even
at this time, Shaw was Socialist enough to defend the action of
the State in both cases. Indeed, he has always been, as he once
told me, somewhat of Morris's opinion that " There may be some
doubt as to who are the best people to have charge of children;
but there can be no doubt that the parents are the worst."
Strange jest of fate, Shaw began his career by joining a society
whose members regarded Socialism as an exploded fallacy
How little did anyone dream that, even then, underground
rumblings of the approaching revolution might be faintly
heard! That recurrent quindecennial cycle of Socialistic up-
heaval of which Karl Kautsky has somewhere spoken, was well-
nigh completed. Within five years Socialism was to burst forth
with fresh impetus, sweep the younger generation along with it,
and plunge the Dialectical and Zetetical Societies into the
" blind cave of eternal night."

One night in the winter of 1879, Lecky dragged Shaw to a
meeting of the Zetetical Society, which then met weekly in the
rooms of the Woman's Protective and Provident League in
Great Queen Street, Long Acre. It will be related elsewhere
why Shaw decided to join the society at once; suffice it to say

Reproduced from the original photo-drawing.

[Facing p. 92

here that he became a frequent attendant upon the meetings of
the society, entering actively, if haltingly, into discussion and
debate. The importance, in its bearing upon Shaw's subsequent
career as a man of affairs and a man of letters, of an acquaintance he formed at this time through the accident of joining the
Zetetical Society, can scarcely be overestimated. A few weeks
after joining the society Shaw's keenest interest was aroused
in a speaker who took part in one of the debates. This speaker
was a young man of about twenty-one, rather below middle
height, with small, pretty hands and feet, and a profile that
suggested, on account of the nose and imperial, an improvement
on Napoleon the Third. I well remember the animated way
in which Mr. Shaw described to me the man and the occurrence.
" He had a fine forehead, a long head, eyes that were built on
top of two highly developed organs of speech (according to the
phrenologists), and remarkably thick, strong, dark hair. He
knew all about the subject of debate; knew more than the lecturer; knew more than anybody present; had read everything
that had ever been written on the subject; and remembered all
the facts that bore on it. He used notes, read them, ticked
them off one by one, threw them away, and finished with a
coolness and clearness that, to me in my then trembling state,
seemed miraculous. This young man was the ablest man in
England—Sidney Webb." Then a trembling novice, yet subsequently to be known as the cleverest man in England, Shaw
to-day does not hesitate to pay full honour to the part Sidney
Webb has played in his career. The extent and value of this
association will reveal itself in due course. Shaw has said and
done a thousand clever things; but, as he once freely confessed
to me, " Quite the cleverest thing I ever did in my life was to
force my friendship on Webb, to extort his, and keep it."

After Shaw had been a member of the Zetetical Society for
about a year, he joined the Dialectical Society, and was faithful
to it for years after it had dwindled into a little group of five
or six friends of Dr. Drysdale, the apostle of Malthus. Shaw
subsequently joined another debating society, the Bedford, presided over by Stopford Brooke, who had not then given up his
pastorate at Bedford Chapel to devote himself exclusively to

literature. During these years, as we shall see more particularly in the next chapter, Shaw was slowly perfecting himself in the art of public speaking. The fascination of the platform grew upon him daily. He not only spoke frequently himself, but also attended public meetings of every sort, learning by precept, experience, and example the secrets of the art of platform speaking. With dogged persistence, he was surely, if slowly, acquiring what he himself has called the coolness, the self-confidence and the imperturbability of the statesman.

During these years he had gradually widened and deepened his knowledge of the subjects which periodically came up for discussion in the various debating societies he had joined. In his boyhood he had read Mill on Liberty, on Representative Government, and on the Irish Land Question. And he was fully the equal of his co-debaters in knowledge and comprehension of the evolutionary ideas and theories of Darwin, Tyndall, Huxley, Spencer, George Eliot, and their school. But of political economy he knew absolutely nothing. It was in 1882 that his attention was first definitely directed into the economic channel.

England and Ireland were greatly stirred up at this time by the arrest of Henry George and James Leigh Joynes as " suspicious strangers " in Ireland (August, 1882). Joynes, a master of Eton, wishing to see something of the popular side of the Irish movement, accompanied George as a correspondent of the London *Times*. George was making an investigation of the situation in Ireland preliminary to his campaign of propaganda in behalf of his Single Tax theories, enunciated in *Progress and Poverty*. The arrest of George and Joynes, on the charge of being agents of the Fenians, was widely commented on in the newspapers of Great Britain and Ireland, and resulted in a Parliamentary questioning. *Progress and Poverty*, pronounced by Alfred Russel Wallace " undoubtedly the most remarkable and important work of the nineteenth century," began to sell by the thousands; it was prominently reviewed in the London *Times* and dozens of other papers; and George felt at last that he was " beginning to move the world." Further encouragement came from the Land Nationalization Society,

which had been founded in London early in 1882, with Alfred
Russel Wallace at its head.* " It contained in its membership," says Mr. Henry George, Jr., in his biography of his
father, " those who, like Wallace, desired to take possession of
the land by purchase and then have the State exact an annual
quit-rent from whoever held it; those who had the Socialistic
idea of having the State take possession of the land with or
without compensation and then manage it; and those who, with
Henry George, repudiated all idea of either compensation or of
management, and would recognize common rights to land simply
by having the State appropriate its annual value by taxation.
Such conflicting elements could not long continue together, and
soon those holding the George idea withdrew and organized on
their own distinctive lines, giving the name of the Land Reform
Union to their organization." While interest was at fever heat,
George was invited by the Land Nationalization Society to
lecture under the auspices of a working men's audience in
Memorial Hall. The bill, a true copy of which lies before me,
reads as follows:

LAND NATIONALIZATION.
MEMORIAL HALL,
FARRINGDON STREET,
On Tuesday, September 5th, 1882.
Under auspices of
THE LAND NATIONALIZATION SOCIETY.
Professor
F. W. NEWMAN
will preside.

George's speech that night was the torch that " kindled the
fire in England "—a fire which he afterwards said no human
power could put out. It was the masses that George was trying
to educate and arouse. It was the masses whose ear he caught
that night.

* Compare *Land Nationalization: Its Necessity and Its Aims,* by Alfred
Russel Wallace. Swan, Sonnenschein and Co., 1892.

At that time, Bernard Shaw eagerly haunted public meetings of all kinds. By a strange chance, he wandered that night into the Memorial Hall in Farringdon Street. The speaker of the evening was Henry George: his speech wrought a miracle in Shaw's whole life. It "kindled the fire" in his soul. "It flashed on me then for the first time," Shaw once wrote, "that 'the conflict between Religion and Science' . . . the overthrow of the Bible, the higher education of women, Mill on Liberty, and all the rest of the storm that raged round Darwin, Tyndall, Huxley, Spencer, and the rest, on which I had brought myself up intellectually, was a mere middle-class business. Suppose it could have produced a nation of Matthew Arnolds and George Eliots!—you may well shudder. The importance of the economic basis dawned on me." * Shaw now read *Progress and Poverty;* and many of the observations which the fifteen-year-old Shaw had unconsciously made now took on a significance little suspected in the early Dublin days of his indifference to land agency.†

Shaw was so profoundly impressed by the logic of Henry George's conclusions and suggested remedial measures that, shortly after reading *Progress and Poverty,* he went to a meeting of the Social Democratic Federation, and there arose to protest against their drawing a red herring across the track opened by George. The only satisfaction he had was to be told that he was a novice: "Read Marx's *Capital,* young man," was the condescending retort of the Social Democrats. Shaw promptly

* Compare Chapter VI. for Shaw's own account of his conversion by Henry George.

† No more significant contradiction between practice and conviction can be found in Shaw's career than lies inherent in the fact that he began life by collecting Irish rents! "These hands have grasped the hard-earned shillings of the sweated husbandman, and handed them over, not to the landlord—he, poor devil! had nothing to do with it—but to the mortgagee, with a suitable deduction for my principal who taught me these arts." Not without its spice of humour, also, is the fact that Shaw is to-day an absentee landlord, having derived from his mother an estate on which her family lived for generations by mortgaging. No wonder that Mr. Shaw contemplates with mingled feelings that process, which he has condemned from a thousand platforms, being carried on in his name between his agents and his mortgagees!

KARL MARX.

HENRY GEORGE.

From a photograph taken in 1882.

went and did so, and then found, as he once said, that his advisers were awestruck, as they had not read it themselves! It was then accessible only in the French version at the British Museum. William Archer has testified to the diligence with which Shaw studied Marx's great work; he caught his first glimpse of Shaw in the British Museum Library, where he noticed a " young man of tawny complexion and attire " studying alternately—if not simultaneously—*Das Kapital*, and an orchestral score of *Tristan and Isolde!*

While Darwin, Huxley, Spencer and their school left a distinct impress upon Shaw's mind, it is nevertheless true that he never became a Darwinian. To-day he is violently opposed to Darwinian materialism; and yet the Shavian philosophy, historically considered, is a natural consequence of that bitter fight against convention, custom, authority, and orthodoxy, inaugurated by Darwin and his followers. But Shaw's sociologic doctrine is a distillation, not of the *Descent of Man* or of the *Data of Ethics*, but of *Das Kapital*. At this crucial period in Shaw's career he was exactly in the mood for Marx's reduction of all the conflicts to the conflict of classes for economic mastery, of all social forms to the economic forms of production and exchange. The real secret of Marx's fascination for him, as he once said, was " his appeal to an unnamed, unrecognized passion—a new passion—the passion of hatred in the more generous souls among the respectable and educated sections for the accursed middle-class institutions that had starved, thwarted, misled, and corrupted them from their cradles." In Marx, Shaw found a kindred spirit; for, like Marx, his whole life had bred in him a defiance of middle-class respectability, of revolt against its benumbing and paralyzing influence. As Shaw once said:

" Marx's ' Capital ' is not a treatise on Socialism; it is a jeremiad against the *bourgeoisie*, supported by such a mass of evidence and such a relentless genius for denunciation as had never been brought to bear before. It was supposed to be written for the working classes; but the working man respects the *bourgeoisie* and wants to be a *bourgeois;*

Marx never got hold of him for a moment. It was the revolting sons of the *bourgeoisie* itself—Lassalle, Marx, Liebknecht, Morris, Hyndman, Bax, all, like myself, *bourgeois* crossed with squirearchy—that painted the flag red. Bakunin and Kropotkin, of the military and noble caste (like Napoleon), were our extreme left. The middle and upper classes are the revolutionary element in society; the proletariat is the conservative element, as Disraeli well knew." *

Some such Marxist passion, one surmises, subsequently carried weight with Shaw in influencing his choice of the Fabian Society as the fit *milieu* for the development and exploitation of his energy and talent. For at heart Shaw is what his plays so abundantly prove him—the revolted *bourgeois*.

Not only did Marx's jeremiad against the *bourgeoisie* awaken instant response in Shaw: it changed the whole tenor of his life. No single book—not the Bible of orthodoxy and respectability, certainly—has influenced Shaw so much as the " bible of the working classes." It made him a Socialist. Although he has since repudiated some of the fundamental economic theories of Marx, at this time he found in *Das Kapital* the concrete expression of all those social convictions, grievances and wrongs which seethed in the crater of his being. He became that most determined, most resistless, and often most dangerous of men to deal with, a man with a mission. " From that hour," I once heard Mr. Shaw say, " I became a man with some business in the world."

During the years 1883 and 1884 Shaw threw himself heart and soul into the exciting task of Socialist agitation and propagandism. His dogged practice in public speaking now began to demonstrate its value with telling effect. While he spent his days in criticizing books in the *Pall Mall Gazette* and pictures in the *World*, he devoted his evenings to consistent and strenuous Socialist propagandism. He accepted invitations to address all

* *Who I Am, and What I Think.*—Part I. In the *Candid Friend,* May 11th, 1901.

sorts of bodies on every day in the week, Sunday not excepted. Remember his confession that he first caught the ear of the British public on a cart in Hyde Park, to the blaring of brass bands. During these years, also, he was coming into close touch with the younger generation destined soon to unite in a solid phalanx as the Fabian Society. Probably no living man has touched modern life at so many points as has Bernard Shaw. In his lifetime he has traversed a very lengthy arc on the circle of modern culture, modern thought and modern philosophy. Sovereign contempt for the laggard is one of his prominent characteristics; he himself has ever been an " outpost thinker " on the firing-line of modern intellectual conflict. Essentially significant because essentially modern, Shaw owes no small share of his ability, his versatility, and his breadth of interests to his voraciously acquisitive, acutely inquisitive intellect. Clever acquaintances, brimming with ideas, and overflowing with combative zeal, furnished grist for the ceaselessly active mill of Shaw's intelligence. No biography which failed to trace the shaping influence exerted upon Shaw's frantically complex career by such men as Hubert Bland, Graham Wallas, Sidney Olivier, Sidney Webb and William Morris, could lay just claim to the title of genuine natural history.

At the Land Reform Union Shaw first met Sidney Olivier, then upper division clerk in the Colonial Office. Sidney Webb and Sidney Olivier, very close friends, were the two resident clerks there. When Webb, at Shaw's persuasion, joined the Fabians, Olivier went with him. There existed a very close relation, not only between the various members of the Fabian Society, but also between many of the advanced societies which came to life at this time. For example, Sidney Olivier, who was secretary of the Fabian Society for several years, and Edward Carpenter's brother, Captain Alfred Carpenter, of the Royal Navy, married sisters; in this way there was a sort of family connection between the Socialist and Humanitarian movements. Olivier had made friends at Oxford with Graham Wallas, who was probably influenced through this connection to become a Fabian. The very intimate relation existing between Shaw, Webb, Olivier and Wallas, and the consequent marked influence upon Shaw's literary career and performance, will be spoken of elsewhere at greater length. It is noteworthy that all of these men possessed literary talents of no mean order. Webb's books have a world-wide reputation. Olivier's play, *Mrs. Maxwell's Marriage*, has been performed by the London Stage Society; and his literary talent has displayed itself, not only in plays, but also in verse, essay and story.* In addition to his ability as a facile public speaker, Graham Wallas also possessed literary talent of no mean order, displayed to best advantage in his book on Francis Place, with its lucid exposition of the way in which politics are "wire-pulled" in England by real reformers.†

Another man of talent, whose very opposition of belief and view-point exerted a sort of stimulating influence upon Shaw, was William Clarke, an Oxford M.A., who contributed the chapter on *The Industrial Basis of Socialism* to *Fabian Essays*. A Whitmanite, with strong feelings of rationalist type, allied in spirit to Martineau, the Unitarians, and their logical outgrowth, the American Ethical Society, Clarke made upon Shaw an ineffaceable impression. Shaw first met this remarkable man at the Bedford Society—a meeting which bore fruit in Clarke's joining the Fabian Society. Clarke had lectured in America, known Whitman, and is remembered as the author of several books. Although a successful lecturer, he had by this time exhausted the interest of lecturing, being much older than the other Fabians. A very unlucky man, he was, in consequence, very poor. It has been often said that in the matter of philanthropy Shaw never let his right hand know what his left was doing; he found a way to relieve Clarke's poverty without even letting Clarke, who quarrelled with everything and everybody, suspect that he was the recipient of benefaction. When the *Daily Chronicle* changed its policy and decided to give a column

---

* Entering the Colonial Office twenty-five years ago, he served as Colonial Secretary of the Island of Jamaica from 1899 to 1904, and on three occasions served as Acting Governor. From 1905 to 1907 he was principal clerk in the West African Department; in April, 1907, he was appointed Governor of Jamaica, to succeed Sir Alexander Swettenham, and he was made a K.C.M.G. on King Edward's birthday in 1907.

† *Life of Francis Place.* Longmans, 1898.

in its pages to Labour, its concerns and interests, the editor, in his search for young blood, hit upon Shaw, who quietly substituted Clarke in his place. Had Clarke ever discovered the truth it might have mitigated the profound moral horror of Shaw he always entertained. How Shaw must have chuckled over the latent comedy! The secret philanthropist regarded as a moral anarchist, a *monstrum horrendum*, by his highly moral beneficiary! To Clarke, an altruist and moralist to the backbone, the dawning of Ibsenism, of Nietzscheism, of Shavianism, seemed to be the coming of chaos. " Yet the fact that I knew his value and insisted on it, and that I could sympathize even with his horror of me," Mr. Shaw once told me, " kept our personal relations remorsefully cordial. The last time I called on him was in the influenza period. He was working madly, as usual. He would have certainly refused to see anyone; but he was alone in the flat, and opened the door for me. With a savage, set face that would have made even Ibsen's mouth look soft by contrast, he said, through his shut teeth: ' I can give you five minutes and that is *all*.' ' My dear Clarke,' I replied, ambling idly into his study, ' I *must* leave in half an hour to keep an appointment; and I have just been thinking how I am to get away from you so soon; for I know you won't let me go.' And it turned out exactly as I said. We began to discuss the Parnell divorce case and the Irish crisis, and I could not get away from him until the hour was nearly doubled." *

The part which the Fabian Society has played in English life, and the share of Bernard Shaw in the task of advancing the principles of Collectivism in the last twenty odd years, alone offer ample material for a book. So diverse in its ramifications is the subject, that it will be possible here to trace the evolu-

* Peculiarly sad are the subsequent details of Clarke's life. After saving about a thousand pounds by frenziedly working away for several years as a journalist, he lost it all again in an unfortunate investment in the Liberator Building Society—the enterprise of the notorious Jabez Balfour. With an assured reputation as a journalist and author, Clarke might have repaired his fortunes. But the first great influenza epidemic almost killed him; and each year thereafter the epidemic laid upon him its increasingly tenacious grip. At last he sought to regain his health by foreign travel, only to die in Herzegovina. Clarke was the first leading Fabian to fall.

tionary advance of Socialism in England only in so far as it directly bears upon Shaw's career.* As we know, Shaw began his real education as a pupil of Mill, Comte, Darwin and Spencer. Converted to Socialism by Henry George and his *Progress and Poverty,* Shaw took to insurrectionary economics after reading *Das Kapital.* Marx's book won his support because it so fiercely " convicted private property of wholesale spoliation, murder and compulsory prostitution; of plague, pestilence and famine; battle, murder and sudden death." For some time before joining any Socialist society, Shaw preached Socialism with the utmost zeal and enthusiasm. The choice of a society lay between the Social Democratic Federation, the Socialist League—both quite proletarian in their rank and file, both aiming at being large working-class organizations—and the Fabian Society, which was middle-class through and through. " When I myself, on the point of joining the Social Democratic Federation, changed my mind and joined the Fabian instead," Shaw once wrote, " I was guided by no discoverable difference in programme or principle, but solely by an instinctive feeling that the Fabian, and not the Federation, would attract the men of my own bias and intellectual habits, who were then ripening for the work that lay before us."

The meetings held at Thomas Davidson's rooms at Chelsea in 1881-1883 furnished the initial impulse to the ethical Socialism in England of the last thirty years. As an immediate outcome of these meetings the Fabian Society sprang into being. In September, 1882, Thomas Davidson, recently returned from Italy, where he had been engaged in writing an interpretation of the ethical philosophy of Rosmini, gathered about him a group of people " interested in religious thought, ethical propaganda, and social reform." Among their number were Messrs. Frank Podmore, Edward R. Pease, Havelock Ellis, Percival Chubb, Dr. Burns Gibson, H. H. Champion, the late William Clarke, Hubert Bland, the Rev. G. W. Allen and W. I.

---

* In this connection, compare *Socialism in England,* by Sidney Webb. Swan, Sonnenschein and Co., 1890.

THE FABIAN SOCIETY,

17, Osnaburgh Street, Regent's Park.

FABIAN TRACTS, No. 2.

A Manifesto.

"For always in thine eyes, O Liberty!
Shines that high light whereby the world is saved
And, though thou slay us, we will trust in thee."

LONDON:
GEO. STANDRING, 8 & 9, FINSBURY STREET, E.C.

1884
Facsimile of Cover of Fabian Tract, No. 2.

Jupp, Miss Caroline Hadden, Miss Dale Owen and Mrs. Hinton. According to Mr. Havelock Ellis, Davidson was convinced of " the absolute necessity of founding practical life on philosophical conceptions; of living a simple, strenuous, intellectual life, so far as possible communistically, and on a basis of natural religion. It was Rosminianism, one may say, carried a step further." The many meetings at Mr. Pease's rooms in Osnaburgh Street and elsewhere finally bore fruit in a series of resolutions proposed by Dr. Burns Gibson.* Certain members of the circle, led by Mr. Podmore, who desired to have a society on more general lines, purposed organizing a second society, not necessarily exclusive of the " Fellowship," on broader and more indeterminate lines, leaving it open to anyone to belong to both societies. At a meeting on January 4th, 1884, these proposals were substantially agreed to. The original name, " The Fellowship of the New Life," was retained by those who originally devised it, and a new organization constituted under the title of " The Fabian Society." †

The Fabian Society, as Shaw has told us in characteristic style, was " warlike in its origin; it came into existence through a schism in an earlier society for the peaceful regeneration of the race by the cultivation of perfection of individual character. Certain members of that circle, modestly feeling that the revolution would have to wait an unreasonably long time if postponed until they personally had attained perfection, set up the banner of Socialism militant, seceded from the regenerators, and established themselves independently as the Fabian

---

* The society was entitled " The Fellowship of the New Life," and its first manifesto was entitled *Vita Nuova*. The following was its original basis, as drawn up by Mr. Maurice Adams, and adopted on November 16th, 1883:

" We, recognizing the evils and wrongs that must beset men so long as our social life is based upon selfishness, rivalry and ignorance, and desiring above all things to supplant it by a life based upon unselfishness, love and wisdom, unite, for the purpose of realizing the higher life among ourselves, and of inducing and enabling others to do the same.

" And we now form ourselves into a Society, to be called the Guild of the New Life, to carry out this purpose."

† Compare *Memorials of Thomas Davidson, the Wandering Scholar*, collected and edited by William Knight. T. Fisher Unwin, London, 1907.

Society." Shaw was not one of the original Fabians; in fact, he knew nothing of the society until its first tract, *Why are the Many Poor?* fell into his hands. For some reason the name of the society struck him as an inspiration. His choice fell upon that society in which he could gratify his desire to work with a few educated and clever men of the type of Sidney Webb.

In the earliest stage of the society the Fabians were content with nothing less than the prompt " reconstruction of society in accordance with the highest moral possibilities." Shaw joined the society on September 5th, 1884, when it was about eight months old, and in the labour-notes *versus* pass-books stage of evolution. Shaw actually debated with a Fabian who had elaborated a pass-book system, the question whether money should be permitted under Socialism, or whether labour-notes would not be a more suitable currency! The next two tracts, numbered 2 and 3, were from Shaw's pen; and although they were, as he now rightly regards them, mere literary *boutades*, they serve as an important link in the history of the evolution of the society.* Tract No. 4, *What Socialism Is*, answering the

---

* Tract No. 2, dated 1884, which is now very rare, has for motto the words of the late John Hay:

> " For always in thine eyes, O Liberty!
> Shines that high light whereby the world is saved;
> And, though thou slay us, we will trust in thee."

Certain sections of this manifesto deserve quotation as illustrative of Shaw's original and characteristic mode of expression:

" That, under existing circumstances, wealth cannot be enjoyed without dishonour, or forgone without misery.

" That the most striking result of our present system of farming out the national land and capital to private individuals has been the division of society into hostile classes, with large appetites and no dinners at one extreme, and large dinners and no appetites at the other.

" That the State should compete with private individuals—especially with parents—in providing happy homes for children, so that every child may have a refuge from the tyranny or neglect of natural custodians.

" That men no longer need special political privileges to protect them against women; and that the sexes should henceforth enjoy equal political rights.

" That the established Government has no more right to call itself the State than the smoke of London has to call itself the weather.

question both from the Collectivist and Anarchist point of view, reveals the early Anarchistic leanings of the society; the tract really contained nothing that had not already been better stated in the famous Communist Manifesto of Marx and Engels. Shaw was especially impressed by the fact that, in *Das Kapital*, Marx had made the most extensive use of the documents containing the true history of the leaps and bounds of England's prosperity, *e.g.*, the Blue Books. This convinced him that a tract stuffed with facts and figures, with careful references to official sources, was what was wanted. Incapable of making such tracts unaided, Shaw at once bethought him of Sidney Webb. That " walking encyclopædia," the student who knew everything and forgot nothing, could do it, Shaw was aware, as well as it could be done. So he brought all his powers of persuasion to bear on Sidney Webb. Picture to yourself the scene—two earnest, enthusiastic, revolutionary young men walking up and down Whitehall, outside the Colonial Office door, holding long and weighty discussions, often prolonged into the wee small hours, concerning the future of Socialism—the keen wit and agile logic of Shaw pitted against the sound judgment and sane conservatism of Webb. In this crucial juncture Shaw's proved the heavier artillery, and Webb became a Fabian. It would be difficult to lay one's finger upon any circumstance of deeper, more permanent, or more salutary effect upon Shaw's whole life. When Sidney Webb joined the Fabian Society there began a new and profoundly significant chapter in the history of Bernard Shaw. The debt Shaw owes to Webb is incalculable, and no one is readier to affirm it than Shaw himself. On various occasions I have heard Mr. Shaw unstintingly ascribe to Mr. Webb the greatest measure of credit for formulating and direct-

" That we had rather face a civil war than such another century of suffering as the present one has been."

Tract No. 3, addressed " To Provident Landlords and Capitalists," urged the proprietary classes to support " all undertakings having for their object the parcelling out of waste or inferior lands among the labouring class, and the attachment to the soil of a numerous body of peasant proprietors." Among the probable results of such a reform was mentioned (section 5): " The peasant proprietor, having a stock in the country, will, unlike the landless labourer of to-day, have a common interest with the landlord in resisting revolutionary proposals."

usable labor
spent labor
stored labor

ing the policy of the Fabian Society for many years. " The truth of the matter," Mr. Shaw once said to me, " is that Webb and I are very useful to each other. We are in perfect contrast, each supplying the deficiency in the other." On the other hand, Mr. Webb assigns the chief credit to Mr. Shaw; and in a personal letter, as well as in conversation, he has assured me that Mr. Shaw has been not simply *a* leading member, but *the* leading member of the Fabian Society practically from its foundation, and that it has always expressed his political views and work. I think we may safely say that Mr. Shaw and Mr. Webb have been mutually complementary—and complimentary.

The immediate result of the acquisition of Webb, the new recruit of the Fabians, was Tract No. 5, *Facts for Socialists,* a tangible proof of Webb's richly-stored mind and well-nourished scholarship. A comparison of this tract with those numbered 2 and 3 is sufficient evidence of the vast practical improvement Webb effected in the publications of the society. From this time forth the tracts and manifestos of the Fabian Society took on character and importance through the fortunate conjunction of Webb's encyclopædic mind and Shaw's literary sense. The next publication of importance was Tract No. 7, *Capital and Land,* a survey of the distribution of property among the classes in England. Drafted by Sidney Olivier, this tract was aimed in reality at the Georgites, who regarded capital as sacred. It exhibits growth of independent thought on the part of the society, and courage in breaking away from the fetters of " mere Henry Georgism."

Eight years later, that official organ of the Gladstonians, the *Speaker,* defined Fabianism as a " mixture of dreary, gassy doctrinairism and crack-brained farcicality, set off by a portentous omniscience and a flighty egotism not to be matched outside the walls of a lunatic asylum." Such denunciatory invective reveals the activity and influence the Fabian Society must have exerted, during those years, in the direction most dreaded by the older Whigs. But many were the lessons learned, the hard knocks received, the follies rejected, before Fabianism was sufficiently dangerous and important to be honoured with the scathing denunciation of the *Speaker.* The Fabian wisdom grew out of the Fabian experience; scientific economics out of insurrectionary anarchism. Decidedly catastrophic in their views at first, the Fabians were not unlike the young Socialist Shaw somewhere describes, who plans the revolutionary programme as an affair of twenty-four lively hours, with Individualism in full swing on Monday morning, a tidal wave of the insurgent proletariat on Monday afternoon, and Socialism in complete working order on Tuesday. After Mrs. Wilson, subsequently one of the Freedom Group of Kropotkinist Anarchists, joined the Fabians, a sort of influenza of Anarchism spread through the society.* In regard to political insurrectionism, the Fabians exhibited no definite and explicit disagreement with the Social Democratic Federation, avowedly founded on recognition of the existence of a class war. All, Fabians and Social Democrats alike, said freely that " as gunpowder destroyed the feudal system, so the capitalist system could not long survive the invention of dynamite "! Not that they were dynamitards; but, as Shaw explains: " We thought that the statement about gunpowder and feudalism was historically true, and that it would do the capitalists good to remind them of it." The saner spirits did not believe the revolution could be accomplished merely by singing the *Marseillaise;* but some of the youthful and insurgent enthusiasts " were so convinced that Socialism had only to be put clearly before the working classes to concentrate the power of their immense numbers into one irresistible organization, that the revolution was fixed for 1889—the anniversary of the French Revolution—at latest." Shaw was certainly not one of the conservative forces; he was outspokenly catastrophic and alarmingly ignorant of the multifarious delicate adjustments consequent upon a widespread social cataclysm. " I remember being asked satirically and publicly at that time," Shaw afterwards wrote, " how long it would take to get Socialism into working order if I had my way. I replied, with a spirited modesty, that a fortnight would be ample for the purpose. When I add that I was frequently complimented on being one of the more reasonable Socialists, you will be able

* Compare Fabian Tract No. 41.

to appreciate the fervour of our conviction and the extravagant
levity of our practical ideas." *

Broadly stated, the Fabians, in 1885, proceeded upon the
assumption that their projects were immediately possible and
realizable, an assumption theoretically as well as practically
unsound. At the Industrial Remunerative Conference they
denounced the capitalists as thieves; while among themselves
they were vehemently debating the questions of revolution,
anarchism, labour-notes *versus* pass-books, and other like futile
and daring projects. The tacit assumption under which they
worked, the purpose of their campaign with its watchwords:
" Educate, Agitate, Organize," was " to bring about a tremendous smash-up of existing society, to be succeeded by complete Socialism." This romantic, almost childlike faith in the
early consummation of that far-off divine event, towards which
the whole of Socialist creation moves, meant nothing more nor
less, as Shaw freely admits, than that they had no true practical
understanding either of existing society or Socialism. But the
tone of the society was changing, gradually and almost imper-
ceptibly, from that of insurrectionary futility to economic practicality. Their tracts and manifestos voiced, less and less frequently, forcible-feeble expressions of altruistic concern and
humanitarian indignation. The practical bases of Socialism,
the Fabians began to realize, were in sore need of being laid.
And there can be no doubt that the frank levity and irreverent
outspokenness, which are the distinguishing traits of Shaw, the
artist, were given the fullest field for development in the early
days of Fabian controversy, when no rein was put on tongue or
imagination. It was at this period, Shaw has told us, that the
Fabians contracted the invaluable habit of freely laughing at
themselves—a habit which has always distinguished them, always
saved them from being dampened by the gushing enthusiasts who
mistake their own emotions for public movements. As Shaw
once expressed it:

* *The Transition to Social Democracy*, an address delivered on September
7th, 1888, to the Economic Section of the British Association at Bath.
Printed in *Fabian Essays*, but first published in *Our Corner*, November,
1888, edited by Annie Besant.

" From the first such people fled after one glance at us, declaring that we were not serious. Our preferences for practical suggestions and criticisms, and our impatience of all general expressions of sympathy with working-class aspirations, not to mention our way of chaffing our opponents in preference to denouncing them as enemies of the human race, repelled from us some warm-hearted and eloquent Socialists, to whom it seemed callous and cynical to be even commonly self-possessed in the presence of the sufferings upon which Socialists make war. But there was far too much equality and personal intimacy among the Fabians to allow of any member presuming to get up and preach at the rest in the fashion which the working-class still tolerate submissively from their leaders. We knew that a certain sort of oratory was useful for ' stoking up ' public meetings; but we needed no stoking up, and when any orator tried the process on us, soon made him understand that he was wasting his time and ours. I, for one, should be very sorry to lower the intellectual standard of the Fabian by making the atmosphere of its public discussions the least bit more congenial to stale declamation than it is at present. If our debates are to be kept wholesome, they cannot be too irreverent or too critical. And the irreverence, which has become traditional with us, comes down from those early days when we often talked such nonsense that we could not help laughing at ourselves." *

No perceptible difference in the various Socialist societies in England was apparent until the election of 1885. When the Social Democratic Federation and that high priest of Marxism, the eloquent H. M. Hyndman, first appeared in the field, they " loomed hideously in the guilty eye of property." Whilst the Fabians numbered only forty, the Federation in numbers and influence was magnified out of all proportion by the imagination of the public and the political parties. The Tories actually believed that the Socialists could take enough votes from the

* Tract No. 41, *The Fabian Society: Its Early History,* by G. Bernard Shaw.

Liberals to make it worth their while to pay the expenses of two Socialist candidates in London.* The Social Democrats committed a huge tactical blunder in accepting Tory gold to pay the expenses of these elections, to say nothing of making the damaging exposure that, as far as voting power was concerned, the Socialists might be regarded as an absolutely negligible quantity. A more serious result of the " Tory money job " to the Federation was the defection of many of its adherents. The Socialist League, in the language of American National Conventions, viewed with indignation and repudiated with scorn the tactics of " that disreputable gang," the S. D. F., as it was currently designated; while the Fabians, more parliamentary in tone, passed the following resolution: " That the conduct of the Council of the Social Democratic Federation in accepting money from the Tory party in payment of the election expenses of Socialist candidates is calculated to disgrace the Socialist movement in England." Certain members of the Federation, under the leadership of C. L. Fitzgerald and J. Macdonald, seceded from it, and in February, 1886, formed a new body called " The Socialist Union," which eked out a precarious existence for barely two years. Far from being reinforced by the secessionists, the Fabians were, on the contrary, only the more inevitably forced to formulate their own principles, to mature their own individual policy. From this time forward, they were classed by the Federation as a hostile body. And, as Shaw says, " We ourselves knew that we should have to find a way for ourselves without looking to the other bodies for a trustworthy lead."

During the years 1886 and 1887, which mark the high tide and recession of Insurrectionism in recent English Socialist history, the sane tacticians, the Fabians, took little or no hand in the revolutionary projects for the relief of the unemployed. The budding economists were not wedded to street-corner agita-

* The main facts of the history of the Fabian Society as here recorded are derived chiefly from Fabian Tract, No. 41, *The Fabian Society: Its Early History,* by Mr. Shaw, and from conversations with Mr. Shaw. Compare, also, *The Fabian Society,* by William Clarke; Preface to *Fabian Essays.* Ball Publishing Co., Boston, 1908.

tions; nor was their help wanted by the men who were organizing church parades and the like. These were years of great distress among the labouring classes, not only in England, but in Holland, in Belgium, and especially in the United States. " These were the days when Mr. Champion told a meeting in London Fields that if the whole propertied class had but one throat he would cut it without a second thought if by doing so he could redress the injustices of our social system; and when Mr. Hyndman was expelled from his club for declaring on the Thames Embankment that there would be some attention paid to cases of starvation if a rich man were immolated on every pauper's tomb." After the 8th of February, 1886, that mad Monday of window-breaking, shop-looting, and carriage-storming memory, Hyndman, Champion, Burns, and Williams were arrested and tried for inspiring the agitation, but were acquitted. " The agitation went on more violently than ever afterwards; and the restless activity of Champion, seconded by Burns' formidable oratory, seized on every public opportunity, from the Lord Mayor's Show to services for the poor in Westminster Abbey or St. Paul's, to parade the unemployed and force their claims upon the attention of the public." Champion gave up in disgust when, impatient of doing nothing but marching hungry men about the streets and making speeches to them, he encountered only refusal of his two proposals to the Federation: either to empower him to negotiate some scheme of relief with his aristocratic sympathizers, or else go to Trafalgar Square and stay there until something should happen. Matters reached a crisis when the police, alarmed by the occasional proposals of incendiary agitation to set London on fire simultaneously at the Bank, St. Paul's, the House of Commons, the Stock Exchange, and the Tower, cleared the unemployed out of the Square. But the agitation for right of meeting grew universal among the working-classes; and finally Mr. Stead, with the whole working-class organization at his back, gave the word " To the Square! " * To the Square they all went, therefore,

* For an interesting account of the early movements of Socialistic consciousness in England, compare *An Artist's Reminiscences*, by the artist, Walter Crane; Chapter " Art and Socialism," pp. 249-338. Methuen and Co., 1907.

Shaw tells us, with drums beating and banners waving, in their tens of thousands, nominally to protest against the Irish policy of the Government, but really to maintain the right of meeting in the Square. With the new Chief Commissioner of Police, however, it was, as one of Bunyan's Pilgrims put it, but a word and a blow. " That eventful 13th of November, 1887, has since been known as ' Bloody Sunday.' The heroes of it were Burns and Cunninghame Graham, who charged, two strong, at the rampart of policemen round the Square and were overpowered and arrested. The heroine was Mrs. Besant, who may be said without the slightest exaggeration to have all but killed herself with overwork in looking after the prisoners, and organizing in their behalf a ' Law and Liberty League ' with Mr. Stead. Meanwhile, the police received the blessing of Mr. Gladstone; and Insurrectionism, after a two years' innings, vanished from the field and has not since been heard of. For, in the middle of the revengeful growling over the defeat at the Square, trade revived; the unemployed were absorbed; the *Star* newspaper appeared to let in light and let off steam; in short, the way was clear at last for Fabianism. Do not forget, though, that Insurrectionism will reappear at the next depression in trade as surely as the sun will rise to-morrow morning." *

Being " disgracefully backward " in open-air speaking, the Fabians had been somewhat overlooked in the excitements of the unemployed agitations. They had only Shaw, Wallas and Mrs. Besant as against Burns, Hyndman, Andrew Hall, Tom Mann, Champion and Burrows, of the Federation, and numerous representative open-air speakers of the Socialist League. The sole contribution of the Fabians to the agitation was a report, printed in 1886, recommending experiments in tobacco culture, and even hinting at compulsory military service as a means of

---

* Shaw's mother was never able to persuade herself, so strong were her aristocratic instincts, that in becoming a Socialist, George had not allied himself with a band of ragamuffins. One day, while walking down Regent Street with her son, she inquired who was the handsome gentleman on the opposite side. On being told that it was Cunninghame Graham, the distinguished *Socialist,* she protested: " No, no, George, that's impossible. Why, that man's a gentleman! "

absorbing some of the unskilled unemployed. Drawn up by Bland, Hughes, Podmore, Stapleton and Webb, this was the first Fabian publication that contained any solid information. In June, 1886, the temper of the society over the social question having cooled to some extent, the Fabians " signalized their repudiation of Sectarianism " by inviting the Radicals, the Secularists, and anyone else who would come, to a great conference, modelled upon the Industrial Remunerative Conference, and dealing with the Nationalization of Land and Capital. Fifty-three societies sent delegates, and eighteen papers were read during the three afternoons and evenings the conference lasted. Among those who read papers were two Members of Parliament, William Morris and Dr. Aveling, of the Socialist League, Mr. Foote and Mr. Robertson, of the National Secular Society. Wordsworth Donisthorpe, Stuart Headlam, Dr. Pankhurst, Mrs. Besant, Edward Carpenter and Stuart-Glennie represented various other shades of Socialist doctrine and belief. The main result of the conference was to make the Fabians known to the Radical clubs and to prove that they were able to manage a conference in a business-like way.

By this time the Fabians had definitely rejected Anarchism, and were agreed as to the advisability of setting to work by the ordinary political methods. The revolutionary hue of the society, however, was not obliterated without many wordy duels with that section of the Socialist League which called itself Anti-Communist, chiefly represented by Mr. Joseph Lane and William Morris.* It finally became necessary to put the matter to a vote in order to determine how many adherents Mrs. Wilson, the one avowed Anarchist among the Fabians, could muster. There ensued a spirited debate over the advisability of the Socialists organizing themselves as a political party " for the purpose of transferring into the hands of the whole working community full control over the soil and the means of production, as well as over the production and distribution of wealth " —a debate in which Morris, Mrs. Wilson, Davis and Tochatti were pitted against Burns, Mrs. Besant, Bland, Shaw, Donald

* Compare *To-Day*, edited by Hubert Bland, for the year 1886.

and Rossiter. The resolution of Mrs. Besant and Bland, in
favour of the organization of such a party, was finally carried,
while Morris's "rider," discountenancing as a false step the
attempt of the Socialists to take part in the Parliamentary contest, was subsequently rejected. The Fabian Parliamentary
League, an organization within the society itself, to which any
Fabian might belong, was now formed in order to avoid a break
with the Fabians who sympathized with Mrs. Wilson. The preliminary manifesto of this body, dated February, 1887, gives
the first sketch of the Fabian policy of to-day.* The League,
Shaw tells us, first faded into a Political Committee of the
society, and then merged silently and painlessly into the general
body. The few branches of the League which Mrs. Besant
formed in the provinces had but a short life, quite to be expected at this time, for, outside Socialistic circles in London,
the society remained unknown.

In connection with Shaw's own individual development, we
shall soon see how the Fabians received their training for public
life and became "equipped with all the culture of the age."
Suffice it to state here that the Fabians had now thoroughly
grounded themselves in the historic, economic and moral bearings
of Socialism. Their rejection of Anarchism and Insurrectionism was not accomplished without the expenditure of many
words, was not unattended by ludicrous results. The minutes
of the tumultuous meeting, signalized by the Besant-Bland-
Morris resolutions and attendant heated debate, closed with the
significant words:

> "Subsequently to the meeting, the secretary received
> notice from the manager of Anderton's Hotel that the
> Society could not be accommodated there for any further
> meetings."

At any rate, even at the cost of being refused a meeting-
place, the Fabians had finally demolished Anarchism in the
abstract "by grinding it between human nature and the theory

* This manifesto, in full, is to be found in Fabian Tract No. 41, pp. 13-14.

of economic rent." They now began to train the artillery of
their culture and economic equipment upon practical politics.
The Fabian Conference of 1886, attesting the repudiation of
sectarianism by the Fabians, had been boycotted by the S. D. F.
In 1888, the Fabians adopted a policy which severed the last
link between the Fabian Society and the Federation. The
Fabians began to join the Liberal and Radical, or even the Conservative, Associations, to become members of the nearest Radical
Club and Co-operative Store, and, whenever possible, to be
delegated to the Metropolitan Radical Federation and the Liberal and Radical Union. By making speeches and moving
resolutions at the meetings of these bodies, and using the Parliamentary candidate for the constituency as a catspaw, the
Fabians succeeded in " permeating " the party organizations.
So adroitly did the Fabians manage their machinery of political
wire-pulling that in 1888 they gained the solid advantage of
a Progressive majority full of ideas " that would never have
come into their heads had not the Fabians put them there," on
the first London County Council. In Shaw's words, in 1892:

" The generalship of this movement was undertaken
chiefly by Sidney Webb, who played such bewildering con-
juring tricks with the Liberal thimbles and the Fabian peas,
that to this day both the Liberals and the Sectarian Socialists stand aghast at him. It was exciting whilst it
lasted, all this ' permeation of the Liberal party,' as it
was called; and no person with the smallest political intelligence is likely to deny that it made a foothold for us in
the press and pushed forward Socialism in municipal
politics to an extent which can only be appreciated by
those who remember how things stood before our campaign. When we published ' Fabian Essays ' at the end
of 1889, having ventured with great misgiving on a sub-
scription edition of a thousand, it went off like smoke;
and our cheap edition brought up the circulation to about
twenty thousand. In the meantime, we had been cramming
the public with information in tracts, on the model of our
earliest financial success in that department, namely, *Facts*

THE SOCIALIST.

From a photograph taken in July, 1891.

[Facing p. 116

for Socialists, the first edition of which actually brought us a profit—the only instance of the kind then known. In short, the years 1888, 1889, 1890 saw a Fabian boom. . . ." *

In the *Political Outlook*, last of the *Fabian Essays*, Hubert Bland wisely predicted that the moment the party leaders had unmasked the Fabian designs, they would rally round all the institutions the Fabians were attacking. They might either put off the Fabians by raising false issues, such as Leaseholds Enfranchisement and Disestablishment of the Church, or, in order to defeat the Fabian candidates, coalesce with their rivals for office—just as, for example, the Republicans and Democrats united in the defeat of Henry George for mayor of New York City. In less than two years, Bland's prediction was verified. When Sidney Webb sought to force to political action a certain " Liberal and Radical " London Member of Parliament, who had unwarily expressed views virtually identical with Socialism, the startled politician discovered that he was not a Socialist and that Webb was. Although the word to " close up the ranks of Capitalism against the insidious invaders " was promptly given, it came too late, for the permeation had gone on too long. But the result was the " show-down " of the Fabian hand, and the call for a " new deal." In fact, the Conference of the London and Provincial Fabian Societies at Essex Hall on February 6th, 1892, was called together, not to celebrate the continuance of the permeation boom, but to face the fact that it was over. The time had come for a new departure. In his address before that conference, Shaw unhesitatingly said: " No doubt there still remains, in London, as everywhere else, a vast mass of political raw material, calling itself Liberal, Radical, Tory, Labour, and what not, or even not calling itself anything at all, which is ready to take the Fabian stamp if it is adroitly and politely pressed down on it. There are thousands of thoroughly Socialized Radicals to-day who would have resisted So-

* Tract No. 41: *The Fabian Society: Its Early History*, by G. Bernard Shaw.

cialism fiercely if it had been forced on them with taunts, threats, and demands that they should recant all their old professions and commit what they regard as an act of political apostasy. And there are thousands more, not yet Socialized, who must be dealt with in the same manner. But whilst our propaganda is thus still chiefly a matter of permeation, that game is played out in our politics. . . . We now feel that we have brought up all the political laggards and pushed their parties as far as they can be pushed, and that we have therefore cleared the way to the beginning of the special political work of the Socialist—that of forming a Collectivist party of those who have more to gain than to lose by Collectivism, solidly arrayed against those who have more to lose than to gain by it." And his final words project no absurdly Utopian dream of striking the shackles from the white slaves of Capital. While expressing undiminished hope for the possibilities of a distant, yet realizable, future, they reveal the sanity of the practical man of affairs, of the realist Shaw has so often magnified and celebrated. " You know what we have gone through, and what you will probably have to go through. You know why we believe that the middle-classes will have their share in bringing about Socialism, and why we do not hold aloof from Radicalism, Trade-Unionism, or any of the movements which are traditionally individualistic. You know, too, that none of you can more ardently desire the formation of a genuine Collectivist political party, distinct from Conservative and Liberal alike, than we do. But I hope you also know that there is not the slightest use in merely expressing your aspirations unless you can give us some voting power to back them and that your business in the provinces is, in one phrase, to create that voting power. Whilst our backers at the polls are counted by tens, we must continue to crawl and drudge and lecture as best we can. When they are counted by hundreds we can permeate and trim and compromise. When they rise to tens of thousands we shall take the field as an independent party. Give us hundreds of thousands, as you can if you try hard enough, and we will ride the whirlwind and direct the storm."

THE CART AND TRUMPET

"I leave the delicacies of retirement to those who are gentlemen first and literary workmen afterwards. The cart and trumpet for me."—*On Diabolonian Ethics.* In *Three Plays for Puritans*, p. xxii.

CHAPTER V

"IF the art of living were only the art of dialectic! If this world were a world of pure intellect, Mr. Shaw would be a dramatist." Mr. Walkley damns the dramatist to deify the dialectician. Many would deny Shaw the possession of a heart; few can deny him the possession of a remarkable brain and a phenomenal faculty of telling speech. The platform orator of to-day—easy, nonchalant, resourceful, instantaneous in repartee, unmatched in *hardiesse*, sublime in audacity—Shaw was once a trembling, shrinking novice. The veteran of a thousand verbal combats was once afraid to raise his voice; the *blagueur*, the "quacksalver" of a thousand mystifications, was once afraid to open his mouth! After all, the "brilliant" and "extraordinary" Shaw is only a self-made man. The sheer force of his will, exerted with tremendous energy ever since he came to man's estate, is the great motor which has carried him in his lifetime "from the seventeenth to the twenty-first century." A scientific natural history of Bernard Shaw's extraordinary career should make clear to all young aspirants that the extraordinariness of that career lies in its ordinariness. "Like a greengrocer and unlike a minor poet," as Mr. Shaw once put it to me, "I have lived instead of dreaming and feeding myself with artistic confectionery. With a little more courage and a little more energy I could have done much more; and I lacked these because in my boyhood I lived on my imagination instead of on my work."

Bernard Shaw has unravelled life's tangles with infinite patience. No cutting of Gordian knots for him. To ignore his training, his dogged persistence, his undaunted "push, pluck and perseverance," is unduly to magnify his natural capacity. Sacrifice the phenomenon and you find the personality; off with the marvel and on with the man. In a letter to me, written in 1904, Mr. Shaw gave due, almost undue, credit to the influence of training:

" It has enabled me to produce an impression of being an extraordinarily clever, original and brilliant writer, deficient only in feeling, whereas the truth is that, though I am in a way a man of genius—otherwise I suppose I could not have sought out and enjoyed my experiences and been simply bored by holidays, luxury and money—yet I am not in the least naturally ' brilliant,' and not at all ready or clever. If literary men generally were put through the mill I went through and kept out of their stuffy little coteries, where works of art breed in and in until the intellectual and spiritual product becomes hopelessly degenerate, I should have a thousand rivals more brilliant than myself. There is nothing more mischievous than the notion that my works are the mere play of a delightfully clever and whimsical hero of the *salons:* they are the result of perfectly straightforward drudgery, beginning in the ineptest novel-writing juvenility, and persevered in every day for twenty-five years."

The combination of supreme audacity with a sort of expansive and ludicrous self-consciousness has enabled Shaw to secure many of his most comic effects. And yet he once said with unreasonable modesty that anybody could get his skill for the same price, and that a good many people could probably get it cheaper. He wrested his self-consciousness to his own ends, transforming it from a serious defect into a virtue of genuine comic force. The apocryphal incident of Demosthenes and the pebbles finds its analogue in the case of Shaw. Only the most persistent and long-continued efforts enabled him to acquire that sublime hardihood in platform speaking which he deprecatingly denominates " ordinary self-possession." When Lecky, in 1879, first dragged him to a meeting of the Zetetical Society, Shaw knew absolutely nothing about public meetings or public order. I remember a talk with Mr. Shaw one day at Ayot St. Lawrence over the morning meal. " I had an air of impudence, of course," said Mr. Shaw, " but was really an arrant coward, nervous and self-conscious to a heartrending degree. Yet I could not hold my tongue. I started up and said something in the debate, and then felt that I had made such a fool of myself (mere vanity; for I had probably done nothing in the least noteworthy) that I vowed I would join the society, go every week, speak every week, and become a speaker or perish in the attempt. And I carried out this resolution. I suffered agonies that no one suspected. During the speech of the debater I resolved to follow, my heart used to beat as painfully as a recruit's going under fire for the first time. I could not use notes; when I looked at the paper in my hand I could not collect myself enough to decipher a word. And of the four or five wretched points that were my pretext for this ghastly practice of mine, I invariably forgot three—the best three." Yet in some remarkable way Shaw managed to keep his nervousness a secret from everyone except himself, for at his third meeting he was asked to take the chair. He bore out the impression he had created of being rather uppish and self-possessed by accepting as off-handedly as if he were the Speaker of the House of Commons. He afterwards confessed to me that the secretary probably got the first inkling of his hidden terror by seeing that his hand shook so that he could hardly sign the minutes of the previous meeting. There must have been something provocative, however, even in Shaw's nervous bravado. His speeches, one imagines, must have been little less dreaded by the society than they were by Shaw himself, yet it is significant that they were seldom ignored. The speaker of the evening, in replying at the end, usually paid Shaw the questionable compliment of addressing himself with some vigour to Shaw's remarks, and seldom in an appreciative vein. Conversant with the political theories of Mill and the evolutionary theories of Darwin and his school, Shaw was, on the other hand, " horribly ignorant " of the society's subjects. He knew nothing of political economy; moreover, he was a foreigner and a recluse. Everything struck his mind at an angle that produced reflections quite as puzzling as at present, but not so dazzling. His one success, it appears, was achieved when the society paid to Art, of which it was stupendously ignorant, the tribute of setting aside an evening for a paper on it by a lady in the " æsthetic " dress of the period. " I wiped the floor with that meeting," Shaw once told me, " and several members confessed to me afterwards that it was this performance that first made them reconsider their first impression of me as a discordant idiot."

Shaw persevered doggedly, taking the floor at every opportunity. Like the humiliated, defiant Disraeli, in his virgin speech in the House of Commons, Shaw resolved that some day his mocking colleagues should hear, aye, and heed him. He haunted public meetings, so he says, " like an officer afflicted with cowardice, who takes every opportunity of going under fire to get over it and learn his business." After his conversion to Socialism, he grew increasingly zealous as a public speaker. He was so full of Socialism that he made the natural mistake of dragging it in by the ears at every opportunity. On one occasion he so annoyed an audience at South Place that, for the only time in his life, he was met with a demonstration of impatience. " I took the hint so rapidly and apprehensively that no great harm was done," Mr. Shaw once said to me; " but I still remember it as an unpleasant and mortifying discovery that there is a limit even to the patience of that poor, helpless, long-suffering animal, the public, with political speakers." Such an incident had never occurred before; and although Shaw has spent his life in deriding the public, he has taken care that such a mortifying experience never occur again. Shaw now began to devote most of his time to Socialist propagandism. An eventful experience came to him in 1883, when he accepted an invitation to address a workmen's club at Woolwich. At first he thought of writing a lecture and even of committing it to memory; for it seemed hardly possible to speak for an hour, without text, when he had hitherto spoken only for ten minutes in a debate. He now realized that if he were to speak often on Socialism—as he fully meant to do—writing and learning by rote would be impossible for mere want of time. He made a few notes, being by this time cool enough to be able to use them. He found his feet without losing his head: the sense of social injustice loosened his tongue. The lecture, called " Thieves," was a demonstration of the thesis that the proprietor of an unearned income inflicted on the community exactly the same injury as a burglar. Fortified by *sæva indig-*

natio, Shaw spoke for an hour easily. From that time forth he considered the battle won.

In March, 1886, Shaw participated in a series of public debates held at South Place Institute, South Place, Finsbury, E.C. Here for the first time he tried his hand, in a fairly large hall, on an audience counted by hundreds instead of scores. " Socialism and Individualism " was the general title of this series of Sunday afternoon lectures.* This was a daring undertaking for Shaw, who had neither the experience nor the *savoir faire* of his colleagues. It was perhaps for this reason that he did not particularly distinguish himself, his opponent giving him as good as he sent. Mrs. Besant, a born orator, was interesting and eloquent, while Webb quite eclipsed Shaw, positively annihilating his adversary. One who knew him well at this initial stage, however, said that if Bernard Shaw knew nothing, he invented as he went along. The lightness of touch, the nimbleness of intellect, lacked complete development. At this time the clever young Irishman had neither memory enough for effective facts, nor presence of mind enough to be an easy winner in debate.

No one has yet measured the all-important influence Sidney Webb has exerted upon Shaw's career, dating from that memorable evening at the Zetetical Society when Shaw gazed in open-mouthed wonder at that miracle of effectiveness and model of self-possession. Shaw's admiration has waxed, not waned, with the passage of time. To-day he regards Webb as one of the most extraordinary and capable men alive. The critic who,

---

* On March 6th, Mrs. Annie Besant (Fabian Society) spoke *versus* Mr. Corrie Grant, subject: " That the existence of classes who live upon unearned incomes is detrimental to the welfare of the community, and ought to be put an end to by legislation." On March 13th, Mr. G. B. Shaw (Fabian Society) *versus* Rev. F. W. Ford, subject: " That the welfare of the community necessitates the transfer of the land and existing capital of the country from private owners to the State." On March 20th, Mr. Sidney Webb (Fabian Society) *versus* Dr. T. B. Napier, subject: " That the main principles of Socialism are founded on, and in accordance with, modern economic science." On March 27th, Mr. H. H. Champion *versus* Mr. Wordsworth Donisthorpe (Liberty and Property Defence League), subject: " That State interference with, and control of, industry is inevitable, and will be advantageous to the community."

SOUTH PLACE INSTITUTE,

SOUTH PLACE, FINSBURY, E.C.

(NEAR MOORGATE STREET AND BROAD STREET STATIONS)

Sunday Afternoon Lectures,

Socialism and Individualism.

A SERIES OF DEBATES

Will take place during MARCH as follows

March 6th.

MRS. ANNIE BESANT *versus* MR. CORRIE GRANT.

(Fabian Society.)

Subject : • That the existence of classes who live upon unearned incomes
is detrimental to the welfare of the Community, and ought to be
put an end to by Legislation."

March 13th.

MR. G. BERNARD SHAW *versus* REV F W FORD.

(Fabian Society.)

Subject " That the welfare of the Community necessitates the transfer
of the land and existing capital of the Country from private
owners to the state.

March 20th.

MR. SIDNEY WEBB *versus* DR. T. B. NAPIER.

(Fabian Society.)

Subject : " That the main principles of Socialism are founded on, and in
accordance with Modern Economic Science."

March 27th.

MR. H. H. CHAMPION

versus

MR. WORDSWORTH DONISTHORPE,

(Liberty and Property Defence League.)

Subject : " That State interference with, and control of industry is
inevitable, and will be advantageous to the Community."

The Chair will be taken each afternoon at 4 o'clock.

The audience are requested to refrain from any interference in the
Debates, which will be confined exclusively to the speakers
announced above.

MR. WALTER HASTINGS

Will give an

ORGAN RECITAL

Each Afternoon from 8-30 to 4 o'clock.

ALL SEATS FREE.   **NO COLLECTION.**

Doors open at 3.20.

CONRAD THIES, Hon. Sec. to Institute Committee.

PROGRAM OF SUNDAY AFTERNOON LECTURES
South Place Institute, South Place, Finsbury, E. C.
March, 1886.

in Disraelian phrase, regards Shaw as " one vast appropriation clause," will find some support for this belief in Shaw's statement that the difference between Shaw with Webb's brains and knowledge at his disposal, and Shaw by himself, is enormous. " Nobody has as yet gauged it," Mr. Shaw once said in a letter to me, " because as I am an incorrigible mountebank, and Webb is one of the simplest of geniuses, I have always been in the centre of the stage whilst Webb has been prompting me, invisible, from the side." Shaw's faculties of acquisitiveness and appropriation are enormously developed, a fact once comically accentuated by him in the frank avowal he once made to me: " I am an expert picker of other men's brains, and I have been exceptionally fortunate in my friends."

It was not without severe training and incessant work that Shaw and his fellow Fabians acquired the equipment in the historic and economic weapons of Social Democracy, comparable to that which Ferdinand Lassalle in his day so defiantly flaunted in the faces of his adversaries. While Stead, Hyndman and Burns were organizing the unemployed agitation in the streets, the Fabians were diligently training themselves for public life. Frank Podmore, a Post Office civil servant, and Edward Reynolds Pease, present secretary of the Fabian Society, two original Fabians, were great friends, and the earliest Fabian meetings were held alternately at Pease's rooms in Osnaburgh Street, and at Podmore's, in Dean's Yard, Westminster.* Certain of

---

* At this time, it is interesting to recall, Pease and Podmore were deeply interested in the Psychical Research Society, which had its office in the Dean's Yard rooms. In this way the Fabians, Shaw in particular, were brought in close touch with the exploits of this society at its most exciting period, when Madame Blavatsky was exposed by the American, R. Hodgson. Compare, for example, Shaw's two book-reviews in the *Pall Mall Gazette*: *A Scotland Yard for Spectres,* being a notice of the *Proceedings of the Society for Psychical Research* (January 23d, 1886), and *A Life of Madame Blavatsky* (January 6th, 1887). On one eventful evening Shaw attended a Fabian meeting, then went on to hear the end of a Psychical Research *séance,* and ended by sleeping in a haunted house with a committee of ghost-hunters. Picture, if you can, Shaw's deep mortification, his intense disgust over having a nightmare on that night of all nights, and waking up in a corner of the room struggling desperately with the ghost.

the Fabians sadly felt the need of solid information and training, in addition to that afforded by the meetings of the society. Thrown upon their individual resources, those most scholarly inclined of the Fabians, a veritable handful, founded the Hampstead Historic Club. First established as a sort of mutual improvement society for those ambitious Fabians wishing to read, mark, learn and inwardly digest Marx and Proudhon, this club was afterwards turned into a systematic history class, in which each student took his turn at being professor. Thus they taught each other what they themselves wished to learn, acquiring the most thorough and minute knowledge of the subject under discussion. In these days Shaw, Webb, Olivier and Wallas were the bravoes of advanced economics—the Three Musketeers and D'Artagnan. As Olivier and Wallas were men of very exceptional character and attainments, Shaw was enabled, as he once expressed it in my presence, to work with a four-man-power equal to a four-hundred-ordinary-man-power, which made his *feuilletons* and other literary performances " quite unlike anything that the ordinary hermit-crab could produce." Mr. Shaw thus explained very quaintly the secret of his success at this period. " In fact the brilliant, extraordinary Shaw *was* brilliant and extraordinary; but then I had an incomparable threshing machine for my ideas—a machine which contributed heaps of ideas to my little store; and when I seemed most original and fantastic, I was often simply an amanuensis with a rather exceptional literary knack, cultivated by dogged practice." And of his three warm friends he freely confessed: " They knocked a tremendous lot of nonsense, ignorance and vulgarity out of me, for we were on quite ruthless terms with one another."

Another associate, one of the Fabian essayists and now a journalist, Hubert Bland, was—and is still—of great value to Shaw and his colleagues, by reason of his strong individuality and hard common sense, and on account of the fact that his views ran counter to Webb's on many lines. Bland lived at Blackheath, on the south side of the river, at this time; and his wife, the very clever woman and distinguished author, " E. Nesbit," was a remarkable figure at the Fabian meetings during the first seven or eight years of its existence. During the era of the Hampstead Historic Club, Bland had a circle of his own at Blackheath; and although Hampstead, lying north of London, was quite out of Bland's district, Shaw and his friends used sometimes to descend on his evening parties. Bland had an utter contempt for the Bohemianism of Shaw and his companions, evincing it by wearing invariably an irreproachable frock-coat, tall hat, and a single eyeglass which infuriated everybody. Mrs. Bland graciously humoured the reckless Bohemianism of the *insouciant* Fabians, and on one memorable occasion stopped them at her door, went for needle and thread, and—perhaps with a faint hope of preserving the *haut ton* of her social evening—then and there sewed up the sleeve of Sidney Olivier's brown velveteen jacket. A *dernier ressort*, for the sleeve was all but torn out! There was some compensation in the fact that, even then, Olivier fully looked the dignified part he was one day to fill. But it is not easy to doubt that the arrant Bohemianism of the luckless Fabians, their reckless disregard of evening dress, must have been very trying to the decorum of Blackheath.

Of fierce Norman exterior and great physical strength, Bland dominated others by force of sheer size. Pugnacious, powerful, a skilled pugilist, and with a voice which Mr. Shaw once accurately described as being exactly " like the scream of an eagle," he made such a formidable antagonist that no one dared be uncivil to him. Just as William Clarke always combated and consequently stimulated Shaw by a diametrically opposite point of view, so Bland exerted a like influence upon Sidney Webb, and indirectly upon Shaw. Strongly Conservative and Imperialist by temperament, Bland stood in sharp contrast to the Millite, Benthamite recruits of the Fabian Society. There were many other clever fellows, many other good friends in Shaw's circle at this time; but through circumstances of time, place and marriage—the changes and chances of this mortal life—they could not be in such close touch with Shaw, Webb, Olivier and Wallas as were these four with one another.

It is not, of course, to be supposed that Shaw was merely the recipient, like Molière always taking his material where he found it. In his own peculiar and, at times, vastly irritating way, he made his personality strongly felt, exerting great influence by sheer force of a sort of perverse common sense. To employ Poe's apt descriptive, he was the Imp of the Perverse made flesh. In the circle of the Fabians there was room for considerable strife of temperaments, and in the other Socialist societies, quarrels and splits and schisms were rather frequent. Unquestionably Shaw's quintessential service to the Fabians lay in his pioneering ideas and his knack of drafting things in literary form and arranging his colleagues' ideas for them with Irish lucidity. A somewhat less conspicuous, yet little less important, service consisted in clearing the atmosphere, in easing off the personal friction which not infrequently produced smoke and at times threatened to kindle a conflagration. This personal friction Shaw managed to eliminate in a most characteristic way: by a sort of tact which superficially looked like the most outrageous want of it. Whenever there was a grievance, instead of trying to patch matters up, Shaw would deliberately betray everybody's confidence after the fashion of Sidney Trefusis, by stating it before the whole set in the most monstrously exaggerated terms. What would have been the result among acquaintances less closely linked by ties of personal friendship it is easy to imagine. The usual result, however, of Shaw's hazardous and tactless outspokenness was that everybody repudiated his monstrous exaggerations, and whatever of grievance there was in the matter was fully explained. Of course, Shaw was first denounced as a reckless mischief-maker, and afterwards forgiven as a privileged lunatic.

Once every fortnight, for a number of years, Shaw attended the meetings of the Hampstead Historic Club; and in the alternate weeks he spent a night at a private circle of economists which subsequently developed into The Royal Economic Society. Fabian, and especially Shavian, Socialism is strictly economic in character, a circumstance due in no small measure to the fact that in this circle of economists the social question was left out and the work kept on abstract economic lines. In speaking of this period, Shaw afterwards confessed:

130

THE CART AND TRUMPET

"I made all my acquaintances think me madder than usual by the pertinacity with which I attended debating societies and haunted all sorts of hole-and-corner debates and public meetings and made speeches at them. I was President of the Local Government Board at an amateur Parliament where a Fabian ministry had to put its proposals into black-and-white in the shape of Parliamentary Bills. Every Sunday I lectured on some subject I wanted to teach to myself; and it was not until I had come to the point of being able to deliver separate lectures, without notes, on Rent, Interest, Profits, Wages, Toryism, Liberalism, Socialism, Communism, Anarchism, Trade-Unionism, Co-operation, Democracy, the Division of Society into Classes, and the Suitability of Human Nature to Systems of Trust Distribution, that I was able to handle Social Democracy as it must be handled before it can be preached in such a way as to present it to every sort of man from his own particular point of view. In old lecture lists of the Society you will find my name down for twelve different lectures or so. Nowadays (1892), I have only one, for which the secretary is good enough to invent four or five different names." *

The only opponents who held their own against the Fabians in debate, men like Levy and Foote, had learned in the harsh school of experience; like the Fabians, they had found pleasure and profit in speaking, in debating, and in picking up bits of social information in the most out-of-the-way places. It was this keen Socialistic acquisitiveness of the Fabians, their readiness to eschew the conventional amusements for the pleasure to be derived from speaking several nights each week, which prepared them for the strenuous platform campaigns of the future. And such fun it was to the Fabian swashbucklers! After being " driven in disgrace " out of Anderton's Hotel, and subsequently out of a chapel near Wardour Street in which they had sought sanctuary, the Fabians went to Willis's Rooms,

* Tract No. 41, *The Fabian Society: Its Early History*, by G. Bernard Shaw.

the most aristocratic and also, as it turned out, the cheapest place of meeting in London. " Our favourite sport," says Shaw, " was inviting politicians and economists to lecture to us, and then falling on them with all our erudition and debating skill, and making them wish they had never been born." On one occasion the Fabians confuted Co-operation in the person of Mr. Benjamin Jones on a point on which, as Shaw afterwards confessed, they subsequently found reason to believe that they were entirely in the wrong and he entirely in the right. The 16th of March, 1888, commemorates the most signal victory of the Fabians in this species of guerrilla warfare. On that night of glorious memory a well-known member of Parliament, now the Secretary of State for War, lured into the Fabian ambuscade, was butchered to make a Fabian holiday. The following ludicrous account of the incident was written by the Individualist, Mr. G. Standring, in *The Radical*, March 17th, 1888. Picture to yourself the scene—a spacious and lofty apartment, brilliantly lighted by scores of wax candles in handsome candelabra, and about eighty ladies and gentlemen, seated around on comfortable chairs, lying in wait for the unsuspecting M.P. The company is composed almost exclusively of members of the Fabian Society—" A Socialist body whose motto is: Don't be in a hurry; but when you *do* go it, go it thick! "

" Such were the surroundings when, on March 16th, Mr. R. B. Haldane, M.P., was brought forth to meet his fate. The hon. gentleman, who is a lawyer and Member for Haddingtonshire, was announced to speak on ' Radical Remedies for Economic Evils,' but one could easily see that this was a mere ruse of war. The Fabian fighters were drawn up in battle array before the Chairman's table, ready for the fatal onslaught.

" Truth to tell, Mr. Haldane did not appear at all alarmed at the prospect of his impending butchery. Erect and manly, he stood at the table, and in calm, well-chosen language showed cause for his belief that Radical principles and Radical methods are sufficient to cure the evils of society. He then critically examined a Fabian pamphlet, ' The True Radical Programme,' and put in demurrers thereto. The hon. and learned gentleman spoke for an hour, and as I sat on my cushioned chair, encompassed round about by Socialists, breathing an atmosphere impregnated with Socialism, I listened, and softly murmured : ' Verily, an angel hath come down from heaven ! '

" As the last words of Mr. Haldane died away, the short, sharp tones of the Chairman's voice told that the carnage was about to commence. After some desultory questioning, Mr. Sidney Webb sprang to his feet, eager, excited and anxious to shake the life out of Mr. Haldane before anyone else could get at him. He spoke so rapidly as to become at times almost incoherent. Mr. Webb seemed to be charged with matter enough for a fortnight, and he was naturally desirous to fire as much of it as possible into the body of the enemy. At length the warning bell of the Chairman was heard, and the attack was continued by Mrs. Annie Besant, who, standing with her back to the foe, occasionally faced round to emphasize a point. Then up rose George Bernard Shaw, and as he spoke, his gestures suggested to me the idea that he had got Mr. Haldane impaled upon a needle, and was picking him to pieces limb by limb, as wicked boys disintegrate flies. Mr. Shaw went over the Radical lines as laid down by his opponent, and this was the burden of his song: That is no good, this is no good, the other is no good—while you leave nine hundred thousand millions, in the shape of Rent and Interest, in the hands of an idle class. Let us nationalize the nine hundred thousand millions, and all these (Radical) things shall be added unto you. Mr. Shaw fired a Parthian shot as he sat down. Mr. Haldane had spoken of education, elementary and technical, as a means of advancing national welfare. Shaw met this with open scorn, and declared that the most useful and necessary kind of education was the education of the Liberal party ! With that he subsided in a rose-water bath of Fabian laughter.

" The massacre was completed by two other members of the Society, and then the Chairman called upon Mr. Haldane to reply. Hideous mockery! the Chairman knew that Haldane was *dead!* He had seen him torn, tossed and trampled underfoot. Perhaps he expected the ghost of the M.P. to rise and conclude the debate with frightful gibberings of fleshless jaws and gestures of bony hands. Indeed, I heard a rustling of papers, as if one gathered his notes for a speech; but I felt unable to face the grisly horror of a phantom replying to its assassins, so I fled."

The three great influences, formative and determinative, whose importance in their bearing upon Shaw's career can scarcely be overestimated, are: first, minute and exhaustive researches into the economic bases of society; second, his persevering efforts as a public man toward the practical reformation of patent social evils; and, third, his strenuous activity persisted in for many years, as a public speaker and Socialist propagandist. His plays are so permeated with the spirit of economic and social research that they may be called, with little exaggeration, clinical lectures upon the social anatomy of our time. Shaw, the public man, the man of affairs, never the literary recluse of the ivory tower, stands revealed alike in criticism and drama. There is more truth than jest in Shaw's statement, generally greeted with derisive scepticism, that his plays differ from those of other dramatists because he has been a vestryman and borough councillor. And there is scarcely a play of Shaw's which does not bear the hall-mark of the facile debater. His weekly *feuilletons,* his literary criticisms, provocative, argumentative, controversial, smack of the arena and the public platform.

This close touch with actual life, this vital association with public effort and social reform, have imparted to Shaw's literary productions a rare, an unique flavour. He has gone down unflinchingly into the pitiless and dusty arena to joust against all comers. Shaw has never lived the literary life, never belonged to a literary club. He has never lived " *l'auguste vie quotidienne d'un Hamlet,*" who, as Maeterlinck asserts, has time to live because he does not act. Shaw has found life in action, action in life. Although he brought all his powers unsparingly to the criticism of the fine arts, he never frequented their social surroundings. When he was not actually writing or attending performances, his time was fully taken up by public work, in which he was fortunate enough to be associated with a few men of exceptional ability and character. From 1883 to 1888, he was criticizing books in the *Pall Mall Gazette* and pictures in the *World*. This left him his evenings free; consequently he did a tremendous amount of public speaking and debating—speaking in the open air, in the streets, in the parks, at demonstrations—anywhere and everywhere. While he never belonged to a literary club, so called, he was a member of several literary societies in London. His intimate acquaintance with Shakespeare was improved by his quiet literary off-nights at the New Shakespeare Society under F. J. Furnival. Elected a member of the Browning Society by mistake, Shaw stood by the mistake willingly enough, and spent many breezy and delightful evenings at its meetings. "The papers thought that the Browning Society was an assemblage of long-haired æsthetes," Shaw once remarked to me; " in truth, it was a conventicle where pious ladies disputed about religion with Furnival, and Gonner and I egged them on." * When Furnival founded the Shelley Society, Shaw, of course, joined that, and became an extremely enthusiastic and energetic member. It was at the Shelley Society's first large meeting that Shaw startled London by announcing himself as, " like Shelley, a Socialist, an atheist, and a vegetarian." † Shaw was afterwards active in forwarding the fine performance of *The Cenci*, given by the Shelley Society, before it succumbed to its heavy printer's bills. Such were Shaw's recreations; but his main business was Socialism. It was first come first served with Shaw. Whenever he received

* The Gonner here referred to is E. C. K. Gonner, M.A., now Brunner Professor of Economic Science at the University College, Liverpool.

† While Shaw has stated publicly numbers of times that he was an atheist, an explanation here is necessary. Shaw has always had a strong sense of spiritual things; his declarations of atheism should always be taken with the context. "If this be religion," he has virtually said in reply to someone's exposition of religion, "then I am an atheist." In the case of Shelley, it is perfectly plain that Shaw meant that he was all these things—a Socialist, an atheist and a vegetarian—in the Shelleyan sense.

an invitation for a lecture, like his own character Morell, he gave the applicant the first date he had vacant, whether it was for a street corner, a chapel, or a drawing-room. He spoke to audiences of every description, from University dons to London washerwomen. From 1883 to 1895, with virtually no exception, he delivered a harangue, with debate, questions, and so on, every Sunday—sometimes twice or even thrice—and on a good many weekdays. This teeming and tumultuous life was passed on many platforms, from the British Association to the triangle at the corner of Salmon's Lane in Limehouse.

In 1888, when he became a critic of music, Shaw was restricted solely to lectures on Sundays, as he could not foresee whether he should have the opera or a concert to attend on week-nights. It is remarkable how much he managed to do, even with this handicap, especially as he had to speak usually on short notice.* At last, as was inevitable with a man burning the candle at both ends, the strain began to tell; Shaw found it impossible to deal with all the applications he received. For an advanced and persistently progressive thinker like Shaw, the unavoidable repetition of the old figures and the old demonstrations in time grew irksome. He felt the danger of becoming, like Morell, a windbag—what George Ade calls a " hot-air machine." By 1895, the machine was no longer by any means in full blast; the breakdown of Shaw's health, in 1898, finished him as a systematic and indefatigable propagandist. His work went on almost uninterrupted, however, although it was no longer explicit propagandism. Indeed, he worked more strenuously than ever on the St. Pancras Vestry, now the St. Pancras Borough Council. Since 1898, Shaw has lectured only occa-

---

* " Take the amusing, cynical, remarkable George Bernard Shaw, whose Irish humour and brilliant gifts have partly helped, partly hindered the (Fabian) Society's popularity. This man will rise from an elaborate criticism of last night's opera or Richter concert (he is the musical critic of the *World*), and after a light, purely vegetarian meal, will go down to some far-off club in South London or to some street corner in East London, or to some recognized place of meeting in one of the parks, and will there speak to poor men about their economic position and their political duties."— William Clarke, in *The Fabian Society and Its Work*. Preface to *Fabian Essays*. Ball Publishing Co., Boston, 1908.

sionally, but often enough for a man who wishes to preserve his health and strength. His labour as head of the Fabian Society, during the years 1906-7, in giving form and definiteness to the policy of that society, was one of the greatest works of his life—a work to which he gave his time and energy without stint. Many of his Fabian colleagues assured me that no one but Bernard Shaw could have accomplished so signal and so sweeping a victory. Within a year or two, he will doubtless resign his arduous duties as head and centre of the Fabian Society. And it is probable, he recently told me, that he will never again undertake another platform campaign.

Shaw's " knack of drafting things," as he calls it, has played no inconsiderable figure in his career. Simultaneously with his desperate attack on the platform, Shaw was acquiring what he denominates the " committee habit." Whenever he joined a society—even the Zetetical—his marked executive ability soon placed him on the committee. In learning the habits of public life and action simultaneously with the art of public speaking, he gained a great deal of valuable experience—experience which cannot be acquired in conventional grooves. The constant and unceremonious criticism of men who were at many points much abler and better informed than himself, developed in Shaw two distinctive traits—self-possession and impassivity. It is certain that his experience as a man of affairs actively engaged in public work, municipal and political, gave him that behind-the-scenes knowledge of the mechanism and nature of political illusion which seems so cynical to the spectators in front.

According to the current view, Shaw has always been a voracious man-eater, like a lion going about seeking whom he might devour. On the contrary, instead of flinging down the gauntlet to any and every one, Shaw never challenged anyone to debate with him in public. To Shaw, it seemed an unfair practice for a seasoned public speaker, and no test at all of the validity of his case—a duel of tongues, of no more value than any other sort of duel. In the eighties, the Socialist League, of which William Morris was the leading figure, made an effort to arrange a debate between Shaw and Charles Bradlaugh, who had graduated from boy evangelism to the rank of the most formidable debater to be found in the House of Commons. In more than one place, but notably in *The Quintessence of Ibsenism,* Shaw has paid the highest tribute to the remarkable qualities of Bradlaugh as thinker and dialectician. The Socialist League challenged Bradlaugh to debate, and chose Shaw as their champion, although he was not even a member of that body. Bradlaugh made it a condition that Shaw should be bound by all the pamphlets and utterances of the Social Democratic Federation, a strongly anti-Fabian body. Had Shaw been richer in experience in such matters, he would undoubtedly have let Bradlaugh make what conditions he pleased, and then said his say without troubling about them. As it was, Shaw proposed a simple proposition, " Will Socialism benefit the English people? " with a simple, general definition of Socialism. But Bradlaugh refused this; and the debate— as Bradlaugh probably intended—did not come off. At the time, Shaw was somewhat relieved over the issue, being very doubtful of his ability to make any great showing against Bradlaugh; he has since privately expressed his regret that the debate did not take place. Bradlaugh was a tremendous debater, and in point of " personal thunder and hypnotism " Shaw would have been, in sporting parlance, outclassed. But to Shaw, whose *forte* is always offence, it would have been a great gratification to tackle Bradlaugh in his own hall—the Hall of Science, in Old Street, St. Luke's. At least Shaw could have had his say.

At a later time, Bradlaugh debated the question of the Eight-Hours' Day with H. M. Hyndman—their second platform encounter. But both sides were dissatisfied, as neither of them stuck to his subject, and the result was inconclusive. A debate on the same question was then arranged between Shaw and G. W. Foote, Bradlaugh's successor as President of the National Secular Society. In this, Shaw's only public set debate with the exception of one in earlier days at South Place chapel, the question was ably and carefully argued by both parties, without rancour, bitterness, or personal abuse.* The debate lasting

---

* In a long contemporary account of the debate, a French newspaper commented approvingly on the high tone maintained throughout, placing

two nights, and presided over by Mr. G. Standring and Mr. E. R. Pease in turn, was held at the Hall of Science, London, on January 14th and 15th, 1891. The verbatim report, which is still procurable, exhibits the best qualities of Shaw as a cool-headed, logical debater. His two speeches, markedly ironical in tone, are frequently punctuated by the bracketed (applause). Mr. Foote closed one of his speeches with the rather effulgent peroration, " Every question must be threshed out by public debate. Let truth and falsehood grapple—whichever be truth and whichever be falsehood; for, as grand old John Milton said, ' Whoever knew truth put to the worse in a free and open encounter? ' "—a sentiment greeted with loud applause. To which Shaw delightfully responded: " I do not know, gentlemen, what a free and open encounter might bring about; but if John Milton asks me whoever saw truth put to shame in such an encounter with falsehood as it has a chance of having in the present condition of society, then I reply to John Milton that George Bernard Shaw has seen it put to shame very often." Shaw maintained that a reduction of hours would raise wages, not prices, and that doing it by law was the only possible way of doing it. His closing words clearly mirror his view of the mission of Socialism, the reason of its existence.

" I can only say, for myself, that the debate has been a pleasant one to me, because of the friendly terms on which Mr. Foote and I stand. I even imagine there is a bond between Mr. Foote and myself that may serve a little to explain this. Mr. Foote and I, on a certain subject— the established religion of this country—entertain the same views. Now, those views have directed our attention very strongly towards the necessity of maintaining the freedom of the individual to hold what views he likes, to have free-dom of speech and association for the purpose of following out all his conclusions, and establishing a genuine culture

the English in sharp contrast with French debates on similar subjects, which were not regarded as unqualified successes unless they broke up in personal encounters, with the attendant imprecations: " *Assassins! A bas les Socialistes! A la lanterne!* "

founded on facts, and not on the dogmas of any church whatsoever. I confess that in the days before I had studied economic questions I was filled with the necessity of individual freedom on these points, and that I also had that strong distrust of the State which Mr. Foote has expressed here to-night. But when my attention was turned to the economic side of the question, I soon became convinced that the real secret of the State's hostility to the advance of reasonable views was that Reason condemned the propertied institutions of this country. Property is the real force that hypocritically expresses itself as Religion. I therefore came to the conclusion that we shall never get out of the mess we are in until the workers come to understand that they are already deprived of individual freedom by the irresistible physical force of the State, and that they can escape from its oppression only by seizing on the political power, and using that very State force to emancipate themselves, and impose their will on the minority which now enslaves them. That is the reason that, just as I urge the importance of individual freedom of speech, so I also urge on the workers that they cannot possibly help themselves by individual action so long as this terrible State is outside them, and ready to cut them down at every point. I believe that they can, by concerted action, not merely in trade unions, but in a united democracy, get complete control of the State, and use its might for their own purposes; and when they once come to understand this, I believe their emancipation will only be delayed until they have learned from experience the true conditions of social freedom." *

There is another feature of Shaw's career as a public speaker which exhibits his attitude towards the work in life he had set before him. Shaw fights for what seems to many less like liberty than licence of speech. He never submitted his intelli-

* *The Legal Eight Hours Question.* A two-nights' public debate between Mr. G. W. Foote and Mr. George Bernard Shaw. Verbatim Report. London: R. Forder, 28, Stonecutter Street, E.C. 1891.

gence, his will, or his power to alien domination. He has never belonged to any political party, rightly considered, never cringed under any lash, never realized in his own experience what he himself has called the only real tragedy: " the being used by personally-minded men for purposes which you recognize as base." It was the determination to remain untrammelled in thought and action which forbade his ever accepting payment for speaking. Very often provincial Sunday Societies invited him to come down for the usual ten guineas fee and give the usual sort of lecture, avoiding politics and religion. Shaw's invariable answer to such requests was that he never lectured on anything but politics and religion, and that his fee was the price of his railway ticket third-class, if the place was further off than he could afford to go at his own expense. The Sunday Society would then " come around " and assure Shaw that he might, on these terms, lecture on anything he liked; and he always *did*. Occasionally, to avoid embarrassing other lecturers who lived by lecturing, the thing was done by a debit and credit entry: that is, Shaw took the usual fee and expenses, and gave it back as a donation to the society. Shaw once related to me the circumstances of a most interesting *contretemps*, which alone would suffice to justify his desire for freedom of speech, his wisdom in arming himself against the accusation of being a professional agitator. " At the election of 1892, I was making a speech in the Town Hall of Dover, when a man rose and shouted to the audience not to let itself be talked to by a hired speaker from London. I immediately offered to sell him my emoluments for five pounds. He hesitated; and I came down to four pounds. At last I offered to take five shillings—half-a-crown—a shilling—sixpence—for my fees, and when he would not take them at that, claimed that he must know perfectly well that I was there at my own expense. If I had not been able to do this, the meeting, which was a difficult and hostile one (Dover being a hopeless, corrupt Tory constituency) would probably have been broken up."

As Mr. Clarence Rook has remarked, London first opened her eyes in wonder over the versatile " G. B. S." when she discovered that in the daytime he preached revolt to the grimy

East from a tub, and in the evening sent William Archer and the cultured West into peals of merriment over his *Arms and the Man*. In those halcyon transpontine days London began to take pains to be present at Shaw's delightful dialectical performances at Battersea. Shaw lectured often in Battersea because it was John Burns' stronghold. Never was Shaw's skyrocketing brilliance more effectively displayed than in one of his orations at the Washington Music Hall, with Clement Edwards in the chair. In this oration he proved that no conclusion could be drawn from a bare profession of Socialism as to what side a man would take on any concrete political issue. In speaking of this remarkable effort, Mr. Shaw recently told me the following incident: " I remember hearing a workman say to his wife as I came up behind them on my way to the station: ' When I hear a man of intellect talk like that for a whole evening, it makes me feel like a WORM.' Which made me feel horribly ashamed of myself. I felt the shabbiest of impostors, somehow, though really I gave him the best lecture I could." With the exception of his two nights' wrestle with G. W. Foote, Shaw's most sustained effort—an oration lasting about four hours—was delivered in the open air on a Sunday morning at Trafford Bridge, Manchester. Shaw takes pleasure in declaring that one of his best speeches, about an hour and a half long, was delivered in Hyde Park in the pouring rain to six policemen sent to watch him, and the secretary of the little society that had invited him to speak. " I was determined to interest those policemen, because as they were sent there to listen to me, their ordinary course, after being once convinced that I was a reasonable and well-conducted person, would be to pay no further attention. But I quite entertained them. I can still see their waterproof capes shining in the rain when I shut my eyes."

Courage and daring, as well as fertility and inventiveness, often enabled Shaw to carry his point or to have his say, in the face of violent and almost invincible opposition. He has more than once actually voted against Socialism in order to forward the motion in hand. And once, in St. James's Hall, London, at a meeting in favour of Woman's Suffrage, he ventured with success upon a curious trick, the details of which he once related to me:

" Just before I spoke a hostile contingent entered the room, and I saw that we were outnumbered, and that an amendment would be carried against us. They were all Socialists of the anti-Fabian sort, led by a man whom I knew very well, and who was at that time worn out with public agitation and private worry, so that he was excitable almost to frenzy. It occurred to me that if they, instead of carrying an amendment, could be goaded to break up the meeting and disgrace themselves, the honours would remain with us. I made a speech that would have made a bishop swear and a sheep fight. My friend the enemy, stung beyond endurance, dashed madly to the platform to answer me then and there. His followers, thinking he was leading a charge, instantly stormed the platform, and broke up the meeting. Then the assailants reconstituted the meeting and appointed one of their number chairman. I then demanded a hearing, which was duly granted me as a matter of fair play, and I had another innings with great satisfaction to myself. No harm was done and no blow struck, but the papers next morning described a scene of violence and destruction that left nothing to be desired by the most sanguinary schoolboy."

Like Ibsen, Shaw has barely escaped the honour of being imprisoned—an honour which, it is needless to say, he never sought. Fortunately for Shaw, the religious people always joined with the Socialists to resist the police. Twice, in difficulties raised by attempts of the police to stop street meetings, Shaw was within an ace of going to prison. The first time, the police capitulated on the morning of the day when Shaw was the chosen victim. The second time Shaw was so fortunate as to have in a member of a rival Socialist society a disputant for the martyr's palm. One can sympathize with Shaw's secret relief when, on a division, his rival defeated him by two votes! One of the most remarkable speakers in England to-day, Bernard Shaw is not simply a talent, a personality: he is a public institution. People flock to his lectures and addresses, and his *bons mots* are quoted in London, New York, Berlin, Vienna and St. Petersburg. He is the most universally discussed man of letters now living. Not since Byron has any British author enjoyed an international audience and vogue comparable to that enjoyed by Bernard Shaw. No one in our time is Shaw's equal in searching analysis and trenchant exposition of the ills of modern society. His ability to see stark reality and to know it for his own makes of him the most powerful pamphleteer, the most acute journalist-publicist since the days of Swift. His indictments of the fundamental structure of contemporary society prove him the greatest master of comic irony since the days of Voltaire. Inferior to Anatole France in artistry and urbanity, Shaw excels him in the strenuousness of his personal sincerity and in the scope of his purpose. Shaw's manner of speaking is as individual, as distinctive, as is his style as an essayist or his fingering as a dramatist. That priceless and inalienable gift which has helped to make Jean Jaurès the leader of modern Socialists—the power of touching the emotions—is a quality which Shaw, like Disraeli before him, wholly lacks. In Shaw there is no spark of the mesmeric force, the hypnotic power of the born orator; he lacks that romance, that power of dramatic visualization, which is a quality of all true oratory. While it is true that people do not " orate " in England as they do in America, still there is a vast difference between the born orator, like Jaurès or Mrs. Besant, and the practised public speaker, like Shaw. All that could be acquired, Shaw acquired. Not Charles Bradlaugh himself had a more thorough training than had Shaw. He is facile, fluent and fertile; he does not leave all his qualities behind him when he mounts the platform. In fine, Shaw has fulfilled to the letter his early vow, solemnly taken the night he joined the Zetetical Society. He has delivered considerably more than a thousand public addresses, and the best of them were masterpieces of their kind. And yet Shaw has only a very ordinary voice; and in order to make himself comfortably heard by a large audience he has to be very careful with his articulation and to speak as though he were addressing the auditor furthest from him.

[Stephen Cribb, Southsea

THE CART AND TRUMPET.

Shaw addressing the dockyard men outside dockyard gate on behalf of Alderman Sanders G. B. S. is annoyed with the interrupter, but is ready with an instant retort.

[Facing p. 144

THE CART AND TRUMPET

With his long, loose form, his baggy and rather *bizarre* clothes, his nonchalant, quizzical, extemporaneous appearance; with his red hair and scraggly beard, his pallid face, his bleak smile, his searching eyes flashing from under his crooked brows; with his general air of assurance, privilege and impudence—Bernard Shaw is the jester at the court of King Demos. Startling, astounding, irrepressible, he fights for opposition, clamours for denial, demands suppression. Shaw was once completely floored by a workman, who rose after he had completed a magnificent pyrotechnic display, and said: " I know quite well that Bernard Shaw is very clever at argument, and that when I sit down he will make mincemeat of everything I say. But what does that matter to me? I still have my principles." Shaw had to admit, as he once told me in speaking of the incident, that this was unanswerable and thoroughly sound at bottom. " Call me disagreeable, only call me something," clamours Shaw; " for then I have roused you from your stupid torpor and made you think a new thought." The incarnation of intellect, not of hypnotism, of reason, not of oratory, this strange image of Tolstoy as he was in his middle years has always made his audience think new thoughts. He has never given the audience what it liked; he has always given it what he liked, and what he thought it needed: a bitter and tonic draught. The successes of the orator who is the mere mouthpiece of his audience have never been his. But he has achieved a more enviable and more arduous distinction; I have heard him say with genuine pride that more than once he has been the most unpopular man in a meeting, and yet carried a resolution against the most popular orator present by driving home its necessity. For the transports which the popular orator raises by voicing popular sentiment Shaw has no use. Of the orator's power of entrancing people and having his own way at the same time he has never had a trace. He is the arch-foe of personal hypnotism, of romance, of sensuous glamour. He has sought the accomplishment of the demand of his will; he never practised speaking as an art or an accomplishment. The desire for that, he once told me, would never have nerved him to utter a word in public. Just as Zola used his journalistic work as a hammer to drive his views into the brain of the public, Shaw used his dialectical skill as a weapon, as a means to the end of making people think. One might truly say of all the things that he has either spoken or written: " *Ils donnent à penser furieusement.*" As a speaker, he first startled and provoked his audience to thought, and then annihilated their objections with the sword of logic and the rapier of wit. His ready answer for every searching query, his instantaneous leap over every tripping barrier, seemed to the novice a proof of very genius. To strange audiences, his readiness in answering questions and meeting hostile arguments seemed astonishing, miraculous. On several different occasions I have heard Mr. Shaw modestly give the explanation of this apparently magic performance. " The reason was that everybody asks the same questions and uses the same arguments. I knew the most effective replies by heart. Before the questioner or debater had uttered his first word I knew exactly what he was going to say, and floored him with an apparent impromptu that had done duty fifty times before." Shaw always carefully thought out the thing for himself in advance, and, which is far more important, had thought out not only an effective, but also a witty answer to the objections that were certain to be raised. This is the secret of Shaw's success in every task which he has undertaken: to think each thing out for himself, and to couch it in terms of scathing satire and fiery wit. His is the sceptical Socratic method pushed to the limit.

Confronted with the point-blank question: " To what do you owe your marvellous gift for public speaking? " Shaw characteristically replied: " My marvellous gift for public speaking is only part of the G. B. S. legend. I am no orator, and I have neither memory enough nor presence of mind enough to be a really good debater, though I often seem to be when I am on ground that is familiar to me and new to my opponents. I learned to speak as men learn to skate or to cycle—by doggedly making a fool of myself until I got used to it. Then I practised it in the open air—at the street corner, in the market square, in the park—the best school. I am comparatively out of practice now, but I talked a good deal to audiences all through the eighties, and for some years afterwards. I should be a really remarkable orator after all that practice if I had the genius of the born orator. As it is, I am simply the sort of public speaker anybody can become by going through the same mill. I don't mean that he will have the same things to say, or that he will put them in the same words, for, naturally, I don't leave my ideas or my vocabulary behind when I mount the tub; but I *do* mean that he will say what he has to say as movingly as I say what I have to say—and more, if he is anything of a real orator. Of course, as an Irishman, I have some fluency, and can manage a bit of rhetoric and a bit of humour on occasion, and that goes a long way in England. But ' marvellous gift ' is all my eye." *

* *Who I Am, and What I Think.* Part I. The *Candid Friend,* May 11th, 1901.

SHAVIAN SOCIALISM

" Of course, people talk vaguely of me as an Anarchist, a visionary, and a crank. I am none of these things, but their opposites. I only want a few perfectly practical reforms which shall enable a decent and reasonable man to live a decent and reasonable life, without having to submit to the great injustices and the petty annoyances which meet you now at every turn."—*George Bernard Shaw: an Interview*. In *The Chap-Book*, November, 1896.

" Economy is the art of making the most of life.
The love of economy is the root of all virtue."
—*The Revolutionist's Handbook*. In *Man and Superman*.

CHAPTER VI

I ONCE heard a Socialist of world-wide renown accuse Bernard Shaw of an inconsistency which, to him, was little short of inexplicable. To every charge of inconsistency, Shaw is always ready with the effective rejoinder: " *l'homme absurde est celui qui ne change jamais.*" To Shaw, the stationary is the stagnant, evolution is progress. That rare literary phenomenon, a master of the comic spirit, Shaw is not only willing to admit for the nonce the inconsistencies in his own make-up: he is positively eager to make thereof genuine comic capital.

To the public, Shaw is his own greatest paradox. What defence, they ask, can be devised for a man rooted in Nietzscheism, who champions the Socialism which Nietzsche mocked? Reconcile the ardent apostle of the levelling democracy of a Social-Democratic Republic with the avowed advocate of the doctrines of Ibsen and Nietzsche, the intellectual aristocrats of this distinctly social era? Identify the agitation for international disarmament, for universal peace, with one who sings of arms and the superman? The Irish Nietzsche, the daring pilgrim in search of a moral Ultima Thule, with one who has forcibly declared the impossibility of anarchism? The evangelist preaching the brotherhood of man with one who repudiates the pacifying sedative: " Sirs, ye are brothers," in the statement that he has no brothers, and if he had, he would in all probability not agree with them? What faith is to be put in the economic grounding of one who, in the course of two or three years, turned from vigorous defence of Marx's value theory to its " absolute demolition, on Jevonian lines, with his own hand "?

It is very difficult to understand Shaw's fundamental philosophy of Socialism without a thorough knowledge of the evolutionary course of his thought. The particular brand of Socialism denominated Shavian is not a bundle of prejudices of

151

an immature youth, but the integration of years of day-by-day observations of life and character, as well as of political and economic science. The diversities of Socialistic faith have been wittily exhibited by Shaw in the opening scenes of the third act of *Man and Superman*. Roughly speaking, there are three kinds of Socialists: theoretical, Utopian and practical. Lassalle and Marx, Liebknecht and Bebel, Guèsde and Jaurès, Hyndman and Kropotkin, Shelley and Morris, George and Bellamy, Shaw and Webb, carry the stamp of the cobweb-spinner, the dreamer, or of the man of affairs. It is Shaw's supreme distinction that, beginning as doctrinaire, he has ended as practical opportunist. He has sought to traverse the chasm between democracy and social-democracy, by the aid of a solid economic structure, rather than by the rainbow bridge of sentimentality and Utopism. No scheme finds favour in his eyes which does not irresistibly commend itself to his intelligence. He has found the " true " doctrine of Socialism in repudiation of the follies of Impossibilism.

Shaw has unhesitatingly given credit to Henry George for the great impetus he gave to Socialism in England, and, in particular, for the important part George played in his own career. In speaking of the memorable evening in 1882, when, under the inspiration of George's stirring and eloquent words, he first began to realize the importance of the economic basis, Shaw recently wrote:*

" One evening in the early eighties I found myself—I forget how and cannot imagine why—in the Memorial Hall, Farringdon Street, London, listening to an American finishing a speech on the Land Question. I knew he was an American, because he pronounced ' necessarily '— a favourite word of his—with the accent on the third syllable instead of the first; because he was deliberately and intentionally oratorical, which is not customary among shy people like the English; because he spoke of Liberty, Jus-

* Letter to Hamlin Garland, as Chairman of the Committee, the *Progress and Poverty* dinner, New York, January 24th, 1905. The letter, dated December, 1904, was kindly lent me by Mr. Henry George, Jr.

tice, Truth, Natural Law, and other strange eighteenth-century superstitions; and because he explained with great simplicity and sincerity the views of the Creator, who had gone completely out of fashion in London in the previous decade and had not been heard of there since. I noticed, also, that he was a born orator, and that he had small, plump, pretty hands.

" Now at that time I was a young man not much past twenty-five, of a very revolutionary and contradictory temperament, full of Darwin and Tyndall, of Shelley and De Quincey, of Michael Angelo and Beethoven, and never having in my life studied social questions from the economic point of view, except that I had once, in my boyhood, read a pamphlet by John Stuart Mill on the Irish Land Question. The result of my hearing the speech, and buying from one of the stewards of the meeting a copy of ' Progress and Poverty' for sixpence (Heaven only knows where I got that sixpence!), was that I plunged into a course of economic study, and at a very early stage of it became a Socialist and spoke from that very platform on the same great subject, and from hundreds of others as well, sometimes addressing distinguished assemblies in a formal manner, sometimes standing on a borrowed chair at a street corner, or simply on the kerbstone. And I, too, had my oratorical successes; for I can still recall with some vanity a wet afternoon (Sunday, of course) on Clapham Common, when I collected as much as sixteen and sixpence in my hat after my lecture, for the Cause. And that all the work was not mere gas, let the feats and pamphlets of the Fabian Society attest!

" When I was thus swept into the great Socialist revival of 1883, I found that five-sixths of those who were swept in with me had been converted by Henry George. This fact would have been far more widely acknowledged had it not been that it was not possible for us to stop where Henry George stopped. . . . He saw only the monstrous absurdity of the private appropriation of rent, and he believed that if you took that burden off the poor man's back, he could help himself out as easily as a pioneer on a pre-empted clearing. But the moment he took an Englishman to that point, the Englishman saw at once that the remedy was not so simple as that, and that the argument carried us much further, even to the point of total industrial reconstruction. Thus George actually felt bound to attack the Socialism he had created; and the moment the antagonism was declared, and to be a Henry Georgeite meant to be an anti-Socialist, some of the Socialists whom he had converted became ashamed of their origin and concealed it; whilst others, including myself, had to fight hard against the Single Tax propaganda."

However carefully other English Socialists have endeavoured to minimize or deny outright the momentous influence of Henry George, certainly Shaw has neither denied nor belittled their debt. " If we outgrew ' Progress and Poverty ' in many ways, so did he himself too; and it is perhaps just as well that he did not know too much when he made his great campaign here; for the complexity of the problem would have overwhelmed him if he had realized it; or, if it had not, it would have rendered him unintelligible. Nobody has ever got away, or ever will get away, from the truths that were the centre of his propaganda: his errors anybody can get away from." And yet Shaw's insularity and sense of British superiority sticks out in the statement that certain of the English Socialists, including himself, regretted that George was an American, and, therefore, necessarily about fifty years out of date in his economics and sociology from the point of view of an older country! The absurdity of such a contention is glaringly patent on comparison of *Progress and Poverty* with the tracts of the Fabian Society during its early period: George was at least fifty years ahead of the English Socialists, instead of the reverse. With that grandiose conceit which is an essential item of his " stock in trade," Shaw has expressed his eagerness to play the part of Henry George to America. " What George did not teach you, you are being taught now by your great Trusts and Combines, as to which I need only say that if you would take them over as national property as cheerfully as you took over the copyrights of all my early books, you would find them excellent institutions, quite in the path of progressive evolution, and by no means to be discouraged or left unregulated as if they were nobody's business but their own. It is a great pity that you all take America for granted because you were born in it. I, who have never crossed the Atlantic, and have taken nothing American for granted, find I know ten times as much about your country as you do yourselves; and my ambition is to repay my debt to Henry George by coming over some day and trying to do for your young men what Henry George did nearly a quarter of a century ago for me."

While Henry George and his *Progress and Poverty* were the prime motors in directing Shaw to Socialism, it was Karl Marx and his *Capital* that first shunted Shaw on to the economic tack. In 1884, the Unitarian minister, Mr. Philip H. Wicksteed, contributed to *To-Day* a criticism of Marx from the point of view of the school of mathematician-economists founded in England on the treatise on Political Economy published by the late Stanley Jevons in 1871.* Mr. Wicksteed, whose writings on Dante and Scandinavian literature are well known, was a remarkable linguist, a popular preacher, and an excellent man. To the fact, however, that he was a mathematician is largely attributable his deep interest in Jevons' theory of value, which scientifically demolished the classical theory of Adam Smith, Ricardo and Cairnes, with its adaptation to Socialism by Hodgskin and Marx. To his mathematical training, also, may be ascribed the lucidity and logical clarity of his application of the Jevonian machinery to Marxian theory. So abject was the deification of Marx by English Socialists at that time that Hyndman, whom Shaw thought should answer the article, poohpoohed Wicksteed as beneath his notice. But the Omniscience

* In the early eighties the monthly magazine *To-Day* was purchased by three Socialists: Henry Hyde Champion, Percy Frost and James Leigh Joynes. Mr. Wicksteed's article, entitled *Das Kapital: a Criticism,* appeared in *To-Day,* New Series, Vol. II., pages 388-409, 1884; publishers, The Modern Press, a printing business conducted by Messrs. H. H. Champion and J. C. Foulger.

and Infallibility of Marx were rudely shaken: Mr. Wicksteed's article had to be answered. Some years later Hyndman accused Shaw of having " rushed in " to defend Marx; but the question here is not of what Mr. Hyndman thinks: it is a question of fact. Shaw was earnestly requested by the proprietors of *To-Day* to answer Mr. Wicksteed; but he replied at once that though he had read *Das Kapital* he was not an economist, and that the reply should come from someone with a real mastery of the subject. At last, after a discussion one day in St. Paul's Churchyard, Frost disconsolately remarked to Shaw that if he wouldn't do it, he supposed he, Frost, must. Suddenly Shaw realized, as he very recently told me, that none of the others, so far as he could see, knew any more about the subject than he himself did; and he consented on the solemn condition that Wicksteed was to be allowed space for a rejoinder. Shaw was not so blind as not to be deeply impressed by his own ignorance of what Carlyle called the " dismal science "; he realized the importance to himself of getting a sound theoretic basis. " I read Jevons," he afterwards wrote, " and made a fearful struggle to guess what his confounded differentials meant; for I knew as little of the calculus as a pig does of a holiday." In his article entitled *The Jevonian Criticism of Marx*, which was more of a counterblast than a thorough analysis and discussion of Mr. Wicksteed's epoch-making article, Shaw had not a word to say in defence of Marx's oversight of " abstract utility." * Quite clever in its Shavian way, Shaw's article did not get at the root of the matter at all, which was not unnatural, considering that he was a novice, and, as he afterwards freely admitted, completely wrong in the bargain. After the appearance of Mr. Wicksteed's brief rejoinder on pages 177-179 of the same volume, the incident was, for some time, closed.

The discussion only whetted Shaw's interest and left him determined to get to the bottom of the economic question. He had been tremendously impressed by the first volume of *Das Kapital*, " the real European book," as he called it, which he had read in the French translation. Even when he was under

* This article appeared in *To-Day*, New Series, Vol. III., pages 22-26, 1885.

this first tremendous impression, his misgivings found expression in a published letter, in which he jocularly pointed out that what Marx had proved was that we were all robbing each other, and not that one class was robbing another. A joke, founded on clever ignorance, may be a poor beginning for a career; yet in this way was Shaw's career as an economist begun. Shaw never doubted, so green was he, that Hyndman or some other leader would at once expose the fallacy in his letter, and teach him something thereby. The fact that nobody did probably started the misgiving that led him to devote so much time and thought to economics.

It was not without many struggles, however, that Shaw was eventually persuaded to see the fallacies in Marx's economics. In the Hampstead Historic Society, that mutual aid association, and in long private discussions with Sidney Webb, Shaw kept at the subject of Marx, defending him by every shift he could think of. All the time, at bottom, Shaw was satisfied neither with his own position nor with Webb's, which was that of John Stuart Mill. He had always mistrusted mathematical symbols since the time of his school days, when a plausible schoolboy used to prove to him by algebra that one equals two—presumably by one of the inadmissible division-by-zero proofs. The boy always began by saying: " Let $x=a$." Shaw saw no harm in admitting that, and the proof followed with apparently rigorous exactness. " The effect was not to make me proceed habitually on the assumption that one equals two," I once heard him say with a boyish laugh; " but to impress upon me that there was a screw loose somewhere in the algebraic art, and a chance for me to set it right some day when I had time to look into the subject." And so, when he saw Jevons' x's, his differentials and his infinitesimals, Shaw at once thought of the plausible boy, and was fired to find that loose screw in Jevonian economics. The difficulty he felt most was that he could not, among Socialists, get into a sufficiently abstract atmosphere to arrive at the pure theory of the thing. It was essential to divorce the discussion absolutely from the social question. Fortunately, yet oddly enough, it was Wicksteed himself who helped Shaw to what he wanted. One of Wicksteed's friends, a prosperous stockbroker named Beeton, began inviting a circle of friends interested in economics to his house. The *To-Day* discussion had established friendly relations between Shaw and Wicksteed; and Shaw secured an entry to this circle and " held on to it like grim death " until after some years it blossomed out into The Royal Economic Society, founded the *Economic Journal*, and outgrew Beeton's drawing-room. Mr. Shaw once remarked to me that his great difficulty was to see through Marx's fallacy in assuming that abstract labour was the unique factor by which the celebrated equation of Value was divisible. " I couldn't, for the life of me," said Mr. Shaw, " see any sense in the equation $2a+3b=8c$. I actually bought an Algebra and tried to recapture any early knowledge I might have had, but it was all gone." And only the other day I ran across this book, *The Scholar's Algebra*, by Lewis Hensley, at a second-hand book-shop in London. Under date " 22-8-87," appears the following, written in Shaw's remarkably neat stenography: " What sudden freak induced me to purchase this book? I saw it offered at a second-hand book-shop in Holborn for one and sixpence. For a time I was puzzled by a notion that the symbols referred to things instead of to numbers. For instance, $2a+3b$ appeared to me as absurd as 2 wrens+3 apples."

In a letter to me Mr. Shaw once related the following story of his economic education—a story which gives the lie to his own strictures on University education. And in conversation he recently admitted to me that this economic training corresponded closely to the highest form of University instruction.* " During those years Wicksteed expounded ' final utility ' to us with a blackboard except when we got hold of some man from

---

* The leading members of this club were Beeton, Wicksteed, Foxwell, Graham Wallas, F. Y. Edgeworth, Alfred Marshall, Edward Cunningham, Charles Wright and Armitage Smith. The club met monthly—from November to June—during the years 1884 to 1889 inclusive, when it came to an end through the formation of what was formally entitled *The Economic Club*, organized mainly at the instance of Alfred Marshall. It may be worthy of mention that Wicksteed dedicated his *Alphabet of Economics* to this club. Shaw joined the club because he wanted to learn abstract economics, and he occasionally contributed something to the programme himself. On November 9th, 1886, for example, he read a paper before the society on the subject of *Interest*.

the ' Baltic ' (The London Wheat Exchange), or the like, to explain the markets to us and afterwards have his information reduced to Jevonian theory. Among university professors of economics Edgeworth and Foxwell stuck to us pretty constantly, and W. Cunningham turned up occasionally. Of course, the atmosphere was by no means Shavian; but that was exactly what I wanted. The Socialist platform and my journalistic pulpits involved a constant and most provocative forcing of people to face the practical consequences of theories and beliefs, and to draw mordant contrasts between what they professed or what their theories involved and their life and conduct. This made dispassionate discussion of abstract theory impossible. At Beeton's the conditions were practically university conditions. There was a tacit understanding that the calculus of utilities and the theory of exchange must be completely isolated from the fact that we lived, as Morris's mediæval captain put it, by ' robbing the poor.' "

In the heated discussions over Marx's economic theories which followed during the next few years, Shaw enjoyed an immense advantage in that nobody else in the Socialist movement had gone through this discipline, which required considerable perseverance and deep scientific conviction. It ended, as Shaw maintains, in his finding out Marx and Hyndman completely as economists. In Shaw's present view Marx was less an economist than a revolutionary Socialist, employing political economy as a weapon against his adversaries: to Marx, the economic theory of Ricardo was simply a " stick to beat the capitalist dog." To Hyndman, doubt of any part of the " Bible of the working classes " was Socialist heresy: the whole issue resolved itself into the question whether Jevons was a Socialist or an anti-Socialist.* No doubt the influence which moved Shaw to devote himself to economic studies was his need of a weapon; but he did not stop to ask whether the steel came from a Socialist foundry or not. " The Marxian steel was always snapping in my hand," he once

---

* As late as 1905 Mr. E. Belfort Bax is found maintaining that Jevons was the mere tool of capitalism, seeking to undermine the Marxian theory of value in the interests of social order and political stability. Compare his article, *Socialism and Bourgeois Culture*, in *Wilshire's Magazine*, 1905.

remarked to me. " The Jevonian steel held and kept its edge, and fitted itself to every emergency. And then, just as one loves a good sword for its own sake, so one loves a sound theory for its own sake." As a literary artist also, accustomed to express himself in terse and pointed phrase, Shaw was fired with determination to extricate the theory from its " damned shorthand " of mathematical symbols, and put it into human language.*

On the appearance of the English translation from the third German edition of *Das Kapital*, by Samuel Moore and Edward Aveling, in 1887, Shaw reviewed it in three consecutive articles.† These articles of Shaw's show that in 1887 his conversion by Wicksteed was complete. In Shaw's article, *Stanley Jevons: His Letters and Journal*, a review of the *Letters and Journal of W. Stanley Jevons*, which appeared in the *Pall Mall Gazette*, May 29th, 1886, he says: " He (Jevons) was far too orthodox in his practical conclusions for those materialists of the science— the revolutionary Socialists—who saw in him a mere ' bourgeois economist,' as their phrase goes. He does not seem to have had any suspicion that Mr. Hyndman and his friends made any economic pretensions at all; but it is remarkable that the most successful attack so far on the value theory of Karl Marx has come from Mr. Philip Wicksteed, a well-known Unitarian minister, who is an able follower of Jevons in economics." Shaw was now the complete Jevonian, had thrown the Marxian theory completely over, and exactly located the step Marx missed. Shaw himself readily admits that Marx came within one step of the real solution. Whilst Marx left Shaw unconvinced as to Marxian economics, he left him profoundly imbued with

* This Shaw achieved with great success in his review, in three parts, of *Das Kapital*, English translation, which appeared in the *National Reformer*.
  † The *National Reformer*, now extinct, then the weekly organ of the National Secular Society, editors, Charles Bradlaugh and Annie Besant; policy, Atheism, Malthusianism and Republicanism. These articles, three in number, under the general heading *Karl Marx and ' Das Kapital,'* appeared in Vol. I., pages 84-86, 106-108, 117, 118. On receiving a cheque for these articles at a rate which he felt sure the *National Reformer* could not afford, Shaw found that the beneficent Mrs. Besant had made a contribution from her private purse, which Shaw characteristically hurled back with indignant gratitude.

Marxian convictions. In Marx, Shaw discerned one who " wrote
of the nineteenth century as if it were a cloud passing down the
wind, changing its shape and fading as it goes; whilst Ricardo
the stockbroker and De Quincey the high Tory, sat comfortably
down before it in their office and study chairs as if it were the
Great Wall of China, safe to last until the Day of Judgment
with an occasional coat of whitewash." While refusing to deify
Marx as a god, Shaw lauds him with what is, for him, the rarest
of panegyrics. " He (Marx) never condescends to cast a
glance of useless longing at the past: his cry to the present is
always, ' Pass by: we are waiting for the future.' Nor is the
future at all mysterious, uncertain, or dreadful to him. There
is not a word of hope or fear, nor appeal to chance or providence, nor vain remonstrance with Nature, nor optimism, nor
enthusiasm, nor pessimism, nor cynicism, nor any other familiar
sign of the giddiness which seizes men when they climb to
heights which command a view of the past, present and future
of human society. Marx keeps his head like a god. He has
discovered the law of social development, and knows what must
come. The thread of history is in his hand."

The point to be grasped, however, is contained in Shaw's
admonition: " Read Jevons and the rest for your economics,
and read Marx for the history of their working in the past, and
the conditions of their application in the present. And never
mind the metaphysics." Shaw stood upon the shoulders of
giants, for Jevons had laid the foundations, and Wicksteed it
was who first pointed out to English Socialists the flaw in
Marx's analysis of wares.* But in that remarkably succinct
and lucid style for which he is justly famous, Shaw elaborately
analyzed the questionable points in the Marxian structure and
explained the latent errors involved, for the comprehension, not
simply of the economist, but of the man-in-the-street. It is
neither possible, nor even desirable, here to give the steps by
which Shaw controverted Marx; reference to Shaw's numerous

---

* These ideas seem to have found expression simultaneously in England
and Austria. Compare *The Theory of Political Economy*, by W. S. Jevons,
London, 1871; *Grundsätze der Volkswirtschaftslehre*, by Anton Menger,
Vienna, 1871.

articles on the subject will give these to the curious. But the conclusions he reached are worthy of enumeration.* In the first place, Shaw objected to Marx's dogmatic assertion of the generally accepted Ricardian theory that " wares in which equal quantities of labour are embodied, or which can be produced in the same time, have the same value "; and for the simple reason that the Jevonian theory called this dogma into question. In the second place, following Wicksteed, Shaw takes Marx to task for first insisting that the abstract labour used in the production of wares does not count unless it is useful, and then contradicting himself by stripping the wares of the abstract utility conferred upon them by abstractly useful work. The logical consequence of admitting abstract utility as a quality of wares produced by abstract human labour is conclusively to disconnect value from mere abstract human labour. Marx thus adroitly begs the question: as Shaw says: " It is as if he (Marx) had proved by an elaborate series of abstractions that liquids were fatal to human life, and had finished by remarking: ' Of course, the liquids must be poisonous.' " Armed with the fact of abstract utility, and the Jevonian weapons of " the law of indifference " and " the law of the variation of utility," Shaw was enabled to prove with mathematical rigour that value does not represent the specific utility of the article, but its abstract utility; and not its total abstract utility, but its final abstract utility—at the " margin of supply," in Wicksteed's phrase—*i.e.*, the utility of the final increment that is worth producing. Translated into terms of labour, this means that the value of the ware represents, not the quantity of human labour embodied in it, but the " final utility," in Jevonian phrase, of the abstract human labour socially necessary to produce it. As Shaw puts it: " Instead of wares being equal in value because equal quantities of labour have been expended on them, equal quantities of labour will have been expended on them because they are of

---

* The question of the validity of the Marxian theory is not now a live subject in England. Mr. Hyndman's defence of the Marxian position is to be found in his *Economics of Socialism,* in which he attempts to demonstrate the " final futility of final utility." It is still a mooted question on the Continent; compare, for example, the works of Böhm-Bawerk, perhaps the most eminent of the " Austrian School " of political economists.

equal value (or equally desirable), which is quite another thing. That slip in the analysis of wares whereby Marx was led to believe that he had got rid of the abstract utility when he had really only got rid of the specific utility, was the first of his mistakes." Under certain ideal conditions, there is a coincidence between " exchange value " and " amount of labour contained "; but as these ideal conditions seldom, if ever, occur in practice, no scientific validity attaches to the Marxian statement that " commodities in which equal quantities of labour are embodied, or which can be produced in the same time, have the same value." Lastly, Shaw insists that if Marx's theory of value were correct, it would refute, not confirm, Marx's theory of " surplus value." The proprietor's monopoly completely upsets those ideal conditions on which Marx's theory of value is based. It can be demonstrated by Jevonian principles that Marx's assumption, that the subsistence wage is the value of the labour force, is untenable, even on Marxian principles. Marx did not see that it is impossible, according to the " law of indifference," for one part of the stock of a commodity available at any given time to have value whilst another part has none, since no man will give a price for that which he can obtain for nothing. Moreover, when he attempts to differentiate labour power from steam power, Marx's logic breaks down. As Shaw says: " Marx's whole theory of the origin of surplus value depends on the accuracy of his demonstration that steam power, machinery, etc., cannot possibly produce surplus value. If Marx were right then a capital of ten thousand pounds, invested in a business requiring nine thousand pounds for machinery and plant, and one thousand pounds for wages (or human labour power), would only return one-ninth of the surplus value returned by an equal capital of which one thousand pounds was in the form of plant and nine thousand pounds in wage capital. As a matter of fact, the ' surplus value ' from both is found to be equal." *

* These conclusions were reached before the third volume of *Capital* appeared. The editor of the first volume, Mr. Frederick Engels, promised that the third volume, when it appeared, would reconcile these and other seeming contradictions. Marx does seem to have modified certain of his theories in the third volume.

Shaw saw plainly enough that the theory of value did not matter in the least so far as the soundness of Socialism was concerned. For, as he once expressed it in a letter to me, " if you steal a turnip the theory of the turnip's value does not affect the social and political aspect of the transaction." But, of course, Hyndman and the few Socialists who had read Marx and nothing else, were furious over Shaw's iconoclastic articles in the *National Reformer.* In view of the fact that the opponents of Socialism continually damaged the cause of the Socialists by alleging that the Socialists' economic basis was Marx's theory and was untenable, with the result that the Socialists persisted in accepting the allegation and defending Marx, Shaw resolutely forced the quarrel into publicity as far as he could. His prime object was to make it clear that the Fabians were quite independent of the Marxian value theory. A heated controversy on the subject in the *Pall Mall Gazette* of May, 1887, engaged in by Shaw, Hyndman, and Mrs. Besant, did not down the ghost of the value theory; for the controversy was reopened in *To-Day* two years later. *An Economic Eirenicon,* by Graham Wallas, was followed by *Marx's Theory of Value,* contributed by H. M. Hyndman, in which, it seems, he merely repeated the old Marxian demonstration without making any attempt to meet the Jevonian attack. Whereupon Shaw " went for " Hyndman in his most aggravating style in an article entitled *Bluffing the Value Theory,* which finished the campaign except for a series of letters in *Justice* by various hands, the tenth of which, in July, 1889, was written by Shaw. There were other letters by Shaw on the same subject, written at different times, which appeared in the *Daily Chronicle.* William Morris never made any pretence of having followed the controversy on its abstract technical side; and perhaps the most amusing feature of the entire campaign was a sort of manifesto which Belfort Bax induced Morris to sign, in which Hyndman, Bax, Aveling and Morris declared that all good Socialists were Marxites! Shaw was once denounced in public meeting by a Marxian Socialist for pooh-poohing Marx as an idiot. His own position, as he himself once remarked to me, lay somewhere between this and that of worshipping Marx as a god. In one of the most re-

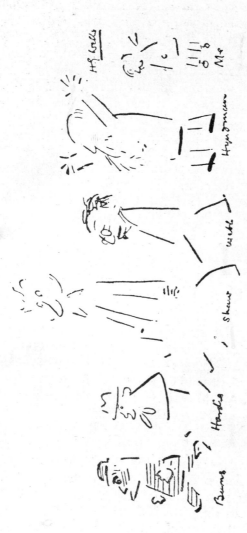

A STUDY OF SIX SOCIALISTS.

From a drawing by H. G. Wells, here reproduced by his permission

[*Facing p.* 164

markable essays ever written by Shaw, entitled *The Illusions of Socialism,* Shaw pointed out why it was that a difficult and subtle theory like that of Jevons could never be as acceptable as a crude and simple labour theory like that of Marx, which seemed to imply that wealth rightly belonged to the labourer.*

From the standpoint of the Marxian religionist, the second heresy of which Shaw is guilty consists in his recognition of the Class War doctrine as a delusion and a suicidal political policy. To Shaw, the form of organization deduced from the Class War doctrine is always the same. " All you have to do is to form a working-class association, declare war on property, explain the economic situation from the platform and at the street corner, and wait until the entire proletariat (made ' class-conscious ' by your lucid lectures) joins you. This being done simultaneously in London, Paris, Berlin, Madrid, Rome, Vienna, etc., etc., nothing remains but a simultaneous movement of the proletarians of all countries, and the sweeping of capitalism into the sea because ' ye are many: they are few.' What can be easier or more scientific? " But a study of the history of Socialism led Shaw to the discovery that the Class War theory had gone to pieces every time it had been invoked. Lassalle attempted to organize the imaginary class-conscious proletariat, only to be disillusioned before the end of the first year by the

---

* In the *Pall Mall Gazette* the following articles appeared: *Marx and Modern Socialism,* by Shaw, May 7th, 1887, page 3; Hyndman's reply, May 11th, page 11; Shaw's rejoinder—*Socialists at Home* (this heading doubtless a jibe of the editor), May 12th, page 11; Hyndman's rejoinder, May 16th, page 2; Mrs. Besant's article on the same subject, May 24th, page 2. In *To-Day,* Vol. XI., New Series, 1889, appeared: *An Economic Eirenicon,* by Graham Wallas, pages 80-86; *Marx's Theory of Value,* by Hyndman, same volume, pages 94-104; Shaw's reply, *Bluffing the Value Theory,* following Hyndman, May, 1889, pages 128-135, was lately reprinted by Eduard Bernstein in *Sozialistische Monatshefte.* Shaw's letter in *Justice* appeared on page 3 of the issue of July 20th, 1889. The fine essay, entitled *The Illusions of Socialism,* quite penetrating in its psychology, although caviare to the ordinary reviewer, originally appeared in German in *Die Zeit* (Vienna), in 1896: No. 108, October 24th, and No. 109, October 31st; later it appeared in English in *Forecasts of the Coming Century,* edited by Edward Carpenter, Manchester: Labour Press, 1897; it afterwards appeared in French in *L'Humanité Nouvelle* (Ghent and Paris), August, 1900, edited by Auguste Hamon, the well-known Socialist and the French translator of Shaw's plays.

" damned wantlessness " of the real proletariat. Owen before him likewise had failed, after apparently converting all Trade-Unionism to his New Moral World. When Marx planned the Socialist side of " The International " in the sixties, he showed his contempt for the trade-union side, with the result: " On the trade-union side a great success. . . . On the Socialist side, futility and disastrous failure, culminating, in 1871, in one of the most appalling massacres known to history." Marx can scarcely be said to have tried to organize the class-conscious proletariat; but the moment his useless vituperation of Thiers, " brilliant as a sample of literary invective, but useless for the buttering of parsnips," made known to English workmen his real opinion of bourgeois civilization, they abandoned him in horror and left the International memberless. In Germany, " Liebknecht made no serious headway until he became a parliamentarian, playing the parliamentary game more pliably than Parnell did, though always ' old-soldiering ' his way with the greenhorns by prefacing each compromise with the declaration that Social Democracy never compromised." In France, Jaurès and Millerand have not so much abandoned the Class War doctrine as wholly neglected and ignored it, thus reducing the old Guèsdist Marxism to absurdity. In England, " the once revolutionary Social-Democratic Federation has been forced by the competition of the quite constitutional Independent Labour Party to give up all its ancient Maccabean poetry, and, after a period of uselessness and surpassing unpopularity as an anti-Fabian Society with a speciality for abusing Mr. John Burns, to settle down into a sort of Ultra-Independent Labour Party, ready to amalgamate with its rival if only an agreement can be arrived at as to which is to be considered as swallowing the other."

Not merely a study of the Class War doctrine from the historical standpoint, but also an examination into the assumptions upon which it rests, have thoroughly convinced Shaw that Socialists have for long been making overdrafts upon their *Capital*. Shaw has never sought to shirk the real point at issue by the quibble of substituting the sort of class-consciousness called snobbery, mighty as is that social force, for the economic class-consciousness of the German formula. In Shaw's interpretation, Hyndman and the Marxists use the term " Class War " to denote a war between all the proletarians on one side and all the property-holders on the other—in Schaeffle's phrase " a definite confrontation of classes "—which will be produced when the workers become conscious that their economic interests are opposed to those of the property-holders. Shaw's position is effectively summed up in his words:

" The people understand their own affairs much better than Marx did, and the simple stratification of society into two classes . . . has as little relation to actual social facts as Marx's value theory has to actual market prices. If the crude Marxian melodrama of ' The Class War; or, the Virtuous Worker and the Brutal Capitalist,' were even approximately true to life, the whole capitalist structure would have tumbled to pieces long ago, as the ' scientific Socialists ' were always expecting it to do, instead of consolidating itself on a scale which has already made Marx and Engels as obsolete as the Gracchi had become in the time of Augustus. By throwing up fabulous masses of ' surplus value,' and doubling and trebling the incomes of the well-to-do middle classes, who all imitate the imperial luxury and extravagance of the millionaires, Capitalism has created, as it formerly did in Rome, an irresistible proletarian bodyguard of labourers whose immediate interests are bound up with those of the capitalists, and who are, like their Roman prototypes, more rapacious, more rancorous in their Primrose partisanship, and more hardened against all the larger social considerations, than their masters, simply because they are more needy, ignorant and irresponsible. Touch the income of the rich, and the Conservative proletarians are the first to suffer." *

In Shaw's opinion, the social struggle does not follow class lines at all, because the people who really hate the capitalist

* *The Class War*, in the *Clarion*, September 30th, 1904.

system are, like Ruskin, Morris, Tolstoy, Hyndman, Marx and Lassalle, themselves capitalists, whereas the fiercest defenders of it are the masses of labourers, artisans, and employees whose trade is at its best when the rich have most money to spend. Socialists like Shaw, who " do not accept the class war," are simply expressing " first, a very natural impatience of crying ' War, War!' where there is no war; and, second, their despair at seeing Socialism, like Liberalism, perishing because it is trying to live on the crop of home-made generalizations so plentifully put forth during the great Liberal boom of 1832-80 by middle-class paper theorists like Malthus, Cobden, Marx, Comte and Herbert Spencer—fine fellows, all of them, but stupendously ignorant of the industrial world." The basic divergence between the Fabian and the " S. D. F." policy is epitomized in Shaw's words: " There is a conflict of interests between those who pay wages and those who receive them; and this is organized by the trade unions. There is another conflict of interests between those workers and proprietors whose customers live on rent (in its widest economic sense), and those whose customers live on wages; but the lines of this conflict run, not between the classes, but right through them, and do not coincide with the lines of the trade union conflict. And any form of Socialist organization, or any tactics toward the trade union movement, based on the theory that the lines of battle *do* run between the classes and not through them, or *do* coincide with the trade union lines of battle, will prove, and always has proved, disastrously impracticable." Shaw exasperatingly said in a recent article * that he refused to agree with anybody on any subject whatsoever. " Let them agree with me if my arguments convince them. If not, let them plank down their own views. I will not have my mouth stopped and my mind stifled." And those mystic forces—historical development and Progress with a large P—in which the Marxists rest their firmest hope, Shaw regards in the spirit of Ingoldsby's sacristan:

* Shaw's position in regard to the Class War is ably set forth in his three articles, under the general heading, *The Class War*, which appeared in the *Clarion*, London; dates: September 30th, October 21st and November 4th, 1904.

SHAVIAN SOCIALISM

"The sacristan he said no word to indicate a doubt;
But he put his thumb unto his nose, and he spread his fingers out."

Th..e are two factors which strongly militate against the
progress of Socialism; the resolute adherence of Socialists to
those theories and policies of Marx which time, experience, and
modern economic science have combined to discredit; and the
tendency of the popular mind to confuse Socialism with
Anarchism.* Shaw's most important negative and destructive
achievements consist in those amazingly clever and interesting
papers in which he attempts to expose Marx's theory of value
as an exploded fallacy, to show that the Class War will never
come, and to demonstrate the impossibilities of Anarchism. In
the *technical* sense of Socialist economics, Shaw occupies the
opposite pole to Individualism and Anarchism. And yet in a
very definite and general sense, Shaw is a thorough-paced individualist and anarchist. If individualist means a believer in the
Shakespearean injunction " To thine own self be true! ", in the
Ibsenic doctrine " Live thine own life! ", then Shaw is an individualist heart and soul. If anarchist means an enemy of convention, of tradition, of current modes of administering justice,
of prevailing moral standards, then Shaw is the most revolutionary anarchist now at large. If, on the other hand, Individualist means one who distrusts State action and is jealous of
the prerogative of the individual, proposing to restrict the one
and to extend the other as far as is humanly possible, then Shaw
is most certainly not an Individualist. If Anarchist means
dynamitard, incendiary, assassin, thief; champion of the *absolute* liberty of the individual and the removal of all govern-
mental restraint; or even a believer, as Communist, in a

* In 1888 Shaw wrote two very clever articles, which so far seem to have
escaped attention, although the disguise is so thin as to be negligible. These
two articles are, respectively, *My Friend Fitzthunder, the Unpractical
Socialist,* by Redbarn Wash—note the anagram—(*To-Day,* edited by Hubert
Bland, August, 1888), and *Fitzthunder on Himself—A Defence,* by
Robespierre Marat Fitzthunder (*To-Day,* September, 1888). These very
amusing papers, both written by Shaw, it is needless to say, constitute a
reductio ad absurdum of the unpractical and revolutionary Socialist; Fitzthunder is evidently a composite picture, made up from a number of Shaw's
Socialist *confrères.*

profound and universal sense of high moral responsibility present in all humanity, then Shaw is a living contradiction of Anarchism.

Shaw opposes Individualist Anarchism since, under such a social arrangement, the prime economic goal of Socialism: the just distribution of the premiums given to certain portions of the general product by the action of demand, would never be attained. As this system not only fails to distribute these premiums justly, but deliberately permits their private appropriation, Individualist Anarchism is, in Shaw's view, " the negation of Socialism, and is, in fact, Unsocialism carried as near to its logical completeness as any sane man dare carry it." The Communist Anarchism of Kropotkin, Shaw also opposes because of his own lack of faith in humanity at large, in the present state of development of the social conscience. If bread were communized, the common bread store obviously would become bankrupt unless every consumer of the bread contributed to its support as much labour as the bread he consumed cost to produce. Were the consumer to refuse thus to contribute, there would be two ways to compel him: physical force and the moral force of public opinion. If physical force is resorted to, then the Anarchist ideal remains unattained. If moral force, what will be the event? The answer reveals Shaw as a confirmed sceptic in regard to the value of public opinion as a moral agent. " It is useless," he avers, " to think of man as a fallen angel. If the fallacies of absolute morality are to be admitted into the discussion at all, he must be considered rather as an obstinate and selfish devil who is being slowly forced by the iron tyranny of Nature to recognize that in disregarding his neighbours' happiness, he is taking the surest way to sacrifice his own." Under Anarchistic Communism, public opinion would no doubt operate as powerfully as now. But, in Shaw's opinion, public opinion cannot for a moment be relied upon as a force which operates uniformly as a compulsion upon men to act morally. Keen, incisive, pitiless, his words descriptive of *public opinion* show how little he is tinged with the poetry, the passion, and the religion which are the very life blood of Socialism.

" Its operation is for all practical purposes quite arbitrary, and is as often immoral as moral. It is just as hostile to the reformer as to the criminal. It hangs Anarchists and worships Nitrate Kings. It insists on a man wearing a tall hat and going to church, on his marrying the woman he lives with, and on his pretending to believe whatever the rest pretend to believe. . . . But there is no sincere public opinion that a man should work for his daily bread if he can get it for nothing. Indeed, it is just the other way; public opinion has been educated to regard the performance of daily manual labour as the lot of the despised classes. The common aspiration is to acquire property and leave off working. Even members of the professions rank below the independent gentry, so-called because they are independent of their own labour. These prejudices are not confined to the middle and upper classes: they are rampant also among the workers. . . . One is almost tempted in this country to declare that the poorer the man the greater the snob, until you get down to those who are so oppressed that they have not enough self-respect even for snobbery, and thus are able to pluck out of the heart of their misery a certain irresponsibility which it would be a mockery to describe as genuine frankness and freedom. The moment you rise into the higher atmosphere of a pound a week, you find that envy, ostentation, tedious and insincere ceremony, love of petty titles, precedence and dignities, and all the detestable fruits of inequality of condition, flourish as rankly among those who lose as among those who gain by it. In fact, the notion that poverty favours virtue was clearly invented to persuade the poor that what they lost in this world they would gain in the next." *

When Shaw attended the International Socialist Congresses in Zurich and in London, he reported them in the *Star* as un-

* Fabian Tract, No. 45: *The Impossibilities of Anarchism*, a paper by Shaw, written in 1888, read to the Fabian Society on October 16th, 1891, and published by the Fabian Society, July, 1893.

sparingly as he would have reported a sitting of Parliament. The Socialists, amazed and indignant at their first taste of real criticism, concluded that Shaw was going over to the enemy. This Fabian policy of unsparing criticism, inaugurated and carried out ruthlessly by Shaw, ended in freeing the Fabians, in great measure, from the illusions of Socialism, and in imparting to their Society its rigidly constitutional character. An incident, which Mr. Shaw once described in a letter to me, gives one some insight into the causes of his reaction against the German Socialists' policy of playing to the galleries by spouting revolutionary rant and hinting catastrophically of impending revolutions.

" At the Zurich Congress I first became acquainted with the leaders of the movement on the Continent. Chief among them was the German leader Liebknecht, a '48 veteran who, having become completely parliamentarized, still thought it necessary to dupe his younger followers with the rhetoric of the barricade. After a division in which an attempt to secure unanimity by the primitive method of presenting the resolution before the Congress to the delegates of the different nations in their various languages in several versions adapted to their views, so that whilst they believed they were all saying ' Yes ' to the same proposition, the wording was really very different in the different translations, and sometimes highly contradictory, it turned out that the stupidity of the English section had baffled the cleverness of the German-Swiss bureau, because the English voted ' No ' when they meant ' Yes,' and upset the apple-cart. Happening to be close to Liebknecht on the platform at the luncheon adjournment, I said a few words to him in explanation of the apparently senseless action of the English. He looked wearily round at me; saw a comparatively young Socialist whom he did not know; and immediately treated me to a long assurance that the German Social Democrats did not shrink from a conflict with the police on Labour Day (the 1st of May); that they were as ready as ever, etc., etc., etc., etc., etc.

I turned away as soon and as shortly as I could without being rude; and from that time I discounted the German leaders as being forty years out of date, and totally negligible except as very ordinary republican Radicals with a Socialist formula which was simply a convenient excuse for doing nothing new.

" When the German leaders visited London in the eighties they treated the Fabian Society as a foolish joke. Later on they found their error; and Liebknecht was entertained at a great Fabian meeting; but to this day the German Socialist press does not dare to publish the very articles it asks me to write, because of my ruthless criticism of Bebel, Singer, and the old tradition of the ' old gang ' generally. My heresy as to Marx is, of course, another horror to the Germans who got their ideas of political economy in the '48-'71 period."

After 1875, let us recall, the old pressure and discontent of the eighteen-thirties descended upon England with renewed force. In 1881, " as if Chartism and Fergus O'Connor had risen from the dead," the Democratic Federation, with H. M. Hyndman at its head, inaugurated the revival of Socialist organization in England. Like those other haters of the capitalist system—the capitalists Ruskin, Morris, Tolstoy, Marx and Lassalle—Hyndman " had had his turn at the tall hat and was tired of it." Shortly after the formation of the Democratic Federation, the Fabian Society, a revolting sect from the Fellowship of the New Life, founded by Professor Thomas Davidson, came into being. Hyndman and his Marxists, Kropotkin and his Anarchists, did not realize, with Shaw, that the proletariat, instead of being the revolutionary, is in reality the conservative element of society. They refused to accept this situation, not realizing that they were confronted by a condition, not a theory. " They persisted in believing that the proletariat was an irresistible mass of Felix Pyats and Ouidas." On the point of joining the Democratic Federation, Shaw decided to join the Fabian Society instead. He did accept the situation, helped, perhaps, as he once said, by his inherited instinct for anti-climax. " I threw Hyndman over, and got to work with Sidney Webb and the rest to place Socialism on a respectable *bourgeois* footing; hence Fabianism. Burns did the same thing in Battersea by organizing the working classes there on a genuine self-respecting working-class basis, instead of on the old romantic middle-class assumptions. Hyndman wasted years in vain denunciation of the Fabian Society and of Burns; and though facts became too strong for him at last, he is still at heart the revolted bourgeois." Prior to the year 1886, there had been no formal crystallization of the Fabian Society into a strictly economic association, avowedly opportunist in its political policy; after September 17th of that year the thin edge of the wedge went in. The Manifesto of the Fabian Parliamentary League contains the nucleus of the Fabian policy of to-day.* The Fabian Society was a dead letter until Shaw, Webb, Olivier and Wallas joined it; from that moment, it became a force to be reckoned with in English life. Almost from the very first, as Mr. Sidney Webb once wrote me, the Society took the colour of Shaw's mordantly critical temperament, and bore the stamp of his personality. The promise of the Fabians lay in their open-mindedness, their diligence in the study of advanced economics, and their resolute refusal of adherence to any formula, however dear to Socialist enthusiasts, which did not commend itself unreservedly to their intelligence. By 1885, it had only forty members; and in 1886, it was still unable to bring its roll of members to a hundred names. In 1900, it boasted a membership of eight hundred, and at present about twenty-six hundred names are found upon its rolls.† It is neither possible nor advisable for me to record the history of the Fabian Society—that may be found in the numerous publications of the Society. But I cannot refrain from stating that the membership increased by forty-three per cent. in the year 1906-7, that this was a year of unprecedented activity; and

---

* Compare the former chapter; complete details are to be found in Fabian Tract No. 41, pages 12-15.

† In the twenty-seventh Annual Report on the work of the Fabian Society (for the year ended March 31st, 1910), the membership is given as 2,627.

that the Society has recently been greatly strengthened by the accession of many well-known men in English public life. There were then *eight* Fabians in the London County Council; and in Parliament, Labour and Socialism have in the last five years been better represented, I believe, than ever before in the history of that body. I have recently talked at length with many of the ablest Socialists in England. The remarkable growth of the Fabian Society and the Socialist representation in English literature, I was told again and again, is not due to any sudden and untrustworthy inflation of Socialist values, but is largely due to the fact that Bernard Shaw, Sidney Webb, Hubert Bland, and their coterie have been planting the seeds for twenty years. Such ideas as are embodied in Mr. Lloyd George's budget and the Old Age Pension Bill are unmistakable marks of that gradual Socialist leavening of English political thought upon which the Fabians have been engaged ever since 1884. " The recent steady influx into the Fabian Society," Mr. Bland said to me energetically, " is a clear proof to my mind that the ideas which have been lurking in the air for a long, long time are at last taking definite shape simultaneously in the minds of a great many people. Such men as Bernard Shaw have brought this thing to pass." *

During the years from 1887 to 1889, the years we are especially concerned with at present, compensation for its paucity of numbers was found not only in the intellectual capacity, but also in the economic inquisitiveness and acquisitiveness of the

* Worthy of record in connection with the new policy of the Fabian Society, although discussion is outside the scope of this work, is the movement inaugurated by Mr. Holbrook Jackson and Mr. A. R. Orage, afterwards joint-editors of the London Socialist organ, *The New Age,* in the foundation of the Leeds Art Club in 1905. " The object of the Leeds Art Club," their syllabus read, " is to affirm the mutual dependence of art and ideas." This movement, supported by a group of able lecturers, proved so successful and so stimulating as to eventuate in the formation of the Fabian Art Group (Bernard Shaw presiding over the initial meeting), the declared object of which is " to interpret the relation of Art and Philosophy to Socialism." Admirable pamphlets and brochures have been published under its auspices; and its meetings, and the Fabian Summer School in Wales, have been addressed by many of the most brilliant and advanced thinkers in England.

leaders in the Fabian Society. This is best revealed in Shaw's sketch of this period:

" By far our most important work at this period was our renewal of that historic and economic equipment of Social-Democracy of which Ferdinand Lassalle boasted, and which has been getting rustier and more obsolete ever since his time and that of his contemporary, Karl Marx. . . . In 1885 we used to prate about Marx's theory of value and Lassalle's Iron Law of Wages as if it were still 1870. In spite of Henry George, no Socialist seemed to have any working knowledge of the theory of economic rent: its application to skilled labour was so unheard of that the expression ' rent of ability ' was received with laughter when the Fabians first introduced it into their lectures and discussions; and as for the modern theory of value, it was scouted as a blasphemy against Marx. . . . As to history, we had a convenient stock of imposing generalizations about the evolution from slavery to serfdom and from serfdom to free wage labour. We drew our pictures of society with one broad line dividing the *bourgeoisie* from the proletariat, and declared that there were only two classes really in the country. We gave lightning sketches of the development of the mediæval craftsman into the manufacturer and finally into the factory hand. We denounced Malthusianism quite as crudely as the Malthusians advocated it, which is saying a great deal; and we raged against emigration, national insurance, cooperation, trade-unionism, old-fashioned Radicalism, and everything else that was not Socialism; and that, too, without knowing at all clearly what we meant by Socialism. The mischief was, not that our generalizations were unsound, but that we had no detailed knowledge of the content of them: we had borrowed them ready-made as articles of faith; and when opponents like Charles Bradlaugh asked us for details we sneered at the demand without being in the least able to comply with it. The real reason why Anarchist and Socialist worked then shoulder to shoulder as comrades and brothers was that neither one nor the other had any definite idea of what he wanted, or how it was to be got. All this is true to this day of the raw recruits of the movement, and of some older hands who may be absolved on the ground of invincible ignorance; but it is no longer true of the leaders of the movement in general. In 1887 even the British Association burst out laughing as one man when an elderly representative of Philosophic Radicalism, with the air of one who was uttering the safest of platitudes, accused us of ignorance of political economy; and now not even a Philosophical Radical is to be found to make himself ridiculous in this way. The exemplary eye-opening of Mr. Leonard Courtney by Mr. Sidney Webb lately in the leading English economic review surprised nobody, except perhaps Mr. Courtney himself. The cotton lords of the north would never dream to-day of engaging an economist to confute us with learned pamphlets as their predecessors engaged Nassau Senior in the days of the Ten Hours' Bill, because they know that we should be only too glad to advertise our Eight Hours' Bill by flattening out any such champion. From 1887 to 1889 we were the recognized bullies and swashbucklers of advanced economics." *

Not without reason have the Fabians been called the Jesuits of the Socialist evangel in England. The "waiting" of the Fabian motto is synonymous, not with inaction, but with unflagging energy.† The Fabians eschewed pleasures and recreations of every kind in favour of public speaking and public instruction; their policy has always been one of education and permeation. In the year ending April, 1889, to take a single example, the number of lectures delivered by members of the Fabian Society alone was upwards of seven hundred. In addi-

* Fabian Tract No. 41, pages 15-16; date, 1892.
† The Fabian motto, suggested by Mr. Frank Podmore, runs: "For the right moment you must wait, as Fabius did most patiently when warring against Hannibal, though many censured his delays; but when the time comes you must strike hard, as Fabius did, or your waiting will be in vain and fruitless."

tion to writing or editing many publications of the Fabian Society, Shaw has delivered, in the last twenty-odd years, considerably more than a thousand public lectures and addresses. Until the close of 1889, the Fabians had confined their propagandist campaign to three directions: publication of manifestos and pamphlets; delivery of public addresses and holding of conferences, and exciting efforts towards the permeation of the Liberal party. In December, 1889, the Fabian Society published the well-known book, *Fabian Essays in Socialism*, edited by Shaw, and containing, in addition to two essays of his own, essays by Sidney Olivier, William Clarke, Hubert Bland, Sidney Webb, Annie Besant and Graham Wallas.* The authors, constituting the Executive Council of the Fabian Society, made no claim to be more than communicative learners: the book was the outcome of their realization of the lack of anything like authoritative, and at the same time popular, presentations of the political, economic, and moral aspects of contemporary Socialism.

In general, it may be said that the Fabians, while strenuously avowing themselves strict evolutionists, are in reality highly revolutionary. The boast of the Fabian Society is freedom from the illusions and millennial aspirations of the great mass of Socialists. It is a society of irreverence and scientific iconoclasm, bowing to the fetishism neither of George nor of Marx. Towards Marx and Lassalle, some of whose views must now be discarded as erroneous or obsolete, the Fabian Society insists on the necessity of maintaining as critical an attitude as these eminent Socialists themselves maintained towards their predecessors St. Simon and Robert Owen. In origin anarchistic and revolutionary as could be desired, in spirit the Fabians remain anarchistic and revolutionary. In principle avowedly orderly and constitutional, in policy frankly opportunist, in practice strictly scientific and economic, the Fabians may be called the realists of the Socialist movement. They have ruthlessly snatched the masks from the faces of the Utopian

* This book has now gone into its seventieth thousand, and has been republished in both Germany and America. It is regarded to-day as the standard text in English for Socialist lecturers and propagandists.

dreamers and romancers.* While the rank and file of the
" S. D. F." have been the very good friends of the Fabians,
the radical differences in their respective policies have precluded
all possibility of amalgamation. As succinctly stated by Shaw:
" The Fabian Society is a society for helping to bring about
the socialization of the industrial resources of the country.
The Social-Democratic Federation is a society for enlisting the
whole proletariat of the country in its own ranks and itself
socializing the national industry." The policy of the one is
fundamentally opportunist; of the other, implacably sectarian.
The Federation counts no man a Socialist until he has joined it,
and supports no man who is not a member; the Fabians advise
concentration of strength to elect that candidate, be he Socialist
or not, who gives the greatest promise of advancing, in greater
or less degree, the general cause of Socialism. The Federation
persistently claims to be the only genuine representative of
working-class interests in England; the Fabians have never
advanced the smallest pretensions in that direction. Its policy
finds ample justification in the recent history of Continental
Socialism. The tactics of the German Socialist Party, in the
last few years, have been " Fabianized " by sheer force of circumstances; to-day, this party is, in great measure, both opportunist and constitutional, the two essential features of Fabian
policy. Sharpened in wit by rigorous persecution, Liebknecht
and his successor Bebel have learned the art of politics through
experience and exigency. In contemporary France is witnessed
the signal triumph of Fabian Socialism. The policy of Jaurès,
although under the frown of the " International," will be continued in France; and Guèsde, despite his barren victory at
the International Socialist Congress at Amsterdam in 1904, will
remain only *vox clamantis in deserto*. The history of the
Fabian Society, which is the history of Shaw, in the last twenty
years, bears evidence that the Fabians have stood in the very
forefront of the battle for collectivist measures, municipal

* Compare Fabian Tract No. 70: *Report on Fabian Policy*, the bomb-
shell thrown by the Fabian Society into the International Socialist Workers' and Trade Union Congress, 1896.

reforms, civic virtue and social progress. As Shaw wrote in 1900:

> " In 1885 we agreed to give up the delightful ease of revolutionary heroics and take to the hard work of practical reform on ordinary parliamentary lines. In 1889 we published ' Fabian Essays ' without a word in them about the value theory of Marx. In 1893 we made the first real attack made by Socialists on Liberalism, on which occasion the Social-Democratic Federation promptly joined in the Liberal outcry against us. In 1896 we affirmed that the object of Socialism was not to destroy private enterprise, but only to make the livelihood of the people independent of it by socializing the common industries of life, and driving private enterprise into its proper sphere of art, invention and new departures. This year we have led the way in getting rid of the traditional association of our movement with that romantic nationalism which is to the Pole and the Irishman what Jingoism is to the Englishman. . . . In short, the whole history of Socialism during the past fifteen years in England, France, Germany, Belgium, Austria and America, has been its disentanglement from the Liberal tradition stamped on Marx, Engels and Liebknecht in 1848, and its emergence in a characteristic and original form of its own, modified by national character, and, in England, calling itself Fabianism when it is self-conscious enough to call itself anything at all." *

Strangely enough, in view of all the facts, it is customary to regard Shaw as a purely destructive and negative spirit. The truth is that Shaw stands for certain definite beliefs, certain undoubted principles. His is the belief of the unbeliever, the principle of the unprincipled, the faith of the sceptic.

Not less important than his destructive achievements has been his constructive work in practical affairs as Vestryman and

* *Socialism and Republicanism,* in the *Saturday Review,* November 17th, 1900.

Borough Councillor. Prior to 1895, roughly speaking, the vestries were ignorantly boasted of as the truest products of a representative democratic government. " The truth of the matter," Mr. Shaw once remarked to me, " is that the vestry, as it was actually elected in those days—a few people getting together when nobody knew of it and at some place of which the public was not notified, and electing themselves members— could scarcely be called a representative democratic body. We Socialists finally began to realize that the way to get at the vestry was to put a programme into their hands. So we sent them all a pámphlet, requesting replies—a pamphlet entitled, ' Questions for Vestrymen,' or something of the sort. The vestrymen were thus forced to the wall and driven to decide upon issues. They actually began to make up their minds on many subjects of which hitherto they had had no conception. Slowly the vestries, under this discipline, began to take on a truly representative character. The *personnel* of the vestry was now permanently altered for the better. Men were elected who not only took an interest in municipal affairs, but likewise were willing to do any amount of hard work. I was ' co-opted '—*i.e.,* chosen by the committee, by agreement with the opposite party, obviously beaten if a vote were taken. So that I was fortunate enough to escape the terrors of a popular election."

It is quite beyond the scope of this book to enter into the details of Shaw's work as Vestryman, afterwards Borough Councillor. Suffice it to say, that he was chosen in 1897, entered at once upon the performance of his duties, and prosecuted them for several terms with great zeal and tireless energy. His various letters to the Press during that period, and occasional reminiscences, show that he was always outspoken and vehement in behalf of all reforms which tended to the betterment of the poorer classes, equalization of public privileges of men and women, better sanitary conditions, and the municipalization of such industries as promise to give the people at large better service and greater value for their money than privately operated concerns. The most tangible result of his work as Vestryman and Borough Councillor is his book, *Municipal*

Trading, which he once told me he regarded as one of the best and most useful things he had ever done.*

At the expiration of his career as Borough Councillor, he stood as the candidate for the Borough of St. Pancras in the London County Council—the seat afterwards occupied by the well-known actor, Mr. George Alexander. " I was beaten," Mr. Shaw recently told me, " because I alienated the Nonconformist element by favouring the improvement of the Church schools. I was convinced that such improvement would lead to the betterment of the education of the children. The Nonconformists were enraged beyond measure by the proposal, looking with the utmost horror upon any measure which tended to strengthen the Church. I remember one rabid Nonconformist coming to me one day, almost foaming at the mouth, and protesting with violent indignation that he would not pay a single cent towards the maintenance of the schools of the Established Church. ' Why, my dear fellow,' I replied, ' don't you know that you pay taxes now for the support of the Roman Catholic Church in the Island of Malta?' Although this staggered the irate Nonconformist for the moment, it did not reconcile his element to the extension of the principle to London. My contention was that under the conditions prevailing at the time, the children were poorly taught and poorly housed, the schools badly ventilated, and the conditions generally unsatisfactory. ' Improve all the conditions,' I said; ' appoint your own inspectors, and in the course of time you will control the situation. Pay the piper and you can call the tune.' But I could not override the tremendous prejudice against the Church, and I was badly beaten." One of Shaw's intimate friends told me not long ago that what lost the seat in the L. C. C. for Shaw was his intrepid assertion, repeated throughout the campaign, that he and Voltaire were the only two truly religious people who had ever lived! Shaw's

* For highly appreciative summaries of *The Common Sense of Municipal Trading* (Archibald Constable and Co.), and of Shaw's article, *Socialism for Millionaires* (first published in the *Contemporary Review* of February, 1896, and afterwards, in 1901, as Fabian Tract No. 107), compare Mr. Holbrook Jackson's monograph, *Bernard Shaw*, pages 114-131.

own account of this, when I taxed him with it, was that he had often pointed out that the religious opinions of the Free Churches (the Nonconformist sects) in England to-day were exactly those of Voltaire, and that what I had been told was quite as near his meaning as most people contrived to get without reading him. And only the other day a well-known politician and a friend of Shaw's made the remark to me that Shaw was an "impossible political candidate," too rash and individualistic in his assertions to avoid alienating many people— even some of the very men who under ordinary circumstances might confidently be relied upon to support a progressive and energetic reformer.

And yet it is noteworthy that as far back as the year 1889 Shaw was asked to stand as a Member of Parliament. Below is given the text of a letter, from Shaw, at 29, Fitzroy Square, W., London, dated March 23rd, 1889, to Mr. W. Sanders, then Secretary of the Election Committee of the Battersea branch of the S. D. F., now a prominent Fabian and recently member of the London County Council. This letter, a copy of which was most kindly given me by Mr. Sanders, was sent in reply to a letter from him to Mr. Shaw asking him to allow his name to be put forward as a candidate for the parliamentary representation of Battersea subsequent to a conference between the Battersea L. and R. Association and the Battersea branch of the S. D. F. Mr. Shaw was mistaken in addressing Mr. Sanders as the Secretary of the Election Committee of the Battersea L. and R. Association.

"DEAR SIR,—

"I wish it were possible for me to thank the Battersea L. and R. Association for their invitation, and accept it without further words. But there is the old difficulty which makes genuine democracy impossible at present—I mean the money difficulty. For the last year I have had to neglect my professional duties so much, and to be so outrageously unpunctual and uncertain in the execution of work entrusted to me by employers of literary labour, that my pecuniary position is worse than it was; and I am at present almost wholly dependent on critical work which requires my presence during several evenings in the week at public performances. Badly as I do this at present, I could not do it at all if I had parliamentary duties to discharge; and as to getting back any of the old work that could be done in the morning, I rather think the action I should be bound to take in Parliament would lead to closer and closer boycotting. As to the serious literary work that is independent of editors and politics, I have never succeeded in making it support me; and in any case it is not compatible with energetic work in another direction carried on simultaneously. You must excuse my troubling you with these details; but the Association, consisting of men who know what getting a living means, will understand the importance of them. As a political worker outside Parliament I can just manage to pay my way and so keep myself straight and independent. But you know, and the Association will know, how a man goes to pieces when he has to let his work go, and then to run into debt, to borrow in order to get out of debt by getting into it again, to beg in order to pay off the loans, and finally either to sell himself or to give up, beaten.

"If the constituency wants a candidate, I see nothing for it but paying him. If Battersea makes up its mind to that, it can pick and choose among men many of whom are stronger than I. And since it is well to get so much good value for the money as can be had, I think poor constituencies (and all real democratic constituencies are poor) will for some time be compelled to kill two birds with one stone, and put the same man into both County Council and Parliament. This, however, is a matter which you are sure to know your own minds about, and it is not for me to meddle in it.

"Some day, perhaps, I may be better able to take an extra duty; for, after all, I am not a bad workman when I have time and opportunity to show what I can do; and I need scarcely say that if the literary employers find that

there is money to be made out of me, they will swallow my
opinions fast enough,
            " I am, dear Sir,
                " Yours faithfully,
                        " G. BERNARD SHAW.
" Mr. W. Sanders."

In many quarters, even among his Socialist *confrères*, Bernard Shaw is regarded as primarily destructive in his proposals.
And yet, at different times and in various places, he has con-
structively outlined his programme of complete Socialism. In
essential agreement with such Collectivists as Émile Vandervelde,
Jean Jaurès and August Bebel, Shaw differs from them only
in regard to the successive mutations in the process of Socialist
evolution. The gradual extension of the principle of the income
tax—*e.g.*, a " forcible transfer of rent, interest, and even rent
of ability from private holders to the State, without compensation," is the scheme of capitalistic expropriation the Collectivists
have in mind. By a gradual process of development, the imposition of gradually increased taxes, the State will secure the
means for investment in industrial enterprises of all sorts. Instead of forcibly extinguishing private enterprises, the State
would extinguish them by successfully competing against them.
Thus, as Proudhon said, competition would kill competition;
in America, Mr. Gaylord Wilshire never tires of exclaiming:
" Let the Nation own the Trusts." If, as Shaw claims, the
highest exceptional talent could be had, in the open market, for
eight hundred pounds, say, nearly half the existing wages of
ability and the entire profits of capital would be diverted from
the pockets of the able men and the present possessors of capital,
and would find its way into the pockets of the State. The vast
sum thus accruing to the State would swell the existing wages
fund, and would be employed in raising the wages of the entire
community. After the means of production have been Socialized, and the State has become the employer, products or
riches will be distributed roughly, " according to the labour
done by each man in the collective search for them." In his
celebrated tilt with Shaw, Mr. W. H. Mallock attacked the

validity of the economics which furnish the substructure of *Fabian Essays*.* Mr. Mallock's contention resolves itself into the assertion that exceptional personal ability, and not labour, is the main factor in the production of wealth. Far from repudiating this assertion, Shaw embraced it, he said, in the spirit of Mrs. Prig: " Who deniges of it, Betsy? " We support and encourage ability, Shaw contends, in order that we may get as much as possible out of it, not in order that it may get as much as possible out of us. Give men of ability and their heirs the entire product of their ability, so that they shall be enormously rich whilst the rest of us remain as poor as if they had never existed, and " it will become a public duty to kill them, since nobody but themselves will be any the worse, and we shall be much the better for having no further daily provocation to the sin of envy." Accordingly, the business of Society is " to get the use of ability as cheaply as it can for the benefit of the community, giving the able man just enough advantage to keep his ability active and efficient. From the Unsocialist point of view this is simply saying that it is the business of Society to find out exactly how far it can rob the able man of the product of his ability without injuring itself, which is precisely true (from that point of view)," though whether it is a " reduction of Socialism to dishonesty or of Unsocialism to absurdity " may be left an open question. " If Mr. Mallock will take his grand total of the earnings of Ability," Shaw asserts, " and strike off from it, first, all rent of land and interest on capital, then all normal profits, then all

* *Fabian Economics,* in the *Fortnightly Review,* February, 1894. Mr. Mallock purposed to show how the defenders of a broad and social Conservatism, as outlined by himself, " may be able, by a fuller understanding of it, to speak to the intellect, the heart, and the hopes of the people of this country (England), like the voice of a trumpet, in comparison with which the voice of Socialism will be merely a penny whistle." Shaw delightfully termed his rejoinder, *On Mr. Mallock's Proposed Trumpet Performance,* which brought forth, in the same magazine, not one, but two rejoinders from Mr. Mallock. In 1909 an attack by Mr. Mallock on Mr. Keir Hardie in the *Times* provoked Shaw to a fierce onslaught on his old opponent, and the Fabian Society presently republished the correspondence and the old *Fortnightly* article under the title, *Socialism and Superior Brains.* The latter, in a shilling edition, is also published by A. C. Fifield, London, in the *Fabian Socialist Series.*

non-competitive emoluments attached to a definite status in the public service, civil or military, from royalty downwards, then all payments for the advantages of secondary or technical education and social opportunities, then all fancy payments made to artists and other professional men by very rich commonplace people competing for their services, and then all exceptional payments made to men whose pre-eminence exists only in the imaginative ignorance of the public, the reminder may with some plausibility stand as genuine rent of ability." And to Mr. Mallock's assertion that " men of ability will not exert themselves to produce income when they know that the State is an organized conspiracy to rob them of it," Shaw characteristically retorts, " Mr. Mallock might as well deny the existence of the Pyramids on the general ground that men will not build pyramids when they know that Pharaoh is at the head of an organized conspiracy to take away the Pyramids from them as soon as they are made."

Shaw holds the fundamentally sound view that " as to the entire assimilation of Socialism by the world, the world has never yet assimilated the whole of any ism, and never will." In that most subtle and distinguished of all his contributions to the Socialist literature of our time, *The Illusions of Socialism*, Shaw has expressed his firm conviction that it is not essential for the welfare of the world to carry out Socialism in its entirety. Unfettered by the dogmas of a political creed, unhampered by the bonds of a narrow partisanship, Bernard Shaw stands forth as a great and free spirit in his prophetic declaration that, long before it has penetrated to all corners of the political and social organization, Socialism will have relieved the pressure to which it owes its elasticity, and will recede before the next great social movement, leaving everywhere intact the best survivals of individualistic liberalism. And far from agreeing with Ibsen in his impossibilist declaration that the State must go, Shaw not only asserts that we must put up with the State, but also expresses no doubt whatsoever that under Social-Democracy the few will still govern. It is a mark of Shaw's British practicality and clear-sightedness that he recognizes in the State a practical instrumentality for effecting

SHAVIAN SOCIALISM

and directing social reform. The State is indispensable as a means for making possible one great consummation: the development of the strong, sound, creative personality. The unsocial man he regards as a " hopelessly private person." The opportunity for the free development of the individual he regards as the fundamental prerequisite and condition for the individual's social and material wellbeing.* " That great joint-stock company of the future, the Social-Democratic State, will have its chairman and directors as surely as its ships will have captains." But this admission involves no endorsement, on Shaw's part, of the State as at present constituted. " Bakounine's comprehensive aspiration to destroy all States and Established Churches, with their religious, political, judicial, financial, criminal, academic, economic and social laws and institutions, seems to me perfectly justifiable and intelligible from the point of view of the ordinary ' educated man,' who believes that institutions make men instead of men making institutions." The State, as at present constituted, Shaw views as simply a huge machine for robbing and slave-driving the poor by brute force. While he laughs at the Individualism expressed in Herbert Spencer's *The Coming Slavery*, at the Anarchy expressed in the word *Liberty*, and in those " silly words " of John Hay on the title-page of Benjamin Tucker's paper, Shaw is, nevertheless, both an individualist and an intellectual anarchist. The alleged opposition between Socialism and Individualism, Shaw has always strenuously maintained, is false and question-begging. " The true issue lies between Socialism and Unsocialism, and not between Socialism and that instinct in us that leads us to Socialism by its rebellion against the squalid levelling down, the brutal repression, the regimenting and drilling and conventionalizing of the great mass of us to-day, in order that a lucky handful may bore themselves to death for want of anything to do, and be afraid to walk down Bond Street without a regulation hat and coat on." Like Ruskin, Morris and

* In his analysis of the situation in his native land, he insisted that Home Rule was a necessity for Ireland, because the Irish would never be content, would never feel themselves free, until Home Rule was granted them. It was not a question of logic, but a question of natural right.

GEORGE BERNARD SHAW

Kropotkin, Shaw sees the whole imposture through and through, " in spite of its familiarity, and of the illusions created by its temporal power, its riches, its splendour, its prestige, its intense respectability, its unremitting piety, and its high moral pretension."

At bottom, it was a deeply religious, a fundamentally humanitarian motive, which drew Shaw into Socialism. The birth of the social passion in his soul finds its origin in the individual desire to compass the salvation of his fellow man. A burning sense of social injustice, a great passion for social reform, directed his steps. In his inmost being he felt his complicity in the social ills of the world. He realized that only by personally seeking to effect the salvation of society could he achieve the salvation of his own soul. The Will to Socialism was thus grounded in a profound individualism: he felt their organic connection. Socialism was the need of the age; and it could only be achieved through the freedom and development of the individual.

That other wit and paradoxer, Mr. Gilbert Chesterton, told the very truth itself when he said that Bernard Shaw " has done something that has never been done in the world before. He has become a revolutionist without becoming a sentimentalist. He has revolted against the cant of authority, and yet continued in despising the cant of revolt." To Shaw, the middle-class origin of the Socialist movement is in nothing so apparent as in the persistent delusions of Socialists as to an ideal proletariat, forced by the brutalities of the capitalist into an unwilling acquiescence in war, penal codes, and other cruelties of civilization. " They still see the social problem," Shaw wittily remarks, " not sanely and objectively, but imaginatively, as the plot of a melodrama, with its villain and its heroine, its innocent beginning, troubled middle, and happy ending. They are still the children and the romancers of politics." *

Shaw finds a sort of sly gratification in the reflection that the world is becoming so familiar with the Socialist, that it no longer fears, but only laughs at him. " I, the Socialist, am

* Socialism at the International Congress, in Cosmopolis, September, 1896.

no longer a Red Spectre. I am only a ridiculous fellow. Good: I embrace the change. It puts the world with me. . . . . All human progress involves, as its first condition, the willingness of the pioneer to make a fool of himself. The sensible man is the man who adapts himself to existing conditions. The fool is the man who persists in trying to adapt the conditions to himself. Both extremes have their disadvantages. I cling to my waning folly as a corrective to my waxing good sense as anxiously as I once nursed my good sense to defend myself against my folly." Shaw is the very man of whom his own Don Juan said: "He can only be enslaved whilst he is spiritually weak enough to listen to reason."

THE ART CRITIC

"Produce me your best critic, and I will criticize his head off."—*On Diabolonian Ethics*. In *Three Plays for Puritans*. Preface, p. xxi.

CHAPTER VII

SHAW'S career as a critic dates from the period of his first acquaintance with Mr. William Archer, in 1885. After living for nine years, according to his own story, on the six pounds of which he is so fond of speaking, Shaw was at last reduced to quite straitened financial circumstances. He eagerly seized the opportunity to become a critic afforded him by Mr. Archer's ingenious kindness. "Our friend, William Archer," Shaw relates, "troubled by this state of things, to which the condition of my wardrobe bore convincing testimony, rescued me by a stratagem. Being already famous as the 'W. A.' of the *World's* drama, he boldly offered to criticize pictures as well. Edmund Yates was only too glad to get so excellent a critic. Archer got me to do the work, resigned the post as soon as I had got firm hold of it, and left me in possession." The years from 1885 to 1889, during which he lived at 29, Fitzroy Square, Shaw devoted in part to criticism of art, contemporary English art in particular; during this period, he once told me, he criticized every picture show in London. He also published many unsigned literary reviews and sallies in the *Pall Mall Gazette;* whilst a number of his criticisms of pictures appeared in unsigned paragraphs, both in the *World*, 1885 to 1888, and in *Truth*, 1889. A few of his *critiques* also appeared in a magazine called *Our Corner*.

I recently read Shaw's critical reviews of this period, especially the complete file of his articles in the *Pall Mall Gazette* from May 16th, 1885, to August 31st, 1888, placed at my disposal by Mr. Shaw. The articles are pertinent and shrewd, but only comparatively few are marked by that peculiar and fantastic humour which has come to be known as Shavian. They embrace every sort of subject from Ouida's novels to the *Life of Madame Blavatsky*, from Grant Allen to W. Stanley Jevons, from Cairo to the Surrey Hills—art, fiction, music, drama, science, theology. Occasionally Shaw took delight in adding to the gaiety and curiosity of his readers by putting forth some Shavian frivolity, under an assumed name. Such, for example, was his letter to the *Pall Mall Gazette* on *The Taming of the Shrew*, dated June 8th, 1888, the earliest instance I have of his so-called " Shakspearean Bull-baiting "—a letter copied innumerable times and in almost every paper in the United Kingdom. It ran as follows:

" To the Editor of the *Pall Mall Gazette*.

" SIR,—They say that the American woman is the most advanced woman to be found at present on this planet. I am an Englishwoman, just come up, frivolously enough, from Devon to enjoy a few weeks of the season in London, and at the very first theatre I visit I find an American woman playing Katharine in *The Taming of the Shrew*— a piece which is one vile insult to womanhood and manhood from the first word to the last. I think no woman should enter a theatre where that play is performed; and I should not have stayed to witness it myself, but that, having been told that the Daly Company has restored Shakspeare's version to the stage, I desired to see with my own eyes whether any civilized audience would stand its brutality. Of course, it was not Shakspeare: it was only Garrick adulterated by Shakspeare. Instead of Shakspeare's coarse, thick-skinned money hunter, who sets to work to tame his wife exactly as brutal people tame animals or children—that is, by breaking their spirit by domineering cruelty—we had Garrick's fop who tries to ' shut up ' his wife by behaving worse than she—a plan which is often tried by foolish and ill-mannered young husbands in real life, and one which invariably fails ignominiously, as it deserves to. The gentleman who plays Petruchio at Daly's—I neither know nor desire to know his name—does what he can to persuade the audience that he is not in earnest, and that the whole play is a farce, just as Garrick before him found it necessary to do; but in spite of his fine clothes, even at the wedding, and his

SHAW'S SECOND HOME IN LONDON.

Fitzroy Square (No. 29).

winks and smirks when Katharine is not looking, he cannot make the spectacle of a man cracking a heavy whip at a starving woman otherwise than disgusting and unmanly. In an age when a woman was a mere chattel, Katharine's degrading speech about

> "'Thy husband is thy lord, thy life, thy keeper,
>   Thy head, thy sovereign: one that cares for thee (with a whip),
>   And for thy maintainance; commits his body
>   To painful labour, both by sea and land,' etc.

might have passed with an audience of bullies. But imagine a parcel of gentlemen in the stalls at the Gaiety Theatre, half of them perhaps living idly on their wives' incomes, grinning complacently through it as if it were true or even honourably romantic. I am sorry that I did not come to town earlier that I might have made a more timely protest. In the future I hope all men and women who respect one another will boycott *The Taming of the Shrew* until it is driven off the boards.

" Yours truly,

" HORATIA RIBBONSON.

" St. James's Hotel, and Fairheugh Rectory, North Devon, June 7th."

In his capacity as art critic, when time was priceless and hundreds of pictures had to be examined critically, Shaw found his knowledge of phonography invaluable. I recently looked over a collection of his art catalogues during a single year, and his phonographic notes give a miniature forecast of the art criticism he is presently to write. Beside the titles of certain pictures often appears a single adjective: " gaudy," " brilliant," " stupid," and the like; beside others, " Wilkie," " Reynolds," and the names of other artists, indicating his detection of resemblance to or imitation of the works of the masters. Beside the mention of a " Lighthouse " picture is pencilled the explanatory note, a mixture of praise and blame: " Too green. Has a lamp lighted. Good subject." One recognizes the Shavian *timbre* in such laconic notes as " Fluffy style "; " What does he mean? " " Very dreadful! " and

"Same old game." And we feel sure that Shaw will "gore and trample" the unfortunate wretches who called forth the damning comments—"wheels awful," "idiotic," and "green blush and pasty face."

During these years, however, from 1885 to 1888 in especial, Socialism was the living centre of all Shaw's interests. His time was principally devoted to the most active form of Socialist propagandism. The literary articles of this period do not possess the piquant interest of the "C. di B." or the "G. B. S." criticisms, which are quite remarkable for epigram, satire, and paradox. Most of them are almost unintelligible now that they can no longer be read with the context of the events of the week in which they appeared. Shaw has always been a leader of forlorn hopes; at this time, willy-nilly, he was on the side of the majority. I remember one day quoting Clarence Rook's remark to the effect that Shaw is like the kite, and can rise only when the *popularis aura* is against him. "No, that is a radical mistake," Mr. Shaw said forcibly. "I have never worked with the sense that everybody is against me. On the contrary, my inspiration springs from a sense of sympathy with my views." Still, one might say that it has always been as a defiant and vexatious personality that Shaw has best succeeded in arousing and challenging clamorous protest. Hermann Bahr insists that Bernard Shaw possesses in rich measure the remarkable and exceptional talent of the great artist-critic: the ability to arouse the whole state, the whole nation, against him. Not only was that opposition, which is the very breath of his nostrils, non-existent: there was no great battle on in the world of art in London comparable to those that were yet to be waged. It is true that the Impressionist movement was struggling for life in London, and while Shaw defended it vigorously, neither its day nor his day was yet come. As an almost totally unknown, comparatively unskilled critic of literature and art, he could scarcely be expected to create the unparalleled sensations which he subsequently achieved as a Shakespearean image-breaker, a champion of Wagner and Ibsen, and the most radical exponent of the newest forms of the New Drama.

THE ART CRITIC

And yet it was during these very years that he developed those remarkable qualities which have won him the title of the most brilliant of contemporary British journalistic critics. On all sides the younger generation, which included Mr. Shaw as one of its most daring and iconoclastic members, rose up in revolt against academicism in style. The New Journalism came into being. "Lawless young men," says Shaw, "began to write and print the living English language of their own day instead of the prose style of one of Macaulay's characters named Addison. They split their infinitives and wrote such phrases as ' a man nobody ever heard of,' instead of, ' a man of whom nobody had ever heard '; or, more classical still, ' a writer hitherto unknown.' Musical critics, instead of reading books about their business and elegantly regurgitating their erudition, began to listen to music and to distinguish between sounds; critics of painting began to look at pictures; critics of the drama began to look at something besides the stage; and descriptive writers actually broke into the House of Commons, elbowing the reporters into the background, and writing about political leaders as if they were mere play-actors. The interview, the illustration, and the cross-heading hitherto looked on as American vulgarities impossible to English literary gentlemen, invaded all our papers; and, finally, as the climax and masterpiece of literary Jacobinism, the *Saturday Review* appeared with a signed article in it. Then Mr. Traill and all his generation covered their faces with their togas and died at the base of Addison's statue, which all the while ran ink." "Don't misunderstand my position," Mr. Shaw once remarked to me. "It is true that I was opposed to academicism in style, not to style itself. I believe in style. I thought that the academicism we had was not good academicism. I was pedantic enough myself when I first began to write—when I wrote my first novel. Afterwards I came to the conclusion that a phrase meant much only after it had been washed into shape in the mouths of dozens of generations. The fact of the matter is that I am extremely sensitive to the *form* of art." Shaw simply repudiated the classical tradition of writing like " a scholar and a gentleman." As far as his scholarship was concerned, he took the greatest pains to dissemble the little he possessed. Moreover, he doubted if it had ever been worth while being a " gentleman," and used every means in his power to discredit this antiquated survival of the age of sentimentalism. He always aimed at accuracy, but scoffed consumedly at the notion of achieving " justice " in criticism. " I am not God Almighty," he said in effect, " and nobody but a fool could expect justice from me, or any other superhuman attribute." He wrote boldly according to his bent; he said only what he wanted to say, and not what he thought he ought to say, or what was right, or what was just. To Shaw, this affected, manufactured, artificial conscience of morality and justice was of no use in the writing of genuine criticism, or in the making of true works of art. For that, he felt that one must have the real conscience that gives a man courage to fulfil his will by saying what he likes. An epigram I once heard him make: " Accuracy only means discovering the relation of your will to facts instead of cooking the facts to save trouble "—is a note of his entire criticism. Shaw sought simply to write as accurately, as frankly, as vividly, and as lightly as possible. He hesitated neither at violating taste, nor at being vexatious, even positively disagreeable. " If I meet an American tourist who is greatly impressed with the works of Raphael, Kaulbach, Delaroche and Barry," he once said, " and I, with Titian and Velasquez in my mind, tell him that not one of his four heroes was a real painter, I am no doubt putting my case absurdly; but I am not talking nonsense, for all that: indeed, to the adept seer of pictures I am only formulating a commonplace in an irritatingly ill-considered way. But in this world if you do not say a thing in an irritating way, you may just as well not say it at all, since nobody will trouble themselves about anything that does not trouble them.".

Mr. H. M. Hyndman, the great English Socialist, once told me that he was really the first person in England to discover Shaw. " In 1883," he explained, " I wrote a letter of recommendation for Shaw to Frederick Greenwood, at that time editor of the *Pall Mall Gazette*. The letter led to nothing, it is true; but that is not material. The point is, that in that letter I compared Shaw to Heine—a comparison for which I have been unmercifully chaffed many times since. Of course, Shaw does not possess Heine's wonderful gift of lyrism; but as iconoclastic critics, they have many qualities in common. In his power to turn up for our inspection the seamy side of the robe of modern life, and make us recoil at the sight, Bernard Shaw is without a peer.

" I have always been inclined to class Bernard Shaw and my dear friend George Meredith together. In enigmatic character and faculty of mystification as to their real opinion, they are remarkably alike."

Of Shaw, in all his criticism, might be quoted his own words descriptive of George Henry Lewes as a critic of the drama: " He expressed his most laboured criticisms with a levity which gave them the air of being the unpremeditated whimsicalities of a man who had perversely taken to writing about the theatre for the sake of the jest latent in his own outrageous unfitness for it."

If the world is convinced that Shaw is only a gay deceiver, he himself has felt from the very beginning that the *rôle* he plays is that of the candid friend of society. " Waggery as a medium is invaluable," he once explained. " My case is really the case of Rabelais over again. When I first began to promulgate my opinions, I found that they appeared extravagant, and even insane. In order to get a hearing, it was necessary for me to attain the footing of a privileged lunatic, with the licence of a jester. Fortunately the matter was very easy. I found that I had only to say with perfect simplicity what I seriously meant just as it struck me, to make everybody laugh. My method, you will have noticed, is to take the utmost trouble to find the right thing to say, and then say it with the utmost levity. And all the time the real joke is that I am in earnest." It is Shaw's supreme distinction that he refuses to view life through the confining, beclouding medium of convention. His primal claim to serious attention is based upon the assertion of his freedom from illusion. If he appears grotesque and eccentric, it is not so much because he expresses himself grotesquely and eccentrically: it is primarily because he scrutinizes life with a more aquiline eyesight than that of the illuded majority. His levity has saved him from martyrdom; for, although it is a very difficult thing to speak disagreeable truths, it is a still more difficult thing to listen to them. Recall the treatment the British public gave to George Moore for his advocacy of realism, to Vizetelly for his championing of Zola, even to Shaw himself for his defence of Ibsen! Shaw has based all his brilliancy and solidity, Mr. Chesterton acutely observes, upon the hackneyed, but yet forgotten, fact that truth is stranger than fiction. And Shaw himself has cleverly put the case in his own paradoxical way. " There is an indescribable levity—not triviality mind, but levity—something spritelike about the final truth of a matter; and this exquisite levity communicates itself to the style of a writer who will face the labour of digging down to it. It is the half-truth which is congruous, heavy, serious, and suggestive of a middle-aged or elderly philosopher. The whole truth is often the first thing that comes into the head of a fool or a child; and when a wise man forces his way to it through the many strata of his sophistications, its wanton, perverse air reassures him instead of frightening him." *

This spritelike quality, this indescribable levity inherent in the final truth of a matter, has communicated itself to Shaw's style in the most intimate way. With the not unnatural result that it is difficult for the average man to believe that opinions advanced with such light-hearted levity carry any of the weight of final truth. It is for this reason that all of Shaw's attempts to write genuine autobiography have been greeted with the most amiable scepticism. Shaw himself is able to speak with more confidence on the folly of writing scientific natural history, because he has tried the experiment, within certain timid limits, of being candidly autobiographical.

"I have produced no permanent impression," he declares, " because nobody has ever believed me. I once told

* *Who I Am, and What I Think.* Part II., in the *Candid Friend,* May 18th, 1901.

a brilliant London journalist * some facts about my family, running to forty-first cousins and to innumerable seconds and thirds. Like most large families, it did not consist exclusively of teetotallers, nor did all its members remain until death up to the very moderate legal standard of sanity. One of them discovered an absolutely original method of committing suicide. It was simple to the verge of triteness, yet no human being had ever thought of it before. It was also amusing. But in the act of carrying it out, my relative jammed the mechanism of his heart— possibly in the paroxysm of laughter which the mere narration of his suicidal method has never since failed to provoke—and if I may be allowed to state the result in my Irish way, he died a second before he succeeded in killing himself. The coroner's jury found that he died ' from natural causes '; and the secret of the suicide was kept not only from the public, but from most of the family.

" I revealed the secret in private conversation to the brilliant journalist aforesaid. He shrieked with laughter and printed the whole story in his next *causerie*. It never for a moment occurred to him that it was true. To this day he regards me as the most reckless liar in London."

Had Shaw ever attempted to write the Rougon-Macquart history of his family in twenty volumes, along the candid lines of the above narrative, it is not improbable that he would thereafter have been permanently and forcibly deprived of his privileges as a lunatic. " I have not yet ascertained the truth about myself," he wrote some years ago. " For instance, am I mad or sane? I really do not know. Doubtless, I am clever in certain directions; my talent has enabled me to cut a figure in my profession in London. But a man may, like Don Quixote, be clever enough to cut a figure and yet be stark mad. A critic recently described me, with deadly acuteness, as having ' a kindly dislike of my fellow-creatures.' Perhaps dread

* Mr. A. B. Walkley, Mr. Shaw lately told me.

would have been nearer the mark than dislike; for man is the only animal of which I am thoroughly and cravenly afraid. I have never thought much of the courage of a lion tamer. Inside the cage he is at least safe from other men. There is not much harm in a lion. He has no ideals, no religion, no politics, no chivalry, no gentility; in short, no reason for destroying anything that he does not want to eat. In the late war, the Americans burnt the Spanish fleet, and finally had to drag men out of hulls that had become furnaces. The effect of this on one of the American commanders was to make him assemble his men and tell them that he believed in God Almighty. No lion would have done that. On reading it and observing that the newspapers, representing normal public opinion, seemed to consider it a very creditable, natural and impressively pious incident, I came to the conclusion that I must be mad. At all events, if I am sane, the rest of the world ought not to be at large. We cannot both see things as they really are."

It was at a somewhat later time that the critics came to treat Shaw as a reckless liar and a privileged lunatic. At this period, he impressed the self-conscious literary clique as a witty, but frivolous, ignoramus, totally incompetent to discuss the high subjects of which he professed such penetrating comprehension. I once had an interesting discussion with Mr. Shaw about the subject of his flippancy. " Do you accept as just the criticism, made in some quarters," I asked Mr. Shaw, " that you and Whistler were very much alike in your attitude towards the general public? "

" Not at all, that is a crude error," replied Mr. Shaw earnestly. " Whistler came to grief because he gave himself up to clever smartness, which is abhorrent to the average Englishman. As for me, I have never for a moment lost sight of my serious relation to a serious public. You see, I had an advantage over Whistler in any case, for at least three times every week I could escape from artistic and literary stuff, and talk seriously on serious subjects to serious people. For this reason—because I persisted in Socialist propagandism—I never once lost touch with the real world."

Shaw's *critiques*, sallies, and reviews were the combination of a laborious criticism with a recklessly flippant manner. Into literature he carried the methods he adopted on the platform, where he tossed off the most diligently acquired, studiously pondered information with all the *insouciance* of omniscience. As a critic, Shaw has ever laboured for the scanty wages of the " intolerable fatigue of thought." In characteristic style, he has gone so far as to declare that good journalism is much rarer and more important than good literature; he has no sympathy with Disraeli's view of a critic as an author who has failed. " I know as one who has practised both crafts," wrote Shaw in 1892, " that authorship is child's play compared to criticism; and I have, you may depend upon it, my full share of the professional instinct which regards the romancer as a mere adventurer in literature and the critic as a highly skilled workman. Ask any novelist or dramatist whether he can write a better novel or play than I; and he will blithely say ' Yes.' Ask him to take my place as critic for one week; and he will blench from the test. The truth is that the critic stands between popular authorship, for which he is not silly enough, and great authorship, for which he is not genius enough." *

While Mr. Shaw was laboriously striving to impart lightness and *insouciance* to his literary style, and to acquire careless *sang-froid* as a platform speaker, he was likewise making the acquaintance of certain distinguished men of his day. His relation and association with William Morris, for example, exercised no noteworthy influence upon his art; but it certainly did no less than accentuate certain distinct traits of his character. Unmistakably, in this way, does this association serve to give us a clearer insight into the *rationale* of Shaw's— popularly-called—idiosyncrasies. On the other hand, it furnishes us a new aspect of Morris from the Shavian point of view.

Readers of the authorized edition of *Cashel Byron's Profession* will recall that William Morris, who, like Shaw, had thrown himself into the Socialist revival of the early eighties, first

---

* *The Author to the Dramatic Critics,* Appendix I. to the first edition of *Widowers' Houses.* London, Henry and Co., Bouverie Street, E.C., 1893.

became curious about Shaw through reading the monthly instalments of *An Unsocial Socialist* as they appeared in the Socialist magazine *To-Day*. Shaw had heard of Morris, to be sure; and had even, years before, once seen him—of all places in the world!—in the Doré Gallery. Yet his notions about Morris were, in reality, of the vaguest. He knew nothing beyond the meagre facts that he was a poet, that he belonged to the Rossetti circle, and that he was associated with Burne-Jones and with what was then called Æstheticism. He had never read a line of Morris's, and, in fact, had taken no definite measure of his calibre. This was the situation when Shaw found himself one evening in Gatti's big restaurant in the Strand at the table with Morris and H. M. Hyndman. Morris belonged to Mr. Hyndman's society, the Democratic Federation, now the Social-Democratic Federation, while Mr. Hyndman himself was the head centre of London Socialism. With naïve simplicity, Morris humbly announced that he was prepared to do whatever he was told and go wherever he was led: that was all he could say. In a letter to me describing the interview, written many years afterwards, Mr. Shaw said that, while it was only snap-judgment—a personal impression across the table—he could not help being " privately tickled by this announcement from an obviously ungovernable man who was too big to be led by any of us."

In ignorance concerning Morris, Shaw was not alone: the other Socialists were in precisely the same predicament. Morris himself said afterwards that it was among his Socialist *confrères* that he first realized he was an elderly duffer. His old Rossettian associates used to call him Topsy; but, as readers of Lady Burne-Jones's *Memorials* will recall, Burne-Jones used to be angry when she applied this embarrassing nickname to Morris before strangers. If Morris was affectionately regarded as a young man by his associates of the " P. R. B.," to his Socialist allies he looked older than he was—sixty at fifty, though a magnificent sixty—a sort of " sixty-years-young " patriarch. Morris and Shaw, after they settled down to the routine of Socialist agitation, were at the opposite poles of the movement. Shaw headed the Fabian

Society, while Morris, after his secession from the S. D. F., organized the Socialist League, which shortly went to pieces— because, as Shaw says, there was only one William Morris; he was afterwards the leading spirit in the Hammersmith Socialist Society. Despite this fundamental difference in viewpoint—for Morris's fundamental conceptions were " Equality, Communism, and the rediscovery under Communism of Art as ' work-pleasure,' " whereas Shaw, as a Fabian, aimed simply at the reduction of Socialism to a constitutional political policy—there was never any personal friction between the two. Indeed, they did a great deal of speaking together in the early days, most of it at the street corner, and often thought themselves lucky if they had an audience of twenty. In after years, we find Morris with the broadest of views endeavouring to settle the differences which arose between the various Socialist sects. By 1893, when he gave his well-known address entitled *Communism* before the Hammersmith Socialist Society, Morris had acquired an intimate knowledge of the attempt to organize Socialism in England which began in the early eighties. " He had himself undertaken and conducted," writes Shaw, " that part of the experiment which nobody else would face: namely, the discovery and combination, without distinction of class, of all those who were capable of understanding Equality and Communism as he understood it, and their organization as an effective force for the overthrow of the existing order of property and privilege. In doing so he had been brought into contact, and often into conflict, with every other section of the movement. He knew all his men and knew all their methods. He knew that the agitation was exhausted, and that the time had come to deal with the new policy which the agitation had shaken into existence. Accordingly, we find him in this (the above-mentioned) paper, doing what he could to economize the strength of the movement by making peace between its jarring sections, and recalling them from their disputes over tactics and programs to the essentials of their cause." *

* Note of the Editor, G. B. Shaw, of Fabian Tract No. 113: *Communism* —a lecture by William Morris, published by the Fabian Society.

None of Morris' Socialist associates were in the least degree hero-worshippers, at least where he was concerned: they never bothered at all about his eminence. " I was not myself conscious of the impression he had made on me," Mr. Shaw once remarked to me, in explaining his feeling for Morris, " until one evening, at a debating society organized by Stopford Brooke, when Morris, in a speech on Socialism in the course of a debate, astonished me by saying that he left the economics to me—' in that respect I regard Shaw as my master.' The phrase meant only that he left that side of the case to me, as he always did when we campaigned together, but though I knew this, still it gave me a shock which made me aware that I had unconsciously rated him so highly that his compliment gave me a sort of revulsion." It was genuine modesty which once prompted Shaw to say that he never liked to call himself Morris's friend, because he was too much his junior and too little necessary or serviceable to him in his private affairs. And yet he enjoyed an unstinted and unreserved intercourse with Morris: one of Shaw's best-known Fabian tracts, *The Transition to Social Democracy*, for example, was written at Morris's mediæval manor-house, Lechlade, on the Thames, and was heartily approved on its historical side by that erudite student of the Middle Ages. Shaw once said that no man was more liberal in his attempts to improve Morris's mind than he was; " but I always found that, in so far as I was not making a most horrible idiot of myself out of misknowledge (I could forgive myself for pure ignorance), he could afford to listen to me with the patience of a man who had taught my teachers. There were people whom we tried to run him down with—Tennysons, Swinburnes, and so on; but their opinions about things did not make any difference, Morris's did." *

Morris greatly enjoyed a number of Shaw's essays, for the prime reason that in those essays Shaw said certain things which Morris wanted to have said. After Shaw's celebrated reply to Max Nordau, Morris suddenly began to talk to Shaw

* Obituary essay: *Morris as Actor and Dramatist*, in the *Saturday Review*, October 10th, 1896. Reproduced in *Dramatic Opinions and Essays*, Vol. II.

about Whistler and the Impressionists in a way which showed that he knew all about them and what they were driving at, though before that Shaw had given Morris up as—on that subject—an intolerant and ignorant veteran of the pre-Raphaelite movement. That this was highly characteristic of Morris from Shaw's standpoint is evidenced by some paragraphs in Shaw's obituary notice of Morris in the *Saturday Review*. " When an enthusiast for some fashionable movement or reaction in art would force it into the conversation, he (Morris) would often behave so as to convey an impression of invincible prejudice and intolerant ignorance, and so get rid of it. But later on, he would let slip something that showed, in a flash, that he had taken in the whole movement at its very first demonstration, and had neither prejudices nor illusions about it. When you knew the subject yourself, and could see beyond it and around it, putting it in its proper place and accepting its limits, he could talk fast enough about it; but it did not amuse him to allow novices to break a lance with him, because he had no special facility for brilliant critical demonstration, and required too much patience for his work to waste any of it on idle discussions. Consequently there was a certain intellectual roguery about him of which his intimate friends were very well aware; so that if a subject were thrust on him, the aggressor was sure to be ridiculously taken in if he did not calculate on Morris's knowing much more about it than he pretended." He thus often presented himself as imperious and prejudiced, because up to a certain point he would neither agree nor discuss, simply giving you up as walking in darkness. But the moment you had worked your way through the subject and come out on the other side, as Shaw expressed it, Morris would suddenly begin to talk like an expert and show all sorts of knowledge— scientific, political, commercial, intellectual-as-opposed-to-artistic, and so on—that you never suspected him of. " He was fond of quoting Robert Owen's rule: ' Don't argue: repeat your assertion,' " Mr. Shaw recently told me; " and mere debating, which he knew to be an intellectual game and not an essential part of the Will-to-Socialism (so to speak), did not interest him enough to make him good at it. But he highly enjoyed hearing anyone else do it cleverly on his side, and was furious when it was done on the other side. In point of command of modern critical language, he was by no means a ready man; and as I was in great practice just then, he would take a prompt from me (if it was the right one) with as much relief and simplicity as if I had found his spectacles for him."

Shaw once said that, as far as he was aware, he shared with Mr. Henry Arthur Jones the distinction of being the only modern dramatist, except the author of *Charley's Aunt*, which bored Morris, whose plays were witnessed by Morris. Shaw did not pretend to claim Morris's visits as a spontaneous act of homage to modern acting and the modern drama, but only as a tribute of personal friendship; for Morris was a " twelfth-twentieth-century artist," exclusively preoccupied with a vision of beauty unrealized upon the modern stage. In a passage in a letter to me, Mr. Shaw has tersely etched the firm figure of the artist and the man, who could not be induced " to accept ugliness as art, no matter how brilliant, how fashionable, how sentimental, or intellectually interesting you might make it."

" Morris's artistic integrity was, humanly speaking, perfect. You could not turn him aside from the question of the beauty and the decency of a thing by bringing up its *interest*, scientific, casuistic, novel, curious, historical, or what not. That was most extraordinary in so clever a man; for he was capable of all the interests. Compared to him Ruskin was not an artist at all: he was only a man whose interest in Nature led him to study Turner, and whose insight into religion gave him a clue to the art of the really religious painters. He would not give two-pence for a rarity or a curiosity or a relic; but when he saw a sanely beautiful thing, and it was for sale, he went into the shop; seized it, held it tight under his arm (it was generally a mediæval book) ; and, after the feeblest and most transparent show of bargaining, bought it for whatever was asked. Once, when he was rebuked for paying eight hundred pounds for something that a dealer

William Morris

would have got for four hundred and fifty pounds, I said, 'If you *want* a thing, you always get the worst of the bargain.' Morris was delighted with my wisdom, and probably spent many unnecessary pounds on the strength of that poor excuse.

" This artistic integrity of his was what made him unintelligible to the Philistine public. When the Americans set to work to imitate his printing, they showed that they regarded him as a fashionably quaint and foolish person; and the Roycroft Shop and all the rest of the culture-curiosity shops of the States poured forth abominations which missed every one of his lessons and exaggerated every one of the practices he tried to cure printers of. In the same way his houses at Hammersmith and Kelmscott were, though quite homely, as beautiful in their domestic way as St. Sophia's in Stamboul; but other people's ' Morris houses ' always went wrong, even when he started them right."

One day Mr. Shaw and I were discussing Morris and the influence he exerted upon Shaw. " What Morris taught me," confessed Mr. Shaw, " was in the main technical—printing, for example.* And I soon came to realize that his most characteristic trait was integrity in the artistic sense. By watching Morris, I first learned that Ruskin wasn't strong as a critic of works of art. In a sense, Ruskin was a naturalist because he understood Turner. And the key to his comprehension of the pre-Raphaelites was his religious sense. And yet he could not discover so glaring an error as Bernardino Luini's employment of the same model for the Virgin and the Magdalen. The trouble with Ruskin was that he invariably fell into egregious blunders when he didn't have his religious clue."

" I learned a great deal from Morris," he added, " because Morris and I worked together in Socialism—and, as a critic, I was intensely interested in the pre-Raphaelite movement."

* In this connection, compare *The Author's View. A Criticism of Modern Book Printing*. By Bernard Shaw. In the *Caxton Magazine*, January, 1902.

It was always a source of regret to Shaw that he never met Burne-Jones, Morris's greatest friend. When Morris died, Shaw wrote obituary articles in the *Daily Chronicle* and in the *Saturday Review*; and when McKail's *Life of Morris* appeared, he reviewed it in the *Daily Chronicle*. Burne-Jones was pleased by the *Saturday Review* article, and wanted to meet Shaw. They made appointment after appointment; but something always occurred—an illness, a journey, or the like—to defeat them. At last they resolved that the meeting *must* come off; and a firm arrangement was made—for a Sunday lunch, it seems—to be kept at all hazards. But Destiny had a card up its sleeve that they did not reckon with. Burne-Jones died the day before; so Shaw never met him as an acquaintance, and only saw him twice, once at an exhibition where he heard him say that a picture attibuted to Morris had been partly painted by Madox Brown, and once at a theatre, where their seats happened to be next one another.

When Shaw became a critic of music in 1888, he began to consider whether he was making enough money by the very hard work of plodding through all the picture exhibitions. At last he counted his gains, and found, to his amazement, that his remuneration for paragraphs at fivepence per line, worked out at—according to his recollection afterwards—less than forty pounds a year; whereas two hundred pounds would not have been at all excessive for the work. " Edmund Yates, when I resigned and told him why," Mr. Shaw once told me, " was as much staggered as I was myself, and proposed a much more lucrative arrangement by which I should divide the work with Lady Colin Campbell. But the division would not have been fair to her; and Yates, recognizing this, did what I asked, which was, to hand the whole department over to Lady Colin, and confine my contributions to music alone."

The period of Shaw's activities as an art critic is memorable less for the quality and value of his criticism than for the revelation of the essential moral integrity of the man so often denounced as the cranky immoralist of this, our time. This, as we shall see, appears most clearly in his relations with W. E. Henley, the story of which, I believe, has never been told in print; yet other crucial instances, equally revelative, are worthy of record. Shaw's experience amply justifies his statement that the public has hardly any suspicion of the rarity of the able editor who is loyal to his profession and to his staff; and that without such an editor even moderately honest criticism is impossible. Take, for example, the case of Shaw and a London paper. Shaw wrote about pictures for the best part of a season until a naïve proposal was made to him that he should oblige certain artist-friends of the editorium by favourable notices, and was assured that he might oblige any friends of his own in the same way. " This proposal was made in perfect good faith and in all innocence," Shaw candidly avers, " it never having occurred to those responsible that art criticism was a serious pursuit or that any question of morals or conduct could possibly arise over it. Of course I resigned with some vigour, though without any ill humour; but some I know were quite sincerely, pathetically hurt by my eccentric, unfriendly and disobliging conduct." During his career as a critic Shaw was repeatedly urged by colleagues to call attention to some abuse which they themselves were not sufficiently strongly situated to mention. He had to resign very desirable positions on the critical staff of London papers; in the case above mentioned, because he considered it derogatory to write insincere puffs; and in another case, " because my sense of style revolted against the interpolation in my articles of sentences written by others to express high opinions of artists, unknown to fame and to me." This second resignation followed the appearance of an Academy notice, written by Shaw in the capacity of art critic to another London paper. This article on an Academy exhibition appeared padded out to an extraordinary length by interpolations praising works which Shaw had never seen—" No. 2,744 is a sweet head of Mrs. —— by that talented young artist, Miss ——," and so on. It is needless to add that Shaw resigned in a highly explosive manner. And so Shaw vanished from the picture galleries. His comment on the conduct of the management of these papers explains his own attitude, testifying conclusively to the rigour of the moral standard to which he always conformed. " They

were no more guilty of corruption," Mr. Shaw expressed the
case to me, " than a man with no notion of property can be
guilty of theft; and to this day they probably have not the
least idea why I threw up a reasonably well-paid job and
assumed an attitude vaguely implying some sort of disapproval of their right to do what they liked with their own
paper."

It was probably at the particular Press view just referred to,
some time after 1889, that Henley's meeting with Shaw occurred. To go back a little, James Runciman, the uncle of
J. F. Runciman, the musical critic, was a Cashel Byronite, and
used to write Shaw letters containing occasional references to
Henley, who also admired *Cashel Byron's Profession*. Between
Runciman, who had known Henley and quarrelled with him, and
Cashel Byron, Shaw got into correspondence with Henley.
Among the various literary and artistic Dulcineas whose championship Henley mistook for criticism, was Mozart. Mr. Shaw
thus explained the situation to me:

" As I also knew Mozart's value, Henley induced me to write
articles on music for his paper, the *Scots Observer*, afterwards
the *National Observer;* and I did write some—not more than
half a dozen—perhaps not so many. Henley was an impossible
editor. He had no idea of criticism except to glorify the masters he liked, and pursue their rivals with quixotic jealousy. To
appreciate Mozart without reviling Wagner was to Henley a
blank injustice to Mozart. Now, he knew I was what he called
a Wagnerite, and that I thought his objections to Wagner
vieux jeu, stupid, ignorant and common. Therefore he amused
himself by interpolating abuse of Wagner into my articles over
my signature. Naturally he lost his contributor; and it was
highly characteristic of him that he did not understand why
he could not get any more articles from me. At the same time
he made the *National Observer* an organ, politically and socially, of the commonest sort of plutocratic and would-be aristocratic Toryism, and clamoured in the usual forcible-feeble
way for the strong hand to ' put down ' the distress which
then—in the eighties—was threatening insurrection. For this
sort of thing I had no mercy. I did not object to tall talk

about hanging myself and my friends who were trying to get something done for the condition of the people; but what moved me to utter scorn was the association of the high republican atmosphere of Byron, Shelley and Keats, and the gallantry of Dumas *père*—another idol of ours—with the most dastardly class selfishness and political vulgarity. When Henley at last pressed me very hard for another article, I wrote him in a perfectly friendly but frankly contemptuous strain, chaffing him rather fiercely as the master of his fate, the captain of his soul, with his head bloody but unbowed, and his hat always off to the police and the upper classes." Shaw always believed that, even then, Henley was simply puzzled, and thought Shaw was only making a senseless literary display of smartness at his expense.

Clearly Shaw was revolted by the atrocious vulgarity of Henley's politics as contrasted with the pretentiousness of his literary attitude. The defence of Henley after his death, to the effect that he knew nothing of politics, and that he placed himself as to the politics of the paper in the hands of his friend Charles Whibley, disarmed Shaw, as I have good reason to know. For Shaw liked Whibley well enough, regarding him as a clever fellow in literary matters, but quite impossible politically. Opinions similar to those quoted below may be found in the only criticism Shaw ever wrote of Henley—a review of his poems in the old *Pall Mall Gazette* under Mr. Stead's editorship. The following quotation from a hitherto unpublished letter to me vividly clarifies the whole matter by defining the grounds of Shaw's criticism of Henley:

" Henley interested me as being what I call an Elizabethan, by which I mean a man with an extraordinary and imposing power of saying things, and with nothing whatever to say. The real disappointment about his much discussed article on Stevenson was not that he said spiteful things about his former friend, but that he said nothing at all about him that would not have been true of any man in all the millions then alive. The world very foolishly reproached him because he did not tell the usual epitaph

monger's lies about 'Franklin, my loyal friend.' But the
real tragedy about the business was that a man who had
known Stevenson intimately, and who was either a penetrating critic or nothing, had nothing better worth saying
about him than that he was occasionally stingy about
money and that when he passed a looking-glass he looked
at it. Which Stevenson's parlour-maid could have told as
well as Henley if she had been silly enough to suppose that
the average man is a generous sailor in a melodrama, and
totally incurious and unconscious as to his personal appearance. But it was always thus with Henley. He
could appreciate literature and enjoy criticism. He could
describe anything that was forced on his observation and
experience, from a tom-cat in an area to a hospital operation. Give him the thing to be expressed, and he could
find its expression wonderfully either in prose or verse.
But beyond that he could not go: the things he said—or
the things he wrote (I know nothing of his conversation)—
are always conventionalities, all the worse because they
are selected from the worst part of the great stock of
conventionalities—the conventional unconventionalisms.
He could discover and encourage talent, and was thus half
a good editor, but he could not keep friends with it; and
so his papers finally fell through."

As in the case of his obituary notices of Sir Augustus Harris
and Sir Henry Irving, Shaw was accused of nothing short of
brutality in his attitude towards Henley, the Cashel Byronite
who had wished to see Shaw's novel dramatized. In the first
place, Henley admired Shaw, and it seemed ungenerous for
Shaw to repay him by a denial of the sort of talent he desired
to excel in. And in the second place, it seemed to Shaw's
detractors that it was doubly ungenerous of a man sound in
wind and limb to disparage a man who was physically a wreck,
fighting bravely against infirmity and pain. I was not surprised to find, on inquiring of Mr. Shaw his real feelings and
attitude in the matter, that he regarded both these reasons as
absurd, sentimental and pointless.

" People have a strong feeling," Mr. Shaw explained, " that if a man has lost his hearing or sight bravely in a noble cause the world is thereby bound in decency to assume for ever after that he had the eye of an eagle and the ear of a hare." He continued, impressively: " I have never belittled a misfortune in that way. Long ago, when a blind poet died, and certain maudlin speeches of his were repeated in print as expressions of the pathos of his darkened existence, I said, also in print, that he always said these things when he was drunk, and that the fact that he was blind may have added to the pity of them, but did not give them any sort of validity.

" In the same way when, in the European revolutionary movement, men came with horrible experiences of prison and Siberian wanderings on them, and women whose husbands had been hanged or committed suicide, I have always had to stand out against the notion that they were the better instead of the worse for their misfortunes, or that they derived any credit or authority whatever from them. Give them the indulgence due to enforced weakness or the help due to unavoidable distress; but don't make them heroes and leaders *ex-officio* because they have been unlucky enough to be lamed.

" And so, I have often conveyed to sentimental people an impression of revolting callousness simply because I know that suffering is suffering, and not merely the acquisition of a romantic halo. Henley's infirmities were to me trifles compared to those which I had encountered in other cases; and in any case, I was trained to look in the face the fact that infirmities disable people instead of reinforcing them. People who learn in suffering what they teach in song usually give very dangerous lessons; and I admire Henley for having no doctrine of that sort. Besides, I have always abhorred the petty disloyalties which men call sparing one another's feelings.

" To make an end of the matter," Mr. Shaw concluded, " Henley, though a barren critic and poet, had enough talent and character to command plenty of consideration. A man cannot be everything. I am as fond of music as Henley was of literature," he added, his grey-blue eyes twinkling brightly; " but I am the worst of players, and have a very poor voice."

The opinion that Shaw's art during this period is less interesting than his life does not necessarily involve any reflection upon the value of his experience as an art critic in giving direction and tendency to the subsequent course of his development. Indeed Shaw has been mainly influenced by works of art in his artificial culture: he has always been more consciously susceptible to music and painting than to literature. It is no idle assertion—one that Shaw is fond of repeating—that Mozart and Michael Angelo count for a great deal in the making of his mind. And, however paradoxical it may sound, the English dramatists after Shakespeare are practically negligible as concerning their influence in the development of his peculiar and highly specialized dramatic genius. His close and familiar daily intercourse with the music masters of the past; his instant recognition of Wagner's overwhelming greatness; his rapturous delight in that king of music-dramatists, Mozart; his dogged attempts, alone and unaided, to master the difficulties of pianoforte playing, which eventuated in his becoming a congenial, sympathetic accompanist—all early marked him as a natural and undiscouragedly persistent lover of music. His individual studies of Italian art, in its history and its expression, while he was still in his teens, his frequent visits to the Dublin Gallery, the many hours passed in London at the priceless picture galleries in Trafalgar Square and Hampton Court, testify with equal force to his spontaneous preoccupation with the best that has been thought and done in the world of art. It would carry one too far afield to pursue the inquiry as to what influence Michael Angelo might possibly have exerted upon the dramas of Bernard Shaw. But there can be little doubt that what Shaw found to wonder at and glorify in Michael Angelo was his passion for anatomy, his devotion to the studiously realistic, and his unlimited mastery of form acquired through "profound and patient interrogation of reality." Shaw, the close, searching student of life, found untold inspiration in the discovery of the genuinely naturalistic spirit in which Michael Angelo worked! Words he once used in speaking to me of the influence of Michael Angelo upon his art are very illuminative. " I never shall forget climbing an enormously high, rickety framework, in company with Anatole France," he remarked, " in order to get a closer look at the Delphic Sibyl. We were close enough to touch it with our hands; and I was surprised to discover that, instead of losing, it gained impressiveness on nearer view. The grand, set face made a tremendous impression upon me. For the first time, I fully realized that Michael Angelo was a great artist, and a great man as well—because his every subject is a person of genius. He never had a commonplace subject. His models are extraordinary people. They are all Supermen and Superwomen.

" Michael Angelo, you see," he continued, " taught me this—always to put people of genius into my works. I am always setting a genius over against a commonplace person."

In the same spirit, Shaw praised Madox Brown as a realist, " because he had vitality enough to find intense enjoyment in the world as it really is, unbeautified, unidealized, untitivated in any way for artistic consumption." The sad, sensuous daydreams of Rossetti, the gentlemanly draughtsmanship of Leighton, the whole romantic trend of English art, with its delicacy of sentiment, its beauty-fancying, its reality-shirking philosophy, found Shaw coldly, cruelly condemnatory. " Take the young lady painted by Ingres as ' La Source,' for example. Imagine having to make conversation for her for a couple of hours." This gives the tone of his criticism. His deepest scorn was aroused by that form of art which sets up " decorative moral systems contrasting roseate and rapturous vice with lilied and languorous virtue, making ' Love ' face both ways as the universal softener and redeemer." The artist who sought to depict life with perfect integrity—in Browning's phrase, " to paint man man, whatever the issue "—the artist who sought to express the veracity and reality of life rather than its imagined beauty and poetry, found in Shaw an unhesitating champion. This passion for unidealized reality was the outcome of long and deliberate study of art works, concerning each of which Shaw deliberately forced himself to form an intelligent and conscious estimate. This was the solid residuum of his studies, rescued from a ruck of sophistication. " I remember once when I was an art critic," wrote Shaw in 1897, " and when Madox Brown's work was only known to me by a few drawings, treating Mr. Frederick Shields to a critical demonstration of Madox Brown's deficiencies, pointing out in one of the drawings the lack of 'beauty' in some pair of elbows that had more of the wash-tub than of 'The Toilet of Venus' about them. Mr. Shields contrived without any breach of good manners to make it quite clear to me that he considered Madox Brown a great painter and me a fool. I respected both convictions at the time; and now I share them. Only, I plead in extenuation of my folly that I had become so accustomed to take it for granted that what every English painter was driving at was the sexual beautification and moral idealization of life into something as unlike itself as possible, that it did not at first occur to me that a painter could draw a plain woman for any other reason than that he could not draw a pretty one." *

Shaw stood forth as a champion of all forms of art—pictorial, fictive and dramatic—which aim at realistic exposure of the sheer facts of life without idealistic falsification and romantic sublimation. He lauded Madox Brown, for example, as he lauded Ibsen, and for the same reason: they both took for their themes "not youth, beauty, morality, gentility and prosperity as conceived by Mr. Smith of Brixton and Bayswater, but real life taken as it is, with no more regard for poor Smith's dreams and hypocrisies than the weather has for his shiny silk hat when he forgets his umbrella." It is no matter for surprise that the unshirking student of sociological conditions should have chosen to write *Widowers' Houses* and *Mrs. Warren's Profession;* it would have been astounding had he not done so. And yet the catholicity of his taste in art enabled him to realize, not simply one aspect of English art, but the real English art-culture of to-day. To Shaw, indeed, the significance of the modern movement in England had its germ in the growing sense of the "naïve dignity and charm" of thirteenth-century work, in a passionate affection for the exquisite beauty of fifteenth-century art. "The whole rhetorical

* *Madox Brown, Watts, and Ibsen.* In the *Saturday Review*, March 13th, 1897.

school in English literature, from Shakespeare to Byron," he once wrote, " appears to us in our present mood only another side of the terrible *dégringolade* from Michael Angelo to Canova and Thorwaldsen, all of whose works would not now tempt us to part with a single fragment by Donatello, or even a pretty foundling baby by Della Robbia." He maintained that William Morris made himself the greatest living master of the English language, both in prose and verse, by picking up the tradition of the literary art where Chaucer left it; that Burne-Jones made himself the greatest among English decorative painters by picking up the tradition of his art where Lippi left it, and utterly ignoring " their Raphaels, Correggios and stuff "; and that Morris and Burne-Jones, close friends and co-operators in many a masterpiece, form the highest aristocracy of English art of our day.*

The only controversial question that came up during Shaw's period as an art critic was raised by the Impressionists; and his reputation, with the select few, for consistency is sustained by the course he adopted. He recognized Impressionism as a new birth of energy in art, a movement in painting which was wholly beneficial and progressive, and in no sense insane and decadent. Despite the fact that the movement, like all new movements in art, was accompanied by many absurdities—exhibition of countless daubs, the practice of optical distortion, the substitution of " canvases which looked like enlargements of obscure photographs for the familiar portraits of masters of the hounds in cheerfully unmistakable pink coats, mounted on bright chestnut horses "—Shaw supported it vigorously because, " being the outcome of heightened attention and quickened consciousness on the part of its disciples, it was evidently destined to improve pictures greatly by substituting a natural, observant, real style for a conventional, taken-for-granted, ideal one." It is needless to say that Shaw did not fall into the Philistine trap and talk " greenery yallery " nonsense about Burne-Jones and the pre-Raphaelite school: his admiration was checked by the sternest critical reservations. He applauded

* Cf. *King Arthur.* In the *Saturday Review,* January 19th, 1895.

the Impressionists for their busy study of the atmosphere, and of the relation of light and dark between the various objects depicted, *i.e.*, of "values." Like Zola in his championship of Monet, Shaw led a miniature crusade in behalf of Whistler, whose pictures at first quite naturally amazed people accustomed to see the "good north light" of a St. John's Wood studio represented at exhibitions as sunlight in the open air—for example, Bouguereau's "Girl in a Cornfield." More than this need not be said: that Shaw never joined the ranks of the *moqueurs* who called Mr. Whistler "Jimmy."

It is worthy of record that Shaw vigorously and ably championed the Dutch school, earnestly advocating the claims of James Maris as a great painter; and he stood up for Van Uhde, not only in defence of his pictures of Christ surrounded by people in tall hats and frock coats, but also in favour of his excellent painting of light in a dry, crisp, diffused way then quite unfashionable. But his most signal art criticism of the last decade, beyond question, has had to do with photography. In 1901, he announced that "the conquest by photography of the whole field of monochromatic representative art may be regarded as completed by the work of this year." His position is based on the dictum that "in photography, the drawing counts for nothing, the thought and judgment count for everything; whereas in the etching and daubing processes where great manual skill is needed to produce anything that the eye can endure, the execution counts for more than the thought." This is no new or sudden notion, derived from the study of some photographic exhibition, but the mature statement of a judgment arrived at over a quarter of a century ago. In *An Unsocial Socialist*, Trefusis astounds Erskine and Sir Charles Brandon with those same remarkable views on photography which to-day, in the mouth of Bernard Shaw, so delight the patrons of the Photographic Salon.*

"It is more than twenty years since I first said in print that nine-tenths (or ninety-nine hundredths, I forget

* Compare *Photography*, October 26th, 1909.

which) of what was then done by brush and pencil would presently be done, and far better done, by the camera. But it needed some imagination, as well as some hardihood, to say this at that time . . . because the photographers of that day were not artists. . . . Let us admit handsomely that some of the elder men had the root of the matter in them as the younger men of to-day; but the process did not then attract artists. . . . On the whole, the process was not quite ready for the ordinary artist, because (1) it could not touch colour or even give colours their proper light values; (2) the Impressionist movement had not then rediscovered and popularized the great range of art that lies outside colour; (3) the eyes of artists had been so long educated to accept the most grossly fictitious conventions as truths of representation that many of the truths of the focussing screen were at first repudiated as grotesque falsehoods; (4) the wide-angled lens did in effect lie almost as outrageously as a Royal Academician, whilst the anastigmat was revoltingly prosaic, and the silver print, though so exquisite that the best will, if they last, be one day prized by collectors, was cloying, and only suitable to a narrow range of subjects; (5) above all, the vestries would cheerfully pay fifty pounds for a villainous oil-painting of a hospitable chairman, whilst they considered a guinea a first-rate price for a dozen cabinets, and two-pound-ten a noble bid for an enlargement, even when the said enlargement had been manipulated so as to be as nearly as possible as bad as the fifty pound painting. But all that is changed nowadays. Mr. Whistler, in the teeth of a storm of ignorant and silly ridicule, has forced us to acquire a sense of tone, and has produced portraits of almost photographic excellence; the camera has taught us what we really saw as against what the draughtsman used to show us; and the telephoto lens and its adaptations, with the isochromatic plate and screen, and the variety and manageableness of modern printing processes, have converted the intelligent artists, smashed the picture-fancying critics, and produced exhibitions such as those now open at the Dudley and New Galleries, which may be visited by people who, like myself, have long since given up as unendurable the follies and falsehoods, the tricks, fakes, happy accidents, and desolating conventions of the picture galleries. The artists have still left to them invention, didactics, and (for a little while longer) colour. But selection and representation, covering ninety-nine-hundredths of our annual output of art, belong henceforth to photography. Someday the camera will do the work of Velasquez and Peter de Hooghe, colour and all; and then the draughtsmen and painters will be left to cultivate the pious edifications of Raphael, Kaulbach, Delaroche, and the designers of the S. P. C. K. But even then they will photograph their models instead of drawing them." *

In a paper Maurice Maeterlinck wrote for Mr. Alvin Langdon Coburn, who kindly gave me a copy, he charges art with having held itself aloof from " the great movement which for half a century has engrossed all forms of human activity in profitably exploiting the natural forces that fill heaven and earth." Maeterlinck lauds the camera as an instrument of thought, proclaiming it the best of mediums, because it serves " to portray objects and beings more quickly and more accurately than can pencil or crayon." Just as Maeterlinck concludes that thought has at last found a fissure through which to penetrate the mystery of this anonymous force (the sun), " invade it, subjugate it, animate it, and compel it to say such things as have not yet been said in all the realm of chiaroscuro, of grace, of beauty and of truth," so Shaw expresses his belief that " the old game is up," and that " the camera has hopelessly beaten the pencil and paint-brush as an instrument of artistic representation."

Shaw is a vigorous champion of the photographic art in its integrity; attempts at imitation of etching or painting draw his hottest fire. The idea of sensitive photographers allowing

* The Exhibitions—I., by G. Bernard Shaw. In the Amateur Photographer, October 1st, 1901.

themselves to be bull-dozed into treating painting, not as an obsolete makeshift which they have surpassed and superseded, but as a glorious ideal to which they have to live up!!! One day Mr. Shaw was showing me some striking examples of his own photographic work—a remarkable picture of Sidney Webb, I recall in especial, an effect got by omitting to do something in taking the photograph. Mr. Shaw remarked that some of the most unique and fantastic pictures he had ever taken were the results of accidents. One day, for instance, he spilled some boiling water over a photograph of himself, which immediately converted it into so capital an imitation of the damaged parts of Mantegna's frescoes in Mantua that the print delighted him more in its ruin than it had in its original sanity. And, in view of his violently-expressed detestation of photographic imitation of painting, it is very refreshing to hear him confess that his own experience as a critic and picture fancier had sophisticated him so thoroughly, that " those accidental imitations of the products of the old butter-fingered methods of picture-making often fascinate me so that I have to put forth all my strength of mind to resist the temptation to become a systematic forger of damaged frescoes and Gothic caricatures."

Mr. Shaw was harshly ridiculed and sharply censured for permitting the exhibition in 1906 of a nude photograph of himself by Alvin Langdon Coburn. In this connection, I recall a conversation with Éduard J. Steichen, who was showing me a collection of his masterly prints, including several nudes. The faces of the nude figures were averted; and Steichen told me, with a laugh, that Shaw had ridiculed him unmercifully for permitting his subjects to call attention to their embarrassment and shame by averting their faces. And in 1901, Mr. Shaw wrote:

" The camera will not build up the human figure into a monumental fiction as Michael Angelo did, or coil it cunningly into a decorative one, as Burne-Jones did. But it will draw it as it is, in the clearest purity or the softest mystery, as no draughtsman can or ever could. And by the seriousness of its veracity it will make the slightest lubricity intolerable. ' Nudes from the Paris Salon ' pass the moral *octroi* because they justify their rank as ' high art ' by the acute boredom into which they plunge the spectator. Their cheap and vulgar appeal is nullified by the vapid unreality of their representation. Photography is so truthful—its subjects are so obviously realities, and not idle fancies—that dignity is imposed on it as effectually as it is on a church congregation. Unfortunately, so is that false decency, rightly detested by artists, which teaches people to be ashamed of their bodies; and I am sorry to see that the photographic life school still shirks the faces of its sitters, and thus gives them a disagreeable air of doing something they are ashamed of." *

One morning in Paris, during the period that Shaw was sitting to Rodin, Coburn, with his camera, caught Shaw coming out of his morning bath; whereupon he laughingly bade Shaw to " be still and look pleasant." " I casually assumed, as near as I could recall it," Mr. Shaw told me, " the pose of Rodin's ' *Le Penseur*.' It was all done in a moment, and although I am not like ' *Le Penseur*,' at least my pose is not unlike his." Mr. Shaw permitted the photograph to be put on exhibition as an object-lesson, so to speak, to the photographic life school; as Steichen expressed it to me: " I believe Mr. Shaw wanted to show the courage of his convictions, by publicly taking the medicine he so unhesitatingly prescribed for others."

It is needless to point out that Bernard Shaw, the analytic critic and clear thinker *par excellence*, would naturally prefer photography to painting. When away from London he is seldom to be seen without a camera slung over his shoulders; and he has been taking pictures, and dabbling away at interesting photographic experiments, for many years. Without talent as an artist himself, but with almost a passion for photography, we need not be surprised to hear him praise the photographer because he is free of " that clumsy tool—the human hand— which will always go its own single way, and no other."

* *The Exhibitions—II.,* in the *Amateur Photographer,* October 18th, 1901.

Steichen and Coburn, he has told me and he has told them, are the two greatest photographers in the world; and he once said to me of Coburn: " Whenever his work does not please you, watch and pray for a while and you will find that your opinion will change." *

To Shaw the true conquest of colour no longer seems far off in the light of Lumière's discoveries, and the day will soon come, he surmises, when work like that of Hals and Velasquez may be done by men who have never painted anything except their own nails with pyro. " As to the painters and their fanciers, I snort defiance at them; their day of daubs is over." He once declared for two photographs of himself against anything of Holbein, Rembrandt, or Velasquez. " When I compare their subtle diversity with the monotonous inaccuracy and infirmity of drawings, I marvel at the gross absence of analytic power and of imagination which still sets up the works of the great painters, defects and all, as standard, instead of picking out the qualities they achieved and the possibilities they revealed, in spite of the barbarous crudity of their methods." There are certain quite definite things the photographer has not yet achieved: Shaw's imagination as a creative dramatist teaches him this, even though he insists that the decisive quality in a photographer is the " faculty of seeing certain things and being tempted by them." Oscar Wilde acutely remarked that in certain modern portraits—Sargent's, notably, I should say— there is often as much of the artist as of the subject. Bernard Shaw insists that in the pictorial and dramatic phases of the photographic art of the future, both the artist and the subject must be imaginative artists, working in conjunction. " As to the creative, dramatic, story-telling painters—Carpaccio, and Mantegna, and the miraculous Hogarth, for example—it is clear that photography can do their work only through a co-operation of sitter and camerist which assimilates the relations of artist and model to those at present existing between playwright and actor. Indeed, just as the playwright is sometimes only a very humble employee of the actor or

* Compare Shaw's article, *Coburn the Camerist,* in the *Metropolitan Magazine,* May, 1906.

actress manager, it is conceivable that in dramatic and didactic photography the predominant partner will not be necessarily either the photographer or the model, but simply whichever of the twain contributes the rarest art to the co-operation. Already that instinctive animal, the public, goes into a shop and says: ' Have you any photographs of Mrs. Patrick Campbell? ' and not ' Have you any photographs by Elliott and Fry, Downey, etc., etc.? ' The Salon is altering this, and photographs are becoming known as Demachys, Holland Days, Horsley Hintons, and so forth, as who should say Greuzes, Hoppners and Linnells. But, then, the Salon has not yet touched the art of Hogarth. When it does, ' The Rake's Progress ' will evidently depend as much on the genius of the rake as of the moralist who squeezes the bulb, and then we shall see what we shall see."

THE MUSIC CRITIC

"CORNO DI BASSETTO" AND "G. B. S."

"Don't be in a hurry to contradict G. B. S., as he never commits himself on a musical subject until he knows at least six times as much about it as you do."—*Music.* In the *World,* January 18th, 1893.

CHAPTER VIII

IN 1888 a gentleman described in the *World* at that time as " a Chinese statesman named Tay Pay," * founded the *Star*, claiming for it the distinction of the first and only halfpenny paper, and ignoring the *Echo*, which early succumbed to the treatment. On the recommendation of Mr. H. W. Massingham, Shaw was placed on the editorial staff as leader writer, on the second day of the paper's existence. At that time the Fabian Society had just invented the municipal modification of Socialism called Progressivism; and the sole object of Shaw, then a " moderate and constitutional, but strenuous Socialist," in joining the *Star* was to foist this new invention upon it as the latest thing in Liberalism. Here Shaw's " impossibilism " broke out worse than ever; and Mr. O'Connor, an Irishman too, and a skilled journalist in the bargain, was not to be taken in. He refused to print the articles. " Then the Fabian Society ordered all its members to write to the *Star*," records Shaw, " expressing indignant surprise at the lukewarmness of its Liberalism and the reactionary and obsolete character of its views. This was more successful; the paper became Progressive, and London rose so promptly to the new programme, that the first County Council election was fought and won on it. The Liberal leaders remonstrated almost daily with T. P., being utterly bewildered by what was to them a most dangerous heresy. But the *Star* articles became more and more Progressive, then ultra-Progressive, then positively Jacobin; and the further they went the better London liked them. They were not, I beg to say, written by me, but by Mr. H. W. Massingham." †

* Mr. T. P. O'Connor.
† In speaking of his first appearance as a journalistic writer—in a " London Letter," written, at the age of fifteen, for a well-known journal in Scarborough—Max Beerbohm once wrote (the *Saturday Review*, January

While the Fabians were thus engaged in " collaring the *Star* by this stage army stratagem," Shaw, to the utter consternation of the Chinese statesman, was writing political leaders for which the country was not ripe by about five hundred years, according to the political computation of the eighties. Too good-natured to do his duty and put Shaw out summarily, Tay Pay, in desperation, proposed that Shaw should have a column to himself, to be headed " Music," and to be " coloured by occasional allusions to that art." It was with a gasp of relief that he heard Shaw's acceptance of the proposition; and so a new career opened for Shaw as " Corno di Bassetto," * a " person now forgotten, but I flatter myself, very popular for a couple of years in the *Star*."

Among Shaw's colleagues on the *Star* at this time were Clement K. Shorter and Richard Le Gallienne. A. B. Walkley, the distinguished dramatic critic of the London *Times*, was then the " *Star* man " in the theatres, and although he was more fastidious and dignified than the incorrigible " Bassetto," he was quite as amusing. " I am far from denying that a man of genius may make even a newspaper notice of the Royal Academy or of a ' Monday Pop.' permanently valuable and delightful," Mr. Archer once said; " all I maintain is that it assuredly takes a man of genius to do so. Mr. Bernard Shaw . . . has to my thinking a peculiar genius for bringing day-by-day musical criticism into vital relation with æsthetics at large, and even with ethics and politics—in a word, with life. . . ." According to his subsequent confession, " The

26th, 1901): " I well remember that the first paragraph I wrote was in reference to the first number of the *Star,* which had just been published. Mr. T. P. O'Connor, in his editorial *pronunciamento,* had been hotly philanthropic. ' If,' he had written, ' we enable the charwoman to put two lumps of sugar in her tea instead of one, then we shall not have worked in vain.' My comment on this was that if Mr. O'Connor were to find that charwomen did not take sugar in their tea, his paper would, presumably, cease to be issued. . . . I quote it merely to show that I, who am still regarded as a young writer, am exactly connate with Mr. Shaw. For it was in this very number of the *Star* that Mr. Shaw, as ' Corno di Bassetto,' made his first bow to the public." This latter statement, although inaccurate, is essentially correct.

* The name of a musical instrument which went out of use in Mozart's time.

"Magnetic, he has the power to infect almost everyone with the delight that
he takes in himself."   (Mr. George Bernard Shaw.)

A Cartoon.   By Max Beerbohm.

[Facing p. 230

Star's own captious critic," as Shaw was denominated at the time, used the word music in a platonically comprehensive sense; for he wrote about anything and everything that came into his head. He once spoke of his column in the *Star*, signed " Corno di Bassetto," as " a mixture of triviality, vulgarity, farce and tomfoolery with genuine criticism." George Henry Lewes' style, as Mr. Archer has shrewdly observed,* reminds one of that of " Corno di Bassetto "; but the dramatic essays of Lewes, Shaw freely confesses, are miles beyond the crudities of Di Bassetto, although the combination of a laborious criticism with a recklessly flippant manner is the same in both. Indeed, Shaw's column in the *Star* was perhaps the most startling evidence of the insurgency and iconoclasm of the New Journalism as represented by the *Star*, its foremost exponent. Imagine a column a week in the sprightly vein of the following:

" I warn others that Offenbach's music is wicked. It is abandoned stuff: every accent in it is a snap of the fingers in the face of moral responsibility, every ripple and sparkle on its surface twits me for my teetotalism, and mocks at the early rising which I fully intend to make a habit of some day. . . . In Mr. Cellier's scores, music is still the chastest of the muses. In Offenbach's she is— what shall I say?—I am ashamed of her. I no longer wonder that the Germans came to Paris and suppressed her with fire and thunder. Here in England how respectable she is! Virtuous and rustically innocent her six-eight measures are, even when Dorothy sings, ' Come, fill up your glass to the brim'! She learned her morals from Handel, her ladylike manners from Mendelssohn, her sentiment from the ' Bailiff's Daughter of Islington.' But listen to her in Paris, with Offenbach. Talk of six-eight time: why, she stumbles at the second quaver, only to race off again in a wild Bacchanalian, Saturnalian, petticoat spurning, irreclaimable, shocking quadrille."

* In his introduction to the *Dramatic Essays of John Forster and George Henry Lewes.*

No more accurate characterization of the work of Di Bassetto can be conceived than is to be found in Shaw's own confession. He secured the privileges he usurped, he says, in two ways: first, by taking care that " Corno di Bassetto " should always be amusing; and, secondly, by using a considerable knowledge of music, which nobody suspected him of possessing, to provide a solid substratum of genuine criticism for the mass of outrageous levities and ridiculous irrelevancies which were the dramatic characteristics of " Bassetto." " I daresay these articles would seem shabby, vulgar, cheap, silly, vapid enough if they were dug up and exposed to the twentieth century light; but in those days, and in the context of the topics of that time, they were sufficiently amusing to serve their turn." *

It will be recalled that Shaw, from his early childhood, had been in close contact with the best that had been thought, felt, and written in music. It was his practice as a boy to whistle to himself the operatic themes he heard continually practised at his home, precisely as a street *gamin* whistles the latest piece of " rag-time." He was introduced to Wagner's music for the first time by hearing a second-rate military band play an arrangement of the *Tannhäuser* march. He thought it a rather commonplace plagiarism from the famous theme in *Der Freischütz*. This boyish impression was exactly the same as that recorded of the mature Berlioz, who was to Shaw at that time the merest shadow of a name which he had read once or twice. Shaw learned his notes at the age of sixteen; and although for a long time thereafter he inflicted untold suffering on his neighbours, he became in time quite a good accompanist. In the early days in London, when he was not laboriously writing five pages a day on one of his novels, Shaw occasionally tried his hand at musical composition, at writing and setting words to music. I have before me now a folded sheet of pink paper, dated " 23d of June, 1883," in Shaw's fine handwriting, on which he had written music for one of Shelley's poems, Rossetti edition, Vol. III., p. 107. On the inside of the folded

* *In the Days of Our Youth.* In the *Star,* February 19th, 1906.

sheet, in Shaw's hand, is copied the poem, headed *Lines*, beginning:

> "When the lamp is shattered,
>   The light in the dust lies dead;
> When the cloud is scattered,
>   The rainbow's glory is shed;
>
> "When the lute is broken,
>   Sweet notes are remembered not;
> When the lips have spoken,
>   Loved accents are soon forgot."

Shaw was deeply interested in a study of Wagner's music, and took great pains in studying Wagner's methods of composition. I have seen Shaw's musical notes made during this period—sheets of stiff paper on which he had written out the musical scores of the various distinct *leit motifs* in the Wagnerian operas—the Ring motive, the Rheingold motive, etc., etc.—with fine marginal stenographic notes in the Pitman system. He once made quite a study of counterpoint; and, as we learned in an earlier chapter, acquired a grounding in "Temperament" through his acquaintance with his friend, James Lecky. When Mr. O'Connor transferred Shaw from the editorial staff to the post of musical critic for the *Star*, believing that he could do no great harm there, his wisdom was justified by the result. All his experience in writing and criticism on the *Star*, combined with his early knowledge of music, filled Shaw's hands with weapons. And when Louis Engel, the "best hated musical critic in Europe," as Shaw calls him, found it necessary to give up his position as musical critic of the *World*, his post fell to "Corno di Bassetto."

At the time when Shaw first entered the lists as a musical critic, he was possessed of the strongest convictions on the subject of music, musicians, and true musical genius. In *Love Among the Artists* Shaw has given expression to his decided views concerning the pedantry of the academic schools, the absurd jargon of conventional musical criticism, and the vacuity and inconsequence of all music, based on method alone, which does not come into being through unaffected enthusiasm for art, and the sincere effort towards the complete realization of personality. The musical criticism which takes the analysis of " Bach in B minor " as its point of departure is there held up to unmeasured scorn. It seems something more than a coincidence that the avoidance of this very subject, with all its implications, should have been the condition on which Shaw began his career as a critic of music. In connection with his appointment as musical critic of the *Star*, Shaw relates this story of Mr. O'Connor: " He placed himself in my hands with one reservation only. ' Say what you like,' he said; ' but for— (here I omit a pathetic Oriental adjuration)—don't tell us anything about Bach in B minor.' It was a bold speech, considering the superstitious terror in which the man who has the abracadabra of musical technology at his fingers' end holds the uninitiated editor; but it conveyed a golden rule." Shaw was in perfect accord with the editor in the belief that " Bach in B minor " is not good criticism, not good sense, not interesting to the general readers, not useful to the student. He fulfilled his part of the contract far more completely than the " Chinese statesman " had any right to expect. Not only did Shaw not tell us anything about " Bach in B minor ": he spent six years of his life in holding the practice up to ridicule and contempt!

Bernard Shaw brought his critical faculty to bear upon music in England during the period when the academic faction held full sway. There was a large reserve of native musical talent in England at this time, but it found nothing like full scope for its development, largely because of the commercial pandering to popular taste. The so-called masters of contemporary music in England were all reared on the methodology of the schools. Dr. Mackenzie, the Principal of the Royal Academy of Music, was probably the leader of the academic faction. Sir George Grove, author of that standard work, the *Dictionary of Musicians*, was an honoured figure in the world of music. Dr. Hubert Parry, at the height of his creative activity, was writing and occasionally conducting his oratorios, such as *Job* and *Judith*. These and other earlier works of his—notably, *L'Allegro ed il Pensieroso* and *Prometheus*—Shaw took the utmost pleasure in declaring to be " without any merit whatsoever," or "the most conspicuous failures," despite their fine feeling, their scrupulous moderation, and other pleasant and perfectly true irrelevancies. At the Albert Hall, Sir Joseph Barnby, Principal of the Royal Choral Society, in his measured and complacent style, was leading those huge, lumbering choirs which are still the pride of Great Britain. Villiers Stanford, that Irish professor ever trifling in a world of ideas, was writing his *Eden*, and other works, which entitled him to a high place in the councils of academicism. Goring Thomas, for his *Golden Web*, and other operas, had already attained a position as a dramatic composer, which, according to Shaw, at least, "placed the production of an opera of his beyond all suspicion as a legitimate artistic enterprise." Arnold Dolmetsch, that rarely fine interpreter of ancient music, was giving those unique viol concerts in the hall of Barnard's Inn and elsewhere which charmed Arthur Symons yesterday as they charmed Bernard Shaw long ago. Gilbert and Sullivan had once more joined forces in *Utopia*, scoring another operatic triumph, somewhat less decisive and conspicuous, it must be confessed, than *Pinafore*, *The Mikado* and *The Pirates of Penzance*. Cowen was winning encomiums as a conductor, and Sterndale Bennett was still a name to conjure with. To the many, Wagner, like Ibsen, was still an offensive impostor. But Ashton Ellis's exhaustive task of translating Wagner's works was slowly proceeding; and Armbruster, that Bayreuth extension lecturer, so to speak, aided by Shaw in the *Star* and in the *World*, was paving the way for a more general comprehension and appreciation of Wagner in England. Paderewski was slowly mounting to the position of the foremost living pianist, and Patti had begun to give her "Farewell Concerts."

In musical criticism, as in all other phases of his strangely diversified career, Shaw is essentially a revolutionary. His attack upon Parry's *Job*, so he always maintained, threatened to call forth a great national protest! He fought for Wagner with the same revolutionary enthusiasm which enlisted him in the cause of Ibsen—and Shaw. He had no tolerance for anything traditional, not even for traditional versions of old airs, for the simple reason that they were always inaccurate. So jealous was he of his critical sense, for fear of its prostitution by irrelevant beauty or factitious romance, that he steadfastly steeled himself against that subtlest of all forces in undermining critical integrity—personal magnetism.

Perhaps the simplest way to arrive at a comprehension of Shaw, the critic of music, is by taking account of his tastes and aversions. For example, Shaw usually viewed Paderewski's performances, at the time when the Polish pianist was first creating such sensations in England, as brutal contests between the piano and the pianist to settle the question of the survival of the fittest. The following description of his sensations on hearing Paderewski is not without its reminder of that once popular *pièce de récitation, How Ruby Played.** " The concerto was over, the audience in wild enthusiasm, and the piano a wreck. Regarded as an immensely spirited young harmonious blacksmith, who puts a concerto on the piano as upon an anvil, and hammers it out with an exuberant enjoyment of the swing and strength of the proceeding, Paderewski is at least exhilarating; and his hammer play is not without variety, some of it being feathery, if not delicate. But his touch, light or heavy, is the touch that hurts; and the glory of his playing is the glory that attends murder on a large scale when impetuously done." Three years later, in 1893, Shaw has reached the conclusion that Paderewski is a weak, a second-hand composer, but an artist whose genuine creative achievements have assured him the title of the greatest of living pianists. " I had rather see Paderewski in his next composition for orchestra drop the piano altogether," Shaw said. " It is the one instrument he does not understand as a composer, exactly because he understands it so well as an executant."

For David Bispham Shaw had the sincerest admiration, and the De Reszkes won his praise because, as he explained it, they sang like dignified men, instead of like male viragoes in the dramatic Italian style. He made a point of insisting, however, that Édouard de Reszke occasionally abused his power by " wilful bawling " for the mere fun of making a thundering

---

* The reference is to Rubinstein.

noise. On hearing Gerster in 1890, he was sufficiently charmed to say: " The old artistic feeling remained so unspoiled and vivid that, if here and there a doubt crossed me whether the notes were all reaching the furthest half-crown seat as tellingly as they came to my front stall, I ignored it for the sake of the charm which neither singer nor opera *(The Huguenots)* has lost for me." Of a concert given in 1893 by " our still adored Patti," whom he calls " now the most accomplished of mezzo-sopranos," he gives the following description:

" It always amuses me to see that vast audience (at Albert Hall) from the squares and villas listening with moist eyes whilst the opulent lady from the celebrated Welsh castle fervently sings: ' Oh, give me my lowly thatched cottage again.' The concert was a huge success: there were bouquets, raptures, effusions, kissings of children, graceful sharings of the applause with *obbligato* players—in short, the usual exhibition of the British *bourgeoisie* in the part of Bottom and the prima donna in the part of Titania. Patti hazarded none of her old exploits as a florid soprano with an exceptional range: her most arduous achievement was ' *Ah, fors e lui*,' so liberally transposed that the highest notes in the rapid traits were almost all sharp, the artist having been accustomed for so many years to sing them at a higher pitch. Time has transposed Patti a minor third down, but the middle of her voice is still even and beautiful; and this with her unsurpassed phrasing and that delicate touch and expressive *nuance* which make her *cantabile* singing so captivating, enables her to maintain what was, to my mind, always the best part of her old supremacy." *

Of that brilliant executant Essipoff, the wife of Leschetizky, Shaw said that if it were possible to believe that she *cared* two straws about what she played, she would be one of the greatest executive musicians of Europe. Hollman was, on the whole

---

* *Music,* signed G. B. S., in the *World,* June 7th, 1893.

and without any exception, in Shaw's opinion, the greatest violoncellist he had ever heard. Joachim's fineness of tone, perfect dignity of style, and fitness of phrasing impressed Shaw as truly magnificent; and when he heard him play Bach's "Chaconne in D minor," he confessed that he came as near as he ever came to calling anything done by mortal artist perfect. Ysaye, that other master-violinist, moved Shaw as much as he moved Symons by the perfectly harmonious blending of his every faculty. Shaw smilingly reminded all readers of the screed of G. B. S. that "Decidedly, if Ysaye only perseveres in playing splendidly to us for twenty-five years more or so, it will dawn on us at last that he is one of the greatest of living artists; and then he may play how he pleases until he turns ninety without the least risk of ever hearing a word of disparagement or faint praise."

In Shaw's view, Mozart is the ideal, the supreme composer. Again and again, throughout his works, Shaw has lavished upon Mozart the finely-tempered praise of the clear-eyed devotee. The critical rating of a composer is overwhelmingly impressive when it is supported by the avowal of personal indebtedness; and Shaw has frequently asserted that Mozart has influenced his dramatic works more than any English dramatist since Shakespeare. I remember discussing Mozart with Mr. Shaw one day; and I took occasion to express my scepticism as to the possibility of any profound influence exerted by Mozart the composer upon Shaw the dramatist. "In a certain sense, Mozart must always have been a model for me," replied Mr. Shaw. "Throughout the entire period of my career as a critic of music, I always thought and wrote of Mozart as a master of masters. The dream of a musician is to have the technique of Mozart. It was not his ' divine melodies ' but his perfect technique that profoundly influenced me. What a great thing to be a dramatist for dramatists, just as Mozart was a composer for composers! First, and above all things else, Mozart was a *master to masters*."

The second part of *Faust* impressed Shaw as the summit of Schumann's achievement in dramatic music; and he was very ready to admit that Schumann had at least one gift which has now come to rank very high among the qualifications of a composer for the stage: a strong feeling for harmony as a means of emotional expression. He always found Brahms to be insufferably tedious when he tried to be profound, but delightful when he merely tried to be pleasant and naïvely sentimental. "Euphuism, which is the beginning and end of Brahms' big works," Shaw remarks in connection with the "Symphony in E minor," "is more to my taste in music than in literature. Brahms takes an essentially commonplace theme; gives it a strange air by dressing it in the most elaborate and far-fetched harmonies; keeps his countenance severely (which at once convinces an English audience that he must have a great deal in him); and finds that a good many wiseacres are ready to guarantee him as deep as Wagner, and the true heir of Beethoven." Dvorak, Bohemia's most eminent creative musician, famed alike for an inexhaustible wealth of melodic invention and a rich variety of colouring, is stamped by Shaw as a romantic composer, and only that. His "Requiem" Shaw found utterly tedious and mechanical, while his "Symphony in G" is "very nearly up to the level of a Rossini overture, and would make excellent promenade music at the summer fêtes." The announcement of a Mass by Dvorak affected Shaw very much as would the announcement of a "Divine Comedy" in ever so many cantos by Robert Louis Stevenson! He regarded Verdi as the greatest of living dramatic composers; and years before Shaw began writing musical criticism, when Von Bülow and others were contemptuously repudiating Verdi, Shaw was able to discern in him a man possessing more power than he knew how to use, or, indeed, was permitted to use by the old operatic forms imposed on him by circumstances.*

For the solemnly manufactured operas of Saint Saëns, Shaw felt not mere distaste, but genuine contempt. As soon, in fact, as he discovered the sort of thing that a French composer dreams of as the summit of operatic achievement, his artistic sympathy with Paris was cut off at the main. Early in his career, he solemnly announces, he gave up Paris as impossible

* In this connection compare Shaw's article: *A Word More about Verdi*, in the *Anglo-Saxon Review*, Vol. VIII., March, 1901.

from the artistic point of view! His characterization of French music is nothing short of Heinesque.

"London I do not so much mind. Your average Londoner is, no doubt, as void of feeling for the fine arts as a man can be without collapsing bodily; but, then, he is not at all ashamed of his condition. On the contrary, he is rather proud of it, and never feels obliged to pretend that he is an artist to the tips of his fingers. His pretences are confined to piety and politics, in both of which he is an unspeakable impostor. It is your Parisian who concentrates his ignorance and hypocrisy, not on politics and religion, but on art. In this unwholesome state of self-consciousness he demands statues and pictures and operas in all directions, long before any appetite for beauty has set his eyes or ears aching; so that he at once becomes the prey of pedants who undertake to supply him with classical works, and swaggerers who set up in the romantic department. Hence, as the Parisian, like other people, likes to enjoy himself, and as pure pedantry is tedious and pure swaggering tiresome, what Paris chiefly loves is a genius who can make the classic voluptuous and the romantic amusing. And so, though you cannot walk through Paris without coming at every corner upon some fountain or trophy or monument for which the only possible remedy is dynamite, you can always count upon the design including a female figure free from the defect known to photographers as under-exposure; and if you go to the opera—which is, happily, an easily avoidable fate—you may wonder at the expensive trifling that passes as musical poetry and drama, but you will be compelled to admit that the composer has moments, carried as far as academic propriety admits, in which he rises from sham history and tragedy to genuine polka and barcarolle; whilst there is, to boot, always one happy half-hour when the opera-singers vanish, and capable, thoroughly trained, hard-working, technically skilled executants entertain you with a ballet. Of course the ballet, like everything else in

Paris, is a provincial survival, fifty years behind English time; but still it is generally complete and well done by people who understand ballet, whereas the opera is generally mutilated and ill done by people who don't understand opera."

Is it any wonder, then, that the " tinpot stage history " of Saint Saëns was the bane of Shaw's existence and the abomination of his critical sense? Or that Offenbach's music struck him as wicked, abandoned stuff? And of Meyerbeer, then still regarded in Paris as a sort of Michael Angelo, he says: " If you try to form a critical scheme of the development of English poetry from Pope to Walt Whitman, you cannot by any stretch of ingenuity make a place in it for Thomas Moore, who is accordingly either ignored in such schemes or else contemptuously dismissed as a flowery trifler. In the same way, you cannot get Meyerbeer into the Wagnerian scheme except as the Autolycus of the piece."

The most significant feature of Shaw's career as a musical critic was his championship of Wagner. Although he had an exalted admiration for Wagner, he was no hero-worshipper, nor in the least degree blind to the defects of Wagner as a composer who failed to preserve philosophic continuity and coherence in his greatest dramatic achievement. The similarity of tastes in music between Wagner and Shaw is a very noticeable feature of the " C. di B." and " G. B. S." criticisms. It was to be expected that Shaw the dramatist would admire Wagner for composing music designed to heighten the expression of human emotion; he realized fully that such music was intensely affecting in the presence of that emotion, and utter nonsense apart from it. Like Wagner, Shaw had a deep love for Beethoven, an intense admiration for Mozart, and a sincere appreciation of the Mendelssohn of the Scotch symphony. And he likewise shared Wagner's sovereign contempt for the efforts of Schumann and Brahms to be " profound."

A German would laugh at the notion that Wagner required any " championing " during the years from 1888 to 1894 inclusive, since the Bayreuth performances began in 1876. The chief novelty in Shaw's Wagner criticisms was his attack on Bayreuth for the various old-fashioned absurdities perpetrated there—the inadequacy of *mise en scène*, the ridiculous unnaturalness and inappropriateness of scenery and dress, and the retention in leading parts of " beer-barrels of singers " who did not know how to sing. The result of Shaw's first visit, in 1889, was an article on Bayreuth for the *English Illustrated Magazine;* a later visit produced an illustrated article in the *Pall Mall Budget.* Besides this, both visits were reported day by day by Shaw in the *Star,* over his signature, " Corno di Bassetto," or " C. di B." Up to that time, in Shaw's opinion, Bayreuth criticism had been either worship or blasphemy. " I threw off all this, and criticized performances of Wagner's works at Bayreuth precisely as I should have criticized performances of Wagner's works at Covent Garden. The effect on pious Wagnerians was as though I had brawled in church."

In his relation of musical critic in England, Shaw took the greatest pains to ascertain the exact bearings of the controversy which had raged round Wagner's music-dramas since the middle of the century. The six years of Shaw's activity as a musical critic fell within the decade of Sir Augustus Harris's greatest operatic enterprises. Shaw spent a large part of his time in making onslaught after onslaught on the " spurious artistic prestige " of Covent Garden. For some seasons he was forced to pay for his own stall; and there were times, Shaw says, when " I was warned that my criticisms were being collated by legal experts for the purpose of proving ' prejudice ' against me, and crushing me by mulcting my editor in fabulous sums. . . . The *World* proved equal to the occasion in the conflict with Covent Garden, and, finally, my invitations to the opera were renewed; the impresario made my personal acquaintance, and maintained the pleasantest relations with me from that time onward. . . ." It is true that Jean de Reszke made his first appearance on any stage on July 13th, 1889, as the hero of *Die Meistersinger;* but it infuriated Sir Augustus Harris to be publicly reminded by Shaw that *Tristan and Isolde,* having been composed in 1859, was perhaps a little overdue. Indeed, it was not until 1896 that *Tristan and Isolde* at last made its way into the repertory of Royal Italian Opera in England. Shaw exhausted himself, in the columns of the *World*, in " apparently hopeless attempts to shame the De Reszkes out of their perpetual Faust and Mephistopheles, Romeo and Laurent, and in pooh-poohed declarations that there were such works in existence as *Die Walküre* and *Tristan*. It was not Sir Augustus Harris who roused Jean de Reszke from his long lethargy, but his own artistic conscience and the shock of Vandyk's brilliant success in Massenet's *Manon*." And when Shaw's successor on the *World*, on the occasion of the death of Sir Augustus Harris in 1896, declared that the great impresario laboured to cast aside the fatuous conventions of the Italian school, and to adopt all that was best in the German stage, Shaw was provoked into a crushing reply. " *Sancta simplicitas!* " he exclaimed. " The truth is that he fought obstinately for the Italian fatuities against the German reforms. He was saturated with the obsolete operatic traditions of the days of Tietjens, whose Semiramide and Lucrezia he admired as great tragic impersonations. He described *Das Rheingold* as ' a damned pantomime '; he persisted for years in putting *Tannhäuser* on the stage with Venusberg effects that would have disgraced a Whitechapel Road gaff, with the twelve horns on the stage replaced by a military band behind the scenes, and with Rotten Row trappings on the horses. . . . It was only in the last few years that he began to learn something from Calvé and the young Italian school, from Wagner, from Massenet and Bruneau, and from Verdi's latest works. In opera, unfortunately, he was soaked in tradition, and kept London a quarter of a century behind New York and Berlin—down almost to the level of Paris—in dramatic music." *

It happens that Shaw's squarest and solidest contributions to Wagnerian criticism were written after his career as musical critic ceased. At the request of Mr. Benjamin Tucker, editor of *Liberty*, a journal of Philosophic Anarchy, published in

---

* *De Mortuis*, signed G. B. S., in the *Saturday Review*, July 4th, 1896.

New York, Shaw wrote a reply to Max Nordau's *Degeneration*, which was then (1895) making a great impression on the American mind. This reply, entitled *A Degenerate's View of Nordau*, was published in a double copy of *Liberty*, especially printed to make room for it; Mr. Tucker sent a copy to every paper in America; and, as Shaw avers, Nordau's book has never been heard of in an American paper since. It was undoubtedly a great piece of journalism in those days for Mr. Tucker to pick out the right man—as Shaw unquestionably was—for that stupendous task; and Shaw still takes an unholy joy in showing how Tucker the crank was able to beat all the big fashionable editors at their own game. Besides being largely imported in England, the article did Shaw a great private service. For when William Morris read it, he at once threw off all reserve in talking to Shaw about modern art, and treated him thenceforth as a man who knew enough to understand what might be said to him on that subject. The article contained, among many other equally able things, an eminently sane and intelligible treatment of the development of modern music, and its relation to Wagner. Mr. Huneker, who regards this as Shaw's finest piece of controversial work, rightly declared that it completely swept Nordau from the field of discussion.*

The other piece of Wagnerian criticism by which Shaw is best known was the subject of a letter Shaw once wrote to the

---

* In the letter Mr. Tucker wrote to Mr. Shaw at Easter, 1895, Shaw once told me, he said that he knew Shaw was the only man in the world capable of tackling Nordau on his various fields of music, literature, painting, etc.: " He said that if I would find out the highest figure ever paid by, say, the *Nineteenth Century* for a single article to any writer, not excluding Gladstone or any other eminent man, he would pay me that sum for a review of ' Degeneration ' for his little paper. This, mind you, from a man who was publishing a paper at his own expense, without a chance of making anything out of it, and with a considerable chance of finding himself in prison some day for telling the truth about American institutions. Mr. Tucker probably worked double shifts and ate half meals for the next two or three years to pay off what the adventure cost him." This essay, somewhat amplified, was recently (February, 1908) published in America by Benjamin R. Tucker, N. Y.—in England by the *New Age* Press, London—under the title, *The Sanity of Art: an Exposure of the Current Nonsense about Artists being Degenerate.*

Bernard Partridge.   *Courtesy of the Artist.*

AHENOBARBUS AT REHEARSAL.

Reproduced from the original water-color, drawn from memory, in 1894.

editor of the *Academy* (October 15th, 1895) : " I see you have
been announcing a book by me entitled, ' The Complete Wagnerite,' " writes Shaw. " This is an error; you are thinking
of an author named Izaak Walton. The book, which is a work
of great merit, even for me, is called, ' The Perfect Wagnerite,' and is an exposition of the philosophy of *Der Ring des
Nibelungen.* It is a G. B. eSsence of modern Anarchism, or
Neo-Protestantism. This lucid description speaks for itself.
As it has been written on what the whole medical faculty and
all the bystanders declare to be my death-bed, it is naturally
rather a book of devotion than one of those vain brilliancies
which I was wont to give off in the days of my health and
strength.—P. S. I have just sprained my ankle in trying to
master the art of bicycling on one foot. This, with two operations and a fall downstairs, involving a broken arm, is my
season's record so far, leaving me in excellent general condition. And yet they tell me a vegetarian can't recuperate! "
In this commentary to what had already been written by
" musicians who are no revolutionists, and revolutionists who
are no musicians," Shaw reads into Wagner far more Socialism than he had ever read into Ibsen. He took pains to base
his interpretation upon the facts of Wagner's life—his connection with the revolution of 1848, his association with August
Roeckel and Michael Bakounin, his later pamphlets on social
evolution, religion, life, art, and the influence of riches—rather
than upon his recorded utterances in regard to the specific
meanings of the " Ring " music-dramas. It is not difficult
to recognize, with Shaw, the portraiture of our capitalistic
industrial system from the Socialist point of view in the slavery of the Niblungs and the tyranny of Alberich: but little
significance attaches to such cheap symbolism. It is more
difficult to identify the young Siegfried with the anarchist
Bakounin on the strength of the latter's notorious pamphlet
demanding the demolition of existing institutions. To the *Ring
of the Niblungs,* Shaw has, so to speak, applied the Ibsenic-
Nietzschean-Shavian philosophy as a unit of measure, and
found it to apply at many points. Siegfried is a " totally un-
moral person, a born Anarchist, the ideal of Bakounin, an

anticipation of the ' overman ' of Nietzsche "—a Germanized Dick Dudgeon or a Teutonic Prometheus. Whenever the philosophy of the " Ring " diverges from the Shavian philosophy, Wagner was " wandering in his mind." Whenever his own explanations do not agree with the *idée fixe* of Shaw, they only prove, as was once claimed by Shaw in the case of Ibsen, that Wagner was far less intellectually conscious of his purpose than Shaw. As an exposition of the Shavian philosophy, the book is worthy of note; as an exposition of the Wagnerian philosophy, it is unconvincing. The book is exceedingly ingenious and in places, brilliant; but it is the work of an ideologue and an a-priorist.

One final word in regard to Shaw's position as a champion of Wagner. While it is of little importance now, still Wagner and anti-Wagner was the great controversy of that time in music until anti-Wagnerism finally became ridiculous in the face of Wagner's overwhelming popularity. In the same way, Ibsen and anti-Ibsen was the great controversy in drama in London after 1889. In both instances, the whirligig of time has brought round its revenges. For some years, even before his death, Ibsen stood unchallenged as the premier dramatist of the age. And now that Wagner's battle is won and over-won, Shaw has the profound gratification of seeing " the professors, to avert the ridicule of their pupils, compelled to explain (quite truly) that Wagner's technical procedure in music is almost pedantically logical and grammatical; that the *Lohengrin* prelude is a masterpiece of the ' form ' proper to its aim; and that his disregard of ' false relations,' and his free use of the most extreme discords without ' preparation,' were straight and sensible instances of that natural development of harmony which has proceeded continually from the time when common six-four chords were considered ' wrong,' and such free use of unprepared dominant sevenths and minor ninths as had become common in Mozart's time would have seemed the maddest cacophony." And in a letter to me, Mr. Shaw said (July 15th, 1905) : " I was on the right side in both instances: that is all. According to the *Daily Chronicle*, Wagner and Ibsen were offensive impostors. As a matter of fact, they

were the greatest living masters in their respective arts; and
I knew that quite well. The critics of the nineteenth century
had two first-rate chances—Ibsen and Wagner. For the most
part they missed both. Second best they could recognize; but
best was beyond them." *

Mr. Shaw's most recent incursion into the field of music
criticism was occasioned by a criticism of Richard Strauss'
Elektra, at the time of its first production in England in
March, 1910, from the pen of the well-known critic of music,
Mr. Ernest Newman. The vigorous controversy between Mr.
Shaw and Mr. Newman that ensued was, of course, quite in-
conclusive, so far as erecting any absolute standards by which
Strauss' greatness as a dramatic composer might be judged.
But it evoked from Mr. Shaw an outburst of enthusiasm un-
paralleled in his career as a critic of music:

> "What Hofmannsthal and Strauss have done is to take
> Clytemnestra and Aegistheus, and by identifying them
> with everything that is evil and cruel, with all that needs
> must hate the highest when it sees it, with hideous domi-
> nation and coercion of the higher by the baser, with the
> murderous rage in which the lust for a lifetime of orgi-
> astic pleasure turns on its slaves in the torture of its
> disappointment and the sleepless horror and misery of its
> neurasthenia, to so rouse in us an overwhelming flood of
> wrath against it and ruthless resolution to destroy it, that
> Elektra's vengeance becomes holy to us; and we come to
> understand how even the gentlest of us could wield the
> axe of Orestes or twist our firm fingers in the black hair
> of Clytemnestra to drag back her head and leave her
> throat open to the stroke.
>
> "That was a task hardly possible to an ancient Greek.

* Is Shaw, the anti-romantic, consistent in championing Wagner, the
head and front of European romanticism? Shaw, the individualist, recognized that Wagner was a great creative force in art; that was sufficient
cause for his championship. It may be interesting in this connection to
consult Julius Bab's acute analysis of Shaw's Wagnerism: *Bernard Shaw*
(S. Fischer, Berlin), pp. 210-214.

. . . And that is the task which Hofmannsthal has achieved. Not even in the third scene of *Das Rheingold,* or in the Klingsor scenes in *Parsifal,* is there such an atmosphere of malignant and cancerous evil as we get here. And that the power with which it is done is not the power of the evil itself, but of the passion that detests and must and finally can destroy that evil, is what makes the work great, and makes us rejoice in its horror. . . .

" That the power of conceiving it should occur in the same individual as the technical skill and natural faculty needed to achieve its complete and overwhelming expression in music, is a stroke of the rarest good fortune that can befall a generation of men. I have often said, when asked to state the case against the fools and money-changers who are trying to drive us into a war with Germany, that the case consists of the single word, Beethoven. To-day, I should say with equal confidence, Strauss. That we should make war on Strauss and the heroic warfare and aspiration that he represents is treason to humanity. In this music-drama Strauss has done for us just what he has done for his own countrymen : he has said for us, with an utterly satisfying force, what all the noblest powers of life within us are clamouring to have said, in protest against and defiance of the omnipresent villainies of our civilization ; and this is the highest achievement of the highest art." *

So often was Shaw mocked by scepticism concerning his talent and by imperviousness to his mood, that he sometimes actually went to the length of tagging one of his Irish bulls with the explanatory parenthesis (" I speak as an Irishman "). If the larger public ever gains a just understanding of Shaw, it will be because they have found this central and directing clue : he speaks as an Irishman. The right to say in jest what is meant in earnest is a right the average Englishman denies ; he agrees with Victor Hugo that " every man has a right to be

* *The 'Elektra' of Strauss and Hofmannsthal.* A letter to the editor of the *Nation* (London), March 19th, 1910.

a fool, but he should not abuse that right." M. Faguet has recently said of Sainte Beuve that he was guided by one of the finest professional consciences the world of literature has ever known. Early in his career, Shaw succeeded in imparting to his readers the conviction that his glaring deficiency was the total lack of a professional conscience. Shaw was preoccupied with the exposition of the eternal comedy. He is that hitherto unknown phenomenon in the history of musical criticism—a musical critic who charged his critical weapon with genuine comic force. The conviction has probably come to every musical critic in some moment of self-distrust that his effort to catch and imprison in written words the elusive spirit of music is, after all, only a more or less humorous subterfuge. In this respect Shaw differs from every other musical critic who ever lived: instead of feeling his criticism to be merely a humorous subterfuge, he actually believed it to be a comically veracious impression of reality.

No view of Shaw's unique attitude as a critic has yet been obtained that is not one-sided, false, or—what is far worse—misleading. The absurdly simple truth is that Shaw always aimed at saying, in the most forcible and witty way possible, exactly what he thought and felt, however absurd, unnatural, or comic these criticisms might sound to the " poor, silly, simple public." To the feelings of other musical critics, to the prejudices of the dry academic schools, or even to the consensus of opinion, crystallized through the lapse of years, he paid no heed whatsoever. He did not feel himself bound by the traditions of any journal, by any obligations, fancied or real, to operatic managers, or by the predilections of his audience. In fact, to put it in a homely way, he was " his own man," feeling free to express his opinions exactly as he chose. And it is perhaps no exaggeration to say that, since 1885, the whole spirit of English criticism, personified in Walkley, Archer and Shaw—an Englishman of French descent, a Scotchman, and an Irishman—has been a spirit of forthrightness, outspoken frankness and unblushing sincerity.

In the matter of individual style, Shaw occupies an absolutely unique position in English literature. He occupied a more unusual *terrain* than had ever been occupied before. Concerning the subjects in which he claimed to be thoroughly versed, he gaily announced himself as an authority. With an air of grandiose condescension, he once confessed that he might be mistaken: " Even I am not infallible—that is, not always." He really meant that he was. " Let it be remembered, that I am a superior person," he characteristically says, " and that what seemed incoherent and wearisome fooling to me may have seemed an exhilarating pastime to others. My heart knows only its own bitterness; and I do not desire to intermeddle with the joys of those among whom I am a stranger. I assert my intellectual superiority—that is all." He was ever sublimely conscious of his own supreme dialectical and critical skill. " Some day I must write a supplement to Schumann's ' Advice to Young Musicians.' The title will be ' Advice to Old Musicians '; and the first precept will run, ' Don't be in a hurry to contradict G. B. S., as he never commits himself on a musical subject until he knows at least six times as much about it as you do.' " If he had been matched in argument with the greatest living critic of the arts—and he was frequently matched against the greatest English critics—he would doubtless have said to him, in the language of the apochryphal anecdote: " All the world's mad save thee and me, John. And sometimes I think thee's a little mad too."

Behind all this " *infernal blague* " lurks the real critic, whose chief conviction is that " Bach in B minor " is not fit subject for enjoyment or criticism. " I would not be misunderstood," Mr. Shaw remarked to me one day, " in regard to my position about analysis and ' analytic criticism.' The analytic criticism I mercilessly condemn is the sort of criticism of Hamlet's soliloquy that reads: ' It is highly significant, in the first place, that Hamlet begins his soliloquy with the infinitive of the verb " To be," etc., etc.' Far from minimizing the function of analysis sanely and appropriately employed in criticism, I attribute my superiority as a critic to my superiority in the faculty of analysis." The inevitable reaction from " absolute music " was the dramatic expression of individuality, *e.g.*, Wagner. The inevitable reaction from " analytic criticism " is the critical expression of individuality, *e.g.*, Shaw. He never hunted out false relations, consecutive fifths and sevenths, the first subject, the second subject, the working out, and all the rest of " the childishness that could be taught to a poodle." His supreme effort was to get away from a discussion of the technology of music to the *nuances* of the music itself, the source of its inspiration, the spirit of its genius. If Shaw should find Wagner an offensive charlatan and his themes cacophonous strings of notes, he would frankly say so, without making any effort to *prove* him so by laying down the first principles of character and composition, and showing that his conduct and his works are incompatible with these principles. The expert, in Shaw's view, should merely give you his personal opinion for what it is worth. Shaw protested against the whole academic system in England, and declared himself its open enemy. " This unhappy country would be as prolific of musical as of literary composers were it not for our schools of music, where they seize the young musician, turn his attention forcibly away from the artistic element in his art, and make him morbidly conscious of its mechanical conditions, especially the obsolete ones, until he at last becomes, not a composer, but an adept in a horribly dull sort of chess played with lines and dots, each player having different notions of what the right rules are, and playing his game so as to flourish his view under the noses of those who differ from him. Then he offers his insufferable gambits to the public as music, and is outraged because I criticize it as music and not as chess."

Shaw made the most persistent effort to encourage the employment of the vernacular in music, as well as in criticism of music. An arrant commonplace, made out of the most hackneyed commonplace in modern music, pleased him more than all the Tenterden Street specialties. " I cry ' Professor ' whenever I find a forced avoidance of the vernacular in music under the impression that it is vulgar. . . . Your men who really can write, your Dickenses, Ruskins and Carlyles, and their like, are vernacular above all things: they cling to the locutions which everyday use has made a part of our common life. The professors may ask me whether I seriously invite them to make their music out of the commonplaces of the comic song writer? I reply, unabashed, that I do."

With the deepest fervour, he continued to preach the doctrine of spontaneity and naturalness. "Why hesitate to perpetrate the final outrage of letting loose your individuality, and saying just what you think in your own way as agreeably and frankly as you can?" His own aim was to reach that truly terrible fellow, the average man—"the plain man who wants a plain answer." If he can only awake the attention of the man in the street and, by expressing himself frankly in everyday language, the quotidian commerce of thought, occasionally even in the vernacular of the street, make clear to that man the appeal that music makes to a critic acutely sensitive to the subtler implications of its highest forms, Shaw is perfectly satisfied with himself and his performance. Accordingly, he aimed, primarily, to make an exact record of the sensations induced by a certain piece of music, or a certain performer, *Don Juan* or De Reszke, Letty Lind or *The Pirates of Penzance*. He made no effort whatsoever to control the current of his humour. He allowed it to play as lightly about Patti, as uproariously about Paderewski, as derisively about Vieuxtemps as his inclination directed. The most solemn symphony excited his risibility to the explosion point, and the latest Mass suggested seaside promenades instead of the life of the world to come.

Shaw's efforts to free musical criticism from the blighting effects of academicism, his advocacy of the free expression of individuality, and his insistence upon the return to nature, both in music and in criticism, brought upon him the scorn and contempt that is always the meed of the would-be reformer. The French public looked up to Francisque Sarcey with a sort of filial veneration, and affectionately dubbed him "uncle." The English public sneered at Shaw's brilliant attacks upon their favourites and their idols, and looked down upon him, not as a reasonable human being, but, as Shaw expressed it, as a mere Aunt Sally. Not only did the critics and the public laugh at his revolutionary zeal, but they regarded him as an amusing incompetent, availing himself of his abundant gift of humour to supply the deficiency of any knowledge of music or of the possession of the faintest critical sense. Analytic criticism was revered, while the individual and impressionistic style of Shaw was immoderately enjoyed as the tricky device of a colossal humbug. Shaw fought against misrepresentation and prejudice with unabated vigour, continually confounding his critics with some unanswerable argument that logically reduced their attacks to nothingness. By apt examples, he often revealed the absurdities of analytic criticism in literature, once confronting his critics with the startling query: " I want to know whether it is just that a literary critic should be forbidden to make his living in this way on pain of being interviewed by two doctors and a magistrate, and haled off to Bedlam forthwith; whilst the more a musical critic does it, the deeper the veneration he inspires. By systematically neglecting it I have lost caste as a critic even in the eyes of those who hail my abstinence with the greatest relief; and I should be tempted to eke out these columns in the Mesopotamian manner if I were not the slave of a commercial necessity and a vulgar ambition to have my articles read, this being the main reason why I write them, and the secret of the constant ' straining after effect ' observable in my style."

Perhaps the most enlightening evidence as to Shaw's position as a critic of music is contained in his recital of an amusing incident. One day, it seems, a certain young man, whose curiosity overswayed his natural modesty, approached Shaw on the subject of the G. B. S. column in the *World*. " At last he came to his point with a rush by desperately risking the question: ' Excuse me, Mr. G. B. S., but *do* you know anything about music? The fact is, I am not capable of forming an opinion myself; but Dr. Blank says you don't, and—er—Dr. Blank is such a great authority that one hardly knows what to think.' Now this question put me into a difficulty, because I had already learnt by experience that the reason my writings on music and musicians are so highly appreciated is that they are supposed by many of my greatest admirers to be a huge joke, the point of which lies in the fact that I am totally ignorant of music, and that my character of critic is an exquisitely ingenious piece of acting, undertaken to gratify my love of mystification and paradox. From this point of view every one of my articles appears as a fine stroke of comedy, occasionally broadening into a harlequinade, in which I am the clown, and Dr. Blank the policeman. At first I did not realize this, and could not understand the air of utter disillusion and loss of interest in me that would come over people in whose houses I incautiously betrayed some scrap of amateurish enlightenment. But the naïve exclamation, ' Oh! you *do* know something about it, then!' at last became familiar to me; and I now take particular care not to expose my knowledge. When people hand me a sheet of instrumental music, and ask my opinion of it, I carefully hold it upside down, and pretend to study it in that position with the eye of an expert. They invite me to try their new grand piano, I attempt to open it at the wrong end; and when the young lady of the house informs me that she is practising the 'cello, I innocently ask her whether the mouthpiece did not cut her lips dreadfully at first. This line of conduct gives enormous satisfaction, in which I share to a rather greater extent than is generally supposed. But, after all, the people whom I take in thus are only amateurs. To place my impostorship beyond question, I require to be certified as such by authorities like our Bachelors and Doctors of Music—gentlemen who can write a ' *Nunc Dimittis* ' in five real parts, and know the difference between a tonal fugue and a real one, and can tell you how old Monteverde was on his thirtieth birthday, and have views as to the true root of the discord of the seventh on the supertonic, and devoutly believe that *si contra fa diabolus est*. But I have only to present myself to them in the character of a man who has been through these dreary games without ever discovering the remotest vital connection between them and the art of music—a state of mind so inconceivable by them—to make them exclaim:

THE MUSIC CRITIC

> "'Preposterous ass! that never read so far
> To know the cause why music was ordained,'

and give me the desired testimonials at once. And so I manage to scrape along without falling under suspicion of being an honest man.

" However, since mystification is not likely to advance us in the long run, may I suggest that there must be something wrong in the professional tests which have been successfully applied to Handel, to Mozart, to Beethoven, to Wagner, and last, though not least, to me, with the result in every case of our condemnation as ignoramuses and charlatans. Why is it that when Dr. Blank writes about music, nobody but a professional musician can understand him; whereas the man-in-the-street, if fond of art and capable of music, can understand the writings of Mendelssohn, Wagner, Liszt, Berlioz, or any of the composers? Why, again, is it that my colleague, W. A., for instance, in criticizing Mr. Henry Arthur Jones' play the other day, did not *parse* all the leading sentences in it? I will not be so merciless as to answer these questions now, though I know the solution, and am capable of giving it if provoked beyond endurance. Let it suffice for the moment that writing is a very difficult art, criticism a very difficult process, and music not easily to be distinguished, without special critical training, from the scientific, technical and professional conditions of its performance, composition and teaching. And if the critic is to please the congregation, who wants to read only about the music, it is plain that he must appear quite beside the point to the organ-blower, who wants to read about his bellows, which he can prove to be the true source of all the harmony." *

* *Music,* in the *World,* February 18th, 1893.

THE DRAMATIC CRITIC

Mac	Beth.
Oth	Ello.
Comedy of Er	Rors.
Merchant of Ve	Nice.
Coriol	Anus.
Midsummer Night's D	Ream.
Merry Wives of Win	Dsor.
Measure for Mea	Sure.
Much Ado about Not	Hing.
Antony and Cleop	Atra.
All's Well that Ends	Well.*

* The conclusive cryptographic proof that Bernard Shaw wrote the plays usually attributed to Shakespeare—discovered by Mr. S. T. James, of Leeds.

CHAPTER IX

WHEN the history of the last quarter of the nineteenth century comes to be written, it will be seen that the name of Bernard Shaw is inextricably linked with five epoch-making movements of our contemporary era. The Collectivist movement in politics, ethics and sociology; the Ibsen-Nietzschean movement in morals; the reaction against the materialism of Marx and Darwin; the Wagnerian movement in music; and the anti-romantic movement in literature and art—these are the main currents of modern thought for which Shaw has unfalteringly sought to open a passage into modern consciousness.

On the death of Mr. Edmund Yates, the editor of the *World*, in 1894, Shaw gave up his " labour of Hercules " as music critic of that paper, and was succeeded by Mr. Robert Hichens. By this time Shaw had only one more critical continent to conquer; but he wanted the right editor, he has told us—" one with the virtues of Yates—and some of his faults as well, perhaps." On Mr. Frank Harris's revival of the *Saturday Review*, it was matter for no surprise that the author of *The Quintessence of Ibsenism* and of four plays besides, should have been offered the post of dramatic critic on that magazine. Shaw did not begin his career as an actor, as is sometimes stated; he never was on the stage, nor ever dreamt of going on it. He has taken part in a copyrighting performance, and once acted at some theatricals, got up for the benefit of an old workman member of the " International," with Edward Aveling, Eleanor Marx, May Morris, and Sidney Pardon, all amateurs; and impersonated a photographer at William Morris's house at one of the *soirées* of the Socialist League. But there is not the remotest foundation for the statement that he began his career as an actor. Although Shaw had written a number of plays, he realized that dramatic authorship no more constitutes a man a critic than actorship constitutes him a dramatic author;

but he rightly judged that a dramatic critic learns as much from having been a dramatic author as Shakespeare or Pinero from having been actors. It was his chief distinction to have touched life at many points; unlike many contemporary dramatic critics, he had not specialized to such an extent as to lose his character as man and citizen, and become a mere playgoer. " My real aim," he asserted in reference to his work on the *Saturday Review*, " is to widen the horizon of the critic, especially of the dramatic critic, whose habit at present is to bring a large experience of stage life to bear on a scanty experience of real life, although it is certain that all really fruitful criticism of the drama must bring a wide and practical knowledge of real life to bear on the stage."

Jowett's characterization of Disraeli as " a curious combination of the Arch-Priest of Humbug and a great man," has a certain appropriateness for Bernard Shaw. That fictitious personage known as G. B. S. is Shaw's most remarkable creation. With characteristic daring, his very first article broke the sacred tradition of anonymity, inviolate till then in the conservative columns of the *Saturday Review*. With the innate instinct of the journalist, he devoted himself to sedulous self-advertisement, creating a traditionary character unrivalled in conceit, in cleverness, and in iconoclastic effrontery. Charged with being conceited, he replied: " No, I am not really a conceited man: if you had been through all that I have been through, and done all the things I have done, you would be ten times as conceited. It's only a pose, to prevent the English people from seeing that I am serious. If they did, they would make me drink the hemlock." Do not make the mistake of concluding, from this confession, that Shaw was merely a ghastly little celebrity posing in a vacuum. If " New lamps for old " is the cry of this ultra-modern fakir, " Remember Aladdin " is the warning of the suspicious populace. Shaw's chief claim for consideration is not merely that he has spent his life in crying down the futility and uselessness of the old lamps, but that with equal earnestness he has advertised the merits of the new. Nowhere is this more clearly shown than in his attitude towards Shakespeare and Ibsen.

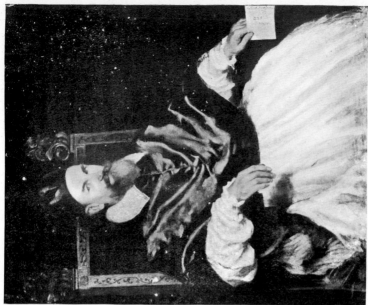

THE MODERN POPE OF WIT AND WISDOM.

After Velasquez.

From the original painting, exhibited in 1907.
(From a photograph by Emery Walker.)

[Facing p. 280

POPE INNOCENT X.

Original in the Doria Palace, Rome.

By Velasquez.

Shaw's incorrigible practice of "blaming the Bard," publicly inaugurated in the *Saturday Review,* is no mere antic in which he indulges for the fun of the thing, but as inevitable an outcome of his philosophy as is his championship of Ibsen. His inability to see a masterpiece in every play of Shakespeare's arises largely from the fact that he knows his Shakespeare as he knows his Bunyan, his Dickens, his Ibsen. It is flying in the face of fact to aver that a man who knew his Shakespeare from cover to cover by the time he was twenty does not like or admire Shakespeare. "I am fond," says Shaw, "unaffectedly fond, of Shakespeare's plays." He looks back upon those delightful evenings at the New Shakespeare Society, under F. J. Furnival, with the most unfeigned pleasure. A careful perusal of his score or more articles on Shakespeare in the *Saturday Review* shows that he has not only studied Shakespeare consistently, and periodically interpreted him from a definite point of view, but that he always fought persistently for the performance of his plays in their integrity. And although he has by no means taken advantage of all his opportunities, yet he has managed to see between twenty and thirty of Shakespeare's plays performed on the stage.

When Shaw first read Mr. Henry Arthur Jones's words: "Surely the crowning glory of our nation is our Shakespeare; and remember he was one of a great school," he almost burst, as he put it, with the intensity of his repudiation of the second clause in that utterance. Against the first clause he had nothing to say; but the Elizabethans Shaw has always regarded chiefly as "shallow literary persons, drunk with words, and seeking in crude stories of lust and crime an excuse for that wildest of all excitements, the excitement of imaginative self-expression by words." Mr. Shaw once defined an Elizabethan as "a man with an extraordinary and imposing power of saying things, and with nothing whatever to say." Indeed, it was not to be expected that the arch-foe of Romance, in modern art and modern life, would be edified with the imaginative and romantic violence of the Elizabethans. Nothing less than a close and, so to speak, biologic study of humanity in the nude can satisfy one who avers that Romance is the root of modern pessimism and the bane of modern self-respect.

To call the Elizabethans imaginative amounted with Shaw to the same thing as saying that, artistically, they had delirium tremens. The true Elizabethan he found to be a " blank-verse beast, itching to frighten other people with the superstitious terrors and cruelties in which he does not himself believe, and wallowing in blood, violence, muscularity of expression and strenuous animal passion as only literary men do when they become thoroughly depraved by solitary work, sedentary cowardice, and starvation of the sympathetic centres." He passes them in review, calling them a crew of dehumanized specialists in blank verse! Webster, a Tussaud laureate; Chapman, with his sublime balderdash; Marlowe, the pothouse brawler, with his clumsy horse-play, his butcherly rant, and the resourceless tum-tum of his " mighty line." Even in this dust-heap, Shaw managed to find some merit and variety. Was not Greene really amusing, Marston spirited and " silly-clever," Cyril Tourneur able to string together lines of which any couple picked out and quoted separately might pass as a fragment of a real organic poem? Though a brutish pedant, Jonson was not heartless; Marlowe often charged his blank-verse with genuine colour and romance; while Beaumont and Fletcher, although possessing no depth, no conviction, no religious or philosophic basis, were none the less dainty romantic poets, and really humorous character-sketchers in Shakespeare's popular style. " Unfortunately, Shakespeare dropped into the middle of these ruffianly pedants (the Elizabethans) ; and since there was no other shop than theirs to serve his apprenticeship in, he had perforce to become an Elizabethan too.

" In such a school of falsehood, bloody-mindedness, bombast, and intellectual cheapness, his natural standard was inevitably dragged down, as we know to our cost; but the degree to which he dragged their standard up has saved them from oblivion." Indeed, Shakespeare, enthused by his interest in the art of acting and by his desire to " educate the public," tried to make that public accept genuine studies of life and character in, for instance, *Measure for Measure* and *All's Well that Ends Well*. But the public would have none of them (traditional evidence, be it noted), " preferring a fantastic sugar doll like Rosalind to such serious and dignified studies of women as Isabella and Helena."

Shakespeare had discovered that " the only thing that paid in the theatre was romantic nonsense, and that when he was forced by this to produce one of the most effective samples of romantic nonsense in existence—a feat which he performed easily and well—he publicly disclaimed any responsibility for its pleasant and cheap falsehood by borrowing the story and throwing it in the face of the public with the phrase ' *As You Like It.*' " Despite Mr. Chesterton's assertion that Shaw has read an ironic snub into the title, and that after all it was only a sort of hilarious bosh, Shaw still maintains, as he did fifteen years ago, that when Shakespeare used that phrase he meant exactly what he said, and that the phrase: " What You Will," which he applied to *Twelfth Night*, meaning " Call it what you please," is not, in Shakespearean or any other English, the equivalent of the perfectly unambiguous and penetratingly simple phrase: " As You Like It."

Shakespeare's popularity, Shaw would have us believe, was due to a deliberate pandering to the public taste for " romantic nonsense." Shaw holds that Shakespeare's supreme power lies in his " enormous command of word-music, which gives fascination to his most blackguardly repartees and sublimity to his hollowest platitudes, besides raising to the highest force all his gifts as an observer, an imitator of personal mannerisms and characteristics, a humorist and a story-teller." No matter how poor, coarse, cheap and obvious may be the thought in *Much Ado about Nothing*, for example, the mood is charming and the music of the words expresses the mood, transporting you into another, an enchanted world.

" When a flower-girl tells a coster to hold his jaw, for nobody is listening to him, and he retorts: ' Oh, you're there, are you, you beauty?' they reproduce the wit of Beatrice and Benedick exactly. But put it this way: ' I wonder that you will still be talking, Signor Benedick: nobody marks you.'

'What! my dear Lady Disdain, are you yet living?' You are miles away from costerland at once." In other words, Shaw insists that a nightingale's love is no higher than a cat's, except that the nightingale is the better musician!

> " It is not easy to knock this into the public head, because comparatively few of Shakespeare's admirers are at all conscious that they are listening to music as they hear his phrases turn and his lines fall so fascinatingly and memorably; whilst we all, no matter how stupid we are, can understand his jokes and platitudes, and are flattered when we are told of the subtlety of the wit we have relished, and the profundity of the thought we have fathomed. Englishmen are specially susceptible to this sort of flattery, because intellectual subtlety is not their strong point. In dealing with them you must make them believe that you are appealing to their brains, when you are really appealing to their senses and feelings. With Frenchmen the case is reversed: you must make them believe that you are appealing to their senses and feelings when you are really appealing to their brains. The Englishman, slave to every sentimental ideal and dupe of every sensuous art, will have it that his great national poet is a thinker. The Frenchman, enslaved and duped only by systems and calculations, insists on his hero being a sentimentalist and artist. That is why Shakespeare is esteemed a master-mind in England, and wondered at as a clumsy barbarian in France." *

Shaw is as far from Taine on the one side as he is from Swinburne on the other—" as far this side bardolatry as Johnson or Mr. Frank Harris." To the idolatrous and insensate worship of Shakespeare which got on Ben Jonson's nerves, which Lamb brought back into fashion, and which has gone to blasphemy and sacrilege in the mouth of Swinburne, Shaw, like Byron before him, declined to subscribe. And for the very

* *Shakespeare's ' Merry Gentlemen,'* in the *Saturday Review*, February 26th, 1898.

good reason that, being primarily an ideologue, he has examined Shakespeare as a man of thought only to find him wanting. Lop away all beauty of form, all grace of mood— in a word, reduce Shakespeare to his lowest terms—and what is the result? Paraphrase the encounters of Benedick and Beatrice in the style of a Blue-book, carefully preserving every idea they present, and it immediately becomes apparent to Shaw that they contain at best nothing out of the common in thought or wit, and at worst a good deal of vulgar naughtiness. Paraphrasing Goethe, Wagner, or Ibsen in the same way, he finds in them original observation, subtle thought, wide comprehension, far-reaching intuition and psychological study. Even if you paraphrase Shakespeare's best and maturest work, you will still get nothing more, Shaw avers, than the platitudes of proverbial philosophy, with a very occasional curiosity in the shape of a rudiment of some modern idea, not followed up. " Once or twice we scent among them an anticipation of the crudest side of Ibsen's polemics on the Woman Question, as in *All's Well that Ends Well,* when the man cuts as meanly selfish a figure beside his enlightened lady-doctor wife as Helmer beside Nora; or in *Cymbeline,* where Posthumus, having, as he believes, killed his wife for inconstancy, speculates for a moment on what his life would have been worth if the same standard of continence had been applied to himself. And certainly no modern study of the voluptuous temperament, and the spurious heroism and heroinism which its ecstasies produce, can add much to *Antony and Cleopatra.*"

Last of all, Shaw goes a step further with the declaration that Shakespeare's weakness lies in his complete deficiency in that highest sphere of thought, in which poetry embraces religion, philosophy, morality, and the bearing of these on communities, which is sociology. " Search for statesmanship, or even citizenship, or any sense of the Commonwealth, material or spiritual, and you will not find the making of a decent vestryman or curate in the whole horde. As to faith, hope, courage, conviction, or any of the true heroic qualities, you find nothing but death made sensational, despair made stage-sublime, sex made romantic, and barrenness covered up by sentimentality and the mechanical lilt of blank-verse." All the truly heroic which came so naturally to Bunyan is missing in Shakespeare. In the words of Whitman, Shaw regards Shakespeare as "the æsthetic-heroic among poets, lacking both in the democratic and spiritual," but never as "the heroic-heroic, which is the greatest development of the spirit." In Shaw's eyes, Shakespeare's "test of the worth of life is the vulgar hedonic test, and since life cannot be justified by this or any other external test, Shakespeare comes out of his reflective period a vulgar pessimist, oppressed with a logical demonstration that life is not worth living, and only surpassing Thackeray in respect of being fertile enough, instead of repeating 'Vanitas vanitatum' at second-hand, to word the futile doctrine differently and better. . . . This does not mean that Shakespeare lacked the enormous fund of joyousness which is the secret of genius, but simply that, like most middle-class Englishmen bred in private houses, he was a very incompetent thinker, and took it for granted that all inquiry into life began and ended with the question: 'Does it pay?' . . . Having worked out his balance-sheet and gravely concluded that life's but a poor player, etc., and thereby deeply impressed a public which, after a due consumption of beer and spirits, is ready to believe that everything maudlin is tragic, and everything senseless sublime, Shakespeare found himself laughing and writing plays and getting drunk at the 'Mermaid' much as usual, with Ben Jonson finding it necessary to reprove him for a too extravagant sense of humour." Like Ernest Crosby, Shaw regards Shakespeare as the poet of courts, of lords and ladies. His fundamental assent is accorded to Tolstoy in his declaration that Shakespeare's quintessential deficiency was his failure to face, fairly and squarely, the eternal question of life: "What are we alive for?" *

It is a task of the merest supererogation to go into the details of Shaw's admiration of Shakespeare's plays, to quote his praise of *Twelfth Night* and *A Midsummer Night's Dream* as

---

* Concerning Shaw's general attitude towards Shakespeare, compare the *Letter from Mr. G. Bernard Shaw* appended to *Tolstoy on Shakespeare.* Funk and Wagnalls Co., 1906.

" crown jewels of dramatic poetry "; of *Romeo and Juliet* with its " lines that tighten the heart or catch you up into the heights "; of *Richard III.*, as the best of all the " Punch and Judy " plays, in which the hero delights man by provoking God, and dies unrepentant and game to the last; of *Julius Cæsar*, in which the " dramatist's art can be carried no higher on the plane chosen "; of *Othello*, which " remains magnificent by the volume of its passion and the splendour of its word-music "; of the " great achievement " of *Hamlet;* and of *Macbeth*, than which " no greater tragedy will ever be written." Not only is Shaw unaffectedly fond of Shakespeare: he pities the man who cannot enjoy him:

> " He has outlived hundreds of abler thinkers, and will outlast a thousand more. His gift of telling a story (provided someone else told it to him first); his enormous power over language, as conspicuous in his senseless and silly abuse of it as in his miracles of expression; his humour; his sense of idiosyncratic character; and his prodigious fund of that vital energy which is, it seems, the true differentiating property behind the faculties, good, bad, or indifferent, of the man of genius, enable him to entertain us so effectively that the imaginary scenes and people he has created become more real to us than our actual life—at least, until our knowledge and grip of actual life begins to deepen and glow beyond the common. When I was twenty I knew everybody in Shakespeare, from Hamlet to Abhorson, much more intimately than I knew my living contemporaries." *

The literary side of the mission of Ibsen in England, as Shaw conceived it, was the rescue of that unhappy country from its centuries of slavery to Shakespeare. The moral side of Ibsen's mission was the breaking of the shackles of slavery to conventional ideals of virtue. And Shaw's iconoclastic cry in the *Saturday Review* was " Down with Shakespeare. Great

* *Blaming the Bard,* in the *Saturday Review*, September 26th, 1896.

is Ibsen; and Shaw is his prophet." * Interrogated in 1892 as to whether Shakespeare was not his model in writing *Widowers' Houses*, Shaw replied with quizzical disdain: " Shakespeare! stuff! Shakespeare—a disillusioned idealist! a rationalist! a capitalist! If the fellow had not been a great poet, his rubbish would have been forgotten long ago. Molière, as a thinker, was worth a thousand Shakespeares. If my play is not better than Shakespeare, let it be damned promptly." And in reviewing his work as a dramatic critic, he said: " After all, I have accomplished something. I have made Shakespeare popular by knocking him off his pedestal and kicking him round the place, and making people realize that he's not a demi-god, but a dramatist." † When he came to judge the works of the two dramatists by the tests of intellectual force and dramatic insight, quite apart from beauty of expression, he found that " Ibsen comes out with a double first-class, whereas Shakespeare comes out hardly anywhere." Shaw recognized only the splendour of Shakespeare's literary gift; whereas, in Ibsen, he hailed the very antithesis of Shakespeare, *i.e.*, a thinker of extraordinary penetration, a moralist of international influence, and a philosopher going to the root of those very questions to the solution of which Shaw's own life has been largely

* As Mr. Will Irwin has it in his *Crankidoxology: Being a Mental Attitude from Bernard Pshaw*:

> I'm bored by mere Shakespere and Milton,
> Tho' Hubbard compels me to rave;
> If *I* should lay laurels to wilt on
> That foggy Shakesperean grave,
> How William would squirm in his grave!

† One day at a reception at the Playgoers' Club, in London, Mr. Osmon Edwards delivered an address on " The superiority of Shaw to Shakespeare." He showed that Shakespeare was a bad dramatist, because he was a great poet; he asserted that his humour was vulgar and his tragedy puerile; and he endeavoured to prove that Shaw was far superior to Shakespeare in his realism, in his critical sense of life, in the depth of his thought, in his stage technique.
At this point, Shaw himself, who was among the audience, rose to his feet and begged to say a few words *in favour of his famous rival*. What a delicious situation—and one not unworthy of Bernard Shaw!
Compare *The English Stage of To-Day*, by Mario Borsa, pp. 152-3. John Lane, London and New York, 1908.

·MAN· AND SUPER -MAN· =

ALL THE WORLD's A STAGE -SOCIETY.

E. T. Reed.]   [*Courtesy of the Artist.*

JOHN BULL'S OTHER PLAYWRIGHT.

A new design for a statue in Leicester Square. Reproduced by the special permission
of the proprietors of *Punch.*

[*Facing p.* 268

devoted. In the dramas of Ibsen, he found epitomized the modern realistic struggle for intellectual and spiritual emancipation, the revolt against the machine-made morality of our sordid, flabby, and hypocritical age. Shaw had begun his career in the strife and turmoil of the Zetetical and Dialectical Societies, debating the questions of Women's Rights, Emancipation, and Married Women's Property Acts. Before he had ever read a line of Ibsen or heard of *A Doll's House*, he had already reached the conclusion, always consistently maintained by him, that Man is not a species superior to Woman, but that mankind is male and female, like other kinds, and that the inequality of the sexes is literally nothing more than a cock-and-bull story, invented by the "lords of creation" for supremely selfish motives. When Ibsen wrote *Ghosts*, his name was unknown to Shaw. But it is undeniable that, in the eighties, Shaw was forging towards precisely similar conclusions. He had felt in his inmost being the loathing of the nineteenth century for itself, and had marked with exultation the ferocity with which Schopenhauer and Shelley, Lassalle and Karl Marx, Ruskin and Carlyle, Morris and Wagner had rent the bosom that bore them. Smouldering within his own breast was that same detestation of all the orthodoxies, and respectabilities, and ideals railed at by these political, social and moral anarchs. Fired by their inspiring example, he had espoused the cause of Socialism, and zealously fought the battle for equality of opportunity, for social justice, for woman's freedom, for liberty of thought, of action, and of conscience. His conscious revolt against a sentimental, theatrical and senselessly romantic age, chivalrously and blindly "holding aloft the banner of the ideal," preceded his acquaintance with *The Pillars of Society* and *The Wild Duck*. A Fabian, almost universally regarded in England as a crack-brained fanatic and doctrinaire, he found years afterwards in *An Enemy of the People* the final expression of his experience that all human progress involves as its fundamental condition a recognition by the pioneer that to be right is to be in the minority. The very keynote of Shaw's own convictions was struck in Ibsen's declaration that the really effective progressive forces of the moment were the revolt of the working-classes against economic, and of the women against idealistic, slavery.

During the entire period of his career as a dramatic critic, Shaw stood forth as an unabashed champion of Ibsen. For many years prior to this period, he had borne the odium of Philistine objurgation; never, even in the blackest hour of British intolerance and insult, did he once flinch from adherence to the Wizard of the North. Much that he wrote in the *Saturday Review* concerning Ibsen and his plays, he had already said—and said better—in *The Quintessence of Ibsenism*, written in the spring of 1890.* Still, the articles in the *Saturday Review* completed Shaw's analysis of Ibsenism, as exhibited in the remaining plays of Ibsen published after 1890; and, in addition, they possessed the advantage of being criticisms of the acted dramas themselves. The brilliant brochure, entitled *The Quintessence of Ibsenism*, contains the heart of Shaw's Ibsen criticism, and is undoubtedly the most notable *tour de force* its author has ever achieved in any line. It is a distinct contribution to that fertile field of modern philosophy farcically and superficially imaged by Gilbert, mordantly

* Cf. preface to *The Quintessence of Ibsenism* for its history and the causes which led to its publication. In July, 1890, Mr. Shaw read his *Quintessence of Ibsenism* in its original form, a study of the socialistic aspect of Ibsen's writings, before the Fabian Society. It is interesting to record what appears to be a reference to this lecture, made by Henrik Ibsen. In a letter to Hans Lien Braekstad (*Letters of Henrik Ibsen,* translated by John Nilsen Laurvik and Mary Morison, pp. 430-1), a Norwegian-English man of letters (since 1887 resident in London), who has done much for the spread of Norwegian and Danish literature in England, Ibsen wrote from Munich, August, 1890, referring to a garbled report of a newspaper interview with him:

"What I really said was that I was surprised that I, who had made it my chief life-task to depict human character and human doctrines, should, without conscious or direct intention, have arrived in several matters at the same conclusions as the social-democratic philosophers had arrived at by scientific processes.

"What led me to express this surprise (and, I may here add, satisfaction), was a statement made by the correspondent to the effect that one or more lectures had lately been given in London, dealing, according to him, chiefly with *A Doll's House.*"

The latter statement appears to be in error; although the correspondent may possibly have had in mind some lectures, delivered by Eleanor Marx, I believe, on *A Doll's House.*

Alvin Langdon Coburn.

G. Bernard Shaw

From the original Lumière autochrome, made in 1908.

[*Frontispiece.*

dramatized by Ibsen, and rhapsodically concretized by Nietzsche. Let us disabuse our minds at once of the idea that this book is either mere literary criticism or a supernally clever *jeu d'esprit*. Not a critical essay on the poetical beauties of Ibsen, but simply an exposition of Ibsenism, it may be described as an ideological distillation of Ibsen in the *rôle* of ethical and moral critic of contemporary civilization. To call *The Quintessence of Ibsenism* one-sided is not simply a futile condemnation: it is a perfectly obvious truth.

To Ibsen, according to Shaw, the pioneer of civilization is the man or woman bold enough to seek the fulfilment of the individual will, hardy enough to prefer the naked facts of life to the comforting illusions of the imagination. Society is composed, in the main, of Philistines who accept the established social order without demur or misgiving; and of a few Idealists, temperamentally dissatisfied with their lot, yet seeking refuge from the spectacle of their own failure in an imaginary world of romantic ideals, and in the self-delusion that to see the world thus is noble and spiritual, whilst to see it as it is is vulgar, brutal and cynical. But sometimes there arises the solitary pioneer, the realist, if you will—a Blake, a Shelley, a Bashkirtseff, a Shaw—who dares to face the truth the idealists are shirking, to chip off the masks of romance and idealism, and to say fearlessly that life needs no justification and submits to no test; that it must be lived for its own sake as an end in itself, and that all institutions, all ideals, and all romances must be brought to its test and stand or fall by their furtherance of and loyalty to it.

Thus to Ibsen: " The Ideal is dead; long live the ideal! " epitomizes the history of human progress. Brand, the heroic idealist, daring to live largely, to will unreservedly, fails because of his inability to realize the unattainability of his ideals in this present life. As Cervantes in *Don Quixote* reduced the old ideal of chivalry to absurdity, so Ibsen in *Peer Gynt* reduces to absurdity the ideal of self-realization when it takes the form of self-gratification unhampered by sense of responsibility. Shaw found it unnecessary to translate the scheme of *Emperor and Galilean* in terms of the antithesis between idealism and realism, since Julian, in this respect, is only a reincarnation of Peer Gynt. After constructing imaginative projections of himself in Brand, Peer Gynt and Julian, Ibsen next turns to the real life around him, to the creatures of *tous les jours*, to continue his detailed attack upon idealism. In *The Pillars of Society*, the Rörlund ideals go down before the realities of truth and freedom; in *A Doll's House*, Helmer's unstable card-house of ideals falls to the ground; and in *Ghosts*, Mrs. Alving offers herself up as a living sacrifice on the altar of the ideal, only to discover the futility of the sacrifice. *An Enemy of the People* exposes the fallacy of the majority ideal, and posits the striking doctrine that to be right is to be in the minority. *The Wild Duck* appears as a wholesale condemnation of the ideal of truth for truth's sake alone. *Rosmersholm* embodies Rebekka's tragic protest against the Rosmersholm ideal " that denied her right to live and be happy from the first, and at the end, even in denying its God, exacts her life as a vain blood-offering for its own blindness." *The Lady from the Sea* presents a fanciful image of the triumph of responsible freedom over romantic idealism grounded in unhappiness, while in *Hedda Gabler* the woman rises from life's feast because she has neither the vision for ideals nor the passion for reality—" a pure sceptic, a typical nineteenth-century figure, falling into the abyss between the ideals which do not impose on her and the realities which she has not yet discovered."

It is needless to follow Shaw's analysis of Ibsenism further, although it might readily be applied to Ibsen's remaining plays. Suffice it to say, that Shaw nowhere denies that Ibsen is an idealist, or that ideals are indispensable to human progress. He has been forced to call Ibsen a realist; in fact, almost to invent new terms, a new phraseology, in order to distinguish between the ideals which have become pernicious through senescence, and the ideals which remain valid through conformity to reality. Out of Ibsen's very longing for the ideal grew that mood of ideal suspiciousness which Brandes, like Shaw, affirmed to be one of his dominant characteristics. Ibsen opposes current political and moral values, strong in the conviction that every end should be challenged to justify the means. Acceptance of Ibsen's philosophy to will greatly, to dare nobly, to be always prepared to violate the code of conventional morality, to find fulfilment of the will as much in voluntary submission to reality as in affirmation of life the eternal—must at once, Shaw rightly indicates, greatly deepen the sense of moral responsibility. " What Ibsen insists on is that there is no golden rule—that conduct must justify itself by its effect upon happiness and not by its conformity to any rule or ideal." *

Shaw's analysis of Ibsenism holds out a large, sane, tolerant standard of life as the inevitable lesson of Ibsen's plays. Lies, pretences, and hypocrisies avail not against the strong man, fortified in the resolution to find himself, to attain self-realization, through fulfilment of the will. However much one may regret that Shaw, by preserving his *postulata* in concrete terms, has to some extent diverted our attention from the whole formidable significance of the Ibsenic drama, it is idle to deny that the book is at once caustically powerful and unflaggingly brilliant. Certainly Shaw has seen Ibsen clearly, even if he has not seen him whole. Ibsen cannot be summed up in a thesis; the curve of his art, as Mr. Huneker says, reaches across the edge of the human soul. " The quintessence of Ibsenism is that there is no formula "—this is Shaw's last assurance to us that he has not reduced Ibsen to a formula. It is impossible for anyone, with greater assurance, to assure us that there is nothing assured.

Comprehension of Shaw's attitude towards Shakespeare and Ibsen is a prerequisite to an accurate judgment of his attitude towards dramatic art in general, and, more particularly, towards the contemporary British stage. Beneath all his criticism lay the belief that the theatre of to-day is as important an institution as the Church was in the Middle Ages. " The apostolic succession from Eschylus to myself," he recently said, in speaking of his *Saturday Review* period, " is as serious and as

---

* This seems to me a very superficial judgment, and one which Shaw himself would doubtless repudiate to-day. How thoroughly inappropriate and erroneous is the use of the word " happiness " in this connection!

continuously inspired as that younger institution, the apostolic
succession of the Christian Church. Unfortunately this Christian Church, founded gaily with a pun, has been so largely
corrupted by rank Satanism that it has become the Church
where you must not laugh; and so it is giving way to that older
and greater Church to which I belong: the Church where the
oftener you laugh the better, because by laughter only can you
destroy evil without malice, and affirm good-fellowship without
mawkishness. When I wrote, I was well aware of what an
unofficial census of Sunday worshippers presently proved, that
church-going in London has been largely replaced by play-going. This would be a very good thing if the theatre took
itself seriously as a factory of thought, a prompter of conscience, an elucidator of social conduct, an armoury against
despair and dullness, and a temple of the Ascent of Man. I
took it seriously in that way, and preached about it instead of
merely chronicling its news and alternately petting and snubbing it as a licentious but privileged form of public entertainment. And this, I believe, is why my sermons gave so little
offence, and created so much interest." * Although plays have
neither political constitutions nor established churches, they
must all, if they are to be anything more than the merest tissue
of stage effects, have a philosophy even if it be no more than
an unconscious expression of the author's temperament. Just
as nowadays all the philosophers maintain intimate relations
with the fine arts, so conversely the great dramatists have at
all times maintained intimate relations with philosophy. William Archer used often to tell Shaw that he (Shaw) had no
real love of art, no enjoyment of it, only a faculty for observing performances, and an interest in the intellectual tendency
of plays. One may retort in Shaw's own words: " In all the
life that has energy enough to be interesting to me, subjective
volition, passion, will, make intellect the merest tool." It is
significant of much that, to Shaw, the play is not the thing,
but its thought, its purpose, its feeling, its execution. Indeed,
he regarded the theatre as a response to our need for a

* *The Author's Apology*—preface to the first English edition of *Dramatic
Opinions and Essays*, by Bernard Shaw.

William Archer

8 Sept 1908

WILLIAM ARCHER.

From the original pencil sketch.

" *sensable* expression of our ideals and illusions and approvals and resentments." In comparing the dramatic standards of Archer and himself, Shaw exhibits a passion for feeling little suspected by his critics: " Every element, even though it be an element of artistic force, which interferes with the credibility of the scene, wounds him, and is so much to the bad. To him acting, like scene-painting, is merely a means to an end, that end being to enable him to make-believe. To me the play is only the means, the end being the expression of feeling by the arts of the actor, the poet, the musician. Anything that makes this impression more vivid, whether it be versification, or an orchestra, or a deliberately artificial rendition of the lines, is so much to the good for me, even though it may destroy all the verisimilitude of the scene."

In a review of the London dramatic season of 1904-5 Mr. Walkley made the following characterization of Shaw:

" After all, we must recall this truth: the primordial function of the artist—whatever his means of artistic expression—is to be a purveyor of pleasure, and the man who can give us a refined intellectual pleasure, or a pleasure of moral nature or of social sympathy, or else a pleasure which arises from being given an unexpected or wider outlook upon life—this man imparts to us a series of delicate and moving sensations which the spectacle simply of technical address, of theatrical talent, can never inspire. And this man is no other than Bernard Shaw." *

In conversation with me, Shaw vehemently repudiated the notion that he was anything so petty as a mere purveyor of pleasure. " The theatre cannot give pleasure," he went so far as to say. " It defeats its very purpose if it does not take you outside of yourself. It may sometimes—and, indeed, often does—give one sensations which are far from pleasant, which may even be, in the last degree, horrifying and terrible. The function of the theatre is to stir people, to make them think, to make them suffer.

" Why, I have seen people stagger out of the Court Theatre

* *Le Temps,* August 28th, 1905.

277

after seeing one of my plays," he said, laughing, " unspeakably indignant with me because I had made them think, had stirred them to opposition, and had made them heartily ashamed of themselves."

In regard to comedy, the field in which he peculiarly excels, Shaw is equally positive in the statement that unless comedy touches as well as amuses him, he is defrauded of his just due. " When a comedy of mine is performed, it is nothing to me that the spectators laugh—any fool can make an audience laugh. I want to see how many of them, laughing or grave, have tears in their eyes." More than once he has insisted that people's ideas, however useful they may be for embroidery, especially in passages of comedy, are not the true stuff of drama, which is always " the naïve feeling underlying the ideas." When Mr. Meredith said, in his *Essay on Comedy*, " The English public have the basis of the comic in them: an esteem for common sense," the remark aroused Mr. Shaw's most vigorous opposition. The intellectual virtuosity of the Frenchman, the Irishman, the American, the ancient Greek, leading to a love of intellectual mastery of things, Shaw acutely observes, " produces a positive enjoyment of disillusion (the most dreaded and hated of calamities in England), and consequently a love of comedy (the fine art of disillusion) deep enough to make huge sacrifices of dearly idealized institutions to it. Thus, in France, Molière was allowed to destroy the Marquises. In England he could not have shaken even such titles as the accidental sheriff's knighthood of the late Sir Augustus Harris." Shaw had realized to his own misfortune that the Englishman's so-called " common sense " always involves a self-satisfied unconsciousness of its own moral and intellectual bluntness, whereas the function of comedy—in particular the comedies written by Shaw himself—is " to dispel such unconsciousness by turning the searchlight of the keenest moral and intellectual analysis right on it." The following paragraph embodies Shaw's rather limited conception of comedy:

" The function of comedy is nothing less than the destruction of old-established morals. Unfortunately, to-day such iconoclasm can be tolerated by our play-going citizens only as a counsel of despair and pessimism. They can find a dreadful joy in it when it is done seriously, or even grimly and terribly as they understand Ibsen to be doing it; but that it should be done with levity, with silvery laughter like the crackling of thorns under a pot, is too scandalously wicked, too cynical, too heartlessly shocking to be borne. Consequently, our plays must either be exploitations of old-established morals or tragic challengings of the order of Nature. Reductions to absurdity, however logical; banterings, however kind; irony, however delicate; merriment, however silvery, are out of the question in matters of morality, except among men with a natural appetite for comedy which must be satisfied at all costs and hazards: that is to say, not among the English play-going public, which positively dislikes comedy." *

It is perfectly apparent that it was Shaw's distinction—a notorious distinction—to be the leading and almost unique representative of a school which was in violent reaction against that of Pinero, generally regarded as the premier British dramatist. Moreover, he lacked the sympathy of his colleagues in dramatic criticism—Clement Scott, the impassioned champion of British sentimentality and ready-made morals, William Archer, the austere patron of young England in the drama, and Walkley, the Gallic impressionist and dilettante. Shaw endured the virulent attacks of Clement Scott with equanimity, if not with positive enjoyment. By his friend Walkley he was taunted, under the classic name of Euthrypho, with being an impossibilist: " Euthrypho hardly falls into Mr. Grant Allen's category of ' serious intellects,' for none has ever known him to be serious, but about his intellect there is, as the Grand Inquisitor says:

> " ' No probable possible shadow of doubt,
> No possible doubt whatever.'

A universal genius, a brilliant political economist, a Fabian

* *Meredith on Comedy*, in the *Saturday Review*, March 27th, 1897.

of the straitest sect of the Fabians, a critic (of other arts than the dramatic) *comme il y en a peu,* he persists, where the stage is concerned, in crying for the moon, and will not be satisfied, as the rest of us have learned to be, with the only attainable substitute, a good wholesome cheese. His standard is as much too high as Crito's (another critic) is too low. He asks from the theatre more than the theatre can give, and quarrels with the theatre because it is theatrical. He lumps *La Tosca* and *A Man's Shadow* together as ' French machine-made plays,' and, because he is not edified by them, refuses to be merely amused. Because *The Dead Heart* is not on the level of a Greek tragedy, he is blind to its merits as a pantomime. He refuses to recognize the advance made by Mr. Pinero because Mr. Pinero has not yet advanced as far as Henrik Ibsen. Half a loaf, the wise agree, is better than no bread; but because it is only half a loaf, Euthrypho complains that they have given him a stone." * Worse than all, Mr. Archer vigorously charged him with the most aggressive hostility towards the contemporary movement in British drama. In one of his *Study and Stage* articles, entitled *Mr. Shaw and Mr. Pinero,* and published August 22d, 1903, Mr. Archer thus condemns Shaw as a dramatic critic: " Just at the time when the English drama began clearly to emerge from the puerility into which it had sunk between the 'fifties and the 'eighties, Mr. Shaw was engaged, week by week, in producing dramatic criticisms. Writing for a sixpenny paper, he had but a limited audience; and, therefore, even his wit, energy and unique literary power (I use the epithet deliberately) could do little to influence the course of events. But all that he could do he did, to discredit, crush and stamp out the new movement. Had he been a power at all he would have been a power for evil. There were moments during that period when I sympathized, as never before or since, with the Terrorists of exactly a century ago. I felt that when a new and struggling order of things is persistently assailed with inveterate and inhuman hostility, it is no wonder if it defends itself with equal relentlessness. If a guillotine had

* *Playhouse Impressions,* article *The Dramatic Critic as Pariah,* pp. 5-6.

been functioning in Trafalgar Square—but do not let us dwell on the horrid fantasy. Those days are over. 'We have marched prospering, not through his presence.' There is still a long fight to be fought before the English theatre becomes anything like the great social institution it ought to be; but even if the movement were now to stop dead (and of that there is not the slightest fear), nothing can alter the fact that the past ten years have given us a new and by no means despicable dramatic literature."

These severe characterizations by the two leading English dramatic critics deserve more than casual notice. Shaw represented *l'école du plein air;* his unpardonable crime consisted in daringly throwing open the windows to let in a fresh and vivifying current of ideas. With Shaw, to dramatize was to philosophize; moreover, he sought to discredit the tradition that the drama is never the forerunner, but always the laggard, in interpretation of the *Zeitgeist.* Far from being the instigator of the crimes and the partner of the guilty joys of the drama, he regarded himself as the policeman of dramatic art; and avowed it his express business to denounce its delinquencies. Firm in the faith that the radicalism of yesterday is the conservatism of to-morrow, he boldly declared: " It is an instinct with me personally to attack every idea which has been full grown for ten years, especially if it claims to be the foundation of all human society. I am prepared to back human society against any idea, positive or negative, that can be brought into the field against it. In this—except as to my definite intellectual consciousness of it—I am, I believe, a much more typical and popular person in England than the conventional man; and I believe that when we begin to produce a genuine national drama, this apparently anarchic force, the mother of higher law and humaner order, will underlie it, and that the public will lose all patience with the conventional collapses which serve for the last acts to the serious dramas of to-day." He found the contemporary English drama lamentably " dating " in ethics and philosophy; their daily observation kept the English dramatists up-to-date in personal descriptions, but there was " nothing to force them to revise the morality they inherited from their grandmothers." But Shaw's high and un-compromising ideal for British drama was no justification for Mr. Archer's charge that Shaw as a dramatic critic was only a paralyzing and sterilizing force. "There is more talent now than ever," wrote Shaw in December, 1895, to take a single example, "more skill now than ever, more artistic culture, better taste, better acting, better theatres, better dramatic literature. Mr. Tree, Mr. Alexander, Mr. Hare have made honourable experiments, Mr. Forbes Robertson's enterprise at the Lyceum is not a sordid one; Mr. Henry Arthur Jones and Mr. Pinero are doing better work than ever before, and doing it without any craven concession to the follies of the British public."

We may, perhaps, best arrive at a notion of Shaw's relation to the British stage by discovering his attitude towards his colleagues in the drama—say Pinero, Jones, Wilde, Grundy, Stevenson and Henley. Pinero he resolutely refused, in the face of popular clamour, to laud as the "English Ibsen." He regarded Pinero as an adroit describer of people as the ordi-nary man sees and judges them, but not as a genuine in-terpreter of character. "Add to this a clear head, a love of the stage, and a fair talent for fiction, all highly cultivated by hard and honourable work as a writer of effective stage plays for the modern commercial theatre; and you have him on his real level." *The Second Mrs. Tanqueray*, hailed as the great-est tragedy of the modern English school, Shaw regarded as not only a stage play in the most technical sense, but even a noticeably old-fashioned one in its sentiment and stage-mechanism; he objected to it on another ground—and quite unreasonably, I think—because it exhibited, not the sexual relations between the principals, but the social reactions set up by this amazing marriage. Shaw was utterly revolted by Pinero's coarseness and unspeakable ignorance in the por-trayal of the feminine social agitation in *The Notorious Mrs. Ebbsmith;* the noble work of such women as Annie Besant, who had worked at Shaw's side for many years, gave the direct lie to Pinero's characterization. "I once pointed out a method of treatment which might have made *The Notorious Mrs. Ebb-*

smith bearable," Mr. Shaw recently remarked to me. " Now
I am of the opinion that nothing could have made it a good
play." Shaw had a vast contempt for Pinero as a moralist
and a social philosopher. " Archer objected to me as a critic,"
he once remarked to me, " because I didn't like *The Profligate*
and *The Second Mrs. Tanqueray.*" But Shaw sincerely admired the Pinero of *The Benefit of the Doubt* and *The Hobby
Horse,* notable as they were for high dramatic pressure or true
comedy, close-knit action or genuine literary workmanship,
humour, fresh observation, naturalness, and free development
of character. Shaw technically defined a " character actor "
as a " clever stage performer who cannot act, and therefore
makes an elaborate study of the disguises and stage tricks by
which acting can be grossly simulated." And he pronounced
Pinero's performance as a thinker and social philosopher to be
" simply character acting in the domain of authorship, which
can impose only on those who are taken in by character acting
on the stage."

The hypothetical " guillotine functioning in Trafalgar
Square," of which Mr. Archer speaks, Shaw insists was re-
served for him, not at all because he did all that he could do
" to discredit, crush, and stamp out the new movement," but
because he would not bow to the fetish of Pinero. One of his
chief heresies consisted in unhesitatingly classing Henry Arthur
Jones as " first, and eminently first, among the surviving fittest of his own generation of playwrights." Ever on the side
of the minority, he regarded *Michael and His Lost Angel* as
" the best play its school has given to the theatre." While
Pinero, in Shaw's eyes, drew his characters from the outside,
Jones developed them from within. Shaw recognized in Jones
a kindred spirit; both believed that " in all matters of the modern drama, England is no better than a parish, with ' parochial '
judgments, ' parochial ' instincts, and ' parochial ' ways of
looking at things." And Shaw accorded Jones the warmest
praise because he was " the only one of our popular dramatists
whose sense of the earnestness of real life has been dug deep
enough to bring him into conflict with the limitations and levities of our theatre."

For Grundy's school of dramatic art, Shaw had absolutely no relish. Indeed, he lamented the vogue of the " well-made piece "—those " mechanical rabbits," as he called them, with wheels for entrails. Henry James's *Guy Domville*, which he regarded as distinctly *du théâtre,* won his sincere praise; and the plays of Henley and Stevenson delighted him with their combination of artistic faculty, pleasant boyishness and romantic imagination, and fine qualities of poetic speech, despite the fact that the authors didn't take the stage seriously— " unless it were the stage of pasteboard scenes and characters and tin lamps." And to Shaw, Oscar Wilde—" almost as acutely Irish an Irishman as the Iron Duke of Wellington "— was, in a certain sense, " our only playwright," because he " plays with everything: with wit, with philosophy, with drama, with actors and audience, with the whole theatre."

The most serious and the most well-founded charge that can be urged against Shaw as a dramatic critic was his impatience with everybody who would not " come his way." It was his habit to damn a play which was not written as he himself would have written it. With characteristic iconoclasm, Shaw expressed his regret that *Michael and His Lost Angel* is a play without a hero—some captain of the soul, resolute in championing his own faith *contra mundum.* " Let me rewrite the last three acts," says the diabolonian author of *The Devil's Disciple,* " and you shall have your Reverend Michael embracing the answer of his own soul, thundering it from the steps of his altar, and marching out through his shocked and shamed parishioners, with colours flying and head erect and unashamed, to the freedom of faith in his own real conscience. Whether he is right or wrong is nothing to me as a dramatist; he must follow his star, right or wrong, if he is to be a hero."

Again, in the latter part of *The Second Mrs. Tanqueray,* Aubrey says to Paula, " I know what you were at Ellean's age. You hadn't a thought that wasn't a wholesome one; you hadn't an impulse that didn't tend towards good. . . . And this was a very few years back." Shaw's comment is highly significant of his attitude. " On the reply to that fatuous but not unnatural speech depended the whole question of Mr. Pinero's rank as a dramatist. One can imagine how, in a play by a master-hand, Paula's reply would have opened Tanqueray's foolish eyes to the fact that a woman of that sort is already the same at three as at thirty-three, and that however she may have found by experience that her nature is in conflict with the ideals of differently-constituted people, she remains perfectly valid to herself, and despises herself, if she sincerely does so at all, for the hypocrisy that the world forces on her instead of being what she is." That " master-hand," of which Shaw speaks, is now well known to the English public through the instrumentality of the Court, the Savoy and the Repertory Theatres. But at the time of writing this, and many another intolerant criticism, Shaw was violently battering away at the gates of tradition, and, Joshua-like, blowing his horn for the fall of the walls of the Jericho of the English stage. In *The Author's Apology* to his *Dramatic Opinions and Essays*, Shaw frankly says:

"I must warn the reader that what he is about to study is not a series of judgments aiming at impartiality, but a siege laid to the theatre of the nineteenth century by an author who had to cut his own way into it at the point of the pen and throw some of its defenders into the moat.

"Pray do not conclude from this that the things hereinafter written were not true, or not the deepest and best things I know how to say. Only, they must be construed in the light of the fact that all through I was accusing my opponents of failure because they were not doing what I wanted, whereas they were often succeeding very brilliantly in doing what they themselves wanted. I postulated as desirable a certain kind of play in which I was destined ten years later to make my mark as a playwright (as I very well foreknew in the depth of my own unconsciousness); and I brought everybody—authors, actors, managers—to the one test: were they coming my way or staying in the old grooves?"

In private, Shaw laughingly declares that the old criticisms of Pinero and Jones were all fudge, that Pinero and Archer were personal friends, and Shaw and Jones personal friends; so that Archer took on the job of cracking up Pinero and Shaw that of cracking up Jones, who were both " doing their blood best " for the drama. Later on the old criticisms proved no bar to the most cordial personal relations between Shaw and Pinero; and the latter's knighthood, unsought and, indeed, undreamt of by himself, was persistently urged on the Prime Minister by Shaw.

Granting all Shaw's unfairness, his confessed partiality and domination by an *idée fixe* for the English stage, it is nevertheless astounding to read Mr. Archer's declaration that Shaw's " critical campaign, conducted with magnificent energy and intellectual power, was as nearly as possible barren of result." On the contrary, it has been remarked that Shaw's dramatic criticisms supply one of the most notable examples of cause and effect modern literary history can show. Far from being barren of result, Shaw's assaults produced an effect little short of remarkable. His theories and principles found free expression in the Court Theatre. Indeed, they may be said in large measure to have created it, controlled it, and achieved its success. To Bernard Shaw and Granville Barker belong the credit for giving London, in the Court Theatre, a school of acting and a repertory—or rather, short-run—theatre such as England had never known before.

It would take me too far afield to attempt to do full justice to the variety and multiplicity of Shaw's functions as a critic of the drama, the stage, and the art of acting. The annoying part of his career, as Mr. W. L. Courtney somewhere says, is that he was more often right than wrong—" right in substance, though often wrong in manner, saying true things with the most ludicrous air in the world, as if he were merely enjoying himself at our expense." He agitated again and again for a subsidized theatre; and fought the censorship with unabating zeal.* He championed Ibsen at all times and in all

* Compare, for example, his ablest and most exhaustive essays on the subject: *The Author's Apology* to the Stage Society edition of *Mrs. Warren's Profession; Censorship of the Stage in England,* in the *North Ameri-*

places, realizing full well, as in the days of his musical criticism, that Sir Augustus Harris's prejudices against Wagner were no whit greater than Sir Henry Irving's prejudices against Ibsen. While he classed Irving as " our ablest exponent of acting as a fine art and serious profession," he considered all Irving's creations to be creations of his own temperament. Shaw took Irving sternly to task for his mutilations of Shakespeare and his inalienable hostility to Ibsen and the modern school. On the day of Irving's death, Shaw wrote: " He did nothing for the drama of the present, and he mutilated the remains of the dying Shakespeare; but he carried his lifelong fight into victory, and saw the actor recognized as the prince of all other artists is recognized; and that was enough in the life of a single man. *Requiescat in pace.*" * Shaw held Irving responsible for the remorseless waste of the modernity and originality of Ellen Terry's art upon the old drama, despite the fact that she succeeded in climbing to its highest summit. Shaw found consolation in the reflection that " if it was denied Ellen Terry to work with Ibsen to interpret the indignation of a Nora Helmer, it was her happy privilege to work with Burne-Jones and Alma-Tadema." † It was only

can *Review,* Vol. CLXIX., pages 251 *et seq.; The Solution of the Censorship Problem,* in the *Academy,* June 29th, 1907; *The Censorship of Plays,* in the *Nation* (London), November 16th, 1907.

* Owing partially to mistakes in re-translation into English, partially to certain statements made therein, Shaw's article in the *Neue Freie Presse* of Vienna (Feuilleton: *Sir Henry Irving, von Bernhard Shaw,* October 20th, 1905, written shortly after Irving's death) aroused a heated discussion and controversy, which raged even in America until the *Boston Transcript* let the disputants down heavily by reprinting the article, which was found to be quite reasonable and absolutely void of the innuendo of which Shaw was accused, namely, that Irving had played the sycophant to obtain a knighthood. It is noteworthy that certain matters as to which Shaw was erroneously supposed to have misrepresented Irving, were solemnly and publicly denied in letters to the *Times,* yet when the time came for biographies of Irving to appear, they contained ample proof that Shaw might have made all the denied allegations had he chosen to do so. For the facts in the case, compare the essay in the *Neue Freie Presse* with the true text of the essay, in the original English, with Shaw's own notes, in the *Morning Post,* London, December 5th, 1905.

† Shaw's fine essay on the art of Ellen Terry also appeared in the *Neue Freie Presse* late in 1905. For the English version of the article, cf. the *Boston Transcript,* January 20th, 1906.

after Irving's death, and after Ellen Terry had reached the age of fifty-eight, that she at last interpreted the Lady Cicely Waynflete of Shaw's own *Captain Brassbound's Conversion.*

After ten years of continuous criticism of the arts of music and the drama, Shaw gave up, exhausted.* The last critical continent was conquered. "The strange Jabberwocky Oracle whom men call Shaw," began to attain to the eminence of the " interview " and the " celebrity at home " column. In his first *feuilleton,* Max Beerbohm, Shaw's successor on the *Saturday Review,* said of him: "With all his faults—grave though they are and not to be counted on the fingers of one hand—he is, I think, by far the most brilliant and remarkable journalist in London." *Plays, Pleasant and Unpleasant,* then just published, were creating unusual interest. Shaw was doubtless influenced thereby to devote himself, as artist, exclusively to the writing of plays. In order to make as much as the stage royalties from *The Devil's Disciple* alone, for example, he would, as he said, have had "to write his heart out for six years in the *Saturday.*" The superhuman profession of journalism began to pall upon him: excellence in it he regarded as quite beyond mortal strength and endurance. "I took extraordinary pains—all the pains I was capable of—to get to the bottom of everything I wrote about. . . . Ten years of such work, at the rate of two thousand words a week or thereabouts —say, roughly, a million words—all genuine journalism, dependent on the context of the week's history for its effect, was an apprenticeship which made me master of my own style." Shaw's income as a journalist began in 1885 at one hundred and seventeen pounds and threepence; and it ended at five hundred pounds. By this time he had reached the age at which one discovers that " journalism is a young man's standby, not an old man's livelihood." Shaw had said all that he had to say of Irving and Tree; and concerning Shakespeare he boasted: "When I began to write, William was a divinity and a bore. Now he is a fellow-creature." But, above all, he had gloriously succeeded in the creation of that most successful

* His *Valedictory* appeared in the *Saturday Review,* May 21st, 1898.

of all his fictions—G. B. S. " For ten years past, with an un-precedented pertinacity and obstination, I have been dinning into the public head that I am an extraordinarily witty, brilliant, and clever man. That is now part of the public opinion of England; and no power in heaven or on earth will ever change it. I may dodder and dote; I may pot-boil and platitudinize; I may become the butt and chopping-block of all the bright, original spirits of the rising generation; but my reputation shall not suffer: it is built up fast and solid, like Shakespeare's, on an impregnable basis of dogmatic reiteration."

THE PLAYWRIGHT—I

"In all my plays my economic studies have played as important a part as a knowledge of anatomy does in the works of Michael Angelo."—Letter to the author, of date June 30th, 1904.

"Plays which, dealing less with the crimes of society, and more with its romantic follies, and with the struggles of individuals against those follies, may be called, by contrast, Pleasant."—*Plays, Pleasant and Unpleasant,* Vol. I., Preface.

CHAPTER X

WHILE resting from the over-exertions of the political campaign at the time of the General Election in 1892, Shaw came upon the manuscript of the partially finished play begun in 1885. "Tickled" by the play, and urged by Mr. Grein, Shaw began work upon it anew. "But for Mr. Grein and the Independent Theatre Society," Shaw confessed, " it would have gone back to its drawer and lain there another seven years, if not for ever." * With this play, *Widowers' Houses,* Shaw made his *début* upon the English stage as a problem dramatist with the avowed purpose of exposing existent evils in the prevailing social order. *Widowers' Houses* is the first native play of the New School in England consciously devoted to the exposure of the social guilt of the community.

In 1885, shortly after the completion of the novels of his nonage, Shaw began this play in collaboration with Mr. William Archer. After learning to know Shaw by sight in the British Museum reading-room, as a " young man of tawny complexion and attire," studying alternately, if not simultaneously, Karl Marx's *Das Kapital* (in French), and an orchestral score of *Tristan and Isolde,* Mr. Archer finally met him at the house of a common acquaintance.

> " I learned from himself that he was the author of several unpublished masterpieces of fiction. Construction, he owned with engaging modesty, was not his strong point, but his dialogue was incomparable. Now, in those days I had still a certain hankering after the rewards, if not the glories, of the playwright. With a modesty in no way inferior to Mr. Shaw's, I had realized that I could not

---

* Compare the account of Mr. Eden Greville, one of Mr. Grein's associates in the Independent Theatre Society, in *Munsey's Magazine,* March, 1906, entitled, *Bernard Shaw and His Plays.*

write dialogue a bit; but I still considered myself a born constructor. I proposed, and Mr. Shaw agreed to, a collaboration. I was to provide him with one of the numerous plots I kept in stock, and he was to write the dialogue. So said, so done. I drew out, scene by scene, the scheme of a twaddling cup-and-saucer comedy vaguely suggested by Augier's *Ceinture Dorée*. The details I forget, but I know it was to be called *Rhinegold*, was to open, as *Widowers' Houses* actually does, in an hotel garden on the Rhine, and was to have two heroines, a sentimental and a comic one, according to the accepted Robertson-Byron-Carton formula. I fancy the hero was to propose to the sentimental heroine, believing her to be the poor niece instead of the rich daughter of the sweater, or slum-landlord, or whatever he may have been; and I know he was to carry on in the most heroic fashion, and was ultimately to succeed in throwing the tainted treasure of his father-in-law, metaphorically speaking, into the Rhine. All this I gravely propounded to Mr. Shaw, who listened with no less admirable gravity. Then I thought the matter had dropped, for I heard no more of it for many weeks. I used to see Mr. Shaw at the Museum, laboriously writing page after page of the most exquisitely neat shorthand at the rate of about three words a minute, but it did not occur to me that this was our play. After about six weeks he said to me: 'Look here: I've written half the first act of that comedy, and I've used up all your plot. Now I want some more to go on with.' I told him that my plot was a rounded and perfect organic whole, and that I could no more eke it out in this fashion than I could provide him or myself with a set of supplementary arms and legs. I begged him to extend his shorthand and let me see what he had done; but this would have taken him far too long. He tried to decipher some of it orally, but the process was too lingering and painful for endurance. So he simply gave me an outline in narrative of what he had done; and I saw that, so far from using up my plot, he had not even touched it. There the matter rested for months and years. Mr. Shaw

Joseph Simpson.]   [Courtesy of the Artist.

BERNARD SHAW.

From the original black and white wash-drawing. Reproduced by permission of the
owner, Mr. J. Murray Allison.

[Facing p. 290

would now and then hold out vague threats of finishing 'our play,' but I felt no serious alarm. I thought (judging from my own experience in other cases) that when he came to read over in cold blood what he had written, he would see what impossible stuff it was. Perhaps my free utterance of this view piqued him; perhaps he felt impelled to remove from the Independent Theatre the reproach of dealing solely in foreign products. The fire of his genius, at all events, was not to be quenched by my persistent application of the wet blanket. He finished his play; Mr. Grein, as in duty bound, accepted it; and the result was the performance of Friday last at the Independent Theatre." *

According to Shaw's account, he produced a horribly incongruous effect by " laying violent hands on his (Archer's) thoroughly planned scheme for a sympathetically romantic 'well-made play' of the type then in vogue," and perversely distorting it into a " grotesquely realistic exposure of slum-landlordism, muncipal jobbery, and the pecuniary and matrimonial ties between it and the pleasant people of 'independent' incomes who imagine that such sordid matters do not touch their own lives." Shortly before the production of *Widowers' Houses*, there appeared an " Interview " with Shaw, purporting to give some idea of the much-mooted play, but leaving the public in doubt as to the seriousness with which this mock-solemn information was to be taken.† " Sir," said Shaw sternly to the interviewer (himself!), " it (my play) will be nothing else than didactic. Do you suppose I have gone to all this trouble to *amuse* the public? No, if they want that, there is the Criterion for them, the Comedy, the Garrick, and so on. My object is to instruct them." And to explain the allusion contained in the title, concerning which speculation was rife, Shaw remarked to the interviewer: " I have been assured that

* Mr. William Archer, writing in the *World* (London), for Wednesday, December 14th, 1892.

† The *Star*, November 29th, 1892. Mr. Archer once told me that there was little doubt that Shaw wrote the " Interview " *in toto*.

in one of the sections of the Bible dealing with the land question there is a clause against the destruction of widows' houses. There is no widow in my play; but there is a widower who owns slum property. Hence the title. Perhaps you are not familiar with the Bible." *

After repeated calls from the audience Shaw made an impromptu speech at the close of the first performance of *Widowers' Houses*. He said that " he wished to assure his listeners that the greeting of the play had been agreeable to him, for had the story been received lightly he would have been disappointed. What he had submitted to their notice was going on in actual life. The action of *Widowers' Houses* depicted the ordinary middle-class life of the day, but he heartily hoped the time would come when the play he had written would be both utterly impossible and utterly unintelligible. If anyone were to ask him where the Socialism came in, he would say that it was in the love of their art on Socialistic principles that had induced the performers to give their services on that occasion. In conclusion, he trusted that, above all, the critics would carefully discriminate between himself and the actors who had so zealously striven to carry out his intentions." According to a contemporary account: " Warm cheers greeted the playwright who thus candidly and gratefully acknowledged the excellent work rendered by the players, whilst still proclaiming that his play was in all particulars the faithful reflex of a sordid and unpitying age."

The play, a nine-days' wonder, was widely paragraphed in the newspapers, and regarded in some quarters as a daring attack on middle-class society. The storm of protest aroused by *Widowers' Houses* almost paralleled the howl of execration evoked by the production of Ibsen's *Ghosts* in England. *Widowers' Houses* was intended as neither a beautiful nor a lovable work. Shaw confessed years afterwards that the play was entirely unreadable except for the prefaces and appendices, which he rightly regarded as good. The art of this play was confessedly the expression of the sense of intellectual and moral

* Matthew xxiii., 14; Mark xii., 38-40; Luke xx., 46-47.

perversity; for Shaw had passed most of his life in big modern towns, where his sense of beauty had been starved, whilst his intellect had been gorged with problems like that of the slums. *Widowers' Houses* is " saturated with the vulgarity of the life it represents "; and, in the first edition of the play, Shaw confesses that he is " not giving expression in pleasant fancies to the underlying beauty and romance of happy life, but dragging up to the smooth surface of ' respectability ' a handful of the slime and foulness of its polluted bed, and playing off your laughter at the scandal of the exposure against your shudder at its blackness."

Like Bulwer Lytton, Stevenson, and other nineteenth-century novelists who turned to the writing of plays, Shaw approached the theatre lacking due appreciation of the difficulties of dramatic art, the perfect artistic sincerity it demands. Writing his play as a pastime, he employed it as a means of shocking the sensibilities of his audience as well as of winging a barbed shaft at its smug respectability. Paying no heed to that golden mean of " average truth," which Sainte Beuve impressed with such high seriousness upon the youthful Zola, Shaw indulges in that extreme form of depicting life, the mutilation of humanity, which Brunetière pronounced to be the vital defect of naturalism. A pair of lovers *dans cette galère!* As Mr. Archer said at the time: " When they are not acting with a Gilbertian *naïveté* of cynicism, they are snapping and snarling at each other like a pair of ill-conditioned curs."

The accusation of indebtedness to Ibsen hurled at Shaw from all sides as soon as his play was produced was promptly squelched by Shaw's vigorous denial. It is worth remarking, however, that " tainted money," that bone of contention in America and the theme of Shaw's later *Major Barbara,* is the abuse which serves as the mark for the satire, both of Ibsen in *An Enemy of the People*, and of Shaw in *Widowers' Houses*. The perverting effect of ill-gotten gains upon the moral sense is the lesson of these two plays. Whereas Shaw was content to uncover the social canker and expose its ravages in all directions, Ibsen, through the instrumentality of Stockmann, holds out an ideal for the regeneration of society.

Widowers' Houses abounds in flashes of insight, in passages of trenchant dialogue, in sardonic exposure of human nature; the keen intellect of the author is everywhere in evidence. Shaw's vigorous Socialism is largely responsible for the clarity and succinctness with which the economic point is driven home; and the discussions of social problems are tense with a nervous vivacity almost dramatic in quality. And yet the structural defect of the play is the loose dramatic connection between the economic elucidations and the general psychological processes of the action.

Before the production of *Widowers' Houses*, Shaw publicly stated that the first two acts were written before he ever heard of Ibsen; and afterwards he asserted that his critics " should have guessed this, because there is not one idea in the play that cannot be more easily referred to half a dozen English writers than to Ibsen; whilst of his peculiar retrospective method, by which his plays are made to turn upon events supposed to have happened before the rise of the curtain, there is not a trace in my work." * Shaw laughed incontinently at those people who excitedly discussed the play as a daringly original sermon, but who would not accept it as a play on any terms " because its hero did not, when he learned that his income came from slum property, at once relinquish it (*i.e.*, make it a present to Sartorius without benefiting the tenants), and go to the goldfields to dig out nuggets with his strong right arm, so that he might return to wed his Blanche after a shipwreck (witnessed by her in a vision), just in time to rescue her from beggary, brought upon her by the discovery that Lickcheese was the rightful heir to the property of Sartorius, who had dispossessed and enslaved him by a series of forgeries unmasked by the faithful Cokane!"

For the sake of its bearing upon Shaw's subsequent career, one important contemporary impression deserves to be placed on record. Five months after the production of *Widowers' Houses*, in a review (published May 4th, 1893) of the Inde-

---

* Appendix I., *Widowers' Houses;* Independent Theatre edition. Henry and Co., London, 1893.

pendent Theatre edition of that play, Mr. William Archer earnestly endeavoured to dissuade Shaw from turning dramatist.

" It is a pity that Mr. Shaw should labour under a delusion as to the true bent of his talent, and, mistaking an amusing *jeu d'esprit* for a work of creative art, should perhaps be tempted to devote further time and energy to a form of production for which he has no special ability and some constitutional disabilities. A man of his power of mind can do nothing that is altogether contemptible. We may be quite sure that if he took palette and ' commenced painter,' or set to work to manipulate a lump of clay, he would produce a picture or a statue that would bear the impress of a keen intelligence, and would be well worth looking at. That is precisely the case of *Widowers' Houses*. It is a curious example of what can be done in art by sheer brain-power, apart from natural aptitude. For it does not appear that Mr. Shaw has any more specific talent for the drama than he has for painting or sculpture."

Shaw's next play, *The Philanderer*, is distinctly a *pièce d'occasion* and should be read in the light of the attitude of the British public toward Ibsen and Ibsenism at the time of its writing. After Miss Janet Achurch's performance as Nora Helmer in *A Doll's House*, in 1889, Ibsen became the target of dramatic criticism; and Shaw's *Quintessence of Ibsenism*, published in 1891, was the big gun, going off when the controversy was at its height. Sir Edwin Arnold made an editorial attack on Ibsen, Mr. Frederick Wedmore echoed his denunciation, and Clement Scott exhausted his vocabulary of vituperation in an almost hysterical outcry against the foulness and obscenity of the shameless Norwegian. *The Philanderer* was written just when the cult of Ibsen had reached the pinnacle of fatuity. From Shaw's picture, one is led to suppose that society, with reference to Ibsen, was roughly divided into three classes: the conservatives of the old guard, regarding Ibsen as a *monstrum horrendum;* the *soi-disant* Ibsenites, glibly conversant with Ibsen's ideas but profoundly ignorant of their meaning; and, lastly, those who really understood Ibsen, this class being made up of two sorts of individuals, those who really intended to adopt Ibsen principles, and those who were keen and unscrupulous enough to exploit Ibsenism solely for the sake of the sustenance it afforded parasitic growths like themselves. The ideal of the " womanly woman " still prevailed in English society. Shaw here readily perceived the possibilities for satire and tragi-comedy, both in the clash of old prejudices with new ideas, and in the mordant contrast discovered by the conflict of the over-sexed, passionate " womanly woman " with the under-sexed, pallidly intellectual philanderer of the Ibsen school. Had Shaw's performance been as able as his perception was acute, *The Philanderer* would have been a genuine achievement instead of a grimly promising failure.

The Philanderer serves as a link between the plays of Shaw's earlier and later manners. Present marriage laws really have very little to do with this play, which concerns itself with a study of social types. Julia is the *fine fleur* of feral femininity; woman's practice of employing her personal charms unscrupulously and man's practice of treating woman as a mere plaything both have a share in the formation of her character. Grace Tranfield is the best type of the advanced woman; she demands equality of opportunity for women, rejects the " lord and master " theory, and fights always for the integrity of her self-respect. Between these two women stands Leonard Charteris, holding the average young cub's cynical ideas about women, sharpened to acuteness through the intellectual astuteness of Bernard Shaw. Charteris, in his bloodless Don Juanism, is the type of the degenerate male flirt—the pallid prey of the *maladie du siècle*. " C'est un homme qui ne fait la cour aux femmes ni pour le bon ni pour le mauvais motif," says M. Filon. " Que veut-il? S'amuser. Seulement—comme on l'a dit des Anglais en général—il s'amuse tristement; il y a dans l'attitude de ce séducteur glacial et dégoûté quelque chose qui n'est pas très viril. On dit la société anglaise infestée de ces gens-là." *

* *M. Bernard Shaw et son Théâtre,* by Augustin Filon. *Revue des Deux Mondes,* November 15th, 1905; p. 424.

PLAYBILL OF *Mrs. Warren's Profession.*

Last "Gastspiel" by the players of the Deutsches Theater and the Kammerspiele in Berlin. Schauspielhaus, Munich. July 31st, 1908. Ninth performance.

PLAYBILL OF *The Philanderer.*

Hebbel-Theater, Berlin. January 3rd, 1909. Sixty-eighth performance.

Upon the mind of any unprejudiced person, I think, *The Philanderer* creates the impression that Shaw's attitude toward women in this play must have been induced by unpleasant personal relations with women prior to the time at which the play was written. Many people paid him the insult of recognizing him in Charteris; and I have even been told that Shaw was temperamentally not dissimilar to Charteris, at that particular period. The play is marked by unnaturalness and immaturity at every turn; but several scenes exhibit great nervous strength. Mr. Robert Loraine once remarked to me that, in his opinion, the first act of *The Philanderer* was unparalleled in its verisimilitude, always making him realize the truth of Ibsen's dictum that the modern stage must be regarded as a room of which one wall has been removed. Mr. Loraine's impression is fully justified by the fact that the scene is a more or less accurate replica of a scene in Mr. Shaw's own life.

As a play, *The Philanderer* is crude and amateurish, revolving upon the pivot of Charteris's satire, and presenting various features in turn—now extravaganza, now broad farce, now comedy, now tragi-comedy. With all its brilliant mental vivisection, the conversation of Charteris is never natural, but supranatural; the utterly gross and caddish indecency of his exposures would never be tolerated for an instant in polite or even respectable society. And yet Mr. Shaw once vehemently assured me: " Charteris is not passionless, not unscrupulous, and a sincere, not a pseudo, Ibsenist "! Cuthbertson is a caricature of Clement Scott; and, in virtually the same words used by Scott in his attacks upon Ibsen, Cuthbertson avows that the whole modern movement is abhorrent to him " because his life had been passed in witnessing scenes of suffering nobly endured and sacrifice willingly rendered by womanly women and manly men." The mannerisms of Craven, " Now really " in especial, are taken directly, Mr. Shaw once told me, from Mr. H. M. Hyndman, the English Socialist leader. Dr. Paramore is the puppet of broad farce, immune to all humane concern through inoculation with the deadly germ of scientific research; while Sylvia is merely the pert little *soubrette*. The inverted Gilbertism of Colonel Craven's: " Do you mean to say that I am expected to treat my daughter the same as I would any other girl? Well, dash me if I will!" faintly strikes the note of Falsacappa, the brigand chief, in Meilhac and Halévy's *The Brigands:* "Marry my daughter to an honest man! Never!" —a phrase with which Mr. W. S. Gilbert afterwards did such execution in *The Pirates of Penzance.*

When *The Philanderer* was published in 1898, the public was puzzled and astounded to read an "attack" on Ibsen by Ibsen's most valiant champion in England! So shocked was Mr. Archer by this "outrage upon art and decency" that he wanted to "cut" his colleague and friend in the street. *The Philanderer* thus laid the foundation of Shaw's reputation as a cynic and a paradoxer. It is chiefly interesting to-day as a foreshadowing and promise of the lines of development of the later dramatist. Superficially, this play mirrors the glaring, even tragic contrast between faddist idealization of Ibsen, and sincere realization of Ibsenism. But, in the light of subsequent events, the play rather teaches that Charteris as male flirt is the model for the sketchy Valentine, that Julia is the Ann Whitefield of a more natural and less self-conscious phase. Throughout the play we are reminded of the brutal laughter of Wedekind, the sardonic humour of Becque, and, in places, even of the dark levity of Ibsen himself. The portrayal of Julia is remarkable, in spite of the damaging error of representing her as fit subject for the police court—mentally arrested in development, victim of violent "brain-storms," unscrupulous, treacherous, deceitful, feline. And yet, by some marvellous trick of subtle art, the author has caused this creature to win our profound sympathy in the end. After all, her love for Charteris is genuine and sincere; and the scene between Grace and Julia, after the latter has accepted Dr. Paramore, is profoundly touching:

> GRACE (*speaking in a low voice to Julia alone*): So you
> have shown him that you can do without him! Now
> I take back everything I said. Will you shake hands
> with me? (*Julia gives her hand painfully, with her
> face averted.*) They think this a happy ending,

Julia—these men—our lords and masters! (*The two stand silent, hand in hand.*)

The human drama of this play, merely sketched though it be, is the conflict in Julia's soul between her violent passion for Charteris and her true impulse toward self-respect. The quintessence of her tragedy is expressed in her last tilt with Charteris. He walks up to congratulate her, proffering his hand.

> JULIA (*exhausted, allowing herself to take it*): You are right. I am a worthless woman.
> CHARTERIS (*triumphant, and gaily remonstrating*): Oh, why?
> JULIA: Because I am not brave enough to kill you.

Shaw's next play, *Mrs. Warren's Profession*, completed his first cycle of economic studies in dramatic form; and at one stroke demonstrated Shaw to be a dramatist of marked powers and ability. Shaw's account of the genesis of this play is an important link in its history. In regard to the title, Shaw says: " The tremendously effective scene—which a baby could write if its sight were normal—in which she (Mrs. Warren) justifies herself, is only a paraphrase of a scene in a novel of my own, ' Cashel Byron's Profession ' (hence the title, *Mrs. Warren's Profession*), in which a prize-fighter shows how he was driven into the ring exactly as Mrs. Warren was driven on the streets." Shaw met the charge of indebtedness to Ibsen and De Maupassant with the statement that, if a dramatist living in the world of multifarious interests, duties and experiences in which he lived has to go to books for his ideas and his inspiration, he must be both blind and deaf. " Most dramatists are," he laconically added. So *Mrs. Warren's Profession* came about in this way:

" Miss Janet Achurch mentioned to me a novel by some French writer as having a dramatizable story in it. It being hopeless to get me to read anything, she told me the story, which was ultra-romantic. I said, ' Oh, I will work out the real truth about that mother some day.' In the following autumn I was the guest of a lady of very distinguished ability—one whose knowledge of English social types is as remarkable as her command of industrial and political questions. She suggested that I should put on the stage a real modern lady of the governing class—not the sort of thing that theatrical and critical authorities imagine such a lady to be. I did so; and the result was Miss Vivie Warren, who has laid the intellect of Mr. William Archer in ruins. . . . I finally persuaded Miss Achurch, who is clever with her pen, to dramatize the story herself on the original romantic lines. Her version is called *Mrs. Daintry's Daughter*. That is the history of *Mrs. Warren's Profession*. I never dreamt of Ibsen or De Maupassant, any more than a blacksmith shoeing a horse thinks of the blacksmith in the next county." *

Of course, one blacksmith cannot possibly know what another blacksmith in the next county is doing. But Shaw was not only aware of what Ibsen was doing and had done: he had actually written a remarkable analysis of Ibsen's plays and, with his utmost critical skill, defended Ibsen's art and philosophy, on the platform and in the press, against the ablest critics in England. As clearly as *Ghosts* does *Mrs. Warren's Profession* reveal the truth of George Eliot's dictum that consequences are unpitying; a true drama of catastrophe, employing Ibsen's peculiar retrospective method, Shaw's play exemplifies, in Amiel's words, the fatality of the consequences which follow every human act. Nora as daughter, instead of Nora as wife, Vivie leaves her home under the same profound conviction of her duty to herself as a human being—a duty infinitely more obligatory than any she may be conventionally imagined to owe to a Magdalen mother, who has educated and

* *Mr. Shaw's Method and Secret*, letter to the editor of the *Daily Chronicle*, April 30th, 1898, signed G. Bernard Shaw. In the first draft, the play was entitled *Mrs. Jarman's Profession*.

purposes to support her out of the profits of a profession which
has its roots in the most hideous of all social evils.*

Mrs. Warren's Profession towers high above his first two
plays, and places Shaw in the front rank of contemporary dramatic craftsmen. Its strength proceeds from the depth displayed in the consideration of the motives which prompt to
action, the intellectual and emotional crises eventuating from the
fierce clash of personalities and the sardonically unconscious self-
scourging of the characters themselves. The scenes are so admirably ordered, the procedure so swift, the situations so
charged with significance that one can find little to wonder at
in Mr. Cunninghame Graham's characterization of *Mrs. Warren's Profession* as " the best that has been written in English
in our generation." Tense, nervous, vigorous, the great scenes
are full of " that suppleness, that undulation of emotional
process," which Mr. Archer pronounces one of the unmistakable
tokens of dramatic mastery. The tremendous dramatic power
of the specious logic with which Mrs. Warren defends her
course; the sardonic irony of the parting between mother and
daughter! Goethe said of Molière that he chastises men by
drawing them just as they are. True descendant of Molière,
whom he once declared to be worth a thousand Shakespeares,
Shaw wields upon vice the shrieking scourge, not of the preacher,
but of the dramatist. Out of the mouths of the characters
themselves proceeds their own condemnation. Devastating in
its consummate irony is the passage in which Mrs. Warren, conventional to her heart's core, lauds her own respectability; and
that in which Crofts propounds his own code of honour:

> CROFTS: My code is a simple one, and, I think, a good one:
> Honour between man and man; fidelity between

* It should be clearly pointed out that Shaw is in no sense indebted to
Ibsen for dissatisfaction with the existent social order. The facts of
Shaw's life disprove the statement of Dr. Georg Brandes (*Bernard Shaw's
Teater,* in *Politikken,* Copenhagen, December 29th, 1902): "What Shaw
chiefly owes to Ibsen, whose harbinger he was, seems to be a tendency
towards rebellion against commonly recognized prejudices, dramatic as well
as social." Shaw's attacks upon modern capitalistic society, both in *Widowers' Houses* and in *Mrs. Warren's Profession,* are the immediate fruits
of his Socialism and his economic studies.

man and woman; and no cant about this or that religion, but an honest belief that things are making for good on the whole.

VIVIE (*with biting irony*): " A power, not ourselves, that makes for righteousness," eh?
CROFTS (*taking her seriously*): Oh, certainly, not ourselves, of course. *You* understand what I mean.

Dr. Brandes called Ibsen's *Ghosts*, if not the greatest achievement, at any rate the noblest action of the poet's career. *Mrs. Warren's Profession* is not only what Brunetière would call a work of combat: it is an act—an act of declared hostility against capitalistic society, the inertia of public opinion, the lethargy of the public conscience, and the criminality of a social order which begets such appalling social conditions. Into this play Shaw has poured all his Socialistic passion for a more just and humane social order.

As an arraignment of social conditions, the play is tremendous. As a work of art, it presents marked deficiencies. Shaw sought to dispose of one charge—that Vivie is merely Shaw in petticoats—in these words: " One of my female characters, who drinks whisky and smokes cigars and reads detective stories and regards the fine arts, especially music, as an insufferable and unintelligible waste of time, has been declared by my friend, Mr. William Archer, to be an exact and authentic portrait of myself, on no other grounds in the world except that she is a woman of business and not a creature of romantic impulse." It is clear that this is not a satisfactory answer to Mr. Archer's charge; but even in more minor details, the play is open to criticism: the futility of Praed, save as a barefaced confidant; the cheap melodrama of Frank and the rifle; the series of coincidences culminating in the Rev. Mr. Gardner's miserably confused " Miss Vavasour, I believe! " at the end of the first act. More important still, as Mr. Archer once pointed out,* there is nothing of the inevitable in the meeting

* *Study and Stage,* by William Archer, in the *Daily News,* June 21st, 1902.

of Frank and Vivie, despite Shaw's assertion that " the children of any polyandrous group will, when they grow up, inevitably be confronted with the insoluble problem of their own possible consanguinity." Had Vivie not happened to take lodgings at that particular farmhouse in Surrey, she would never have seen or heard of Frank, and the " inevitable " would never have happened. But this single lapse of logic, together with the other defects mentioned, are comparatively venial faults—which Shaw probably classes among those " relapses into staginess " betraying, as he confessed, " the young playwright and the old playgoer in this early work of mine."

It is the predominance of a certain hard, sheer rationalism, and a defiant, irresponsible levity in places, which mars the artistic unity of the play, and denies it the exalted rank to which it well-nigh attains. At the fundamental morality of the play there is no cause to cavil. Instead of maintaining an association in the imagination of the spectators between prostitution and fashionable beauty, luxury and refinement, as do *La Dame aux Caméllias*, *The Second Mrs. Tanqueray*, *Iris*, *Zaza* and countless other modern plays, *Mrs. Warren's Profession* exhibits the life of the courtesan in all its arid actuality, and inculcates a lesson of the sternest morality. It is because she is what she is that Mrs. Warren loses her daughter irrevocably. In general, the logic of the play is unimpeachable; but the rationalist character imparted to the conversations of the principal characters by their persistence in arguing everything out logically gives the play a sort of glacial rigidity. The principal defect of the play is the discrepancy between the tragic seriousness of the theme and the occasional depressing levity of its treatment. Consonance between theme and tone is the prime requisite of a work of art. This remarkable play falls just short of real greatness because its whimsical, facetious, irrepressible author was unable to discipline himself to artistic self-restraint. *Mrs. Warren's Profession* is calculated to produce an almost unendurable effect because, as Mr. Archer wisely says, Bernard Shaw is " the slave of his sense of the ridiculous."

The close of the year 1893 marks the beginning of a new

phase in the evolution of Shaw's art as a dramatist. As Brunetière said to the Symbolists, so the English public said to Mr. Grein and his supporters of the Independent Theatre Society: " Gentlemen, produce your masterpieces ! " Shaw eagerly took up the case; and rather than let it collapse, he " manufactured the evidence." His first play met with a *succès de scandale;* his second failed of production; and his third, the expected " masterpiece," was debarred by the censorship. The union of economics and Socialism in thesis-plays met with no favour at the hands of the British public. Shaw was forced to relinquish for the time being his purpose of reforming the public through the medium of the stage. His original disavowal of any intent to amuse the public went for naught in default of a platform from which to deliver instruction.

Shaw's social determinism, as M. Auguste Hamon once expressed it to me, is " absolute ": his fundamental Socialism throws the blame, not upon Trench, Charteris, Crofts and Mrs. Warren, as *individuals,* but upon the *prevailing social order,* the capitalistic *régime,* which offers them as alternatives, not morality and immorality, but two sorts of immorality.* Upon each individual in his audience, whether in the study or in the theatre, Shaw threw the burden of responsibility for defective social organization, and for those social horrors which can only be mitigated, and, perhaps, ultimately abolished, by public opinion, public action and public contribution. Mr. Shaw once described this play to me as a faithful presentment of the " economic basis of modern commercial prostitution." But the managers well knew that the public was averse to being forced to face the unpleasant facts set forth in Shaw's three " unpleasant " plays. The rigour of the censorship and prevailing theatrical conditions in London were hostile to Shaw's initial efforts.

" You cannot write three plays and then stop," Shaw has

---

* Compare *The Author's Apology,* the preface to the Stage Society edition of *Mrs. Warren's Profession* (Grant Richards, London, 1902), pp. xxvii. and xxviii. in especial; and also *Mainly About Myself,* the preface to Vol. I. of *Plays, Pleasant and Unpleasant,* pp. xxix-xxxi. in the American edition (H. S. Stone and Co., Chicago, 1902).

explained. Accordingly, for obvious reasons, social determinism ceased to be the motive force of Shaw's dramas; and he began to write plays concerned more particularly with the comedy and tragedy of individual life and destiny. Shaw did not cease to be a satirist, did not desist from his effort to startle the public out of its bland complacency: he merely diverted for the time being the current of his satire from social abuses to the shams, pretences, illusions and self-deceptions of individual life. Having learned to beware of solemnity, Shaw makes the satiric jest his point of departure. From this time forward he occupies and operates upon a new plane. He has ceased to be purely the social scavenger. Bernard Shaw's comedy of manners and of character now enters into the history of British drama.

Arms and the Man—obviously deriving its title from the *Arma virumque cano* of the opening line of Virgil's *Æneid*—is one of Shaw's most delightful comedies—a genuine comedy of character and yet *theatrical* in the true sense, Dr. Brandes has called it. Not the least of its virtues is the implicitness of its philosophy; perhaps this is one reason why Mr. Shaw (as he lately remarked to me) now considers it a very slight and immature production! From one point of view, this play may be regarded as a study of the psychology of the military profession.* From another point of view—the standpoint of the regular playgoer—the play has for its dramatic essence the collision of romantic illusion with prosaic reality.

To many people the play appeared as a " damning sneer at military courage," an attempted demonstration of the astounding thesis that heroism is merely a sublimated form of cowardice! When King Edward—then Prince of Wales—witnessed a performance of the play, he could not be induced to smile even once; and afterwards it was reported that " his Royal Highness regretted that the play should have shown so disrespectful an attitude toward the Army as was betrayed by

---

* Compare *La Psychologie du Militaire Professionel,* by Auguste Hamon, which appeared in November, 1893. I have no reason to believe that Shaw was under any indebtedness to this book in writing *Arms and the Man.*

PLAYBILL OF *Arms and the Man*.
Avenue Theatre, London. April 21st, 1894. First production on any stage.

the character of the chocolate-cream soldier." * Bluntschli is a natural realist, to whom long military service has taught the salutary lesson that bullets are to be avoided, not sought; that the main object of the efficient soldier is not the bubble reputation at the cannon's mouth, but practical success and the preservation of life. Shaw had never seen service, never participated in a battle—save the battle of Trafalgar Square. But he happened to be a modern realist with a tremendous fund of satire and fantasy. And although he had to get his data at second hand, he experienced no difficulty in finding abundant material, to authenticate his presentment of the common-sense soldier, in great realistic fiction such as Zola's *La Débâcle*, in classic autobiography such as Marbot's *Memoirs*, and in the recorded experiences of English and American generals, notably Lord Wolseley and General Horace Porter. People were inclined to laugh Shaw's play out of court as an exercise no more serious than that of a " mowing down military ideals with volleys of chocolate creams." Yet Shaw knew a man who lived for two days in the Shipka Pass on chocolate; while some years later, during the Boer war, Queen Victoria presented every soldier in the British army with a ration of chocolate—chocolate which Liebig pronounced the most perfect food in the world. The idea of an officer carrying an empty pistol! And yet Lord Wolseley mentions two officers who seldom carried any weapons, and one of them was Gordon. Bluntschli's hysterical condition in the first act finds its analogue in General Porter's account describing the condition of his troops after a battle. And Bluntschli's delightful description of a cavalry charge finds its analogue, not in the Tennysonian *Charge of the Light Brigade*, but in the account of this charge as given by the popular historian Kinglake; and, as a matter of fact, Shaw's description

---

* Compare the reminiscences on the Avenue Theatre production, by Mr. Yorke Stephens, who played the part of Bluntschli; *Music and the Drama,* in the *Daily Chronicle,* November 6th, 1906. It was at the *première* at the Avenue Theatre that Shaw, called before the audience, found himself disarmed by lack of opposition. A solitary malcontent in the gallery began to boo: Bernard was himself again. Looking up at the belligerent oppositionist, he said with an engaging smile: " My friend, I quite agree with you—but what are we two against so many? "

was taken almost verbatim from an account given privately to a friend of Shaw's by an officer who served in the Franco-Prussian war. The catalogue might easily be extended; suffice it to say that, *irrespective of the totality of impression,* there can be no question of the credibility of the separate incidents in the play, which furnished such ready targets for critical marksmanship.*

From the dramatic side, *Arms and the Man* is far less a " realistic " comedy than a satiric exposure of the illusions of warfare, of love, of romantic idealism. Of course, Shaw imparts an air of pleasing likelihood to the racial traits or characters, and the local colour of the scenes; and, as Dr. Brandes has remarked, in Bernard Shaw's choice of themes one feels the mental suppleness of the modern critic, with his ability to throw himself sympathetically into different historic periods and into the minds of different races. In *Arms and the Man,* " the whole environment is characteristic, the people of most refinement being proud of washing themselves ' almost every day,' and of owning a ' library,' the only one in the district. Everything smacks of the Balkan Peninsula, even to the waiting-maid and the man-servant, with their half-Asiatic mingling of forwardness and servility." † To be accurate, Shaw sketches in his *milieu* with the very lightest of strokes. Bluntschli might just

---

* Compare Shaw's brilliant article, *A Dramatic Realist to His Critics,* in the *New Review,* September, 1894, appearing two months after the close of the run of *Arms and the Man* at the Avenue Theatre. In *A Word about Stepniak,* in *To-Morrow,* February, 1896, Mr. Shaw says: " He (Stepniak) studiously encouraged me to think well of my own work, and went into the questions of Bulgarian manners and customs for me when I was preparing my play *Arms and the Man* for the stage as if the emancipation of Russia was a matter of comparatively little importance. . . . To him I owe the assistance I received from that Bulgarian admiral in whose existence the public, regarding Bulgaria as an inland State, positively declined to believe."

† *Der Dramatiker Bernard Shaw:* in *Gestalten und Gedanken,* by Georg Brandes, München-Langen, 1903. " Human nature is very much the same, always and everywhere," Shaw explained. " And when I go over my play to put the details right I find there is surprisingly little to alter. *Arms and the Man,* for example, was finished before I had decided where to set the scene, and then it only wanted a word here and there to put matters straight. You see, I know human nature "!

as well have served in a war between Peru and Chili, or Greece and Turkey; while for all practical purposes, the scene might just as well have been laid along the coasts of Bohemia. I have long contended that *Arms and the Man* was not a play, but a light opera; and now comes Oscar Straus to compose the music for the libretto adapted from Shaw's Bulgarian fantasy.

Mr. Shaw once told me that his two friends, Sidney Webb, the solid and the practical, and Cunninghame Graham, the hidalgesque and fantastic, suggested the contrast between Bluntschli and Saranoff. " The identity," he explained, " only lies on the surface, of course. But the true dramatist must always find his contrasts in real life." And it will be recalled that the rodomontade placed with such ludicrous effect in the mouth of the Bulgarian braggadocio, had actually been used, with equally telling effect, by Mr. Cunninghame Graham in a speech in the House of Commons. Shaw promptly stole the potent phrase, " I never withdraw," for the sake of its perfect style, and used it as a cockade for Sergius the Sublime. The great charm of the play consists in the disillusionment of the romantic Raina and the sham-idealist Saranoff by the practical realism of the common-sense Bluntschli. A Bulgarian Byron, Sergius is perpetually mocked by the disparity between his imaginative ideals and the disillusions which continually sting his sensitive nature. And the true tragedy of the idealist, in the Shavian frame of mind, is summed up in his words, " Damnation! mockery everywhere! Everything that I think is mocked by everything that I do." And Shaw himself has said:

" My Bulgarian hero, quite as much as Helmer in *A Doll's House*, was a hero shown from the modern woman's point of view. I complicated the psychology by making him catch glimpse after glimpse of his own aspect and conduct from this point of view himself, as all men are beginning to do more or less now, the result, of course, being the most horrible dubiety on his part as to whether he was really a brave and chivalrous gentleman, or a humbug and a moral coward. His actions, equally of course, were hopelessly irreconcilable with either theory. Need I add that if the straightforward Helmer, a very honest and ordinary middle-class man misled by false ideals of womanhood, bewildered the public and was finally set down as a selfish cad by all the Helmers in the audience, *a fortiori* my introspective Bulgarian never had a chance, and was dismissed, with but moderately spontaneous laughter, as a swaggering impostor of the species for which contemporary slang has invented the term ' bounder '? " *

Arms and the Man has laid its hold upon the modern imagination, and has been produced all over the world. What more delightful than to have seen Bluntschli interpreted by the actors of our generation—by Mansfield, with his quaintly dry cynicism, by Jarno, with a humour racy of the soil, by Mantzius, with scholarly accuracy, by Sommerstorff, with a touch of romance!—by Loraine, Nhil, Stephens, Daly. It is quite true that the play is loose in form, oscillating between comedy and fantastic farce, and that even now it is already beginning to " date." But its fantasy, its satire, and its genial philosophy will amply suffice to give it a long lease on life.† Shaw's own confidence in his power as a dramatist and in the future of the play is humorously expressed in characteristic style in the fol-

---

* From Shaw's preface to Mr. Archer's *The Theatrical World of 1894,* pp. xxvii-xxviii. In view of the interest manifested in *Arms and the Man* at the time of its first production in 1894, Mr. Archer requested Mr. Shaw to say something about it in this preface.

† *Arms and the Man* has, most appropriately, furnished the " book " for a comic opera, entitled *The Chocolate Soldier,* written by Bernauer and Jacobson, music by Oscar Straus, the popular composer. It was to be expected that there would be many " comic " attractions in the adaptation of Mr. Shaw's play. Of course, all the complications, such as the incident of the incriminating photograph, are multiplied by three: Nicola disappears and Louka makes way for Mascha, now the cousin of Raina. In the end all are happily mated. In consequence of the " comic variations " from the original play, Mr. Shaw insisted that the programme contain a frank apology for this " unauthorized parody of one of Mr. Bernard Shaw's comedies." First successfully produced at the Theater des Westens, Berlin, 1909, *The Chocolate Soldier,* both for the borrowed, if parodied, cleverness, and the delightful music, has since won great popularity through the productions of Mr. F. C. Whitney (English version by Mr. Stanislaus Stange), in New York (May, 1910) and London (September, 1910).

lowing letter written in response to an apologetic note from his American agent, Miss Elisabeth Marbury, accompanying a meagre remittance for royalties on *Arms and the Man:*

> " RAPACIOUS ELISABETH MARBURY,
>
> " What do you want me to make a fortune for? Don't you know that the draft you sent me will permit me to live and preach Socialism for six months? The next time you have so large an amount to remit, please send it to me by instalments, or you will put me to the inconvenience of having a bank account. What do you mean by giving me advice about writing a play with a view to the box-office receipts? I shall continue writing just as I do now for the next ten years. After that we can wallow in the gold poured at our feet by a dramatically regenerated public."

Arms and the Man is an injunction to found our institutions, in Shaw's little-understood phrase, not on " the ideals suggested to our imagination by our half-satisfied passions," but on a " genuinely scientific natural history."

A distinguished dramatic critic once said to me that he regarded all of Shaw's works as derivative literature. Shaw's first three plays were traced to Ibsen, to De Maupassant, to Strindberg; and won for him the flattering title of the " second-hand Brummagem Ibsen " (William Winter)! And after witnessing two acts of *Arms and the Man* at the Avenue Theatre, Mr. Archer began to have a misgiving that he had wandered by mistake into The Palace of Truth. The relation of the art of Bernard Shaw to the art of W. S. Gilbert is one of much delicate intricacy; and deserves more than casual mention. Shaw has declared that those who regard the function of a writer as " creative " are the most illiterate of dupes, that in his business he knows *me* and *te*, not *meum* and *tuum*, and that he himself is " a crow who has followed many plows." In a vein of mocking acknowledgment, Shaw once spoke of the seriousness with which he had pondered the jests of W. S. Gilbert. A careful critical examination of the methods of Shaw and Gilbert reveals the undoubted resemblance, as well as the fundamental dissimilarity, of these two satiric interpreters of human nature.*

One particular incident in *Arms and the Man* seems to derive directly from an incident in Gilbert's *Engaged*. The scene in which Nicola advises Louka, his betrothed, to gain a hold over Sergius, marry him ultimately, and so " come to be one of my grandest customers, instead of only being my wife and costing me money," is but a paraphrase and inversion of that ludicrous scene in *Engaged*, in which " puir little Maggie Macfarlane " advises her lover, Angus Macalister, to resign her to Cheviot-Hill for the princely consideration of two pounds. Aside from this one minor similarity, *Arms and the Man* is very different from a Gilbert play. For purposes of general comparison, turn once more to *Engaged*—which will serve as well as any of the works of Gilbert—for this passage:

> CHEVIOT-HILL (*suddenly seeing her*): Maggie, come here. Angus, do take your arm from around that girl's waist. Stand back, and don't you listen. Maggie, three months ago I told you I loved you passionately; to-day I tell you that I love you as passionately as ever; I may add that I am still a rich man. Can you oblige me with a postage-stamp?

Here, not only is the comic note struck by the juxtaposition of two essential incongruities: in addition, the farcicality of the idea stamps it as impossible. It is an admirable illustration of that exquisite sense of quaint unexpectedness, evoked by the

---

* Shaw has been charged with indebtedness, not only to W. S. Gilbert, but to earlier topsy-turvyists. In April, 1906, there appeared in the *New York Tribune* a " deadly parallel " between *Arms and the Man* and *Used Up*, adapted from the French by Charles Mathews in 1845. As a matter of fact, the passage cited—Bluntschli's proposal for the hand of Raina (compared with Sir Charles Coldstream's for the hand of Lady Clutterbuck)—is neither an imitation of Mathews, nor a triumph of eccentric invention, but a paraphrase, Shaw unqualifiedly asserts, of an actual proposal made by an Austrian hotel proprietor for the hand of a member of Mr. Shaw's own family.

plays of both Gilbert and Shaw. Take now a scene of somewhat cognate appeal in *Arms and the Man*. In both scenes the bid is for sudden laughter, through the startle of surprise. Bluntschli flatly tells Raina to her face that he finds it impossible to believe a single thing she says.

> RAINA (*gasping*): I! I!!! (*She points to herself incredulously, meaning, " I, Raina Petkoff, tell lies! " He meets her gaze unflinchingly. She suddenly sits down beside him, and adds, with a complete change of manner from the heroic to the familiar.*) How did you find me out?
>
> BLUNTSCHLI (*promptly*): Instinct, dear young lady. Instinct, and experience of the world.
>
> RAINA (*wonderingly*): Do you know, you are the first man I ever met who did not take me seriously?
>
> BLUNTSCHLI: You mean, don't you, that I am the first man that has ever taken you quite seriously?
>
> RAINA: Yes, I suppose I do mean that. (*Cosily, quite at her ease with him.*) How strange it is to be talked to in such a way! . . .

Gilbert employs a device of the simplest mechanism, giving merely the shock of unexpected contrast. Shaw's spiritual adventure is an excogitated bit of psychology, of intellectual content and rational crescendo. It is the Shavian trick of putting into dialogue the revealing, accusatory words seldom spoken in real life.

This calls to mind a resemblance—with a difference—between Shaw and Gilbert. In Gilbert's *The Palace of Truth* each character indulges in frank self-revelation. Enchanted by the spell of a certain locality, everyone is compelled to speak his whole thought without disguise, under the delusion that he is only indulging in the usual polite insincerities. All this self-analysis and self-exposure goes for naught but to evoke laughter; for, lacking either profound insight into human nature or cynical distrust of humanity, Gilbert is incapable of trenchant generalization. In Shaw's plays, people play the game of " Truth " for all there is in it; and perhaps Shaw's greatest capacity is the capacity for generalization. Shaw's incomparable superiority to Gilbert consists in his acute perception and subtle delineation of the comic, and often tragic, inconsistencies of genuine human character. Shaw has succeeded in revealing certain subconscious sides of human nature that usually remain hidden because dramatists fail to put into the mouths of their creations the real thoughts that clamour for expression. One almost always hears their superficial selves speaking solely through the voluble medium of society or the reticent medium of self.

Not only in philosophic grasp, but also in imagination, does Shaw excel Gilbert; an incident will suffice to explain. Mr. John Corbin once told me that in comparing Shaw and Gilbert, he had instanced to Mr. Henry Arthur Jones the play of *Pygmalion and Galatea*, as showing that, after all, Gilbert had a heart and an imagination for beauty. "Ah, yes!" replied Mr. Jones. "But Gilbert never could have written that line in *Cæsar and Cleopatra:*

> CÆSAR: What has Rome to show me that I have not seen already? One year of Rome is like another, except that I grow older, whilst the crowd in the Appian way is always the same age."

Philosophically speaking, Gilbert's characters accept without question the current ideals of life and conduct; and make ludicrous spectacles of themselves in the effort to live up to them. Shaw's creations discover the hollowness and vanity of these same current ideals, and gain freedom in escape from their obsession. As Mr. Walkley once put it: " Gilbertism consists in the ironic humour to be got out of the spectacle of a number of people hypocritically pretending, or naïvely failing, to act up to ideals which Mr. Gilbert and his people hold to be valid. . . . Shavianism consists in the ironic humour to be got out of the spectacle of a number of people trying to apply the current ideas only to find in the end that they won't work." * Let us

---

* *Mr. Bernard Shaw's Plays,* in *Frames of Mind* (Grant Richards, London, 1889), p. 47.

have done with rating of Shaw as a cheap imitator of Gilbert. It is quite true that Gilbert anticipated Shaw by many years in the use of the device of open confession—the characters naïvely " making a clean breast " of things; but the device was handed on to Shaw for legitimate use instead of for farcical misuse. In any deep sense, Shaw owes nothing to Gilbert; and his paradoxes, unlike Gilbert's, are the outcome of a profound study of human nature and of contemporary civilization. " Gilbert would have anticipated me," Mr. Shaw once assured me, " if he had taken his paradoxes seriously. But it does not seem to have occurred to him that he had found any real flaw in conventional morality—only that he had found out how to make logical quips at its expense. His serious plays are all conventional. Most of the revolutionary ideas have come up first as jests; and Gilbert did not get deeper than this stage."

Arms and the Man is the first of four plays which I class in a category by themselves—the plays constructed in the loose and variegated comedic form, presumably designed to be " popular " and to amuse the public, fantastically treated, and imbued with a mild philosophy held strictly implicit.* These four plays are *Arms and the Man, You Never Can Tell, How He Lied to Her Husband* and *Captain Brassbound's Conversion*. In *You Never Can Tell* Shaw deliberately made concessions to that coy monster, the British public. Thitherto he had in large measure disdained the task of complying with the demands of London audiences for a popular comedy, combining his oft-praised cynical brilliancy and his talent for " giving furiously to think," with his unquestioned ability to amuse. Shaw's realization of the truth of Molière's words: " *C'est une étrange entreprise que celle de faire rire les honnêtes gens,*" did not in the least deter him from embarking upon this perilous undertaking. In *You Never Can Tell* he gave himself up wholly to the hazardous task, tentatively inaugurated in *Arms and the Man*, of attempting to amuse that public which had so persistently refused, so defiantly scorned, his instruction. *You Never Can Tell* was Shaw's propitiatory sacrifice to recalcitrant

* By this method of treatment, chronology is of necessity sacrificed to logic.

London. Strange to say, this deliberate concession to popular demand even his most lenient censors refused to validate.* London, matching Shaw for whimsicality, was no whit propitiated by his proposal of a *mariage de convenance* with that doubtful character, public opinion. Shaw has taken Shakespeare himself to task for pandering to public taste in a play coolly entitled *As You Like It*. When the " Dramatist of Donnybrook Fair," as Mr. Corbin calls him, sets out to write *As You Like It*, what is the result? " You Never Can Tell!" It was nine years before Shaw was able to change his tentative and dubious, " You Never Can Tell!" into a triumphant, " I told you so!"

" I think it must have been in the year 1895," one reads in some reminiscences by Mr. Cyril Maude, the well-known English actor, " that the devil put it into the mind of a friend of mine to tempt me with news of a play called *Candida*, by a writer named Bernard Shaw, of whom until then I had never heard." †
Mr. Maude wrote to Shaw, suggesting that he be allowed to see the play in question. In characteristic vein, the author replied that the play would not suit the needs of the Haymarket Theatre, offering, however, to write a new play instead; which Mr. Maude protests he never asked Shaw to do, yet to which he interposed no objection. Whereupon Shaw took a chair in Regent's Park for the whole season, and sat there, in the public eye, we are told, writing the threatened play.

It was not until the winter of 1897 that this play, *You Never Can Tell*, came into Mr. Maude's hands. It was accepted, and actually put into rehearsal. From that very moment things began to go wrong. Shaw proposed impossible casts, dictated

---

* Preferring to see Shaw fail seriously rather than succeed farcically, Mr. Archer sternly admonished him to "quit his foolishness"; and Mr. Shaw's former champion of Independent Theatre days, Mr. J. T. Grein, gently but firmly advised him never again to send up any more such *ballons d'essai.*

† *The Haymarket Theatre* (Grant Richards, London, 1903). Chapter XIV. (from which the above and following quotations are taken), Mr. Maude says, " was sent to me as an aid to the completion of this work. It professes to deal with that period of our management when we rehearsed a piece by the brilliant Mr. Bernard Shaw. The writer, I am assured, is well fitted to deal with that period. I leave it to the reader to judge, and to guess its authorship." Needless to say that the author was Bernard Shaw himself!

to each actor in turn, equalled his own John Tanner in endless and torrential talk. Actor after actor, led by the genial Jack Barnes, withdrew in fatigue and disgust. One day Shaw insulted the entire cast and the entire profession by wanting a large table on the stage, on the ground that the company would fall over it unless they behaved as if they were coming into a real room instead of, as he coarsely observed, " rushing to the float to pick up the band at the beginning of a comic song."

After a first reading of the manuscript, Mr. Maude's misgivings had been aroused to such an extent that he went to Shaw and plainly told him that certain lines would have to be cut out.

" Oh, no! " replied Shaw. " I really can't permit that."

" But in this shape," protested the alarmed actor-manager, " the play can never be produced."

" My dear fellow, you delight me," was the truly Shavian reply.

It was unbearable to the cast to be lectured and grilled unmercifully by a red-headed Mephistopheles dressed like a " fairly respectable carpenter " in a suit of clothes that looked as though it had originally been made of brown wrapping paper. The rehearsals continued, however, with the entire cast in a state of the most profound dejection.

" The end came suddenly and unexpectedly. We had made a special effort to fulfil our unfortunate contract. . . . We were honestly anxious to retrieve the situation by a great effort, and save our dear little theatre from the disgrace of a failure.

" Suddenly the author entered, *in a new suit of clothes!!* " Nobody who had seen Shaw sitting there day after day in a costume which the least self-respecting plasterer would have discarded months before could possibly have understood the devastating effect of the new suit upon the minds of the spectators. " That this was a calculated *coup de théâtre* I have not the slightest doubt." Shaw played the part of benevolent rescuer, and the play was withdrawn. " I met him in Garrick Street not long ago and noticed that he still wore the suit which he had purchased in 1897 in anticipation of the royalties on *You Never Can Tell!* "

" The only thanks that people give me for not ' boring

them,'" Shaw once said, " is that they laugh delightedly for three hours at the play that has cost many months of hard labour, and then turn round and say that it is no play at all and accuse me of talking with my tongue in my cheek. And then they expect me to take them seriously!" No one can accuse Shaw of taking the world seriously in *You Never Can Tell*. Never was more playful play, more irresponsible fun. It is all a pure game of cross-purposes, a contest of intellectual motives, a conflict of ideas and sentiments.

This play is especially interesting to me because it was the first of Shaw's plays I saw produced, and led me to a study of his works. And yet I should be the last to deny that it is a farce, in which fun as a motive takes precedence over delineation of character. The characters are no more faithful to actuality than is the dialogue to ordinary conversation. Indeed, the play is almost a new *genre*, differing from the ordinary farce, in which action predominates over thought, in the respect that here thought, or rather vivacious mentalization, takes precedence over everything—the antics are psychical, not physical. Shaw maintains, not that the play is a comedy, but that it is cast in the ordinary practical comedy form. I take this to mean that Shaw has utilized the stock characters and devices of ordinary comedy—not to mention those of farce, burlesque and extravaganza!—purely for his own ends, giving them a fresh and unique interest by animating them with the infectious mirth of his own personality. At last Shaw has found that loose, variegated, kaleidoscopic comedic form which freely admits of the intrusive antics of the Shavian whimsicality.

There is not a single play of Shaw's that starts nowhere and never arrives; and here the fault is not that the play has no meaning, but that it has too many meanings. And it is perhaps just as well that there is no clear line of thought-filiation running through the play. It is quite possible, as Hervieu would say, to " disengage " one, or even several motives, interlinked with one another, from the play. Shaw, however, seems content to put everyone on the defensive, to search out the weak points in their armour, and to give to each in turn the *coup de grâce*.

The play is notable in two respects—for its treatment of the emotions and for the figure of William. Valentine is the imperfect prototype of John Tanner. His sole equipment is his tongue; instead of a conscience and a heart, he has only a brain. George Ade would have called him " Gabby Val, the conversational dentist." Gloria succumbs to the scientific wooing of the new " duellist of sex "; her armour of frigid reserve, the heritage of twentieth-century precepts, melts before the calculated warmth of Valentine's advances. After allowing her to belong to herself for years, Nature now seizes her and uses her for Nature's own large purposes. And Valentine, but now the triumphant victor in the duel of sex, realizes when it is too late that, after all, he is only the victimized captive. All comedies end with a wedding, because it is then that the tragedy begins! The real distinction of the play consists in Shaw's portrayal of his conception of love as it exhibits itself in the contemporary human being. As Mr. Walkley has put it, love, in Shaw's view, is not, as with Chamfort, the *échange de deux fantaisies*, but the *échange de deux explications*. With Shaw, the symbol of love is not a Cupid blindfold, but the alertest of Arguses. His intellectual reflection of the erotic illusion exhibits neither tender sentiment, emotive abandon, nor sexual passion. Shaw's lovers, as Mr. Desmond MacCarthy has pertinently put it, " instead of using the language of admiration and affection, in which this sexual passion is so often cloaked, simply convey by their words the kind of mental tumult they are in. Sexual infatuation is stripped bare of all the accessories of poetry and sympathy. It is represented as it is by itself, with its own peculiar romance, but with none of the feelings which may, and often do, accompany it." *

The one really admirable figure in the play is the immortal William. A master figure of classic, rather than modern, comedy, he suggests, with exquisite subtlety, the graceful unobtrusiveness that dignifies his calling. Whenever he loses sight of his menial position long enough to utter one of his kindly bits of philosophy, it is always to fade back again into the

* *The Court Theatre, 1904-1907,* by Desmond MacCarthy (A. H. Bullen, London, 1907), p. 57.

and laid the foundations of Shaw's—and Daly's—success in America.

On July 14th, 1905, in a booth in Regent's Park, London, for the benefit of the Actors' Orphanage, was " performed repeatedly, with colossal success," a " tragedy," entitled *Passion, Poison and Petrifaction; or The Fatal Gazogene*, written by Shaw at the request of Mr. Cyril Maude. It is an extravagant burlesque on popular melodrama, and the main incident of the " tragedy " is the petrifaction of the hero caused by swallowing a lot of lime as an antidote to the poison administered to him by the jealous husband of his *inamorata*, Lady Magnesia Fitztollemache. " The play has a funny little history," Mr. Shaw told me, " having its origin in a story I once made up for one of the Archer children. In the early days of William Archer's married life I was down there one night, and one of the children asked me to tell him a story. 'What about?' I asked. 'A story about a cat,' was the eager reply. It seems that at one time my aunt was interested in making little plaster-of-paris figures; and one day the cat came along, and, thinking it was milk, lapped up some of the moist plaster-of-paris. And so the sad result, as I told the Archer children, was that the poor cat petrified inside. 'And what did they do with the cat?' one of the children asked. 'Well, you see,' I replied, ' one of the doors of the house would never stay shut, so my mother kept the cat there ever afterwards to hold the door shut.' The funny part of it all was that Mrs. Archer said that she had caught me in a lie—and to her own children at that. To this day she never believes a single thing I say!"

" *Passion, Poison and Petrifaction* is, of course, the most utter nonsense," Shaw continued. " But, would you believe it,"— with a chuckle—" it was recently successfully produced in Vienna, and seriously praised as a characteristic play of the brilliant Irish dramatist and Socialist, Bernard Shaw!" *

Slightest of all three is *The Interlude at The Playhouse*,

---

* *Passion, Poison, and Petrifaction; or the Fatal Gazogene;* originally appeared in *Harry Furniss's Christmas Annual* for 1905 (Arthur Treherne and Co. Ltd., Adelphi, London), pp. 11-24, with illustrations by Mr. Harry Furniss.

written for Mr. and Mrs. Cyril Maude, and delivered by them at the opening of The Playhouse, Mr. Maude's new theatre, on Monday, January 28th, 1907.* The little piece extracts all the comedy to be got out of the embarrassment of an actor-manager over having to deliver a certain speech, and the solicitude of his wife in making an appeal to the audience on his behalf, but without his knowledge, for sympathy and encouragement. The genuine delicacy and lightness of touch with which the situation is handled, and the absence of Shavian intrusiveness, unite in making of the interlude a little gem, quite perfect of its kind.

The last of the comedies of character is *Captain Brassbound's Conversion*, classified by Shaw as one of the *Three Plays for Puritans*. This play might never have been written, but for the fact that Ellen Terry made no secret of the fact that she was born in 1848. When her son, Gordon Craig, became a father, Ellen Terry, according to Shaw, said that now no one wo... ver write plays for a grandmother! Shaw immediately wr... *Captain Brassbound's Conversion* to prove the contrary. And... even years later Ellen Terry portrayed Lady Cicely Way... te with a charm, a waywardness, and a grace that gave pleasure to thousands in England and America.

Just as, in *The Devil's Disciple*, Shaw reduces the melodramatic form to absurdity, so in *Captain Brassbound's Conversion* does he reduce to absurdity the melodramatic view of life. The scene of the play is an imaginary Morocco, a second-hand, fantastic image vicariously caught for Shaw by Mr. Cunninghame Graham. Not only did Shaw want to write a good part for Ellen Terry: he also wanted to write a good play. So he wrote a whimsical fantasy, half melodrama, half extravaganza, conditioned only by his own mildly philosophic bent and the need for developing Lady Cicely's character. The result, as he is fond of saying, is simply a story of conversion —a Christian tract!

The protagonist, the pirate Brassbound, orders his life upon

* The text of this dainty little interlude is to be found in the *Daily Mail*, January 29th, 1907. Mr. and Mrs. Maude were playing in *Toddles* at the time.

the principle that, as Bacon puts it, " revenge is a sort of wild justice." He is imbued with mediæval concepts of right and wrong. In opposition to him, he discovers his opposite—a cool, tactful, unsentimental woman of the world, disarming all opposition through her Tolstoyism. With sympathetic interest, she soon wins from Brassbound the secret of his life, and with quiet and delicious satire, opens his eyes to the pettiness of his mock-heroics, the absurdity of the melodramatic view-point—the code of the Kentucky feud, the Italian vendetta. The revulsion in Brassbound is instant and complete: he is wholly disarmed by the discovery that, instead of being the chosen instrument for the wild justice of lynch-law, he is only a ridiculous twopence coloured villain.

" My uncle was no worse than myself—better, most likely," is his final confession to Lady Cicely. " Well, I took him for a villain out of a story-book. My mother would have opened anybody else's eyes: she shut mine. I'm a stupider man than Brandyfaced Jack even; for he got his romantic nonsense out of his penny numbers and such-like trash; but I got just the same nonsense out of life and experience."

Lady Cicely Waynflete is the most charming woman that Shaw has ever drawn. Shaw has intimated that he found in the friendship of Ellen Terry, who served as the model for Lady Cicely, the " best return which could be expected from a gifted, brilliant and beautiful woman, whose love had already been given elsewhere, and whose heart had witnessed thousands of temptations." * In speaking of the character of Lady Cicely Waynflete, Miss Florence Farr once said: " As a sex, women must be

---

* The figure of Lady Cicely Waynflete possesses an unique interest in view of the fact conveyed in the following record of Ellen Terry's: " At this time (1897), Mr. Shaw and I frequently corresponded. It began by my writing to ask him, as musical critic of the *Saturday Review* (!), to tell me frankly what he thought of the chances of a composer-singer friend of mine. He answered ' characteristically,' and we developed a perfect fury for writing to each other. Sometimes the letters were on business, sometimes they were not, but always his were entertaining, and mine were, I suppose, ' good copy,' as he drew the character of Lady Cicely Waynflete in *Brassbound* entirely from my letters. He never met me until after the play was written." *From Lewis Carroll to Bernard Shaw*, in *McClure's Magazine*, September, 1908.

for ever grateful to Miss Ellen Terry for teaching Mr. Shaw
that lesson about woman." Nothing could be simpler or more
effective than the secret of command possessed by this charming woman. She knows that to go straight up to people, with
hand outstretched and a frank "How d'ye do?" is all that is
needed to win their confidence. The dastardly sheikh, into
whose hands she is about to be delivered, is stupefied and "almost
persuaded," when she assures her friends that he will treat her
like one of Nature's gentlemen: "Look at his perfectly splendid
face!" Combining as she does the temperament of Ellen Terry
with the genial *esprit* of Bernard Shaw, Lady Cicely is a thoroughly delightful and unique type of the eternal feminine. She
is just at the "age of charm," her actions are unhampered by
sentiment, and her chief attractions are frank *naïveté*, the trait
of attributing the best of qualities to other people, and an
innocent assumption of authority that quietly pinions all opposition. She always manages to do just what she likes because
she is bound by no ties to her fellow-creatures, save the bonds
of sympathy and innate human kindness. In one respect is
she a true Shavienne: toward law, convention, propriety,
prejudice, she takes an attitude of quaintly humorous scepticism. What a delicious touch is that when Sir Howard protests
that she has made him her accomplice in defeating justice!
"Yes," is her delightfully feminine reply: "aren't you glad
it's been defeated for once?"

The moral of this charming but very slight and superficially
fantastic play is that revenge is not wild justice, but childish
melodrama, and that the justice of the courts of law, enforced
by melodramatic sentences of punishment, is often little else
than a very base sort of organized revenge. The fable is rather
trivial; and the long arm of coincidence puts its finger into
the pie more than once, playing that part of timely interven-
tion at which Shaw is so fond of railing. The mixture of
Shavian satire with Tolstoyan principles is both novel and
piquant; and the mildly Ibsenic ending is a good "curtain"—
Brassbound discovering at last the secret of command, *i.e.*,
selflessness and disinterested sympathy, and Lady Cicely ec-

statically felicitating herself upon her escape from—the bonds of love and matrimony.

One other feature of the play is the hideous language of the cockney, Felix Drinkwater, *alias* Brandyfaced Jack. It takes quite an effort, even with the aid of the key which Shaw has considerately appended, to decipher the jargon of this unhappy hooligan, " a nime giv' us pore thortless lads baw a gint on the *Dily Chronicle*." In Drinkwater, Shaw sought to fix on paper the dialect of the London cockney, and he once told me that he regarded this as the only accurate effort of the kind in modern fiction. Interested in the study of phonetics through his acquaintance and friendship with that " revolutionary don " and academic authority, Henry Sweet of Oxford, Shaw put his knowledge to work to represent phonetically the lingo of the Board-School-educated cockney. " All that the conventional spelling has done," Shaw once said in one of his numerous journalistic controversies, " is to conceal the one change that a phonetic spelling might have checked; namely, the changes in pronunciation, including the waves of debasement that produced the half-rural cockney of Sam Weller, and the modern metropolitan cockney of Drinkwater in *Captain Brassbound's Conversion*. . . . Refuse to teach the Board School legions your pronunciation, and they will force theirs on you by mere force of numbers. And serve you right!"

THE PLAYWRIGHT—II

"I have, I think, always been a Puritan in my attitude towards Art. I am as fond of fine music and handsome buildings as Milton was, or Cromwell, or Bunyan; but if I found that they were becoming the instruments of a systematic idolatry of sensuousness, I would hold it good statesmanship to blow every cathedral in the world to pieces with dynamite, organ and all, without the least heed to the screams of the art critics and cultured voluptuaries."—*Why for Puritans?* Preface to *Three Plays for Puritans,* p. xix.

"I do not satirize types. I draw individuals as they are. When I describe a tub, Archer and Walkley say it is a satire on a tub."—Conversation with the author.

CHAPTER XI

CÆSAR AND CLEOPATRA, unique in Bernard Shaw's theatre, alike in subject matter and *genre*, warrants individual consideration. To an interviewer, on April 30th, 1898, Shaw related that he was just in the middle of the first act of a new play, in which he was going " to give Shakespeare a lead." Unlike Oscar Wilde, who once said that the writing of plays for a particular actor or actress was work for the artisan in literature, not for the artist, Shaw freely confessed that he wrote *Cæsar and Cleopatra* for Forbes Robertson, " because he is the classic actor of our day, and had a right to require such a service from me." * Asked if he had not been reading up " Mommsen and people like that," Shaw replied, " Not a bit of it. History is only a dramatization of events. And if I start telling lies about Cæsar, it's a hundred to one that they will be just the same lies that other people have told about him. . . . Given Cæsar and a certain set of circumstances, I know what would happen, and when I have finished the play you will find I have written history." †

In an opening scene of rare beauty and mystery, Cæsar discovers the child-truant Cleopatra reclining between the paws of her " baby-sphinx." What possibilities, what previsions are packed in this prophetic hour, which witnesses the meeting of these two supreme representatives of two alien worlds, two diverse civilizations! From the sublime we are hurled down to the ridiculous. Cæsar, dreamer and world-conquerer, apos-

---

* *Bernard Shaw and the Heroic Actor,* in *The Play,* No. 62, Vol. X. In this same article Shaw says: " No man writes a play without any reference to the possibility of a performance: you may scorn the limitations of the theatre as much as you please; but for all that you do not write parts for six-legged actors or two-headed heroines, though there is great scope for drama in such conceptions."

† *Mr. Shaw's Future: A Conversation,* in the *Academy,* April 30th, 1898. This interview is signed " C. R."—presumably Clarence Rook.

trophizing the sphinx in the immemorial moonlight of Egypt, is suddenly feazed out of countenance by a childish voice: " Old gentleman!—don't run away, old gentleman." It is the voice of Shaw to his public: " I may take unpardonable liberties with you; but—don't run away."

In the main, Shaw follows, as far as time, place and historical events go, such facts of history as are to be found in Plutarch and in *De Bello Gallico;* in every other respect the play is modern, colloquially modern, in tone and in spirit. Shaw approaches his theme under the domination of an *idée fixe:* scorn of tradition and of the science of history. The notion that there has been any progress since the time of Cæsar is absurd! Increased command over Nature by no means connotes increased command over self; if there has been any evolution, it has been in our conceptions of the meaning of greatness. When Shaw wrote his celebrated preface *Better than Shakespeare?* he had a very definite claim to make; that his Cæsar and Cleopatra are more credible, more natural, to a modern audience, than are the imaginative projections of a Shakespeare. Shaw maintains that, in manner and art, nobody can write better than Shakespeare, " because, carelessness apart, he did the thing as well as it can be done within the limits of human faculty." But Shaw did profess to have something to say by this time that Shakespeare neither said nor dreamed of. " Allow me to set forth Cæsar in the same modern light," pleads Shaw, in speaking of the hero-restorations of Carlyle and Mommsen, " taking the same liberty with Shakespeare as he with Homer, and with no thought of pretending to express the Mommsenite view of Cæsar any better than Shakespeare expressed a view that was not even Plutarchian. . . ." * " Shakespeare's Cæsar is the *reductio ad absurdum* of the real Julius Cæsar," Mr. Shaw once remarked to me; " my Cæsar is a simple return to nature and history."

Are there many cases in dramatic psychology, asked M. Filon, as interesting as the *liaison* which would have had " Cæsarion " as result? But in *Cæsar and Cleopatra,* there is no battle of

---

* *Better than Shakespeare?* Preface to *Three Plays for Puritans.*

IN CONSULTATION

From the original monochrome, made at 10, Adelphi Terrace, London, W.C.,
August, 1907.

[*Facing p.* 332

love, no dramatic conflict. Shaw might have produced a drama of the nations, in which the cunning intrigues of Egypt are matched against the forthrightness and efficiency of the Romans; or a drama of passion, charged to the full with poetic imagination. But he has availed himself neither of the historic sense, in which he appears to be deficient, nor of the romantic violence of poetic imagination, against which he rages with puritanical fervour. Shaw calls the play a "history"; certainly it is not a "drama" in the technical sense.* And yet, despite the numerous *longueurs* of the play, the pyrotechnic flashes of wit which only barely suffice to conceal the fact that the action is marking time, the exciting incidents which separately give a semblance of activity to the piece, there is a genuine thread of motive connecting scene with scene.

Cæsar and Cleopatra is, from one point of view, a study in the evolution of character; and this play, and *Major Barbara,* are the only exceptions to Shaw's theatre of static character. The psychological action of the piece consists in the evolution, under the guiding hand of Cæsar, of the little Egyptian sensualist, in the period of plastic adolescence. Cæsar has the weak fondness of an indulgent uncle for the adolescent Cleopatra, with her strange admixture of childish *mauvaise honte* and regal covetousness. Realizing with the instinct of a king-maker Cleopatra's dangerous possibilities as a ruler, Cæsar exercises upon her the plastic and determinative force of an architect of states. Slowly the little Cleopatra learns her lesson, glories in her newly-won power, tyrannizes inhumanly over all about her, and eventually—with well-nigh disastrous effects to herself—endeavours to teach her teacher the true secret of dominion.

From another point of view, this play is the portrait of a hero in the light of Shavian psychology—a hero in undress

---

* In Berlin the play was given in its entirety at the Neues Theater; in London, at the Savoy Theatre, it proved quite feasible to give the play omitting the entire third act. And yet the third act, according to M. Jean Blum (*Revue Germanique,* November-December, 1906), contains the dramatic climax! Compare also, *Dramatische Rundschau,* by Friedrich Düsel, *Westermann's Monatshefte,* June, 1906.

costume, in his dressing-gown as he lived, with all his trivial vanities and endearing weaknesses. The halo of the "pathos of distance," surrounding the head of the demi-god, wholly fades away; and there stands before us a real man, shorn of the romantic, the histrionic, the chivalric, it is true, but a real man, every inch of him, for all that. Shaw clearly draws the distinction:

"Our conception of heroism has changed of late years. The stage hero of the palmy days is a pricked bubble. The gentlemanly hero, of whom Tennyson's King Arthur was the type, suddenly found himself out as Torvald Helmer in Ibsen's *Doll's House*, and died of the shock. It is no use now going on with heroes who are no longer really heroic to us. Besides, we want credible heroes. The old demand for the incredible, the impossible, the super-human, which was supplied by bombast, inflation, and the piling of crimes on catastrophes and factitious raptures on artificial agonies, has fallen off; and the demand now is for heroes in whom we can recognize our own humanity, and who, instead of walking, talking, eating, drinking, making love and fighting single combats in a monotonous ecstasy of continuous heroism, are heroic in the true human fashion: that is, touching the summits only at rare moments, and finding the proper level of all occasions, condescending with humour and good sense to the prosaic ones as well as rising to the noble ones, instead of ridiculously persisting in rising to them all on the principle that a hero must always soar, in season or out of season." *

Mr. Forbes Robertson recently said that he regarded *Cæsar and Cleopatra* as a "great play," representing very truly what one would imagine Cæsar said, thought and felt. "Possibly the play is before its time—some people have said such curious things about it. There are scenes of wonderful brilliancy and beauty, and I myself see nothing farcical about the play, as

---

* *Bernard Shaw and the Heroic Actor*, in *The Play*, No. 62, Vol. X.

some people seem to suggest. I see a great wit and humour; and, as Mr. Shaw points out, by what right are we to presuppose that Cæsar had no sense of humour? He meets this amusing little impudent girl, and is very much amused with her, and interested in her, quite naturally as a human being. Why should one expect him to go strutting about, with one arm in his toga and the other extended, spouting dull blank verse?" Indeed, Shaw's Cæsar is a remarkable personality—in practice a man of business sagacity; in politics, a dreamer; in action, brilliant and resourceful; in private, a trifle vain and rhetorical—boyish, exuberant, humorous. When Pothinus expresses amazement that the conqueror of the world has time to busy himself with taxes, Cæsar affably replies: "My friend, taxes are the chief business of a conqueror of the world."

Like Mirabeau, he had no memory for insults and affronts received, and "could not forgive, for the sole reason that— he forgot." He answers to Nietzsche's *differentia:* "Not to be able to take seriously for a long time, an enemy, or a misfortune, or even one's own misdeeds—is the characteristic of strong and full natures, abundantly endowed with plastic, formative, restorative, also obliterative force." Cæsar's policy of clemency is constantly thwarted by the murderous passions of his soldiers; the murder of Pompey he contemns as a stroke of unpardonable treachery and revenge, the removal of Vercingetorix very much as Talleyrand regarded the execution of the Duc d'Enghien: it was worse than a crime, it was a blunder. Sufficient unto himself, strong enough to dispense with happiness, Cæsar is—to use a phrase of Mr. Desmond MacCarthy's— "content in the place of happiness with a kind of triumphant gaiety, springing from a sense of his own fortitude and power." Cæsar is a thoroughly good fellow, prosaically, patho-comically looking approaching old age in the face and wearing his conqueror's wreath of oak leaves—to conceal his growing bald spot. Were Rome a true republic, Cæsar would be the first of republicans; he values the life of every Roman in his army as he values his own, and makes friends with everyone as he does with dogs and children. "Cæsar is an important public man," as Mr. Max Beerbohm puts it, "who knows that a little chit of a girl-queen has taken a fancy to him, and is tickled by the knowledge and behaves very kindly to her, and rather wishes he were young enough to love her." But when he is again recalled to Rome, Cleopatra concerns him no more. Cæsar is the Shavian type of the naturally great man—great, not because he mortifies his nature in fulfilment of duty, but because he fulfils his own will." *

Cæsar and Cleopatra, to employ a phrase of the elder Coquelin, is a " combination of the most absolute fantasy with the most absolute truth." One feels at times that it belongs in the category of *Orphée aux Enfers* and *La Belle Hélène,* and only needs the music of Offenbach to round it out. Shaw shatters the illusion of antiquity with a multitude of the stock phrases of contemporary history: " Peace with honour," " Egypt for the Egyptians," " Art for Art's sake," etc., etc.† True to Shakespearean practice, Shaw revels in anachronisms, and goes so far as to assert that this is the only way to make the historic past take form and life before our eyes. If Shakespeare makes a clock strike in ancient Rome, Shaw shows a steam engine at

* Cf. *Genealogy of Morals* (Translated by William A. Hausemann, the Macmillan Co.), where Nietzsche points out that in the case of " noble men," prudence is far less essential than the " perfect reliableness of function of the regulating, *unconscious* instincts or even a certain imprudence, such as readiness to encounter things—whether danger or an enemy, or that eccentric suddenness of anger, love, reverence, gratitude and revenge by which noble souls at all times have recognized themselves as such."

† *Cæsar and Cleopatra,* in respect to its revolt against the dogmas of classical antiquity, against the accepted conventions in the reconstitution of past epochs, has been classed by Herr Heinrich Stümcke with the *Cäsar in Alexandria* of Mora and Thoele's *Heidnischen Geschichten.* In a skit, *Cäsar (ohne Cleopatra),* by the German dramatic critic, Alfred Kerr, and dedicated " an Bernard Shaw mit freundlichen Grüssen," this feature is wittily satirized, in these two verses:

" Könnt ich den Zweck des Blödsinns ahnen!
Ich führte manchen schweren Streich,
Bezwang mit Mühe die Germanen—
Trotzdem kommt Sedan und das Reich.

" Ein Zauberer, ihr grossen Götter,
Ist jener nordische Poet;
Herr Arnold Rubek bleibt mein Vetter:
Dich, Leben! Leben! spur ich spät. . . ."

work in Alexandria in 48 B.C.! If Shakespeare puts a billiard table in Cleopatra's palace, Shaw alludes to the ancient superstition of table-rapping in the year 707 of the Republic! Shaw gives free play to his abounding humour, having long since learned that nothing can be accomplished by solemnity. "Whenever I feel in writing a play," he frankly confesses, " that my great command of the sublime threatens to induce solemnity of mind in my audience, I at once introduce a joke and knock the solemn people from their perch." The eighteenth-century Irishman, with his contempt for John Bull, peeps out here and there; and when Cleopatra asks Britannus, Cæsar's young secretary from Britain, if it were true that he was painted all over blue, when Cæsar captured him, Britannus proudly replies: " Blue is the colour worn by all Britons of good standing. In war we stain our bodies blue; so that though our enemies may strip us of our clothes and our lives, they cannot strip us of our respectability."

In *Cæsar and Cleopatra* Shaw has created something more or less than drama—a tremendous fantasy surcharged and interpenetrated with deep imaginative reality. In certain plays of which I shall now speak, Shaw shows that he can play the dramatist, pure and simple, and write with a concentration of energy, a compression of emotive intensity, that seem very foreign to the prolixity and discursiveness of his later manner. The stern artistic discipline to which he nearly succeeded in schooling himself in *Mrs. Warren's Profession,* once more exhibits itself in *The Man of Destiny, Candida* and *The Devil's Disciple.* The essential fact that these plays have proved popular *stage* successes in the capitals of the world—New York, London, Berlin, Vienna, Dresden, St. Petersburg, Buda-Pesth, Brussels, etc.—is in itself testimony to the fact that—always allowing for the refraction of the Shavian temperament—Bernard Shaw is a true dramatist, capable of touching the deeper emotions and appealing to universal sentiments.

In speaking of his earliest works, Shaw airily refers to those " vain brilliancies given off in the days of my health and strength." Perhaps something of their diffuseness, and the lack of concentrative thought evident in their construction, are explained, not alone by reference to Shaw's *intransigéance*, but in part by the conditions under which they were written. A bit of reminiscence voiced by the great English comedian, Sir Charles Wyndham, is illuminating:

"I shall never forget the first time Shaw called to see me. In those days he would not have a bit of linen about him. He wore soft shirts and long, flowing ties, which, with his tawny hair and long, red beard, gave him the appearance of a veritable Viking. Well, he came in and sat down at the table. Then he put his hand into his right trousers pocket and slowly drew out a small pocket memorandum-book; then he dug into the left side-pocket and fished out another of the little books, then still another and another. Finally, he paused in his explorations, looked at me and said:

"'I suppose you're surprised to see all these little pocket-books. The fact is, however, I write my plays in them while riding around London on top of a 'bus.'" *

The How and Where of the composition of such plays might well account for much inconsequence and aerial giddiness!

The Man of Destiny has an origin not a little unique. Many plays are written for some one great actor or actress—few are written for two. And yet, according to Shaw's own confessions, *The Man of Destiny* was written for Richard Mansfield and Ellen Terry—Mansfield serving as the model for Napoleon, Terry as the model for the Lady. At this time, Shaw had seen Mansfield only in *Dr. Jekyll and Mr. Hyde* and *Richard III.*; and once in 1894 had chatted with him for an hour at the Langham. The impression he received was so strong, the suggestion of Napoleon so striking, that he resolved to write a play about Napoleon based on a study of Mansfield.†

* The *New York Times*, November 20th, 1904.

† "Mansfield was always especially sympathetic with the character of Napoleon, and, indeed—however extravagant the statement may seem at first glance—his personality comprised some of the attributes of that character—stalwart courage, vaulting ambition, inflexible will, resolute self-

In a letter to Mansfield (September 8th, 1897), Shaw says: "I was much hurt by your contemptuous refusal of *A Man of Destiny*, not because I think it one of my masterpieces, but because Napoleon is nobody else but Richard Mansfield himself. I studied the character from you, and then read up Napoleon and found that I had got him exactly right." * Shaw frequently corresponded with Ellen Terry during the days he was writing *The Man of Destiny;* he saw her numberless times on the stage, but had never actually met her when he wrote *The Man of Destiny*. Shaw escaped the " illusion " of the Lyceum, created by " Irving's incomparable dignity and Terry's incomparable beauty "—simply because " I was a dramatist and needed Ellen Terry for my own plays. . . . I had tried to win her when I wrote *The Man of Destiny*, in which the heroine is simply a delineation of Ellen Terry—imperfect, it is true, for who can describe the indescribable! " †

The Man of Destiny, Shaw, in fact, confesses, was written chiefly to exhibit the virtuosity of the two principal characters; and it must be confessed that their virtuosity is so pervasively dazzling as occasionally to distract attention from the dramatic procedure. The unnamed possibilities of the situation have been exploited in the subtlest fashion. This little " fragment " is a dramatic *tour de force;* the rapid shifting of victory from one side to the other, the excitingly unstable equilibrium of the balance of power, the fierce war of wills are of the very essence of true drama. The serious underlying issue, the struggle of Napoleon for a triumph that spells personal dishonour, is a dramatic motive sanctioned by that great classic example, the *Œdipus Rex*. Unlike Sophocles, whose listeners knew in advance the story of the ill-fated king, Shaw withholds from the spectator any foreknowledge of the outcome; but the grow-

confidence, great capacity for labour, iron endurance, promptitude of decision, propensity for large schemes, and passionate taste for profusion of opulent surroundings."—William Winter's *Life and Art of Richard Mansfield*, Vol. I., pp. 222-223; Moffat, Yard and Co., New York, 1910.

* *Richard Mansfield: The Man and the Actor,* by Paul Wilstach, p. 264; Charles Scribner's Sons, New York, 1909.

† *Ellen Terry*, by Bernard Shaw. *Neue Freie Presse,* January, 1906; English translation, *Boston Transcript,* January 20th, 1906.

ing curiosity of Napoleon, instantaneously inducing like inquisitiveness on the part of the spectator, is one of the chief factors of interest in the play. Early in the development of the action, the purpose of the letter is readily guessed by anyone familiar with such Napoleonic history as is recorded, for example, in the *Memoirs of Barras*.*

As Shaw's Cæsar is his interpretation of the great man of ancient history, so Napoleon is his interpretation of the great man of modern history. Shaw's Napoleon is a strange mixture of noble and ignoble impulses. He is strangely imaginative—a dreamer in the great sense, with a touch of the superstition of a Wallenstein, a great faith in his star. A ravenous beast at table, he feverishly gorges his food, while his hair sweeps into the ink and the gravy; his absolute obliviousness to surroundings is the mask of tremendous energy of purpose. Gravy answers the purpose of ink, a grape hull marks a strategic point on the map: the mark, not the material, is Napoleon's concern. And it is the *imprévu* of his decisions that so often puts his adversaries to rout. M. Filon protests against Shaw's portrait of Napoleon as a mere repetition of the caricatures of Gillray and the calumniating distortions of the historian Seeley; but Shaw's Napoleon is, in great measure, not the Napoleon of the glorified Bonapartist chromo, but the Napoleon post-figured by his later career. Le Petit Caporal is the ancestor of the Emperor Napoleon I.; and in this early phase, Napoleon may be best described in the sneering characterization of the Lady as " the vile, vulgar Corsican adventurer." Says Mr. John Corbin: " The final sensation of the character is of vast unquenchable energy and intelligence, at once brutally real and sublimely

* On account of the vagueness of the story in certain details, Mr. John Corbin has taken Shaw to task for not stating " who the Lady is and why she was so heroically bent on rescuing Napoleon from himself." It suffices to know that she is Josephine's emissary, sent to intercept the incriminating letter. Her duel with Napoleon is a heroic effort, not to " rescue Napoleon from himself," but, by playing upon his boundless ambition, to prevent him from discovering the extent of Josephine's perfidy, and to rescue Josephine from the consequences of her indiscretion. That the Lady in the end proves faithless to her trust merely transposes the key from tragedy to comedy; and the dramatic excellence of the play is no whit impaired by this characteristically Shawesque conclusion.

theatrical. And is not this the great Napoleon? By virtue of this mingling of seemingly opposed but inherently true qualities this Man of Destiny, for all the impertinences and audacities of Mr. Shaw's pyrotechnics, may be reckoned the best presentation of Napoleon thus far achieved in the drama, as it is certainly by far the most delightful." I asked Mlle. Yvette Guilbert one day if she thought *The Man of Destiny* would succeed in Paris. " I rather fear not," she replied. " Shaw's portrait is too true to the original to suit the French! " *

Towards the close of *The Man of Destiny*, Napoleon, taking for his text the famous phrase: " The English are a nation of shop-keepers," launches forth into a perfect torrent of irrelevant histrionic pyrotechnics. " Let me explain the English to you," he says, and in Shaw's most Maxim-gun style, proceeds to summarize the history of England in the nineteenth century, in a half-critical, half-prophetic philippic, beginning with discussion of the views of the Manchester School, of British industrial and colonial policy, and of Imperialism, and concluding with allusions to Wellington and Waterloo! In reading the play, this passage appears to be a gross irrelevancy and an absurd anachronism; but on the stage the speech appears to be quite in character with Shaw's Napoleon. Still, this passage calls attention to Shaw's most obvious and most deliberately committed fault: self-projection through the medium of his characters. Shaw identifies himself with his work as possibly no other dramatist before him has ever done. I rejoice in Shaw as M. Filon rejoices in Dumas *fils;* selfless reserve, abdication of personality, are as impossible for Shaw as for Dumas *fils*, and I freely confess that what I enjoy most in Shaw's plays is— Shaw.

Sir Charles Wyndham was once asked his opinion of the plays of Bernard Shaw. " Shaw's works are wonderful intellectual studies, but," he replied firmly, " they are not plays! " And he continued: " At one time I saw a great deal of Shaw and

---

* I believe that Shaw's Napoleon has never been adequately interpreted save possibly by Max Reinhardt in Berlin. The impersonation I saw at the Court Theatre, London, in June, 1907, was an egregious failure.

had great hopes of him as a dramatist. But he wouldn't come down to earth, he wouldn't be practical. When he had just completed *Candida* he came and read it to me. I told him it was 'twenty years too soon for England.' Well, he put it on at a special *matinée,* and it was much applauded. Then Shaw went out and addressed the audience. 'I read the play to Wyndham,' he said in his speech, 'and he told me it was twenty years too soon. You have given the contradiction to that statement.'" *Candida* has been played on some of the greatest stages of Europe, as well as all over England and America, and leading critics have praised it as one of the most remarkable plays of this generation.*

Candida is an acute psychological observation upon the emotional reverberations in the souls of three clearly imagined, exquisitely realized characters; its connection with pre-Raphaelitism, as Mr. Shaw confessed to me, is purely superficial and extrinsic. Aside from its association with a certain stage in Shaw's own development, the character of Marchbanks might just as well have been linked with the name of Shelley,† or with

* Mr. W. K. Tarpey, who called *Candida* "one of the masterpieces of the world," relates that some time at the end of 1894, or beginning of 1895, Shaw fell into a calm slumber; in a vision an angel carrying a roll of manuscript appeared unto him. To Shaw, who was no whit abashed, the angel thus spoke: "Look here, Shaw! wouldn't it be rather a good idea if you were to produce a work of absolute genius?" Shaw granted that the idea was not half a bad one, although he did not see how it could be carried out. Then the angel resolved his doubts: "I've got a good play here, that is to say, good for one of us angels to have written. We want it produced in London. The author does not wish to have his name known." "Oh!" replied Shaw, "I'll father it with pleasure; it is not up to my form, but I don't care much for my reputation." Shaw undertook the business side of the matter, put in the comic relief, and named the play *Candida: a Mystery!*

† Mr. Arnold Daly was in the habit of opening the third act of *Candida* by reading the familiar verses of Shelley to an unnamed love:

> "One word is too oft profaned
>   For me to profane it;
> One feeling too falsely disclaimed
>   For thee to disclaim it.
> One hope is too like despair
>   For prudence to smother,
> And pity from thee more dear
>   Than that from another.

the Celtic Renascence of to-day; but the whole atmosphere of the play makes it inconceivable at any time in the world's history save in the age of Ibsen. It bears marked resemblances to *The Comedy of Love* and *The Lady from the Sea*. *Candida* portrays the conflict between prose convention and poetic anarchy, concretely mirroring that conflict of human wills which Brunetière announced as the criterion of authentic drama. " Unity, however desirable in political agitations," Shaw once wrote, in reference to this play, " is fatal to drama, since every drama must be the artistic presentation of a conflict. The end may be reconciliation or destruction, or, as in life itself, there may be no end; but the conflict is indispensable: no conflict, no drama."

In striking contrast to many of Shaw's plays which are marked by a hyper-natural, almost blatant psychology, *Candida* reveals in Shaw a mastery of what may be termed profound psychological secrecy. " This is the play in which Bernard Shaw has tried to dig deepest, and has used his material with the greatest economy," wrote Dr. Brandes, in 1902. " The quietude of the action, which works itself out purely in dialogue, is here akin to Ibsen's quietude. . . . There is great depth of thought in this play, and a knowledge of the human soul which penetrates far below the surface." A domestic drama—little more than a " scene from private life "—*Candida* is the latest form of Diderot's invention, the *bourgeois* drama. Abounding in scenes and situations tense with emotional and dramatic power, it is stamped with the finish and restraint of great art. The characters in this play, so chameleon-like in its changing lustres, at every instant turn toward the light new facets of their natures. We catch the iridescent and ever-varying tints of life; and over all is a sparkle of fine and subtle humour, lightening the tension of soul-conflicts with touches of homely veracity.

> " I can give not what men call love,
>   But wilt thou accept not
> The worship the heart lifts above
>   And the heavens reject not,
> The desire of the moth for the star,
>   Of the night for the morrow,
> The devotion to something afar
>   From the sphere of our sorrow? "

The " auction scene " of the third act is transcendentally real, making an almost imperceptible transition from verisimilitude to fantasy.* Indulging his penchant for dialectic, Shaw here turns advocate, and argues the case with all the surety of the lawyer, the art of the *littérateur.* Men and women do not guide their actions in accordance with the dictates of pure reason; as Alceste says to Philinte in *Le Misanthrope:*

> " 'Tis true my reason tells me so each day;
> Yet reason's not the power to govern love."

And, after all, the auction scene is merely the *scène à faire,* leaving the situation absolutely unchanged. As Shaw himself once confessed: " It is an interesting sample of the way in which a scene, which should be conceived and written only by transcending the ordinary notion of the relations between the persons, nevertheless stirs the ordinary emotions to a very high degree, all the more because the language of the poet, to those who have not the clue to it, is mysterious and bewildering, and, therefore, worshipful. I divined it myself before I found out the whole truth about it."

Candida well justifies its sub-title of a *Mystery* in the number of astounding interpretations given it by the critics. In France it was regarded as a new solution of the Feminist problem. Candida remains as the free companion of a weak man, we are told by certain foreign critics, because " she understands that she has a duty to fulfil to her big baby of a husband, who could no longer succeed in playing his *rôle* in society without the firm hand which sustains and guides him." M. Maurice Muret, who

---

* In a notable *conférence* on *Candida* at the Théâtre des Arts, in Paris, preceding a production of that play, during the latter part of May, 1908, Mme. Georgette Le Blanc-Maeterlinck said: " La situation du mari n'est pas neuve, mais elle se présente ordinairement au troisième acte, et elle est toujours tranchée sans que la conscience intervienne, elle est tranchée par la jalousie, par la douleur et la mort. Ici, nous avons affaire à des intelligences meilleures, à des êtres qui essayent de se conduire d'après leur raison et leur volonté la plus haute. . . . C'est leur effort de sagesse qui les rend absolument illogiques, les soustrait à l'analyse et les rend presque inadmissibles à la lecture; mais c'est parce qu'ils sont illogiques, comme nous tous, qu'ils sont si vivants, si curieux en scène."—*Le Figaro,* May 30th, 1908; also *L'Art Moderne,* September 20th and 27th, 1908.

THEATRE DES ARTS

(THÉATRE DES BATIGNOLLES)

78, Boulevard des Batignolles, 78

METRO : VILLIERS-ROME

Tous les Soirs, à 9 heures

CANDIDA

Pièce en 3 actes, de Bernard SHAW

Version française d'Augustin et Henriette HAMON

VERA SERGINE

DIMANCHES ET FÊTES

MATINEE A 2 HEURES

Tous les Soirs à 9 heures

CLAPIN, Alençon-Paris — Imprimerie spéciale pour Publicités théatrales et Tournées artistiques

PLAYBILL OF *Candida*.

Théâtre des Arts, Paris. Director: Robert d'Humières. May 7th, 8th, 9th, 1908. Twenty-five subsequent performances. Shaw's only play to be produced in France to date.

wrote me that he was induced to read *Candida* by laudatory
articles in the German Press after Agnes Sorma's production
in Berlin, has thus betrayed his comic misunderstanding:
" From the mass of *femmes revoltées* who encumber the contemporary drama, the personage of Candida stands out with
happy distinction. Feminist literature has produced nothing
comparable to this exquisite figure. A tardy, but brilliant revenge of the *traditional* ideal upon the new ideal, is this victory
of *la femme selon Titien* over the Scandinavian virago, this triumph of Candida over Nora "!* And one of the most eminent
of German dramatic critics, after Lili Petri's production in
Vienna, said in an open letter to Shaw: " It is not virtue; not
prosaically *bourgeois*, nor vaguely romantic, feeling; nor even
the strength of this Morell, but simply his weakness, which
chains Candida to his side: because he needs her, the woman
loves him more than the young poet, who may perhaps recover
from his disappointment and learn to live without her. Shaw,
Bernard, Irishman! I abjure thee! "

Not only with such interpretations, but even with Shaw's own
dissection of his greatest play, I find it quite impossible to sympathize or to agree. Shaw seems merely to be taking a fling at
the " Candidamaniacs," as he called the play's admirers; his
" analysis " strikes me as a batch of Shavian half-truths, rather
than a fair estimate of the play's true significance. In answer
to Mr. Huneker's question *à propos* of Candida's famous
" shawl " speech, Shaw wrote:

" Don't ask me conundrums about that very immoral
female Candida. Observe the entry of W. Burgess: ' You're
the lady as hused to typewrite for him? ' ' No.' ' Naaow:
she was younger? ' And therefore Candida sacked her.
Prossy is a very highly selected young person indeed, devoted to Morell to the extent of helping in the kitchen, but
to him the merest pet rabbit, unable to get the slightest
hold on him. Candida is as unscrupulous as Siegfried:

* *De Nora à Candida*, by Maurice Muret; *Journal des Débats*, No. 544,
June 24th, 1904, pp. 1216-1218.

Morell himself sees that ' no law will bind her.' She seduces Eugene just exactly as far as it is worth her while to seduce him. She is a woman without character in the conventional sense. Without brains and strength of mind she would be a wretched slattern or voluptuary. She is straight for natural reasons, not for conventional ethical ones. Nothing can be more cold-bloodedly reasonable than her farewell to Eugene. ' All very well, my lad; but I don't quite see myself at fifty with a husband of thirty-five. It is just this freedom from emotional slop, this unerring wisdom on the domestic plane, that makes her so completely mistress of the situation.

" Then consider the poet. She makes a man of him by showing him his own strength—that David must do without poor Uriah's wife. And then she pitches in her picture of the home, the onions, and the tradesmen, and the cossetting of big baby Morell. The New York *Hausfrau* thinks it a little paradise; but the poet rises up and says: ' Out, then, into the night with me '—Tristan's holy night. If this greasy fool's paradise is happiness, then I give it to you with both hands, ' life is nobler than that.' That is the ' poet's secret.' The young things in front weep to see the poor boy going out lonely and broken-hearted in the cold night to save the proprieties of New England Puritanism; but he is really a god going back to his heaven, proud, unspeakably contemptuous of the happiness he envied in the days of his blindness, clearly seeing that he has higher business on hand than Candida. She has a little quaint intuition of the completeness of his cure: she says: ' He has learnt to do without happiness.' " *

Candida quickly divines that Marchbanks is " falling in love with her," and whilst fully conscious of her charms, she is equally conscious of the evil that may be wrought by unscrupulous use of them. She has too much respect for Marchbanks' passion to insult him with virtuous indignation. Her maternal insight

* *The Truth about Candida,* by James Huneker, *Metropolitan Magazine,* August, 1904.

enables her to sympathize with him in his aspirations and in his struggles.

It is quite true that Candida's standards are instinctively natural, not conventionally ethical: " Put your trust in my love, James, not in my conscience," is her eminently sound point of view. It is her desire to save Eugene from future pain, to show

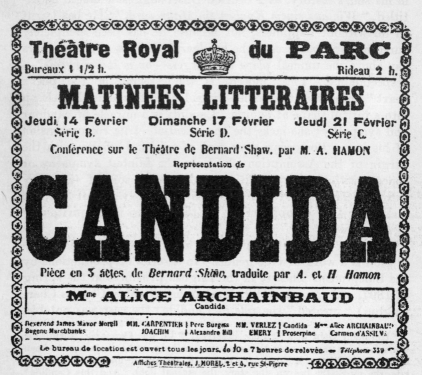

PLAYBILL OF *Candida.*

Théâtre Royal du Parc, Brussels. Preceded by a *conférence* on *The Theatre of Bernard Shaw,* by M. A. Hamon. Four " Matinées Littéraires," February 7th, 14th, 17th, 21st, 1907. First production of any of Shaw's plays in the French language.

him quite gently the hopelessness of his passion, that leads her to " seduce " him into perfect self-expression, to make clear to him that he is a " foolish boy " and that her love is not the inevitable reward for the triumph of his logic. Marchbanks' magnificent bid of " his soul's need " does not win her, because she loves Morell. Taught by Candida to recognize the difference between poetic vision and prosaic actuality, Marchbanks realizes that his hour has struck: it is the end of his youth. He has made the inevitable Shavian discovery that service, not happiness, is the nobler aim in life; and this episode in his soul's history, as Friedrich Düsel suggests, should be entitled, " *Wie aus einem Knaben ein Mann wird.*" He has learnt to do without happiness, not because he has been completely cured of love, but because he has learnt that his own love soars far above the unideal plane of Burgess—or is it *bourgeois?*—respectability. This, indeed, is the " secret in the poet's heart "; otherwise the golden-winged god of dreams shrivels up into a pitiful shape of egoism. Candida is a miracle of candour and sympathy; she lacks the one essential—true comprehension of his love. Possessing some sort of spiritual affinity with the Virgin of the Assumption, she lacks the faintest sympathy or concern with the art of Titian; feeling some sort of sympathy with Marchbanks and what is to her his comedy of calf-love, she lacks any true comprehension of the fineness and spirituality of his passion.*

Whatever interpretation may be adopted, this drama of disillusion is a work of true genius. In a series of productions by the Independent Theatre in the English provinces in the spring of 1897, and again in 1898, Janet Achurch (Mrs. Charles Charrington) " created " the *rôle* of Candida; the cast was notable,

---

* Hermann Bahr has acutely observed: " In the Germanic world, the woman wields power over the man only so long as he feels her to be a higher being, almost a saint: so Candida is the transcendent, the immaculate, the pure—the heaven, the stars, the eternal light. And this Candida? There is no doubt that she is an angel. The only question is in which heaven she dwells. There is a first heaven, and a second heaven, and so on up to the seventh heaven. In the seventh heaven, as you well know, Shaw, dwell only the poets; and of the seventh heaven must the woman be, before the worshipful Marchbanks will once kneel to her, if, indeed, it can be said that a poet ever kneels. But your beloved Candida is of a lower heaven—a lesser alp, a thousand metres below, in the region of the respectable *bourgeoisie*. There is she the saint the Germanic mannikin needs. There she shines—shines for the Morells, the good people who inculcate virtue and solve social questions every Sunday. And it is there that she belongs."

the parts of Morell and Marchbanks being taken by Mr. Charles Charrington and Mr. Courtenay Thorpe respectively. Doubtless Janet Achurch's interpretation of Candida as the serene *clairvoyante* remains unequalled to-day, even by Agnes Sorma or Lili Petri. The play has been patronizingly spoken of as an amusing little comedy; Oliver Herford, the humorist, hailed it with great enthusiasm as a " problem-farce "! But *Candida* has always appealed to me, as to Mr. Gilbert Chesterton, " not only as the noblest work of Mr. Shaw, but as one of the noblest, if not the noblest, of modern plays: a most square and manly piece of moral truth."

The Devil's Disciple is the fourth and last play in the category of authentically dramatic pieces, ranking just below *Candida* in the subtlety of its character-delineation and the magnetic force of its appeal. The play had its genesis in a conversation between Shaw and that remarkable romantic actor, William Terriss. In Shaw's words:

" One day Terriss sent for me, and informed me that since witnessing the production of *Arms and the Man* he regarded me as one of the ' greatest intellectual forces of the present day.' He proposed to combine my intellect with his knowledge of the stage in the construction of a play. Whereupon he gave me one of the most astounding scenarios I ever encountered. . . . When I endeavoured with all my reasoning powers to convince this terrible Terriss that such a scenario contained far too much action and far too little delineation of character, he declared firmly: ' Mister Shaw, you have convinced me.' With these words, and without the slightest hesitation, he threw the whole scenario into the fire with the attitude and decision of a man who well knows that he has another draft lying in his desk. Nevertheless, the fact that he greeted me as a great intellectual force and yet had implied that I was incapable of writing a popular melodrama delighted me beyond words, and I resolved to get together all the trite episodes, all the stale situations, which had done such good service in the last ten years in trashy plays, and combine them in a

new melodrama, which should have the appearance of
a deeply thought-out, original modern play. The result of
it all was *The Devil's Disciple*." *

The spontaneity and naturalness which characterize the dialogue of Shaw's plays are the results, in part, of his habit of
writing his plays on scraps of paper at odd times. And in the
case of *The Devil's Disciple*, Shaw achieved the incomparable
feat of writing a brilliant play and " looking pleasant " at one
and the same time! " A young lady I know," relates Shaw,
" wanted to make a portrait of me, sitting on the corner of
a table, which is a favourite attitude of mine. So I wrote the
play in a notebook to fill up the time."

In that mock-modest preface, *On Diabolonian Ethics*, Shaw
has confessed his indebtedness to literary history and openly
acknowledged his thefts from the past. But in one place he
quietly asserts that he has put something original into this play.
" *The Devil's Disciple* has, in truth, a genuine novelty in it.
Only, that novelty is not any invention of my own, but simply
the novelty of the advanced thought of my own day." How
can one express more succinctly the end and aim of the modern
dramatist? Goethe once said that the great aim of the modern
intelligence should be to gain control over every means afforded
by the past, in order thereby to enable himself to exhibit those
features in which the modern world feels itself new and different
and unique. A remarkably subtle travesty upon melodrama,
The Devil's Disciple is a picture of life seen through the refractory temperament of a thoroughly modern intelligence.

The veiled satire underlying *The Devil's Disciple* is found in
the fact that, whilst speciously purporting to be a melodrama,
by individual and unique treatment the play gives the lie to the
specific melodramatic formula. The comprehension of the dual
rôle made this play as presented by Richard Mansfield peculiarly
appreciated by American audiences; in England, the play was
absurdly misunderstood, as related in one of Shaw's prefaces.

* *Vornehmlich über mich selbst,* in Program No. 88 of the Schiller Theater, Berlin. This *Plauderei* appeared originally in the Vienna *Zeit* in
February, 1903, shortly before the production of *Teufelskerl* in Vienna.

If we consider the crucial moments of the play, we observe the brilliant way in which Shaw has combined popular melodrama for the masses and Shavian satire upon melodrama for the discerning few. How the hardened old playgoer chuckles over his prevision of the situation that is to result after Dick is arrested and led off to prison! Of course, the minister will come back, Judith will waver between love for her husband and desire to save the noble altruist, the secret will be torn from her at last, her husband will prepare to go and take Dick's place. She will adjure him to save himself, but he will remain firm as adamant. What a tumult of passions, what a moving farewell, every eye is moist—the genuine *scène à faire!* What a sense of exquisite relief when Shaw has the minister take the natural, the businesslike, and not the melodramatic course! Again, in the third act, when Judith, like a true Shakespearean heroine, disregards the convention of feminine fastidiousness in order to penetrate to the profoundest depths of Dick's heart, the melodramatic formula is clear: Dick will kneel at Judith's feet, pour out his burning love for her, the two will revel in the ecstasies of *la grande passion.* Reality is far subtler and more complex than melodrama—not a game of heroics, but a clash of natures, says Shaw.

" You know you did it for his sake," charges Judith, " believing he was a more worthy man than yourself."

" Oho! No," laughs Dick in reply; " that's a very pretty reason, I must say; but I'm not so modest as that. No, it wasn't for his sake."

Now she blushes, her heart beats painfully, and she asks softly: " Was it for my sake? " " Perhaps a little for your sake," he indulgently admits; but when, emboldened by his words, she romantically charges him to save himself, that he may go with her, even to the ends of the earth, he takes hold of her firmly by the wrists, gazes steadily into her eyes, and says:

" If I said—to please you—that I did what I did ever so little for your sake, I lied as men always lie to women. You know how much I have lived with worthless men—aye, and worthless women too. Well, they could all rise to some sort of goodness and kindness when they were in love. That has taught me to set very little store by the goodness that only comes out red-hot. What I did last night, I did in cold blood, caring not half so much for your husband or for you as I do for myself. I had no motive and no interest: all I can tell you is that when it came to the point whether I would take my neck out of the noose and put another man's into it, I could not do it. I don't know why not: I see myself as a fool for my pains; but I could not, and I cannot. I have been brought up standing by the law of my own nature; and I may not go against it, gallows or no gallows. I should have done the same thing for any other man in the town, or any other man's wife. Do you understand that?"

"Yes," replies the stricken Judith; "you mean that you do not love me."

"Is that all it means to you?" asks the revolted Richard, with fierce contempt.

"What more—what worse—can it mean to me?" are Judith's final words.

Last of all, Shaw indulges in his most hazardous stroke of satire in the scene of the military tribunal. Imagine the cloud of romantic gloom and melodramatic horror that the author of *La Tosca* would have cast over this valley of the shadow of death! Shaw ushers in an exquisite and urbane comedian to irradiate the gathering gloom with the sparks of his audacious speech and the scintillations of his heartless wit. Thus Shaw elevates the plane of the piece into a sublimated atmosphere of sheer satire.

In *The Devil's Disciple*, Shaw succeeds in humanizing the stock figures of melodrama, revealing in them a credible mixture of good and evil, of reality and romance. In life itself, Shaw finds no proof that a rake may not be generous, nor a blackguard tender to children, nor a minister virile and human. All mothers are not angels, all generals are not imposing dignitaries, all British soldiers are not Kitcheners in initiative or Gordons in heroism. That Dick scoffs at religion and breaks the social code does not prove that he is either naturally vicious or depraved. In the stern asceticism of his nature, he is a more genuine Puritan than his self-righteous mother. Under every trial is he always valid to himself, obedient to the law of his own nature; he might have chosen for his device the words of Luther: " *Ich kann nicht anders.*" The play was written for Richard Mansfield; and Mr. Shaw once told me that the part of Dudgeon was modelled upon Mansfield himself. On the stage, Dudgeon is usually represented either as the melodramatic type of hero, with white soft shirt and bared neck—*e.g.*, Karl Wiene, in Vienna; or as the gay debonair rake, counterpart of the best type of those fascinating blades of Sheridan and the other writers of earlier English comedy—*e.g.*, Richard Mansfield, in America. As a matter of fact, Dick is neither a conventional stage hero nor a dashing rake. " Dick Dudgeon is a Puritan of the Puritans," says Shaw. " He is brought up in a household where the Puritan religion has died and become, in its corruption, an excuse for his mother's master-passion of hatred in all its phases of cruelty and envy. In such a home he finds himself starved of religion, which is the most clamorous need of his nature. With all his mother's indomitable selfishness, but with pity instead of hatred as his master-passion, he pities the devil, takes his side, and champions him, like a true Covenanter, against the world. He thus becomes, like all genuinely religious men, a reprobate and an outcast." Unfortified by the power of a great love, unconsoled by hope of future reward, Dick makes the truly heroic sacrifice with all the sublime spirit of a Carton or a Cyrano. Of such stuff are made not stage, but real heroes. " He is in one word," says Mr. J. T. Grein, " a man, spotted it is true, but a man, and, as such, perhaps the most human creature which native fancy has put on our modern stage."

In *The Devil's Disciple*, as Hermann Bahr maintains, Shaw virtually asserts the modern dramatic principle that every situation of adventitious character, every external adventure which meets the hero like a vagabond upon the highway, is undramatic; the sole aim of modern drama is representation of the inner life, and all things must be transposed into the key of spiritual significance.* This principle is exemplified in the

* *Rezensionen. Wiener Theater, 1901-1903,* by Hermann Bahr; article *Ein Teufelskerl,* pp. 440-453.

three leading characters. Like Raina in *Arms and the Man*, Judith learns by bitter experience to distrust the iridescent mirage of romance. Sentimental, spoiled, romantic, this re-fined Lydia Languish does not know whether to hate, to admire, or to love the fascinating, devil-may-care rake. In the briefest space of time, her husband has become in her eyes a coward and a poltroon. Her heart is in a tumult of emotions: like a willow she sways between duty to her husband and love for the dashing Dudgeon. And when she puts all to the touch, she discovers that her romance is only a pretty figment of her fancy, powerless before the omnipotent passion of obligation to self. And when her husband appears in the nick of time, and proves to be a hero after all, her love floods back to him. Dick must promise that *he will never tell!* Surely the figure of the minister's young wife, says Heinrich Stümcke, is one of the most delicate creations of the English stage. " In the recital of Judith's relations with Dick," writes Dr. Brandes, " there is convincing irony, and rare insight into the idiosyncrasies and subtleties of the feminine heart."

Among the minor excellences of the play, the figure of Burgoyne stands out in striking relief. In Shaw's view, his Burgoyne is not a conventional stage soldier, but " as faithful a portrait as it is in the nature of stage portraits to be "—whatever that may mean! In reality, Shaw's Burgoyne interests us, not at all as an historical personage, but as a distinct dramatic creation. " Gentleman Johnny," suave, sarcastic, urbane—the high comedian with all the exquisite grace of the eighteenth century—delights us by exchanging rare repartee with Dick over the banal topic of the latter's death. Burgoyne's speech of Voltairean *timbre*, quite in the key of De Quincey's *Murder as a Fine Art*—beginning with " Let me persuade you to be hanged "—is the finest ironical touch in English drama since Sheridan. " The historic figure of the English General Burgoyne," says Dr. Brandes, " though he holds only a subordinate place in the play, stands forth with a fresh and sparkling vitality, such as only great poets can impart to their creations." Shaw once modestly averred that " the most effective situation on the modern stage occurs in my own play—*The Devil's Dis-*

ciple." I have always had the feeling that the first act of this play, although actually delaying the beginning of the " love story " until the second act, is the most remarkable act Shaw has ever written—a *genre* picture eminently worthy of the hand of a Hogarth or a Dickens. And, to quote Dr. Brandes once more, " I consider *The Devil's Disciple* a masterpiece, whether viewed from the psychological or the dramatic standpoint. Well acted, it ought to create a *furore.*"

THE PLAYWRIGHT—III

" I find that the surest way to startle the world with daring innovations and originalities is to do exactly what playwrights have been doing for thousands of years; to revive the ancient attraction of long rhetorical speeches; to stick closely to the methods of Molière; and to lift characters bodily out of the pages of Charles Dickens."—*Prophets of the Nineteenth Century* (Unpublished), by G. Bernard Shaw.

" I have honour and humanity on my side, wit in my head, skill in my hand, and a higher life for my aim."—G. Bernard Shaw, in the *New York Times,* September 25th, 1905.

CHAPTER XII

MAN AND SUPERMAN inaugurates another cycle of Shaw's theatre, and first presents Shaw to the world as a conscious philosopher. By reason of its bi-partite nature—it is sub-entitled *A Comedy and a Philosophy*—this play furnishes the natural link between Shaw the dramatist and Shaw the creator of a new form of stage entertainment. It is worth recalling that at the time this play appeared Shaw had not yet won the favour of the " great public " in England. He had, however, won the attention and the enthusiastic, yet tempered, praise of one of the ablest dramatic critics in England. Mr. William Archer pronounced *Mrs. Warren's Profession* a " masterpiece—yes, with all reservations, a masterpiece," and as each one of Shaw's plays appeared, he discussed it in the fullest and most impartial way, bespoke for it the attention of the British public, and roundly berated the managers of the large West End theatres for letting slip through their fingers the golden opportunities afforded by the brilliant works of the witty Irishman.* For that matter, Shaw was not wanting in appreciative students of his plays among the dramatic critics of the day; and even Mr. Max Beerbohm and Mr. A. B. Walkley, though temperamentally Shaw's opposites, took the liveliest interest in the Shavian drama.

Indeed, it was Mr. Walkley who asked Shaw to write a Don Juan play; and the fulfilment of this request was *Man and Superman*. *Ab initio*, Shaw realized that there are no modern English plays in which the natural attraction of the sexes for one another is made the mainspring of the action. The popular contemporary playwrights, thinking to emulate Ibsen, had produced plays cut according to a certain pattern, *i.e.*, plays preoccupied with sex, yet really devoid of all sexual interest. In plays, of which *The Second Mrs. Tanqueray* is the type illustration, the

---

* In a subsequent volume will be indicated in detail Mr. Archer's intimate relation to the growth of popular interest in Shaw's plays.

woman through indiscretion is brought in conflict with the law which regulates the relation of the sexes, while the man by marriage is brought in conflict with the social convention that discountenances the woman. Such dramas, portraying merely the conflict of the individual with society, Shaw had railed at in the preface to his *Three Plays for Puritans;* such " senseless evasions " of the real sex problem serve in part to explain Shaw's partial lack of sympathy with Pinero during Shaw's *Saturday Review* period. Shaw was in no mind to treat his friend Walkley to a lurid play of identical import; nor did the Don Juan of tradition, literature and opera, the libertine of a thousand *bonnes fortunes,* suit his wants any better. The prototypic Don Juan of sixteenth-century invention, Molière's persistently impenitent type of impiety, and Mozart's ravishingly attractive enemy of God had all served their turn; whilst in Byron's Don Juan, Shaw saw only a vagabond libertine, a sailor with a wife in every port. Even that spiritual cousin of Don Juan, Goethe's Faust, although he had passed far beyond mere love-making to altruism and humanitarianism, was still almost a century out of date.

This *reductio ad absurdum* process finally gave Shaw the clue to the mystery; the other types being perfected, and in a sense exhausted, a Don Juan in the philosophic sense alone remained. The modern type of Don Juan " no longer pretends to read Ovid, but does actually read Schopenhauer and Nietzsche, studies Westermarck, and is concerned for the future of the race instead of for the freedom of his own instincts." Confronted with the stark problem of the duel of sex, Shaw solved it with the striking conclusion that Man is no longer, like Don Juan, the victor in that duel. Though sharing neither the prejudices of the homoist nor the enthusiasms of the feminist, Shaw found it easy to persuade himself that woman has become dangerous, aggressive, powerful. The *rôles* established by romantic convention, and evidenced in the hackneyed phrase " Man is the hunter, woman the game," are now reversed: Woman takes the initiative in the selection of her mate. Thus is Don Juan reincarnated; once the headlong huntsman, he is now the helpless quarry. *Man and Superman,* in Shaw's own

HUDSON THEATRE

HENRY B. HARRIS   MANAGER

The Attractions for this Theatre furnished by Charles Frohman.

WEEK BEGINNING MONDAY EVENING, MAY 21, 1906.
Evenings at 8.20.   Matinees Wednesday and Saturday at 2.15.

CHARLES DILLINGHAM Presents

Robert Loraine

AND COMPANY

IN BERNARD SHAW'S COMEDY,

MAN AND SUPERMAN

Characters.

(In order of their first appearance.)

ROEBUCK RAMSDEN.......................Mr. LOUIS MASSEN
PARLOR MAID.......................Miss PAULINE ANTHONY
OCTAVIUS ROBINSON.......................Mr. ALFRED HICKMAN
JOHN TANNER.......................Mr. ROBERT LORAINE
MISS ANN WHITEFIELD.......................Miss IDA CONQUEST
MRS. WHITEFIELD.......................Miss LOIS FRANCES CLARK
MISS SUSAN RAMSDEN.......................Miss SALLIE WILLIAMS
MISS VIOLET ROBINSON.......................Miss NELLIE THORNE
HENRY STRAKER.......................Mr. EDWARD ABELES
HECTOR MALONE, Jr.......................Mr. CHARLES GOTTHOLD
HECTOR MALONE, Sr.......................Mr. J. D. BEVERIDGE

Synopsis of Scenery.

ACT I.—Roebuck Ramsden's study in his house, Portland Place, London,
W. A Spring morning.

ACT II.—Carriage drive of Mrs. Whitefield's country home, Richmond,
Surrey, England. Next day

ACT III.—The garden of a villa in Granada, Spain. Four days later

Time—The present.

The play staged under the direction of MR. ROBERT LORAINE.

Manager for Mr. Dillingham, MR. FRED G. LATHAM.

PROGRAM OF *Man and Superman.*
Hudson Theatre, N. Y. May 21st, 1906. Second Season.

words, is "a stage projection of the tragi-comic love chase of the man by the woman."

Shaw's solution of the problem was generally regarded as audaciously novel and original. And yet, as Shaw points out in the Dedicatory Epistle, and as I have indicated in a former chapter, the notion is very far from novel. Beaumont and Fletcher's *The Wild Goose Chase* furnishes the interesting analogy of Mirabell, a travelled Italianate gentleman and cynical philanderer, pursued by Oriana, the "witty follower of the chase," who employs a number of more or less crude and coarse artifices to entrap him; when the ingenuity of the dramatists is exhausted, Mirabell succumbs to Oriana's wiles.* And those who have a passion for attributing all Shaw's ideas to Nietzsche, might find some support in that passage in *A Genealogy of Morals:* "The philosopher abhors *wedlock* and all that would fain persuade to this state, as being an obstacle and fatality on his road to the *optimum.* Who among the great philosophers is known to have been married? Heraclitus, Plato, Descartes, Spinoza, Kant, Schopenhauer—they were not; nay, we cannot even so much as *conceive* them as married. A married philosopher is a figure *of comedy.* . . ."

The attitude toward woman exhibited by Shaw in *Man and Superman* has won for him the appellation, "the most ungallant of dramatists." Mr. Huneker has ventured to assert that Shaw is "practically the first literary man who has achieved the feat of making his heroines genuinely disagreeable persons." Now to Wilde and to Strindberg, woman is an inferior being, the history of woman being the history of tyranny in its harshest form, *i.e.,* the tyranny of the weak over the strong. Shaw is quite as far from misogyny on the one hand as from gynolatry on the other. From the beginning of his literary career, Shaw

---

* This parallel was called to my attention by Professor William Lyon Phelps, of Yale University. Compare, for example, Tanner's long outburst against the chains of wedlock with Mirabell's, "I must not lose my liberty, dear lady, and like a wanton slave cry for more shackles," etc., etc. In reply to a question of mine in regard to indebtedness, Mr. Shaw replied: "Why, I never thought of such a thing! As a matter of fact, the old English comedies are so artificial and mechanical, that I always forget them before I have finished reading them."

has been imbued with the conviction that, to use his own words, "women are human beings just like men, only worse brought up, and consequently worse behaved." In Shaw's plays it is a toss-up between the men and the women as to which are the worse behaved. The women in Shaw's plays seem always deliberately to challenge the conventional ideal of the womanly Woman. As a dramatist, Shaw rebelled from the very first against the long-established custom of making all heroines perfect, all heroes chivalrous and gallant, all villains irretrievably wicked. Stock characters, in Shaw's view, must be swept off from dramatic art along with romance, the womanly woman, the ideal heroine, and all the other useless lumber that so fatally cumbered the British stage. In Shaw's first play, he confessedly " jilted *the* ideal lady for *a* real one," and predicted that he would probably do it again and again, even at the risk of having the real ones mistaken for counter-ideals. Shaw has kept his promise, and has been jilting the ideal lady ever since.

M. Filon finds Shaw's " *galerie de femmes* " nothing short of astonishing in the veracity and vitality of the likenesses. Ann Whitefield, whom Shaw once pronounced his " most gorgeous female," is really one of his least successful portraits. " As I sat watching *Everyman* at the Charterhouse," says Shaw, " I said to myself, ' Why not Everywoman? ' Ann was the result; every woman is not Ann; but Ann is Everywoman." Thus the play takes on the character of a " morality," and purports to adumbrate a deep, underlying truth of nature. Unfortunately, Shaw is not a flesh painter; Ann is not a successful portrait of a woman who is ." an unscrupulous user of her personal fascination to make men give her what she wants." She is deficient in feminine subtlety—the obscurer instincts and emotions of sex. The strong, heedless, unquestioning voice of fruitful nature voices its command, not through the passion of a " mother woman," but through the medium of the comic loquacity of a laughing philosopher ! * In the master works of that sovereign

* Compare the novel, *The Confounding of Camellia,* by Anne Douglas Sedgwick, concretely imaging the thesis of Shaw's play. The pursuit of man is portrayed in its natural colours, the pursuer and temptress being a seductive siren who exploits all the intricate wiles and complex arts of personal fascination to ensnare her struggling prey.

student of human nature, Thomas Hardy, the Life Force holds
full sway; Wedekind's *Erdgeist* reveals the omnivorous, man-
eating monster, devouring her human prey with all the ferocity
of a she-lioness. Inability to portray sexual passion convincingly is a limitation of Shaw's art. And yet in the present
instance we must not forget that, as Mr. Archer reminds us,
" no doubt the logic of allegory demanded that the case should
be stated in its extremest form, and that the crudest femineity
should, in the end, conquer the alertest and most open-eyed mas-
culinity." While concerned with the problem of sex, *Man and
Superman* remains a drama of ideas. And it is difficult to
avoid the conclusion that, had the Life Force in Ann been supreme, Maeterlinck would have been vindicated by her in his
fine saying: " The first kiss of the betrothed is but the seal
which thousands of hands, craving for birth, have impressed
upon the lips of the mother they desire."

Man and Superman is the most pervasively brilliant of all
Shaw's comedies. And in spite of the fact that the idea-plot
is intricate and requires to be disengaged from the action-plot
the comedy, as I saw it produced in both New York and London, gave rise to an almost unbroken burst of merriment on the
part of the audience. It is customary to identify Shaw with
Tanner; and in the first production of *Man and Superman* at
the Court Theatre, Tanner (Mr. Granville Barker) was " made
up " to represent Shaw. As a matter of fact, Mr. Shaw once
told me that in Tanner, with all his headlong loquacity, is
satirized Mr. H. M. Hyndman, the great Socialist orator. One
other detail in the play is noteworthy—the extrinsically irrelevant incident which leaves everyone at the end of the first act
" cowering before the wedding-ring." It is an illustration of
a curious device once or twice employed by Shaw—a sort of
comic " sell " of the audience, appearing beside the mark because its relation with the action is ideological, not dramatic.
In general, the effect of *Man and Superman* is to make one
wish that Shaw would write a comedy of matrimony furnishing
the lamentable spectacle pictured by Nietzsche of the married
philosopher. Mr. Robert Loraine has actually written a clever
sketch upon this theme, entitled *The Reformer's Revenge; or,*

the Revolutionist's Reconcilation to Reality; * and Mr. William
Archer publicly urged Shaw to complete his " Morality " and
(following the precedent of *Lord Dundreary Married and Settled*) give us *John Tanner Married and Done For.*

The play just discussed is the society comedy, as it appears
in the printed book, with the omission of the Shavio-Socratic
scene in hell, and one or two alterations and omissions in the
printed play itself. The dream in hell—Act III. of the printed
book—is the ultimate form of Shaw's drama of discussion, and
has actually been successfully presented at the Court Theatre,
London. When I saw it produced there, I was surprised to note
the favour with which it was received, the brilliancy and wit
of the dialogue compensating in great measure for the absence
of all action and the exceptional length of the speeches. At
last Shaw's dream of long speeches, Shavian rhetoric, and a
pit of philosophers was realized. Upon the average popular
audience, the effect would doubtless have been devastating; and
even under the most favourable circumstances, the audience was
partially seduced into appreciative interest by well-executed
scenic effects, exquisite costumes specially designed by Charles
Ricketts, and a long synopsis of *Don Juan in Hell,* especially
prepared by the author.†

* *The Actor's Society Monthly Bulletin,* Christmas, 1905.

† " As this scene may prove puzzling at a first hearing," reads the leaflet,
" to those who are not to some extent skilled in modern theology, the Management have asked the Author to offer the Court audience the same
assistance that concert-goers are accustomed to receive in the form of an
analytical programme." Follows the synopsis:

" The scene, an abysmal void, represents hell; and the persons of
the drama speak of hell, heaven and earth, as if they were separate
localities, like 'the heavens above, the earth beneath, and the waters
under the earth.' It must be remembered that such localizations
are purely figurative, like our fashion of calling a treble voice 'high'
and the bass voice 'low.' Modern theology conceives heaven and hell,
not as places, but as states of the soul; and by the soul it means, not
an organ like the liver, but the divine element common to all life, which
causes us 'to do the will of God' in addition to looking after our
individual interests, and to honour one another solely for our divine
activities and not at all for our selfish activities.

" Hell is popularly conceived not only as a place, but as a place
of cruelty and punishment, and heaven as a paradise of idle pleasure.
These legends are discarded by the higher theology, which holds that

The year 1904 marks a turning-point in the career of Bernard Shaw. The average age at which artists create their greatest work is forty-six to forty-seven, according to Jastrow's table; and so, practically speaking, *John Bull's Other Island* is chronologically announced as Shaw's *magnum opus*. In the technical, no less than in the popular sense, this path-breaking play registers the inauguration of a new epoch in Shaw's career. In this new phase we find him breaking squarely with tradition, and finding artistic freedom in nonconformity. A true drama of national character, *John Bull's Other Island* portrays the conflict of racial types and exhibits its author as a descendant of Molière, a master of comic irony, and at heart a poet.

this world, or any other, may be made a hell by a society in a state of damnation: that is, a society so lacking in the higher orders of energy that it is given wholly to the pursuit of immediate individual pleasure, and cannot even conceive the passion of the divine will. Also that any world can be made a heaven by a society of persons in whom that passion is the master passion—a 'communion of saints' in fact.

"In the scene represented to-day hell is this state of damnation. It is personified in the traditional manner by the devil, who differs from the modern plutocratic voluptuary only in being 'true to himself'; that is, he does not disguise his damnation either from himself or others, but boldly embraces it as the true law of life, and organizes his kingdom frankly on a basis of idle pleasure seeking, and worships love, beauty, sentiment, youth, romance, etc., etc.

"Upon this conception of heaven and hell the author has fantastically grafted the seventeenth century legend of Don Juan Tenorio, Don Gonzalo, of Ulloa, Commandant of Calatrava, and the Commandant's daughter, Dona Ana, as told in the famous drama by Tirso de Molina and in Mozart's opera. Don Gonzalo, having, as he says, 'always done what it was customary for a gentleman to do,' until he died defending his daughter's honour, went to heaven. Don Juan, having slain him, and become infamous by his failure to find any permanent satisfaction in his love affairs, was cast into hell by the ghost of Don Gonzalo, whose statue he had whimsically invited to supper.

"The ancient melodrama becomes the philosophic comedy presented to-day, by postulating that Don Gonzalo was a simple-minded officer and gentleman who cared for nothing but fashionable amusement, whilst Don Juan was consumed with a passion for divine contemplation and creative activity, this being the secret of the failure of love to interest him permanently. Consequently we find Don Gonzalo, unable to share the divine ecstasy, bored to distraction in heaven; and Don Juan suffering amid the pleasures of hell an agony of tedium.

"At last Don Gonzalo, after paying several reconnoitring visits to hell under colour of urging Don Juan to repent, determines to settle there permanently. At this moment his daughter, Ana, now full of

Originally designed for production by Mr. W. B. Yeats under the auspices of the Irish Literary Theatre, this play was found unsuited both to the resources of the new Abbey Theatre and to the temper of the neo-Gaelic movement.* Temperamentally incapable of visionarily imagining Ireland as "a little old woman called Kathleen ni Hoolihan," Shaw drew a bold and uncompromising picture of the real Ireland of to-day; and the sequel was the production of the play, not at the Abbey, but at the Royal Court Theatre, London. That interesting experiment in dramatic production inaugurated by Messrs. J. E. Vedrenne and H. Granville Barker at the Royal Court Theatre in 1904, furnishes material for the most interesting chapter in the history of the development of the contemporary English

years, piety, and worldly honours, dies, and finds herself with Don Juan in hell, where she is presently the amazed witness of the arrival of her sainted father. The devil hastens to welcome both to his realm. As Ana is no theologian, and believes the popular legends as to heaven and hell, all this bewilders her extremely.

"The devil, eager as ever to reinforce his kingdom by adding souls to it, is delighted at the accession of Don Gonzalo, and desirous to retain Dona Ana. But he is equally ready to get rid of Don Juan, with whom he is on terms of forced civility, the antipathy between them being fundamental. A discussion arises between them as to the merits of the heavenly and hellish states, and the future of the world. The discussion lasts more than an hour, as the parties, with eternity before them, are in no hurry. Finally, Don Juan shakes the dust of hell from his feet, and goes to heaven.

"Dona Ana, being a woman, is incapable both of the devil's utter damnation and of Don Juan's complete supersensuality. As the mother of many children, she has shared in the divine travail, and with care and labour and suffering renewed the harvest of eternal life; but the honour and divinity of her work have been jealously hidden from her by man, who, dreading her domination, has offered her for reward only the satisfaction of her senses and affections. She cannot, like the male devil, use love as mere sentiment and pleasure; nor can she, like the male saint, put love aside when it has once done its work as a developing and enlightening experience. Love is neither her pleasure nor her study: it is her business. So she, in the end, neither goes with Don Juan to heaven nor with the devil and her father to the palace of pleasure, but declares that her work is not yet finished. For though by her death she is done with the bearing of men to mortal fathers, she may yet, as Woman immortal, bear the Superman to the Eternal Father."

* In W. B. Yeats's Collected Works, Vol. IV., p. 109 (London: Chapman and Hall, 1908), appears a statement (dated 1903), with reference

drama.* The companies trained by Mr. Barker, an able actor and already a promising dramatist, wrought something very like a revolution in the art of dramatic production in England. The unity of tone, the subordination of the individual, the general striving for totality of effect, the constant changes of bill, the abolition of the " star " system—all were noteworthy features of these productions. There were given nine hundred and eighty-eight performances of thirty-two plays by seventeen authors; seven hundred and one of these performances were of eleven plays by one author—Bernard Shaw. Plays of other authors—notably of Mr. Barker himself—were produced, and often with noticeable success. But in the main the whole undertaking may be regarded as a monster Shaw *Festspiel*, prolonged over three years. Mr. Barker, Mr. Galsworthy, the late Mr. Hankin, Miss Elizabeth Robins and Mr. Masefield, all came prominently into public notice as dramatists of the " new " school. The Court was not, in the strict sense, a repertory theatre; rather it furnished a tentative compromise between the *théâtre à coté* and the actor-managed theatre backed by a syndicate of capitalists. The Vedrenne-Barker enterprise did the imperatively needed pioneer work of breaking ground for the repertory theatre idea; created a public of intelligent playgoers with literary tastes, who had long since lost interest in the theatre of commerce; developed a whole " school " of playwrights, with Mr. Barker at their head; and brought to the English public at large a belated consciousness of the greatness of Bernard Shaw.

Coming at a political *Sturm und Drang* period, *John Bull's Other Island* achieved an immediate and immense success. Leading figures in public life, including Mr. Arthur Balfour and the late Sir Henry Campbell-Bannerman, again and again heard the play with unmitigated delight; and, finally, King Edward

to " the play which Mr. Bernard Shaw has promised us." The appended footnote reads: " This play was *John Bull's Other Island*. When it came out in the spring of 1905, we felt ourselves unable to cast it without wronging Mr. Shaw. We had no Broadbent, or money to get one."

* In a subsequent volume, dealing with the dramatic movement inaugurated by Mr. Shaw, the production of his plays at the Court Theatre will be fully discussed.

From the original monochrome, made in 1908.

[*Facing p.* 368

" commanded " a special performance. The gods of English
society, upon whose knees ever rests the ultimate fate of the
British artist, suddenly awoke at last to the realization of the
fact that a genius was living in their midst. *John Bull's Other
Island* marked a new stage in Shaw's career; for whilst the play
itself is the *fine fleur* of Shavian dramaturgy, the characters
are set firmly upon solid ground. In Shaw's former plays, as
a rule, the locality was not strikingly material, the characters
often supra-natural, and the ideas deftly bandied about at
times, much as a juggler manipulates glass balls. This new
play exhibited nothing short of a new type of drama. Emotion
is subsidiary to idea, action is less important than character,
and conflict of ideas replaces the conflict of wills of the dramatic
formula.

In the Shavian *Anschauung*, the action and reaction of national types inevitably takes precedence over the purely human
problem of the love story. The study in emotional psychology
is the incidental underplot to the larger study of England *versus*
Ireland; here we see the line of cleavage between Shaw and the
conventional dramatist. Shaw's hand, so deft in the handling
of national types, the portrayal of racial traits, failed him in
the delicate task of the exhibition of vital emotion. " I do
not accuse Mr. Shaw of dealing in symbols," says Mr. John
Corbin, " but I shall not, I am sure, misinterpret him radically
in saying that *Nora* is *Kathleen ni Hoolihan*—the embodiment
of his idea of Ireland. The real drama of the piece centres
in the story of how the Irishman loses Nora and the Briton
wins her. . . . In his heart Larry loves his countrywoman,
as she has always loved him, and she has no real affection for
the Briton. Here lies the comic irony of the *dénouement*, the
very essence of Shaw's comment on his problem." * The " real
drama," one rather feels, is the death struggle of nations. Ireland and England are the antagonist and protagonist, respectively, of the drama; and the dramatic characters, in a broad
sense, are both individualized human beings and concrete impersonations of racial traits. It seems to me quite improbable that

* *Bernard Shaw and His Mannikins*, in the *New York Sun*, October 15th,
1905.

John Bull's Other Island will " cross frontiers " as readily as many of Shaw's other plays. For, despite the signal merits of the character-drawing, the problem is essentially unique, and, as the title implies, peculiar to the British Isles.

Roscullen, the scene of the play, is a segment of the living Ireland, and here are encountered all those conflicting elements which have made a hopeless enigma of the Irish question for so many generations. In this miniature Ireland we find jostling each other the dreamer and the bigot, the superstitious and the unilluded. Instead of the great landowner, there is a group of small proprietors, who treat their employees and tenants with a harshness and industrial cruelty that can only result in the latter's ruin. Religion continues to be the dominant force in the community; and the clergy exhibit that profound political sagacity and that unscrupulousness in playing upon the superstition of the credulous peasants which are such defining marks of the Roman Catholic priesthood. Ireland's sense of her oppression and bitter wrongs has not succeeded in destroying her sense of humour, her passion for mysticism, and her native charm. These qualities we observe in the ineffable merriment of the peasants over the comic spectacle of Broadbent as an unconscious humorist; in the fascinating figure of the Irish St. Francis, chatting amicably with the grasshopper and breaking his heart over Ireland; and in Nora Reilly, quintessence of graceful coquetry, *larmoyant* piquancy and Celtic charm.

Thomas Broadbent, Shaw's conception of the typical Englishman, approximates quite closely to Napoleon's description of the Englishman in *The Man of Destiny*. To Mr. A. B. Walkley's characterization of *John Bull's Other Island* as a " Shavian farrago," Shaw replied, " Walkley is too thorough an Englishman to be dramatically conscious of what an Englishman is, and too clever and individual a man to identify himself with a typical averaged English figure. I delight in Walkley: he has the courage of his *esprit;* and it gives me a sense of power to be able to play with him as I have done in a few Broadbent strokes which are taken straight from him." * And

* *George Bernard Shaw: A Conversation,* in *The Tatler,* November 16th, 1904.

374

in a letter to Mr. James Huneker, of date January 4th, 1904, Shaw says, " I tell you, you don't appreciate the vitality of the English. . . . Cromwell said that no man goes farther than the man who doesn't know where he is going." In that you have the whole secret of the " typical averaged English figure." Endowed with the stolid density and exaggerated self-confidence of the average Englishman, Broadbent resolves to study the apparently insoluble Irish question " on the ground "; but his incurable ignorance of Ireland's plight stands revealed in his declared faith that the panacea for all of Ireland's ills is to be found in the " great principles of the great Liberal party." Ireland irresistibly appeals to his sentimentalities through its traditional charms—the Celtic melancholy, the Irish voice, the rich blarney, the poetic brogue. " Of the evils you describe," he says to Keegan, " some are absolutely necessary for the preservation of society and others are encouraged only when the Tories are in office." . . . " I see no evils in the world— except, of course, natural evils—that cannot be remedied by freedom, self-government, and English institutions. I think so, not because I am an Englishman, but as a matter of common sense." With blundering shrewdness, Broadbent announces himself as a candidate for the parliamentary seat, on the ground that he is a Home Ruler, a Nationalist, and Ireland's truest friend and supporter. " Reform," he announces, " means maintaining these reforms which have already been conferred on humanity by the Liberal party, and trusting for future developments to the free activity of a free people on the basis of these reforms." In Shaw's description, he (Broadbent) is " a robust, full-blooded, energetic man in the prime of life, sometimes eager and credulous, sometimes shrewd and roguish, sometimes portentously solemn, sometimes jolly and impetuous, always buoyant and irresistible, mostly likable, and enormously absurd in his most earnest moments."

Broadbent is a great comic figure, destined to take high rank in the portrait-gallery of English letters. His foil, the Irishman, Larry Doyle, without being less interesting, is less convincingly portrayed. Doyle is cursed with the habitual self-questioning and disillusionment of the self-expatriated

Irishman. Realizing the charm of Ireland's dreams and the brutality of English facts, Doyle longs discontentedly for " a country to live in where the facts are not brutal and the dreams not unreal." His hope for a Greater Ireland is based on his own dream of Irish intellectual lucidity mated with English push, the Irishman's cleverness and power of facing facts grafted on the Englishman's indomitable perseverance and high efficiency. And yet, he has absorbed the English view of his own race; this " clear-headed, sane Irishman," so " hardily callous to the sentimentalities and susceptibilities and credulities," if we accept Shaw's estimate of the typical Irishman, thus describes his own countrymen:

" Oh, the dreaming! the dreaming! the torturing, heart-scalding, never-satisfying dreaming, dreaming, dreaming, dreaming! No debauchery that ever coarsened and brutalized an Englishman can take the worth and usefulness out of him like that dreaming. An Irishman's imagination never lets him alone, never convinces him, never satisfies him; but it makes him that he can't face reality, nor deal with it, nor handle it, nor conquer it: he can only sneer at them that do, and be ' agreeable to strangers,' like a good-for-nothing woman on the streets. It's all dreaming, all imagination. He can't be religious. The inspired churchman that teaches him the sanctity of life and the importance of conduct is sent away empty, while the poor village priest that gives him a miracle or a sentimental story of a saint has cathedrals built for him out of the pennies of the poor. He can't be intelligently political: he dreams of what the Shan Van Vocht said in '98. If you want to interest him in Ireland you've got to call the unfortunate island Kathleen ni Hoolihan and pretend she's a little old woman. It saves thinking. It saves working. It saves everything except imagination, imagination, imagination; and imagination's such a torture that you can't bear it without whiskey."

A noticeable feature of the play's construction is its slow beginning; the first act might more properly be called a pro-

logue. The remainder of the play, although it has little or no
story worth recounting, is constructed with unusual care; the
interest inheres chiefly in the dialogue and the traits of the
principal characters. When Shaw was charged with throwing
all attempt at construction overboard, he vehemently replied:

" I never achieved such a feat of construction in my life.
Just consider my subject—the destiny of nations! Consider my characters—personages who stalk on the stage
impersonating millions of real, living, suffering men and
women. Good heavens! I have had to get all England and
Ireland into three hours and a quarter. I have shown the
Englishman to the Irishman and the Irishman to the Englishman, the Protestant to the Catholic and the Catholic
to the Protestant. I have taken that panacea for all the
misery and unrest of Ireland—your Land Purchase Bill—
as to the perfect blessedness of which all your political
parties and newspapers were for once unanimous; and I
have shown at one stroke its idiocy, its shallowness, its
cowardice, its utter and foredoomed futility. I have shown
the Irish saint shuddering at the humour of the Irish
blackguard—only to find, I regret to say, that the average
critic thought the blackguard very funny and the saint
very unpractical. I have shown that very interesting psychological event, the wooing of an unsophisticated Irish-
woman by an Englishman, and made comedy of it without
one lapse from its pure science. I have even demonstrated
the Trinity to a generation which saw nothing in it but
an arithmetical absurdity. I have done all this and a dozen
other things so humanely and amusingly that an utterly
exhausted audience, like the wedding guest in the grip of
the Ancient Mariner, has waited for the last word before
reeling out of the theatre as we used to reel out of the
Wagner Theatre at Bayreuth after *Die Götterdämmerung*.
And this they tell me is not a play. This, if you please,
is not constructed." *

* *George Bernard Shaw: A Conversation*, in *The Tatler*, November 16th,
1904.

Not the least noticeable feature of the play is the omission of the character which, in former plays, appeared as Shaw in disguise. The characters are sharply individualized, each is a personality as well as a type. Moreover, Shaw has seized the situation with the hand of a master; we discern an Irish Molière revelling in the comic irony of character-reactions, and observing the rigid impartiality of the true dramatist. This very fairness allows Shaw a free play of intellect that partisanship would have stifled; every situation is transfused with the Shavian ironic consciousness. I once asked Mr. William Archer which play he regarded as Shaw's *magnum opus*. " I suppose *Man and Superman* is Shaw's most popular play," said Mr. Archer, " but I have always regarded it, somehow, as beneath —unworthy of—Shaw. I should be inclined to rate *John Bull's Other Island* as Shaw's greatest dramatic work." I remember remarking to Mr. Shaw one day that *John Bull's Other Island* revealed greater solidity of workmanship and greater self-restraint than any of his former plays. " Yes, that is quite true," replied Mr. Shaw; " my last plays, beginning with *John Bull*, are set more firmly upon the earth. They have ceased to be fantastic, and tend to grow more solid and more human." The cleverest and truest remark about *John Bull* was made by W. B. Yeats: " *John Bull's Other Island* is the first play of Bernard Shaw's that has a genuine geography."

While no character in the play can be called essentially Shavian, it is noteworthy that Keegan, the unfrocked parish priest, is the " ideal spectator "; in his mouth Shaw places his own poignant criticisms penetrating to the heart of the situation. At last the mystic in Shaw's temperament utters his noble message. And the true poet, vaguely shadowed forth in that essentially romantic figure Marchbanks, speaks from the heart of Bernard Shaw in the accents of Keegan, the mystic:

" In my dreams heaven is a country where the State is the Church and the Church the people: three in one and one in three. It is a commonwealth in which work is play and play is life: three in one and one in three. It is a temple in which the priest is the worshipper and the wor-

THE FIRST PERFORMANCE IN THIS COUNTRY

CANDIDA

A Play, in Three Acts.

By GEORGE BERNARD SHAW

Play Staged by Mr. Daly, who wishes to express his thanks to Messrs Shubert and Evans for the theatre, and to Mr. Dillingham for the scenery.

CHARACTERS.

REV. JAMES MAVER MORELL.........DODSON MITCHELL

EUGENE MARCHBANKS.............ARNOLD DALY

MR. BURGESS ....HERBERT CARR

LEXV MILL........................F NEWTON-LINDO

PROSERPINE ....LOUISE CLOSSER

CANDIDA ....DOROTHY DONNELLY

SCENE—Sitting-room in the house of the Rev. James Maver Morell, opposite Victoria Park, London, East End.

ACT I.—Morning.

ACT II.—Afternoon.

ACT III.—Evening.

PROGRAM OF *Candida.*

The Princess Theatre, New York. Director: Arnold Daly. December 8th, 1903. The first professional performance in the United States.

The Princess Theatre

BROADWAY & TWENTY-NINTH STREET

NEW YORK

Management
Sam S. Shubert

Messrs. Sam S. & Lee Shubert & Chas. E. Evans, Lessees

shipper the worshipped: three in one and one in three. It is a godhead in which all life is human and all humanity divine: three in one and one in three. It is, in short, the dream of a madman."

In *Major Barbara*, Shaw's next play, we discover a reversion to the earlier economic tone of *Mrs. Warren's Profession* combined with a more specific elaboration of the "Shavian dramaturgy." This "Discussion in three acts" has aroused so much discussion as to its meaning and purpose that the story of its genesis may throw some light upon its obscurities. Mr. Shaw once related to me the circumstances under which the germ ideas of the play first took form in his mind. It seems that, while spending some time at his county place, Ayot St. Lawrence, in Hertfordshire, he formed an acquaintance with a young man who was a near neighbour, Mr. Charles McEvoy, the author of a play entitled *David Ballard*, produced under the auspices of the London Stage Society. At the close of the War between the States in America, Mr. McEvoy's father, who had fought on the side of the Confederacy, and was a most gentle and humane man, established a factory for the manufacture of torpedoes and various high-power explosives. The idea of this grey-haired gentleman, of peculiarly gentle nature and benignant appearance, manufacturing the most deadly instruments for the destruction of his fellow-creatures appealed to Shaw as the quintessence of ironic contrast. Here, of course, we have the germ idea of Andrew Undershaft. The contrast of the mild-mannered professor of Greek with the militant armourer occurred to Shaw as the result of his acquaintance with a well-known scholar, Professor Gilbert Murray, admirably kodaked by Shaw in the stage description: "Cusins is a spectacled student, slight, thin-haired and sweet voiced. . . . His sense of humour is intellectual and subtle, and is complicated by an appalling temper. The lifelong struggle of a benevolent temperament and a high conscience against impulses of inhuman ridicule and fierce impatience has set up a chronic strain which has visibly wrecked his constitution. He is a most implacable, determined, tenacious, intolerant person, who, by

mere force of character, presents himself as—and actually is
—considerate, gentle, explanatory, even mild and apologetic,
capable possibly of murder, but not of cruelty or coarseness."

In 1902, when *Mrs. Warren's Profession* was produced in
London, Shaw said in the *Author's Apology* affixed to the
Stage Society edition of that play, " So well have the rescuers
(of fallen and social outcasts) learnt that Mrs. Warren's defence of herself and indictment of society is the thing that most
needs saying, that those who know me personally reproach
me, not for writing this play, but for wasting my energies
on ' pleasant plays ' for the amusement of frivolous people,
when I can build up such excellent stage sermons on their own
work." *Major Barbara* marks a return to Shaw's earlier preoccupation with economic themes and is a profound study of
some of the greatest social and economic evils of the contemporary capitalistic *régime*. In conversation, Mr. Shaw gave me
the reasons which led him to write this play.

" For a long time," he said, " I had had the idea of the
religious play in mind; and I always saw it as a conflict between
the economic and religious views of life.

" You see, long ago, I wrote a novel called *Cashel Byron's
Profession*, in which I showed the strange anomaly of a profession which has the poetry and romance of fighting about it
reduced to a perfectly and wholly commercial basis. Here we
see the pressure of economics upon the profession of prize-
fighting.

" After a while, I wrote a play which I called *Mrs. Warren's
Profession*. I showed that women were driven to prostitution,
not at all as the result of excessive female concupiscence, but
because the economic conditions of modern capitalistic society
forced them into a life from which, in another state of society,
they would have shrunk with horror. Here we see the pressure
of economics upon the profession of prostitution.

" Finally, there came *Major Barbara*. Perhaps a more suitable title for this play, save for the fact of repetition, would
have been *Andrew Undershaft's Profession*. Here we see the
pressure of economics upon the profession of dealing in death
and destruction to one's fellow-creatures. I have shown the

conflict between the naturally religious soul, Barbara, and Undershaft, with his gospel of money, of force, of power and his doctrine not only that money controls morality, but that it is a crime not to have money. The tragedy results from the collision of Undershaft's philosophy with Barbara's."

Major Barbara is Shaw's presentment, as Socialist, of the problem of social determinism. Undershaft began as an East Ender, moralizing and starving, until he swore that he would be a full-fed free man at all costs. " I said, ' Thou shalt starve ere I starve '; and with that word I became free and great." As in the case of Mrs. Warren, " Undershaft is simply a man who, having grasped the fact that poverty is a crime, knows that when society offered him the alternative of poverty or a lucrative trade in death and destruction, it offered him not a choice between opulent villainy and humble virtue, but between energetic enterprise and cowardly infamy." The doctrine of the direct functionality of money and morality is no new doctrine. Colonel Sellers maintained that every man has his price. Becky Sharp averred that any woman can be virtuous on five thousand pounds a year. The penniless De Rastignac on the heights of Montmartre, shaking his fist at the city that never sleeps, bitterly exclaimed: " Money *is* morality." Shaw has declared again and again in the public prints and on the platform, that money controls morality, that money is the most important thing in the world, and that all sound and successful personal and social morality should have this fact for its basis. So Undershaft, asked if he calls poverty a crime, replies:

" The worst of crimes. All the other crimes are virtue beside it: all the other dishonours are chivalry itself by comparison. Poverty blights whole cities: spreads horrible pestilences; strikes dead the very souls of all who come within sight, sound or smell of it. What you call crime is nothing: a murder here and a theft there, a blow now and a curse then: what do they matter? they are only the accidents and illnesses of life: there are not fifty genuine professional criminals in London. But there are millions of poor people, abject people, dirty people, ill-fed, ill-clothed people. They poison us morally and physically: they kill the happiness of society; they force us to do away with our own liberties and to organize unnatural cruelties for fear they should rise against us and drag us down into their abyss. Only fools fear crime: we all fear poverty. Pah! you talk of your half-saved ruffian in West Ham; you accuse me of dragging his soul back to perdition. Well, bring him to me here; and I will drag his soul back again to salvation for you. Not by words and dreams; but by thirty-eight shillings a week, a sound house in a handsome street, and a permanent job. In three weeks he will have a fancy waistcoat; in three months a tall hat and a chapel sitting; before the end of the year he will shake hands with a duchess at a Primrose League meeting, and join the Conservative party. . . . It is cheap work converting starving men with a Bible in one hand and a slice of bread-and-butter in the other. I will undertake to convert West Ham to Mahommedanism on the same terms. . . . I had rather be a thief than a pauper. I had rather be a murderer than a slave. I don't want to be either; but if you force the alternative on me, then, by Heaven! I'll choose the braver and more moral one. I hate poverty and slavery worse than any other crime whatsoever. And let me tell you this. Poverty and slavery have stood up for centuries to your sermons and leading articles: they will not stand up to my machine guns. Don't preach at them: don't reason with them. Kill them."

Now it is patent on reflection that poverty *per se* is not a crime, but frequently an incentive to crime; poverty is an evil that must be remedied by social reforms.* The casuistry of Undershaft's arguments lies in the assumption that good ends

---

* Several years ago, in a public address, Mr. Andrew Carnegie made the remarkable statement: "You hear a good deal these days about poverty. People wish it abolished. The saddest day civilization will ever see will be that in which poverty does not prevail. Fortunately we are assured that the poor are always to be with us. It is upon the evil of poverty that virtue springs"!

justify the worst of crimes; but the very strongest case can
be made out against this materialist Socialism, inasmuch as it
leaves out of consideration all sense of individual integrity and
personal honour. The implication of *Major Barbara* is that the
summum bonum vitæ is not virtue, or honour, or goodness, or
personal worth, but material well-being, if not worldly prosperity. Undershaft expresses the doctrine of those industrial
captains of the predatory rich class whom Mr. Roosevelt has
entitled " malefactors of great wealth." Mr. John D. Rockefeller is publicly quoted as preaching to his Sunday School
class that it is every man's *religious* duty to make as much
money as he possibly can—adding the sardonic parenthesis,
" honestly, of course." Undershaft, whose motto is " Unashamed," finds the parenthesis superfluous—his expressed doctrine is to acquire money at all hazards—*recte si possit, si non,
quocumque modo rem*. He would displace the Christian doctrine of submission with the Shavian doctrine of self-assertion.
If the present practice of the Christian religion is found inadequate to modern social conditions, Undershaft asserts, why,
scrap the Christian morality, and try another—the Undershaft
morality, say, *faute de mieux*. But with that comic irony which
never deserts Shaw even in treating the characters most akin
to himself in temperament, he betrays the discrepancy in Undershaft's position: the lack of connection between his " tall
talk " and his perfectly legitimate actions. There is no evidence that Undershaft employed dishonest means in the acquisition of his wealth, or committed any violence in the furtherance of his commercial ambition. Lady Britomart acutely
pricks the bubble in the assertion that she could not get along
with Undershaft because he gave the most immoral reasons for
the most moral conduct!

Shaw suffered the customary fate of the dramatist in having
Undershaft's Nietzschean doctrine of the " will to power " laid
at his own door. It is an historic fact that Shaw once dis-
suaded a mob from going on another window-smashing excursion
in the West End, by convincing them of its futility: and yet
in the preface to *Major Barbara* he says, " The problem being
to make heroes out of cowards, we paper apostles and artist

magicians have succeeded only in giving cowards all the sensations of heroes whilst they tolerate every domination, accept every plunder, and submit to every oppression." As a Fabian, Shaw is a strict advocate of procedure by constitutional means; he constitutionally agitated for Old Age Pensions, threatening the Liberal Party all the while with speedy dissolution if this measure were not carried into effect. It is quite evident that in *Major Barbara*, Shaw is endeavouring to awake public thought and arouse public sentiment in England upon the momentous problems of poverty and the unemployed. To rich and poor alike, he quite consistently and impartially preaches Socialism, finding this to be most effectively accomplished by putting in the mouths of his dramatic characters extremes of opinion expressed in the extremest ways. Shaw advises the malefactor of great wealth, after acquiring a swollen fortune, to turn Socialist and, emulating the examples of Carnegie and Rhodes in educational and other fields, to employ his wealth in improving the conditions of life for the working classes.* To the poor, Shaw points out the inadequacy of the " paper apostles and artist magicians," and the imperative necessity of militant opposition to oppression, revolt against subjection and poverty. In speaking of Undershaft's " hideous gospel," Sir Oliver Lodge pertinently says, " Perhaps, after all, it is only the wealthy cannon-maker's gospel that is being preached to us; why should we take it as the gospel of Shaw himself? Shaw must have a better gospel than that in the future, and some day he will tell it us, but not yet. As yet, perhaps, it has not dawned clearly on him. . . . In nearly all Bernard Shaw's writings . . . the background of strenuous labour, of poverty and overwork, which constitutes the foundation of modern society, is kept present to the consciousness all the time, is borne in upon the mind even of the most thoughtless: it is not possible to overlook it, and that is why his writings are so instructive and so welcome." †

* In the Fabian tract, *Socialism for Millionaires,* Shaw preaches much the same gospel to the millionaire. This paper was first published in the *Contemporary Review,* February, 1896.

† '*Major Barbara,*' *G. B. S., and Robert Blatchford,* by Sir Oliver Lodge; in the *Clarion* (London), December 29th, 1905.

From the dramatic standpoint, *Major Barbara* is the most remarkable demonstration yet given by Shaw of the vitality of a type of entertainment in complete contradistinction to the classical model. Shaw has created a form of stage representation, not differing externally from the conventional form of drama, in which material action attains its irreducible minimum, and the conflict takes place absolutely within the minds and souls of the characters. *Major Barbara* consists in a succession of logical demonstrations, flowing from conflicting reactions set up in the souls of the leading characters by the simplest actions, externally trivial but subjectively of vital significance. In this play Shaw fully justifies his cardinal tenet of dramatic criticism that *illumination of life* is the prime function of the dramatist, and that the life of drama is not merely the passion of sexual excitement, but the *social, religious and humanitarian passions.* The drama of the future will concern itself with the passion of humanity for all great ends.

Major Barbara is epoch-making in virtue of its theme: the evolutional struggle of the religious consciousness in a single personality. The stage upon which the drama is enacted is the soul of the Salvation Army devotee. " Since I saw the Passion Play at Oberammergau," said Mr. W. T. Stead in writing of *Major Barbara*, " I have not seen any play which represented so vividly the pathos of Gethsemane, the tragedy of Calvary." * I do not see how anyone can read this story of a soul's tragedy, or see the play upon the stage, without a quickening of the nobler emotions, and a realization that Bernard Shaw is a man of profound feeling and of sentiment, in the best sense. The second act is the acme of great art, alike in the validity of its emotive power and the marvellous portraiture of true practical Christianity in the character of Major Barbara. The sanity and sweetness of her noble nature, the positive divination of her religious sense which inspires her to sink self and go straight to the heart of the religious problem, are revelations in the art of character-portrayal. Her loss of faith appears insufficiently motived in the play; her conversion in the last act is

---

* *Impressions of the Theatre.—XIV. Mr. Bernard Shaw's ' Major Barbara,'* in the *Review of Reviews* (London), January 27th, 1906.

even less convincing. Undershaft's intellectuality dominates Barbara's emotionality; slight reflection might well have convinced her that the Salvation Army accepted Undershaft's and Bodger's " tainted money " without explicit or tacit obligation of any sort whatsoever.* But perhaps she saw—as Shaw intends us to see—that the Salvation Army is foredoomed to failure so long as its chief means of support is derived from the very class against which it animadverts. If the Salvation Army goes so far as actually to threaten the incomes of the predatory rich, it will at once discover that its means of support derived from that quarter, will be forthcoming no longer.

Not without its significance is the fact that, in *Major Barbara*, leading dramatic critics found fantastic and absurd what leading publicists found momentous and profound. To Mr. Walkley, *Major Barbara* was a " farrago," to Mr. Archer, a play in which there are " no human beings." On the other hand, Sir Oliver Lodge and Mr. W. T. Stead were immensely impressed with this play as a vital study of contemporary religious and social manifestations. These contrasted views tend to emphasize the facts that the plot of *Major Barbara* is quite obviously fantastic, and Undershaft a mystic whose ideas are dangerously unpractical. And yet the separate characters in the play, with the exception of Undershaft—and even in his case, we should remember that no character is impossible in a world which holds a Bernard Shaw—are all perfectly natural and perfectly comprehensible. Shaw's practically unlimited acquaintance with all ranks of society enables him to exhibit characters so diametrically diverse as Bill Walker and Major Barbara, Lady Britomart and Mrs. Baines, Undershaft and

---

* Commissioner Nicol, of the Salvation Army, has pointed out that a " real " Barbara, before sending in her resignation, would have consulted General Booth as to the Army's policy in the matter of accepting " tainted money." He relates (the *Star,* November 29th, 1905), that General Booth accepted one hundred pounds from the Marquess of Queensberry for his " Darkest England " project. A Christian friend was astonished that he took the " dirty money." Said the General: " We'll wash it clean in the tears of the widow and orphan, and consecrate it on the altar of humanity for Humanity's good." It is quite clear that Shaw's " Barbara " prefers to do her own thinking; if she had let General Booth do it for her, there would have been no play.

Cusins, Lomax and " Snobby " Price. The play's greatest faults are the fantastic plot, the exaggerated discursiveness degenerating toward the close into rather wearisome prolixity, and the lack of conviction inspired by Barbara's " conversion " to Undershaftism at the close. The seriousness of the theme is everywhere lightened by the brilliancy of the dialogue, the deadly accuracy of the paradoxes, and the satiric portraiture of social types. But Shaw's incorrigible dialecticism leaves something to be desired; and we feel toward Shaw the playwright much as Lady Britomart felt towards Undershaft. " Stop making speeches, Andrew," she says. " This is not the place for them "; to which Undershaft (*punctured*) replies: " My dear, I have no other way of conveying my ideas."

Shaw recently asserted that the " way to get the real English public into the theatre was to give them plenty of politics, to suffuse the politics with religion, and have as many long speeches as possible. I knew this because I was in the habit of delivering long speeches to British audiences myself." At the Court Theatre, and later at the Savoy, Shaw drew the real English public to the theatre with the politics of *John Bull's Other Island*, the religion of *Major Barbara*, and the long speeches of these two and *Man and Superman*. In his next play, which he told me he regarded as his most human and most rational drama, Shaw's active and long-continued interest in modern medicine found full vent. " The theme of my new play is modern serumpathy; and the hero is a doctor," he wrote me while engaged upon the first act of *The Doctor's Dilemma*.

One day in the summer of 1906, during a visit to the Shaws at Mevagissey on the seacoast of Cornwall, Mr. Granville Barker told Mrs. Shaw about a friend of his, a Dr. W——, who had recently been treated for tuberculosis at a London hospital. Mrs. Shaw was struck by the recital, which prompted the consideration of the vast pains often taken by medical scientists to preserve the lives of people who, unlike Dr. W——, were quite useless to the world. Such people, whose constitutions were hopelessly undermined, should not be dabbled over for endless time to no purpose: it was agreed that they ought to be put into the lethal chamber.

"Why, yes," exclaimed Mrs. Shaw in a moment of inspiration, "there's a play in that!"

Mr. Shaw replied: "Sure enough, I believe you are right. Hand me my tablet and I will go to work on it at once." The necessary writing materials were immediately handed him; this was the beginning of *The Doctor's Dilemma*.

Upon the leading motive of the play hinges the principal criticism which might be directed against Shaw as a realist. Almost everyone is inclined to maintain that, whereas problems of the most serious ethical significance confront even the most ordinary practitioner, the dilemma in which Ridgeon finds himself placed is one that would never arise in actual experience. The truth of the matter is that the play is based upon an actual incident; and Mr. Shaw once related the story to me in detail. One day he was at St. M——'s Hospital, London, visiting a famous physician, Sir A—— W——. The size of the hospital admitted of only a few patients for treatment, say fifteen all told. In the course of the conversation, an assistant came in to report to the head of the hospital that some unknown man had made an urgent request to be taken in as a patient at the hospital. "Is he worth it?" asked the eminent physician. "This gave me the clue to *The Doctor's Dilemma*, you see," explained Mr. Shaw. "A choice between those worthy and those unworthy to be treated, and presumably saved, was an ethical question inevitably arising in virtue of the cramped facilities of the hospital. The question whether the patient was physically worthless or not was in no sense an inhuman question; and my own treatment, you see, is in no sense either freakish or inhuman."

After Ibsen's death Shaw wrote a critical appreciation of Ibsen's work, in the course of which he said: "Ibsen seems to have succumbed without a struggle to the old notion that a play is not really a play unless it contains a murder, a suicide, or something else out of the *Police Gazette*. . . . The Brand infant and Little Eyolf are as tremendously effective as a blow below the belt; but they are dishonourable as artistic devices, because they depend on a morbid horror of death and a morbid enjoyment of horror." * Loyally championing Ibsen and the fundamental principles of drama—for the above quotation appeared to be nothing short of an attack upon tragedy—Mr. William Archer characterized Shaw's charge as " the æstheticism of the fox without a tail . . . the instinctive self-justification of the dramatist fatally at the mercy of his impish sense of humour." In a challenging tone he went on to aver that Shaw " eschews those profounder revelations of character which come only in crises of tragic circumstance. He shrinks from that affirmation and consummation of destiny which only death can bring. Death is, after all, one of the most important incidents of life, not only to him or her who dies, but to those who survive. . . . If, in Mr. Shaw's own phrase, ' the illumination of life ' is the main purpose of drama, what illuminant, we may ask, can be more powerful than death? . . . It is not the glory but the limitation of Mr. Shaw's theatre that it is peopled by immortals." †

A few weeks later—as Mr. Archer himself has recorded ‡— a paragraph appeared in the *Tribune*, " from an unexceptionable source," announcing the practical completion of *The Doctor's Dilemma*. This was its substance:

> " Mr. Bernard Shaw has been taking advantage of his seaside holidays in Cornwall to write a new play. . . . It is the outcome of the article in which Mr. William Archer penned a remarkable dithyramb to Death, and denied that Mr. Shaw could claim the highest rank as a dramatist until he had faced the King of Terrors on the stage. Stung by this reproach from his old friend, Mr. Shaw is writing a play all about death. . . . He has not evaded the challenge by a quip; the play is in five acts, with the fatal situation in the correct position—at the end of the

---

* *Ibsen,* by G. Bernard Shaw; in the *Clarion,* June, 1906.

† *About the Theatre,* by William Archer; in the *Tribune* (London), July 14th, 1906.

‡ *About the Theatre: ' The Doctor's Dilemma '* by William Archer; in the *Tribune* (London), December 29th, 1906.

fourth. The death scene will be unlike any ever before represented."

The conversation at Mevagissey and the incident at the hospital in London prior thereto were the real clues to the creation of *The Doctor's Dilemma*. Mr. Archer's " challenge," as Mr. Shaw assured me, happened to fit in conveniently with his already formulated dramatic plan. When the play was actually produced, Mr. Archer triumphantly declared that Shaw had ingeniously evaded his challenge to " keep a straight face long enough to write a scene of pathos or of tragedy." He explained that " death, of all things, requires to be approached in humility of spirit, and that humility has been omitted from Mr. Shaw's moral equipment. He must always be superior to every character, every emotion, every situation he portrays. . . . If the ' King of Terrors' thinks he can perturb or overawe the cool, clear, quizzical intelligence of G. B. S., his majesty is very much mistaken. . . . As he (Mr. Shaw) is superior to life, there is no reason in the world why he should not be superior to death." * In a later article Mr. Archer maintained that Shaw had " doctored " the situation of Dubedat's death. Moreover, Mr. Archer gave his case away in the words: " He has not treated death soberly, seriously, naturally, or, in a word, with a straight face. He has chosen an extremely exceptional case, and has treated it realistically in outward detail; ironically in spirit and effect. It was not realism I demanded —it was poetry!" † Now, to expect a man quintessentially an ironic and comedic dramatist to throw around death a halo of imaginative poetry is to commit the critical blunder of complaining of one author that he does not write like another— say, that Shaw does not write like Shakespeare. If there is anything that Shaw abhors, it is the spectacle of death made stage-sublime. And it is quite unreasonable not to expect a man

* This very able and profound discussion, in which Mr. Archer gave the very fairest exposition of his real opinion of Shaw as personality and dramatist, revealed the fundamental issues of the vexed question at issue without in the least settling them.

† *About the Theatre: The Dissolution of Dubedat,* by William Archer; in the *Tribune* (London), January 19th, 1907.

who does not believe in personal immortality to be " superior to death "; and Shaw once said, as I have remarked elsewhere, that he was looking for a race of men who were not afraid to die. Death is approached in *The Doctor's Dilemma* with neither awe nor humility; not by the doctors who are professionally callous, or by the amoral atheist, Dubedat. We are made to realize Jennifer's anguish during Dubedat's dissolution; her action following Dubedat's death—the action of a Ouida or a Laurence Hope—is both logical and psychological. It is quite true that Shaw has not complied with Mr. Archer's unreasonable and extravagant request; but he has treated the scene, allowing for the indispensable " heightening for dramatic effect," with acute psychological penetration, with wonderful art, and with absolute consistency to his own view of life—an eminently honest and square course to pursue.

Various other incidents in the play, branded unqualifiedly by numerous critics as impish, in execrable taste, or frankly impossible, are based upon actual occurrences; the names of the parties concerned and the details are quite well known to others besides Shaw himself. For example, Dubedat's disgraceful suggestion about the worthless cheque, which of necessity must eventually be paid by Jennifer to avert Dubedat's disgrace, is an exact record of a similar proposal once made to Shaw himself by a man whose name, because of its association with that of one of the greatest thinkers of the nineteenth century, is known all over the world. Dubedat's lack of any sense of obligation to finish pictures paid for before execution is paralleled in an episode in the life of a well-known sculptor. The incident of the reporter's suggestion to interview the artist's widow five minutes after bereavement on " How it feels to be a widow," is founded on fact. " A few years ago," Shaw recounts, " when Mrs. Patrick Campbell's husband died in South Africa, a leading London paper sent a man up on the instant to interview her. Of course, she didn't see him, and next morning the editor of the paper in his story of the death actually expressed grieved surprise at her lack of hospitality." There is a scene in the play in which Dubedat attempts to justify his conduct on the ground that he is a disciple of Bernard Shaw,

whom he calls " the most advanced man now living." To remove any misapprehension in the public mind on the subject,
Shaw recently told the following story:

> " Some people have thought that by allowing the im-
> moral artist to say he was my disciple, I have virtually
> admitted that all my disciples die immoral and that im-
> morality is what my teachings amount to. Of course, that
> is not what I meant. The incident, as I say, was founded
> on fact. About six months ago a scampish youth tried
> to blackmail his own father, and the old gentleman, a
> most respectable person, was actually forced to prosecute
> him. At his trial the youth excused himself just as the
> dying artist in my play attempted to excuse himself—
> by asserting that he was a ' follower of Bernard Shaw.'
> Then the youth said some irreligious things that scandal-
> ized the judge, and finally got sent to prison, where he
> actually expected me to go to visit him and act as a sort
> of chaplain to him." *

Lastly, there is the creed of the dying artist, beginning with
the words: " I believe in Michael Angelo, Velasquez, and Rembrandt "—universally deplored as impossible, to say nothing of
its being in execrable taste. " This creed of the dying artist,"
Shaw found himself forced to explain, " which has been repro-
bated on all hands as a sally of which only the bad taste of
a Bernard Shaw could be capable, is openly borrowed with
gratitude and admiration by me from one of the best known
prose writings of the most famous man of the nineteenth century.
In Richard Wagner's well-known story, dated 1841, and translated under the title, *An End in Paris*, by Mr. Ashton Ellis
(Vol. VII. of his translation of Wagner's prose works), the
dying musician begins his creed with ' I believe in God, Mozart
and Beethoven.' " †

* The *New York Times*, December 30th, 1906.
† ' *The Doctor's Dilemma*,' in the *Standard* (London), November 22d,
1906. Shaw's comment is characteristic: " It is a curious instance of the
enormous Philistinism of English criticism that this passage should not

In *The Doctor's Dilemma* medical quackery and humbug are portrayed with a satiric verve truly Molièresque. The long first act does little to further the action beyond indicating that " to put a tube of serum into Bloomfield-Bonington's hands is murder—simple murder," and suggesting that Ridgeon has a temporary " idiosyncrasy " to fall in love with the first pretty woman that comes along. The real purpose of the first act is to portray the state of modern medical science; the quackeries of M. Purgon and Mr. Diafoirus come at once to mind, and one feels that the picture drawn by Shaw is done much as Molière would have done it, had he been alive to-day. In Dubedat Mr. Max Beerbohm has discovered a strong resemblance to the Roderick Hudson of Henry James. One catches here and there, too, a suggestion of the Oscar Wilde who said: " If one love art at all, one must love it beyond all things in the world, and against such love the reason, if one listened to it, would cry out. There is nothing sane about the worship of beauty. It is something entirely too splendid to be sane. Those of whose lives it forms the dominant note will always seem to the world to be pure visionaries." This figure of a clever young artist, of rare charm of temperament and phenomenal executive skill, who came to an early, untimely end through disease had several prototypes in actual life; but on the whole Dubedat must be regarded as a composite picture, and not a portrait." Dubedat raises the eternal question as to how far genius is a morbid symptom.* The most notable

only be unknown among us, but that a repetition of its thought and imagery sixty-five years later should still find us with a conception of creative force so narrow that the association of Art with Religion conveys nothing to us but a sense of far-fetched impropriety." It is needless to remark that Dubedat omits God's name for the obvious reason that he does not believe in God.

* Shaw recently said: " I do not see how any observant student of genius from the life can deny that the Arts have their criminals and lunatics as well as their sane and honest men . . . and that the notion that the great poet and artist can do no wrong is as mischievously erroneous as the notion that the King can do no wrong, or that the Pope is infallible, or that the power which created all three did not do its own best for them. In my last play, *The Doctor's Dilemma*, I recognized this by dramatizing a rascally genius, with the disquieting result that several highly intelligent and sensitive persons passionately defended him, on the ground, apparently,

PLAYBILL of *Arms and the Man.*
Schauspielhaus, Frankfurt. October 6th, 1906. First performance at this theatre.

PLAYBILL of *The Doctor's Dilemma.*
Schauspielhaus, Cologne. January 23d, 1910. One hundred and sixty-first performance.

passage in the play is the discussion between Sir Colenso Ridgeon and Sir Patrick Cullen as to the worthlessness of Dubedat, and the value of Blenkinsop.

" Well, Mr. Saviour of Lives," asks Sir Patrick, " which is it to be—that honest man, Blenkinsop, or that rotten blackguard of an artist, eh? "

" It's not an easy case to judge, is it? " queries Ridgeon. " Blenkinsop's an honest, decent man; but is he any use? Dubedat's a rotten blackguard; but he's a genuine source of pretty and pleasant and good things."

" What will he be a source of for that poor innocent wife of his, when she finds him out? "

" That's true. Her life is a hell."

" And tell me this: Suppose you had this choice put before you: Either to go through life and find all the pictures bad, but all the men and women good, or to go through life and find all the pictures good and the men and women rotten. Which would you choose? "

" That's a devilish difficult question, Paddy. The pictures are so agreeable, and the good people so infernally disagreeable and mischievous, that I really can't undertake to say off-hand which I should prefer to do without."

" Come, come! none of your cleverness with me: I'm too old for it. Blenkinsop isn't that sort of good man; and you know it."

" It would be simpler if Blenkinsop could paint Dubedat's pictures."

" It would be simpler still if Dubedat had some of Blenkinsop's honesty. The world isn't going to be made simpler for you, my lad: you must take it as it is."

that high artistic faculty and an ardent artistic imagination entitled a man to be recklessly dishonest about money, and recklessly selfish about women, just as kingship in an African tribe entitles a man to kill whom he pleases on the most trifling provocation. I know no harder practical question than how much selfishness one ought to stand from a gifted person for the sake of his gifts or the chance of his being right in the long run."—*The Sanity of Art: An Exposure of the Current Nonsense about Artists being Degenerate,* by Bernard Shaw, pp. 11-12; The *New Age* Press (London), 1908. This brochure is also published by Benjamin R. Tucker, New York.

After further discussion, Sir Patrick finally poses the issue in clear-cut terms:

" It's a plain choice between men and pictures."

" It's easier to replace a dead man than a good picture," parries Ridgeon.

" Colly, when you live in an age that runs to pictures and statues and plays and brass bands, because its men and women are not good enough to comfort its poor aching soul, you should thank Providence that you belong to a high and great profession, because its business is to heal and mend men and women."

" In short, as a member of a high and great profession, I am to kill my patient."

" Don't talk wicked nonsense. You can't kill him. But you can leave him in other hands."

" In B. B.'s, for instance, eh? " queries Ridgeon, looking at Sir Patrick significantly.

" Sir Ralph Bloomfield-Bonington is a very eminent physician."

" He is," accedes Ridgeon.

" I'm going for my hat," adds Sir Patrick, with conclusive finality.

Whilst all the characters are admirably drawn and sharply individualized, Shaw's inspiration is singularly displayed in making of Jennifer a native of Cornwall, that land of rhapsodic faith and splendid religious enthusiasm. She is a true child of nature, impulsive and romantic, to whom belief in Dubedat's genius, much more than love for his personality, has become nothing short of a religion. To engarb herself in the " purple pall of tragedy," the instant Dubedat is dead, is a perfectly characteristic action. " Jennifer is an impossible person to live with, I grant you," Mr. Shaw once remarked to me, " but it is clear to me that her impulsiveness and her unquestioning fidelity to Dubedat's memory must find immediate expression in fulfilment of the dying injunction of her King of Men. Even if I had been writing a novel, in which the treatment is more leisurely "—this in answer to my question—" I should have made her act precisely as she did."

The first three acts of *The Doctor's Dilemma* are as able in treatment and solid in workmanship as anything Shaw has ever achieved. The pervasive comic irony is tremendous; and if in the latter part of the play there is a regrettable drop into farce-comedy, one should remember that this is a fault shared in by the plays of Sheridan and Molière. The anti-climax of the epilogue is banal—" a sell " of the true Shavian brand. It is exceedingly amusing to the dispassionate onlooker to note the discomfiture of the dismayed audience over the discovery that the enigmatic author regards the identity of Jennifer's second husband as a quite pointless secret between Jennifer and Bernard Shaw! *

" I have just finished a crude melodrama in one act—the crudity and melodrama both intentional," Mr. Shaw wrote me on March 15th, 1909, " which I should say will be played by Tree if it were not that my plays have such an extraordinary power of getting played by anybody in the world rather than by the people for whom they were originally intended." Even then, it seems, Mr. Shaw dimly foresaw the banning of his play by the King's Reader of Plays, and the enforced alteration of plans for its production entailed by that decision. Promised initial production by Sir (then Mr.) H. Beerbohm Tree, " the first of our successful West End managers to step into the gap left by the retirement of Messrs. Vedrenne and Barker from what may be called National Theatre work with his Afternoon Theatre," *Blanco Posnet* was driven away to far-off Dublin, where it first saw the light of production. Upon no play of Shaw's, with the single exception of *Mrs. Warren's Profession*, are we so fully " documented "—primarily due in both cases to the interdict of the Censorship. Fortunately a letter which Shaw wrote to Tolstoy in the autumn of 1909 gives a detailed account of the genesis of the play. Tolstoy had been reading Shaw's plays, and evinced much interest in the plot of *Blanco Posnet* as it had come to his ears. He expressed a wish to

* I have had the privilege of reading Mr. Shaw's copy of *The Doctor's Dilemma*. Consideration of *Getting Married, Misalliance* and *The Dark Lady of the Sonnets,* all unpublished in English at this time (November, 1910), is postponed for a subsequent edition of the present work.

read the play, says Mr. Aylmer Maude in his biography of Tolstoy, " because, as he said, to many people the working of man's conscience is the only proof of the existence of a God." * When Mr. Maude repeated this conversation to Mr. Shaw, the latter sent Tolstoy a copy of the play with the following letter (quoted in part):

" MY DEAR COUNT TOLSTOY,—I send you herewith, through our friend, Aylmer Maude, a copy of a little play called *The Showing Up of Blanco Posnet.* ' Showing up ' is American slang for unmasking a hypocrite. In form it is a very crude melodrama, which might be played in a mining camp to the roughest audience.

" It is, if I may say so, the sort of play you do extraordinarily well. I remember nothing in the whole range of drama that fascinated me more than the old soldier in your *Power of Darkness.* One of the things that struck me in that play was the feeling that the preaching of the old man, right as he was, could never be of any use—that it could only anger his son and rub the last grains of self-respect out of him. But what the pious and good father could not do, the old rascal of a soldier did as if he was the voice of God. To me that scene where the two drunkards are wallowing in the straw, and the older rascal lifts the younger one above his cowardice and his selfishness, has an intensity of effect that no merely romantic scene could possibly attain; and in *Blanco Posnet* I have exploited in my own fashion this mine of dramatic material which you were the first to open up to modern playwrights.

" I will not pretend that its mere theatrical effectiveness was the beginning and end of its attraction for me. I am not an ' Art-for-Art's sake ' man, and would not lift my finger to produce a work of art if I thought there was nothing more than that in it. It has always been clear to me that the ordinary methods of inculcating honourable conduct are not merely failures, but—still worse—they

* *The Life of Tolstoy: Later Years,* by Aylmer Maude; Constable and Co., 1910.

actually drive generous and imaginative persons into a dare-devil defiance of them. We are ashamed to be good boys at school, ashamed to be gentle and sympathetic instead of violent and revengeful, ashamed to confess that we are very timid animals instead of reckless idiots, in short, ashamed of everything that ought to be the basis of our self-respect. All this is the fault of the teaching which tells men to be good without giving them any better reason for it than the opinion of men who are neither attractive to them, nor respectful to them, and who, being much older, are to a great extent not only incomprehensible to them, but ridiculous. Elder Daniels will never convert Blanco Posnet: on the contrary, he perverts him, because Blanco does not want to be like his brother; and I think the root reason why we do not do as our fathers advise us to do is that we none of us want to be like our fathers, the intention of the Universe being that we should be like God."

It is inconceivable that this play should have been banned by the Censorship.* It is a story of religious conversion, told with sincerity and depth of conviction. So far is it from being irreverent that it may, with truth, be described as the most

* The Censor objected to two passages; the second passage Mr. Shaw was perfectly willing to alter, but not so the first—Blanco's story of his conversion, so reminiscent of the style of Job, in which he describes how God "caught him out at last." This first passage, which Mr. Shaw rightly considered to embody the crux and central meaning of the play, he refused point-blank to alter. The play was next promised production by the Abbey Theatre, Dublin. A certain passage which was subject to misinterpretation was willingly altered by Mr. Shaw at the suggestion of Lady Gregory; and the phrase, "Dearly beloved brethren," and the use of the word "immoral" in description of Feemy's relations with the men of the village, were omitted in deference to the wishes of the Lord-Lieutenant. The directors of the Abbey Theatre, Lady Gregory and Mr. W. B. Yeats, were warned by the Lord-Lieutenant that their patent for the theatre might be withdrawn in case the play offended popular and religious sentiment in Ireland. Despite these warnings, the play was successfully produced on August 25th, 1909. "The audience took it in a very friendly manner," wrote the dramatic critic of the *Times* (London), "laughing heartily at its humours, passing over its dangerous passages with attentive silence, calling loudly but in vain for the author at the close." There was no sensation and no excitement—and no cause for any. The *Irish Times* said that if ridicule were as deadly in

sincerely religious of all of Shaw's plays. " Like flies to wanton boys are we to the Gods," says Shakespeare: " they kill us for their sport." Like pawns in the great game of life are we to God, says Shaw; He uses us for His own great purpose. " There's no good and bad," says Posnet in his puncheon-bench sermon; " but by Jiminy, gents, there's a rotten game, and there's a great game. I played the rotten game; but the great game was played on me; and now I'm for the great game every time. Amen." It is the final expression in Shaw of that neo-Protestantism which had already found more or less adequate expression in *The Devil's Disciple* and *Major Barbara*. It needs no exposition here—especially after Shaw's expository letter to Tolstoy.* One word only as to the play's " crudity." To an American, familiar with the scenes and conditions described, its pseudo-realism is grotesque in its unreality. Fortunately the import of the play is in no wise impaired by the fact that Shaw has been unsuccessful in assimilating Bret Harte.

During the latter part of March, and the month of April, 1909, Mr. Shaw, accompanied by Mrs. Shaw, went for his health on a motoring tour through Algeria. His next play, which he

England and Ireland as it is in France, the Censorship would be " blown away in the shouts of laughter that greeted *Blanco Posnet.*" In September, 1909, the play was once again presented to the Censor for consideration—in the meantime the author having rewritten an important passage after it had been tested in rehearsal. Miss Horniman wished to produce it at her Repertory Theatre in Manchester. " What the Censorship has actually done," said Mr. Shaw in comment on the decision, " exceeds the utmost hopes of those who, like myself, have devoted themselves to its destruction. It has licensed the play, and endorsed on the licence specific orders that all its redeeming passages shall be omitted in representation. I may have my insolent prostitute, my bloodthirsty, profane backwoodsmen, my atmosphere of coarseness, of savagery, of mockery, and all the foul darkness which I devised to make the light visible; but the light must be left out. I may wallow in filth, ferocity and sensuality, provided I do not hint that there is any force in Nature higher and stronger than these." Subsequently the play was successfully produced under the auspices of the Incorporated Stage Society, at the Aldwych Theatre, London, December 5th and 6th, 1909, by the Irish National Theatre Society's Company from the Abbey Theatre, Dublin.

* For detailed and excellent expositions of the purport of the play—particularly helpful at the time of the banning by the Censorship—compare *The Incorrigible Censorship*, in the *Nation*, July 29th, 1909; and an open letter to the *Spectator* of September 4th, 1909, by George A. Birmingham.

had been requested to write on the chosen subject by Mr. Forbes Robertson, was written at odd moments during this trip. The play, described by Mr. Shaw as an " ordinary skit," was aptly entitled *Press Cuttings: A Topical Sketch compiled from the Editorial and Correspondence Columns of the Daily Papers*. In form, it is very like, though superior in characterization, to a Paris *revue*; Julius Bab has pronounced it vastly above the contemporary German *Witzblatt*. Its appearance just at the time when the activities of the " militant " suffragettes were at their height, was peculiarly *à propos*. Once again, the Censorship intervened to ban one of Shaw's plays—this time on the ground that Mr. Shaw was guilty, not of blasphemy, but of employing " personalities, expressed or implied." The Civic and Dramatic Guild was immediately created to evade the interdict of the Censorship, and the play was produced for the first time at the Royal Court Theatre, London, on July 9th, 1909.* The indignation aroused among dramatic authors and critics by the banning of two of Mr. Shaw's plays in succession at last focussed the opposition to the Censorship; and the dissatisfaction with its operation, which had made itself felt vigorously, but more or less intermittently, for a number of years thitherto, finally crystallized. A special committee, from both Houses, was appointed by Parliament, to examine into and report on the operation of the Censorship, and, if necessary, to make recommendations as to its powers and functions for the future. Many sittings were held, and a large number of the leading men of letters in Great Britain, including Mr. Shaw himself, actors, theatre-managers, bishops, men of various shades of opinion, gave evidence before the committee. One result of the sittings of that committee † has been the establishment of

* The play was subsequently produced successfully at the Gaiety Theatre, Manchester, October 18th, 1909, and at the Kingsway Theatre, London, June 21st, 1910, at a benefit *matinée* organized by the Actresses' Franchise League. The Reader of Plays allowed the production of the play after the change of the names of " Balsquith " and " Mitchener " to " Johnson " and " Bones," respectively.

† *Report of the Joint Select Committee of the House of Lords and the House of Commons on the Stage Plays (Censorship), together with the Proceedings of the Committee, and Minutes of Evidence;* Eyre and Spottiswoode, 1909. The many questions which intimately concern the free devel-

NATIONAL UNION OF WOMEN'S SUFFRAGE SOCIETIES

A BENEFIT MATINEE

Organised by THE ACTRESSES' FRANCHISE LEAGUE

Will be given on Tuesday, June 21st, at 2.30 p.m,

AT

THE KINGSWAY THEATRE

"HOW THE VOTE WAS WON"

By CICELY HAMILTON and CHRISTOPHER ST. JOHN

WITH AN ENTIRELY STAR CAST.

"PRESS CUTTINGS"

By GEORGE BERNARD SHAW.

Recitation by Miss MAXINE ELLIOTT

The following Artistes are kindly giving their services—

Miss LILIAN BRAITHWAITE
Miss ADELINE BOURNE
Miss ALICE CRAWFORD
Miss MARIANNE CALDWELL
Miss POLLIE EMERY
Miss DI FORBES
Miss MAUD HOFFMAN
Miss AURIOL LEE

Miss LILLAH McCARTHY
Miss EDYTH OLIVE
Miss NELLA POWYS
Miss BEATRICE FORBES ROBERTSON
Miss AGNES THOMAS
Miss HAIDEE WRIGHT
Miss MAY WHITTY
etc.

Mr LESLIE FABER
Mr O. P HEGGIE

Mr. EDWARD RIGBY
Mr. BEN WEBSTER
and Others

AFTER THE MATINEE A RECEPTION

Will be held in the Foyer of the Theatre, by

Miss GERTRUDE ELLIOTT

(Mrs. FORBES ROBERTSON, President of the Actresses' Franchise League).

TICKETS · Stalls, 10s. 6d. Dress Circle, 7s. 6d. and 5s.
Upper Circle, 4s., 3s. and 2s. Pit, 2s. 6d.

Can be obtained from the Offices of the National Union of Women's Suffrage Societies, Parliament Chambers, Great Smith Street; and the Actresses' Franchise League, Adelphi Terrace House.
Tea Tickets for the Reception (of which a limited number only will be issued), 2s. each

D. A. & S., Ltd., London

PLAYBILL OF *Press Cuttings*.

The Kingsway Theatre, London. June 21st, 1910. National Union of Women's Suffrage Societies. Direction of Actresses' Franchise League.

an advisory board in connection with the Censorship. In many quarters hopes are expressed that a Bill will be passed by Parliament for the purpose of ameliorating the hardships of dramatic authors under the present operation of the Censorship, and of giving greater encouragement to the free development of a national English drama in the future.

Press Cuttings is the most perfectly amusing thing Shaw has written in many years. It recalls the days of delightful irresponsibility, which seemed to have passed for ever—the days of *Arms and the Man* and *You Never Can Tell.* The adverse decision of the Censorship is inconceivable, in the light of the sanction of Mr. Barrie's *Josephine,* in which Mr. Chamberlain and Mr. Balfour were " caricatured," and even a number of their public utterances put in the mouths of the characters obviously impersonating them. Mr. Shaw's Balsquith (Balfour-Asquith) and Mitchener (Milner-Kitchener) bear not the faintest resemblance to any of the personages suggested by their names—representing merely, in a light of broadly farcical-comedy, a prime minister and a head of the army. From the situation arising from reversing the *rôles* of man and woman, due to the agitation of the " militant suffragettes "—woman developing all the " manly " qualities of pugnacity and overbearing insolence, man developing the " womanly " qualities of timidity and indecision—Shaw has extracted a comedy that is breezily, devastatingly comical. But, even in a topical sketch, Shaw from time to time " puts away childish things " and shows us the serious sides of several subjects. Those who indulge in

opment of the national drama in England, arising in connection with the investigation of the Censorship, fall outside the scope of the present work. They will be considered in detail in a subsequent volume dealing with the movements in dramatic art associated with Mr. Shaw's name. Mr. Shaw, desiring to have his full views on the Censorship included in the printed report, had a volume printed at his own expense which he filed with the committee. The committee decided by vote not to allow this printed evidence to be printed in their report. This volume, entitled *Statement of the Evidence in Chief of George Bernard Shaw before the Joint Committee on Stage Plays (Censorship and Theatre Licensing),* printed privately and marked " Confidential," constitutes a remarkable indictment against the Censorship, and an elaborate exposition of grounds for the abolition of the Censorship as at present constituted.

the futile claim that men are more useful to the world than women will find food for serious reflection in the passage in Shaw's play in which General Mitchener tries to excuse himself for giving way to profanity. He is sternly reproved by the Irish charwoman, Mrs. Farrell—admirably played by that remarkable character-actress, Miss Agnes Thomas.

"When a man has risked his life on eight battlefields, Mrs. Farrell," pleads the General in extenuation, "he has given sufficient proof of his self-control to be excused a little strong language."

"Would you put up with strong language from me," queries Mrs. Farrell pertinently, "because I've risked me life eight times in childbed?"

"My dear Mrs. Farrell," expostulates the General, "you surely would not compare a risk of that harmless kind to the fearful risks of the battlefield?"

"I wouldn't compare risks run to bear livin' people into the world to risks run to blow them out of it," replies Mrs. Farrell conclusively. "A mother's risk is jooty; a soldier's is nothin' but divilment."

The popular hysteria in the fear of German invasion is reflected with great cleverness in the discussions between Mitchener and Balsquith, and Mitchener's vigorous asseveration caps the climax.

"Let me tell you, Balsquith, that in these days of aeroplanes and Zeppelin airships the question of the moon is becoming one of the greatest importance. It will be reached at no very distant date. Can you, as an Englishman, tamely contemplate the possibility of having to live under a German moon?"

Shaw's admirable art in character-creation is portrayed in the figure of the orderly, a very minor part. In a brief scene or two, he shows us a definite, clear-cut character, full of humour, consistency and point. The orderly, with the sharpened vision of common sense, has penetrated the great drawback to military service in England. The National Service League might well ponder Shaw's words: "With regard to military service, the only real objection to it in this country is the fact that at present the man who enlists as a soldier loses all his civil rights and becomes simply an abject slave. Sooner than submit to such conditions, which are wholly unnecessary and mischievous, the country, I consider, would be perfectly justified in resisting any such measure by violent revolution.

" On the other hand, there is no reason why a man should not be compelled to do military service just as he is compelled to serve on a jury or to pay his taxes, provided that his civil rights are unimpaired."

THE TECHNICIAN

"Like all dramatists and mimes of genuine vocation, I am a natural-born mountebank."—*On Diabolonian Ethics.* Preface to *Three Plays for Puritans.*

CHAPTER XIII

THE drama is the casual, not the inevitable, vehicle for the exposition of Bernard Shaw's theories of conduct. This dramatist of " genuine vocation," as he once denominated himself, was literally " called " to the post of dramatist for the New Movement. He was a " pressed " man, a conscript in the service of the theatre. It is hardly an exaggeration to say that Shaw entered the ranks and took up arms against a sea of twaddle, not initially impelled by the inner, imperious necessity for creative expression, but fired with the desire to prove that he could write plays. According to his own statement, he proceeded to manufacture the evidence. At one time or another throughout his varied career he has employed almost every conceivable medium—novelistic, journalistic, critical, artistic, propagandist—for the communication of his unique and peculiar views. For the last eighteen years the drama has afforded him the most popular instrument for the wide diffusion of his brilliance. The drama has never been the supreme interest of his career; nor, indeed, as he recently told me, has it played any very absorbing part in his life until within the last nine or ten years. The American " discovery " of Shaw as a " new " dramatist amused him immensely, even awoke in him a sense of slight disappointment. He had rather hoped that he would not be " found out " until some years after his death! At last he saw that he must reconcile himself to the inevitable and make the best of the matter, since it could not be helped! " To me," he said in a letter to me, after the *Candida* furore in New York, " all the fuss about Candida is only a remote ripple from the splashes I made in the days of my warfare long ago."

Whether or not the drama has played a very absorbing part in Shaw's own life, it is certain that this is the field in which he has been most strikingly successful in making a world-wide reputation. Until *Candida* created such a stir in New York, he was regarded in America as a phenomenally clever dilettante in novelism, in art, music, and dramatic criticism; in fact, as anything but a dramatist. He was all but unheard of on the Continent until his plays gained admittance to the broadly catholic repertory of the German Theatre.* To-day Georg Brandes writes of him, not as a critic, a novelist, or a Socialist, but as the leader of the most modern, most advanced drama in England. Julius Bab pronounces Shaw the greatest spiritual phenomenon since Nietzsche, the greatest literary success since Ibsen. The time has come for a serious consideration of the question whether he is a good dramatist, a bad dramatist, or, in fact, whether, in the last analysis, he is a dramatist at all. Remarkable as it may appear, it is the last question upon which some of the acutest dramatic critics are divided. Moreover, it remains vivid that Shaw has made some distinct and original contributions to dramatic theory and practice. If Shaw were to paint a portrait or model a piece of sculpture, there is no doubt that he would produce a work presenting evidence of a keen and searching intelligence. Upon the drama, from the questions of prefaces, stage-directions, and technique down to that of punctuation, Shaw has left the marks of an adroit and sagacious ratiocinative faculty.

In his search for a field other than fiction and criticism for the free play of his " abnormally normal vision," Shaw's eye fell upon the stage. He recognized that the existing popular drama of the day is " quite out of the question for cultivated people who are accustomed to use their brains." Looking about

* Almost all of Bernard Shaw's plays have been produced at the most distinguished and artistic theatres of German Europe. In gaining the German stage, he won a leading position in world-drama. Compare, for example, the statement of Herr Carl Hagemann in his recent book *Aufgaben des Modernen Theaters:* " Neben den anerkannten Vertretern der Bühne der Lebenden (Ibsen, Hauptmann, Schnitzler und andere—im Musikdrama: Wagner), müssen auch die Jüngeren und Jüngsten erschienen (alle die Wedekind, Hoffmannsthal, Vollmoeller, Eulenberg, Wilde, Shaw, Strindberg—im Musikdrama Strauss, Schillings, Humperdinck, Weingartner, Pfitzner, Blech, Siegfried Wagner)." Hermann Bahr recently said that a Shaw *première* is as great an event in Berlin as a Hauptmann *première.*

him, he soon perceived that under present conditions the modern theatre creates the drama, despite the fact that the reverse is the ideal state of affairs. No one more than the idealistic Shaw deplores the present vogue of the musical comedy, the problem play which substitutes sensuous ecstasy for intellectual validity, and the well-made piece in which the plot is hatched by the stage-setting. To him, as to another, modern dramas may be classified under a few heads: neurotic, erotic, Pinerotic, and tommyrotic. The whole difficulty has arisen through the drama of the day being written " for the theatre instead of from its own inner necessity." The only way to reform the theatre was by constructive effort. Realizing that reformation and regeneration could come only from within, and more especially from the man of abnormally normal vision, George Bernard Shaw—he set to work to effect the needed reforms.

Piquancy was imparted to the situation by the fact that Shaw was one of those restless modern spirits who are out of patience with the existing status, not only in the drama, but in the world at large. By his own confession, he ran counter to all conventional standards.* An Irishman by birth, an Englishman by adoption, he pretended to patriotism neither for the land of his nativity nor for the country to which it owed its ruin. A humanitarian, he detested warfare of any kind; a vegetarian, he abhorred the slaughter of animals, in sport or in the butcher's yard. An enthusiastic Ibsenist, he paralleled the Master in having no respect for popular morality, no admiration for popular heroics, no belief in popular religion. An art critic, he had no taste for popular art; a Socialist, profoundly imbued with an enthusiasm for social truth as an instrument of social reform, he was out of patience with the lagging snail-pace at which the world moved. The times were out of joint; but, unlike Hamlet, as Mr. Norman Hapgood suggests, he deemed it no cursèd spite that he was born to set them right.

It is not to be wondered at that the acutely individualized

* The following characterization closely follows his own words in *Mainly about Myself*, preface to *Plays, Pleasant and Unpleasant*, Vol. I.

Shaw should feel the necessity of outlining his unusual, almost
unparalleled frame of mind. As a public speaker, his aim had
always been, not to awake the primitive feelings of the mob, but
to make each individual in his audience think new thoughts:
elucidation, not oratory, was the keynote of his public speeches.
As a critic he had sought to speak out his whole thought without disguise: he dallied with no professional phraseology. He
addressed the man who knew nothing of technique; accordingly, he wrote in the vernacular of every day. Clarity, lucidity and wit were the standards at which he aimed. In like
manner, his sincere effort toward the constructive achievement
of the " New Drama " necessitated the most elaborate elucidation of his views, aims and methods. As Mr. Walkley has
pointed out, Bernard Shaw is nothing if not explanatory. By
prefaces, appendices and epilogues, he endeavours to raise the
intellectual standard of public opinion, which to him represents the will of the ignorant majority as opposed to that of
the discerning few. It is matter for no surprise that such a
strange phenomenon as Shaw should have led the critics astray.
Few men in their lifetime have been so fundamentally misunderstood, so farcically misrepresented: Beyle, Shelley, Wilde,
naturally come to mind. Shaw resolved to fight against misrepresentation with the many effective weapons, the use of
which, from long and arduous practice, he had so well learned.
The haughty aloofness of an Ibsen with his " *Quod scripsi,
scripsi,*" the unconscious self-forgetfulness of a Browning in
the oft-recorded anecdote of " *me und Gott,*" the lofty injunction of a Goethe " *Bilde, Kunstler, rede nicht,*" weighed with
him not at all. The man who had first caught the ear of the
British public on a cart in Hyde Park, to the blaring of brass
bands, was not the man soon to forget his lesson. Shaw has
never discarded the trumpet and the cart-wheel declamation.
This is not merely the device to attract attention for the moment, but to win a hearing long enough to awaken thought
upon the views he so adroitly and wittily expounds. He writes
prefaces and appendices because he believes that an author
should not merely allow his works to speak for themselves, but
should present their claims to intelligent consideration with his

utmost literary skill. Shaw avers that, like Dryden, he writes prefaces because he can. The crass ignorance, the unspeakable fatuity of his critics have driven him to it. Shaw writes prefaces not only because he can: he writes them because he must.

The rare and ancient custom of preface-writing is now almost a lost art. Shaw is virtually the only modern dramatist who writes expository and critical prefaces. His prefaces are little masterpieces of essay-writing. After *The Quintessence of Ibsenism*, they measure the high-water mark of Shaw's supreme talent as a polemist, a dialectician, a gorgeous and extravagant paradoxer. " In finely polyglot style " *j'en* chortle, as chortled Stevenson over the admirable Bashville. Inimitable, incomparable are these prefaces, vitally animate with the fantastic humours of the prankish Max, the solemn absurdities of Mark Twain, the mordant irony of Henry Becque. Shaw turns a paradox as dexterously as Chesterton, bubbles with self-persiflage as delightfully as Whistler, mocks the stolid British Philistine with an exasperating acuity for which we have to go to Heine to find a parallel. William Archer has said that one of the prefaces of Dumas *fils* might have been the product of collaboration between Isaiah, Tolstoy and Bernard Shaw. Any of the prefaces of Bernard Shaw might have been the product of a collaboration between Dumas *fils*, Friedrich Nietzsche, and that great American showman, P. T. Barnum.

Shaw's incorrigible practice of writing prefaces is the perfectly logical outcome of his point of view. The direct corollary of this practice is Shaw's distinctly original contribution to the technology of modern realistic drama in the matter of ample elucidative and descriptive stage directions. For reasons similar to those that actuated Gerhart Hauptmann to draw plans and write pages of stage directions to compel a clear visualization of the scenes of his early social drama, *Vor Sonnenaufgang*, Shaw describes in lucid and illuminating stage directions of considerable length the traits, qualities and characteristics of the people and places that play determining parts in his dramas. From the standpoint of the dramatic critic, he long ago recognized the bankruptcy of the old school of acting. Its technique was wholly inadequate for the interpretation of the plays of Ibsen and the modern school of realistic dramatists. A new fingering of the dramatic keyboard was demanded. The sophistication of the actor's consciousness by romance could be obviated only by the most cunning portraiture of each character. To aid the actor in every possible way to realize unusual states of mind and apparently aberrant views of ethical conceptions, Shaw drew the most tersely descriptive character sketches of the sort of person he meant the actor to incarnate. These little thumb-nail sketches are marvels of character-drawing in miniature. The German Shaw, Hermann Bahr, has paralleled, if not followed, Shaw in describing each personage, as he appears, with photographic minuteness, but with nothing like the piquancy and originality of his predecessor. Shaw has always fulminated against the romancer's habit of announcing his hero as a man of extraordinary genius, and yet totally failing to reinforce this announcement in his subsequent speech and action. Shaw complains even of Ibsen that he has left entirely too much to the reader's and the actor's imagination and insight. Is Borkman a real Napoleon of Finance or only an hallucinated impostor? What reason have we to believe, barring the author's statement, that Lövborg was actually a creative genius, that Allmers was in the least degree capable of a masterwork on Human Responsibility, or that Solness was an architect of exceptional original power? When interrogated as to his meaning, for example, Ibsen haughtily replies: "What I have said, I have said." But, as Shaw pertinently indicates, what he hasn't said, he hasn't said. Whether uniformly successful or not, Shaw, as practical playwright, has made a definite contribution to modern realistic drama by conscientiously seeking to remedy in his own plays the defect he has discovered in Ibsen, the consummate craftsman of the age. Shaw's descriptions, not only of the characters, but of the scenes in which these characters are set, are little essays in social criticism. The description of the dentist's operating-room in *You Never Can Tell*, or of Ramsden's study in *Man and Superman*, is at once the epitome and the indictment of an entire social era, of a phase of ethical or industrial evolution. It intrigues the fancy, as Whistler used to say, to make the ludicrous, if futile, inquiry whether the fate of heroes, the destiny of humanity, depend upon the upholstery of the chairs, the ornaments upon the mantel-shelf, or the pattern of the wall-paper!

Among contemporary dramatists, Bernard Shaw is an exponent of that modern movement of which, as Mr. Chesterton has recently reminded us, Robert Browning, among modern poets, was the fount and origin—the school whose chief characteristic is the apotheosis of the insignificant. Like Browning, Shaw has " ceased to believe certain things to be important and the rest to be unimportant." He has resolved to distil the quintessence of the unessential. By the cultivation of subjective intensity, Maurice Maeterlinck has opened our eyes to the miracle of the commonplace, the treasure of the humble. By examining the neglected, George Gissing has revealed the importance of the trivial. With an imaginative insight that subsequently finds verification in real life, Henrik Ibsen depicts a soul's tragedy in a married woman's loss of her dolls. In conformity with the realistic logic of his race, Paul Hervieu traces the finger of fate in the colour of a woman's bonnet. Realizing those queer mental experiences that the ordinary observer would not see or could not describe, George Meredith illumines the obscurity of fugitive and subconscious sensations. Bernard Shaw arraigns a social era in his description of a parlour because he has learnt the supreme importance of detail, the mystery and immensity of little things.

Shaw was driven to the expedients of preface and exhaustive stage-direction not alone by the false critical interpretations of his plays, by the actor's failure to divine the *rationale* of his characters, and by the evolutionary trend of modern realistic art. He also felt the necessity of falling back upon his own literary expertness in order to restore the English drama to anything like its former level of estimation in English literature. In that barren period of dramatic unproductivity, approximately speaking, from 1835 to 1885, the habit of reading plays, which had obtained in England from the time of Shakespeare to that of Sheridan Knowles, fell into " innocuous desuetude." Against the notion that plays are essentially unreadable, a legacy of that period of England's abject servitude to France in the realm of the drama, Shaw has justly and finely protested as an author, as a dramatic critic, as a dramatist. With Fontenelle and the younger Dumas, he was united in the belief that "the spectator can give only success, it is the reader who confers renown." He has employed his powers of literary expression in all their vigour and vitality to make his plays, as published and readable artistic productions, worthy of competition with such elaborate fiction as that of Bourget, James, or D'Annunzio. Shaw's discouraging experience in the effort to have his own plays published brought the subject forcibly to his attention. As late as 1896, every publisher who was approached with a view to publishing a play, Shaw asserts, at once said: "No use: people won't read plays in England."

Shaw rightly lays the blame for the passing of the printed play as a marketable commodity at the doors, not of the publisher, but of the playwright, on account of the absurd jargon in which stage directions are customarily couched. There is a sign-language, a scenic chirography pertaining peculiarly to the stage; it is essential, as Mr. Brander Matthews recently said, that the playwright who wishes his play to be generally read "should translate it out of the special dialect of the stage folk into the language of the people." And a number of years ago Shaw wrote: "I suggest that it is the fault of the playwrights who deliberately make their plays unreadable by flinging repulsive stage technicalities in the face of the public, and omitting from their descriptions even that simplest common decency of literature, the definite article? I wonder how many readers Charles Dickens would have had, or deserved to have, if he had written in this manner:

> (SYKES *lights pipe—calls dog—loads pistol with newspaper, takes bludgeon from R. above fireplace and strikes* NANCY.) NANCY: Oh, Lord, Bill! (*Dies.* SYKES *wipes brow—shudders—takes hat from chair O. P.—sees ghost, not visible to audience—and exit L. U. E.)*"

In this sort of thing, "literary people trying their hand at the drama for the first time revel as ludicrously as amateur actors

revel in flagrant false hair, misfitting tunics and tin spears."
The abuse, as Mr. William Archer has pointed out, arose at
the time when the drama ceased to be regarded as literature.
Plays designed for " intending performers," amateur and professional, were often printed from the actual prompt-books used
in the theatre. Even when this was not the case, they were
closely modelled after the prompt-books.

Shakespeare and Ibsen, to mention two obvious examples,
suffer from this very deficiency. " What would we not give,"
asks Shaw, " for the copy of *Hamlet* used by Shakespeare
at rehearsal, with the original ' business ' scrawled by the
prompter's pencil? . . . It is for want of this (realistic) process of elaboration that Shakespeare, unsurpassed as poet,
story-teller, character draughtsman, humorist and rhetorician,
has left us no intellectually coherent drama, and could not
afford to pursue a genuinely scientific method in his studies
of character and society. . . ." The literary product of two
years of Ibsen's life, exhibiting exhaustive knowledge not only
of the character of the individuals represented, but also of their
personal history and antecedents, reads to the actor-manager,
Shaw declares, exactly like a specification for a gas-fitter! It
is an " insult " to an exceptionally susceptible, imaginative,
fastidious person like Shaw. Frankly speaking, Ibsen in this
respect occupies a position intermediate between Pinero, with
his dry enumeration, and Shaw, with his breezy loquacity.
Shaw swings to the furthest extreme, making his stage-directions piquant and facetious essays for the edification of the
reader—discursive, argumentative, polemical, historical, psychological, or social essays, varying in length from two lines
to five pages. With characteristic adroitness, Shaw has defended one of his own stage-directions which has been rebuked
as a silly joke. " It runs thus: ' *So-and-So's complexion fades
into stone-gray, and all movement and expression desert his
eyes.*' This is the sort of stage-direction an actor really wants.
Of course, he can no more actually change his complexion to
stone-gray than Mr. Forbes Robertson can actually die after
saying, ' The rest is silence.' But he can produce the impression suggested by the direction perfectly. *How* he produces

it is his business, not mine. This distinction is important, because, if I wrote such a stage-direction as ' *turns his back to the audience and furtively dabs vaseline on his eyelashes,*' instead of ' his eyes glisten with tears,' I should be guilty of an outrage on both actor and reader. Yet we find almost all our inexperienced dramatic authors taking the greatest pains to commit just such outrages."

The issue, however, is not to be confused by any such defence, however adroit. In fact, in this particular instance Shaw makes a valid defence of a stage-direction with which no fault can be found save that of literary over-accentuation. Shaw has followed one safe rule in his stage-directions: " Write nothing in a play that you would not write in a novel "; but the converse: " Write everything in a play that you would in a novel," would be fatal. The great fictionist does not write: " A keen pang shot through the mother's heart; for she saw at a glance that her child had not many more chapters to live." Similarly the dramatic author should not tell the public that " part of the stage is removed to represent the entrance to a cellar." Shaw is perfectly correct in saying that " a dramatist's business is to make the reader forget the stage and the actor forget the audience, not to remind them of both at every turn, like an incompetent ' extra gentleman ' who turns the wrong side of his banner towards the footlights." But Shaw's practice of obtruding the refractory lens of his own temperament between the reader and the characters of the drama is open to very serious objection. The prime incident in the history of the production of *Candida* in both New York and Vienna was the animated discussion over the concluding sentence, which Georg Brandes regarded as wholly superfluous: " James and Candida embrace. But they do not know the secret in the poet's heart." Shaw was so much amused by the futile guesses of the Candida-maniacs that he wrote to Mr. James Huneker a Shavian *exposé* of the " secret in the poet's heart." A spurious interest was thus tacked on to the play on account of Shaw's proposition of a riddle of which he alone claimed knowledge of the solution. Again, Shaw goes to the length of explaining dubious and laconic remarks of his characters, thus totally destroying the realistic illusion that this conversation is actually taking place. The following illustration from *The Devil's Disciple* seems to be a sort of first aid to the actor: "*Judith smiles, implying 'How stupid of me!'* . . ." At one point in the trial of Dick Dudgeon, Burgoyne remarks: "By the way, since you are not Mr. Anderson, do we still——eh, Major Swindon?" [*Meaning "do we still hang him?"*] When the party breaks up at the close of the first act of the same play, Shaw pauses to give us the following historical and social reminder: "Mrs. Dudgeon, now an intruder in her own home, stands erect, crushed by the weight of the law on women. . . . For at this time, remember, Mary Wollstonecraft is as yet only a girl of eighteen, and her Vindication of the Rights of Women is still fourteen years off." The vital defect of Shaw's method is epitomized in that single word "remember." He might just as well write "Gentle Reader" and be done with it. And yet Shaw is not alone in this defect; Bahr not infrequently strikes the personal note, and some of D'Annunzio's stage directions are little poems in themselves—delightful, but not strictly artistic. Shaw has done genuine service to the modern English drama by his conscientious effort to make his plays readable, to write not mere drama, but genuine literature. Through his long training as dramatic critic, he learned to effect the complete visualization of the painted sets of the stage, thus preserving intact, in that respect, the illusion of reality. He has replaced the old stocks and stones of *French's Acting Edition* by personal and scenic descriptions, imaginatively, vividly, humorously—in a word, artistically—rendered. But he has not avoided the intrusion of the personality of the dramatist; he has imported into the English drama that pleasant vice of English fiction: imperfect objectivity. Mr. Archer states the plain common-sense of the matter when he says that stage-directions should be clear, adequate, and helpful, but that they should always be *impersonal*.[*] With all Shaw's praiseworthy efforts to create the realistic illu-

[*] Cf. *Shaw on Stage Directions*, by William Archer, in the *Daily News*, December 28th, 1901.

sion of life by making us forget that his characters are only
fictions of the stage, he occasionally destroys that illusion by
making us remember that they are only the puppets of Bernard
Shaw.

However original and iconoclastic Shaw may be in respect
to interpretative prefaces and artistically cast stage-directions,
in the matter of dramatic construction and technique he has
been notably rigorous, rather than careless, in his attempt at
realistic representation. In minor matters of punctuation, it
is true, he has freely gratified his own preferences and likings—
using spaced letters for emphasis, omitting commas and apos-
trophes whenever no doubt as to the sense is involved, avoiding
quotation marks for titles and, indeed, in Biblical fashion, dis-
pensing with punctuation on every possible occasion. All these
things are merely matters of taste. But the conventional
technique of the drama, the customs, tricks and devices of
stage-craft, he ordinarily accepts without question. In *Widowers' Houses* in its first form, he made the explicit division
into scenes; since that time, he has made each of his plays, as
far as scenes go, a continuous whole, unbroken save only by
division into acts, and by a succession of asterisks where a
lapse of time is to be understood. In this respect, he
has carefully preserved his rule of writing down nothing that
might remind the reader of an actual stage or a theatric
representation.*

The incidents, plot, construction and technical details of
drama Bernard Shaw manipulates for his own purposes, giving them novelty, piquancy, and charm by the essentially modern use he makes of them. As for indebtedness to Ibsen for
his technique, he vigorously scorns the idea. " It is quite the
customary thing to say, nowadays," Mr. Shaw once remarked
to me, " that Ibsen revolutionized the technique of English
drama. I cannot, for the life of me, find the least evidence
of such a thing. The objective side of Ibsen's technique is a
part of the common stock of modern dramatic realism. The
symbolic side of Ibsen's technique is incommunicable—peculiar

---

* In Herr Siegfried Trebitsch's translations of Shaw's plays into German is found the explicit division into scenes.

to Ibsen alone. The technique of such a play as *John Gabriel Borkman*, for example, is inextricably bound up with the dramatic genius which devised it." Shaw asserts that his own plays have all the latest mechanical improvements. In his plays there are no " asides," no impossible soliloquies, no long-winded recitals in the second act of what has taken place in the first, no senseless multiplication of doors and windows, no incessant stream of letters and telegrams. Shaw revolted against many of the technical practices of Ibsen. " Go back to Lady Inger," he recently wrote, " and you will be tempted to believe that Ibsen was deliberately burlesquing the absurdities of Richardson's booth; for the action is carried on mostly in impossible asides." And he said to me, in discussing the use of the soliloquy, " I do not in the least object to the soliloquy provided it does not exceed the time-limit a rational man might be supposed to observe in talking aloud. But if there is anything that drives me wild, it is to hear Brown come down to the footlights, and begin: ' I wonder where Jones can be! He promised to meet me here at half-past four. Can it be possible that he is still suffering from remorse for the murder of his father-in-law? etc., etc.' Deliver me from the soliloquy used solely as a first aid to ignorant audiences." In his *Saturday Review* period, Shaw insisted that, " What most of our critics mean by mastery of stage-craft is recklessness in the substitution of dead machinery and lay figures for vital action and real characters." And in his notable essay on Ibsen, in 1906, he clearly sets forth his dramatic ideal.

" What we might have learned from Ibsen was that our fashionable dramatic material was worn out as far as cultivated modern people are concerned, that what really interests such people on the stage is not what we call action—meaning two well-known and rather short-sighted actors pretending to fight a duel without their glasses, or a handsome leading man chasing a beauteous leading lady round the stage with threats, obviously not feasible, of immediate rapine—but stories of lives, discussion of conduct, unveiling of motives, conflict of characters in talk, laying bare of souls, discovery of pitfalls—in short, illumination of life. . . ." *

" All this talk about the dramatist proceeding according to rule and only making a coherent story which begins at the beginning of the play," Mr. Shaw remarked to me one day, " is the most mistaken and harmful notion in the world. A dramatist finds himself in the grip of a situation or a complex of character of which he must make the most and the best that he can. Take Ibsen, for example. Not infrequently he finds himself compelled, for the sake of giving coherence and validity to his characters, to introduce a long recital by some character, without which the play would lack a vital part of the dramatic structure. Not that I defend such technique. I instance it merely to show that even a craftsman like Ibsen is driven occasionally to such expedients."

" It seems to me," I remarked, " that, whereas some of your plays are notable for their first acts—*The Philanderer* and *Arms and the Man,* for instance—because you seem to be concerned chiefly with exposition of the plot and not with brilliant Shavian divagations, in certain others you wholly concern yourself in the first act with the careful setting-up of a complex *milieu,* the elaboration of an environment out of which the principal character emerges. In certain other plays, the method is somewhat the same, but the purpose and the result quite different. The first act of *The Devil's Disciple,* for instance, is like a picture of Hogarth. By minutely delineated portrayal of Dick's home, his training and environment—all the influences and surroundings of his youth, you explain and thus justify his revolt. The first act isn't a part of the plot— it is, however, an indispensable phase of the situation. From the first act there emerges one remarkable character, Dick Dudgeon; this act makes him comprehensible—that is its fundamental purpose. But in *The Doctor's Dilemma* the case is quite different; the hour-long first act is vital only in the sense of acquainting us with the single fact that, to turn a patient

---

* *Ibsen,* by G. Bernard Shaw, in the *Clarion,* June 1st, 1906. Also published in *Die Neue Rundschau,* December, 1906.

SHAW'S COUNTRY HOUSE AT AYOT ST, LAWRENCE.

[*Facing p.* 418

over to Bloomfield-Bonington for treatment is to commit murder."

"Yes, you are quite right about *The Devil's Disciple*," replied Mr. Shaw. "You have stated precisely the significance of that first act. Unquestionably, the drama is the art of preparation and this method is as legitimate a means of preparation as many others, and certainly much more effective. There is no reason in the world why the drama should be debarred as a medium for the painting of *genre* pictures."

"As for the first act of *The Doctor's Dilemma*," he continued, "it is true, as you say, that the story really doesn't begin until nearly the end of the long first act. But you must remember that the hero of my play is no one single character, but modern medical science. You see, I have been absolutely modern in my treatment of medicine, and I have devoted this first act to a complete exposition of the present state of modern medicine."

"The real truth of the matter," he went on to explain, greatly interested in his subject, "is that in my first acts I have often put many things I can't afford to waste my time with later on. When an audience first enters a theatre, it comes absolutely fresh and is prepared to stand a great deal from the dramatic author—a great deal which is not, strictly speaking, germane to the carrying-on of the plot of the 'story'—provided it is cast in a sufficiently entertaining and diverting form. The average audience is so accustomed to the conventional, wearisome piling up of one detail upon another —mere mechanical exposition until the middle of the second act—that my method, by which I furnish forth a complete social and psychological *milieu* in as entertaining a fashion as I can, is quite a relief."

One may say in general that, not without reason does Shaw claim to have cast his plays always in the ordinary practical comedy form in use at all the theatres. There are, however, two marked features in which his dramas, as tone pictures and as realistic transcripts of life, are strikingly unique and distinctive. In the first place, Shaw runs counter to the conventional standpoint of the emotion-racked critic by refusing to preserve the medium in which plays are customarily cast. Most of his plays deserve a twin appellation: tragi-comedy, farce-comedy, burlesque-extravaganza, and the like. In some of them the key is transposed so frequently as to defy brief classification. Shaw is intent upon opening our eyes to points of view, not accidentally variant, but purposely divergent from the conventional form. He scorns the attitude of the romance-riddled melodramatist, and is utterly impatient of the Fitch mood or the Belasco sentimentalism. If you have tears, Mr. Fitch seems to say, prepare to shed them now. Holding the blunderbuss of sentimentality and emotionalism to our heads, Mr. Belasco bids us stand and deliver. In Shaw's hands, the play is now comedy, now tragedy, now audacious satire—everything by turns and nothing long. Once catch the distinction between the vital spirit of Shaw and the demoralizing rant of the sentimentalists, and you have gained an insight into Shaw's philosophy of will that clarifies and illumines the motive and purpose of those creations of his that are customarily classed as eccentrics, perverts, madmen, bounders, or cads.[*]

We must, however, take account not only of the virtues, but also of the defects of Shaw's qualities. His ability to play the *rôles* of the acrobat, the trapeze-performer, the clown, even the stern ringmaster, has occasionally seduced him from the strait and narrow path of true drama. The statement that

---

[*] "About the plays of Shaw," writes Hermann Bahr, "we are never quite sure in what category they belong, whether they are farces, comedies, or plays: for they summon death and the devil, threaten the hero's life and happiness, and, in the midst of the greatest danger, indulge in such audacious wit that we are not always sure whether to shudder or to laugh. By degrees, however, it dawns upon us that this has happened to us once before, namely, in life itself, which so intermingles hope and despair, the previsions of destiny and the absurdities of chance, necessity and free will, law and whim, favour and spite, that it is peculiarly the experience of our time to question whether our existence be tragic, against which view our daily life warns us; or a senseless jest, to which our pride will never submit; or a pleasant, disturbed dream, which, again, is too weighty, too terrible a burden for our consciousness. This very uncertainty in the elements of our primitive feelings, Shaw expresses with a mad, malicious joy. Indeed, one might say, first and foremost, that Shaw is the poet of our uncertainty." *Rezensionen. Wiener Theater, 1901-3,* by Hermann Bahr: article, *Bernard Shaw.*

Shaw's serious plays are exceedingly good *pastiches* of Ibsen is perhaps an exaggeration of Mr. Max Beerbohm in his *rôle* of licensed jester. In reality there is no doubt that the strict compression demanded by the Ibsenic form gave Shaw no legitimate opportunity for the free play of his irresponsible humour. His appearance as jester was often a manifest intrusion. *Mrs. Warren's Profession* just missed being a masterpiece because Shaw was incapable of artistic self-sacrifice. The occasional lapse from tragic seriousness to a tone of almost revolting levity robbed the play of its dignity as a tragedy. Mr. Archer was severely shocked by *Mrs. Warren's Profession* when he saw it on the stage; in the study he had called it " a masterpiece—yes, with all reservations, a masterpiece." Mr. Grein, who wished to produce the play in the Independent Theatre series, sternly renounced Shaw after seeing it played by the Stage Society. It is clear, then, why such plays as *Arms and the Man* and *You Never Can Tell* are genuine successes, theatric as well as dramatic. They are least disturbed by rapid transitions, their large and loose comedic form giving considerable room for Shaw's kaleidoscopic changes. Shaw's farce-comedies are the natural and spontaneous expressions of Shaw's peculiar comedic talent, the sports of his own humorous imagination. Shaw's compositions are chameleons which are always most interesting and attractive when they take the changing colours of his own temperament.

In any classification according to form, Shaw's plays are very difficult to catalogue. We have seen in the first place that Shaw purposely runs counter to the conventional standpoint of the dramatic critic. In *Widowers' Houses* he jilts the ideal heroine; in *The Philanderer* he blasts the womanly woman; in *Arms and the Man* he knocks the romantic notion of war, and of the stage, so to speak, into a cocked hat. In *You Never Can Tell* he tilts against the Old Man and the New Woman; in *The Devil's Disciple* he reduces the melodramatic formula to absurdity; in *John Bull's Other Island* he explodes that outworn fiction, the stage Irishman; in *Major Barbara* he exposes the evils of charity; in *The Doctor's Dilemma* medical quackery is the target for his ridicule. All this he does in the most fantastic and variable forms—farce, melodrama, burlesque, extravaganza, comedy, allegory—any one, but usually a diverting combination and succession of these forms. In fact, he has almost succeeded in inventing a new form of drama. This second characteristic of Shaw's plays, as Professor Hale has remarked, is almost a note of Shaw's dramaturgy.* His plays are frequently fantastic criticisms of life, cast in the most photographically realistic form. In the guise of severely natural transcripts of life, many of his plays, at bottom, are critical judgments of humanity on a satiric plane of pure fantasy. If neo-realism is "merely the presentation of the ultimate facts of life in any way you like," then Bernard Shaw is the high-priest of neo-realism. In him we discern the marvellous versatility of the modern critic, capable of making himself at home in any nationality and in any age. But whether he is giving us an Offenbachian Egypt, a comic-opera Bulgaria, a melodramatic America, or an imaginary Morocco, the result is the same: a portrayal of human nature, a criticism of life, penetrating, engaging, true. As Dr. Max Meyerfeld, the German champion of Wilde, has tersely put it, Bernard Shaw possesses the supreme faculty of the critic: "*in fremden Seelengehäuse hineinzuschlupfen.*"

Shaw spent nearly four years of his life continuously in saying to British dramatists, "That's not the way to do it." He has spent a considerable part of his life in the last eighteen years in saying to the world, by concrete and constructive achievement, "This is the way to do it." Bernard Shaw is to be reckoned as one of the most suggestive and certainly the most brilliant of all the critics of the modern British stage, understanding the word critic in its broadest sense. His prime distinction consists not only in the cleverness of his critical attacks upon the stage, past and present, but also in the notable effort he has made, by actually writing plays, to elevate its plane. Every phase of his activities as dramatic critic and dramatic author has been vital with the force of powerful

---

* *Dramatists of To-Day*, by E. E. Hale, Jr.: article, *Bernard Shaw*.

originality. His *feuilletons* in the *Saturday Review* easily won him the title of the most brilliant of contemporary British journalistic critics. If he did not set a precedent, he almost rediscovered a lost art in writing those masterpieces of egotistical, combative, polemical, controversial criticism, the prefaces, appendices and epilogues to his plays. A genuine contribution to dramaturgy is his innovation of ample stage-directions so-called: penetrating character sketches of places as well as people, revelative hints to the actor, brief clarifying essays to elucidate each dramatic situation. His effort to make plays readable, to write literature instead of specifications, is worthy of emulation, and eventually his method, in certain modified forms, will doubtless be generally adopted. His practice of casting fantastic situations in rigidly realistic form strikes quite a novel note in dramaturgy despite Shaw's oft-repeated assertion that, after all, he is a very old-fashioned playwright.

THE DRAMATIST

"The function of comedy is nothing less than the destruction of old-established morals."—*Meredith on Comedy,* by G. B. Shaw, in the *Saturday Review,* March 27th, 1897.

CHAPTER XIV

THERE can be no new drama, as Mr. Stuart-Glennie has pointed out, without a new philosophy. Drama can never be the same again since Ibsen has lived. The drama of the future, in Shaw's view, can never be anything more than the play of ideas.

Whether as yet accurately formulated in standard works of dramatic criticism or not, the fact remains that a clear and demarcative line of division runs across the drama of to-day. On one side of this line falls that vast majority of plays— serious drama, comedy, melodrama, farce—which accord more or less rigidly with the established canons and authoritative traditions of dramatic art. On the other side falls the persistently crescent minority of plays which break away from the old conventions and set up new precedents for formulation by the Freytag of the future. In the first class are found those works of art which are founded upon emotion, live solely in and for the dramatic moment, and treat of the universal themes of time and age, character and destiny, life and death. They receive their impulse from eternal and enduring, rather than from topical or transitory, aspects of human life; and draw their inspiration as much—if not more—from the literature of the past as from the human pageant of the present. In the second class are found those works which start into life through the quickening touch of the contemporary, which seek an interpretation of society through the illuminative, transmutative intermediaries of all that is newest, most vitally fecund, most prophetic in the science, sociology, art and religion of to-day; and which endeavour, through faithful portraiture of the present, to detect and reveal the traits and qualities of human nature in its permanent and immutable aspects. The authors of such works find their themes chiefly

431

in the crucial instances of to-day, the conflict of humanity with current institutions, of human wills with existent circumstances, and they have for their end a humanitarian ideal: the exposure of civic abuse, the redress of social wrong, and the regeneration, redemption and reform of society—not less than artistic fidelity to fact, satiric unmasking of human folly, and veritistic embodiment of human passion. To the one class belong Shakespeare, Calderon, Schiller, Rostand; to the other, Charles Reade, Ibsen, Gorki, Brieux. It is a fundamental characteristic of Bernard Shaw that he belongs to the second class—in this respect he is sealed of the tribe of Rousseau, Dumas *fils*, Zola and Tolstoy.

Through the powerful social thrust of modern art there has forged to the front a new and disquieting force. As an isolated phenomenon, this has occasionally made its appearance in the past; but as a distinct genus it may justly be regarded as a creation of the new social order. To scoff at, rather than to study, to dismiss cavalierly rather than to examine conscientiously, this new force, were as short-sighted and senseless as to deny its existence. We are in duty bound to consider and to weigh, carefully and critically, the claims of this " dramatist of the future " as opposed to the classic virtues of the dramatist working frankly in the manner of tradition. The dramatist who conforms to popular and critical standards is an artist facile in revealing either character in action or action in character, invariable in interpreting life from the side of the emotions, and resolute in imaging drama as a true conflict of wills—in a word, the artist gifted with what the French so aptly term *la doigté du dramaturge*. He recognizes the drama as the most impersonal of the arts, and sedulously devotes himself to the realization of Victor Hugo's dictum that dramatic art consists in being somebody else. On the other hand, the new type of dramatist—the dramatist of the future, if you will—is no less an artist than the other; his primal distinction is his demand for that large independence of rules and systems which Turgenev posited as the indispensable requisite of great art. Just as Zola enlarged the conception of the function of the novel, sublimating it into a powerful and far-reaching instrument for social and moral propagandism, so this new dramaturgic iconoclast demands the stage as an instrumentality for the exposition, diffusion, and wide dissemination of his views and theories—upon standards of morality, rules of conduct, codes of ethics, and philosophies of life. With him there is no question of importing the methods of the Blue Book into the drama; nor would he, in any broad sense, idly shirk what Walter Pater terms the responsibility of the artist to his material. He accepts the natural limitations, not the mechanical restrictions, of his art; he does not seek to appropriate the privileges, while refusing to shoulder the responsibilities, of his medium. His distinction arises from the discovery of the hackneyed, but ever alarming and heretical truth, that life is greater than art. For art's sake alone he refuses to exist, with strange perversity insisting that he lives not for the sake of art, but for the sake of humanity.

In reply to the question: " Should social problems be freely dealt with in the drama? " Shaw characteristically said: " Suppose I say yes, then, vaccination being a social question, and the Wagnerian music drama being the one complete form of drama in the opinion of its admirers, it will follow that I am in favour of the production of a Jennerian tetralogy at Bayreuth. If I say no, then, marriage being a social question, and also the theme of Ibsen's *A Doll's House*, I shall be held to condemn that work as a violation of the canons of art." As a matter of fact, Shaw believes that every social question furnishes material for drama—the conflict of human feeling with circumstances—since institutions are themselves circumstances. On the other hand, every drama by no means involves a social question, since human feeling may be in conflict with circumstances which are not institutions. The limitation of drama with a social question for motive is that, ordinarily, it cannot outlive the solution of that question. It is true that some of the best and most popular plays are dramatized sermons, pamphlets, satires, or Blue Books: Gilbert's *Trial by Jury*, a satire on breach of promise; Sheridan's *School for Scandal*, a dramatic sermon; Reade's *Never Too Late to Mend*, a dramatic pamphlet; and so on. The greatest dramatists, however, abjure political and social themes, rooting their dramas in the firm soil of human nature and elemental feeling. The reason for this is that, as a rule, social questions are too temporal, too transient to move the great poet to the mightiest efforts of his imagination. Shaw maintains that the general preference of dramatists for subjects in which the conflict is between man and his apparently inevitable and eternal, rather than his political and temporal, circumstances, is due in the vast majority of cases to the dramatist's political ignorance, and in a few—Goethe and Wagner, for example—to the comprehensiveness of their philosophy.

The era of the drama of pure feeling, in Shaw's opinion, is now past. Every great social question, owing to the huge size of modern populations and the development of the Press, takes on the character of a world-problem. *Les Misérables* is the pure product of our epoch; Zola is the colossal champion of social justice and social reform, Ibsen the arch-enemy of social, as well as moral, abuse. William Morris left house decoration for propagandism; Ruskin resigned *Modern Painters* for modern pamphleteering; Carlyle began by studying German culture and ended with railing against English social crime. The poets are following Shelley as political and social agitators, the drama is becoming an arena for discussion, because the machinery of government is becoming so criminally tardy in its settlement of the perpetually increasing number of social questions: the poet must put his shoulder to the wheel. " The hugeness and complexity of modern civilizations and the development of our consciousness of them by means of the Press," Mr. Shaw maintains, " have the double effect of discrediting comprehensive philosophies by revealing more facts than the ablest man can generalize, and at the same time intensifying the urgency of social reforms sufficiently to set even the poetic faculty in action on their behalf. The resultant tendency to drive social questions on to the stage, and into fiction and poetry, will eventually be counteracted by improvements in social organization which will enable all prosaic social questions to be dealt with satisfactorily long before they become grave enough to absorb the energies which claim the devotion of the dramatist, the story-teller, and the poet." *

Shaw has placed on record his belief that subjects such as age, love, death, accident, personality, abnormal greatness of character, abnormal baseness of character give drama a permanent and universal interest independent of period and place, and will keep a language alive long after it has passed out of common use. It is not the drama of profound and elemental human feeling against which Shaw rails, but the drama designed solely for the obsession of the senses. His most vehement attack is directed against plays pleasurably appealing to animal passions and sensual appetites. To Bernard Shaw, as Benjamin de Casseres has indelicately expressed it, romantic love is lust dressed in Sunday clothes. The voluptuous appeal of the romantic drama is utterly abhorrent to him. The flaccid sentimentalities, the diluted sensualities of the modern plays which he dubs aphrodisiacs, totally fail to impose on him. Sitting at such plays, he says, we do not believe: we make believe. His own plays, he has spared no pains to tell us, are built " to induce, not voluptuous reverie, but intellectual interest, not romantic rhapsody but humane concern. . . . The drama of pure feeling is no longer in the hands of the playwright; it has been conquered by the musician, after whose enchantments all the verbal arts seem cold and tame. . . . The attempt to produce a genus of opera without music—and this absurdity is what our fashionable theatres have been driving at for a long time past without knowing it—is far less hopeful than my own determination to accept problem as the normal material of the drama." †

Cervantes abolished chivalry; let us have done with it, is Shaw's insistent clamour. Romance died with Schopenhauer; let sentiment expire with Shaw. " The thing that Mr. Shaw calls romance," says Mr. Gilbert Chesterton, " is simply the fullness of life, the boiling over of the pot of existence. Things

---

* *The Problem Play: A Symposium (V.),* by G. Bernard Shaw, in the *Humanitarian,* May, 1895.

† *The Author's Apology,* Preface to the Stage Society's edition of *Mrs. Warren's Profession,* p. xxii.

are so good in general that men have, in order to keep pace with the great cataract of beneficence, to call them good in particular. This great and ancient tide of exultation, which makes the tree green, the sunset splendid, the woman beautiful, the flag a thing to be saved at any cost, is, of course, a fact as square and solid as a beefsteak or St. Paul's Cathedral. . . . But Mr. Bernard Shaw has, for all practical purposes, denied the existence of this elemental tendency, and it is not, therefore, strange that he finds the world a moon-struck and half-witted place." * In his plays, indeed, Shaw does not sound these deep and eternal notes of the human symphony. He has fallen into the curious error of confounding contempt for romance with denial of its existence. It is all very well to deplore the eternal idealization of the sexual instinct; it is a totally different matter to represent life as devoid of the ecstasies and raptures of lovers, the pangs of despisèd love, the tyranny of romantic passion.

Temperamentally and philosophically, Shaw is the very antithesis of the romantic. He has consistently sought to reveal and exalt the creative forces in life and art; to awaken the individual to alerter consciousness and to sharpen his preference for actuality over illusion, for reality over appearance. To that romance which seeks to mask the facts of life with the roseate mists of sentiment, the golden halo of illusion, Shaw has proved an inveterate foe. Upon Nordau in his philistine and romantic struggle to uphold a hypothetical standard of normality and to pollute those clear streams of creative energy in art to which we owe the masterpieces of our epoch— upon Nordau Shaw retorted with such splendid force and energy that no one who realizes the issues involved can withhold his gratitude for that triumphant service to the creative spirit of art and of humanity.

One of Bernard Shaw's fundamental claims to attention consists in his effort toward the destruction, not only of romance, but of all the false ideals and illusions which obsess the soul of man. He has assumed the function of tearing the mask of

* *The Meaning of Mr. Bernard Shaw*, by G. K. Chesterton, in the *Daily News*, October 30th, 1901.

GEORGE BERNARD SHAW.

[*Facing p.* 430

idealism from the face of fact. And yet it is a mark of his catholicity of view, that in his attack upon illusions he is neither so blind nor so narrow as not to realize their far-reaching and oftentimes beneficent effect. Thus he says:

" Suppress that phase of human activity which consists in the pursuit of illusions, and you suppress the greatest force in the world. Do not suppose that the pursuit of illusions is a vain pursuit: on the contrary, an illusion can no more exist without reality than a shadow without an object. Unfortunately the majority of men are so constituted that reality repels, while illusions attract them."

With acute psychologic insight, Shaw draws the distinction between two classes of illusions: those which flatter and those which are indispensable. By flattering illusions he understands those which encourage us to make efforts to attain things which we do not know how to appreciate in their simple reality; either they reconcile us to our lot, or else to actions we are obliged to take contrary to the dictates of conscience. These are, indeed, deplorable consequences in the eyes of the humanitarian meliorist who believes that to be reconciled to one's lot is the worst fate that can befall mankind, and who once said that the one real tragedy in life is the being used by personally-minded men for purposes which you yourself recognize to be base.

The *métier* of Bernard Shaw is the destruction, not of the indispensable illusions which support the social structure and ultimately make for the uplift of humanity, but of those treacherously flattering illusions which ensnare men in the toils of an existence for which they have not the requisite passion, courage, faith, endurance and self-restraint. " In my plays," Shaw wrote in the Vienna *Zeit*, " you will not be teased and plagued with happiness, goodness and virtue, or with crime and romance, or, indeed, with any senseless thing of that sort. My plays have only one subject: life; and only one attribute: interest in life." * It is a mistake of the German dramatic critic, Heinrich Stümcke, to aver that the quintessence of Shaw is *nil admirari*. It would be far nearer the truth to say that he wonders at everything in this demented, moon-struck world. The law of contrasts is the *motif* of his art. He is never so brilliant as in the portrayal of opposites.

With the transcendent egotism of the genius, he unhesitatingly claims to see more clearly than humanity at large, to have ever fought illusion, denied the ideal, and scorned to call things by other than their real names.† Thus we see him always in search of what Walter Pater was fond of calling *la vraie vérité,* challenging the old formulas with the new ideas, transvaluing moral values with Nietzschean fervour, and bidding humanity stand from behind its artificial barriers of custom, law, religion and morality, and dare to speak and live the truth. In his capacity of realistic critic of contemporary civilization, he is neither surprised nor confounded to encounter scepticism on all hands. Indeed, he is wise enough to expect it, since he has observed that, when reality at last presents itself to men nourished on dramatic illusions, they have lost the power to recognize it.

Bernard Shaw, as Alfred Kerr has put it, is a distinct ethical gain for our generation. His prime characteristic as a propagandist—and his deficiency as a dramatist—is found

---

* Prospectus of the Schiller-Theater, Berlin. *Vornehmlich über mich selbst,* von Bernard Shaw. This " Plauderei " appeared in the Vienna *Zeit* in February, 1903, shortly before the production of *Teufelskerl (The Devil's Disciple)* in Vienna.

† The celebrated account Shaw once gave of his visit to an ophthalmic surgeon clearly sets before us his conception of the nature and value of his critical faculty: " He tested my eyesight one evening, and informed me that it was quite uninteresting to him because it was ' normal.' I naturally took this to mean that it was like everybody else's; but he rejected this construction as paradoxical, and hastened to explain to me that I was an exceptional and highly fortunate person optically, ' normal ' sight conferring the power of seeing things accurately, and being enjoyed by only about ten per cent. of the population, the remaining ninety per cent. being abnormal. I immediately perceived the explanation of my want of success in fiction. My mind's eye, like my body's, was ' normal '; it saw things differently from other people's eyes, and saw them better."—*Mainly About Myself,* Preface to *Plays, Pleasant and Unpleasant,* Vol. I., p. 11.

in his assertion that the quintessential function of comedy is the destruction of old-established morals. Hence it is that his plays are conceived in a militant spirit—in the Molièresque key of *Les Précieuses Ridicules*, or the Ibsenic key of *An Enemy of the People*. His drama may roughly be defined as the conflict of the Shavian *Ausschauung* with conventional dogma. Like Brieux, he has ingeniously employed the drama as a means of giving lectures. He frankly confesses that his object is to make people uncomfortable, to make them thoroughly ashamed of themselves. "Molière and I are much alike," he once remarked to me; "we both attack pedantry." * Shaw does not wish to drain the drama of all feeling; he merely wishes to make feeling subsidiary to logic. He regards the portrayal of emotion, not as an end in itself, but as an incentive to thought. "You cannot witness *A Doll's House* without *feeling*," he once said, "and, as an inevitable consequence, thinking." He wishes to set up, in the minds of his audience, a train of reflections and meditations which may alter their own lives, which may influence the whole world. For, as Emerson says, "To think is to act." Shaw's object is to create a true drama of ideas, having for its normal material "problem, with its remorseless logic and iron framework of fact." He would have intellect predominate over sentiment; will engineered by idea, and not unreasoning passion, the controlling factor. Bernard Shaw is frequently charged with being devoid of feeling. Shaw is less influenced by or concerned with mere personal feeling than anyone I have ever known; but his whole being is vibrant with passion for the welfare of society. If social pity is the underlying motive of the later Russian novelists, social indignation seems to be the guiding principle of Bernard Shaw. To him, social thought has become a genuine passion.

The quintessence of the Shavian drama is the Shavian phi-

---

* At various times, in essays published in Europe and in America, I have called attention to the resemblance between Shaw and Molière, dubbing Shaw the Molière of our time. Recently, M. Auguste Hamon has made a detailed comparison of the two comic dramatists in the *Nineteenth Century and After: Un Nouveau Molière*, July, 1908.

losophy. Shaw's theatre may be defined as an effort to depict naked instincts upon the stage; this is the meaning of his "scientific natural history." He has sought to project instinctive temperaments, alive and potent, before our very eyes. The inspiring words of Zola at the funeral of Edmond de Goncourt might well have served as the motto for his principal figures: "Ah! to have intellectual courage! To tell the truth and the whole truth, even if it cost one peace and friends; never to consider any convention, to go to the end of one's thought, careless of consequence. Nothing is rarer, nothing is finer, nothing is grander." Unhampered by such scrupulousness as that of Mark Twain, who declared that it was immodest to tell the naked truth in the presence of ladies, Shaw's leading characters are ever in quest of truth and freedom. They seek truth in unflinching recognition of facts, freedom in emancipation from slavery to the false idealism of romantic convention. They are libertines, in the original and not the perverted sense of the word, with judgment unbiassed by traditional influence or contemporary prejudice. They are natural, not so much in the sense of being perfect replicas of contemporary men and women—for they are often little more than personified aspects of Shavianism—as in the sense of being in a state of nature in regard to whim, eccentricity, fancy, impulse, passion. There is a sort of complex and advanced juvenility about Shaw's characters; they are the *enfants gâtés* of modern drama. In them are concretely delineated the outlines of the Shavian philosophy: "Duty is the thing one should never do," "Virtue consists, not in abstaining from vice, but in not desiring it," "Sentimentality is the error of supposing that quarter can be given or taken in moral conflicts." The difference between moral and right, for these Shavians, is the difference between doing what you ought to do and what you want to do. Shakespeare's "To thine own self be true" is insufficient; the modern sociologist knows that it is imperative to realize, not only what you are, but where you are. After studying the possibilities, not the restrictions, of their environment, the Shavian characters go straight ahead and do what they choose. Shaw outranks Ibsen himself in the individualistic injunction "Live your own life."

In his own admirable way, Shaw has given us a succinct exposition of his conception of the Shavian drama. Asked if he wrote plays to make fun of people, Shaw replied, more in sorrow than in anger:

"People talk all this nonsense about my plays because they have been to the theatre so much that they have lost their sense of the unreality and insincerity of the romantic drama. They take stage human nature for real human nature, whereas, of course, real human nature is the bitterest satire on stage human nature. The result is that when I try to put real human nature on the stage they think that I am laughing at them. They flatter themselves enormously, for I am not thinking of them at all. I am simply writing natural history very carefully and laboriously; and they are expecting something else. I can imagine a Japanese who had ordered a family portrait of himself, and expected it to be in the Japanese convention as to design, being exceedingly annoyed if the artist handed him a photograph, however artistic, because it was like him in a natural way. He would accuse the photographer of making fun of him and of having his tongue in his cheek.

"But there is a deeper reason for this attitude of mind. People imagine that actions and feelings are dictated by moral systems, by religious systems, by codes of honour and conventions of conduct which lie outside the real human will. Now it is a part of my gift as a dramatist that I know that these conventions do not supply them with their motives. They make very plausible *ex post facto* excuses for their conduct; but the real motives are deep down in the will itself.

"And so an infinite comedy arises in everyday life from the contrast between the real motives and the alleged artificial motives; and when the dramatist refuses to be imposed upon, and forces his audience to laugh at the

441

imposture, there is always a desperate effort to cover up the scandal and save the face of the conventional by the new convention that whoever refuses to play the conventional game is a cynic and a satirist, a *farceur*, a person whom no one takes seriously." *

The supreme difficulty in any criticism of Bernard Shaw as dramatist is to draw the many fine distinctions between his critical expositions of his dramatic system and the actual qualities of the dramas themselves. It is primarily incumbent upon the interpreter of Shaw to indicate with sufficient clearness the discrepancy between theory and practice, between purpose and performance. No objection need be raised to Shaw's definitions. " Drama is no mere setting up of the camera to Nature," he says: " it is the presentation in parable of the conflict between Man's will and his environment: in a word, of problem." But what is one to make of Sir Charles Wyndham's assertion that Shaw's dramatic works are wonderful intellectual studies, but not plays? The dramas are undoubtedly manufactured after the usual pattern, with divisions called acts; figures like people walk back and forth and engage each other in conversation; the mechanical illusion is complete. What is it, then, that gives an air of unreality to all this mimic show?

Bernard Shaw possesses in rich measure the genius of the stage-director, the pliability and suppleness of the critic of modern civilization. The effects he produces, quite often, are tremendous. But capitally and congenitally, Shaw is lacking in that quality ordinarily recognized as natural dramatic genius. In his plays we look almost in vain for those crucial emotional conjunctures, those climacteric soul-crises, which dramatic critics announce to be the criteria of authentic drama—the *scène à faire* of a Sarcey. Just as Oscar Wilde may be said to have invented the comedy of conversation, so Bernard Shaw may be said to have invented the drama of discussion. The tendency to prolixity and discursiveness has

* *Our Saturday Talk.—VI.,* Mr. Bernard Shaw, in the *Saturday Westminster Gazette,* November 26th, 1904.

steadily grown upon him; at last he has thrown off all disguise and deliberately set to work to create a dramatic system based on dialectic. Two noteworthy features of his career are his attacks upon conventional cant and Shakespearean rhetoric. And all the time, he has been creating, for his own part, both a Shavian cant and a Shavian rhetoric. " I find that the surest way to startle the world with daring innovations and originalities," he recently said, " is to do exactly what playwrights have been doing for thousands of years; to revive the ancient attraction of long rhetorical speeches; to stick closely to the methods of Molière; and to lift characters bodily out of the pages of Charles Dickens." The defining characteristic of his plays is their argumentative and controversial character. They are expository lectures, in dramatic form, on the Shavian philosophy. Mr. Archer once said that Shaw's keen and subtle intellect has built for itself a world of its own, in which it sits apart, inaccessible; this world is not the real earth, but

> "Composed just as he is inclined to conjecture her,
> Namely, one part pure earth, ninety-nine parts pure lecturer."

Instead of the indispensable conflict of wills, we often seem to have merely a war of wits, in which the cleverest dialectician wins. Aristophanes and Shaw have certainly one point in common: the plays of both are dramatized debates. Instead of touching each other's emotions, Shaw's characters often seem merely to arouse each other's combative interest. Just as Victor Hugo gives a passion apiece to each of his characters and lets them fight it out, so Shaw gives a philosophy apiece to each of his characters and lets them argue it out. His comedies exhibit with tremendous comic irony the exposure of non-Shavians by Shavians. One day Huxley in jest described Herbert Spencer's idea of a tragedy as " a deduction killed by a fact." In a moderate, a partial, sense, this might serve as a just criticism of the theatre of Bernard Shaw.

There is a certain fanciful sort of resemblance between a play of Shaw's and a meeting of his own Borough Council: the meeting is called to order, there is argument and discussion *pro* and *con,* a resolution is moved, seconded, carried.

Shaw is positively judicial in his fairness, even to the extent of creating the impression that his characters are vocalized points of view. With consummate shrewdness, Shaw has fully realized that if the dramatist take sides in a dramatic wrangle, he is lost. A sense of the most absolute fairness and impartiality pervades and dominates his plays. Every character has his say without let or hindrance; and the whole play is signalized by the "honesty of its dialectic." Shaw does not disclaim the fullest responsibility for the opinions of all his characters, pleasant and unpleasant. "They are all right from their several points of view; and their points of view are, for the dramatic moment, mine also. This may puzzle the people who believe that there is such a thing as an absolutely right point of view, usually their own. It may seem to them that nobody who doubts this can be in a state of grace. However that may be, it is certainly true that nobody who argues with them can possibly be a dramatist, or, indeed, anything else that turns upon a knowledge of mankind. Hence it has been pointed out that Shakespeare had no conscience. Neither have I, in that sense." *

This quality of anxious self-explanation in his characters, this "Let me make clear to you my philosophy of life," produces upon the reader and spectator two distinct impressions: first an "overwhelming impression of coldness and inhuman rationalism"; and, second, the impression that the characters are replicas or mouthpieces of Shaw himself. The resemblance is still further enhanced through the instrumentality of one of Shaw's most diverting traits as a humorist: his idiosyncrasy for self-mockery and self-puffery. There is nothing, not even himself, about which Shaw will not jest; for, to use an Oscarism, he respects life too deeply to discuss it seriously. He is a master of that art of burlesque which, in Brunetière's harsh characterization, consists "in the expansion of the ego in the joyous satisfaction of its own vulgarity." One of the truest words, spoken in jest, is Shaw's confession that the main obstacle to the performance of his plays has been—himself!

* *Man and Superman: Epistle Dedicatory to Arthur Bingham Walkley,* p. xxvi.

THE DRAMATIST

In contradistinction to the classic formula—that the drama should be the most impersonal of the arts—Shaw's drama may be defined as a revelation of the personality of Bernard Shaw. "We must agree with him," concludes M. Filon, "and accept —or reject—the dramatic work of Mr. Shaw as it is, namely, as the expression of the ideas, sentiments and fantasies of Mr. Shaw." *

In fine, I should say that Bernard Shaw is a striking instance of the unusual combination of critical and creative faculties. Sometimes the dramatist, he is always the critic. While Shaw can make one laugh, it is seldom that he can make one weep. He unites within himself the power both to construct and to dissect. With Shaw—the *Richter und Dichter* of German characterization—rationality precedes creation. His richly constructive fancy seldom imagines what his cooler reason has not already perceived. In his plays, there is scarcely a hint of what he himself somewhere described as "the stirring of the blood, the bristling of the fibres, the transcendent, fearless fury which makes romance so delightful." Shaw is always perfectly aware of himself; Coventry Patmore would have denied him the title of true genius. As someone has cleverly said: "Shaw's eye has never yet in a fine frenzy rolled." If he had ever listened to the horns of elfland faintly blowing, he would doubtless have said afterwards that Kosleck of Berlin could have done it better. If he had ever heard the morning stars sing together and the sons of God shout for joy, the experience would probably have elicited the coolly critical remark that the *ensemble* effect was not as good as at Bayreuth, and that the shouting was not as ear-splitting as the "wilful bawling" of the De Reszkes.

This coolly critical attitude, which Shaw manages to transfer to his characters, gives them the appearance of beings peculiarly rationalistic and bloodless. In their veins, as Mr. Archer once said of the leading characters in *Widowers' Houses*, there seems to flow a sort of sour whey. Shaw has almost succeeded in eliminating the Red Corpuscle from Art.

* *M. Bernard Shaw et son Théâtre,* by Augustin Filon; *Revue des Deux Mondes,* November 15th, 1905.

His characters seem to be devoid of animal passions; their pallid ratiocinations can more aptly be described as vegetable passions.

In the case of Shaw, I often receive the impression that inspiration is replaced by excogitation, imagination by what Rossetti called fundamental brain-work. Lessing's phrase, "dramatic algebra," is not a wholly inappropriate term for his plays. A partial explanation of this phenomenon may perhaps be found in the speech I heard him deliver at the Vedrenne-Barker dinner. "One hears a lot of talk these days about the New School of Shavian playwrights—Granville Barker, St. John Hankin, and the rest. I sincerely hope they will not try to imitate my style and method. There is only one Bernard Shaw, and that one is quite sufficient. I find a striking analogy between the case of the old Italian masters and myself. When they began to work, they found that the human form had been neglected and ignored. Forthwith they began to paint works which appeared to be anatomical studies, so emphasized was the figure. I found myself in much the same situation when I first began to write for the stage. I found that the one thing which had been neglected and ignored by British dramatists was human nature. So I began to put human nature barely and nakedly upon the stage, which so startled the public that they declared that my characters were utterly unnatural and untrue to life. But I have gone on and on exposing human nature, more and more in each succeeding play. If my imitators continue to reveal human nature so ruthlessly, I am afraid I shall have done more harm than good." * The greatest artist, according to Shaw's own definition, is "he who goes a step beyond the demand, and, by supplying works of a higher beauty and a higher interest than have yet been perceived, succeeds, after a brief struggle with its strangeness, in adding this fresh extension of sense to the heritage of the race." It is a mark of Shaw's high purpose, of the sociologic significance of the man, that he employs art

* Response to the toast: *The Authors of the Court Theatre,* by G. Bernard Shaw, at the Vedrenne-Barker Dinner, Criterion Restaurant, London, July 7th, 1907.

SHAW'S PRESENT HOME IN LONDON,

10, Adelphi Terrace, W.C.

[*Facing p.* 440

merely as one of a number of means by which he can put his ideas into effect. Doubtless because of his belief that philosophic content is the touchstone of real greatness in art—that Bunyan is greater than Shakespeare, Blake than Lamb, Ibsen than Swinburne, Shaw than Pinero—his plays have something of the rigidity of theses. Shaw's plays not infrequently suffer from the malady of the *à priori*. Sometimes they are even stricken down with what Wagner called the incurable disease of thought.

Shakespeare created a drama of human nature in which the actions of the characters are their own commentary. Maeterlinck created a drama of shadow in which the characters are most articulate in their silence. Shaw has created a drama of discussion in which his characters have not the strength to hold their tongues. Shakespeare's characters are self-unconscious characters; Maeterlinck's, subconscious; Shaw's, self-conscious. Mr. Holbrook Jackson remarks that " Shaw's drama is the only consistently religious drama of the day—it is as relentless in its pursuit of an exalted idea as were the ancient Moralities and Mysteries." But Mr. Jackson fails to draw the conclusion that, for this reason, Shaw's characters often take on the guise of intellectual abstractions. The Frenchman calls them *hommes-idées;* the German, *Gedanken-puppen.* Shaw's plays are pitched on a plane of transcendental realism. His supreme gift as a dramatist, someone has wisely said, is to produce an impression of life more real than reality itself. His power of penetrative insight at times appears to be something almost like divination. The soul of his wit is laconic brevity and marvellous astuteness in character exposure. His dialogue is the most entertaining, the most diverting, that has been written since the days of Sheridan. He has succeeded in interpreting life with so precise and so illuminating a medium that he frequently transcends the bounds of plausibility, probability, or even possibility, without the lapse being noted. Many, perhaps the majority, of his leading characters, operate upon a plane of fantasy; the psychological impossibility of their actions is concealed by the intellectual credibility of their ideas. They appear as the mouthpieces of his theories, as replicas of his personality, or as changing aspects of his own temperament. Or else, in the later plays, they appear as embodied forces of Nature, as allegorical personifications of modern Moralities. Shaw is constitutionally opposed to " holding the kodak up to Nature "; he believes in making the chaos of Nature intelligible by intelligent choice of material. His *métier*, then, is interpretation, not observation. As a consequence, he gives us life interpreted in strict accordance with Shavian sophistication. In large part, he depicts human beings not as they really are, but as they might be supposed to be if animated by the Shavian philosophy modified to suit the needs of their individual temperaments.

Quite a number of Shaw's leading characters, and the majority of the subsidiary characters, are marvellously natural studies in contemporary psychology. Unhampered by the *impedimenta* of Shavianism, they move freely and naturally along the beaten paths of humanity. Now and then, we are whisked away to the realm of fantasy; or else we have only to shut our eyes and open our ears to hear Shaw's ironical laughter echo through their speeches. But, on the whole, we are not deceived in believing that Bernard Shaw's plays are all stages in his search for the essential reality of things. Along the pathway, he has left many vivid, many brilliant, many comprehensible, some complex, and all essentially modern figures. Sartorius, kind-hearted and inhumane; the unwomanly " womanly woman," Julia; Mrs. Warren, reptilianly fascinating and repulsive, her mother-love slain by the relentless sword of her profession; Crofts, upholding a hideously immoral standard of honour before our sickened gaze; Bluntschli, genial, droll expositor of the prose and common sense of life; Marchbanks, anæmic, asthenic—a visionary penetrating to the truth beneath all disguises and learning the lesson of life in the black hour of disillusionment; Morell, the stupid, good-natured, self-centred parson; Candida, the maternal *clairvoyante;* Dudgeon, the fascinating dare-devil, resolute in fulfilment of the law of his own nature; Judith, the sentimental and *larmoyante;* Lady Cicely, ingenuous, tactful, feline, irresistible; Cleopatra, subtly evolving from a kittenish minx into a tigerish and vengeful tyrant; the boyish, energetic, humane Cæsar, large in humour and in comic perception; Broadbent, the typical, stolid Englishman, blunderingly successful because he doesn't know where he is going; Keegan, the gentle and the bitter, *vox clamantis in deserto*, interpreting a new trinity for the worship of the coming age; Sir Patrick Cullen, quintessence of gruff and kindly common sense; the immortal William, deferential and urbane; and how many more!—a group of finely imagined, subtly conceived, *essentially* real, if not always credibly human, beings.

Shaw is a marvellous portrait painter, a Sargent in his insight into human nature and into contemporary life. He is a wit of the very first rank, a satirist to be classed with Voltaire, Renan and Anatole France. The static drama he has created enlarges our conception of the function of the drama. The new dramatic system of Shaw's creation, in the words of M. Filon, subordinates the development of the sentimental action to the painting of characters and the discussion of ideas. Like Molière, Shaw has stamped his characters in the idea, and made of them the necessary exponents of contemporary philosophy, the inevitable interpreters of contemporary life.

Capitally and fundamentally, Bernard Shaw's drama is socially deterministic. His characters are what they are, become what they become, far less on account of heredity or ancestral influence than on account of the social structure of the environment through which their fate is moulded. Economist as well as moralist, Shaw attributes paramount importance to the economic and political conditions of the *régime* in which his characters live and move and have their being. His drama has its true origin in the conflict between the wills of his characters and the social determinism perpetually at work to destroy the freedom of their wills. The germ idea of his philosophy is rooted in the effort to supplant modern social organization by Socialism through the intermediary of the free operation of the will of humanity.

ARTIST AND PHILOSOPHER

" It was easy for Ruskin to lay down the rule of dying rather than doing unjustly; but death is a plain thing, justice a very obscure thing. How is an ordinary man to draw the line between right and wrong otherwise than by accepting public opinion on the subject; and what more conclusive expression of sincere public opinion can there be than market demand? Even when we repudiate that and fall back on our own judgment, the matter gathers doubt rather than clearness. The popular notion of morality and piety is to simply beg all the more important questions in life for other people; but when these questions come home to ourselves, we suddenly discover that the devil's advocate has a stronger case than we thought: we remember that the way of righteousness or death was the way of the Inquisition; that hell is paved, not with bad intentions but with good ones."—An Essay on Modern Glove Fighting appended to *Cashel Byron's Profession.*

CHAPTER XV

IT is worthy of record that Bernard Shaw does not *claim* to be a great novelist, or a great dramatist, or a great critic. As Mr. Chesterton says, Shaw is very dogmatic, but very humble. Indeed, Mr. Shaw once wrote me that he does not *claim* to be great: either he is or he is not great, and that is an end of the matter! But it is highly significant that Shaw does specifically claim to be a philosopher. Shaw's philosophical ideas have generally been regarded by English and American critics either as of undoubted European derivation, or else as fantastic paradoxes totally unrelated to the existing body of thought. " I urge them to remember," Shaw remonstrates, " that this body of thought is the slowest of growths and the rarest of blossomings, and that if there is such a thing on the philosophic plane as a matter of course, it is that no individual can make more than a minute contribution to it." Whilst it is undoubtedly true that Shaw's philosophy has been partially shared in by many forerunners, nevertheless, he has made his own " minute contribution " to the existing body of thought. Bernard Shaw is an independent thinker and natural moralist, with a clearly co-ordinated system of philosophy. Let us critically endeavour, then, in the language of political economy, to award Shaw his merited " rent of ability."

Shaw's fundamental postulate is that morality is not a stagnant quality, the same yesterday, to-day and for ever, but transitory and evolutional. Morality flows: " What people call vice is eternal; what they call virtue is mere fashion." A celebrated French critic once declared: " *La morale est purement géographique.*" Shaw goes far beyond this in the assertion that morality is a creature of occasion, conditioned by circumstance. And why is it that morality comes to be regarded as not in itself a fixed quantity, a solid substratum of human consciousness, but a concomitant fluxion of civilization?

It is because, historically considered, progress connotes repudiation of custom: social advance takes effect through the replacement of old institutions by new ones. " Since every institution involves the duty of conforming to it, progress must involve the repudiation of an established duty at every turn." History shows us a world strewn with the wrecks of institutions whose laws, upheld for a time as fixed, were eventually broken by the triumphant assertion of the crescent will of man. This phenomenon is not to be confused with that in which an institution is burst simply by the natural growth of the social organism. The phenomenon of which we are speaking involves a deliberate assertion of self-constituted authority on the part of the individual in defiance of established and generally accepted customs.*

" The ideal is dead; long live the ideal! " is the epitome of all human progress. It is the note of nineteenth century literature. For the first time in history the devil began to get his due. Men ceased to be always on the side of the angels; a new day was dawning, the day of the saintly anarch, the *advocatus diaboli.* Shaw has given us a brief history of the movement:

> " Formerly, when there was a question of canonizing a pious person, the devil was allowed an advocate to support his claims to the pious person's soul. But nobody ever dreamt of openly defending him as a much misunderstood and fundamentally right-minded regenerator of the race until the nineteenth century, when William Blake boldly went over to the other side and started a devil's party. Fortunately for himself, he was a poet, and so

---

* Shaw's philosophy has many points of contact with the Pragmatism of Schiller and James. Shaw sees in truth and justice, not abstract principles external to man, but *human passions,* which have, in their time, conflicted with higher passions as well as with lower ones. With James he is at one in the belief that " Truth has its palæontology, and its ' prescription' and may grow stiff with years of veteran service and petrified in men's regard by sheer antiquity"; and with Schiller's " humanistic " doctrine that " to an unascertainable extent our truths are man-made products too." To Shaw, as to James, "' the right' is only the expedient in the way of our behaving."

passed as a paradoxical madman instead of a blasphemer. For a long time the party made little direct progress, the nation being occupied with the passing of its religion through the purifying fire of a criticism which did at last smelt some of the grosser African elements out of it, but which also exalted duty, morality, law and altruism above faith; reared ethical societies; and left my poor old friend the devil (for I, too, was a Diabolonian born) worse off than ever. Mr. Swinburne explained Blake, and even went so far as to exclaim: ' Come down and redeem us from virtue '; but the pious influences of Putney reclaimed him, and he is now a respectable, Shakespeare-fearing man. Mark Twain emitted some Diabolonian sparks, only to see them extinguished by the overwhelming American atmosphere of chivalry, duty and gentility. A miserable spurious Satanism, founded on the essentially pious dogma that the Prince of Darkness is no gentleman, sprang up in Paris, to the heavy discredit of the true cult of the Son of the Morning. All seemed lost, when suddenly the cause found its dramatist in Ibsen, the first leader who really dragged duty, unselfishness, idealism, self-sacrifice, and the rest of the anti-diabolic scheme to the bar at which it had indicted so many excellent Diabolonians. The outrageous assumption that a good man may do anything he thinks right (which in the case of a *naturally* good man means, by definition, anything he likes), without regard to the interests of bad men or of the community at large, was put on its defence, and the party became influential at last.

"After the dramatist came the philosopher. In England, G. B. S.; in Germany, Nietzsche." *

The whole anarchistic spirit of our time is summed up in the words of a character in one of Ibsen's plays: " The old beauty is no longer beautiful; the new truth is no longer true."

* *Giving the Devil His Due:* a review, by Bernard Shaw, of Vols. I. and II. of the works of Friedrich Nietzsche. Supplement to the *Saturday Review,* May 13th, 1899.

Every age has its dominant accepted ideas and forms; but, as Georg Brandes has said: "besides these, it owns another whole class of quite different ideas, which have not yet taken shape, but are in the air, and are apprehended by the greatest men of the age as the results which must now be arrived at." The ideas of the evolutionary trend of human ideals, of the triumphant hypocrisy of current morality, of the necessity for challenging and repudiating the code of the human herd were in the air: they were slowly being arrived at. We hear Chamfort's contemptuous assertion: "*Il y a à parier que toute idée publique—toute convention reçue—est une sottise; car elle a convenue au plus grand nombre.*" We see William Blake performing the ceremony of the *Marriage of Heaven and Hell;* the Pirate King in W. S. Gilbert's *Pirates of Penzance* repudiates *bourgeois* respectability in his reply to Frederic's urgent request to accompany him back to civilization: "No, Frederic, it cannot be. I don't think much of our profession, but, contrasted with respectability, it is comparatively honest. No, Frederic; I shall live and die a pirate king." In *The Man that Corrupted Hadleyburg,* Mark Twain posits a new reading of the Lord's Prayer: "Lead us (not) into temptation"; he arraigns the morality of custom in *Was It Heaven or Hell?* Nietzsche works his way, through the "outer fortifications, the garb and masquerade; the occasional incrustation, petrification, dogmatization" of the ideal, to a position beyond good and evil, from which he transvalues all moral values.*

With Ibsen, the disciple as well as the master of his age, the newer ideas gained currency through the medium of the drama. The individualist Stockmann, in *An Enemy of the*

---

* "'Is here,' someone will ask, 'an ideal being erected, or an ideal being broken down?' But have ye ever really asked yourselves sufficiently as to how dearly the erection of *all* ideals on earth were paid for? How much reality had to be slandered and misconceived for this purpose; how much falsehood sanctioned; how much conscience confused; how much 'God' sacrificed each time? In order that a sanctuary may be erected, *a sanctuary must be broken down:* this is the law—name me an instance in which it is violated!" Friedrich Nietzsche, *Genealogy of Morals,* translated by William A. Hausemann, p. 122 (Macmillan).

People, preaches the salutary sermon of the "saving remnant" in his passionate declamation: "The majority is never right! That's one of the social lies a free, thinking man is bound to rebel against. Who make up the majority in any given country? Is it the wise men or the fools? I think all must agree that the fools are in a terribly overwhelming majority all the world over. . . . What sort of truths do the majority rally round? Truths that are decrepit with age. When a truth is as old as that, then it's in a fair way to become a lie." Ibsen is one with Saint Augustine in the belief that it matters not so much what we are as what we are becoming. "Neither our moral conceptions nor our artistic forms," he once said, "have an eternity before them. How much in duty are we really bound to hold on to? Who can afford me a guarantee that up yonder on Jupiter two and two do not make five?" And at a dinner at the Grand Hotel, Stockholm, he concretized this tenet of modern faith in the words: "It has been asserted on various occasions that I am a pessimist. So I am to this extent—that I do not believe human ideals to be eternal. But I am also an optimist, for I believe firmly in the power of those ideals to propagate and develop." In like manner Zola declared that there was always a contest between men of unconquerable temperaments and the herd: "I am on the side of the temperaments, and I attack the herd." How fiercely Schopenhauer and Shelley, Lassalle and Karl Marx, Ruskin and Carlyle, Morris and Wagner railed at all the orthodoxies, the respectabilities and the ideals! Heine tilted against the Philistine, "the strong, dogged, unenlightened opponent of the chosen people, of the children of light," with an *élan* equalled only by the detestation of Carlyle for the snobbery which he denominated "respectability in its thousand gigs." The literature of the age resounded with the "rattle of twentieth century tumbrils."

Nietzsche has declared that the good taste, the "honesty," of a psychologist consists nowadays, if in anything, in his opposing the shamefully permoralized language by which as by a phlegm all modern judging on men and things is covered. His aim must be to "re-discover" the incarnate innocence in moralistic mendaciousness, to stagger the complacency of the illuded, ever " holding aloft the banner of the ideal," to divorce the imagined life from the real. Mr. W. S. Gilbert was the first modern English dramatist to satirize the morality of custom; but his philosophy was a mere farcical masquerade and sham. " He would put forward a paradox," Shaw has justly observed, " which at first promised to be one of those humane truths which so many modern men of fine spiritual insight, from William Blake onward, have worded so as to flash out their contradictions of some weighty rule of our systematized morality, and would then let it slip through his fingers, leaving nothing but a mechanical topsy-turvitude." *

Bernard Shaw has identified the function of comedy with the destruction of old-established morals. In play after play, from *Mrs. Warren's Profession* and *Arms and the Man* to *The Devil's Disciple* and *Man and Superman,* he has mordantly and fiercely attacked that " inmost feminism which delights in calling itself idealism," that Philistine respectability which vaunts itself on its " morality of custom," and the genuine British narrowness, with its humdrum conservatism, its slavery to routine, its stupid distrust of new ideas and fear of bold thinking. Like Ibsen, he is always an outpost thinker, having no tolerance for conservatism—the attitude of " the little narrow-chested, short-winded crew that lie in our wake." He has lived in passionate defiance of the precept:

> " Be not the first by whom the new is tried,
> Nor yet the last to lay the old aside."

The step from the premiss that morality is a variable function of civilization to the conclusion that salvation lies alone

* To take a single example, consult *My Dream,* from *The Bab Ballads and Songs of a Savoyard,* the first two stanzas of which read:

> The other night, from cares exempt,
> I slept—and what d'you think I dreamt?
> I dreamt that somehow I had come
> To dwell in Topsy-Turvydom.

> Where vice is virtue—virtue, vice;
> Where nice is nasty—nasty, nice;
> Where right is wrong and wrong is right;
> Where white is black and black is white.

in revolt was inevitable. Historically considered, the stages in the growth of man's spirit may be classified under three heads: Faith, Reason, Will. First came the age of Faith: man accepted the precepts of the Bible as the revelation of God's voice. Faith in the Bible became the criterion of righteous intention, and for a time the authority of the Church reigned supreme. After a while came the age of free-thought, of Reason; the free-thinker begins to " find reasons for not doing what he does not want to do; and these reasons seem to him to be far more binding on the conscience than the precepts of a book of which the divine inspiration cannot be rationally proved." Faith was dethroned by Reason, and rationalist " free-thinking " soon came to mean " syllogism worship with rites of human sacrifice."

The great error of the Rationalists is latent in Voltaire's reply to the plea of the poetaster that he must live: " *Je n'en vois pas la nécessité.*" " The evasion was worthy of the Father of Lies himself," Shaw has it; " for Voltaire was face to face with the very necessity he was denying—must have known, consciously or not, that it was the universal postulate—would have understood, if he had lived to-day, that since all human institutions are constructed to fulfil man's will, and that his will is to live even when his reason teaches him to die, logical necessity, which was the sort Voltaire meant (the other sort being visible enough) can never be a motor in human action, and is, in short, not necessity at all." In the course of time came Schopenhauer to re-establish the old theological doctrine that reason is no motive power; that the true motive power in the world—otherwise life—is will, and that the setting up of reason above will is a damnable error.

Shaw has warned us that acceptance of the metaphysics of Schopenhauerism by no means involves endorsement of its philosophy. To Shaw, the cardinal Rationalist error into which Schopenhauer fell consisted in making happiness the test of the value of life. Shaw is the most vigorous possible combatant of the pessimist conclusion that life is not worth living, and that " the will which urges us to live in spite of this is necessarily a malign torturer, the desirable end of all things being the Nirvana of the stilling of the will, and the consequent setting of life's sun ' into the blind cave of eternal night.' " The keynote of the Shavian philosophy is *the pursuit of life for its own sake. Life is realized only as activity that satisfies the will: that is, as self-assertion. Every extension or intensification of activity is an increase in life.* Quantity and quality of activity measure the value of existence. Shaw has refused to acknowledge the validity of the will of the official theologians, because their God stands outside man and in authority above him. He accepted Schopenhauer's view of the will as a " purely secular force of nature, attaining various degrees of organization, here as a jelly-fish, there as a cabbage, more complexly as an ape or a tiger, and attaining its highest form, so far, in the human being." This was Shaw's key to the works of two great artists, Wagner and Ibsen, notably, *The Ring* and *Emperor and Galilean.*

It is the idlest nonsense to say of Shaw, in Oscar Wilde's phrase, that he has the courage of other people's convictions. Shaw's most conspicuous trait is his courage in challenging and defying other people's convictions. Instead of clinging to the pessimism of Schopenhauer, he has been bold enough to " drop the Nirvana nonsense, the pessimism, the rationalism, the theology, and all the other subterfuges to which we cling because we are afraid to look life straight in the face and see in it, not the fulfilment of a moral law or the deductions of reason, but the satisfaction of a passion in us of which we can give no account." Claiming for himself the faculty of unilluded vision, he conceives it his mission to tear away the veils with which we persist in hiding realities and to call things by their true names, instead of the false names with which we are content to dupe ourselves. Mr. Walkley once said: " Mr. Shaw takes up the empty bladders of life, the current commonplaces, the cant phrases, the windbags of rodomontade, the hollow conventions and the sham sentiments; quietly inserts his pin, and the thing collapses with a pop." But Shaw regards this as a cheap job which any man might do and which Mr. Walkley himself excels in. "It is not the bubbles and bladders that require some tackling," Mr. Shaw once observed to me; "it is the solid brass that has to be assayed and proved to be base metal."

In many places, in varying ways, Shaw has given pungent expression to the opinion so well advanced in Meredith's words: "Our world is all but a sensational world at present, in maternal travail of a soberer, a braver, a bright-eyed." The clarity of Shaw's vision has saved him from the cheap crudeness of pessimism: unlike Ibsen, plenty of "sound potatoes" have come under his observation. His position is clearly expressed in his own words:

"Now to me, as a realist playwright, the applause of the conscious, hardy pessimist is more exasperating than the abuse of the unconscious, fearful one. I am not a pessimist at all. It does not concern me that, according to certain ethical systems, all human beings fall into classes labelled liar, coward, thief, and so on. I am myself, according to these systems, a liar, a coward, a thief, and a sensualist; and it is my deliberate, cheerful and entirely self-respecting intention to continue to the end of my life deceiving people, avoiding danger, making my bargains with publishers and managers on principles of supply and demand instead of abstract justice, and indulging all my appetites, whenever circumstances commend such actions to my judgment. If any creed or system deduces from this that I am a rascal incapable on occasion of telling the truth, facing a risk, forgoing a commercial advantage, or resisting an intemperate impulse of any sort, then so much the worse for the creed or system, since I have done all these things, and will probably do them again. The saying, ' All have sinned ' is, in the sense in which it was written, certainly true of all the people I have ever known. But the sinfulness of my friends is not unmixed with saintliness: some of their actions are sinful, others saintly. And here, again, if the ethical system to which the classifications of saint and sinner belong, involves the conclusion that a line of cleavage drawn between my friends' sinful actions and their saintly ones will coincide exactly with one drawn between their mistakes and their successes (I include the highest and the widest sense of the two terms), then so much the worse for the system; for the facts contradict it. Persons obsessed by systems may retort: ' No; so much the worse for your friends '—implying that I must move in a circle of rare blackguards; but I am quite prepared not only to publish a list of friends of mine whose names would put such a retort to open shame, but to take any human being, alive or dead, of whose actions a genuinely miscellaneous unselected dozen can be brought to light, to show that none of the ethical systems habitually applied by dramatic critics (not to mention other people) can verify their inferences. As a realist dramatist, therefore, it is my business to get outside these systems. . . . The fact is, though I am willing and anxious to see the human race improved, if possible, still I find that, with reasonably sound specimens, the more intimately I know people the better I like them; and when a man concludes from this that I am a cynic, and that he who prefers stage monsters —walking catalogues of the systematized virtues—to his own species, is a person of wholesome philanthropic tastes, why, how can I feel toward him except as an Englishwoman feels toward the Arab, who, faithful to *his* system, denounces her indecency in appearing in public with her mouth uncovered." *

The destruction of the principle of alien authority carries with it the necessity for the creation of the individual standard. The dethronement of rationalism, be it observed, involves no repudiation of logic and intellect as guides to everyday life. " Ability to reason accurately is as desirable as ever, since it

* *A Dramatic Realist to His Critics,* in the *New Review* (London), July, 1894.

is only by accurate reasoning that we can calculate our actions so as to do what we intend to do—that is, to fulfil our will." Instead of accepting the nude, anarchistic formula of Maurice Barrés, for example, " *Fais ce que tu veux*," Shaw may be understood to enjoin: " Form your moral conscience and act as it directs you." *

A development in our moral views must first appear insane and blasphemous, Shaw has time and again warned us, to people who are satisfied, or more than satisfied, with the current morality. Henri Beyle was for long, and still is, much misunderstood for the simple reason that the characters he created evolve their own standard, pursue their cherished ideals with unfaltering determination, and brook no interference, make no compromise, until they have won and established their self-respect. All the while insisting on the prudence necessary to discover the way for the will, Shaw has unhesitatingly taken the supreme step, realizing always that " Every step in morals is made by challenging the validity of the existing conception of perfect propriety of conduct. . . . Heterodoxy in art is at worst rated as eccentricity or folly: heterodoxy in morals is at once rated as scoundrelism, and, what is worse, propagandist scoundrelism, which must, we are told, if successful, undermine society and bring us back to barbarism after a period of decadence like that which brought Imperial Rome to its downfall."

The time comes, however, when the voice of instinctive temperament makes itself heard and heeded. In the past the younger generation waited, but with a divine impatience, until " they were old enough to find their aspirations toward the fullest attainable activity and satisfaction working out in practice very much as they have worked out in the life of the race; so that the revolutionist at twenty-five, who saw nothing for it but a clean sweep of all our institutions, found himself, at

---

* This morality is no new thing under the sun; Maurice Maeterlinck has declared that our morality of to-day has nothing to add to this injunction, found in the *Arabian Nights:* " Learn to know thyself! And do thou not act till then. And do thou then only act in accordance with all thy desires, but having great care always that thou do not injure thy neighbour."

forty, accepting and even clinging to them on condition of a few reforms to bring them up to date." To-day the younger generation is loud in its demands, imperious in its insistence. They are outspoken in their scepticism concerning the infallibility of their parents, they insist that their " spiritual pastors and masters " speak humanly, and not dogmatically, of morality, and are determined to try all pontifical wisdom by the touchstone of experience. They formulate their heresy as a faith, and Shaw is the arch-heretic of them all. Ibsen would abolish the State and inaugurate a bloodless revolution: a revolution of the spirit of man; Hauptmann poetizes the Nietzschean ideal in *Die Versunkene Glocke;* Sudermann challenges the equity of parental authority in *Heimat.* With all the appearance of profound wisdom and abstract justice, Maeterlinck teaches that the preservation of virtue and adherence to conventional moral standards may be the quintessence of selfishness and egotism. Tolstoy preaches an impossible ideal of celibacy, and Shaw would abolish marriage because it is the " most licentious of human institutions." Modern literature from Ibsen and Nietzsche to Bourget and Shaw is a " long litany in praise of the man who wills." Men to-day contemn the " slavery to duty and discipline which has left so many soured old people with nothing but envious regrets for a virtuous youth." Moral heroism is the toast of the epoch—" the heroism of the man who believes in himself and dares do the thing he wills." It finds complete expression in Henley's best known poem, with its clamant finale:

> " I am the master of my fate,
> I am the captain of my soul."

The philosophy whose pæan is glorification of the man whose standards are within himself, whose actions are controlled by his will, carries with it certain inevitable and shocking consequences. It is the clearest proof of Shaw's consistency that he has never swerved one jot from the course marked out by himself. He accepts the disagreeable consequences along with the rest, neither blinking nor shirking them. Georg Brandes epitomized his doctrine in the words: " To obey one's senses is to have character. He who allows himself to be guided by his own passions has individuality." Shaw has avowed that he regards this as excellent doctrine, both in Brandes' form and in the older form: " He that is unjust, let him be unjust still; and he that is filthy, let him be filthy still; and he that is righteous, let him be righteous still; and he that is holy, let him be holy still." Shaw is fundamentally an optimist; he identifies all life with the will itself. This will, this Life Force, he refuses to regard as naturally malign and devilish. His life-work may be said to consist in an attack upon the conception that passions are necessarily base and unclean; his art works are glorifications of the man of conviction who can find a motive, and not an excuse, for his passions; whose conduct flows from his own ideas of right and wrong; and who obeys the law of his own nature in defiance of appearance, of criticism, and of authority. This abrogation of authority, this repudiation of systematized morality is the step which the strongest spirits in all history have taken; it is the inevitable step for the naturally good man, who can breathe only in an atmosphere of truth and freedom. Emancipation comes only when man fulfils his duty to himself; but one's duty to oneself, as Shaw has reminded us, is no duty at all, since a debt is cancelled when the debtor and creditor are the same person. " Its payment is simply a fulfilment of the individual will, upon which all duty is a restriction."

The obverse of the medal is not so clear: What will happen in the case of a person of ungovernable temper, of unbridled passions? The whole philosophy of his position, with all its appalling consequences, Shaw has expounded in that most remarkable of all his philosophical essays, entitled, *A Degenerate's View of Nordau.*

> " If ' the heart of man is deceitful above all things, and desperately wicked,' then truly, the man who allows himself to be guided by his passions must needs be a scoundrel, and his teacher might well be slain by his parents. But how if the youth, thrown helpless on his passions, found that honesty, that self-respect, that hatred

of cruelty and injustice, that the desire for soundness and health and efficiency, were master passions—nay, that their excess is so dangerous to youth that it is part of the wisdom of age to say to the young: ' Be not righteous overmuch: why shouldst thou destroy thyself?' . . . The people who profess to renounce and abjure their own passions, and ostentatiously regulate their conduct by the most convenient interpretation of what the Bible means, or, worse still, by their ability to find reasons for it (as if there were not excellent reasons to be found for every conceivable course of conduct, from dynamite and vivisection to martyrdom), seldom need a warning against being righteous overmuch, their attention, indeed, often needing a rather pressing jog in the opposite direction. The truth is that passion is the steam in the engine of all religious and moral systems. In so far as it is malevolent, the religions are malevolent too, and insist on human sacrifices, on hell, wrath and vengeance. You cannot read Browning's ' Caliban upon Setebos, or Natural Theology on the Island ' without admitting that all our religions have been made as Caliban made his, and that the difference between Caliban and Prospero is that Prospero is mastered by holier passions. And as Caliban imagined his theology, so did Mill reason out his essay on ' Liberty ' and Spencer his ' Data of Ethics.' In them we find the authors still trying to formulate abstract principles of conduct—still missing the fact that truth and justice are not abstract principles external to man, but human passions, which have, in their time, conflicted with higher passions as well as with lower ones."

It is one of Shaw's disconcerting theories—after Blake— that " the road of excess leads to the palace of wisdom "; the law of the stern asceticism of satiety is that " you never know what is enough unless you know what is more than enough." In amplifying this idea Shaw once said: " When Blake told men that through excess they would learn moderation, he knew that the way for the present lay through the Venusberg, and that the race would assuredly not perish there as some individuals have, and as the Puritan fears we all shall unless we find a way round. Also, he no doubt foresaw the time when our children would be born on the other side of it, and so be spared that fiery purgation."

It is not *mal à propos* that the arms of the Shaw family should have borne the motto, in Latin: " Know thyself." Shaw insists upon the salutary virtue of experience, its reforming and educative effect. " If a young woman, in a mood of strong reaction against the preaching of duty and self-sacrifice and the rest of it," Shaw once wrote, " were to tell Mr. Herbert Spencer that she was determined not to murder her own instincts and throw away her life in obedience to a mouthful of empty phrases, I suspect he would recommend the ' Data of Ethics ' to her as a trustworthy and conclusive guide to conduct. Under similar circumstances I should unhesitatingly say to the young woman: ' By all means do as you propose. Try how wicked you can be; it is precisely the same experiment as trying how good you can be. At worst, you will only find out the sort of person you really are. At best, you will find that your passions, if you really and honestly let them all loose impartially, will discipline you with a severity your conventional friends, abandoning themselves to the mechanical routine of fashion, could not stand for a day.' As a matter of fact, I have seen over and over again this comedy of the ' emancipated ' young enthusiast flinging duty and religion, convention and parental authority, to the winds, only to find herself becoming, for the first time in her life, plunged into duties, responsibilities and sacrifices from which she is often glad to retreat, after a few years' wearing down of her enthusiasm, into the comparatively loose life of an ordinary respectable woman of fashion." It is not a case of after satiety, moderation; after Venus, Saint Elizabeth; after Bohemianism, the convent. This is not what happens, except to ordinary loose livers. What happens, according to Shaw, is, that when we cast off all moral restraint we find Saint Elizabeth and the convent drawing us more passionately to them than Venus and the Bohemians. The true trend of the movement, it scarcely need be remarked, has been mistaken by many of its supporters as well as by its opponents. " The ingrained habit of thinking of the propensities of which we are ashamed as ' our passions,' " Shaw has shrewdly remarked, " and our shame of them and of our propensities to noble conduct as a negative and inhibitory department called our conscience, leads us to conclude that to accept the guidance of our passions is to plunge recklessly into the insupportable tedium of what is called a life of pleasure. Reactionists against the almost equally insupportable slavery of what is called a life of duty are, nevertheless, willing to venture on these terms. The ' revolted daughter,' exasperated at being systematically lied to by her parents on every subject of vital importance to an eager and intensely curious young student of life, allies herself with really vicious people and with humorists who like to shock the pious with gay paradoxes, in claiming an impossible license in personal conduct. No great harm is done beyond the inevitable and temporary excesses produced by all reactions; for the would-be wicked ones find, when they come to the point, that the indispensable qualification for a wicked life is not freedom, but wickedness." *

In the present state of the world's civilization, the universal application of the Shavian philosophy is neither possible nor desirable. Like Nietzsche, Shaw has evolved a philosophy for the *naturally good man*, for the strong man who realizes that freedom connotes, not license, but responsibility. His error inheres in the statement that no great harm would be done by people claiming an impossible license in personal conduct beyond the inevitable and temporary excesses produced by all reactions. Far from being temporary and negligible, the consequences that would result, were every person permitted to give a personal unrestricted interpretation of his own instincts, would be lasting and irremediable. The average sensual man,

---

* Compare also the notable passage, embodying a similar view, in Max Stirner's *The Ego and His Own* (Benjamin R. Tucker, N. Y., 1907), p. 212, beginning: " ' What am I? ' each of you asks himself. An abyss of lawless and unregulated impulses, desires, wishes, passions, a chaos without light or guiding star! . . ."

George Bernard Shaw.
From a photograph by Alvin Langdon Coburn made in 1906.

" the mean sensual man," as Granville Barker translates it—for whom passion means merely sexual lust, would take every advantage of the loopholes for self-indulgence offered by the Shavian programme. Were every man a Martin Luther, a William Blake, a Bernard Shaw; were every woman a Mary Wollstonecraft, a Candida Burgess, the world might, indeed, be clear of cant, of hypocrisy, of moralistic mendaciousness, of idealistic sophistication!

Mr. Shaw once went so far as to assure me that the universal application of the Shavian philosophy does actually take place. As a matter of fact, the vast majority of people do not do what they please, but, aside from scruples of conscience, find it vastly more convenient and satisfactory to conform to prevailing standards of right and wrong. Indeed, the limits to the application of the Shavian philosophy are given by Shaw himself when he tells us that " the men in the street have no use for principles, because they can neither understand nor apply them; and that what they can understand and apply are arbitrary rules of conduct, often frightfully destructive and inhuman, but at least definite rules enabling the common stupid man to know where he stands, and what he may do and not do without getting into trouble." That is, most people can and actually do fulfil their desires only within the limits prescribed by the prevailing code of morality. Most men are neither philosophers nor moralists. Under present circumstances, as Shaw himself admits, the number of people who can think out a line of conduct for themselves is very small, and the number who can afford the time for it still smaller.

" Nobody can afford the time to do it on all points. The professional thinker may on occasion make his own morality and philosophy as the cobbler may make his own boots; but the ordinary man of business must buy at the shop, so to speak, and put up with what he finds on sale there, whether it exactly suits him or not, because he can neither make a morality for himself nor do without one. This typewriter with which I am writing is the best I can get; but it is by no means a perfect instrument; and I have not the smallest doubt that in fifty years' time the authors of that day will wonder how men could have put up with so clumsy a contrivance. When a better one is invented, I shall buy it: until then I must make the best of it, just as my Protestant and Roman Catholic and Agnostic friends make the best of their creeds and systems. This would be better recognized if people took consciously and deliberately to the use of the creeds as they do to the use of typewriters. Just as the traffic of a great city would be impossible without a code of rules of the road which not one wagoner in a thousand could draw up for himself, much less promulgate, and without, in London at least, an unquestioning consent to treat the policeman's raised hand as if it were an impassable bar stretched half across the road, so the average man is still unable to get through the world without being told what to do at every turn, and basing such calculations as he is capable of on the assumptions that everyone else will calculate on the same assumptions. Even your man of genius accepts a thousand rules for every one he challenges; and you may lodge in the same house with an Anarchist for ten years without noticing anything exceptional about him. Martin Luther, the priest, horrified the greater half of Christendom by marrying a nun, yet was a submissive conformist in countless ways, living orderly as a husband and father, wearing what his bootmaker and tailor made for him, and dwelling in what the builder built for him, although he would have died rather than take his Church from the Pope. And when he got a Church made by himself to his liking, generations of men calling themselves Lutherans took that Church from him just as unquestionably as he took the fashion of his clothes from his tailor. As the race evolves, many a convention which recommends itself by its obvious utility to everyone passes into an automatic habit, like breathing; and meanwhile the improvement in our nerves and judgment enlarges the list of emergencies which individuals may be trusted to deal with on the spur of the moment without reference to regulations, but there will for many centuries to come be a huge demand for a ready-made code of conduct for general use, which will be used more or less as a matter of overwhelming convenience by all members of communities." *

The final effect of the philosophy of Ibsen, of Nietzsche, of Shaw is to substitute *conscience* for *conformity*.† With the dramatists of the Restoration, as Meredith has reminded us, morality was a duenna to be circumvented; with Shaw, morality is a mere convenience, like etiquette at a dinner-table or drill on a parade-ground. " For too long a time man regarded his natural bents with an ' evil eye,' " writes Nietzsche, " so that in the end they became related to ' bad conscience.' A reverse experiment is *in itself* possible—but who is strong enough for it? " Readiness to override tradition, to act unconventionally, to violate the current code of morality requires moral courage of the very highest order. The sense of moral responsibility is infinitely deepened. " Before conversion the individual anticipates nothing worse in the way of examination at the judgment bar of his conscience," wrote Shaw before he had ever heard of Nietzsche, " than such questions as: Have you kept the commandments? Have you obeyed the law? Have you attended church regularly; paid your rates and taxes to Cæsar; and contributed, in reason, to charitable institutions? It may be hard to do all these things; but it is still harder not to do them, as our ninety-nine moral cowards in the hundred know. And even a scoundrel can do them all and yet live a worse life than the smuggler or prostitute, who must answer ' No ' all the way through the catechism. Substitute for such a technical examination one in which the whole point to be settled is, Guilty or Not Guilty?—one in which there is no more and no less respect for chastity than for incontinence, for subordination than for rebellion, for legality than for illegality,

---

* *A Degenerate's View of Nordau,* in *Liberty,* July 27th, 1895.
† Mr. Shaw has recently pointed out that Professor A. K. Rogers, in his *Mr. Bernard Shaw's Philosophy (Hibbert Journal,* July, 1910), has failed to note the " trumpery (!) distinction between instinct and conscience " which Shaw had drawn in *Man and Superman.*

for piety than for blasphemy, in short, for the standard virtues than for the standard vices, and immediately, instead of lowering the moral standard by relaxing the tests of worth, you raise it by increasing their stringency to a point at which no mere pharisaism or moral cowardice can pass them." One of John Tanner's epigrams was "Liberty means responsibility. That is why most men dread it." All the stock excuses of the average man vanish before the inexorable fact of this responsibility: "'The woman tempted me'; 'The serpent tempted me'; 'I was not myself at the time'; 'I meant well'; 'My passion got the better of my reason'; 'It was my duty to do it'; 'The Bible says that we should do it'; 'Everybody does it,' and so on. Nothing is left but the frank avowal: 'I did it because I am built that way.' Every man hates to say that. He wants to believe that his generous actions are characteristic of him, and that his meannesses are aberrations or concessions to the force of circumstances." Most men are lacking in the "vigilant open-mindedness," the splendid moral courage of an Ibsen; few men are willing to face the fearful responsibility entailed by revolt against the will of the majority. Only a master impulse, a ruling passion will drive them to it. Shavianism means liberty with a string to it; while knocking off the fetters of alien authority, it forges upon one the iron band of liberty with responsibility.* Shavianism is the philosophy for the reformer who is driven by the "passion of a great faith"; in the words of Nietzsche, it is "the privilege of the fewest." The keynote of Shaw's philosophy he has sounded in the perfect epigram, "The golden rule is that there is no golden rule." But, as Mr. Chesterton rightly reminds us, the saying can be simply answered by being turned around. "That there is no golden rule is itself a golden rule, or, rather, it is much worse than a golden rule. It is an iron rule, a fetter on the first movement of a man."

* It is worthy of note that Nietzsche has defined freedom as the will to be responsible for oneself. Compare also *The Ego and His Own*, pp. 237-238 (Benjamin R. Tucker, N. Y.), the passage beginning: "To be *a* man is not to realize the ideal of Man, but to realize *oneself*, the individual. . . ."

The battle-cry of Shaw's life is the Nietzschean command: "Forward, march! our old morality, *too*, is a *piece of comedy*." Originality in regard to moral notions he regards as the true diagnostic of the first order in literature, the distinction that "sets Shakespeare's *Hamlet* above his other plays, and that sets Ibsen's work as a whole above Shakespeare's work as a whole." Bunyan, Blake, Hogarth and Turner (these four apart and above all the English classics), Goethe, Shelley, Schopenhauer, Wagner, Ibsen, Morris, Tolstoy and Nietzsche, he has told us, are among the writers whose peculiar sense of the world he recognizes as more or less akin to his own. While granting to Dickens and Shakespeare the "specific genius of the fictionist and the common sympathies of human feeling and thought in pre-eminent degree," he yet insists that in spite of their combination of sound moral judgment with light-hearted good-humour, they are concerned with the diversities of the world instead of with its unities. His highest meed of praise goes to the artist-philosopher who identifies himself with the purpose of the world. He classes himself with writers of the "first order," so called, because he has recognized and proclaimed in all his works that the rules of code-morality and the "need for them produced by the moral and intellectual incompetence of the ordinary human animal, are no more invariably beneficial and respectable than the sunlight which ripens the wheat in Sussex and leaves the desert deadly in Sahara, making the cheeks of the ploughman's child rosy in the morning and striking the ploughman brainsick or dead in the afternoon; no more inspired (and no less) than the religion of the Andaman Islanders: as much in need of frequent throwing away and replacement as the community's boots."

The prime reason for the accusation that in his plays Shaw ignores all human feeling is not as simple as it seems. It is not enough to say it is because he is judicially impartial or even that he ignores stage logic. Humanity may possibly move by clockwork in Shaw's plays, as Mr. Arthur Symons once said; but even if it did, there must be some key which sets the machine in motion. That key is not intellect, but will;

against which systems, creeds, conventions, every sort of formalism is ineffective and impotent. " Take care to get what you like or you will be forced to like what you get "; that is the creed of all his characters; or, in the words of Ann Whitefield: " The only really simple thing to do is to go straight for what you want, and grab it." It is his view that " people imagine that their actions and feelings are dictated by moral systems, by religious systems, by codes of honour and conventions of conduct which lie outside the real human will." As a dramatist, he recognizes that these conventions do not supply them with their motives, but merely serve as very plausible *ex post facto* excuses for their conduct. He has sought to reveal to us real people with real motives which are deep down in the will itself. It was Sainte Beuve's aim, as he himself phrased it, to set forth " the natural history of the intellect." One might say of Shaw, the dramatist, that his aim is to set forth the natural history of the human will. " Far from ignoring idiosyncrasy, will, passion, impulse, whim, as factors in human action, I have placed them so nakedly on the stage that the elderly citizen, accustomed to see them clothed with the veil of manufactured logic about duty, and to disguise even his own impulses from himself in this way, finds the picture as unnatural as Carlyle's suggested painting of Parliament sitting without its clothes."

It is this unmasking of all the ideals, this shattering of all the illusions, this demolition of the romantic cast of life which makes Shaw appear as a cynic, representing human creatures as frauds, impostors, poseurs, cads, bounders, hypocrites and humbugs. It is difficult to convince some people, especially women, that Shaw is not a cynic and pessimist. Like Schopenhauer, Shaw is a pure metaphysiologist. It is the inevitable result of his disbelief in the validity of custom-made morality that he should appear as a cynic, and the characters of his plays as frauds and shams. But he has deliberately averred: " It is not my object in the least to represent people as hypocrites and humbugs. It is conceit, not hypocrisy, that makes a man think he is guided by reasoned principles when he is really obeying his instincts." And in explaining his view of the world-comedy, he has shown that, as a dramatist, he pretends to be, not the historian, but the naturalist of his age.

" It is this premature search for a meaning that produces the comedy. We are not within a million years, as yet, of being concerned with the meaning of the world. Why do we recognize that philosophy is not a baby's business, although its facial expression so strongly suggests the professional philosopher? Because we know that all its mental energy is absorbed by the struggle to attain ordinary physical consciousness. It is learning to interpret the sensations of its eyes and ears and nose and tongue and finger tips. It is ridiculously delighted by a silly toy, absurdly terrified by a harmless bogey, because it cannot as yet see things as they really are. Well, we are all still as much babies in the world of thought as we were in our second year in the world of sense. Men are not real to us; they are heroes and villains, respectable persons and criminals. Their qualities are virtues and vices; the natural laws that govern them are gods and devils; their destinies are rewards and expiations; their conditions are innocence and guilt—there is no end to the amazing transubstantiations and childish imaginings which delight and terrify us because we have not yet grown up enough to be capable of genuine natural history. And then people come to you with their heads full of these figments, which they call, if you please, ' the world,' and ask you what is the meaning of them. The answer is, that they have not even an existence, much less a meaning. The blank incredulity of men to that reply, and their absurd attempts to act on their illusions, are as funny as the antics of a baby: that is what you call the world-comedy. But when they try to force others to act on them, when they ostracize, punish, murder, make war, impose by force their grotesque religious and hideous criminal codes, then the comedy becomes a tragedy. And only the dramatist sees through it; all the rest, the Army, the Navy, the Church, and the Bar are busy bolstering up the imposture.

The dramatic faculty is nothing more nor less than a little more than common forwardness in natural history, a little more than common freedom from illusion, or, to put it as the average dupe sees it, and as Ruskin flatly expressed it concerning Shakespeare, a little less than common conscience. . . . If the playgoer could see the dramatist's mind, all the dramatists would be hanged, just as all the men and women of forty would be massacred by all the youths and maidens of twenty, if these young ones only knew." *

The world-comedy, in Shaw's eyes, consists in the imaginative self-delusion, the moralistic sophistication of man; the world-tragedy in the bankruptcy of what we delight in calling progress with a P.

Progress, from Shaw's point of view, means increased command over self; this lamentable desideratum is the cause of his scepticism. But let us observe the open-minded, clear-eyed consistency of Shaw. While heartily subscribing to the metaphysics of Schopenhauer, he yet as heartily refuses to accept his pessimistic philosophy. At one with Darwin and Huxley in their scientific, realistic, yet anarchistic challenge of the validity of Biblical theology, Shaw, by his deliberate rejection of their materialistic views, occupies the opposite pole of conviction. It is useless to pretend to a " generation which has ceased to believe in heaven and has not yet learned that the degradation by poverty of four out of every five of its number is artificial," that the " pessimism of Koheleth, Shakespeare, Dryden and Swift can be refuted if the world progresses solely by the destruction of the unfit, and yet can only maintain its civilization by manufacturing the unfit in swarms of which that appalling proportion of four to one represents but the comparatively fit survivors." To Shaw, progress means, not an effect of the survival of the fittest brought about by the destruction of the unfit, but the growth of the spirit of man. He has refused to accept the Darwinian theory of evolution,

* *Who I Am, and What I Think,* Part II., in *The Candid Friend,* May 18th, 1901.

since it " only accounted for progress at all on the hypothesis of a continuous increase in the severity of the conditions of existence—that is, on an assumption of just the reverse of what was actually taking place "—a fact which escaped Huxley. He finds in the world no signs of progress in the humanitarian and ethical sense; only a few more discoveries in physics. And even the much-trumpeted " increased command over nature," harnessing continents, circling the globe, and so on, as an argument for progress vanishes before the inevitable query as to whether a negro of to-day using a telephone is superior to George Washington. Shaw rails at the " theistic credulity " of Voltaire as he rails at the " tribal soothsayings " of Huxley. As he recently wrote me: " I have not escaped from a literal belief in the Book of Genesis only to fall back into the gross blindness of seeing nothing in the world but the result of natural selection operating on a chapter of accidents, which is popular Darwinism."

In that most whimsical and witty essay, entitled, *The Conflict Between Science and Common Sense,* Shaw declares that he has " found out " the man of science: " In future my attitude towards him will be one of more or less polite incredulity. Impostor for impostor, I prefer the mystic to the scientist— the man who at least has the decency to call his nonsense a mystery, to him who pretends that it is ascertained, weighed, measured, analyzed fact." In a sense, Shaw's part in the humanitarian campaign against vivisection, modern science generally, vaccination, education, flogging, " cannibalism," and so on, are all part of his attitude as a " mystic." He has no faith in the scientist with his specious invitation: " My friend, by a diabolically cruel process I have procured a revoltingly filthy substance. Allow me to inject this under your skin, and you can never get hydrophobia, or enteric fever, or diphtheria, etc. I have even a very choice preparation, of unmentionable nastiness, which will enable you, if not to live for ever (though I think that quite possible), at least to renew in your old age the excesses of your youth." While the average man, with incomprehensible credulity, jumps at the bait, Shaw refuses to be so easily duped. While science has taught him that dirt is " only matter in the wrong place," his own common sense has taught him that " disease is only matter in the wrong condition, and that to inject matter in the wrong condition into matter in the right condition (healthy flesh, to wit) is to put matter in the wrong place with a vengeance." In the public prints, in his novels and plays, notably, *Cashel Byron's Profession* and *The Philanderer,* Shaw has fulminated as vigorously against vivisection as against vaccination. From the first he perceived that the vivisector was " just the same phenomenon in science as the dynamiter in politics, and that to all humane men both methods of research and reform, effective or not, were eternally barred, precisely as highway robbery is barred as a method of supporting one's family." His persistent vegetarianism is not based upon a scientific inquiry into the amount of hydrocarbons, uric acid, or what not deleterious stuff there may be in meat, but in his perfectly natural and humane distaste for the shedding of blood. " I have not the slightest doubt myself," he once said, " that a diet of nice tender babies, carefully selected, cleanly killed and tenderly cooked, would make us far healthier and handsomer than the haphazard dinners of to-day, whether carnivorous or vegetarian. . . . There is no objection whatever to a baby from a nitrogenous point of view. Eaten with sugar, or with beer, it would leave nothing to be desired in the way of carbon. My sole objection to such a diet is that it happens to be repugnant to me. I prefer bread and butter." Shaw's " three centuries " of life have taught him, mainly, to regard " men's principles as excuses for doing what they want to do." And in the moral sphere, he contends that " the world remains as dependent as ever on pure dogmatic, instinctive recoil from suffering on the one hand, and pure dogmatic, instinctive love of inflicting it on the other. Common to both these temperaments, and to the compound temperament in which they struggle for mastery, is the timid perception that society can only exist through a compact to live and let live. . . . All sorts of virtuously indignant persons, clamouring for all sorts of vulgar retaliations, from the kicking of a cad to the humiliation of a minister by an election defeat, are indulging the destructive in-

stincts under cover of solicitude for the common weal, as unmistakably as the scientist who, with a thousand humane
departments of research open to him, deliberately prefers
cruel experiments, and pleads that the man who ascertains how
long it takes to bake a dog to death confers as great a boon
on humanity as the man who discovers the Röntgen rays and
their application to surgery. The cruel (loving to read the
description of his experiments), the selfish (hoping for cures),
the sportsman (anxious to be kept in countenance), and the
cowardly (seeking an excuse for tolerating an evil they dare
not attack) will accept his excuse: the humane will not. The
final conflict is not between the excuses in their logical disguise
of scientific arguments, but between the cruel will and the
humane will."

A leading cause for Shaw's "divine discontent" with
progress, with moral systems, with institutions, with "regi-
mentation," with flogging in the navy, vaccination, science,
cannibalism, and a thousand other things, is his loss of faith
in education. He has lost his illusions on the subject. Education and culture, he maintains, are for the most part "nothing but the substitution of reading for experience, of literature
for life, of the obsolete fictitious for the contemporary real."
He sees Masters of Art as "patentees of highly questionable
methods of thinking, and manufacturers of highly questionable, and for the majority but half valid, representations of
life." This is the natural attitude for one who said only the
other day that "great communities are built by men who sign
with a mark: they are wrecked by men who write Latin verses."
The ruthless repression which we practise on our fellow creatures whilst they are still too small to defend themselves, he
insists, ends in their "reaching their full bodily growth in a
hopelessly lamed and intimidated condition, unable to conceive
of any forces in the world except physically coercive and socially conventional ones." "Modern" education, he declares,
"differs from Dr. Johnson's education only in substituting
Jenner and Pasteur for Plato and Euripides as academic idols,
and replacing the recognition of a purpose in the world, and
the investigation of that purpose, by a conception of the uni-

verse as the accidental result of a senseless raging of mechanical forces, and by a boundless credulity, not outdone in
dirt, cruelty, and stupidity, by any known savage tribe, as
to the possibility of circumventing these forces by nostrums
and conjurations." The hope of the world lies in the development of individuality and self-reliance. Real live learning
would soon flourish on the boundless basis of human curiosity
and ambition.*

Bernard Shaw is not a materialist or natural selectionist,
but in direct line of descent, astounding as the contrast may
appear, from Schopenhauer, Lamarck and Samuel Butler.
Shaw does not subscribe to the belief that goodness implies
that " man is vicious by nature, and that supreme goodness is
supreme martyrdom." A fundamental tenet of his philosophic
faith is the conviction that " progress can do nothing but make
the most of us all as we are." This conviction has more or
less consciously animated him all through his career. Within
his secret soul, Shaw has always cherished a radiant and
gorgeous hope for humanity, always unconsciously trod the
rainbow bridge from the real to the ideal. In his heart, he has
whispered Ibsen's thought, " The expression of our own individuality is our first duty." A dream of human perfectibility
has lured him on: the dearest foe of this arrant realist has ever
been—an ideal. As a youth he revelled in the Shelley of
Prometheus Unbound; young manhood found him working
upon the hypothesis of the Economic Man. In *The Quintessence of Ibsenism,* Shaw sang of the new man, the sovereign
individual—in Nietzsche's phrase, " the possessor of a long in-
frangible will, who has, in his possession, his *standard of valuation.*" He had found out the impossibilities of anarchism
before he came to Wagner; his clearer vision and enlarged
horizon enabled him to realize that " the individual Siegfried
has come often enough, only to find himself confronted with
the alternative of government or destruction at the hands of
his fellows who are not Siegfrieds." At last he began to
realize that " it is necessary to breed a race of men in whom

* Compare *Does Modern Education Ennoble?* by G. Bernard Shaw; in
Great Thoughts, October 7th, 1905.

A PLASTER BUST OF SHAW.

Made in forty minutes.

[*Facing p.* 474

the life-giving impulses predominate before the New Protestantism becomes politically practicable." The matured form of his ideal is the ethical man, convinced of the bankruptcy of education and progress, inspired with the faith of the world-will, and resolved, not to adopt a new philosophy, but to develop and perfect the human species. " To rise above ourselves to ourselves "—that is the creed of the new faith, of the humanitarian artificial selectionist concerned even more for the future of the race than for the freedom of his own instincts. Every phase in Shaw's career, it cannot be too strongly insisted upon, is the legitimate and logical outcome of his Socialism. His philosophy is the consistent integration of his empirical criticisms of society and its present organization, founded on authority and based upon Capitalism. And to the Socialist, nothing is necessary for the realization of Utopia but that man should will it. " Man will never be that which he can and should be," wrote Wagner, " until by a conscious following of that inner natural necessity, which is the only true necessity, he makes his life a mirror of nature, and frees himself from his thraldom to outer artificial counterfeits. Then will he first become a living man, who now is a mere wheel in the mechanism of this or that Religion, Nationality or State." The fact faced by the Shavian philosophy is that Man does not effectively will perfection. The quintessence of Shavianism is that " he never will until he becomes Superman." *

The cardinal point in the New Theology as enunciated by Bernard Shaw is the identification of God with the Life Force. " There are two mutually contradictory ideas which cut across each other in regard to the relative powers of God and Man," Mr. Shaw once said to me in the course of a long discussion of his religious views. " According to the popular conception, God always creates beings inferior to Himself: the creator must be greater than the creature. I find myself utterly unable to accept this horrible old idea, involving as it does the belief that all the cruelty in the world is the work of an omnipotent God, who, if He liked, could have left cruelty out

---

* The substance of Shaw's philosophy—as, indeed, he once told me—is embodied in Act III. of *Man and Superman*.

of creation. If God could have created anything better, do you suppose He would have been content to create such miserable failures as you and me?

"As a matter of fact," he continued, "we know that in all art, literature, politics, sociology—in every phase of genuine life and vitality—man's highest aspiration is to create something higher than himself. So God, the Life Force, has been struggling for countless ages to become conscious of Himself —to express Himself in forms higher and ever higher up in the scale of evolution. God does not take pride in making a grub-worm because it is lower than Himself. On the contrary, the grub is a mere symbol of His desire for self-expression."

To Bernard Shaw, the universe is God in the act of making Himself. At the back of the universe, according to his mystical conception, there is a great purpose, a great will. This force behind the universe is bodiless and impotent, without executive power of its own; after innumerable tentatives—experiments and mistakes—the force has succeeded in changing inert matter into the amœba, the amœba into some more complex organism; this again into something still more complex, and finally has evolved a man, with hands and a brain to accomplish the work of the Will. Man is not the ultimate aim of the Life Force, but only a stage in the scale of evolution. The Life Force will go still further and produce something more complicated than Man, that is, the Superman, then the Angel, the Archangel, and last of all an omnipotent and omniscient God.*

Shaw has startled and shocked many people during his lifetime by asserting vehemently that he was an atheist.† And so indeed he is, if orthodoxy connotes belief in the early-Victorian God of cruelty and barbarity—the Almighty Fiend of Shelley's characterization. The idea of God as a cruel Designer, vindictive in punishment of the unbeliever, then held full sway.

---

* For the sake of making himself easily understood, Shaw frequently expresses his neo-theological conceptions in the familiar phraseology of orthodox religion. Shaw's practice of personifying God, when in reality he mentally identifies "God" with a mystical and impersonal "Force," is a practice which many people quite justly condemn.

† *Cf.* Shaw's open letter to G. W. Foote, in *The Freethinker,* November 1st, 1908.

" Neither science on the one hand, nor the moral remonstrances of Shelley and his school on the other, were able to shake the current belief in that old theology that came back to the old tribal idol, Jehovah." Then came Darwin with his theory of natural selection, involving the corollary that all the operations of the species can be accounted for without consciousness, intelligence or design. After rapturously embracing Darwinism for six weeks, Samuel Butler turned upon Darwin and rent him—he had discovered that Darwin had actually banished mind from the universe.* Butler saw clearly that natural selection had no moral significance, that it did away not only with the necessity for purpose and design in the universe, but actually with the necessity for consciousness.

Philosophically and scientifically, Shaw derives directly from Schopenhauer, Lamarck and Butler. He recognizes purpose and will in the world because he is himself conscious of purpose and will. Woman brings children into the world, not for herself or for her husband, but to fulfil the end in view of which the Life Force has created her. Man produces great works just as woman brings men into the world, with travail and pain; man is continually engaged in doing things which do not benefit him. He works just as hard when there is no chance of profit as when there is. Shaw, then, is a confirmed Neo-Lamarckian in the view that " where there's a will there's a way." Just as Lamarck, with his theory of functional adaptation, virtually maintained that living organisms changed because they wanted to, so Shaw believes that there is a purpose in the universe; identifies his own purpose with it, and makes the achievement of that purpose an act, not of self-sacrifice for himself, but of self-realization. In Shaw's view, Schopen-

* In this connection it is interesting to read Shaw's review of Samuel Butler's *Luck or Cunning?* published under the heading " Darwin Denounced," in the *Pall Mall Gazette,* May 31st, 1887. At this time, Shaw committed himself neither to Lamarck nor to Butler, but was content to define the issues of the controversy. Certainly his interest was aroused, and years later his support was won, by Butler's protest against natural selection as—to use Butler's own words—" a purely automatic conception of the universe as of something that will work if a penny be dropped into the box."

hauer's treatise on the World as Will is the complement to Lamarck's natural history; for Will is the driving force of Lamarckian evolution.*

Bernard Shaw's religion is the expression of his faith in Life and in the Will. He regards man as divine because, actually, he is the last effort of the Will to realize itself as God. And yet he does not believe in the doctrine of personal immortality. " I have a strong feeling that I shall be glad when I am dead and done for—scrapped at last to make room for somebody better, cleverer, more perfect than myself," Mr. Shaw once remarked to me. " This, I believe, is the clue to my views on immortality. The idea of personal salvation is intensely repugnant to me when it is not absurd. Imagine Roosevelt, the big brute, preserving his personality in a future state and swaggering about as a celestial Rough Rider! Or imagine me in heaven, giving forth all sorts of epigrams and paradoxes, startling Saint Peter with my iconoclasm, being paragraphed in the *Eternal Herald* and cartooned in the *Æon Review!* No, I think the trouble has come about through imagining that there are only two attributes—eternal life and utter extinction at death. I believe neither of these theories to be correct. Life continually tends to organize itself into higher and better forms. There is no such thing as personal immortality; and death, as Weismann says, is only a means of economizing life. The vital spark, the Life principle within us, goes on in spite of personal annihilation.

" As I told Mrs. Besant the other night," he added, " I am looking for a race of men who are not afraid to die."

A popular error into which many able critics fall is involved in the oft-repeated assertion that Shaw derives his philosophy directly from Ibsen, Strindberg, Stirner and Nietzsche. It is quite true that *The Quintessence of Ibsenism* might have been written by an ardent disciple of Nietzsche; and yet the first time Shaw ever heard Nietzsche's name was from a German mathematician, a Miss Borchardt, who had read Shaw's brochure on Ibsen, and who told him she knew where he had

* Compare *The Philosophy of Bernard Shaw,* by Archibald Henderson, in the *Atlantic Monthly,* February, 1909.

got it all. On being asked where, she replied " From Nietzsche's *Jenseits von Gut und Böse*." Shaw at once understood and appreciated the title, and thereafter took an interest in Nietzsche; but he could not read much of the few English translations that were attempted except Thomas Common's book of selections; the German originals he never even attempted to read. " If all this talk about Schopenhauer and Nietzsche continues," Shaw laughingly said to me one day, " I really will have to read their works, to discover just what we have in common. This habit of referring every idea of mine to Schopenhauer and Nietzsche comes about partly because, to people without philosophy, all philosophies seem the same, and partly because I have often referred to them to remind my readers that what they called my eccentricities and paradoxes are part of the common European stock." As for Stirner, I have never heard Mr. Shaw mention Stirner. I recall no mention of Stirner in all of Shaw's works, and I have no reason to believe that Shaw is indebted to him in the slightest degree. It is quite true that, like Stirner, Shaw is an intellectual anarch; but he has no real sympathy for Stirner's " Eigentum," for the reason that though Shaw is an individualist, he is likewise a constitutional collectivist. He sees no real conflict between Individualism and Socialism, and has actually given the striking definition: " Socialism is merely Individualism rationalized, organized, clothed and in its right mind." Shaw has been accused of indebtedness to Strindberg also; the truth is, that he has all along been perfectly familiar with the idea of hatred of woman-idolization through the writings and conversation of Mr. Ernest Belfort Bax, whose essays attacking *bourgeois* morality were published before Strindberg, or Nietzsche, for that matter, had been heard of in England. But although Shaw has read very little of the marvellously prolific Strindberg, he admires him greatly, and once told me that he thought Strindberg would prove to be " the noblest Roman of us all." Nietzsche's view of Christianity as a slave-morality was advanced in England by Mr. Stuart-Glennie, a Scotch historical philosopher, still living and much neglected, in what appealed to Shaw as a far more sensible way, Stuart-

Glennie regarding it as the means by which the white races
(the Supermen) enslaved the dark races and mean whites, while
Nietzsche regarded it as an imposition by the slaves themselves.* Shaw, Stuart-Glennie and Bax are all Socialists; if
" the physiologist of the mind " would seek to trace in Shaw's
work early influences upon his philosophy, he must look for
them in the works of Stuart-Glennie and Bax, rather than in
the works of Nietzsche and Strindberg. And as for Shaw's
strange complex of Socialism and individualism, I personally
find it to be a mean between the extravagant individualism of
Max Stirner, the intellectual anarchy of Elisée Reclus, and
the practical collectivism of Jaurès and Vandervelde.

The English critics, however, continue to refer Shaw's philosophy to Nietzsche and Schopenhauer, " knowing nothing
about them," as Shaw says, " except that their opinions, like
mine, are not those of the *Times* or the *Spectator*." Indeed,
Shaw is an unwilling impostor as a pundit in the philosophy
of Schopenhauer and Nietzsche. What, for example, could be
more foreign to the Shavian philosophy than Nietzsche's repudiation of Socialism, his admiration of the Romans, or his
notions about art? Shaw's Superman is mere man to Nietzsche;
whilst Nietzsche's Superman is God to Shaw. " Nietzsche's
erudition I believe to be all nonsense," Shaw recently remarked
to me. " I think he was academic in the sense of having a
great deal of second-hand book-learning about him, and don't
care for him except when he is perfectly original—that is,
when he is dealing with matters which a peasant might have
dealt with if he had brains enough, and had had the run of a
library. You feel how clever and imaginative he is, and how
much he has derived from writers of genius and from his own
humanity about men and nations; but there is a want of actual
contact knowledge about him; he is always the speculative university professor or the solitary philosopher and poet, never
quite the worker and man of affairs or the executive artist in

---

* Compare *A Genealogy of Morals,* translated by William A. Hausemann; Alexander Tille's Introduction, pp. xvi. and xviii. For Shaw's general confession of indebtedness to others, compare the preface to *Major
Barbara—First Aid to Critics.*

solid materials. It annoys me to see English writers absolutely ignoring the work of British thinkers, and swallowing foreign celebrities—whether philosophers or opera-singers—without a grain of salt. It shows an utter want of intellectual self-respect; and the result of it is that Nietzsche's views, instead of being added solely to the existing body of philosophy, are treated as if they were a sort of music-hall perfomance."

Bernard Shaw is endowed with that persistent strain of British practicality which makes him employ philosophy as an instrumentality for the achievement of the purposes of life. In a word, Shaw is fundamentally an ethicist: philosophy to him means a guide for life. His metaphysic is basically moralistic, consisting of a series of postulates in respect to conduct.

In the manuscript of an unfinished work which Mr. Shaw once loaned to me, I discovered a notable passage which throws a flood of light upon Shaw's philosophy as an index to his entire life and career. Perhaps it may distil the quintessence of the Shavian philosophy:

"The man who is looking after himself is useless for revolutionary purposes. The man who believes he is only a fly on the wheel of Natural Selection, of Evolution, or Progress, or Puritanism, or ' some power not ourselves, that makes for righteousness ' is not only useless, but obstructive. But the man who believes that there is a purpose in the universe, and identifies his own purpose with it, and makes the achievement of that purpose an act, not of self-sacrifice for himself, but of self-realization: that is the effective man and the happy man, whether he calls the purpose the will of God, or Socialism, or the religion of humanity. He is the man who will combine with you in a fellowship, which he may call the fellowship of the Holy Ghost or you may call Democracy, or the Parliament of Man, or the Federation of the World, but which is a real working, and if need be fighting, fellowship for all that. He is the man who knows that nothing intelligent will be done until somebody does it, and who will place the doing of it above all his other interests.

" In short, we must make a religion of Socialism. We must fall back on our will to Socialism, and resort to our reason only to find out the ways and means. And this we can do only if we conceive the will as a creative energy, as Lamarck did; and totally renounce and abjure Darwinism, Marxism, and all fatalistic, penny-in-the-slot theories of evolution whatever."

THE MAN

"Like all men, I play many parts, and none of them is more or less real than the other. . . . I am a soul of infinite worth. I am, in short, not only what I can make out of myself, which varies greatly from hour to hour, and emergency to emergency, but what you can see in me."—Bernard Shaw's review of G. K. Chesterton's *Bernard Shaw.*

"Many people seem to imagine that I am an extraordinary sort of person. The fact of the matter is that ninety-nine per cent. of me is just like everybody else."—Remark of Bernard Shaw to the author.

"This is the true joy in life: the being used for a purpose recognized by yourself as a mighty one; the being thoroughly worn out before you are thrown on the scrap-heap; the being a force of nature, instead of a feverish, selfish little clod of ailments and grievances, complaining that the world will not devote itself to making you happy."—*Man and Superman. Epistle Dedicatory to A. B. Walkley.*

CHAPTER XVI

BERNARD SHAW looks down upon contemporary life from many windows. The world is caught in the drag-net of his infinite variety: few escape. To each man, Shaw comes in a different capacity. The world at large knows little, astoundingly little, of Shaw the man. That is why, after detailing the various features of his literary and public career, I have put last the study of his personality. From the preceding chapters the reader may have constructed a more or less imaginary portrait. In this chapter is portrayed Shaw, if not as in himself he really is, certainly as one who knows him really sees him.

It may not be devoid of interest to think of Shaw at several stages of his career. During the epidemic of 1881, he caught small-pox which, as he expressed it, " left him unmarked, but an anti-vaccinationist for ever." The next few years Shaw passed " in desperate want and despair," as an acquaintance has expressed it. While this statement is somewhat exaggerated, certainly the clothes he wore at this period gave it colour: tawny trousers, extraordinarily, unbelievably baggy; a long, *soi-disant* black cut-away coat, and a tall silk hat, which had been battered down so often that it had a thousand creases in it from top to crown. " My clothes turned green," Shaw has confessed, " and I trimmed my cuffs to the quick with a scissors, and wore my tall hat with the back part in front, so that the brim should not bend double when I took it off to an acquaintance."

Despite the loyal protest of the Secretary of the Fabian Society, who once wrote me vehemently asserting that Shaw always wore perfectly normal and conventional clothes, it must be admitted that Shaw has been associated throughout his life with queer sartorial tastes. The notorious velvet jacket which he wore during the days of his activity as a critic of the drama, furnished the *casus belli* in Shaw's war with the theatre managers. Shaw refused point-blank to obey the iron-clad regulation that occupants of stalls must wear evening clothes. The irrepressible conflict was precipitated one night, according to a story which Shaw vehemently denies, when Shaw was stopped at the door of the theatre by an attendant.

" What do you object to? " asked Shaw; " the velvet jacket? "

The attendant nodded assent.

" Very well," exclaimed Shaw, no whit abashed, " I will remove it." And the next instant he was striding up the aisle in his shirt sleeves.

" Here, that won't do! " shouted the attendant in great alarm, hurrying after Shaw and stopping him with great difficulty.

" Won't do? " cried Shaw, with fine assumption of indignation. " Do you think I am going to take off any more? "

And with that he promptly redonned his velvet jacket and turning on his heel, left the house. Shaw finally won the battle and enjoyed his triumph in face of the objection of managers and the indignation of the fashionable and wealthy theatregoers.

Shaw's snuff-coloured suit and flannel shirt made him a marked figure in London during the 'nineties. He wore it so long that it finally came to look, as one of his acquaintances said, as if it were made of brown wrapping paper. So much a part of his individuality had it become that, when he finally discarded it, some friends of Shaw's, seeing it depending from a nail, exclaimed—so well had it retained its shape—" Good heavens! he's done it at last! "

Of peculiar, almost unique, interest is the record of Shaw's physical proportions and qualities, taken in the Anthropometric Laboratory arranged by Francis Galton, F.R.S., at the International Health Exhibition on August 16th, 1884. This was just twenty days before Shaw joined the Fabian Society. According to this chart, numbered 3,655, Shaw's anthropometric properties were as follows:

Colour of eyes, blue-grey.

EYESIGHT.

Greatest distance in inches of reading "Diamond" type—
Right eye, 23; left eye, 27.

Colour sense (goodness of)—Good.

JUDGMENT OF EYE.

Error per cent. in dividing a line of 15 inches—in three parts,
1½; in two parts, ½.

Error in degrees of estimating squareness—¼.

HEARING.

Keenness can hardly be tested here owing to the noises and
echoes.

Highest audible note—Between 30,000 and 40,000 vibrations
per second.

BREATHING POWER.

Greatest expiration in cubic inches—298.

STRENGTH.

Of squeeze in lbs. of—right hand, 83; left hand, 80.

Of pull in lbs.—57.

SPAN OF ARMS.

From finger tips of opposite hands—5 feet 11.7 inches.

HEIGHT.

Sitting, measured from seat of chair—3 feet 1.8 inches.

Standing in shoes........................6 feet 0.8 inch

Less height of heel......................   0.7 inch
_____

Height without shoes.....................6 feet 0.1 inch.

WEIGHT.

In ordinary indoor clothing in lbs.—142.

The social, physical, mental and moral measurements of the
man, at different periods of his life, have been taken by a thousand hands. Not the least interesting of these is the record
of a chirological expert in the *Palmist and Chirological Review*,
July, 1895.* Shaw is inclined to believe in palmistry to the

* The journal of the Chirological Society, edited by Mrs. K. St. Hill and
Mr. Charles F. Rideal.

extent of regarding the hand to be as good an index of character as the face. He once laughingly remarked to me that the following chirological study possessed a curious interest, because it was such a remarkable *mélange* of acute character-analysis and hopeless, utter nonsense.

Omitting technical details—the specific *indicia* of specific traits—the hands of Shaw yielded the following " results." The author, dramatist, musician and critic is betrayed by the long conical hands—the smallness of which for so tall a man indicates that the subject will be given to jumping to conclusions on insufficient grounds in matters of opinion. The subject is very unconventional and independent, especially in thought, and adaptable to people and circumstances. His will is very strong, and he is obstinate in opinion, very argumentative, dogmatic, and unconvincible. He is not only fond of books and reading, but also has a great love of rule and power over others. His temperament is a curious compound of caution and liberality, very dependent upon moods for their expression. The dramatic power he possesses is that of the dramatist, not of the actor; he is gifted with great power in carrying out ideas and turning circumstances to his advantage, due in no small measure to his remarkable power of words, whether for speaking or writing. While not entirely tactful, he is constantly scheming and planning; but he is usually more successful in handling plots than persons. Great energy, both physical and mental, and cultivated self-control are distinguishing marks of the man; to these traits are superadded much aggressiveness and high moral courage. He is endowed with a great sense of fun, remarkable wit, immense wealth of imagination and extreme eccentricity of ideas. The subject makes his own career in the world, and tries to carry out to some extent his eccentric ideas; but as a rule, his actions are directed by his accurate knowledge of the world. In many respects, the subject is very genuine and sincere; but along with this goes an incurable tendency to pose for effect. His fame will steadily grow with the years; and it is predicted that he will accomplish fine artistic work, if he will leave the practical side of things to others, and stick to art as he should.

He can make or mar his own career as he chooses; he possesses the power to turn circumstances to his own advantage. In a large sense, he is the master of his fate.

Did the analysis stop here, Mr. Shaw might almost be justified in believing it impossible to derive such accurate information solely from a superficial knowledge of his public career. Unfortunately, the palmist indulged in certain other characterizations which are doubtless included in Mr. Shaw's category of " utter nonsense." According to the palmist, Mr. Shaw has a very good opinion of himself, due to vanity, not to self-confidence, in which he is conspicuously lacking. He is very susceptible to criticism, but harsh in his criticism of others; very apprehensive of consequences, changeable and uncertain in his moods. Quiet in temper, he is, nevertheless, very revengeful and vindictive, imbued not only with a great power of hatred, but also with utter mercilessness in carrying it out. His temperament is very hard, and, in a refined manner, cruel. He has an extreme disregard for truth, all notions and opinions being coloured by fancy until facts are completely lost sight of, thus showing the subject to be utterly wanting in practical common sense in his opinions and ideas. He is neither passionate nor benevolent; but he has a laudable tendency to idealize his friends. It is a very unlucky temperament in affairs of the heart; his nature has little if any faculty for attachment. He imagines himself in love, and the more obstacles and impossibilities in the way of his suit, the more he will delight in it; he imagines the object of his attachment perfect, and will endeavour, contrary to all rules and observances, to live in his castles in the air, and when they dissolve he will throw it all away, perfectly heedless of consequences to himself or others, and start on a new ambition, or an entirely different line. " That this has already happened once in his life," adds the chirologist, " is shown by the bar line, now fading, from the upper Mars across to Head and Heart." *Il ne manquait que ça!*

Let us now skip another eleven, or rather twelve, years, and take a look at Bernard Shaw as he is to-day. Many people seem to regard Shaw as too funny to be true—as fanciful as

Pierrot, as imaginary as Harlequin, as remote as the Man in the Moon. In reality, he is the most unmistakable sort of person. The nervous, almost boyish swing of his gait, the length and lankiness of his figure, the scraggly reddish-brown beard, heavily tinged, or rather edged, with grey, the high and noble brow, the quizzical geniality of his expression, the sensitive mouth and the challenging directness of his grey-blue eyes—all proclaim the original of a Coburn print, or a Max Beerbohm cartoon. The balance between conventionality and *bizarrerie*, between the serious thinker and the sardonic wit, is symbolized in eyebrows and moustaches, one of each cocking humorously upward, the other gravely preserving the level of dignity. This gives him, when he is in a gay mood, the air of a genial Celtic Mephistopheles; and even when his face is in repose this hirsute peculiarity imparts a sort of quaint *diablerie* to his expression. The delicate texture and excessive pallor of his skin gives the note of distinction to his face; and his eyes, whether turned full upon you with level gaze or dancing with the light of irrepressible humour, are his most distinctive feature. The frame for an artist's sketch of his profile would be a vertically elongated rectangle—a curious cephalic conformation ready made to the hand of the cartoonist.

Mr. Gilbert Chesterton's description, in his book, *The Ball and the Cross*, of the sane professor of psychology whose ideas are wilder than those of the lunatics under his charge, gives a rather startling picture in semi-caricature—with slight variations—of the man Shaw: " The advancing figure walked with a stoop, and yet, somehow, flung his forked and narrow beard forward. That carefully cut and pointed yellow beard was, indeed, the most emphatic thing about him. When he clasped his hands behind him, under the tails of his coat, he would wag his beard at a man like a big forefinger. It performed almost all the gestures; it was more important than the glittering eye-glasses through which he looked, or the beautiful, bleating voice in which he spoke. His face and neck were of a lusty red, but lean and stringy; he always wore his expensive gold-rim eye-glasses slightly askew upon his aquiline nose, and he always

Joseph Simpson.] [Courtesy of the Artist.

G. B. S. (A Cartoon).

Reproduced from *Three Living Lions*.

showed two gleaming foreteeth under his moustache, in a smile
so perpetual as to earn the reputation of a sneer."

The extravagant braggart and arrant *poseur* of the Shavian
myth vanishes in the presence of the real Shaw. His playful
pretence of vanity is a source of great amusement to himself
and his friends. Socially, it is an admirable resource in the
art of entertainment. " I have never pretended that G. B. S.
was real," said Shaw the other day: " I have over and over
again taken him to pieces before the audience to show the trick
of him. And even those who, in spite of that, cannot escape
from the illusion, regard G. B. S. as a freak. The whole point
of the creature is that he is unique, fantastic, unrepresentative,
inimitable, impossible, undesirable on any large scale, utterly
unlike anybody that ever existed before, hopelessly unnatural,
and void of real passion. Clearly such a monster could do no
harm, even were his example evil (which it never is)." " The
G. B. S. you know," he laughingly remarked to me one day,
with a rapid shrug of the shoulders and a deprecatory wave
of the hand, " is merely a family joke with a select circle.
G. B. S. sometimes gets on my nerves; but he is a great source
of amusement to a small but highly enlightened audience. Of
course, there are lots of people in the world who regard me as
a huge joke; and perhaps I am as much responsible for the
G. B. S. legend as anybody else. But the vast majority of
my readers," he added, " are serious persons who regard me
as a serious person who has something serious to impart."

As an instance of the multiplicity of diverse impressions
which Bernard Shaw succeeds in evoking, consider his letter
to P. F. Collier and Son. Unknown to Shaw, his story, *Aërial
Football*, was published during a period within which the best
story submitted was to receive a prize of one thousand dollars. Shaw's letter in " acknowledgment " of Collier's cheque
evoked a thousand different expressions of opinion—ranging
between the opinion at one end of the scale that Shaw, as a
great man of letters, was entirely justified in his indignant
protest at being placed involuntarily in the position of competing for a money prize in a fiction contest, and the opinion
at the other end of the scale that Shaw was playing a spec-

tacular and sensational prank, and indulging in a rather expensive form of advertisement. Shaw's letter speaks for itself:

" SIR,—What do you mean by this unspeakable outrage? You send me a cheque for a thousand dollars, and inform me that it is a bonus offered by Messrs. P. F. Collier and Son for the best story received during the quarter in which my contribution appeared. May I ask what Messrs. P. F. Collier and Son expected my story to be?

" If it were not the best they could get for the price they were prepared to pay, they had no right to insert it at all. If it was the best, what right have they to stamp their own contributors publicly as inferior when they have taken steps to secure the result beforehand by paying a special price to a special writer?

" And what right have they to assume that I want to be paid twice over for my work, or that I am in the habit of accepting bonuses and competing for prizes?

" Waiving all these questions for a moment, I have another one to put to you. How do Messrs. P. F. Collier and Son know that my story was the best they received during the quarter? Are they posterity? Are they the verdict of history? Have they even the very doubtful qualification of being professional critics?

" I had better break this letter off lest I should be betrayed into expressing myself as strongly as I feel. I return the cheque. If you should see fit to use it for the purpose of erecting a tombstone to Messrs. P. F. Collier and Son, I shall be happy to contribute the epitaph, in which I shall do my best to do justice to their monstrous presumption.

" G. BERNARD SHAW."

In quite good humour the editor of *Collier's Weekly* assured Mr. Shaw that the award was a mistake. The " responsible " readers were out of town, and the sporting editor, who was a devotee of football, a vegetarian, a Socialist, a misanthrope, a misogynist—in short, a true disciple of G. B. S.—made the award. Of course, on receipt of Mr. Shaw's letter the sporting editor was summarily discharged!

The fantastic phenomenon "G. B. S.," accredited by popular superstition, after a long campaign on Shaw's part in the interest of creating and fostering the legend, is a phenomenon that obviously never could, never did, nor ever will, exist under the heavens. Indeed, it is one of Mr. Shaw's foibles to insist that he is short of many accomplishments which are fairly common, and in some ways an obviously ignorant, stupid and unready man. Certainly it is not a little strange that with all his remarkable knowledge of modern art, music, literature, economics and politics, he speaks no language but his own, and reads no foreign language, save French, with ease. I remember hearing someone ask Rodin whether Shaw really spoke French. "Ah! no!" replied Rodin, with his genial smile and a faint twinkle of the eyes; "Monsieur Shaw does not speak French. But somehow or other, by the very violence of his manner and gesticulation, he succeeds in *imposing* his meaning upon you!" Shaw is fond of relating the incident which laid the foundation for his reputation as an Italian scholar. "Once I was in Milan with a party of English folk. We were dining at the railway restaurant, and our waiter spoke no language other than his own. When the moment came to pay and rush for the train, we were unable to make him understand that we wanted not one bill, but twenty-four separate ones. My friends insisted that I must know Italian, so to act as interpreter, I racked my memory for chips from the language of Dante, but in vain. All of a sudden, a line from *The Huguenots* flashed to my brain: '*Ognuno per se: per tutti il ciel*' ('Every man for himself: and heaven for all.') I declaimed it with triumphant success. The army of waiters was doubled up with laughter, and my fame as an Italian scholar has been on the increase ever since."

As a rule, foreign critics rate Shaw higher as a thinker and philosopher than as wit and dramatist. The painters and sculptors likewise represent him as a personality of tremendous intellectual force. The bust by Rodin—intermediate as a work

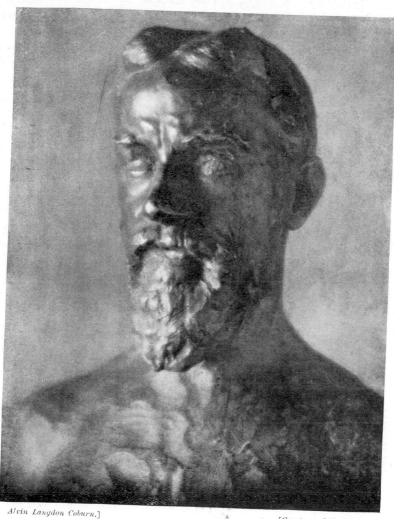

Alvin Langdon Coburn.]　　　　　　　　　　　*[Courtesy of the Sculptor.*

A BUST OF SHAW.

By Auguste Rodin.

From the bronze original owned by Bernard Shaw.　A marble replica is in the
Municipal Gallery of Modern Art, Dublin.

[*Facing p.* 492 　: ...

of art between his busts of Puvis de Chavannes and J. P. Laurens in the Musée de Luxembourg—reveals the thoughtful student, of philosophic insight and tremendous cerebration. Rodin, who finds Shaw " charming," recently said to Mrs. John van Vorst: " He is perhaps a ' fraud,' as you Americans put it. But the first victim of Bernard Shaw's charlatanism is Bernard Shaw himself. Susceptible to impressions as are all artists, and a philosopher at the same time, he cannot do otherwise than deceive himself. The cold reason which he could, were it unhampered, apply to the problems of this life, is modified, reduced to vapour, by his delicate temperamental sensitiveness and by his keen Irish sense of humour. It is, in fact, to his Irish blood that Bernard Shaw, as we know him, is due. With the cold Anglo-Saxon current only in his veins, he would have proved the ' bore ' *par excellence* who tries to divert us while reforming society, to win our applause by mere idol-breaking." * Also, in the Hon. Neville S. Lytton's portrait of Shaw, after the Innocent X. of Velasquez, there is portrayed the modern pope of wit and wisdom.† And the redoubtable logician, the philosophic satirist, is admirably bodied forth in that remarkable photograph of Shaw—the masterpiece in portraiture of Alvin Langdon Coburn.‡

The real Bernard Shaw is one of the most genial and delightfully entertaining of men. In his London quarters, at Adelphi Terrace, or in the quiet retreat of Ayot St. Lawrence, in Hertfordshire, he is easy, hospitable and unaffectedly natural.§ In his manner, the combination of light spontaneity with a sort

---

* *Rodin and Bernard Shaw,* by Mrs. John van Vorst; in *Putnam's Monthly and the Critic,* February, 1908.

† Unfortunately this portrait has a somewhat flouting and cynical expression, produced chiefly by the protruding under-lip. In answer to a question of mine on the subject, in which I pointed out that the feature was untrue to life, Mr. Lytton replied: " The unfortunate expression to which you refer does not represent my interpretation of Bernard Shaw's character or attitude towards the world, but is the result of my effort to accentuate the likeness of Shaw to the original of Velasquez. Personally, I am a great admirer of Bernard Shaw."

‡ The photogravure facing page 468.

§ One night about eleven o'clock, just after finishing the discussion of certain portions of the present work, I remember asking Mr. Shaw how

of effusive shyness is peculiarly engaging. There is something strikingly transitory about his presence: one always feels that he has just managed to catch Shaw " on the fly." While he not infrequently plays up to his reputation for gay self-puffery, in such innocent diversions, for example, as ecstatically admiring the Rodin bust or rhapsodizing over Coburn's prints of him, it is always quite obviously with the humorous consciousness that his listener is sharing in the imposture. The genius of proverbial classification writes like an angel and talks like Poor Poll; Shaw possesses the unique distinction of talking, whether in his own home or upon the public platform, as trenchantly and as brilliantly as he writes. Unlike many celebrated *raconteurs,* whose ability consists almost solely in pouring forth a flood of polished anecdote and personal reminiscence, Shaw talks with apparent ease and equal wit upon any and every subject that comes to hand, from Richard Wagner to Anthony Comstock, from spiritualism to bicycling, from German philosophy to women's clothes. One is amused to discover that his extreme acuteness in analyzing subjects upon which he is an authority is equalled only by his marvellous glibness in talking of things of which he can really know little or nothing. Far from taking his cue from Coleridge or Wilde and monopolizing the conversation for hours at a time, he makes an attentive and appreciative listener, instantaneously responsive to clever characterization or thoughtful analysis. A great tease and joker, he is perpetually telling upon his friends devastatingly comic stories which they vehemently deny *in toto.* When he is not poking fun at your views or drawing your fire by carefully directed sarcasm, he is entertaining you with some humorous episode in his own life—a tilt with Anatole France, perhaps, a bit of repartee with which he turned the

he happened to take the place in Hertfordshire. "Come with me and I will show you," he said; and we wandered across the common in the moonlight over to the old English church, redolent of mystery and sanctity. Shaw pointed to the inscription on a tomb near by: "Jane Eversley. Born, 1815. Died, 1895. Her time was short." "I thought," said Shaw, "that if it could be truthfully said of a woman who lived to be eighty years old that her time was short, then this was just exactly the climate for me."

tables on Gilbert Chesterton, or an illiterate person's joke on Shaw which for the time being completely floored him.

I remember hearing him say that Anatole France and he, among others, were once dining together in Paris, and with great brilliance France spoke uninterruptedly for a long time about the strange type of men called geniuses. At the conclusion, Shaw said: "Yes, I know all about them, for I myself am a genius." France, who knew virtually nothing of Shaw, was taken aback for only a moment. "*Mais oui, monsieur,*" he replied, "*et une courtisane se nomme une marchande de plaisir!*"

Simplicity and unostentation are the keynotes of Shaw's home life. The ornate, the gaudy, the useless are banished from his scheme of things. In his wife, a gracious person of great sweetness, he has both a charming companion and an enthusiastic supporter in all his multifarious activities. Mr. Shaw's retirement from the journalistic lists was signalized by his marriage to Miss Charlotte Frances Payne-Townshend, who nursed him back to health and strength—and matrimony—after a serious accident. "I was very ill when I was married," Mr. Shaw once wrote, "altogether a wreck on crutches and in an old jacket which the crutches had worn to rags. I had asked my friends, Mr. Graham Wallas, of the London School Board, and Mr. Henry Salt, the biographer of Shelley and De Quincey, to act as witnesses, and, of course, in honour of the occasion they were dressed in their best clothes. The registrar never imagined I could possibly be the bridegroom; he took me for the inevitable beggar who completes all wedding processions. Wallas, who is considerably over six feet high, seemed to him to be the hero of the occasion, and he was proceeding to marry him calmly to my betrothed, when Wallas, thinking the formula rather strong for a mere witness, hesitated at the last moment and left the prize to me."

Shaw is the quintessence of vital energy. He rushes hither and thither, from one task to another, with a feverish, almost frenzied activity. " Bernard Shaw reminds me of a locomotive of the most modern type," said one of his intimate friends, " perfectly adjusted and running with lightning speed—an engine of tremendous power and efficiency." One is liable to receive a first impression that Shaw is a delicate and anæmic sort of person—an impression fostered by the mackintosh and gloves he habitually wears and the umbrella he is fond of carrying. Once you have seen the man in action, and realized his abundant vitality and apparently inexhaustible store of nervous energy, you are not surprised to note, in Coburn's nude portrait of Shaw, in the casually affected pose of Rodin's *Le Penseur*, very massive shoulders and strong muscular development in arms and back. " Mr. Bernard Shaw is New York incarnate," once wrote Miss Florence Farr. " Both of them are feverish devotees at the altar of work. Empty Mr. Shaw and New York of work and hurry, the man has a headache and closes his eyes in pain; he feels no reason for existence; and the city is a desolation. To Mr. Shaw, as to New York," she pointedly added: " ' doing nothing ' is hell and damnation." *

As a conversationist, Mr. Shaw is the most witty and delightful person imaginable. " Shaw is just a great big boy," one of his intimate friends said to me, " who enjoys life and the world and himself to the fullest extent." His enjoyment of his own anecdotes, witticisms, and strokes of repartee is irresistibly contagious; you howl with merriment, even when the joke is on you—and untrue to boot, as it often is. Brevity is the soul of his wit; and yet his stories pour forth in a perfect flood, and the coming of the " point " is duly heralded. The bubbling, chuckling note in his voice, the hands rubbed together with lightning-like rapidity, his body convulsively rocking back and forth in his chair—then the " point " with a rush, fol-

---

* Shaw suffers from periodical headaches, which come about once a month, and last a day. "Don't you ever suffer any ill effects from the terrible hardships you have to undergo in the bleak northern latitudes? " Shaw inquired one day of Fridtjof Nansen, the great Arctic explorer. "Yes," replied Nansen, "I suffer with the most frightful headaches." "Have you never tried to discover a cure for the headache? " asked Shaw. "Why, no! " replied Nansen. "I never thought of such a thing! " "Well, my dear fellow," said Shaw, "that is the most astonishing thing I have ever heard. Here you have spent a lifetime trying to discover the North Pole, that nobody in the world cares tuppence about, and you have never even tried to discover a cure for the headache, which the whole world is crying for."

lowed by his mirthfully expressive: "Well, you know——!";
he fairly doubles up, his head is thrown back, his body shakes
from head to foot, and his eyes dance and glitter like the sea
when struck full by the rays of the sun. His habit is to turn
his light batteries of genial sarcasm, satire and irony upon
those things which he perceives to be the especial objects of
your respect, admiration, or veneration; he invariably depre-
ciates and even ridicules those works of his own which you
express an especial liking for. In private conversation, as well
as on the platform, he is frequently engaged in drawing your
fire and "putting you to your trumps"; and he once laughingly remarked to me that nothing delighted him more than
to create around him a miniature reign of terror.* Less
strongly opinionated persons than himself, when challenged in
this way, are occasionally frightened into concealing or belying
their real views. I once heard one of Shaw's acquaintances say
with much harshness: "The astuteness and acumen of Bernard
Shaw is little short of miraculous. His power of making people
say precisely what he wants to hear, and at the same time
what they don't necessarily believe, is truly phenomenal, almost
diabolic." He always keeps his temper and seldom goes beyond sharp, but good-humoured banter; but when attacked
upon some fundamental point in which his convictions are
profoundly engaged or the meaning of his life fundamentally
misinterpreted, he becomes a dangerous dialectic antagonist
who unmasks upon his opponent all the batteries of his keen
satire, cutting logic and mordant wit.†

* The delightful way in which Lady Randolph Churchill "squelched"
him on the occasion of one of his terrorizing utterances is eminently worthy
of quotation. In answer to her invitation to a luncheon party, Shaw
wrote: "Certainly not! What have I done to provoke such an attack on
my well-known habit?" To which she replied: "Know nothing of your
habits; hope they are not as bad as your manners." Shaw then wrote her
a long letter of "explanation"—leaving the victory with the lady.—
Reminiscences of Lady Randolph Churchill, in the *Century Magazine*, September, 1908.

† Perhaps the most interesting feature of the Adelphi Terrace quarters
is the inscription cut in the enamel headboard of the mantelpiece—an
inscription vitally characteristic of Shaw, the freethinker and *intransigéant*
—taken from the walls of Holyrood Palace:

"*Thay say. Quhat say thay? Lat thame say!*"

GEORGE BERNARD SHAW

As a platform speaker and mob orator, Bernard Shaw is unique alike in his incisive, metallic utterance and in the mystifying directness of his paradoxes. It is genuinely amusing to watch him—the head and front of Fabianism—at a meeting of the Fabian Society. Here he is truly Sir Oracle: his opinion controls the policy of the society, as it has done for many years. While the speaker is addressing the society, Mr. Shaw is usually seated to the front and at the right of the platform, his eye-glasses depending from the hook upon the breast of his coat, his head bowed slightly forward, the fingers of his right hand lightly resting across his lips. This striking figure, with face of deadly pallor, eyes of steel blue, and general appearance of patient, amused tolerance, is here the chief justice of the court, the critic of highest authority. When he does not agree with the speaker, he shakes his head with all the naïve assumption of infallibility; and when some point is made which supports or clinches some well-known argument of his own, he gravely nods with equal *sang-froid*—the air of the sage encouraging promising youth. When he rises to speak, he dabbles with no graceful preliminaries, but plunges at once *in medias res*, and, with long forefinger upraised, sharply and mercilessly drives home his paradoxical point with all the deadly accuracy of the practised duellist. Whilst Shaw uses the rapier of cold logic in debate, and is merciless in penetrating the joints in his opponents' armour, he is scrupulously fair and just. His audiences, even at the Fabian meetings, seldom fully endorse, or even seem to understand thoroughly, the full significance and implication of his position; the applause at the close of one of his speeches is, not infrequently, less vigorous and unanimous than at the beginning. And after the meeting is over, one may observe groups of excited Fabians, scattered here and there, vehemently debating as to what Bernard Shaw really meant, and as to whether, after all, what he said was to be taken *au grand sérieux!*

It is a strange and inexplicable mystery that, whenever a man makes a genuine effort to disencumber himself of all traditional sentiment and contemporary prejudice, and to express himself with perfect *naïveté* and impartiality, the British pub-

506

"A PROPHET, THE PRESS, AND SOME PEOPLE."

Reproduced from the original water-colour.

[Facing p. 498

lic immediately concludes that he is a frivolous jester. Mr. William Archer, however, is of opinion that Shaw is far less free from sentiment than he appears. " I suspect Bernard Shaw of being constitutionally an arrant sentimentalist, whose abhorrence of sentiment is as the shrinking of the dipsomaniac from the single drop of alcohol which he knows will make his craving ungovernable! " If this humorous conjecture be correct, the mania is assuredly a furtive one. On occasion Bernard Shaw enjoys to the full playing with his public and flaunting a red rag at the British Bull, named John; when he chooses he airily plays to perfection the parts of *jongleur* and *matador* rolled into one. " It is an astounding thing that people so thoroughly fail to understand me," Mr. Shaw remarked to me one day. " All that is necessary is discrimination, a strong sense of humour, and ability to occupy my point of view for the time being. Of course, I get no end of fun out of fluttering the dove-cotes. I love to leave fire and desolation in my path— to create the impression that I am a terrible fellow to deal with. The great difficulty with most people is to distinguish between my moods—when I am joking, and when I am serious; they can't see how anyone can joke about serious things. I am continually being asked all sorts of silly questions, and I am human enough "—this with a twinkle in the grey-blue eyes and an expressive wave of the hand—" to enjoy mystifying people who labour under the misfortune of being born without a sense of humour. Why, only the other day some innocent had the temerity to ask me if I were really serious in all that I said, wrote and did.

" ' My dear sir,' I replied, with the air of all earnestness and conviction, ' if you really believe me to be serious, it is unnecessary for me to assure you of the fact. If you do not believe me to be serious, it is equally unnecessary to assure you of something you would not believe.' "

It is related that on one occasion a student just beginning his studies as a naturalist, walked into a bookstore and ignorantly asked: " Have you any books by the great Buffoon (meaning Buffon, of course)? " Whereupon the clerk, with-

507

out the slightest hesitation, presented the applicant with the latest work of Bernard Shaw!

I have been interested to discover, through acquaintance with Bernard Shaw and the late Mark Twain, that their views as to the fundamental nature of man are in many respects identical. Their thoroughly human, wise views of man, his failings and limitations, might easily be regarded as cynical by thoughtless persons; in reality, their " cynicism " is nothing more nor less than a profound knowledge of human nature. Shaw, who has the very highest admiration for Mark Twain, both as sociologist and humorist, once said: " Of course, he is in very much the same position as myself. He has to put matters in such a way as to make people who would otherwise hang him believe he is joking." Shaw was once asked why he was always so cynical; to which he replied, without hesitation or embarrassment, that he could not account for his cynicism—that it must be accepted as the primary and original product of his own genius. " I am not a cynic at all," Mr. Shaw once told me, leaning forward in his chair and speaking with convincing earnestness, " if by cynic is meant one who disbelieves in the inherent goodness of man. Nor am I a pessimist, if by pessimist is meant one who despairs of human virtue or the worth of living. But all this babble about the search for happiness does not impose on me in the slightest degree. Remember the incident of Napoleon:

" ' Could I be what I am, little one, cared I only for happiness? '

" Life is worth living for its own sake, and for the sake of the general welfare of humanity. It is a common error to mistake a penetrating critic for a confirmed cynic. I owe my success as a critic, not to any quality of cynicism, but to a searching power of analysis."

Strangely enough, this advocate of life for its own sake is charged in many quarters, and notably by Mr. Gilbert Chesterton, with being feelingless, rationalistic and a Puritan of the Puritans. It is quite true that in matters of food, drink, dress and sanitation, Shaw is scientifically hygienic and Puritanical—if Puritanical be the just word for this attitude of mind. In his views concerning the relations of the sexes, there is no evidence to show that he is one whit more Puritanical than George Meredith, who advocated marriages limited to a specified time. Mr. Shaw one day told me a good story about an argument he had with Mr. Gilbert Chesterton. " Chesterton *would* insist upon calling *me*, the author of *Mrs. Warren's Profession* and *Man and Superman*, a Puritan," explained Shaw. " ' Of course, Shaw, I admire your hard and frigid Puritanism,' said Chesterton, ' but, for Heaven's sake, indulge in a little frivolity now and then. Fling away, if only for the moment, your terrible burden of duty.' ' My dear Chesterton,' I replied, ' you cannot deceive me by declaring me to be a Puritan. You pretend to be attacking Puritanism when you say that, despite my splendid love of truth, my deficiency in fully comprehending truth springs from a neglect of the great gaieties out of which Romance is born. What you call an attack on Puritanism is nothing but a veiled defence of excess.' " " And do you know," added Shaw—clearly exhibiting the irreconcilability of the two philosophies of life—" Chesterton— Chesterton, our English Rabelais—actually admitted it ! "

Most persistent of all these accusations made against Shaw is that he is a case of intellect almost pure, without feelings and without heart. Were it fitting, I could cite many instances of Mr. Shaw's generosity, benevolence and philanthropy—true stories which have come to me without my seeking and without Mr. Shaw's knowledge. I happen to know that Shaw has the utmost abhorrence for " those abominable bastard Utopias of genteel charity, in which the poor are first robbed and then pauperized by way of compensation, in order that the rich man may combine the idle luxury of the protected thief with the unctuous self-satisfaction of the pious philanthropist." Shaw is continually engaged in assisting people in various ways— frequently without their knowledge and always in such a way as to avoid the radical error of permitting them to suffer in self-respect. Shaw believes in helping other people to help themselves. He will take any amount of trouble for a friend, and he has materially assisted innumerable people who had not one iota of claim upon his time or his services. His courtesy is of the truest sort, without affectation or pretence; and one of his acquaintances recently said: " My memory of the cheerful and easy grace of Bernard Shaw's instant considerateness and simple courtesy, when he believed himself to be unobserved and unrecognized, remains with me as among the most delightful impressions I have ever collected of a large mind taking pleasant and friendly cognizance of the importance of the little everyday acts of good-fellowship which make this world a less irksome place to sojourn in than it would otherwise be." If Shaw has deeply angered many people by his unrestrained outspokenness, he has also given many people both pleasure and happiness, by his generosity, his brilliant wit, and his sanity of spirit. Recall one of the finest of his maxims: " We have no more right to consume happiness without producing it than we have to consume wealth without producing it."

I once asked Mr. Shaw what answer he had to make to the statement that he was a bloodless, passionless, intellectual machine. His answer made upon me a more profound impression than anything that has ever occurred in my association with him.

" Look here," he replied, the utmost earnestness moulding his expression, " real feeling is the most difficult thing in the world to recognize. A parable will serve. Two men are walking down the crowded Strand, gazing at the vast throng of people as they hurry along with a thousand different aims. To one, the spectacle signifies nothing more than the ordinary metropolitan aspect of the greatest city in the world. The other sees in the spectacle a company of men and angels ascending and descending an endless ladder which reaches from earth to heaven. The one passes a starving child whose face is pinched with the cold; he shudders with discomfort, draws his greatcoat tighter around him, and, after giving the child a penny, passes on, thanking God that he is not as other men are. The other man regards the little waif with infinite compassion, his heart goes out in profoundest sympathy, and his whole being protests against the social system which makes such things possible. And he devotes his life, not to giving pennies to individual sufferers, but to exposing the conditions which produce such horrors and to agitating for such reforms as will mitigate these horrors, and eventually render them impossible."

The close and searching student of Bernard Shaw's work and personality cannot fail to detect, beneath the surface, the profound and passionate sentiment which runs through his entire life. In his fierce reaction against the puerile sentimentalities, the fraudulent romance, the loathsome eroticism of modern art and life, one can detect the spur of real sentiment and passion. The pure love of man and woman, physically congruent and temperamentally compatible, he regards as the ideal condition for the progressive evolution of the race. And he once assured me of his conviction that such marriages, eventuating in children sound in mind and body, were best from every possible standpoint; but that in actual experience, marriages of this sort are in a hopeless minority. Shaw's fundamental Socialism prompts him to batter down the social barriers which set off the aristocrats from the common people—those barriers which result in the aristocracy feeding upon its own vitality, breeding and in-breeding, until the sexual product is hopelessly anæmic and degenerate. Stronger, better, saner men and women, Shaw believes, would be bred through the intermarriage of the duchess and the navvy; he strongly advocates the experiment, not simply for the sake of breaking down the social barriers, but primarily for the cause of the ultimate betterment of the race.

It is Shaw's chief distinction that, for the sake of sentiment, he would deny sentiment. "I verily believe," a distinguished author once remarked to me, "that Mr. Shaw lives in mortal terror of the public for fear it will discover his great secret: the possession of a warm heart." His reaction is not against the sentiment which civic virtue and personal integrity bespeak, but against the popular clap-trap, romanticized notion of sentiment which to the unilluded goes by the name of sentimentality. Bernard Shaw is a man of tremendous sentiment— social and humanitarian sentiment. Sociologic thought and social service are the ruling moral passions of his life.

"The final ideal for civic life," he said in a public address not long ago, "is that every man and every woman should set before themselves this goal—that by the labour of their lifetime they shall pay the debt of their rearing and their education, and also contribute sufficient for a handsome maintenance during their old age. And more than that: why should not a man say: ' When I die my country shall be in my debt.' Any man who has any religious belief will have the dream that it is not only possible to die with his country in his debt but with God in his debt also."

The germ of Shaw's philosophy of life may be found in these words:

" I am of the opinion that my life belongs to the whole community, and as long as I live it is my privilege to do for it whatsoever I can.

" I want to be thoroughly used up when I die, for the harder I work, the more I live. I rejoice in life for its own sake. Life is no ' brief candle ' for me. It is a sort of splendid torch, which I have got hold of for the moment; and I want to make it burn as brightly as possible before handing it on to future generations."

APPENDIX

GENEALOGICAL CHART OF THE SHAW FAMILY

OF COUNTIES TIPPERARY, KILKENNY AND DUBLIN, TOGETHER WITH OTHER
LINEAL ANCESTORS OF

GEORGE BERNARD SHAW

INDEX

Abbey Theatre, Dublin, 400-1.
Academy, 246, 287.
Achurch, Janet, 299, 304, 353-4.
Actors' Society Monthly Bulletin, The, 369.
Adams, Maurice, 104.
Addison, Joseph, 199.
Ade, George, 136.
Adelphi Terrace, 20.
Admirable Bashville, The. See G. B. Shaw.
Aldwych Theatre, 401.
Alexander, George, 183, 282.
Allen, Grant, 279.
Allen, Rev. G. W., 102.
Alma-Tadema, Sir L., 287.
Amateur Photographer, 226.
Anderton's Hotel, 115, 131.
Angelo, Michael, 31, 46, 90, 153, 218-9, 225, 243, 291, 393.
Archer, William, 20, 75, 84, 90, 91, 142, 251, 297, 306, 315, 327, 333, 369, 413, 417, 443; and Cashel Byron's Profession, 61, 76; first sees Shaw, 97; and Shaw's career as a critic, 195; and Shaw's musical criticisms, 232-3; and Shaw's dramatic criticisms, 279 et sqq., 286; collaborates with Shaw, 293, 295; and Shaw as a dramatist, 299; and Mrs. Warren's Profession, 307-8, 363, 425; and Arms and the Man, 316-17; and You Never Can Tell, 325; and Shaw's greatest work, 378; and Major Barbara, 387; and The Doctor's Dilemma, 390 et sqq.; and stage directions, 419; and Widowers' Houses, 445; and Shaw's sentiment, 507.
Arms and the Man. See G. B. Shaw.
Arnold, Matthew, 96.
Arnold, Sir Edwin, 299.
Art Moderne, L', 348.
Atlantic Monthly, The, 484.
Augier, E., 294.
Author, The, 91.

Aveling, Dr., 114, 160, 164, 261.
Avenue Theatre, 312 et sqq., 316.

Bab, Julius, 85, 249, 402.
Bach, 236, 240, 252.
Bahr, Hermann, 198, 353, 358, 410, 414, 424.
Bakunin, Michel, 98, 189, 247.
Balfour, Right Hon. A. J., 372, 404.
Ball Publishing Co., 111.
Barker, Granville, 286, 368, 371-2, 388, 398, 446.
Barnby, Sir Joseph, 237.
Barrie, J. M., 404.
Barry, James, 200.
Bashkirtseff, Marie, 5, 273.
Bax, Belfort, 51, 98, 164, 485-6; his article, Socialism and Bourgeois Culture, 159.
Beaumarchais, 23.
Beaumont and Fletcher, 264, 366.
Bebel, F. A., 152, 180, 186.
Beerbohm, Max, 231, 288, 339, 363, 394, 425, 496.
Beethoven, 18, 23-4, 73, 153, 240, 243, 250, 257, 393.
Beeton, 158.
Bell, Chichester, 34-5, 44.
Bellamy, Edward, 152.
Bellini, 18.
Bennett, Sterndale, 237.
Berlioz, 234, 257.
Bernstein, Eduard, 165.
Besant, Mrs. Annie, 52, 92, 109, 113 et sqq., 125, 133, 144, 160, 165, 178, 283, 484.
Beyle, Henri, 20, 412, 463.
Birmingham, George A., 401.
Bispham, David, 238.
Bizet, 24, 61.
Blake, William, 447, 454 et sqq., 466, 469, 473.
Bland, Hubert, 67, 99, 102, 114 et sqq., 128-9, 169, 175, 178.
Bland, Mrs. Hubert, 128-9.
Blavatsky, Madame, 127.
Blum, M. Jean, 337.
Booth, General, 387.

515

Borchardt, Miss, 484.
Borsa, Mario, 270.
Boston Transcript, 287.
Bouguereau, W. A., 222.
Bourget, Paul, 416, 464.
Bradlaugh, Charles, 137-8, 144, 160, 176.
Braekstad, Hans L., 272.
Brahms, 241, 243.
Brandes, Dr. Georg, 306, 307, 311, 313, 347, 359-60, 418, 464.
Brentanos, 54-5.
Brieux, Eugène, 432, 439.
Brooke, Stopford, 15, 93, 208.
Brown, Ford Madox, 212, 219-20.
Browning, Robert, 31-2, 40, 219, 412, 415, 466.
Browning Society, 135.
Bruneau, 245.
Brunetière, Ferdinand, 307, 309.
Bryant, D. Sophia, 37-8.
Bülow, Hans Von, 241.
Bunyan, John, 268, 447, 473.
Burne-Jones, Sir Edward, 206, 212, 221, 225.
Burne-Jones, Lady, 206.
Burns, Right Hon. John, 112 *et sqq.*, 127, 142, 166, 174.
Burrows, 113.
Butler, Samuel, 480, 483.
Byron, Lord, 143, 215, 364.

Cæsar and Cleopatra. *See* G. B. SHAW.
Cairnes, J. E., 155.
Calderon, 432.
Calvé, Mme., 245.
Campbell-Bannerman, Sir Henry, 372.
Campbell, Lady Colin, 212.
Campbell, Mrs. Patrick, 228, 392.
Candida. *See* G. B. SHAW.
Candid Friend, The, 42, 60, 98, 147, 202, 476.
Captain Brassbound's Conversion. *See* G. B. SHAW.
Carlyle, Thomas, 253, 271, 336, 434, 457, 474.
Carnegie, Andrew, 383, 385.
Carpaccio, 227.
Carpenter, Captain Alfred, 99.
Carpenter, Edward, 50, 99, 114.
Carroll, Rev. William George, 15.
Cashel Byron's Profession. *See* G. B. SHAW.
Caxton Magazine, 211.

Cellier, Alfred, 233.
Century Magazine, 505.
Chamberlain, Right Hon. Joseph, 404.
Chamfort, Nicholas, 456.
Champion, Henry Hyde, 48, 51, 52-3, 102, 112 *et sqq.*, 125, 155.
Chap-Book, The, 29, 57, 149.
Chapman and Hall, 47.
Chapman, George, 264.
Charrington, Charles, 354.
Charrington, Mrs. *See* ACHURCH.
Chaucer, 221.
Chesterton, Gilbert K., 9, 190, 202, 354, 413, 415, 435, 436, 453, 472, 489, 496, 503, 508-9.
Chopin, 23, 25.
Christian Socialist, The, 47.
Chubb, Percival, 102.
Civic and Dramatic Guild, 402.
Clarion, The, 385, 390, 422.
Clarke, M.A., William, 100 *et sqq.*; his *The Fabian Society*, 111, 129, 136.
Clerk, The, 22.
Cobden, Richard, 168.
Coburn, Alvin L., 224 *et sqq.*, 496, 501 *et sqq.*
Collier and Son, P. F., 498-9.
Colvin, Sidney, 53.
Comedy Theatre, 295.
Common Sense of Municipal Trading, The. *See* G. B. SHAW.
Common, Thomas, 485.
Comte, Auguste, 102, 168.
Constable and Co., Archibald, 55, 183, 399.
Contemporary Review, 183, 385.
Corbett, James J., 72.
Corbin, John, 319, 321, 344, 373.
Correggio, 221.
Courtney, W. L., 63, 80, 81, 177, 286.
Court Theatre, 277, 285, 286, 324, 345, 368-9, 371-2, 388, 402.
Cowen, Sir Fred, 237.
Crane, Walter, his *An Artist's Reminiscences*, 112.
Crawford, Rev. William, 16.
Criterion Theatre, 295.
Cunningham, Edward, 158.
Cunningham, W., 159.

Daily Chronicle, The, 100, 164, 212, 248, 305, 312, 331.
Daily News, The, 75, 91, 419.

INDEX

Daly, Arnold, 315, 326, 346.
D'Annunzio, Gabriel, 416, 419.
Dark Lady of the Sonnets, The. See G. B. SHAW.
Darwin, Charles, 92, 94, 96, 102, 123, 153, 261, 476, 483; his *Descent of Man,* 97.
Davidson, Thomas, 102-4, 173.
Davis, 114.
Day, Holland, 228.
Delaroche, Paul, 200, 224.
Della Robbia, 221.
Demachy, 228.
De Quincey, Thomas, 51, 153, 161, 359, 503.
De Reszke, Édouard, 238, 445.
De Reszke, Jean, 238, 245, 445.
Devil's Disciple, The. See G. B. SHAW.
Dialectical Society, 92-3, 271.
Dickens, Charles, 41, 253, 361, 416, 443, 473.
Die Zeit, 165.
Disraeli, Benjamin, Earl of Beaconsfield, 98, 124, 144, 205, 262.
Doctor's Dilemma, The. See G. B. SHAW.
Dolmetsch, Arnold, 237.
Donald, 114.
Donatello, 221.
Don Giovanni, 18, 23.
Donisthorpe, Wordsworth, 114, 125.
Donizetti, 18, 23.
Don Juan in Hell. See G. B. SHAW.
Dramatic Opinions and Essays. See G. B. SHAW.
Dryden, John, 476.
Drysdale, Dr., 93.
Dublin, Shaw born at, 3; Shaw's early life in, 3 *et sqq.*
Dumas, Alexandre, 61, 67.
Dumas, Alexandre *fils,* 413.
Düsel, Friedrich, 337.
Dvorak, 241.

Echo, The, 231.
Economic Club, The, 158.
Economic Journal, The, 158.
Edgeworth, F. Y., 158-9.
Edison, Thomas A., 44.
Edward VII., 311, 372.
Edwards, Clement, 142.
Edwards, Osmon, 270.
Eliot, George, 92, 94, 96, 305.
Ellis, Alexander, 91.
Ellis, Ashton, 393.

Ellis, Havelock, 102.
Emerson, Ralph Waldo, 3, 439.
Engel, Louis, 235.
Engels, Friedrich, 106, 163, 167, 181.
English Illustrated Magazine, 244.
English Land Restoration League, The, 47, 99.

FABIAN ESSAYS IN SOCIALISM. See G. B. SHAW.
Fabian Society, The, 39, 47, 52, 56, 89 *et sqq.,* 173 *et sqq.,* 231, 280.
Faguet, Émile, 84, 250.
Farr, Florence, 329, 504.
Faust, 18.
Fellowship of the New Life, The. See THE FABIAN SOCIETY.
Figaro, Le, 348.
Filon, Augustin, 300, 336, 344-5, 367, 445, 449.
Fitzgerald, C. L., 111.
Fontenelle, 416.
Foote, G. W., 114, 131, 138 *et sqq.,* 482.
Ford, Rev. F. W., 125.
Fortnightly Review, The, 24, 60, 187.
Foxwell, 158-9.
France, Anatole, 144, 449, 502-3.
Freethinker, The, 482.
Freiligrath, Ferdinand, 51.
Frost, Percy, 155-6.
Funk and Wagnalls Co., 268.
Furniss, Harry, 327.
Furnival, Dr. F. J., 135.

GAIETY THEATRE, MANCHESTER, 402.
Galsworthy, John, 372.
Galton, Sir Francis, F.R.S., 492.
Garcke, Emil, 91.
Garland, Hamlin, 152.
Garrick, David, 196.
Garrick Theatre, 295.
George, Henry, 47-8, 50, 56, 90, 117, 153 *et sqq.,* 176, 178; his *Progress and Poverty,* 94, 96, 102, 152, 154-5, 178.
George, Henry, Jr., 95, 152.
George, Right Hon. Lloyd, 175.
Gerster, 239.
Gestalten und Gedanken, 313.
Getting Married. See G. B. SHAW.
Gibson, Dr. Burns, 102, 104.
Gilbert, Sir W. S., 237, 303, 316 *et sqq.,* 433, 456 *et sqq.;* his *Palace of Truth,* 318 *et sqq.*

INDEX

Gissing, George, 415.
Godard, J. G., 91.
Goethe, 23, 306, 364, 412, 434.
Goncourt, Edmond de, 440.
Gonner, E. C. K., 135.
Gordon, General, 312.
Gorki, Maxim, 432.
Gounod, 18, 24.
Graham, Cunninghame, 113, 306, 314, 328.
Grant, Corrie, 125.
Great Thoughts, 480.
Greene, Robert, 264.
Greenwood, Frederick, 200.
Gregory, Lady, 400.
Grein, J. T., 293, 295, 309, 321, 358.
Greuze, 228.
Greville, Eden, 293.
Grove, Sir George, 236.
Grundsätze der Volkswirtschaftslehre, 161.
Grundy, Sydney, 282, 284.
Guèsde, 152, 166, 180.
Guilbert, Yvette, 345.
Gurly, Lucinda Elizabeth. *See* Mrs. G. C. Shaw.
Gurly, Walter Bagenal, 7.

Hadden, Caroline, 104.
Hagemann, Herr Carl, 410.
Haldane, Right Hon. R. B., 132 *et sqq.*
Hale, Professor, 426.
Hall, Andrew, 113.
Hals, Franz, 227.
Hamon, Auguste, 165, 309-10, 353, 439.
Hampstead Historic Club, 128 *et sqq.*, 157.
Handel, 18, 23, 233, 257.
Hankin, St. John, 372.
Hapgood, Norman, 325, 411.
Hardie, Keir, 187.
Hardy, Thomas, 55, 368.
Hare, Sir John, 282.
Harper and Brothers, 54-5.
Harper's Bazaar, 85.
Harris, Frank, 261, 266.
Harris, Sir Augustus, 216, 245, 278, 287.
Hart, Sir Robert, 16.
Hauptmann, Gerhart, 413, 464.
Hausemann, William A., 340, 456, 486.
Hawthorne, Nathaniel, 25.
Hay, John, 189.

Haydn, 36.
Haymarket Theatre, 321.
Headlam, Rev. Stewart, 48, 114.
Hebbel Theater, 301.
Heine, Heinrich, 3, 47, 201, 413, 457.
Helmholtz, Hermann Von, 44.
Henderson, Archibald, 484.
Henley, W. E., 53, 212, 214 *et sqq.*, 282.
Henry and Co., 205, 298.
Hensley, Lewis, his *The Scholar's Algebra*, 158.
Herwegh, Georg, 51.
Hibbert Journal, 471.
Hichens, Robert, 261.
Hinton, Horsley, 228.
Hinton, Mrs., 104.
Hodgskin, 155.
Hodgson, R., 127.
Hogarth, William, 227-8, 422, 473.
Holbein, 227.
Hollman, 239.
Holmes, Oliver Wendell, his *Autocrat of the Breakfast Table*, 89.
Hooghe, Peter de, 224.
Hope, Laurence, 392.
Hoppner, John, 228.
Horniman, Miss, 401.
How He Lied to Her Husband. See G. B. Shaw.
Hudson Theatre, 365.
Hughes, 114.
Hugo, Victor, 23, 59, 250, 432, 434, 443.
Humanitarian League, The, 49.
Humanitarian, The, 435.
Huneker, James G., 84-5, 246, 275, 350, 366, 375, 418.
Huxley, Thomas, 92, 94, 96-7, 443, 476-7.
Hyndman, H. M., 98, 110, 112-3, 127, 138, 152, 156-7, 159, 160, 164-5, 167 *et sqq.*, 173-4, 200, 206, 302, 368; his *Economics of Socialism*, 162; his *Marx's Theory of Value*, 164-5.

Ibsen, Henrik, 14, 25, 39, 59, 90, 143, 198, 237, 247, 299 *et sqq.*, 415, 432, 447, 455, 460, 471, 480; Shaw compared to, 61-2, 304, 316, 420 *et sqq.*, 458; his *Love's Comedy*, 78, 347; his *Little Eyolf*, 81; his *The Master Builder*, 81; the controversy on, 248-9; Shaw's championship of, 263, 272 *et sqq.*, 305,

INDEX

Ibsen, Henrik—*continued.*
389-90; his mission, 269; Shaw's admiration for, 270; his *A Doll's House*, 271, 274, 299, 314, 338, 433, 439; his *Peer Gynt*, 273; his *Emperor and Galilean*, 273, 460; his *The Pillars of Society*, 271, 274; his *An Enemy of the People*, 274, 297, 439, 456-7; his *Ghosts*, 274, 296, 305, 307; his *The Wild Duck*, 274; his *Rosmersholm*, 274; his *The Lady from the Sea*, 274, 347; his *Hedda Gabler*, 274; criticized by Shaw, 303; his death, 389; and stage directions, 417-18.

Immaturity. *See* G. B. SHAW.

Independent Theatre Society, 293, 295, 309, 321.

Ingersoll, Robert G., 92.

Ingres, Jean, 219.

Interlude at the Playhouse, The. *See* G. B. SHAW.

Ireland, its irreligion, 8-9; National Gallery of, 19, 31; land agency in, 21; described in *John Bull's Other Island*, 372 *et sqq.*

Irish National Theatre Society, 401.

Irish Times, The, 400.

Irrational Knot, The. *See* G. B. SHAW.

Irving, Sir Henry, 216, 287 *et sqq.*

Irwin, Will, 270.

JACKSON, HOLBROOK, 11, 175, 447.

James, Henry, 64, 284, 394, 416, 454.

James, S. T., 259.

Jaurès, Jean, 144, 152, 166, 180, 186, 486.

Jefferies, Richard, 51.

Jevons, Stanley, 155-6, 159 *et sqq.*; his *Letters and Journal*, 160; his *Theory of Political Economy*, 161.

Joachim, Joseph, 240-1.

John Bull's Other Island. *See* G. B. SHAW.

Johnson, Dr., 479.

Jones, Benjamin, 132.

Jones, Henry Arthur, 210, 257, 263, 282 *et sqq.*

Jonson, Ben, 264, 266.

Journal des Débats, 350.

Jowett, Benjamin, 262.

Joynes, James Leigh, 48, 50-1, 90, 94, 155.

Jupp, W. I., 104.

Justice, 164-5.

KAULBACH, WILHELM VON, 200, 224.

Keats, John, 40, 215.

Kerr, Alfred, 340, 438.

Kingsway Theatre, The, 402, 403.

Knight, William, his *Memorials of Thomas Davidson,* 104.

Knowles, Sheridan, 415.

Kropotkin, Prince, 98, 108, 152, 170, 173.

LAMARCK, JEAN, 480, 483-4, 488.

Lamb, Charles, 6, 266, 447.

Land Nationalization Society, 95.

Land Reform Union. *See* ENGLISH LAND RESTORATION LEAGUE.

Lane, John, 270.

Lane, Joseph, 114.

Lassalle, Ferdinand, 98, 127, 152, 165, 168, 173, 176, 178, 271, 457.

"Law and Liberty League," 113.

Lecky, James, 90 *et sqq.*, 122, 235.

Leeds Art Club, 175.

Lee, George J. V., 17-8, 22, 37.

Le Gallienne, Richard, 232.

Leighton, Sir Frederick, 219.

Leschetizky, 239.

Le Temps, 277.

Levy, 131.

Lewes, George H., 201, 233.

Liberty, 189, 246.

Liebknecht, Wilhelm, 98, 152, 166, 172-3, 180-1.

Lind, Letty, 254.

Linnell, John, 228.

Lippi, Fra Filippo, 221.

Liszt, Abbé, 23, 257.

Lodge, Sir Oliver, 385.

Lohengrin, 35.

London Stage Society, 380.

Longfellow, Henry W., 24.

Loraine, Robert, 43, 302, 315, 368.

Love Among the Artists. *See* G. B. SHAW.

Lucrezia Borgia, 18.

Luther, Martin, 469-70.

Lyceum Theatre, 282, 343.

Lytton, Hon. Neville S., 501.

Lytton, Lord, 297.

MACAULAY, THOMAS B., 199.

MacCarthy, Desmond, 324, 339.

McClure's Magazine, 329.

Macdonald, J., 111.

McEvoy, Charles, 380.

McKail, J. W., 212.

McKee, Rev. T. A., 16.

INDEX

Mackenzie, Sir Alexander, 236.
Macmillan Co., The, 340, 456.
McNulty, Edward, 34; his *Misther O'Ryan, The Son of a Peasant* and *Maureen*, 33.
Maeterlinck, Maurice, 134, 224, 368, 415, 463-4.
Mainly About People, 1.
Mallock, W. H., 59, 60, 186-7.
Malthus, Thomas R., 92-3, 168.
Man and Superman. See G. B. SHAW.
Mann, Tom, 113.
Man of Destiny, The. See G. B. SHAW.
Mansfield, Richard, 54, 315, 342-3, 355, 358.
Mantegna, 46, 225, 227.
Marbot, his *Memoirs*, 312.
Maris, James, 222.
Marlowe, Christopher, 264.
Marshall, Alfred, 158.
Marston, John, 264.
Marx, Eleanor, 261, 272.
Marx, Karl, 50, 79, 90, 128, 151-2, 159, 173, 176, 178, 181, 261, 271, 457; his *Das Kapital*, 96 *et sqq.*, 106, 155 *et sqq.*, 160 *et sqq.*, 293.
Masefield, John, 372.
Massenet, Jules, 245.
Massingham, H. W., 231.
Mathews, Charles, 317.
Matthews, Brander, 416.
Maude, Aylmer, his *Life of Tolstoy*, 399.
Maude, Cyril, 321, 328.
Maupassant, Guy de, 304-5, 316.
Melba, Mme., 24.
Mendelssohn, 18, 24, 233, 243.
Menger, Anton, 161.
Meredith, George, 46-47, 77, 201, 278, 461, 471, 509; his *Essay on Comedy*, 278.
Merimée, Prosper, 24.
Methuen and Co., 112.
Metropolitan Magazine, 227, 351.
Meyerbeer, 24, 243.
Meyerfeld, Dr. Max, 43, 426.
Millerand, 166.
Mill, John Stuart, 91-2, 94, 96, 102, 123, 153, 157, 466.
Milton, John, 139.
Mirabeau, 339.
Misalliance. See G. B. SHAW.
Modern Press, The, 155.

Moffat, Yard and Co., 343.
Molière, 23, 130, 270, 278, 306, 320, 361, 364, 370, 378, 394, 439, 443, 449.
Mommsen, Theodor, 336.
Monet, Claude, 222.
Moody and Sankey, 10-11, 27, 33.
Moore, George, 202.
Moore, Samuel, 160.
Moore, Thomas, 243.
Morning Leader, 91.
Morris, May, 261.
Morris, William, 90, 98, 152, 173, 261, 271, 434, 457, 473; makes Shaw's acquaintance, 52; and *Cashel Byron's Profession*, 74; on parents and children, 92; his influence on Shaw, 99, 205; and the Fabian Society, 114-5; and the Socialist League, 137; and the value theory, 164; Shaw's ignorance of, 206; his Socialist views, 207; Shaw's obituary notice of, 209, 212; his artistic integrity, 210-11; his mastery of English, 221; and Shaw's article on Nordau, 246.
Mozart, 18, 24, 32, 36, 90, 214, 218, 240, 243-4, 248-9, 257, 364, 393.
Munsey's Magazine, 293.
Muret, M. Maurice, 349-50.

NANSEN, FRIDTJOF, 504.
Napier, Dr. T. B., 125.
Napoleon, 342 *et sqq.*, 508.
Napoleon III., 93.
Nation, 250, 287, 401.
National Observer, 214.
National Reformer, 160, 164.
National Secular Society, 114, 160.
National Service League, 405.
Nesbit, E. *See* MRS. H. BLAND.
Neue Freie Presse, 287, 343.
New Age, The, 175, 246, 396.
Newman, Ernest, 249.
Newman, Professor F. W., 95.
New Review, The, 313, 462.
New Shakespeare Society, 135, 263.
New York Herald, 54.
New York Sun, 373.
New York Times, 342, 361, 393.
New York Tribune, 317.
Nicol, Commissioner, 387.
Nietzsche, 20, 39, 81, 90, 151, 247, 261, 273, 339, 413, 455 *et sqq.*, 464, 468, 471 *et sqq.*, 480, 484 *et*

INDEX

Nietzsche—*continued.*
  sqq.; his *Genealogy of Morals,* 340,
  364, 456, 486.
Nineteenth Century, 246, 439.
Nordau, Max, 35, 246, 436.
North American Review, 286-7.

O'CONNOR, FERGUS, 173.
O'Connor, T. P., 231, 232, 235-6.
Offenbach, 233, 243, 340.
Olivier, Sir Sydney, 48, 99, 107,
  128-9, 174; his play, *Mrs. Max-*
  well's Marriage, 100; his career,
  100.
One and All, 43.
Orage, A. R., 175.
Ouida, 392.
Our Corner, 52, 109, 195.
Owen, Miss Dale, 104.
Owen, Robert, 178, 209.

PADEREWSKI, I. J., 237-8, 254.
Pall Mall Budget, 244.
Pall Mall Gazette, 48, 50-1, 98, 127,
  135, 160, 164-5, 195-6, 200, 215,
  483.
Palmist and Chirological Review,
  493.
Pankhurst, Dr., 114.
Pardon, Sidney, 261.
Parker, Dr. H. R., 16.
Parnell, Charles Stewart, 101.
Parry, Sir Charles H. H., 236-7.
Passion, Poison and Petrifaction.
  See G. B. SHAW.
Pater, Walter, 433, 438.
Patmore, Coventry, 445.
Patti, Adelina, 237, 239, 254.
Pease, Edward R., 102, 104, 127, 139.
Pepys, Samuel, 45.
Phelps, William L., 366.
Philanderer, The. See G. B. SHAW.
Photography, 222.
Pinero, Arthur Wing, 3, 279 *et sqq.,*
  364, 447.
Plançon, P., 24.
Play, The, 335, 338.
Playhouse, The, 327.
Plays for Puritans. See G. B.
  SHAW.
Plays, Pleasant and Unpleasant.
  See G. B. SHAW.
Podmore, Frank, 102, 104, 114, 127,
  177.
Poe, Edgar Allan, 5, 24, 130.
Pope, Alexander, 59, 243.

Porter, General Horace, 312.
Praxiteles, 32.
Proudhon, P. J., 128, 186.
Psychical Research Society, The,
  127.
Public Opinion, 11, 33.
Putnam's Monthly, 501.

QUEENSBERRY, MARQUESS OF, 387.
Quintessence of Ibsenism. See G. B.
  SHAW.

RABELAIS, 201, 509.
Radical, The, 132.
Raphael, 208, 221, 224.
Reade, Charles, 432-3.
Reclus, Elisée, 486.
Reinhardt, Max, 345.
Rembrandt, 227, 393.
Renan, Ernest, 449.
Repertory Theatre, 285.
Review of Reviews (London), 386.
Revue des Deux Mondes, 300, 445.
Rhodes, Cecil, 385.
Ricardo, David, 155, 159, 161.
Richards, Grant, 55, 309, 319, 321.
Robertson, Forbes, 282, 335, 338, 402,
  417.
Robertson, John Mackinnon, 45, 114.
Robins, Elizabeth, 372.
Rockefeller, John D., 384.
Rodin, Auguste, 226, 500-1, 504.
Roeckel, August, 247.
Rogers, Professor A. K., 471.
Rook, Clarence, 141, 198, 335.
Roosevelt, Theodore, 384, 484.
Rossetti, D. G., 219, 446.
Rossini, 18.
Rossiter, 115.
Rostand, Edmond, 432.
Rousseau, J. J., 5.
Runciman, James, 214.
Runciman, J. F., 214.
Ruskin, John, 7, 168, 210-11, 253,
  271, 434, 451, 457.

SAINTE BEUVE, CHARLES A., 251, 297,
  474.
Saint Saëns, Camille, 241, 243.
St. Simon, Claude H., Comte de, 178.
Salt, Henry, 48 *et sqq.,* 90, 503.
Sanders, W., 184.
Sargent, J. S., 227, 449.
Saturday Review, The, 53, 181, 199,
  208-9, 212, 220-1, 231, 245, 261 *et*
  sqq., 266, 269, 272, 275, 279, 288,
  364, 421, 427-9, 455.

INDEX

Savoy Magazine, The, 14.
Savoy Theatre, 285, 337, 388.
Scheffer, Ary, 24.
Schiller, Friedrich, 23, 432, 454.
Schiller Theater, 355.
Schopenhauer, 81, 271, 364, 366, 435, 457, 459, 473-4, 476, 480, 483 et sqq.
Schumann, 23, 240, 243, 252.
Scott and Co., Walter, 53, 179.
Scott, Clement, 279, 299, 302.
Scott, Sir Walter, 61, 67.
Scribner's Sons, Charles, 343.
Sedgwick, Anne D., her Confounding of Camellia, 367.
Shakespeare, William, 26, 55, 74, 81, 135, 196, 341, 391, 417, 447, 473, 476; his plays criticized by Shaw, 262 et sqq., 288, 321; Shaw's preface on, 336.
Shaw, Agnes, 22, 25.
Shaw, Frederick, 10.
Shaw, George Bernard, his birth, 3; his complex characteristics, 4; on autobiographies, 5-6; his parentage and ancestry, 6 et sqq.; his early life, 8 et sqq., 39; on church going, 8-9, 11-12 et sqq.; enters his uncle's office, 10; on Moody and Sankey, 10-11, 27, 33; his dislike of snobbery, 14-5, 21, 35, 41; his education, 15 et sqq.; his great love of music, 18-9, 22 et sqq., 36-7, 216; his early love of art, 19; enters Mr. Townshend's office, 20; his original musical technique, 23, 218; goes to London, 25; his religious training, 26; his asceticism, 26-7; choosing a profession, 31 et sqq.; his friendship with Edward McNulty, 33-4; and Chichester Bell, 34-35, 44; first introduction to Wagner's music, 35, 234; his resemblance to his mother, 38-9; his struggles in London, 39 et sqq.; his dress, 40-1, 491-2; on poverty, 41-2, 46; on the artistic temperament, 43; first literary earnings, 43, 47; his egotism, 44-5; his Immaturity, 46-7; and land nationalization, 47-8; makes new friends, 47 et sqq.; his vegetarianism, 49, 471; and the Salts, 48 et sqq.; on Shelley and Wagner's principles, 49-50; and the death of J. L. Joynes, 50-51; publication

of his novels, 51 et sqq.; becomes acquainted with William Morris, 52; on Cashel Byron's Profession, 52; his Plays, Pleasant and Unpleasant, published, 54; his plays, Arms and the Man and The Devil's Disciple, produced, 54; on American publishing, 54 et sqq.; on novel-writing, 59, 60; Stevenson on, 61; and Ibsen, 61-2, 297 et sqq., 316, 420 et sqq.; his The Irrational Knot, 62 et sqq.; his Love Among the Artists, 65 et sqq.; his Cashel Byron's Profession, 69, 71 et sqq.; on the education of children, 70-1; his The Admirable Bashville, 74 et sqq.; his An Unsocial Socialist, 77 et sqq.; his attitude towards women, 80 et sqq.; as a novelist, 83 et sqq.; his versatility, 89, 409, 424; various influences on, 90, 99, 100; his friendship with Lecky, 90 et sqq.; studies phonetics, 91; joins the Zetetical Society, 92-3; joins the Dialectical Society, 93; on Sidney Webb, 93; practices public speaking, 94; his admiration for Henry George, 96; studies Marx, 97-8; and the Darwinian School, 97; an enthusiastic Socialist, 98 et sqq., 385; and William Clarke, 100-1; and the Fabian Society, 102 et sqq., 173 et sqq., 279-80, 385; Sidney Webb's great influence on, 106-7, 125-7; his powers of oratory, 121 et sqq., 412, 505-6; his early training for public speaking, 121 et sqq.; and the Hampstead Historic Club, 128 et sqq.; his love of debating, 130-1, 135; and Mr. Haldane, 133-4; and literary societies, 135; his strenuous work, 136-7; and Bradlaugh, 138; debates with G. W. Foote, 138 et sqq.; his independent attitude, 140-1; his appearance, 145, 338; his Socialistic philosophy, 151 et sqq., 188 et sqq.; his letter to Hamlin Garland, 152; influence of Henry George on, 153 et sqq.; studies economics, 155 et sqq.; and Wicksteed, Jevons and Marx, 155 et sqq.; attends International Socialist Congress at Zurich, 171; as a Vestryman and Borough

Shaw, George Bernard—*continued.*
Councillor, 181 *et sqq.*; on municipal trading, 182-3; invited to stand for Battersea, 184-5; his career as an art critic, 193 *et sqq.*; his criticism of the *Taming of the Shrew*, 196-7; and the New Journalism, 199; compared to Heine and Meredith, 201; his affected levity, 201 *et sqq.*; compared with Whistler, 204; his opinion of criticism, 205; William Morris's influence on, 205, 208, 211; Morris's appreciation of, 208; his obituary of Morris, 209 *et sqq.*; his integrity as an art critic, 212-13; becomes a musical critic, 212; and Henley, 214 *et sqq.*; his admiration for Michael Angelo, 218-9; and Madox Brown, 219-20; and the Impressionists, 221; and the Dutch school, 222; and photography, 222 *et sqq.*; photographed by A. L. Coburn, 225 *et sqq.*; as a music critic, 231 *et sqq.*; on the staff of the *Star*, 231 *et sqq.*; his *nom-de-plume* of Corno di Bassetto, 232 *et sqq.*; on Offenbach, 233, 243; his admiration for Wagner, 235; on some modern composers, 236 *et sqq.*; on Paderewski, 238; on Patti and Bispham, 238-9; on Hollman, Essipoff, Joachim and Ysaye, 239, 240; on Mozart, 240; on Saint Saëns and Meyerbeer, 243; on Beethoven, Mendelssohn, Schumann and Brahms, 243; his championship of Wagner, 243 *et sqq.*; his Bayreuth criticisms, 244; on Covent Garden Opera, 244-5; on Strauss' *Elektra*, 249-50; his attitude as a critic, 251 *et sqq.*; dramatic critic on the *Saturday Review*, 261 *et sqq.*; his aim as dramatic critic, 262, 427; on Shakespeare, 263 *et sqq.*; on modern problems, 271; champions Ibsen, 272 *et sqq.*; on Church and Stage, 276-7; on comedy, 278 *et sqq.*; leading critics on, 279 *et sqq.*; on Pinero, 282 *et sqq.*; on some modern playwrights, 283; on Irving and Ellen Terry, 287-8; his income from journalism, 288; as a playwright, 293 *et sqq.*; his first play produced, 293 *et sqq.*;

Archer's article on, 293 *et sqq.*; and the writing of *Mrs. Warren's Profession*, 305-6; his new phase as a dramatist, 309 *et sqq.*; and W. S. Gilbert, 316 *et sqq.*; and Cyril Maude, 321-2, 327-8; and Arnold Daly, 326-7; and Ellen Terry, 328 *et sqq.*, 343; and Richard Mansfield, 342-3; Sir Charles Wyndham on, 346; Dr. Brandes on, 347; and William Terriss, 354; William Archer's admiration for, 363, 378, and the modern drama, 363 *et sqq.*, 413 *et sqq.*; his *magnum opus*, 370 *et sqq.*; Walkley's criticism on, 374, 460-1; and politics at the theatre, 388; and the plot of the *Doctor's Dilemma*, 391 *et sqq.*; his letter to Tolstoy, 399; as a technician, 409 *et sqq.*; his world-wide reputation, 409-10; his prefaces, 413; his descriptive powers, 414; and stage directions, 417 *et sqq.*; his defects, 424-5; a *résumé* of his plays, 425-6, 448-9; as a dramatist, 431 *et sqq.*; and the problem play, 433 *et sqq.*; G. K. Chesterton on, 436; on illusions, 436 *et sqq.*; philosophy of his plays, 439 *et sqq.*, 481; as artist and philosopher, 453 *et sqq.*; on Schopenhauer, 459; his optimism, 459 *et sqq.*; on self-knowledge, 467 *et sqq.*; and science, 477; on vivisection, 178-9; on progress, 480; his atheism, 482; his religion, 484; alleged influences on, 484 *et sqq.*; Sir Francis Galton's anthropometric chart, 492-3; his characteristics, 494-5, 501 *et sqq.*; as he is to-day, 495; his prize story, 498-9; foreign critics on, 500-1; his marriage, 503; his energy, 503; as a conversationist, 504; his Puritanism, 508-9; his kindness of heart, 509-10; on marriage, 511-12.

Shaw, G. B., his works:—
Cashel Byron's Profession, 32, 51 *et sqq.*, 61, 71 *et sqq.*, 205, 304, 381, 451, 478.
Common Sense of Municipal Trading, The, 183.
Dramatic Opinions and Essays, 208, 276, 285.

INDEX

Shaw, George Bernard—*continued.*
Fabian Essays in Socialism, 178.
Immaturity (Unpublished), 46-7.
Irrational Knot, The, 45, 52, 55, 62 *et sqq.*
Love Among the Artists, 52, 54, 67 *et sqq.,* 85, 235.
Perfect Wagnerite, The, 247.
Quintessence of Ibsenism, 138, 272-3, 299, 413, 480, 484.
Unsocial Socialist, An, 51, 54, 77, 81-2, 206, 222.
Shaw, G. B., Pamphlets, Articles, etc.:—
Aërial Football (Collier's Weekly), 498.
Author to the Dramatic Critics (Widowers' Houses), 205.
Author's View, The (Caxton Magazine), 211.
Authors of the Court Theatre, The, 446.
Blaming the Bard (Saturday Review), 269.
Bluffing the Value Theory, 164-5.
Censorship of Plays (The Nation), 287.
Censorship of the Stage in England (North American Review), 286-7.
Class War, The (Clarion), 167-8.
Coburn the Camerist (Metropolitan Magazine), 227.
Conflict Between Science and Common Sense, 51, 477.
Darwin Denounced (Pall Mall Gazette,) 483.
Das Kapital (National Reformer), 160.
Degenerate's View of Nordau, A, 465, 471.
De Mortuis (Saturday Review), 245.
Diabolonian Ethics, On (Three Plays for Puritans), 119, 355.
Does Modern Education Ennoble? (Great Thoughts), 481.
Dramatic Realist to His Critics (New Review), 313, 462.
Elektra of Strauss and Hoffmansthal (Nation), 250.
Ellen Terry (Neue Freie Presse), 343.
Exhibitions, The (Amateur Photographer), 226, 228.
Fabian Essays, 109, 116, 136

Fabian Society Tracts, The, 87, 105 *et sqq.,* 110, 111, 115, 131, 171, 174, 177, 183, 207-8, 385.
Failures of Inept Vegetarians (Pall Mall Gazette), 50.
Fitzthunder, My Friend (To-Day), 169.
Fitzthunder on Himself (To-Day), 169.
Giving the Devil His Due (Saturday Review), 455.
Haymarket Theatre, The (Chap. XIV.), 321.
Ibsen (The Clarion), 390, 422.
Illusions of Socialism, The, 165, 188.
Impossibilities of Anarchism, The, 171.
In the Days of Our Youth (Star), 234.
King Arthur (Saturday Review), 221.
Life of Madame Blavatsky, A (Pall Mall Gazette), 127, 195.
Madox Brown, Watts and Ibsen (Saturday Review), 220.
Marx and Modern Socialism (Pall Mall Gazette), 165.
Meredith on Comedy (Saturday Review), 278-9, 429.
Morris as Actor and Dramatist (Saturday Review), 208.
Music (The World), 239, 257.
Notes on the Clarendon Press Rules for Compositors and Readers (The Author), 91.
On Going to Church (Savoy Magazine), 14.
On Mr. Mallock's Proposed Trumpet Performance (Fortnightly Review), 60, 187.
Our Saturday Talk (Westminster Gazette), 442.
Phonetic Spelling; a Reply to Some Criticisms (Morning Leader), 91.
Plea for Speech Nationalization, A (Morning Leader), 91.
Prefaces:—
Author's Apology (Dramatic Opinions and Essays), 276.
Author's Apology (Mrs. Warren's Profession), 286, 309, 435.
Better than Shakespeare? (Three Plays for Puritans), 336, 364.

524

Shaw, George Bernard—continued.
First Aid to Critics (Major Barbara), 486.
Mainly About Myself (Plays, Pleasant and Unpleasant), 309, 411, 438.
Problem Play (Humanitarian), 435.
Religion of the Pianoforte, The (Fortnightly Review), 24, 50.
Sanity of Art, The, An Exposure of the Current Nonsense About Artists Being Degenerate, 246, 396.
Scotland Yard for Spectres, A (Pall Mall Gazette), 127.
Shakespeare's Merry Gentlemen (Saturday Review), 266.
Shaw, Bernard, 489.
Shaw Abashed, Bernard (Daily News), 75.
Shaw, George Bernard: A Conversation (The Tatler), 374.
Shaw and the Heroic Actor, Bernard (The Play), 335, 338.
Shaw as a Clerk, Bernard (The Clerk), 22.
Shaw, Letter from Mr. G. Bernard (Tolstoy on Shakespeare), 268.
Shaw's Method and Secret, Mr. (Daily Chronicle), 305.
Shaw's Works of Fiction, Mr. Bernard (Novel Review), 80.
Socialism and Republicanism (Saturday Review), 181.
Socialism at the International Congress, 190.
Socialism for Millionaires (Contemporary Review), 183, 385.
Socialists at Home (Pall Mall Gazette), 165.
Solution of the Censorship Problem (Academy), 287.
Spelling Reform v. Phonetic Spelling (Daily News), 91.
Stanley Jevons: His Letters and Journal (Pall Mall Gazette), 160, 195.
Sunday on the Surrey Hills (Pall Mall Gazette), 48.
Theatrical World (Archer's), 315.
Transition to Social Democracy, 208.
Valedictory (Saturday Review), 288.

Who I Am, and What I Think (Candid Friend), 42, 60, 98, 147, 202.
A Word About Stepniak (To-Morrow), 313.
A Word More About Verdi (Anglo-Saxon Review), 241.
Shaw, G. B., his plays:—
Admirable Bashville, The, or Constancy Unrewarded, 74 et sqq.
Arms and the Man, 54, 142, 311, 313 et sqq., 320, 359, 404, 422, 425, 458.
Cæsar and Cleopatra, 335 et sqq., 340.
Candida, 54, 85, 326, 341, 346 et sqq., 409-10, 418.
Captain Brassbound's Conversion, 91, 288, 320, 328 et sqq.
Dark Lady of the Sonnets, 398.
Devil's Disciple, The, 54, 288, 328, 341, 354 et seq., 401, 419, 422-3, 425, 438, 458.
Doctor's Dilemma, The, 389 et sqq., 422-3, 425.
Don Juan in Hell (Man and Superman), 369 et sqq.
Getting Married, 398.
How He Lied to Her Husband, 320, 326.
Interlude at the Playhouse, The, 327.
John Bull's Other Island, 15-16, 34, 370 et sqq., 388, 425.
Major Barbara, 297, 337, 380, 381, 382, 384 et sqq., 401, 425, 486.
Man and Superman, 27, 81-2, 152, 363 et sqq., 368, 378, 388, 414, 444, 458, 471, 481, 489, 509.
Man of Destiny, The, 341 et sqq., 374.
Misalliance, 398.
Passion, Poison and Petrifaction; or the Fatal Gazogene, 327.
Philanderer, The, 51, 299 et sqq., 422, 425, 478.
Plays for Puritans, 27, 119, 193, 328, 333, 336, 364, 407.
Plays, Pleasant and Unpleasant, 49, 54, 288, 291, 309, 411.
Press Cuttings, 402, 404.
Showing-up of Blanco Posnet, 27, 398 et sqq.
Warren's Profession, Mrs., 220, 286, 304 et sqq., 341, 363, 380 et sqq., 398, 425, 458, 509.

INDEX

Shaw, George Bernard—*continued.*
Widowers' Houses, 22, 205, 220, 270, 293 *et sqq.,* 420, 425, 445.
You Never Can Tell, 320, 321 *et sqq.,* 404, 414, 425.
Shaw, G. B., Books and Articles on:—
Archer, William, *Shaw's Phonetic World-English,* 91; *About the Theatre,* 390; *Shaw on Stage Directions,* 419; Article in *The World,* 295.
Bab, Julius, *Bernard Shaw,* 249.
Bahr, Hermann, *Bernard Shaw,* 424.
Brandes, Georg, *Der Dramatiker Bernard Shaw,* 313.
Chesterton, G. K., *The Meaning of Mr. Bernard Shaw,* 436.
Corbin, John, *Bernard Shaw and His Mannikins,* 373.
Filon, Augustin, *M. Bernard Shaw et son Théâtre,* 300, 445.
Greville, Eden, *Bernard Shaw and His Plays,* 293.
Hale, E. E., Jr., *Dramatists of To-Day (Bernard Shaw),* 426.
Hamon, Auguste, *Un Nouveau Molière,* 439.
Henderson, Archibald, *The Philosophy of Bernard Shaw,* 484.
Huneker, James, *Bernard Shaw and Woman,* 84-5; *The Truth About Candida,* 351.
Irwin, Will, *Crankidoxology, Being a Mental Attitude from Bernard Pshaw,* 270.
Jackson, Holbrook, *Bernard Shaw,* 183.
Play, The, *Bernard Shaw and the Heroic Actor,* 335, 338.
Rogers, Professor A. K., *Mr. Bernard Shaw's Philosophy,* 471.
Rook, Clarence, *Mr. Shaw's Future,* 335.
Stead, W. T., *Impressions of the Theatre (Major Barbara),* 386.
Terry, Ellen, *From Lewis Carroll to Bernard Shaw,* 329.
Walkley, A. B., *Mr. Bernard Shaw's Plays,* 319.
Shaw, Mrs. G. B., 388-9, 401, 495.
Shaw, George Carr (G. B. Shaw's father), 6 *et sqq.,* 20, 22.
Shaw, Mrs. George Carr (G. B. Shaw's mother), 7, 8, 17; her mu-
sical talent, 17 *et sqq.,* 22, 36 *et sqq.*
Shaw, Lucy Carr, 22, 26.
Shaw, Sir Robert, 33.
Shelley, P. B., 32, 40, 48 *et sqq.,* 90, 92, 152-3, 215, 234, 271, 273, 346, 412, 434, 457, 473, 480, 482, 503.
Shelley Society, 135.
Sheridan, Richard B., 3, 40, 433.
Shields, Frederick, 220.
Shorter, Clement K., 232.
Showing-up of Blanco Posnet. See G. B. SHAW.
Sims, George R., 43.
Smith, Adam, 155.
Smith, Armitage, 158.
Social Democratic Federation, 96, 102, 108, 110 *et sqq.,* 138, 173, 206.
Socialist League, 137-8, 207, 261.
Socialist Society, Hammersmith, 207.
Sozialistische Monatshefte, 165.
Speaker, The, 107.
Spectator, The, 401, 486.
Spencer, Herbert, 92, 94, 96-7, 102, 168, 443, 467; his *The Coming Slavery,* 189.
Standard Elocutionist, The, 34.
Standard, The, 393.
Standring, G., 132, 139.
Stanford, Sir Charles V., 237.
Stange, Stanislaus, 72, 315.
Stapleton, 114.
Star, The, 113, 171, 231 *et sqq.,* 237, 295, 387.
Stead, W. T., 112-3, 215, 386-7.
Steichen, Éduard J., 225.
Stephens, Yorke, 312.
Stevenson, R. L., 85, 241; letters of, 53, 61, 73, 215-16, 282, 297.
Stirner, Max, his *The Ego and His Own,* 468, 472, 484 *et sqq.*
Stone and Co., H. S., 54, 309.
Straus, Oscar, 314, 315.
Strauss, Richard, his *Elektra,* 250.
Strindberg, August, 316, 366, 484 *et sqq.*
Stuart-Glennie, J. S., 114, 431, 485-6.
Stümcke, Herr Heinrich, 340, 438.
Sullivan, Sir Arthur, 237.
Sweet, Henry, 91, 331.
Swift, Jonathan, 3, 60, 476.
Swinburne, Algernon C., 266, 447, 455.
Symes, Rev. —, 48.
Symons, Arthur, 237, 240, 473.

INDEX

TAINE, HIPPOLYTE, 266.
Taming of the Shrew, The, 196-7.
Tarpey, W. K., 346.
Tatler, The, 377.
Tennyson, Alfred, Lord, 8, 24; his Charge of the Light Brigade, 312.
Terriss, William, 354.
Terry, Ellen, 287-8, 328 et sqq., 342-3.
Théâtre des Arts, 348-9.
Théâtre Royal du Parc, 353.
Thomas, Agnes, 405.
Thomas, Goring, his Golden Web, 237.
Thomson, James, 51.
Thoreau, 50.
Thorpe, Courtenay, 354.
Thorwaldsen, Bertel, 221.
Times, The, 94, 187, 232, 287, 400, 486.
Titian, 200.
Tochatti, 114.
To-Day, 51 et sqq., 114, 155-6, 158, 165, 206.
Tolstoy, Leo, 145, 168, 173, 268, 398-9, 401, 413, 464, 473.
Tourneur, Cyril, 264.
Townshend, Uniacke, 10, 20, 33-4.
Traill, H. D., 199.
Trebitsch, Herr Siegfried, 420.
Tree, Sir H. Beerbohm, 282, 288, 398.
Treherne and Co., A., 327.
Tribune, The, 390, 391.
Trollope, Anthony, 39, 41.
Trovatore, Il, 18, 24.
Truth, 195.
Tucker, Benjamin R., 189, 245-6, 396, 468.
Turner, J. M. W., 210-11, 473.
Twain, Mark, 10, 38, 413, 440, 456, 508.
Tyndall, Professor, 35, 44, 94, 96, 153.

Unsocial Socialist, The. See G. B. Shaw.
Unwin, T. Fisher, 104.

VANDERVELDE, EMILE, 186, 486.
Van Uhde, 222.
Vasa-Theater, 326.
Vaudeville Magazine, 11.
Vedrenne, J. E., 371-2, 398, 446.
Velasquez, 200, 224, 227, 393.
Verdi, 18, 23, 241, 245.

Victoria, Queen, 312.
Vieuxtemps, Henri, 254.
Vizetelly, Henry, 202.
Voltaire, 144, 183-4, 449, 459, 477.
Vorst, Mrs. John van, 501.

WAGNER, RICHARD, 24, 69, 73, 81, 90, 198, 214, 241, 257, 271, 447, 457, 473, 481, 502; his Tannhäuser, 23, 234, 245; Shaw's first acquaintance with music of, 35, 234; his ascetic temperament, 49; his Tristan und Isolde, 97, 244, 293; Shaw's admiration for, 218, 243; Shaw studies music of, 235; Shaw's defence of, 237; Shaw's criticisms on, 244 et sqq., 252-3; his Die Meistersinger, 244; his Die Walküre, 245; his Das Rheingold, 245, 250; his Ring of the Niblungs, 247, 460; his Lohengrin, 248; his Parsifal, 250; his Götterdämmerung, 377; his story, An End in Paris, 393; his philosophy, 434.
Walkley, Arthur Bingham, 20, 121, 203, 232, 279, 324, 333, 363, 364, 374, 387, 412, 444, 460, 489; his Frames of Mind, 319.
Wallace, Alfred Russel, 94; his work on Land Nationalization, 95.
Wallace, Vincent, 24.
Wallas, Graham, 99, 100, 113, 128-9, 158, 174, 178, 503; his Life of Francis Place, 100; his An Economic Eirenicon, 164-5.
Warren's Profession, Mrs. See G. B. Shaw.
Washington, George, 477.
Webb, Sidney, 90-1, 93, 99, 102, 105 et sqq., 114, 116-7, 125 et sqq., 133, 152, 157, 174-5, 178, 225, 314.
Weber, his Der Freischütz, 234.
Webster, John, 264.
Wedmore, Frederick, 299.
Wesley College, Dublin, 15-6, 34.
Wesley College Quarterly, 16.
Westermann's Monatshefte, 337.
Whibley, Charles, 215.
Whistler, J. McNeill, 204, 222-3, 413-4.
Whitcroft, Ellen, 7.
Whitman, Walt, 50, 243, 268.
Whitney, F. C., 315.
Wicksteed, Philip H., 155 et sqq., 160 et sqq.; his Alphabet of Economics, 158.

527

INDEX

Widowers' Houses. *See* G. B.
  Shaw.
Wilde, Oscar, 3, 227, 282, 284,
  366, 394, 412, 426, 442, 460,
  502.
Williams, 112.
Willis's Rooms, 131.
Wilshire, Gaylord, 186.
Wilshire's Magazine, 159.
Wilson, Mrs., 108, 114-5.
Winter, William, 343.
Wollstonecraft, Mary, 419, 469.
Wolseley, Lord, 312.
World, The, 98, 135-6, 195, 231, 237,
  239, 244-5, 255, 257, 261, 295.

Wright, Charles, 158.
Wyndham, Sir Charles, 342, 345-6,
  442.

Yates, Edmund, 195, 212, 261.
Yeats, W. B., 371, 378, 400.
You Never Can Tell. *See* G. B.
  Shaw.
Ysaye, Eugen, 240.

Zeit, Die, 431.
Zetetical Society, The, 91 *et sqq.*,
  122, 144, 271.
Zola, Emile, 40, 59, 84, 146, 202, 297,
  432, 440, 457; his *La Débâcle,* 312.

REVIEWS,

from Foreign Journals of Opinion, of

"George Bernard Shaw: His Life and Works"

By

ARCHIBALD HENDERSON, M. A., Ph. D.,

of The University of North Carolina

"The book is a most remarkable achievement."—George Bernard Shaw, in the *Morning Post* (London), May 3, 1911.

"Mr. Shaw is explored from every point of view. . . . Newspaper files have been ransacked, forgotten controversies between dramatic critics or different kinds of Socialists have been unearthed, profound researches made into contemporary literature suggesting parallels and illustrations, stray thoughts gathered up and traced in their development from childhood to middle age. . . .
"We cannot praise Mr. Henderson too highly. We know of nothing in the literature of biography that is so exhaustively complete."—*Westminster Gazette* (London), April 22, 1911.

"Its comprehensiveness gives it the importance of an historical document. . . . It is something more than a chronicle of the life of Mr. Bernard Shaw, it is a remarkable chronicle of English revolutionary movements during the last twenty-five years. . . . In the sixteen chapters of his book, Dr. Henderson tells the history of the idea movements of the last quarter of a century *apropos* of Bernard Shaw. . . . The reader who cannot find instruction and entertainment within its covers lacks the art of reading."—Holbrook Jackson, in the *Bookman* (London), May, 1911.

"Dr. Henderson's authorized and critical biography . . . is indispensable. . . . The fullest, the best informed, and the most carefully studied account of Bernard Shaw that has yet been published. . . . The book will rank immediately after Mr. Shaw's own works as material for students of the advanced tendencies of which in this country the author of *John Bull's Other Island* is the most conspicuous representative. . . ."
—*The Scotsman* (Edinburgh), April 13, 1911.

"A biography that could scarcely be bettered. . . . It is full, minute, and exact. Biographer and autobiographer have joined forces, and the result is a masterly study of the most complicated personality of our time. . . . The author has spared no pains in verifying his references and arranging his materials. Here you have Shaw in his quiddity. . . . Dr.

i

Reviews of "George Bernard Shaw: His Life and Works"

Henderson out-Boswells Boswell in his enormous pertinacity, his prodigious fidelity. He has not left a crumb for other biographers."—James Douglas, in the *Star* (London), April 15, 1911.

"It would be hard to find anyone perfectly equipped for the task (of writing Shaw's biography). Mr. Granville Barker . . . would have shown a more intelligent sympathy in Mr. Shaw's ideals. But we should have had as much Barker as Shaw. Our lily would have been painted. Mr. Archer might have seized the opportunity to set up that guillotine for which he once sighed. Mr. Webb would have been unreliable once inside the theatre. We might have had a score of articles from various writers, each qualified to speak on one aspect of Mr. Shaw, but we should then have been like children with the pieces of a puzzle, unable to fit them together. No, Professor Henderson is not easily dethroned. . . .
"The book is almost a history of the last quarter of the nineteenth century, and . . . it has not a dull moment."—*Evening Standard and St. James's Gazette* (London), April 11, 1911.

"At length comes the really big thing, . . . and following precedent, it comes from the home of big things, America. Dr. Henderson . . . is not only elaborate in his interpretation of our leading dramatist and controversialist, but comprehensive as well. His book is . . . a mine in which all future students of George Bernard Shaw will be forced to dig and delve. . . . Nothing is impossible to this amazingly energetic American professor. . . . Professor Henderson is an interpreter of modern ideas. He feels that we are in the midst of a remarkable intellectual awakening, and he is impelled . . . to give his complex and multiplex period a coherent voice. . . .
"Professor Archibald Henderson is the modern counterpart of the old chronicler; they saw the romance and significance of events, he sees the romance and significance of ideas; he is a Hakluyt of ideas, of personalities. . . . His interests and his enthusiasms embrace the hemispheres."—*Black and White* (London), April 22, 1911.

"Ce livre n'est pas seulement une étude magistrale sur la personnalité la plus compliquée de notre temps, il est aussi un exposé fort complet des divers mouvements d'idées qui ont agité l'Angleterre en ces derniers vingt-cinq ans. . . . Mr. Henderson mérite qu'on lui sache gré des six ans de labeur qu'il a consacrés à ce livre, qui restera un document des plus précieux."—Henry D. Davray, in the *Mercure de France* (Paris), June 16, 1911.

"The reader's astonishment when the book is laid down is not at its length but at its brevity. . . . Here things regain their true proportions, and much of our astonishment and admiration for the book, its author, and its hero are due to this. . . . Nowhere does Dr. Henderson's critical faculty show to greater advantage than in his deductions as to the general aim of the plays. . . . Dr. Henderson is a critic before he is a biographer. There is nothing of the attitude of a Boswell in his work. . . . There remains the possibility that others may gauge the results of Shaw's secret with more acumen than he himself. There is no probability, however, that this will ever be done with more discretion, discernment, and distinction than by Mr. Henderson."—*Manchester Courier* (England), April 11, 1911.

Reviews of " George Bernard Shaw: His Life and Works "

" An elaborate and detailed history of Bernard Shaw and his effects as a dramatist, Socialist, and general revolutionary. . . . George Bernard Shaw is looked at, sounded, discussed, examined, and appraised from every point of view. . . . It is a well into which all future students of Bernard Shaw will have to dip their buckets. . . . The biographical chapters are brimming over with lively anecdote. . . . In the three chapters devoted to Shaw as a dramatist, Mr. Henderson gives a critical analysis of the plays of G. B. S. which is as penetrating as it is painstaking, and will easily give him a front seat among Bernard Shaw's commentators. . . . Shaw's . . . biographer has succeeded, and it is no small praise to say that throughout the whole of his book you feel that you are in the presence of a living personality. . . ."—*T. P.'s Weekly* (London), April 21, 1911.

" This notable book . . . is a long one, but we have noticed very few faults either in fact or of taste in reading it. . . . Nothing in it is so salutary as the final impression it leaves of the power to which a man can attain through the old-fashioned virtues of energy, industry, and determination. . . . As critic, political thinker, and dramatist, Mr. Shaw has managed to do a great deal of splendid work . . . ; and Dr. Henderson gives us a capital picture of it all."—*Pall Mall Gazette* (London), April 11, 1911.

" A record which, in completeness, is unique among the *Men of Our Time*. What would we not give to know as much of some of the mighty intellects of the past! "—*Daily Graphic* (London), April 11, 1911.

" Acknowledgment should be made of Dr. Henderson's critical sanity. . . . A most interesting and weighty book. It is the nearest thing to that ideal autobiography which Mr. Shaw will never write, and is a worthy tribute to a man of whom this country ought to be proud."—George Sampson, in the *Daily Chronicle* (London), April 11, 1911.

" The large and exceedingly handsome volume . . . deals with its distinguished subject in every variety of aspect, while managing to remain itself both interesting and entertaining."—*Punch* (London), May 10, 1911.

" Mr. Henderson's book is full of good things. . . . He analyses and explains, watches and reports, exploits the whys and retails the wherefores. . . . He is a searchlight. . . ."—*Sketch* (London), May 3, 1911.

" Mr. Henderson's criticism of the plays of George Bernard Shaw is, indeed, acute and painstaking to an extraordinary degree."—*Lloyd's Weekly* (Liverpool), April 30, 1911.

" Mr. Henderson's illuminating Life. . . . His task has been carried out with remarkable thoroughness."—*Globe* (London), April 12, 1911.

" Dr. Henderson has done his work with the Boswellian thoroughness and assiduity. He has tracked Mr. Shaw down through the files of remote and forgotten newspapers; he has ransacked libraries; he has unearthed and pumped Mr. Shaw's friends and critics in all countries; he has zealously studied the social movements in which his hero was involved, and got the atmosphere of the London intellectual cliques as if he had lived his life among them instead of being a Professor in an American University. Finally, he has compelled Mr. Shaw himself to take an interest in the work, to contribute to it, criticise it, and thoroughly overhaul it, so much so indeed as to lead to the suggestion that it

iii

should be called a biography and autobiography. . . . If he (Dr. Henderson) has not given us the verdict which history will pronounce on his subject . . . , he has pronounced the verdict of the clever people of to-day."
—R. A. Scott-James, in the *Daily News* (London), April 11, 1911.

" A document of value. Immense pains have been taken by the author and by Mr. Shaw to bring together within its covers as many of the facts about Mr. Shaw's life and character and opinion as Mr. Shaw wishes to be generally known. . . . Best of all the chapters is that called ' The Cart and Trumpet,' the record of the days when his personal force was in full flood."—*Outlook* (London), April 22, 1911.

" The chapters which tell of the rise of the Socialistic spirit in London, dating as it does from about 1880, of the genesis of the Fabian Society, and of various controversies upon economic matters, are capital reading and form valuable contributions to the history of the period. . . . Another excellent feature is the portion of the book dealing with the brilliant Vedrenne-Barker seasons at the Court Theatre—seasons which made theatrical history rapidly and forced both the critics and the public to sit up and look around."—*Wilfred L. Randall,* in the *Academy* (London), April 29, 1911.

" We are agreeably surprised to find a critic who can consider the Shavian drama without going to extremes of laudation or disapproval. Mr. Henderson has found the golden mean."—*Irish Times* (Dublin), May 12, 1911.